DICTIONARY OF HERESY TRIALS IN AMERICAN CHRISTIANITY

Edited by
George H. Shriver

GREENWOOD PRESS
Westport, Connecticut • London

Library of Congress Cataloging-in-Publication Data

Dictionary of heresy trials in American Christianity / edited by
    George H. Shriver.
        p.   cm.
    Includes bibliographical references and index.
    ISBN 0-313-29660-X (alk. paper)
    1. Heretics, Christian—United States—History—Dictionaries.
    2. Heresy (Trials)—United States—History—Dictionaries.   3. United
    States—Church history—Dictionaries.   I. Shriver, George H.
    BR517.D5   1997
    273'.9'0973—dc21   96-53522

British Library Cataloguing in Publication Data is available.

Library of Congress Catalog Card Number: 96-53522
ISBN: 0-313-29660-X

First published in 1997

Greenwood Press, 88 Post Road West, Westport, CT 06881
An imprint of Greenwood Publishing Group, Inc.

Printed in the United States of America

The paper used in this book complies with the
Permanent Paper Standard issued by the National
Information Standards Organization (Z39.48-1984).

10 9 8 7 6 5 4 3 2 1

In memory of
Max Gray Rogers
and
Robert K. Gustafson

Contents

Trials and Denominations

Preface

This volume presents the stories of 50 formal or informal heresy trials in the history of American Christianity. The trials are arranged alphabetically, although chronologically the trials range from the early colonial period to recent contemporary time. Each entry attempts an objective, historical, and analytical presentation of the major aspects of the individual's or institution's story of contextual heresy. Four institutions and more than 46 individuals appear here. Most entries contain less than 4,000 words, and only a minimum of internal parenthetical notes is to be found—mainly for longer quotations. A selected bibliography follows the entire group of trials, along with an appendix identifying the trials by denominational family. Since so many of these trials and persons touch one another, an asterisk (*) has been used for cross-referencing trials found in the book.

Edited volumes have their own set of interesting and sometimes sticky problems, but I must pay the highest compliments and sincerest appreciation to the 40 writers who have joined with me in this effort. We have indeed been a team and a community at work. A special word and mention must be made of Dr. Robert Gustafson and Dr. Max Gray Rogers. To my knowledge, their last scholarly efforts are those found in this volume. Dr. Gustafson's widow mailed his entry to me a few weeks after his death, and Dr. Rogers sent his entry only two months prior to his death. Their commitment to the team and the project may serve as an inspiration to all of the rest of us poor pilgrims of God who struggle along the academic road.

The mechanics of putting things together has been made easier for me by David Martin, Bradley M. Winn, and especially Peggy Smith, typist par excellence. My wife Cathy and others have endured my sometimes rough temperament. Special friends Henry Bowden and Martin Marty have shared ideas and prodding remarks. And Alicia Merritt at Greenwood Press has been patient and creatively encouraging. What more can an editor ask for? Well, for an excellent production editor and copyeditor—so, kudos to Bridget Austiguy-Preschel and Susan Badger for superior assistance.

Perhaps the most important card of thanks must go to those deeply committed Christians and their bewildering offspring who have been called "heretic" at some point in their careers. Without them, this book would not exist.

Introduction

The image of the heretic has been one of the most abused images in the history of the Christian Church. The course of American Christianity in its setting of apparent freedom has not changed this situation. Professors, ministers, and laypersons alike in America have suffered grievous formal and informal trials that have often resulted in loss of position as well as loss of ordination and/or membership in a particular religious communion. At times, entire institutions have died or seen such alteration of their essence that their history has indeed been "broken." From the earliest period of the Founding Fathers to the last decade of the twentieth century, there have been heretics and trials on the American religious scene.

Originally in early Christian history, the words *heresy* and *heretic* referred simply to "choice." One person chooses a particular opinion, while another prefers the contrary, or at least a variant. But in the course of Christian history, as soon as truth became identified with a particular propositional statement or canonized viewpoint, such variant choice was deadly business. Political orthodoxy entered the picture. Variant opinion then became deadly not only for the ideas but also for the persons. The pages of Western religious history are marred in every chapter by the story of the persecution of the heretic—from Arius to twentieth-century American individuals of various stripe. The Christian heretic, then, is one who has deviated within the fold of Christian faith from some established or generally accepted doctrine or set of doctrines. In brief, the heretic is one who has challenged a rather closed and canonized system of orthodoxy. Interestingly enough, probably the greatest heretic in Western religious history was Martin Luther himself, the father of the Protestant movement. This observation makes another immediate point—namely, the contextuality of heresy, for Martin Luther believed he was far more orthodox in relation to the essence of the faith than those who condemned him.

The heretic has always paid some kind of penalty, even when his or her career has taken a turn for the best as a result of some formal or informal trial. The pilgrimage of the heretic has been courageous but costly. Generally, penalties on these courageous people have been imposed after some kind of trial, either formal or informal. Even medieval inquisitors held trials—farcical as they sometimes were. Too often, the Thomistic rationale was followed: If society imposes the death penalty on one who murders a physical body, how much more responsible is it to rid itself of one who damns the soul for eternity? The simple logic cannot be denied, given the assumptions.

Protestantism made no improvement on this score to medieval Catholicism. It even raised other issues as the ostensible reasons for trial and penalty. Sedition was a favorite charge against heretics by the magisterial reformers. By doing this, the reformers actually rejected in part the very principle of Protestantism that they themselves had discovered. Openness to the fresh and renewing hand of God, which had been at the heart of their attack upon Roman Catholic institutionalism, was partially rejected in their own persecution of "seditionists" and heretics.

The American religious scene brought no end to the trials of heretics; it brought even greater complexity, owing to the increasing fragmentation of religion in America. One certainly would expect to find victims in the intolerant colonial period but would perhaps expect a cessation of trials in the national period with its commitment to religious liberty and then to academic freedom. This was definitely not the case, however. Instead of one or a few orthodox opinions, there were numerous orthodoxies and attendant trials. In fact, this century has witnessed some of the most insidious trials in American religious history. These trials have not always been exactly formal ones.

Carl F. H. Henry was not exactly correct in his judgment several decades ago when he said: "Heresy trials became an oddity in contemporary church history, not because of an absence of heresy, but because of the lack of zeal to prosecute heretics." In the contemporary period, one has witnessed more than enough misplaced zeal in regard to the so-called heretic. Heretics and heresy trials, then, are not relics from the medieval past. Some of the most intriguing and revealing cases have appeared on the American scene as late as the nineteenth and twentieth centuries.

But what of the heretic and his or her image in the American religious tradition? Unfortunately, no precise definition nor description can really be given. In addition, the denominational complexity in America further confuses the issue. An accused heretic in a conservative or fundamentalist denomination might be considered a conservative and orthodox Christian in another, more mainline denomination. One must not oversimplify with populist rhetoric when dealing with and trying to define the American religious heretic. Reducing the heretic to a stereotype or common denominator results in absolute distortion. The heretic does not hate Jesus, despise the church, or corrupt the youth. The heretic is not a wicked person nor un-American. Heretics do not conceive of their task as that of troublemaker, nor are they obsessed with arrogance and an infallibility complex. These are some of the false images and populist rhetoric often used to discredit them even before they have spoken or written, however.

These accusations have more often than not been used by their opponents, unfortunately. These opponents, often motivated politically, have used the word *heretic* as a battle cry for others to rally around the orthodox flag. Sadly enough, the battle cry has more often than not intentionally obscured the real issues and led to false simplifications. The heresy hunters have also often allowed themselves to pervert Christian ethics in their pursuit of their goal of discrediting persons they have labeled "heretics." Denominational leadership and political power structures have too often been arrogant and judgmental with those they should have tried most to understand. As a result, heretics have suffered, and denominations have paid a heavy price of forestalled self-criticism and examination.

A more useful image of the heretic in Christian history as well as in the American religious tradition would be conveyed by the use of the word *saint*. Without a manual of religious history as program guide, it would be very difficult to tell the saints from most of the heretics in Western religious history. For example, compare the heretic Peter Waldo with Saint Francis of Assisi. Both have been the most religious of persons in their own generation. Need we remind ourselves that in the beginning Christianity itself was a Jewish heresy? And may not those who experience Christianity at its deepest and innermost levels be called "heretics"?

This new image pictures the heretic as a creative precursor of new ideas in a particular context—whether within a single denomination or within a complete generation. What these folks are about does not lead to "peace in Zion" but is rather generative of a healthy restlessness. They are avant-gardists who attempt to lead their denominations to fresh assessments and interpretations within the context of self-criticism. The heretic thus becomes a healthy cathartic agent. For him or her personally, however, there is a haunting loneliness as he or she passes through valleys of shadow, often with unspeakable burdens. Can it not be said that the heretic, more than others, enters into the mysticism of Gethsemane suffering? It is not then so strange to observe that the interrogation of Jesus on that morning of the last day of his life was the "prototype of all heresy trials!"

The last decade of the twentieth century has witnessed a renewed interest in heresy and trials in several quarters in the United States. The lead article of *The Christian Century* of 12 April 1995 was entitled "Can We Talk About Heresy" in a kind of point/counterpoint format. Thomas Oden of

Drew University Theological School presented the case of the confessing church movement within the United Methodist Church that wishes to examine the issue of heresy with implications for those who choose their "own personal will over against the truth." Oden would once again urge boundaries in theology. Lewis Mudge of the San Francisco Theological Seminary gave the counterpoint and argued that "the way the church has handled alleged doctrinal deviance has often been heretical itself." Instead of boundaries interpreted arbitrarily by leadership, Mudge sees each age discerning "the 'pattern' of faith anew"—a rediscovery and rearticulation of faith. And at opposite ends of the spectrum, the Protestant Episcopal Church and the Southern Baptist Convention have wrestled with heresy issues. The Protestant Episcopal Church in mid-1996 refused to entertain heresy charges against Bishop Walter Righter for his ordination of a gay man as a deacon. On the other hand, in the wake of the political takeover of the Southern Baptist Convention by militant fundamentalists, there were numerous informal heresy trials, especially of seminary professors, as these fundamentalists "cleansed" their theological schools of heresy.

Samuel Laeuchi's *The Serpent and the Dove* has an excellent chapter entitled "The Heresy of Truth." There he observes that "there is an infinite gap between orthodoxy as dynamic search for authentic response and orthodoxy as an established formula." The Protestant principle is indeed described in the first section of this statement, while an orthodox interest in defining the circumference of doctrine is identified in the last few words. Those who would define circumference must not be too naive about or insensitive to the numerous abuses in Christian history in defining this circumference. Indeed, so many of the historically judged heretics were far more committed Christians than their accusers and condemners! The *history* of heresy and heretics must not be overlooked by those who wish to reintroduce doctrinal parameters. Some voices in this effort decry an environment of hypertoleration. The counterpoint of other voices decries an environment of hyperintoleration in which no one's dynamic search for authentic response to God in Christ is equal to that of those who define and enforce the circumference of Christian truth. Unfortunately, as the entries in this book clearly illustrate, those who have tried to define orthodoxy have been influenced and motivated by many other factors than simply the search for Christian truth. Politics, jealousies, power struggles, anti-intellectualism, miscommunication, limits of knowing, grudges, personal animosities, confusion of ethics with doctrine—all these and more have played roles in the decisions made concerning so-called heretics. In addition, where there exists multifaceted pluralism, there is the simple fact of contextualism.

Up to the present time, there has been no attempt to gather under one cover the essence of the stories of the major heresy trials in the history of American Christianity. The selection made here is not all inclusive, but it is believed that these are the *major* trials among the various denominations. There are no Afro-American trials here. Eugene Lowe and I searched in vain for such a major trial but without success. This in itself is worthy of reflection. Certainly there is a constellation of reasons for this, and one major one is a preoccupation with practice instead of theological dissent. Is heresy generally the form that dissent takes where there is spiritual monopoly, and this kind of monopoly is not found in Afro-American traditions? Whatever the reasons are, we were unable to discover any records of a major formal or informal trial. It is evident, however, from the selection herein that no one denomination has dominated these trials, although the Presbyterians and Baptists are far out front. A cross section of major denominations is to be seen—at least 11 communions are represented. More than Forty-six individuals and four institutions make this point vividly. Although the four institutions best illustrate the search for academic freedom in American religious education, all of the trials in one way or another contribute to this subject as well.

Further, the word *informal* is as valid as *formal* as a description of heresy trials. Many denominations simply do not have the machinery in place for a formal trial, and even those that do have sometimes employed an informal methodology in dealing with what they consider to be heresy. Informal trials have at times led to even more devastating results than formal trials. Indeed, the generalization may hold true that within the context of formal trial procedures there is less likely to be a gross miscarriage of justice.

P. T. Forsyth once said that a "live heresy is better than a dead orthodoxy," and someone else has perceptively observed that there is no heresy in a dead religion! The presentations in this volume will describe a number of heretics and their trials as well as the lively orthodox churchpersons who tried them. We leave the reader to the decisions as to who are the most valid heirs of the faith of Jesus the Christ.

Andover Theological Seminary
(1886–1892)

In 1886 a long-standing controversy among New England Congregationalists led to the heresy trial of five professors: Egbert Coffin Smyth,* William J. Tucker, George Harris, Edward Y. Hincks, and John W. Churchill.
The Board of Visitors, who heard the case, convicted Egbert Coffin Smyth,
president of the faculty and editor of the *Andover Review*, and dismissed
the charges against the other four. Since Andover Seminary's constituting
documents permitted the appeal of the decisions of the Visitors to the Massachusetts state court, Smyth appealed the verdict. In 1891 the Massachusetts Supreme Court set aside his conviction. Their argument was that the
Visitors acted improperly in denying the Board of Trustees the right to legal
counsel at the original hearing. Since the Trustees both hired and paid
Smyth, they had full standing as a party to the proceedings. A second trial
in 1892 before the Visitors resulted in the dismissal of the charges without
prejudice to either the professor or his accusers.

The basic charge against the Andover professors was that they had
taught contrary to the Andover Creed. To support this allegation, the complainants—Joshua Wellman, Orpheus Lanphear, J. J. Blaisdell, and Henry
M. Dexter (the so-called Committee of the Alumni)—brought 16 specific
accusations. These included assertions that the five faculty members had
departed from the traditional doctrine of biblical authority, taught an unorthodox understanding of the knowledge of Christ during Jesus' earthly
ministry, and maintained the doctrine of a second probation after death.
On the Atonement, always a controverted point in New England, the complainants maintained that the faculty had taught that Christ's Atonement
was primarily his identification with humanity and not his sacrificial death.
In addition, the complainants alleged that the professors taught that sinners

were unable to repent without knowledge of Christ and maintained that the new theology was better than the old.

The outline of the Andover affair is simple, but the actual course of events had many interwoven personal, institutional, and theological twists. For most of the nineteenth century, orthodox Congregationalists debated missions, theological orthodoxy, the centrality of the Scriptures, professional education for clergy, and the role of boards and agencies. However, after 1870, changes in the great intellectual atmosphere exacerbated existing theological tensions and created new ones. Under the impact of modern science, biblical criticism, and newer understandings of human potential, the traditional Calvinism of New England eroded, leaving a theological void. Dissenters no longer directed questions at this or that part of the Calvinist system; with the erosion of its foundations, they now doubted the system itself and speculated about its eventual replacement.

ANDOVER'S CONTENTIOUS HISTORY

Andover Seminary's origins almost predestined the school's future role as a center of controversy and dissension. When Harvard elected Henry Ware as Hollis Professor of Divinity in 1805, the orthodox Calvinists began searching for an alternative means to educate their ministers. Since they had the support of the Board of Phillips Academy, Andover, they planned to locate their ministerial school on that school's campus. Meanwhile, the Hopkinsians or Consistent Calvinists, followers of Samuel Hopkins, a disciple of Jonathan Edwards, were also planning a school to perpetuate their system of doctrine. After prolonged negotiations, the orthodox Calvinists and the Hopkinsians agreed to establish one theological school that would have representatives of both factions on its faculty. The founders established a complicated system of governance, designed to preserve the power of both groups. For legal purposes, the school was under the Trustees of Phillips Academy, who had full fiduciary responsibilities, including the right to hire the faculty. In addition, the Hopkinsians secured a Board of Visitors, composed of three members, who had the responsibility of overseeing the theological and moral conduct of the professors on the Associate Foundation. All faculty were initially bound to the Westminster standards. In addition, the founders required those on the Associate (Hopkinsian) Foundation to subscribe to an additional confessional statement, known as the Andover Creed, that contained the principal points of Consistent Calvinist doctrine.

When the Theological Institute in Phillips Academy opened in 1808, the school succeeded beyond everyone's expectations. Instead of the expected handful of candidates, the school founded itself with a growing student body that soon numbered 100. As its early faculty struggled with this success, they filled out the founder's vision of the school. Under its powerful systematic theologians Leonard Woods and Edwards Amasa Park, the Andover school was a center for rigorous Hopkinsianism or Consistent Calvinism. Both Woods and Park labored to fill in the details of the system created by Jonathan Edwards and Samuel Hopkins. But at the same time, such teachers as Moses Stuart, who was deeply influenced by European biblical studies, made the school a leader in scriptural exegesis and Semitic languages. Further, the school's students and faculty helped establish the American Board of Commissioners for Foreign Missions, the largest and arguably best of the nineteenth-century sending agencies. Andover supplied almost half of the total number of American missionaries that served before the Civil War and a healthy proportion thereafter.

Janus-like, Andover faced in two directions. Seen from one perspective, the foundations of the school were very narrow. The founding documents bound the faculty to a narrow confessionalism, and the Associate faculty members subscribed an even narrower creed every five years. This school was a citadel of orthodoxy, perched on Zion's hill. Yet, from another view, Andover was a remarkably free institution, open to the newest currents of scholarly thought at home and abroad. Early on the school developed ties to leading German scholars and collected their works in its library. The school's press, located nearby, published grammars and lexicons for the principal Semitic languages. Disputes arose early between those who considered the school from these two different perspectives.

The school dismissed the irascible James Murdoch, who appealed his case to the state courts (7 Pick. 303 1829). A dispute over subscription, the Norris Case, resulted in the Associate (Hopkinsian) faculty having to subscribe only to the Creed and ending their requirement to subscribe to the Westminster documents (12 Mass. 546). Other controversies did not lead to court action. Critics questioned Moses Stuart's orthodoxy, even as he sought to defend the faith against Unitarianism. In the 1840s, Daniel Dana publicly accused Edwards Amasa Park of departing from the Associate Creed, although little came of it except embarrassment.

The rhythm of faculty appointments at Andover was similar to that of other nineteenth-century seminaries. Boards looked for young people at the beginning of their careers and expected them to stay for their whole career. The advantages of this system were many. Since American graduate education was in its infancy, faculty members could use their early years at a school to teach themselves their subjects, and popular teachers could develop a popular following. In 1880, when Edwards Amasa Park retired, he was only the second person to hold the Abbot chair. Since most faculty members began their service together in their twenties, they often retired within a few years of each other as older persons. Thus, schools changed almost overnight. This pattern of appointment also meant that when faculty changes did occur, the seminary often skipped a whole generation of thought and reflection. A school's public, consequently, might see evolutionary changes in the development of thought as theological and institutional revolutions.

THE BIRTH OF A NEW THEOLOGY

Unfortunately, the generation that was skipped at Andover was a remarkably fruitful one. During the 1850s and 1860s, the tendency of American scholars to look toward Germany for models became more pronounced. The nineteenth-century German university blended teaching and research in such a way as to make possible considerable intellectual advance. The progress of biblical studies demonstrated the productivity of the new professional scholarship. By 1870, German scholars had replaced the traditional understanding of such issues as the authorship and date of particular books with a new critical canon. The newer biblical studies passed almost unconsciously into the American scholarly mainstream. When Charles Augustus Briggs* published his monumental *Biblical Study* in 1883, he was seemingly unaware of how far he had traveled from traditional biblical orthodoxy. The same unconscious process was true of other advanced critics in this same decade.

Simultaneously, other theological changes occurred. German theologian Isaac Dorner, who had inherited Schleiermacher's mantle as the leader of the mediating school, was especially popular with visiting Americans, including Newman Smyth,* who translated his teacher's works for American readers. Dorner was a thoroughgoing Romantic who believed that Christianity had developed organically since the time of the apostles. Hence, the original kernel of Christian faith was always generating new doctrinal and institutional forms. Dorner was also noted for two theological innovations. In his Christology, Dorner argued for a thoroughly kenotic position that maintained that Christ set aside such divine powers as omniscience and omnipotence during Jesus' earthly life. Hence, Jesus shared the common assumptions of his day about such matters as physical causation and such human limitations as ignorance of the future. Dorner also taught the controversial doctrine that God might give those who did not have a chance to confess Christ in their earthly life an opportunity to do so in the life to come.

In America, most theologians were more directly indebted to Horace Bushnell,* pastor of the North Church in Hartford. Bushnell studied theology at Yale under Nathaniel Taylor, but he had deep doubts about the validity of traditional theology. During a period of deep despair, Bushnell read English Romantic Samuel Taylor Coleridge and found his faith reborn. Bushnell's religion, however, was far from orthodox. The Hartford pastor believed that religious language was inherently symbolic and, hence, that a theologian might reconcile even the most apparently contradictory propositions by taking a more comprehensive view of their meaning. Anthropology was one area where such a comprehensive view was possible. In his *Christian Nurture* (1847), Bushnell argued that few Christians needed to pass through an agonizing conversion since the influence of a Christian family and government would lead them naturally to faith. The Atonement was another. In his *Vicarious Sacrifice* (1866), Bushnell argued that Christ's solidarity with humankind was at the heart of his mission. For many, however, the most important contribution that the Sage of Hartford made was to recast theology in an optative mood and make it a vehicle for hope.

In his early career, Andover's Edwards Amasa Park sought a middle ground between traditional doctrine and these innovations in his "Theology of the Intellect and of the Feelings" (1850). As he aged, Park became more opposed to the new directions. After 1860, he spent much of his time railing against these doctrinal innovations in alliance with Enoch Pond of Bangor, George Broadman of Chicago, and Israel Dwinell of Pacific Theological Seminary. It was a losing battle. Congregationalists installed Theodore Munger, among the most able liberals, in North Adams, Massachusetts, in 1877, and the new theology clearly influenced such younger Andover faculty as Egbert Smyth. When Park retired in 1881, he was thoroughly committed to an antiliberal position.

NEWMAN SMYTH'S ELECTION

In 1881 the Andover Trustees elected Newman Smyth as Park's successor in the Abbot professorship. Smyth, the brother of Egbert Smyth, Andover's professor of church history, was among the most advanced Congregational theologians. He had spent two years in Germany studying at the Universities of Berlin and Halle. Smyth's two recent books, *Old Faiths in a New Light* (1879) and *The Orthodox Theology of To-day* (1883), both advocated the new theology and argued that the old theology was less than Christian. The two studies, however, also demonstrated that Newman Smyth was among the most capable theological writers in America. The books were skillfully written and carefully researched.

Smyth's appointment became part of the debate over second probation or the belief that those who had never heard of Christ would have a chance to believe in him after death. Many supporters of missions believed that this new doctrine would remove the primary motive behind the missionary movement. The appointment went to the Visitors, where some members raised serious questions about Smyth's election. Although the Visitors apparently expected the Trustees to withdraw the nomination, the Trustees stood firm. Forced to act, the Visitors finally did so but in an unclear fashion. While the Visitors found Smyth orthodox, they turned down his appointment because Smyth "seems to conceive of thought poetically rather than speculatively" and, hence, would not be an effective teacher. The justification was weak. Smyth's problem was not his vagueness; instead, he was clear, all too clear, on the issues in dispute.

The rejection of Smyth drew a line in the sand. The Andover Trustees, who were primarily governors of a boy's academy, may not have understood the theological issues involved. Yet they were deeply aware of the need for academic freedom and intellectual quality. Consequently, they began to raise money for a new chair of apologetics that would not be on the Associate Foundation and, hence, not subject to the veto of the Visitors. Before the Trustees could arrange this appointment, Newman Smyth accepted the pastorate of the Center Church in New Haven, where he served until his retirement in 1908. Smyth became the nation's leading theological interpreter of science and an ecumenical pioneer.

THE CONTROVERSY DEEPENS

The Trustees countered the rejection of Smyth by electing George Harris in his place in 1882. Harris, while a lesser intellect than Newman Smyth, held many of the same theological opinions, especially on such topics as second probation, and no one accused him of Romantic fantasies. The Visitors, blocked in by their declaration that Smyth was orthodox, had no choice but to confirm Harris. But the controversy did not end with this action. Park answered Harris's inaugural address with a 96-page refutation and began to work behind the scenes to advise those who were dissatisfied with the appointment. Park's study of the Associate Creed of the Seminary, published in 1883, affirmed that no one could subscribe to both the Creed and the new theology. One year later, Park published *A Declaration of Faith, Written on Request of the Pilgrim Congregational Church*, which highlighted the fundamental theological doctrines that he believed the new theologians ignored or denied.

The Andover faculty was not idle either. In 1884 they began the publication of a monthly, the *Andover Review*, designed to set forth their interpretation of current religious and intellectual issues. The *Review*, clearly a replacement for Park's *Bibliotheca Sacra*, was frankly polemical. When the editors were asked whether they would accept articles by either James Freeman Clarke, the noted Unitarian writer on world religions, or William G. T. Shedd, a leading conservative scholar, they replied negatively. The primary focus of each issue of the *Review* was the editorial that addressed a particular issue from the faculty's perspective. In 1889 the faculty published *Progressive Orthodoxy*, a collection of the most representative of these editorials.

THE TRIAL ITSELF

The 1886 charges against the five faculty members were a conservative counterattack on the authors and editors of the *Review*. The actual process was messy, perhaps reflecting the difficulty of both sides in holding a heresy trial near the end of the nineteenth century. With both sides represented by distinguished counsel, the procedures began with demands for the clarification of the charges and for an explicit statement of the authority of the Visitors over the procedures. The hearing on the substance of the charges began on 28 December 1886 and lasted until 3 January 1887.

The central issue was the meaning of subscription to the Andover Creed. Interestingly enough, since one purpose of the Creed was to confound the Unitarian heresy, the defense argued that the Creed was a progressive document that pointed toward the future perfection of theology as a science. They argued that the reason that the founders made the Creed unchangeable was to prevent retrogression to an earlier stage of theological reflection! A far more cogent approach was the frank statement that the Creed could not be taken that literally in the present. Professor William Jewitt Tucker reminded the Visitors that when he had signed the Creed, he had said: "The Creed which I am about to read, and to which I shall subscribe, I fully accept as setting forth the truth against the errors which it was designed to meet. No confession so elaborate, and with such intent may assume to be the final expression of truth, or an expression equally fitted in language or tone to all times" (Tucker, *My Generation*, 210).

The complainants did not stress the doctrine of second probation, despite its prominence in the contemporary press. Instead, Joshua Wellman, who spoke for the Committee of Alumni, stressed the question of biblical authority. Wellman was particularly upset by an article in the *Review*—"The Bible as a Theme for the Pulpit"—that argued that ministers should gradually introduce their congregations to their advanced thinking about the Bible to avoid controversy. Although Wellman was careful not to charge the faculty with urging ministers to save their positions, even at the cost of their honor, he inferred it. Wellman did not understand the article's intent. Egbert Smyth, its author, believed that he was cautioning pastors to avoid harsh and undiplomatic expositions of the new scholarship. Although Wellman's implicit charge of duplicity missed the mark, he had a point. The new theologians were not always forthcoming about the implications of their theological changes, and they may not have realized the full implications of some of their positions.

The trial ended on a strange note that lacks explanation. The Visitors found Egbert Smyth, the president of the faculty as well as its intellectual leader, guilty and found the rest innocent. The rumor was that Julius Steelye, the chair of the Visitors and president of Amherst College, wanted to find all the accused innocent, while Joshua Marshall of Lowell had wanted to find them all guilty. In this scenario, William T. Eustus had refused to vote except on the one case where he was physically present to hear the arguments of both sides. Since the only one that Eustus had heard was Smyth, he voted for Smyth's conviction.

This explanation sounds both too simple and too complicated. The Visitors had approved all the accused faculty earlier, and nothing that they had said or done had happened in a corner. If they were guilty in 1887, they were guilty in 1883 or 1884 as well, and the Board had not acted then. One suspects (although without any evidence) that the Visitors may have wanted a test case to establish their authority and to determine the legally binding nature of the Creed. Since Smyth immediately appealed to the Massachusetts Supreme Court, as he had the right to do under the Andover documents, this was, in any event, the result of their decision.

The years between the trial and the appellate decision were filled with controversy in New England. In some ways, the case of William Noyes eclipsed the trial of his teachers. Noyes graduated from Andover Seminary in 1887, and shortly thereafter, the American Board turned him down for missionary appointment because of his views on second probation. Noyes became the assistant pastor at the Berkeley Avenue Congregational Church, an institutional church with close ties to Andover Seminary. While serving, he so impressed the congregation with his devotion to missions that they called an ecclesiastical council, ordained him as a missionary, and sent him to Japan without the support of the American Board. Noyes periodically applied for support until the Board accepted him in 1893.

The formal adjudication of the appeal did not occur until 1891, perhaps because the judges were waiting for public opinion to form. In many ways, the court's final decision was almost a refusal to rule on the substantial issues. Although they upheld the Visitor's right to try Smyth for violating the Creed, they sent the case back to the Visitors because the Trustees, who hired Smyth and paid his salary, had not been represented by legal counsel. Although the Visitors held a second trial in 1892, the situation was different. The emotions that had fueled the original trial had dissipated, and the membership of the Board of Visitors had changed. The Board dismissed the charges against Smyth without prejudice to him or to their right to judge whether a professor taught in harmony with the Associate Creed.

THE AFTERMATH OF THE TRIAL

The trial and appeal did not stay the course of reform at Andover. Part of the Andover tradition had been that the structure of theological education depended on a school's theological affirmations, and the new faculty shared that assumption. Originally, Andover's faculty had required a year or part of a year for an intense study of each of the theological disciplines. Thus, students studied the Bible in the first year, systematic theology in the second, and church history and preaching in the third. In 1871–1872, the seminary shifted to a program that had the students studying each discipline during each academic year. The Andover faculty moved from this form steadily toward individual courses with assigned credits—similar to the pattern in universities. Further, they took advantage of the freedom that the course system permitted to introduce a limited elective system and a graduate program. Since the new theology stressed the presence of God within human life and experience, the elective program came to include courses in sociology and ethics. The new curriculum expanded the biblical program, traditionally tied to a rigorous program of Greek and Hebrew exegesis, to include work in biblical archeology, biblical history, and biblical theology. Further, the school made some tentative beginnings toward a program of field education. These changes recast theological education. Where the earlier theological program sought to make its students masters of a fixed body of divinity, the new Andover curriculum aimed at the mission of the church to the world. In terms of method, the new course of studies was a movement from erudition to research.

The changes in the curriculum reflect one of the deeper issues in the Andover trial. The older picture of the professional as the person of erudition who was able to recall the details of a subject or text was giving way to the ideal of the professional able to apply knowledge in a given area. In higher education, the real professional was the researcher who could add to the world's body of knowledge. Likewise, in ministry, the real professional was the person who could apply the gospel to concrete human situations. If the Andover liberals won their case in part because of the willingness of people to recognize their academic expertise, their curriculum was an attempt to extend similar professional thinking to the work of the ministry.

The effect of the trial on Andover Seminary is hard to determine. Despite the high quality of its academic program, the school's enrollment went into decline. In 1908, Andover Seminary moved to Cambridge, where it affiliated with the Harvard Divinity School. When the Boards of these two schools proposed a formal merger in 1922, determined opposition and future court cases led to the dissolution of the Harvard connection. In 1931, Andover affiliated with Newton, a Baptist seminary in suburban Boston.

BIBLIOGRAPHY

An Historical Statement, a Careful Summary of the Arguments of the Respondent Professors, and the Full Text of the Arguments of the Complainants and Their Council: Together with the Decision of the Board of Visitors, Furnishing the Nearest Available Approach to a Complete History of the Whole Matter. Boston: Stanley and Usher, 1887.

Meyerhoff, Stephen. "Andover Seminary: The Rise and Fall of an Evangelical Institution." The Presbyterian 8 (1982): 13–24.

Rowe, Henry. History of Andover Seminary. Newton, MA: Andover-Newton, 1933.

Smyth, Egbert Coffin. In the Matter of the Complaint against Egbert C. Smyth and

Others, Professors of the Theological Institution in Phillips Academy, Andover. The Andover Defense. Defense of Professor Smyth, Arguments of Professor Theodore W. Dwight, with the Statements of Professors Tucker, Harris, Hincks, and Churchill. Boston: Cupples, Upham & Company, 1887.

Thompson, J. Earl. "The Andover Liberals as Theological Educators." *Andover-Newton Theological Quarterly* 8 (March 1968): 202–222.

Tucker, William Jewitt. *My Generation: An Autobiographical Interpretation.* Boston: Houghton Mifflin Company, 1919.

Wellman, Joshua. "The Question at Issue in the Andover Case. Arguments of Rev. Dr. Joshua W. Wellman and Orpheus T. Lanphear, complainants in the Andover Case." Prepared for the hearing before the Board of Visitors, 1 September 1892.

Williams, Daniel Day. *The Andover Liberals: A Study in American Theology.* New York: Octagon Books, 1970.

Glenn T. Miller

Albert Barnes
(1798–1870)

In the late 1820s, the Presbyterian Church began to debate the usage and theology of the "new measures" being used by revivalists in the Ohio Valley and western New York, who became known as "New School" Presbyterians. Since the Presbyterian Church is a voluntary organization, some tolerance for doctrinal differences had developed. To settle disputes over doctrine, the Presbyterians turned to the one thing they could agree on: polity. Although there were more famous revival preachers, Albert Barnes became the focus of the debate in the New Jersey–Pennsylvania area. This entry will explore the background and circumstances that led to the "Old School" Presbyterians' trial of Barnes for heresy twice.

EARLY YEARS

Albert Barnes was born in Rome, New York, on 1 December 1798, the son of a local businessman ("Life and Labors," 1). His father is variously listed as being a tanner, mechanic, or gentleman farmer (Barnes, *Three-Score and Ten*, 57). Barnes recalls his heritage as having parents who were "virtuous and industrious, and entered on my course [in life] with the advantage which was to be derived from their counsels and example" (Barnes, *Three-Score*, 28–29). Albert attended the local school, then entered Fairfield Academy to prepare for a legal career ("Life and Labors," 1). He read widely and became intellectually convinced of the truth of Christianity as a moral system. Later he transferred to Hamilton College, where he was converted during his senior year. "A classmate, recently converted, stated to me in simple words, and with no appeal to me personally, his own feelings on the subject of religion, described the change which had occurred in his mind, and left me. His words went to my heart" (Barnes, *Three-Score*, 63). This experience convinced Barnes that intellectual assent was not true religion. A deeper conviction was necessary to save the soul. One of the great aims of his ministry became leading intellectuals to a "better foundation of hope" and securing their eternal destiny (Barnes, *Three-Score*, 64).

Albert enrolled in Princeton Seminary, bastion of the "Old School" Presbyterians. He was licensed to preach on 23 April 1823, following completion of his studies. Barnes's ordination took place when he was installed as pastor of the Presbyterian Church in Morristown, New Jersey ("Life and Labors," 3). He would spend five years laboring in this parish, gaining preaching and pastoral skills.

Two incidents were influential in Barnes's development while he pastored in Morristown. He heard some of the revival preachers while visiting friends in the northern part of the state. This moved him to pursue a different type of preaching as he tried to reach the intellectuals in his parish.

The second incident came as Albert sought materials for the Sabbath schools. He found a lack of plain and simple commentary that could be used by teachers. He had begun preparing brief notes on Matthew's gospel when he learned that the Rev. James Alexander, of Trenton, New Jersey, was doing similar work for the American Sunday-School Union. Due to Alexander's delicate health, he turned the project over to Barnes (Barnes, *Three-Score*, 52). Albert thus began his long writing career by seeking to meet a need he perceived in his parish. Many of his works remain in print today as *Barnes' Notes on the New Testament*. Barnes was content with preaching, pastoring, and writing in Morristown.

FIRST PRESBYTERIAN CHURCH, PHILADELPHIA

Southwest of Morristown was the major metropolis of Philadelphia, with its historic roots as the center of Presbyterianism. The Rev. James Wilson had pastored the First Presbyterian Church in Philadelphia for 20 years. Several bouts of ill health caused Wilson to take some extended time away from parish duties. The country air did not restore his vigor, and he tried to resign as pastor. The congregation did not accept his resignation (Wilson, "Letters"). With his health failing, Wilson wrote to the Session, requesting they secure a copastor. Wilson was willing to serve in a subordinate position and at little or no salary (Wilson, "Letters").

The position of pastor was offered to several leading preachers. Each refused to come to First Church due to doubts about leaving their present positions. These disappointments were followed by a series of ministers declining even to fill the pulpit for a Sunday preaching engagement at First Church.

Desperation appeared in the form of letters and petitions to the Session over the preaching. Wilson was clearly unable to continue much longer, and pulpit supply prospects were very thin. It was during this time that Albert Barnes came to the attention of the Session. After soliciting several letters of recommendation, they contacted him and found him agreeable to moving. A congregational meeting was held on 22 March 1830, during which the letters were read and Barnes was elected pastor, without ever having preached before them. There were 55 members present; 54 members voted for Barnes ("Session Minutes"). Barnes would be installed as pastor on 25 June 1830 while Wilson gratefully retired to the country. The congregation would stand united behind Albert Barnes in the next six years as he was tried for heresy (Barnes, *Three-Score*, 33).

"THE WAY OF SALVATION"

In keeping with the revival style of preaching and his own desire to reach the intelligentsia, Albert Barnes had preached a sermon on salvation before the Morristown church on 8 February 1829. The reactions were so positive that Barnes decided to expand and publish the sermon to provide in one place "the leading doctrines of the Bible respecting God's way of saving men" (Barnes, *Salvation*, ix). He claimed no originality, seeking only to provide a skeletal outline emphasizing both the sovereignty of God and the duty of humanity to unqualified surrender to God (Barnes, *Salvation*, x).

The sermon received wide circulation in New Jersey and Pennsylvania. It probably was read by the search committee of First Church, Philadelphia. It was definitely read by Charles Hodge, Ashbel Green, and others connected with Princeton Seminary. These Old School men were displeased with the doctrinal exposition Barnes had given. They took no action until Barnes was issued the call to First Church, Philadelphia.

The call would need the approval of the Philadelphia Presbytery, of which Ashbel Green was a member. He sought to prevent Barnes's transfer and installation, being joined by 12 other members of the Presbytery. In typical Presbyterian fashion, Green fought against Barnes's doctrine through polity maneuvers. Green claimed it was improper to approve the call since Barnes had never preached before the congregation and only 50 of the 220 members had voted for it. He raised the further problem of erroneous doctrine contained in the sermon that supported his call ("Complaint," 2–4).

FIRST HERESY TRIALS

The Philadelphia Presbytery debated whether it was proper to question someone doctrinally prior to admission into the Presbytery. The first vote taken permitted the reading of the sermon and doctrinal debate. Later in the day, the Presbytery found that it had acted too quickly. They decided they first should admit Reverend Barnes, then allow Dr. Green to proceed with charges of unsound faith. This action was promptly appealed to the Synod by Green and the other 12 men as an infringement of their rights as Presbyters ("Complaint," 8–13).

The Synod of Philadelphia took up Barnes's case at its meeting in Lancaster on 29 October 1830. Barnes was allowed to explain and defend his sermon in answer to five charges of heresy. The charges were: (1) denying the fundamental doctrine of original sin; (2) holding Atonement sentiments in direct opposition to doctrinal standards (i.e., Westminster Confession); (3) attributing too much to human ability; (4) omitting justification by the imputed righteousness of Christ; and (5) lack of adherence to Presbyterian standards (*Answer*, 53–82).

In his defense, Barnes carefully considered each charge as it applied to the sermon "The Way of Salvation." He laid out detailed arguments refuting the charges made by Dr. Green. Barnes showed he believed in original sin, the Atonement, and justification by Christ's righteousness. Although he disagreed with Green's interpretation of the doctrinal and Presbyterian standards, Barnes demonstrated how he in fact held those tenets, albeit in different terms than the Old School and Dr. Green (*Answer*, 51–89). Barnes relied heavily upon the diversity allowed within the Presbyterian polity for his justification.

The Synod found Albert Barnes guilty of the charges. The case was then appealed to the General Assembly in 1831. Once again, the Presbyterians dealt with doctrinal squabbles by appeals to polity issues. The Assembly first referred the case to its Judicial Committee. The committee did not resolve the substantive issues. Instead, it proposed a procedure for hearing the case by the whole Assembly. The entire record of the Presbytery trial was read before the Assembly and discussed. After listening for two days, the Assembly was ready to vote. However, it decided instead to refer the entire matter to a select committee (1831 *Minutes of the General Assembly*, 319ff). The members of the committee and other actions of the Assembly favored the Old School party. It is likely the Old School felt a turning of the Assembly members and were concerned that they were going to be defeated. Thus, taking the polity route, they moved again to refer the case out to a select committee. This gained time, and the Old School party still had another chance to convince a small group that Barnes's sermon was heretical.

The select committee worked over the weekend and returned with resolutions Monday afternoon. They felt it was unnecessary for the Assembly to go into the various minute details of the case. Instead, three resolutions were proposed: (1) Barnes's sermon had some unguarded and objectionable passages, but Barnes had given satisfactory explanations. The Presbytery "ought to have suffered the whole to pass without further notice." (2) The Presbytery of Philadelphia should suspend further proceedings against Albert Barnes. (3) To promote peace in the Philadelphia Presbytery, it should be divided into parts (1831 *Minutes of the General Assembly*, 329). The resolutions passed, and the Assembly gave thanks in prayer for the harmonious end of the case, although it would be another year before the Philadelphia Presbytery was divided (1832 *Minutes of the General Assembly*, 361).

BARNES IN PHILADELPHIA

Albert Barnes was relatively young (31 years old) when he became pastor at the First Church. While still trying to settle into his pastoral duties, he became almost immediately the focus of the Old School–New School debate. One source of support for Barnes was the inherited goodwill from the previous pastor, James Wilson, and the pastoral relationship with the congregation. Barnes's opinions were readily endorsed, and Wilson acted as mentor to the young pastor. The congregation drew around him in a united front until the trials were resolved in his favor. Barnes eventually saw the General Assembly give sanction to the views for which he struggled (Barnes, *Three-Score and Ten*, 32–34).

While national debates swirled around him, Barnes found time to continue working on the "Notes," which were his commentaries for Sunday school teachers. Each day he would arise before 6:00 A.M. and write. Stopping at 9:00 A.M., Albert would take up his pastoral duties, having already put in a solid three hours in his study. Thus, working steadily, Barnes would write commentaries on the entire New Testament and five Old Testament books. His published works would amount to 1 million volumes in circulation before his death. He attributed his ability to work to a divine guidance of his life and a simple response to pastoral needs (Barnes, *Three-Score and Ten*, 63–65).

Albert Barnes also grew close to the people in his congregation. He exhorted them to be active in their community. One particular passion he shared with them was the temperance movement. He had made a decision early in his ministry to refrain from any drink and to urge temperance upon his congregation (Barnes, *Three-Score*, 38–46). He preached on the subject, wrote pamphlets, and engaged in public debate wherever the opportunities presented themselves. It was a cause that would suffer defeat toward the end of his pastorate in 1859 (Barnes, *Three-Score*, 46–47). Barnes's greatest success was the production of his commentaries.

"NOTES ON ROMANS"

Albert Barnes had begun writing about the Book of Romans in November 1826 (Barnes, "Notes"). He sensed the need for congregational material on the New Testament. No printed material being available, Barnes began making notations verse by verse with the intention of publishing it for Sunday schools (Barnes, *Three-Score*, 52). Although these early "Notes" were never published, they reflect the preliminary systematic thinking of Barnes on Romans.

Beginning in 1826 through 1828, Albert Barnes was wrestling with the concepts for which he would later be tried. He did not adopt the Princetonian position that the Old School held and wanted declared as the sole orthodox position for the Presbyterian Church. Barnes did, however, remain within the pale of Presbyterian orthodoxy, holding such views as: (1) justification is more than simple pardon for sin; (2) humans can only do good through divine grace and mercy; and (3) faith comes from the heart as well as the intellect. Barnes based his interpretation upon exegesis of the Scriptures. He sought to follow the same method Charles Hodge was using. His alleged heresy was the result of coming to different conclusions than the Princetonians.

The political maneuvering of the Old School against Barnes continued as they carefully reviewed his published material. With the "Notes" on Romans, they found enough substance to undertake a second heresy trial. It was anticipated that the doctrines set forth in the "Notes" could be openly debated without reference to Barnes himself or any nuance he might make on the offensive passages (Stansbury, *Trial*, 154). The prosecution was undertaken by the Rev. Dr. George Junkin, president of Lafayette College, Philadelphia. Junkin felt justified in bringing heresy charges since the 1831 General Assembly had found Barnes's sermon "unguarded and objectionable" (Junkin, *Vindication*, 11). Junkin saw the "Notes" as holding the same unguarded and objectionable views as the earlier sermon.

George Junkin accused Albert Barnes of heresy on ten points from his "Notes" on Romans. Junkin first notified Barnes of his disagreements in a letter informing him of the intention to press charges. Barnes replied promptly, only to find Junkin had already filed charges (Stansbury, *Trial*, 95). The Second Presbytery of Philadelphia held a trial considering the heresy charges at length. Since the Second Presbytery was entirely New School men, it is not surprising that Barnes was found innocent of heresy in June 1835 (*Appendix*).

In a twist of polity, Junkin promptly appealed to the Synod of Philadelphia, where he was a member, although the Second Presbytery and Albert Barnes were at the time part of the Synod of Delaware. The Synod of Philadelphia took up the case in October and considered first the polity question of its jurisdiction in the matter. Finding that the Delaware Synod had been dissolved between the Presbytery trial and this Synod's meeting, it decided it did have jurisdiction to hear the case. Barnes did not agree and stated he would appeal to the next General Assembly (Stansbury, *Trial*, 28–35). The Synod of Philadelphia, made up primarily of Old School men, ignored Barnes's statement and proceeded to trial despite the polity problems raised by Barnes and other New School members.

During this trial before the Synod of Philadelphia in October 1835, Albert Barnes claimed that any offensive language in his "Notes" on Romans was inadvertent on his part. From a polity standpoint, Barnes argued that he should not be tried for heresy when there was no intention on his part to write in language that might be offensive to others. He also argued that Junkin had not come to him with the alleged errors prior to filing charges and allowed him the opportunity of correction (Stansbury, *Trial*, 95).

Quotations taken by Junkin in his prosecution are from the 1834 edition of Barnes's "Notes," which was the third edition (Stansbury, *Trial*, 94). During the Synod trial, Barnes initially offered his fourth edition as proof of his willingness to alter the offensive language (Stansbury, *Trial*, 67). As discussion progressed in the trial, Barnes withdrew the offer of the new edition and ultimately refused to be tried by the Synod on procedural grounds (Stansbury, *Trial*, 69). The Second Presbytery, which conducted the original trial on the "Notes" on Romans, then refused to turn over their minutes to the Synod when demanded at the trial (Stansbury, *Trial*, 39). After lengthy debate the Synod again decided to continue with the trial de novo.

There were ten charges George Junkin made before both the Second Presbytery and the Synod. According to both sides, the charges presented by Junkin at the Synod trial were exactly the same as those presented at the Second Presbytery's trial (Stansbury, *Trial*, 64). The first, third, and fourth charges relate to human ability and sinful actions. Junkin accused Barnes of holding that sin is voluntary, that people are able to keep God's commandments, and that faith is an intellectual act of the mind. The second, fifth, sixth, and seventh charges revolve around Barnes's views of Adam's relationship to people today. It was claimed he held that Adam was ignorant of the possible effects of his sin, that Adam was not the federal head nor was his sin imputed to his descendants, and that humans are not guilty because of Adam's sin. The eighth charge asserts that Barnes denied that Christ suffered the penalty for human sins. The ninth and tenth charges accuse Barnes of heresy due to his views on justification. Junkin claimed Barnes denied that Christ's righteousness was imputed for human justification and that justification meant simply a divine pardon (Stansbury, *Trial*, 103–152).

In his written defense, which was presented at the Second Presbytery's trial, Barnes gave a detailed response to the charges. Barnes held a defined role for the Holy Spirit prior to any human action or ability. Only after the releasing of the bonds of sin by the Holy Spirit can a person respond to an invitation to put one's faith and trust in Jesus Christ. Contrary to Junkin's charges, Barnes did not hold faith as solely an act of the mind; divine intervention and heart faith are also necessary.

Adam's imputed sin was another area of contention for Junkin. Barnes held that human freedom allowed God to hold humans accountable for sin that they commit, even when they do not have the ability to act otherwise. Barnes thus wanted to maintain the tension between the free will of people and the sovereignty of God. "But liberty is a negative idea and must be admitted to render man accountable, whilst he is dependent for every good. God as a sovereign may give or withhold and is holy, wise and just" (Barnes, "Notes," chap. 9, v. 11). Junkin's charge against Barnes was grounded in the concept that Barnes held that humans could choose not to sin, contrary to the Old School doctrine of imputation of Adam's sin. Barnes took the other side, contending that humans only do good when God chooses. The choice rests solidly with God in his sovereignty and not in any human capacity.

Junkin drew evidence from Barnes's "Notes" on Romans, which showed disbelief in the doctrine of penal substitution by Christ. Junkin wanted this view of the Atonement because it showed the injustice of Christ's death and thus its supreme value (Stansbury, *Trial*, 143–145). Barnes argued instead for an Atonement theory that attributes Christ's merit earned in dying on the cross (Stansbury, *Trial*, 238–245). While these Atonement theories are different, both had been held to be within orthodoxy for the Presbyterian Church. Junkin and the Old School wanted only penal substitution Atonement held as orthodox.

Junkin's charge about justification as only pardon and not re-creation was refuted in Barnes's analysis of Romans, chapter 3. Barnes made the claim that Romans was arguing to two different audiences: Gentiles and Jews. Barnes asserted that the Gentiles are *not* wholly excused by ignorance, and the privileges of the Jews did not offer a defense (Barnes, "Notes," chap. 3, v. 26). Thus, he denied Junkin's charge of justification being simply pardon. Both Jews and Gentiles needed to be made new creatures through justification; pardon was insufficient to restore human ability to be righteous.

The Synod of Philadelphia did not hear Barnes's defense, although they did call upon Barnes to present it. He had left the meeting and would not return for procedural and tactical reasons: Wanting to preserve his right of appeal on the jurisdictional issue, he did not want to remain and possibly waive his rights. The Synod asked if someone else would defend Barnes, and no one came forward (Stansbury, *Trial*, 152). After a roll call discussion, the vote was taken, and Barnes was found guilty of heresy on all Junkin's charges (Stansbury, *Trial*, 237).

1836 GENERAL ASSEMBLY

Albert Barnes promptly appealed the Synod's decision to the General Assembly of 1836. As grounds for the appeal, he cited primarily polity errors: no jurisdiction, parole testimony, insufficient evidence, and lack of method for retraction of his erroneous views. Barnes also included substantive issues of justice, personal harm to himself, and the chilling effect this decision would have upon other ministers.

The 1836 Assembly took up the appeal and complaint of Albert Barnes and the Synod of Philadelphia during its fourth day of business. The entire proceedings of the Synod trial were read over the next two days. The Assembly then voted to hear Barnes's defense as published, despite protests by Junkin and the committee defending the Synod of Philadelphia. They also heard Barnes orally for parts of three days on why the verdict of the Synod should be overturned. Dr. Junkin then replied with his arguments in favor of the Synod decision. A roll call vote was held that acquitted Albert Barnes of heresy 134 to 96 (1836 *Minutes of the General Assembly*, 251–68).

One of the direct results of this acquittal was that the Old School would organize for the 1837 General Assembly. They met a week prior to the Assembly and plotted their strategy. The 1837 Assembly would take action against the New School men, excising them from the Presbyterian Church. Again, the ground of attack was polity. The Plan of Union from 1801 was disavowed and four Synods dissolved. The Old School had mustered a majority sufficient to "kick out" over 40 percent of the Presbyterian Church. The split in the church would last through the Civil War until 1869. Even then, the reunion of the Old and New Schools could not be accomplished until Albert Barnes withdrew his commentary series from the official publishing house of the Presbyterian Church.

BIBLIOGRAPHY

Answer to the Protest against the Leave Granted by the Presbytery of Philadelphia to the First Presbyterian Church to Prosecute a Call for Mr. Barnes to Become Their Pastor. New York: Leavitt, Lord, & Co., 1836.

Appendix to the Book of Records of Second Presbytery of Philadelphia. By Thomas Eustace, Stated Clerk. 30 June 1835. This *Appendix* contains the final judgment in Barnes's heresy trial in 1835 before the Second Presbytery. The Department of History, Presbyterian Church (USA), also holds the minutes of a different Second Presbytery of Philadelphia that was created by the Synod after the General Assembly created its Second Presbytery in 1832 on the basis of affinity to certain theological tenets.

Barnes, Albert. "Advertisement to the First Edition." *The Way of Salvation.* New York: Leavitt, Lord & Co., 1836.

———. *Life at Three-Score.* Philadelphia: Parry and McMillan, 1859.

———. *Life at Three-Score and Ten.* Philadelphia: Henry B. Ashmead, Book and Job Printer, 1869.

———. "Notes on Theological Subjects from the Book of Romans, 1827–28." Presently held by the Presbyterian Department of History. These are two small notebooks, approximately 3½" × 5". They are handwritten beginning November 1826. The manuscript pages are not numbered; however, there are notations as to which verse Barnes is writing about. The inside front cover has notations about the authorship, date, place, and so on of the letter to the Romans.

"Complaint Re: Albert Barnes." Handwritten manuscript signed by Ashbel Green and others, held by the Department of History, Presbyterian Church (USA), Philadelphia.

Hodge, Charles. *Systematic Theology*. Grand Rapids: Wm. Eerdmans, 1940.

Junkin, George. *Vindication, Containing a History of the Trial of the Rev. Albert Barnes, by the Second Presbytery, and by the Synod of Philadelphia*. Philadelphia: Wm. S. Martien, 1836.

"Life and Labors of Rev. Albert Barnes with Some of His Views on Temperance and Slavery; Also Poetic Tributes to This Illustrious Personality." No author is listed on this typed manuscript dated 1870, held by the Department of History, Presbyterian Church (USA), Philadelphia.

Memorial Services on the Occasion of the Death of Rev. Albert Barnes. Philadelphia: Jas. B. Rodgers, Co., 1871. Address by Rev. Wm. B. Stevens. Pamphlet held by the Department of History, Presbyterian Church (USA), Philadelphia.

Minutes of the General Assembly of the Presbyterian Church in the United States of America. Philadelphia: Presbyterian Board of Publication, 1821–1837.

"Session Minutes, 1807–1909." April–June 1829. Record Group 35, box 1, folder 11, held by the Department of History, Presbyterian Church (USA), Philadelphia.

Stansbury, Arthur. *Trial of Albert Barnes before the Synod of Philadelphia in Session at York, October 1835, on a Charge of Heresy, Preferred Against Him by the Rev. George Junkin; with All the Pleadings and Debate*. New York: Van Nostrand & Dwight, 1836. Also Appendices: "The Appeal of Mr. Barnes" and "Defense of Albert Barnes."

Wilson, James. "Letters between James Wilson and the Session of First Church, dating May and June, 1828." Record Group 35, box 1, folder 5, held by the Department of History, Presbyterian Church (USA), Philadelphia.

———. "Letter, James Wilson to Session, First Presbyterian Church." Dated 6 January 1829. Record Group 35, box 1, folder 5, held by the Department of History, Presbyterian Church (USA), Philadelphia.

Daryl Fisher-Ogden

Edward Beecher
(1803–1895)

Edward Beecher, the third child and second son of the Rev. Lyman* and Roxana (Foote) Beecher, was born at East Hampton, Long Island, on 27 August 1803. His most notable siblings were Catharine, William Henry, Mary Foote, Harriet [Stowe], Henry Ward, Charles, Isabella, Thomas, and James. An ordained Congregational minister, he served as the first president of Illinois College at Jacksonville. He died on 28 July 1895.

Edward finds a place in this dictionary of heresy trials even though we have no record of his having been formally charged and brought to trial. A Beecher descendant and biographer, Lyman Beecher Stowe uses the term *heretic* in connection with three members of the Lyman Beecher family: Edward's father, Lyman Beecher, is labeled "near heretic"; Edward's eldest sister, Catharine Beecher, is labeled "Puritan heretic"; and younger brother Charles has the distinction of being labeled simply "the heretic." Edward, on the other hand, is labeled by Stowe as "the scholar." A careful reading of the data, however, including especially the data about Lyman, Catharine, and Charles, suggests that the scholar is implicated in the "heretical" tendencies of his father and his siblings.

Edward was raised in a staunch Calvinist household and appears to have considered himself a true heir of Calvin throughout his long life. Both his personal faith journey and his theological evolution can be seen as vintage Beecher. As one account of the Beecher family's story insightfully and impishly observed, humanity has its saints and its sinners—and then there are the Beechers. The story of this prolific and famous family is required reading for anyone who wants to understand any individual member of the family. (See the entry on Lyman Beecher in this dictionary.)

Edward himself was never formally tried for heresy, but his controversial theological explorations were intimately connected to the heresy trials of his father Lyman and his youngest brother, Charles. His own faith journey, as well as the faith journeys of his sisters Catharine and Harriet, also played a significant role in his evolving theological position.

Lyman Beecher was tried for heresy but was exonerated; Charles was tried and found guilty. In both trials, the theology that reached its fullest expression in Edward's *The Conflict of Ages* was actually in the dock, albeit proleptically in Lyman's case. Edward's two sisters struggled with the doctrines inherited with the family's cherished Calvinism vis-à-vis their respective passions: Catharine with the eternal destiny of the soul of her free-thinking fiancé at the time of his unexpected death; Harriet with the role of the Christian in a society attempting to come to grips with slavery. Edward's personal and sociotheological struggles were similarly intertwined with the Beecher family's Calvinist heritage, independence of mind, active social conscience, individual strengths of will, and, in most cases, longevity—outliving many of their critics.

In other words, to understand Edward's relationship to the trials of Lyman and Charles, and the struggles of Catharine and Harriet, we need to understand how Edward's theology was related to his emerging understanding of the political, social, as well as theological trends of his time. These trends, in turn, must be seen in the context of the Beecher family's colorful and illustrious story.

Edward Beecher is regularly recognized by Beecher biographers as the premier scholar of the family. While every member of the family appears to have been endowed with above-average intelligence and strength of will, it was the Yale-educated Edward who sharpened and employed his mental skills in ways that drew him into public attention in scholarly circles. The pivotal work in this regard was *The Conflict of Ages; or, The Great Debate on the Moral Relations of God and Man*. While this work was not published until 1853, the basic themes of this controversial treatise have been identified as being already in place within his evolving theological system as early as the 1830s. The second most notable avenue for Edward's articulations was the respected religious journal *Congregationalist*, which he cofounded and served as editor in chief in its early years.

From Lyman to Charles, including Henry Ward, the Beechers endeavored to bring their Calvinist heritage into meaningful dialogue with issues and events of their respective times. Underlying most of the theological controversy surrounding the Beechers was the suspicion on the part of Old School Calvinists of their day that the Beechers were sitting too loose with certain "central tenets" of the Calvinist doctrines in their efforts to address issues claiming public attention. At issue were some central Calvinist themes: predestination and human free will; the capacity of God the Father to suffer. Charges of Pelagianism, Arminianism, and even Unitarianism were commonly leveled by critics who suspected that the Beechers were free-thinking or modernist wolves parading in Calvinist ("sheep's" does not seem to fit the Beechers) clothing. Lyman's assailants charged him with heresy, slander, and hypocrisy. C. H. Rammelkamp, writing in the *Dictionary of American Biography*, elaborates that Beecher was accused "of heresy because his interpretation of the Westminster Confession differed from theirs, of slander because he maintained that his views were those of a large body of evangelical Christians, of hypocrisy because he pretended that his doctrines squared with the Scriptures and the Confession."

While most of the Beechers pressed ahead in their respective areas of concern without bothering to reconcile their actions and their words with the "central tenets" of their Calvinist heritage, Edward did not settle for a solution based on avoidance. His passion was consistency in thought, word, and deed—even when he found it expedient to understate his evolving convictions regarding how to reconcile his inherited theological tradition with the practical demands of addressing the issues of his day. But even this avenue of understatement had a consistency: He presented his case in ways that, in his mind, would enable him to maintain relations with disagreeing parties on all sides. His biographers seem to agree that the primary catalyst for Edward's earliest efforts at reconciling his Calvinist heritage and his nineteenth-century social conscience was his involvement with the antislavery efforts of Elijah P. Lovejoy and the events at Alton, Illinois, which came to a head with Lovejoy's death at the hands of his opponents. (See E. Beecher's account of these events in his *Alton Riots* [1838].)

These eminently political events were, in Edward's mind, inherently theological. Indeed, as several students of Edward's life and writings note, Edward's Calvinism did not allow him to separate politics and theology (see especially Merideth, *The Politics of the Universe: Edward Beecher, Abolition, and Orthodoxy*). The sovereign God of the Beechers' Calvinism rules all human events—and therein lies the agony and the ecstasy of Edward's theological tour de force and the springboard for his cutting-edge theological explorations that would be embraced by his brother Charles and lead to Charles's being found guilty of heresy.

Most of the Beechers found in slavery a central example of the societal expression of human sin. And yet there were "good Christians" who practiced slavery and many more who allowed it to continue. How does one reconcile the obvious twistedness of the human condition (Calvinism's "total depravity") with the goodness and justice (Edward tended to prefer the phrase "honor and right") of an all-sovereign God without having the blame for that depravity coming to rest in the lap of the creator God?

Conflict of Ages is Edward's meticulous and intimidating answer to that riddle. Here Edward culls from the history of the Church evidence that his solution to the riddle is neither original nor heretical. Beginning with the biblical writers, moving through the major theological giants of the ages, and addressing the then-current heated debates among the parties in his own day—especially the Old Schoolers, New Schoolers, and the Unitarians—Edward seeks to document that his way of reconciling the "conflict of ages" is consistent with the theological positions of the recognized "orthodox" ancestors of the nineteenth-century Calvinists. He goes out of his way to acknowledge the sincerity, intelligence, and piety of opponents, asking only that they grant to him the same courtesies.

But his father, while acknowledging the weight of the evidence that Edward presents, warned Edward that few would enter his camp: "Edward, you've destroyed the Calvinistic barns, but I hope you don't delude yourself that the animals are going into your little theological hencoop." The reason was simple enough: Preexistence of souls, which is fundamental both to Edward's theological resolution of the age-old conflict between human depravity and divine goodness and justice and to his efforts to reconcile the disputing parties of his day, was *not* to be accepted as "orthodox," in spite of the amount of evidence presented and the intricate logic employed in *Conflict of Ages*.

While the nature of the entries in this dictionary precludes any adequate exposition of either Edward's thesis or the literature produced by his supporters and opponents in response to *Conflict of Ages*, the main lines of this thesis warrant inclusion. Edward presents several summary statements throughout *Conflict of Ages*:

> I shall proceed to present what is certainly a possible mode of removing all conflict between the moving powers of Christianity; that is, between those thorough views of innate human depravity, and subjection to the powers of evil, which are recognized as true and scriptural by men of a profound Christian experience, and the highest principles of honor and right, which a well-ordered mind intuitively perceives to be true, and obligatory upon God as well as upon men. (198)

Edward demonstrates that efforts on all sides of this conflict in his own day were presenting false resolutions to the age-old conflict because they ended up letting go of either one or the other of "the moving powers of Christianity": They play loose either with the reality of human depravity (e.g., most Unitarian schemes) or with the justice and honor of God (e.g., most Calvinists). By positing the preexistence of souls, Edward claims that these polarized positions are harmonized:

> [B]y supposing the preexistent sin and fall of man, the most radical views of human depravity can be harmonized with the highest views of the justice and honor of God. The doctrines of the innate depravity of man, and his exposure to corrupt social organizations, and to the power of evil spirits, sustain entirely different relations to the principles of honor and right, as we reject, or as we adopt, the idea of preexist-

ence. If we reject it, the alleged facts and the principles come into immediate and inevitable conflict. (198)

In a dictionary of heresy trials, it would be inappropriate to leave unexamined the obvious question raised by the above data: Why was Lyman
Beecher acquitted, Charles Beecher found guilty, and Edward, the "brains
of the outfit," never even brought to trial?

The data surrounding Lyman Beecher's heresy trial suggest that the
charges brought against him were rooted more in spite or even jealousy
than in theological substance—although Lyman's New School theology
was indeed suspect in Old School circles. Court after court in the church
system acquitted Lyman, until finally his accusers gave up their threatened
endless round of appeals. Another element in his acquittal may well have
been his refusal to accept Edward's views regarding preexistence of souls.
Charles's account of this period in the Beecher family story makes it clear
that Lyman "had no place in his system for this new revelation—The great
champions of evangelical faith, Taylor, Goodrich, Stuart and others heed
not—he [Edward] must be silent, as became his youth. He must be 'dead
and his life hid with Christ in God' " (quoted in Merideth, *The Politics of
the Universe*, 490).

While Edward did not exactly keep silent regarding the views that led to
his being suspected of pushing beyond the acceptable Calvinist boundaries,
he was circumspect and subtle enough to avoid head-on confrontations in
most public settings—that is, until the publication of *Conflict of Ages*. But
that work, as already noted, was so daunting for most readers that the field
was left to specialists, most of whom delighted more in the debates than
in leveling charges of heresy.

Not so with Charles. Apparently when he was only 14, he had "instantly
as by a kind of intuition" accepted Edward's views regarding preexistence
of souls. When he reached maturity, his convictions found public voice
among nonspecialists. Charles, unlike Edward, refused to muffle his tones.
Charles's "questionable theology" combined with his passionate antislavery
statements (from pulpit as well as beyond) resulted in his being convicted
of heresy in a formal church court. Even though his conviction was later
overturned, primarily as a result of his manifest piety and effectiveness as
a minister, the stigma of the conviction never fully disappeared.

Thus it was that Edward Beecher, chief proponent of the "heretical"
doctrine of the preexistence of souls, and participant in some controversial
antislavery movements, was never brought to trial for the "crimes" that so
influenced a younger brother for whom both trial and conviction were a
reality. And thus it is that Edward Beecher appears in a dictionary of heresy
trials.

BIBLIOGRAPHY

Material on Edward Beecher is rather limited. Prior to the publication in 1934 of Lyman Beecher Stowe's *Saints, Sinners, and Beechers* (Indianapolis: Bobbs-Merrill, 1934), the main sources were:

Bateman, Newton and Selby, Paul. *Historical Encyclopedia of Illinois*. Chicago: Munsell Publishing Company, 1906.

Beecher, Edward. *The Conflict of Ages; or, The Great Debate on the Moral Relations of God and Man*. Boston: Phillips, Sampson and Co., 1853.

———. *Narrative of Riots at Alton, in Conjunction with the Death of Rev. Elijah P. Lovejoy*. Alton, IL: G. Holton, 1838. (Commonly listed as *Alton Riots*.)

Bungay, George W. *Off-Hand Takings; or, Crayon Sketches of the Noticeable Men of Our Age*. New York: Robert M. De Witt, 1854.

Congregational Year Book. London: Published for the Union by Jackson and Walford, 1896.

Johnson, Allen, ed. *Dictionary of American Biography*. New York: Charles Scribner's Sons, 1929.

Record of the Meetings of the Class of 1822, Yale College, etc. (1869). No other data available. But see information under first *Summary* listing.

Sturtevant, Julian Monson. *An Autobiography*. Edited by J. M. Sturtevant, Jr. New York: Fleming, 1885.

Summary of the Record of the Class of 1822, Yale College, to the Year 1860. New Haven: R. Hayes, printer [1860]. Available through Microfiche, Woodbridge, CT. Research Publications International, 1990.

Summary of the Record of the Class of 1822, Yale College, to the Close of 1879 (1879). No other data available. But see previous *Summary* listing.

By far the most extensive treatment of Edward Beecher, with a complete bibliography of Edward Beecher's works, is:

Merideth, Robert. *The Politics of the Universe: Edward Beecher, Abolition, and Orthodoxy*. Nashville: Vanderbilt University Press, 1963.

Robert L. VanDale

Lyman Beecher
(1775–1863)

Lyman Beecher achieved immortality in American Protestantism, not only by reason of his own accomplishments but as the patriarch/colossus of the Beecher dynasty. Large but not atypical for that era, the Beecher family was nurtured in turn by three wives, Roxanna Foote, Harriet Porter, and Mrs. Lydia Jackson, the first two managing to bear him thirteen children before their untimely deaths. Two children died in infancy, two by their own hand, and two, Henry Ward Beecher and Harriet Beecher Stowe, attained a degree of prominence that could be said to have outstripped that of their renowned father.

In his mature years, Lyman's position as president of Lane Theological Seminary in Cincinnati, Ohio, and the perceived threat of his popularizing a brand of "modified" Calvinism known as the New Haven Theology, derived from Nathaniel W. Taylor, led to his trial on charges of heresy by the Cincinnati Presbytery. Old School Presbyterians, fearing New School rejection of the more orthodox form of Calvinism, regarded it as an affirmation of Pelagianism, if not outright Arminianism, and determined not to allow Presbyterianism in the West to be led down such a slippery slope.

Lyman was born in New Haven, Connecticut, on 12 October 1775 of sturdy blacksmith stock. The death of his tubercular mother almost immediately after his birth caused him to be reared by an aunt, for whom, in gratitude, his first child was named, and an uncle in the rural surroundings of Guilford, Connecticut. Farm life gifted Lyman with a love of nature and the Puritan virtues of diligence and hard work, but it also inspired him to rely on his intellectual talents rather than his inherited brawn for his future success. His foster parents conceded that college, rather than the plow, was indeed his best vocational choice.

Yale College exerted an influence upon Beecher's life far beyond his academic preparation. Timothy Dwight, successor to Ezra Stiles as president, had doubtless inherited revivalistic impulses from his grandfather, Jonathan Edwards, and resolved to bring salvation and piety to Yale undergraduates in addition to improving their minds. Lyman described the campus scene at Yale as follows:

> Before he came college was in a most ungodly state. The college church was almost extinct. Most of the students were skeptical and rowdies were plenty. Wine and liquors were kept in many rooms; intemperance, profanity, gambling, and licentiousness were common. . . . That was the day of the infidelity of the Tom Paine school. . . . [M]ost of the class before me were infidels, and called each other Voltaire, Rousseau, D'alembert, etc. (Cross, *Autobiography*, 1:27)

President Timothy Dwight's influence on the reputation of the college and on the student body was profound. Beecher remembered that his sermons and lectures were "a continual course of education and a continual feast." There was in him "a pith and power of doctrine there that has not been since surpassed, if equaled" (Mussey, *Yankee Life*, 94). From Yale, where approximately one third of the students were converted, revivals spread to other college campuses and added to the success of the Second Great Awakening. Beecher's conversion under Dwight's relentless evangelistic crusade at Yale was followed by an equally significant influence on his developing religious opinions, the emergence of the New Haven Theology, a departure from the strict Edwardsean Calvinism as developed by Nathaniel W. Taylor. Though Taylor was somewhat younger than Beecher, the two were to become warm friends and theological allies.

Taylor's views and the opposition they spawned were at the heart of the later Old School and New School controversy among Presbyterians. While insisting that he was not rejecting the Westminster Confession, he nevertheless came to modify the "harsh decrees" of Calvinism to the extent that its implied determinism was softened if not outright rejected. While not embracing Arminianism totally, Taylor held that humankind is more free and responsible than orthodox Old School Presbyterians would allow. The influence of Taylorism on Beecher was at the heart of his presumed and, in his position, influential heresy at Lane. His final, "side by side" (Ahlstrom, *Religious History*, 421) resting place with Taylor in the cemetery in New Haven symbolized their theological, as well as personal, connectedness.

Beecher's first pulpit, a difficult "internship" of approximately 12 years, was the Presbyterian Church in East Hampton, Long Island, which he was ordained to serve in 1799. Before his ordination, Beecher was subjected to the typical examination before the Presbytery at Middletown. Theological hairsplitting emerged as a problem, not with regard to his own views but among various members of the Presbytery itself. Beecher recalled:

> At eight o'clock Presbytery began examination and continued till one. Resumed at two p.m. and concluded in about an hour. There was nothing difficult in the examination, except what arose from difference of sentiment between the examiners on several subjects, on which they disputed through the candidate. (Cross, *Autobiography*, 1:79)

At the tender age of 24, he was already a committed revivalist, all five feet seven inches of him! His characterization of his early sermons indicates that, early on, he gained experience and at least some confidence that success would ultimately crown his efforts:

> I did not attack infidelity directly. Not at all. That would have been cracking a whip behind a runaway team—made them run the faster. I always preached right to the conscience. Every sermon with my eye on the gun to hit somebody. Went through the doctrines; showed what they didn't mean; what they did; then the argument; knocked away objections, and drove home on the conscience. They couldn't get up their prejudices, because I had got them away. At first there was winking and blinking from below to gallery, forty or fifty exchanging glances, smiling, and watching. But when that was over, infidelity was ended. (Cross, *Autobiography*, 1:68)

No hint of incipient heterodoxy was in evidence at the beginning of his ministry; indeed, he could not have been more acceptable in his opposition to the pervasive evils of the day. In addition to the usual targets of pulpit oratory—intemperance, gambling, Sabbath breaking, and the like—an event of national prominence and shame occurred that added yet another in Lyman's mind: dueling.

In 1804, Alexander Hamilton had been gunned down in a test of honor and animosity by Aaron Burr. Some have questioned whether the effect would have been the same had the more respected Hamilton been the better marksman; nevertheless, a shocked nation seemed potentially responsive to reexamining the legitimacy of such practice. Beecher's antidueling sermon "The Remedy for Dueling: A Sermon Delivered Before the Presbytery of Long Island, at the Opening of Their Session, at Aqueboque, April 6, 1806" (Cross, *Autobiography*, 1:105; Henry, *Unvanquished Puritan*, 57, 64) as well as his successful resolution in the Synod that antidueling societies be formed served to elevate him to national prominence.

Life at East Hampton was marked by his marriage to the first of his three wives (his father David outlasted five), Roxanna Foote, and the birth of his first six children. Financial exigency, poor health, during which for almost a year he did not preach, as well as only moderate success meant that when the more promising Congregational Church at Litchfield, Connecticut, invited him in 1810 to be their minister, he shifted not the substance of his vigorous revivalistic efforts but only the location.

The change from a Presbyterian to a Congregational pulpit was not a radical one. Since both denominations embraced the theology of Calvin, their chief point of contention lay in church polity, a difference regarded as slight. Indeed, in 1801 the Plan of Union between the two denominations was enacted, which allowed a mixed congregation to select a minister of either persuasion, especially on the frontier as it moved westward from the original 13 colonies. The church at East Hampton itself had formerly been Congregational in its denominational ties.

Though concerns about money were to plague Lyman all his days, the increased annual salary at Litchfield—$800—allowed some relief, but a growing family meant that the respite would only be temporary. His beginning salary at East Hampton had been $300 annually plus firewood—his predecessor having been allowed the dubious bonus of 25 percent of the whales found stranded on the beach. Beecher remarked, "That is the only case I ever knew of a minister's being paid in whales" (Cross, *Autobiography*, 1:67). Judge Tapping Reese, a prominent lawyer and founder of its local Law School, was instrumental in securing Lyman's appointment, especially after reading a copy of his well-received sermon "The Government of God Desirable."

Since colonial days, church life in Connecticut had been characterized by an establishment of religion that made Congregationalism the officially recognized religion, supported in part by tax funds. Dissenters were tolerated, but religious liberty was limited at best. Beecher arrived at Litchfield in the middle of growing agitation for disestablishment, and he gave his best efforts to defeat it, convinced that the Church would suffer without state support. The First Amendment had been enacted to forbid a federal establishment of religion but did nothing to strike down such arrangements at the state level. "Congress shall make no law respecting an establishment of religion," the First Amendment declared, but Connecticut and other states already had. One by one, individual states overturned the Standing Order.

The first domino to fall was Virginia with the passage of Jefferson's bill for Religious Freedom in 1785. Massachusetts was the last holdout until 1833, and in between, Connecticut, convinced by Baptists and other assorted dissenters, voted for disestablishment on 15 September 1818. Reflecting on the changed circumstances, Beecher, a reluctant convert to church-state separation, concluded:

> It was as dark a day as ever I saw. The odium thrown upon the ministry was inconceivable. The injury done to the cause of Christ, as we then supposed, was irreparable. For several days I suffered what no tongue can tell for the best thing that ever happened to the State of Connect-

icut. It cut the churches loose from dependence on state support. It threw them wholly on their own resources and on God. . . . They say ministers have lost their influence; the fact is, they have gained. By voluntary efforts, societies, missions, and revivals, they exert a deeper influence than ever they could by queues and shoe buckles, and cocked hats and gold-headed canes. (Cross *Autobiography*, 1:418)

At Litchfield, another enemy to be engaged was alcohol. While Puritanism was never synonymous with teetotalism, there developed an increasing concern that intemperance ruled the land. Beecher's reminiscences include the observation that even among ministers, especially at ordinations, the problem was rampant. Primarily because of his efforts, the Connecticut Society for the Reformation of Morals was founded in 1813, and its existence led to the establishment of similar organizations elsewhere. Both Timothy Dwight and Beecher adopted the radical position of advocating total abstinence rather than mere temperance. In 1826, Beecher's "Six Sermons on the Nature, Occasions, Signs, Evils, and Remedy of Intemperance" offered the theological defense of this position, which had a significant influence on the developing temperance movement (Ahlstrom, *Religious History*, 426; Henry, *Unvanquished Puritan*, 94).

During these years, Lyman was also instrumental in the formation of the American Bible Society. In a meeting in New York on 18 May 1816, representatives of several local and state Bible societies, having determined to create a "general Bible institution for the circulation of the Holy Scriptures without note or comment," created a committee composed of 11 prominent persons for this purpose. Included among them was Beecher, who later described the causes that led to its founding:

The first cause, no doubt, was the existence and prosperous operations of the British and Foreign Bible Society. The second was the foreign missionary spirit that was awakened a few years anterior, and the organization of the Foreign Missionary Society. The primary agent in this movement, I am well assured, was the Rev. Samuel J. Mills, in whose heart the fire of foreign missions first burned for several years. In his travels West and South he had the organization of an American Bible Society at heart, and, though a man of little promise in appearance, was distinguished by strong and increasing love to God and man, added to a profound wisdom, indefatigable industry, and unparalleled executive power in the excitement and combination of minds in benevolent organizations. (Smith et al., *American Christianity*, 1:552–553)

Continuing financial difficulties in Litchfield—the family attempted to reduce the burden by taking in boarders—as well as a general feeling of "mission accomplished" caused Lyman to respond favorably when the Hanover Street Congregational Church in Boston in 1826 extended an invitation to him to become its minister. His most formidable foe in Boston was neither infidelity nor intemperance but the enemy from within, Unitarianism. The radical wing of Congregationalism, it rejected not only orthodox Calvinistic views but the doctrine of the Trinity as well. The upper middle class tended to be Unitarians, and Harvard, especially after the appointment of the liberal Henry Ware, sent Unitarian ministers into New England to advance its cause. Harriet Beecher Stowe described the pervasive hold of Unitarianism over New England as follows: "All the literary men of Massachusetts were Unitarian. All the trustees and professors of Harvard College were Unitarians. All the elite of wealth and fashion crowded Unitarian churches" (Cross, *Autobiography*, 2:82).

Beecher championed Trinitarian orthodoxy through sermons, pamphlets, and occasional letters to the denominational publication the *Christian Spectator* but especially through efforts toward revival. Unitarians, he declared, "will gain the victory if we are left without revivals, but they will perish by the breath of His mouth and the brightness of His coming if revivals prevail" (Weisberger, *River*, 78).

Another perceived enemy of true religion for Beecher and for the majority of Americans at the time was "popery." The prevailing mood of the country was characterized by the fear that militant Catholicism would prevail unless resisted on all fronts. Beecher both reflected the sentiments of the day and, in some measure, contributed to them. Not only anti-Catholic sermons from responsible pulpits but scandalous tracts purporting to be "confessions" of young girls "trapped" in Catholic convents fanned the flames of antagonism, suspicion, and "Know-Nothing" feeling.

Beecher's sermons may well have had an indirect responsibility for the tragic burning of an Ursuline convent in Charlestown, Massachusetts, on 11 August 1834. Though regret for the incident was expressed far and wide, Roger Williams's* ideal for complete religious liberty in colonial Rhode Island was yet to become a national reality. In the same year of the Ursuline tragedy, Beecher, newly appointed president of Lane Theological Seminary in Cincinnati, wrote his *Plea for the West*, which, in addition to pleas for funds for this strategic seminary, included a lengthy tirade against what was regarded as an evident Catholic conspiracy to capture the West:

"The spirit of the age," which Bonaparte says dethroned him, is moving on to put an end in Europe to Catholic domination, creating the necessity of making reprisals abroad for what liberty conquers at home. . . . Clouds like the locusts of Egypt are rising from the hills and plains of Europe, and on the wings of every wind, are coming over to settle down upon our fair fields; while millions, moved by the noise of their rising and cheered by the news of their safe arrival and green pastures, are preparing for flight in an endless succession. . . . No design! How does it happen that their duty, and the analogy of their past policy, and their profession in Europe, and their predictions and exultation in this country, and their deeds, should come together accidentally with such admirable indications of design? (Quoted in Ahlstrom, *Religious History*, 562)

Whatever Beecher's other commendable insights, ecumenicity was clearly not among them.

Lane Seminary in Cincinnati, jointly launched by both Congregationalists and Presbyterians as a consequence of the Plan of Union, seemed an unpromising arena for an inveterate New Englander such as Beecher. The invitation to become its first president was compelling, however, and in 1832, he moved to the West to spend the last major period of his ministry. In addition to teaching and laboring to ensure the success of the fledgling institution, Beecher was to become engaged in two major controversies that were to consume his energies during this period: abolition and orthodoxy. The first raised questions regarding the "correctness" of his ethics, the second, his theology.

Theodore Weld was a late-twenty-ish seminary student in the entering class at Lane. An intransigent "immediate" abolitionist who had been converted to the manumission of the slaves by Charles Grandison Finney, the firebrand revivalist and later president of Oberlin College, he became the leader of a student movement to enlist the seminary in the cause. Nothing less than total commitment would be acceptable. Colonization, the repatriation of Negroes to Africa, had seemed to some to achieve the twin results of "solving" the problem of slavery while assisting in the Christian evangelization of the continent as well. Indeed, Beecher considered himself an abolitionist as well as a colonizationalist, "without perceiving in myself any inconsistency" (Cross, *Autobiography*, 2:242). Colonization, however, represented a misguided solution to the problem; indeed, it more than smacked of racism to abolitionists.

Beecher—himself an opponent of slavery and, ironically, the father of Harriet Beecher Stowe, whose *Uncle Tom's Cabin* was widely regarded as the catalyst for emancipation—embraced moderation, a position, in the minds of Lane students, that was not acceptable. Harriet later described her father preaching so passionately against slavery that he brought tears from "the hardest faces of the old farmers in his congregation." Likewise, she informed Frederick Douglass that his prayers on the subject "indelibly impressed my heart and made me what I am from my very soul, the enemy of all slavery" (quoted in Henry, *Unvanquished Puritan*, 279). But Beecher was now a practical administrator who did not regard "immediate" abolition as the only Christian position.

Lane students were virtually unanimous in their conviction that Beecher, the faculty, and trustees not only were unsympathetic to their cause but denied them the right to pursue it. The students made impossible demands;

the conservative trustees, in Beecher's absence, passed restrictive measures that he was unable to rescind, and a mass exodus of students resulted.

To Oberlin, Finney, and a more congenial abolitionist atmosphere they departed. "The exodus continued until of the forty students originally in theology, only three remained and but five of the sixty in the literary department from the preceding year" (Henry, *Unvanquished Puritan*, 189). Beecher's opposition to slavery was not enough; his perceived conservative accommodationism—no doubt to preserve the school's endowment— meant that increasing the enrollment of a depleted seminary was a formidable task. This, the death of his second wife, Harriet Porter, and a new problem, a heresy trial, all but consumed him during these years.

Presbyterians might be pleased to be regarded as among the most thoroughly committed guardians of orthodox Christianity, were it not for the fact that they have received the dubious distinction of arranging one of the largest number of heresy trials in American Protestantism in order to achieve that end. For the president of the new seminary to be charged with heresy is indicative of the degree to which Old Order Presbyterians in the West viewed the seriousness of "Taylorite" attempts to modify, if not reject, classic Calvinism. The chief accuser was Joshua Lacy Wilson, venerable minister of the First Presbyterian Church in Cincinnati and ministerial colleague of Beecher, since the presidency of Lane carried a joint appointment as minister of the Second Presbyterian Church. That Beecher was not a true Presbyterian, Plan of Union or no, and did not accept the Westminster Confession at face value, Wilson was intent on proving.

The source of Wilson's animosity toward Beecher—whether he entertained an ambition to be the seminary's first president, only to be thwarted by an "outsider"—is impossible to assess. That he feared the invasion of the New Haven Theology is certain. Having first voted in favor of Beecher's appointment, Wilson quickly mounted an organized attack on Beecher's departure from Calvinist orthodoxy, and, in consequence of which, he resigned his office not only as president of the board but also as a trustee member.

That Beecher was essentially a Congregationalist and not a Presbyterian should not have mattered, given the Plan of Union. But both parties to the plan were becoming increasingly restive by reason of its provisions and results, and in 1837, it was dissolved. Even so, an enthusiastic, if naive, supporter of Beecher had concluded that he saw "no difficulty in having the preacher Presbyterianized" (Henry, *Unvanquished Puritan*, 213). "Presbyterianized," in some measure, he became but not without difficulty.

The chief thrust of Wilson's attack was that Beecher's theology represented a departure from the Westminster Confession of Faith, especially his contention that "man" was not totally passive in the process of salvation, possessing the ability to resist as well as embrace God's proffered grace. If "free will" was regarded as the "whore" by both Jonathan Edwards and

Roger Williams, did this not, at the very least, characterize a woman of "easy virtue"?

Beecher's views, however unacceptable to Wilson and Old School Presbyterians, were not newly formed and should have been known long before his appointment at Lane. As early as his first pastorate at East Hampton, his sermon "The Government of God Desirable" had concluded that although God governs the world "as a part of his moral kingdom," persons are "still entirely free and accountable for all the deeds done in the body." God, furthermore, will "send to hell none who are not opposed to Him, and to holiness, and to heaven; none, who are not, by voluntary sin and rebellion, unfitted for heaven and fitted for destruction as eminently as saints are prepared for glory" (Cross, *Autobiography*, 1:116–117).

Beecher as well as Taylor contended that these views were not foreign to true Edwardsean Calvinism and could be squared (though not without difficulty) with the Westminster Confession. Wilson, convinced otherwise, launched a defense of orthodoxy and brought formal charges of heresy, slander, and hypocrisy against Beecher in 1835. Wilson charged him with "heresy, on the ground that he differed from the Westminster standards; slander, on the ground that he claimed to represent true evangelical Christianity; and hypocrisy, on the ground that he claimed to agree substantially with the Scripture and the Westminster Confession" (Ahlstrom, *Religious History*, 459).

In his sermon "The Faith Once Delivered to the Saints," Beecher insisted "that men are free agents, in the possession of such faculties, and placed in such circumstances, as render it practicable for them to do whatever God requires and that all men are invited sincerely . . . to return to God, with an assurance of pardon and eternal life if they comply" (Cross, *Autobiography*, 1:412–413). This made his acceptance by the Presbytery and his fitness to serve as Lane's president impossible in Wilson's mind. Beecher's defense was straightforward: "I do not say that I have not taught the doctrines . . . but I deny their being false" (Henry, *Unvanquished Puritan*, 220).

Concerning the trial, the *Autobiography* states: "We can not . . . go into the details of the trial, nor is it necessary" (2:264). Sufficient details are provided, however, to present a picture of Beecher as a valiant, embattled contender for the faith. The weeklong trial required Beecher to continually defend his views regarding total depravity, the nature and extent of human freedom, and original sin. Beecher rejected the criticism that his theology tended to "modify the Calvinistic system in its essential parts and in its vital interests" (Cross, *Autobiography*, 2:133). His contention was that he was the defender, not the opponent, of Calvinism: "Calvin was as bad as I am. . . . The doctrine for which I am to be turned out . . . is not new divinity, but old Calvinism" (Henry, *Unvanquished Puritan*, 221). This served, at least in part, to convince the Presbytery that the charges of heresy were unfounded. The decision for acquittal read: "Resolved, that in the opinion of this presbytery the charges of J. L. Wilson, D.D., against Lyman Beecher, D.D., are not sustained" (222).

Unhappy with the result, Wilson appealed the decision for acquittal to the Synod. The minutes of the Synod reveal that they saw nothing in Wilson's conduct "which ought to infer censure," nor did they find any major flaw in Beecher's theology that would "justify any suspicion of unsoundness in the faith." They were, however, inclined to express the opinion that on certain Calvinistic points

> Dr. Beecher has indulged a disposition to philosophize, instead of exhibiting in simplicity and plainness these doctrines as taught in the Scriptures; and has employed terms and phrases, and modes of illustration calculated to convey ideas inconsistent with the Word of God and our Confession of Faith, and that he ought to be, and he is hereby admonished to be more guarded in future. (Cross, *Autobiography*, 2:270)

The decision for acquittal, though not unanimous, represented a vindication of Beecher's theology and allowed him to get on with addressing the pressing needs of the seminary. He continued to serve both the congregation of Second Presbyterian Church in Cincinnati until his resignation in 1843 and Lane Theological Seminary until 1850. His declining years were largely spent with his son Henry Ward in Brooklyn, where he died in 1863. Unable or unwilling to write his own autobiography, the work was completed as a result of his son Charles's editorial efforts and is the most important source of reminiscences regarding his life and times. Beecher's own most important works include: *A Plea for the West* (1832), *Views in Theology* (1836), and his collected *Works* in three volumes (1852–1853).

Was Lyman Beecher truly a heretic or a practical evangelist willing to adapt earlier creeds to existing realities? In comparison to practically all of his children, who were radically independent thinkers (e.g., Charles and Edward embraced the notion of the preexistence of souls), he was a thoroughgoing traditionalist. In terms of a strict Old School Presbyterian reading of the Westminster Confession, Beecher was guilty as charged. But yesterday's heresy may become tomorrow's orthodoxy, and to Beecher, along with Nathaniel W. Taylor and others, is due the credit for moving Calvinism, in its Congregational and Presbyterian forms, into its mainline, "modified" version that represents today's orthodoxy.

BIBLIOGRAPHY

Ahlstrom, Sydney E. *A Religious History of the American People*. New Haven: Yale University Press, 1972.

Cross, Barbara M., ed. *The Autobiography of Lyman Beecher*. 2 vols. Cambridge, MA: Harvard University Press, 1961.

Henry, Stuart C. *Unvanquished Puritan: A Portrait of Lyman Beecher*. Grand Rapids, MI: Eerdmans, 1973.

Mussey, Barrows, ed. *Yankee Life: By Those Who Lived It*. New York: Alfred A. Knopf, 1947.

Smith, H. Shelton, Robert T. Handy, and Lefferts A. Loetscher, eds. *American Christianity: An Historical Interpretation with Representative Documents*. 2 vols. New York: Charles Scribner's Sons, 1960.

Weisberger, Bernard A. *They Gathered at the River*. Boston: Little, Brown, 1958.

Bernard H. Cochran

Borden Parker Bowne
(1847–1910)

THE CONTEXT

At the time of Borden Parker Bowne's birth, during the bleak winter of 1847, new winds of sectionalism and individualism were blowing across the young American nation. Andrew Jackson had inaugurated a new democracy during his term as president, rapid changes were occurring in the economic life of the country, and demographic patterns were being altered by westward expansion. Religiously, new and strange sects were arising, reforms and new thoughts were developing, and established churches were being victimized by internal strife. Schism splintered the Presbyterians in 1837–1838; Lyman Beecher,* the distinguished president of Lane Seminary, was charged with heresy in 1835; Union Theological Seminary was founded by the liberal wing of the General Assembly in 1836; from 1835 to the Civil War the Protestant Episcopal Church was riven with strife; the conservative Missouri Synod of the Lutheran Church was formed in 1846; Mormonism was steadily gaining strength; the American Anti-Slavery Society was formed in 1833; in 1845, the Southern Baptist Convention was organized; and in 1844, a Plan of Separation, resulting in the division of this communion, was drawn up at the Methodist Episcopal Church's General Conference. Altogether, these were halcyon times for churches and theologians.

Bowne's father, Joseph, was a justice of the peace in Leonardville, New Jersey, and a strong abolitionist "when it cost something to speak against slavery" (McConnell, *Borden Parker Bowne*, 9; McConnell's biography is the definitive work on Bowne, and this and subsequent historical data are largely dependent upon this source). His mother, Margaret, was described by Bishop McConnell as "a character of straight-forward simplicity with a marked vein of mystic piety." His boyhood was spent on the family farm; at 17, he went to live with friends in Brooklyn, and for a time, he worked as a teamster. Bowne matriculated at New York University in September 1867 and was licensed to preach just one month later at the Navesink (Methodist) Church. He graduated with a B.A. degree in January 1871, was elected to Phi Beta Kappa, and was named valedictorian of his class. In 1872, he entered the New York East Conference of the Methodist Episcopal Church and was ordained deacon and appointed to the church in Whitestone, Long Island. After one year in this station, he took the opportunity to travel and study in Europe—chiefly in Paris, Halle, and Göttingen—and his thought was permanently influenced through his work with Hermann Lotze. Bowne was called to Boston University in 1876 and remained there until his death on 1 April 1910.

Six years before his death, Bowne was indicted for heresy by fellow Methodist minister George A. Cooke and tried before a "Select Number" of the New York East Conference. In the more than nine decades since, scant attention has been given to the anatomy of the trial itself. If only because his indictment, trial, and acquittal constitute the last significant investigation by (what is now) the United Methodist Church into the alleged heresy of one of its ministers, it deserves attention and careful treatment. This entry attempts to bring together fugitive (and sometimes unrelated) references and citations in order to reconstruct substantively the facts relating to the trial. Of three actions against Bowne—two in 1904 and one in 1908—there is record (beyond that included in the Conference *Minutes*) *only* of the second set of charges and the Conference's decision. Except as it contributes to the mystery of the missing trial transcript, the absence of detailed record of these charges is insignificant. That extensive record of the second action is missing, for example, might be explained by the fact that a committee of three reported to the Conference that "there is nothing in the charges presented demanding their consideration by the Conference" (*Minutes*, 1904, 28). The Conference refused to entertain the third action "by a unanimous rising vote" (*Minutes*, 1908, 17). Suspicion that the trial transcript may have been deliberately removed is given credibility inasmuch as it was of such considerable size and that it was certainly available 18 years after the trial when Elliott excerpted portions for his article in the *Methodist Review*.

THE PRETEXT

The first set of allegations resulted in the trial that is the subject of this entry. Failing to gain a conviction on these specifications, Cooke introduced new charges against Bowne on Friday, 8 April 1904, at the same Annual

Conference. Four years later, in the New York East Annual Conference of 1908, Cooke again presented charges, which were summarily disposed.

In 1895, nine years before his own trial, when appointments to the faculty of the Boston University School of Theology were reviewed every five years by the bishops of the Methodist Church, Bowne's colleague in Old Testament, Professor Hinckley Gilbert Thomas Mitchell,* was threatened with dismissal because he had taught the new "higher criticism" of the Bible. When Mitchell's tenure was jeopardized again in 1900, Bowne was actively involved in galvanizing support for Mitchell. In the short run, his efforts met with success; but in 1905, the year after Bowne's vindication of heresy charges, Mitchell's appointment was not renewed. There is no textual evidence to show that Bowne's trial in 1904 was in any way related to his defense of Mitchell in 1900; nevertheless, it is not unreasonable to suppose that the same group that opposed Mitchell also found objection to Bowne. The central issue in the Mitchell case had to do with the nature of biblical revelation—an issue that also appears in the charges against Bowne. In retrospect, the most significant development to eventuate from these contretemps, however, was the action of the Judiciary Committee of the 1908 General Conference that relieved the bishops of responsibility for the orthodoxy of professors in the Methodist theological schools!

Although the specific allegations against him are preserved in George Cooke's pamphlet, the particulars of Bowne's trial remain ambiguous owing chiefly to the absence of a trial transcript. It is, however, clear that the Presiding Elder of Bowne's district had a list of charges in hand "several months before the assembling of the Conference"; but these were somehow defective and therefore dismissed. A corrected set was resubmitted on 26 February 1904, approximately five weeks prior to the Conference. Bowne himself was aware of Cooke's charges against him as early as 26 December 1903.

THE TEXT

In five specifications, Bowne was charged with teaching (1) doctrines that are contrary to the Methodist Episcopal Church's Articles of Religion and (2) doctrines that are contrary to the established standards of the Methodist Episcopal Church.

It was alleged in *The First Specification* that Bowne denied the doctrine of the Trinity and the moral attributes of the Deity as these are described in the first and fourth Articles of Religion. These articles assert that there is "but one living and true God" in whose unity "there are three persons, of one substance, power, and eternity" and that the Holy Ghost "is of one substance, majesty, and glory with the Father and the Son." In the absence of any document from Cooke that isolates the particulars with which he charged Bowne, it is clear from the fragments of Bowne's testimony that he was accused of Unitarianism. But citations as corroborative evidence from Bowne's *Theism*, his *Metaphysics*, and his testimony reported in the *Methodist Review* confirm the judgment that these writings do not support the charge that Bowne was a unitarian.

There is, in fact, no discussion of the Trinity in these volumes. Instead, Bowne deals with questions of cosmology, ontology, epistemology, and psychology—matters that, no doubt, tend to shape one's doctrine of the Trinity; but precisely *how* this would be accomplished is not the subject of Bowne's work in either *Theism* or *Metaphysics*. It is arguable that the emphasis in Bowne's writings lay upon the unity of God; but fairness to Bowne would also require it to be said that this emphasis was sponsored by a commitment to make it impossible to think of God at all except by thinking at once of Father, Son, and Spirit. Bowne's works *The Christian Revelation* (1898), *The Christian Life* (1899), and *The Atonement* (1900) constitute variations on this central theme and lend further credibility to the conclusion that Bowne was innocent of the charge of Unitarianism.

Bowne's testimony during his trial puts the matter in a positive way: "There *is* a Trinitarian argument. I am a Trinitarian of the Trinitarians. I published a sermon in Zion's Herald on the Incarnation, in which I set forth that our Lord had existed before his incarnation. . . . All this argument, which was meant as Trinitarian, and which is Trinitarian, is brought here as proof that I am a Unitarian" (Elliott, "Orthodoxy," 402). While this is not a substantive answer to the charge, it clearly hints at how a solid argument might proceed.

According to George Elliott, who has provided the only extant fragments of the transcript, the longest time in the trial was consumed with *The Second Specification*, which held (1) that Bowne's teaching on miracles tended "to weaken if not destroy faith in large portions of the Old and New Testaments" and (2) that his views on the inspiration of the Bible contradict the Bible itself and the fifth Article of Religion, "The Sufficiency of the Holy Scriptures for Salvation." The pages cited in *The Christian Revelation*, and offered in support of this charge, indicate that the fundamental question for Bowne about the doctrine of revelation was not with the reality of revelation but with the "manner of conceiving it." Methodology was the issue.

Bowne argued that what is needed is some guiding principle for interpretation, a hermeneutic. The Christian revelation, he said, "is not the Bible, though it is in the Bible. It consists essentially in certain ways of thinking about God, his character, his purpose in our creation, and his relation to us." The Christian revelation therefore cannot be reduced to abstract speculative theology any more than it can be thought to consist of a text in ethics or anything other than a self-revelation of God himself. In sum, the character of revelation is not constituted as truth *about* God but as encounter with the very God himself. On this point, Bowne was doubtless ahead of his own time, anticipating the work of several renowned twentieth-century theologians—including Karl Barth, Emil Brunner, Rudolf Bultmann, and William Temple.

What appears to be further at stake is whether the general truthfulness of the biblical record accords with history and experience. If the Bible helps us to God, its religious use is warranted; but as a book, it is functional only and not to be worshiped or glorified for its own sake. "There are a few persons," said Bowne, "who say that they take the Bible just as it reads; but that only means that they take their interpretation for the Bible. . . . There is no such thing as a hard-and-fast interpretation of such language. What we find in it will depend very much on ourselves, and on the pre-suppositions which we bring with us" (Bowne, *The Christian Revelation*, 91–92). Bowne applied the same logic to other phenomena that are supposed to be miraculous: "Here [in the Christian revelation] we have, not indeed a God whom we understand, but one whom we can trust while we do not understand. I do not think that Christianity removes many, if any, of the intellectual difficulties we feel in contemplating life and the world; it rather outflanks them by a revelation of God which makes it possible to trust and love him, notwithstanding the mystery of his ways" (Bowne, *The Christian Revelation*, 36–38).

Bowne's views were undoubtedly advanced and liberal for his time, but none of the documents submitted in evidence against him shows him to be at variance with Article Five. What is demonstrated is a hermeneutical conflict that in no way jeopardizes the authority of Scripture but only a particular approach to its interpretation. According to Bowne, the church itself is witness to this claim: It existed before it had a Bible, and it continues because of the truth expressed in Scripture, not because of some doctrine of inspiration and authority. With this matter decided, the final three specifications were treated meagerly and summarily.

Both the excerpt of trial testimony that Elliott provides and quotations in a pamphlet by Cooke make it clear that *The Third Specification* focused on Bowne's repudiation of substitutionary and penal theories of the Atonement. Methodist interpretation had been traditionally in terms of a substitutionary theory, and although *Methodist* and *Wesleyan* are not synonymous terms, examination of John Wesley's sermons supports the contention that, on this point, Bowne had in fact diverged from accepted Methodist teaching in his rejection of substitution and ransom. All the same, it was the question of the appropriate theory—and not the fact—of Atonement that dominated this portion of the trial.

Bowne's claim was that no quasinaturalistic rite can save us, not even Christ's Atonement when it is interpreted and celebrated so woodenly as to become a merely mechanistic transaction. "For all practical purposes," he said, "all we need is to become the disciples of our Lord, trusting in his promises and the Father whom he revealed. With this practical discipleship we shall receive all the benefits of the Savior's work without any theory; and without this discipleship we are lost, whatever our theory" (Bowne, *The Atonement*, 152). Cooke could have pursued a more vigorous course here; had he done so, it is difficult to imagine how the Select Number could have failed to convict Bowne on this charge. Of all the specifications, it is in his teaching on the Atonement that he appears most vulnerable.

The Fourth Specification consists of Cooke's charge that Bowne taught views of the "divine government and of the future of souls" that were not consonant with Jesus' teaching on "the future punishment of the wicked and the future reward of the righteous." Most likely, the elements of this indictment posited (1) Bowne's alleged universalism and (2) his rejection of an impersonally conceived divine sovereignty. There is no direct reference in any of Bowne's cited writings to the first of these and no demonstrable proof of the second. Here again, what appears is a basic conflict between Cooke and Bowne who hold different views regarding biblical interpretation and divine activity. Bowne argued for what we today would call an "existential" hermeneutic; Cooke defended a thoroughgoing biblical literalism. The documentary evidence supports, beyond any reasonable doubt, the verdict of the Select Number.

The final charge, *The Fifth Specification*, alleged that Bowne's teaching on the Christian life did not represent "the views of the Methodist Episcopal Church as expressed in our standard works of theology." Cooke apparently held the view that salvation is instantaneous, cataclysmic, and intensely individualistic. The selections cited from both *Theism* and *The Christian Life* show that Bowne advanced what is essentially an evolutionary view of Christian experience. While he did not insist that a sudden and unambiguous experience of salvation is impossible, he did argue that when the experience is viewed in its entirety, one will see a great variety of psychological and historical factors that shape and give substance to the event itself. What therefore appears to be at issue here is the claim that salvation does not occur *in vacuo* but is profoundly oriented both socially and interpersonally.

A CONCLUDING NOTE

The Select Number, by unanimous vote taken by ballot, found that the five specifications and charges that Bowne was "disseminating doctrines contrary to the Articles of Religion and our standards of doctrine" could not be sustained. Four years later, in what appears to be a personal vendetta, Cooke again lodged charges against Bowne—this time alleging defamation of character, intimidation, and hypocrisy. On the motion of James M. Buckley, "the Conference refused to entertain them by a unanimous rising vote." That Cooke may have been motivated by something less than a dispassionate search for ministerial integrity is further suggested by the fact that at the same 1908 Conference he twice brought charges against James M. Buckley, Bowne's defense counsel in the trial of 1904! Neither set of charges against Buckley was sustained. The analysis of the anatomy of these proceedings that is offered here leads to several conclusions.

First, while Bowne was surely in advance of the popular theological constructions of his own time, he was clearly within traditional limits at four of the five points on which he stood accused. Second, Bowne should have been challenged more forcefully on the doctrine of Atonement and the indictment either sustained or the defendant reprimanded for advocating a view that was at variance with then-accepted Methodist teaching. Third, given the time devoted to the trial and the seriousness of the charges, the judgment that the trial was viewed with a measure of amusement may not be descriptively accurate. Fourth, that the official record of the trial transcript, available 18 years after the trial, is now entirely missing—save for Elliott's excerpts—raises serious questions about the Methodist Episcopal Church's institutional interests in this last trial of one of its ministers for heterodoxy.

In the end, and taking a rather synoptic view, Bowne's innocence overall would have to be defended. He was plainly a liberal churchman and a forward-thinking theologian, and while these traits in and of themselves have often been taken as sufficient reason for accusations of heresy, it is far from demonstrated fact in the case of Borden Parker Bowne.

SELECTED BIBLIOGRAPHY

Bowne is credited with having written 17 books and over 130 articles. The bibliography cited here consists of entries particularly relevant to the charges made against him by George Cooke.

Bowne, Borden Parker. *The Atonement*. Cincinnati: Curts & Jennings, 1900.
———. *The Christian Life*. Boston: Christian Witness, 1899.
———. *The Christian Revelation*. Cincinnati: Jennings & Pye; New York: Eaton Mains, 1898.
———. *Metaphysics: A Study in First Principles*. New York: Harper & Brothers, 1882.
———. *Philosophy of Theism*. New York: Harper, 1887.
———. *Studies in Christianity*. Boston and New York: Houghton Mifflin Co., 1923. Copyright 1909.
———. *Studies in Theism*. New York: Phillips & Hunt; Cincinnati: Hitchcock & Walden, 1880.
———. *Theism*. New York: American Book Co., 1902. This is a revision of *Philosophy of Theism*.
Buckley, James M. "The Acquittal of Professor Bowne." *Christian Advocate* 79 (14 April 1904): 571–573. Reprinted in *Zion's Herald* 16 (20 April 1904): 489f.
Cooke, George A. *The Present and the Future of Methodism: An Examination of the Teachings of Prof. Borden P. Bowne*. Boston: Cusman Press, n.d.

Elliott, George. "The Orthodoxy of Bowne." *Methodist Review* 105 [Fifth Series, 38] (May–June 1922): 399–413.

McConnell, Francis John. *Borden Parker Bowne, His Life and His Philosophy.* New York: Abingdon Press, 1929. The 14-page excerpt of Bowne's trial transcript is reproduced in the chapter "The Defender of Biblical Research."

New York East Conference, The Methodist Episcopal Church. *Minutes.* 1904, 1908.

Steinkraus, Warren. "Five Letters of Bowne to James Mudge." *Personalist* 46 (summer 1965): 342–347.

Trotter, F. Thomas. "Methodism's Last Heresy Trial." *Christian Advocate* 4 (31 March 1960): 9–10.

The search for data has been arduous and often frustrating. Attempts to discover the full transcript have been futile despite communications with officials of the (Methodist Episcopal) New York East Conference, area universities and schools, various New England historical and genealogical societies, public and private libraries, the morgues of contemporary newspapers, magazines and journals, and pastors and archivists of Methodist Churches that served as sites for various deliberations. Correspondence with the four surviving members of the Conference at which Bowne was tried produced good wishes for my research and interest in it but only very vague recollections dimmed by more than a half-century removal from the proceedings. For whatever reason, Bowne's widow saw fit to destroy virtually all of his papers. A mysterious trunk, allegedly containing a copy of the trial transcript together with related materials, was believed to exist as late as the mid-1960s, but strenuous efforts to discover its whereabouts proved to be ineffectual. In sum, there is nowhere extant a substantial collection of Bowne materials. For fuller discussion of these bibliographic difficulties, see my "Borden Parker Bowne: Heresy at Boston," in George H. Shriver, ed., *American Religious Heretics* (Nashville: Abingdon Press, 1966), 148–154. There are apparently permanent lacunae in the transcript. Contemporary editor James M. Buckley reported, "The stenographic report would make a book of two hundred and forty pages" ("The Acquittal of Professor Bowne," *Christian Advocate* 79 [14 April 1904]: 571), but as I have noted, the whereabouts of such a document is presently unknown. Fourteen pages of the transcript, dealing mainly with the first three of the five specifications of heresy, are reproduced in George Elliott, "The Orthodoxy of Bowne," *Methodist Review* 105 [Fifth Series, 38] (May–June 1922): 399–413. To my knowledge, this is the only extant fragment of the trial transcript. Investigations further to my bibliographic searches in the early and mid-1960s have not produced additional documentary evidence. Before my 1966 essay, the most recent treatment of Bowne's adversity, very brief and written for a popular audience, is F. Thomas Trotter's "Methodism's Last Heresy Trial," *Christian Advocate* 4 (31 March 1960): 9–10.

Harmon L. Smith

Charles Augustus Briggs
(1841–1913)

PART I

Nineteenth-century American religious thought witnessed the emergence of an unusual form of scholasticism known as Princeton theology. Distinguished by its view of verbal inspiration and textual inerrancy, this position quickly found itself juxtaposed to the critical historical methodology of biblical interpretation. The struggle between these two points of view climaxed in the last decade of the nineteenth century. The man most closely associated with the critical method of biblical study was Charles Augustus Briggs.

A native of New York City, Briggs was born on 15 January 1841. Following three months' service with the New York 7th Regiment in the Civil War, he enrolled in the Union Theological Seminary in October 1861. On 19 October 1865, Briggs married Julie Valentine of Trenton, New Jersey, and New York City.

Briggs's desire to study abroad was realized in the summer of 1866. The next three years were spent at the University of Berlin with Isaac August Dorner, E. W. Hengstenberg, Emil Roediger, and H.G.A. Ewald. After one semester under Hengstenberg, Briggs turned aside from the study of the Pentateuch and only returned to that discipline during his last year abroad under H.G.A. Ewald of Göttingen.

The state of his parents' health required that Briggs return home in July 1869. On 30 June 1870, Briggs was installed as pastor of the First Presbyterian Church of Roselle, New Jersey. In January 1874, he accepted the position of provisional professor at Union Theological Seminary, thus beginning a relationship of almost 40 years that would profoundly affect the destinies of both the man and the institution. Two years later, he was elected Davenport Professor of Hebrew and Cognate Languages.

Largely at Briggs's instigation, the *Presbyterian Review* was founded as a joint venture of the faculties of Princeton and Union Seminaries. Under the coeditorship of Briggs and Professor A. A. Hodge of Princeton, the *Review* during the span from 1880 to 1889 became the most comprehensive journal of religion of that time.

Early on in this joint effort the issue of biblical criticism was raised in the form of the heresy trial of W. Robertson Smith in Scotland. American opponents of Smith's views insisted that the question be raised in the *Review*. A series of eight articles was agreed upon with four pro and four con. The first article, prepared by Hodge and B. B. Warfield under the title "Inspiration," was the embodiment of Princeton theology. Here Hodge defined inspiration as "the superintendence by God of the writers in the entire process of their writing, which accounts for nothing whatever but the absolute infallibility of the record in which the revelation, once generated, appears in the original autograph" (Hodge, "Inspiration," 225–226). Hodge wrote that all affirmations of Scripture "are without error, when the *ipsissima verba* of the original autographs are ascertained and interpreted in their natural and intended sense (238).

Warfield contended: "A proved error in Scripture contradicts not only our doctrine but the Scripture claims and, therefore, its inspiration in making those claims" (245).

Briggs in the second article dismissed both the doctrine of verbal inspiration and the notion of original autographs. Instead, he acknowledged the presence of errors and inconsistencies in the biblical text. For Briggs, verbal inspiration itself endangered rather than reinforced the doctrine of inspiration.

Francis L. Patton, who had succeeded A. A. Hodge in 1882 as coeditor of the *Review*, resigned that position in 1888 in order to become president of Princeton College. As his successor, the Princeton faculty chose B. B. Warfield.

The General Assembly of 1889 posed the question to all of its Presbyteries: "Do you desire a revision of the Confession of Faith? If so, in what respects, and to what extent?" Three schools of thought quickly emerged in response to that question: one in support of revision; one opposed to revision; and a third that urged the adoption of a new and simple consensus creed. Union Seminary joined the party of revision. Princeton led the forces opposed to revision.

Initially, Briggs opposed the revision movement as "premature and impracticable." He argued that "the statements of the Calvinistic system in the Westminster symbols are the most cautious, firm, and carefully guarded that can be found, and I would not trust any set of divines now living to revise them or improve them" (Briggs, "The General Assembly," 467). Briggs's proposal was "simply to emend the strictness of the formula of subscription" (470). As the controversy continued to grow, Briggs was drawn into the party supporting revision.

The working relationship between the coeditors of the *Review* steadily deteriorated. On 22 September 1889, Briggs resigned as coeditor. The Union faculty decided to discontinue their support of the *Review*.

Just prior to his resignation, Briggs published a defense of the revision movement entitled *Whither? A Theological Question for the Times*. Briggs cited the fourth chapter of the Confession of Faith dealing with Creation as being most in need of revision. Modern science had ruled out any Creation period of six days of 24 hours each. As a result of *Whither?* Briggs came to be identified as a leading proponent of the revision movement.

The Presbyterian Union of New York arranged a debate on the revision issue and invited Francis Patton and Briggs to represent their respective positions. Briggs was convinced that this event served to draw the ire of the antirevisionists upon Union Seminary and himself. During the 1880s Briggs had gained recognition for both his support of biblical criticism and his views favoring the revision movement. This had increasingly aroused the suspicion of the conservative faction of the Presbyterian Church.

In November of 1890, Union's Board of Directors transferred Briggs to the newly proposed Edward Robinson Chair of Biblical Theology. Briggs was dissuaded by the donor of the chair from focusing his inaugural address on the topic of biblical geography. Instead, he was urged to speak on a topic more attuned to the issues of revision and biblical criticism. Briggs warned that such a topic would only arouse the hostility of the ultraconservatives.

Briggs said of the address, which was entitled the *Authority of Holy Scripture*: "The aim of the address was to maintain and to assert in the strongest terms the divine authority of Holy Scripture in connection with a full recognition of the results of modern Biblical criticism and modern thought in all departments" (Prentiss, *Union Theological Seminary*, 332). Briggs insisted that there was no position expressed in that address that had not been published previously.

In his inaugural address delivered on 20 January 1891 in the Seminary's Adams Chapel, Briggs proclaimed that God had made his presence known to men of every age through "three great fountains of divine authority— the Bible, the Church and the Reason." He then posed six barriers that had restricted the human approach to the Scriptures. These included superstition, verbal inspiration, authenticity of the Scriptures, inerrancy, violation of the laws of nature (required for all miracles), and minute prediction (predictive prophecy).

Briggs had some very pointed comments to make regarding each of these. Minute prediction or "predictive prophecy" Briggs contended was always secondary to human redemption. Prophecies were often unfulfilled or withdrawn by God in order to advance redemption. In connection with redemption, Briggs expanded his comments to affirm his belief in progressive sanctification, a middle state between justification (which occurred at the time of death) and final judgment. While denying the doctrines of purgatory and second probation, Briggs urged that redemption required progressive sanctification in order that each individual might prepare for final judgment.

The reaction to the address both in the secular and in the religious press exceeded anything Briggs had anticipated. At its April meeting, the Presbytery of New York appointed a seven-member committee to study the address and determine what, if any, action should be taken. At the May meeting, the majority report signed by four members specified three areas in which the inaugural ran counter to the Confession of Faith. These were (1) equating the Bible, the church, and the reason as coordinate fountains of divine authority; (2) rejecting the inerrancy of the original autographs of Holy Scripture; and (3) holding that progressive sanctification after death was both biblical and church doctrine.

The minority report recommended that no action be taken regarding the inaugural, noting that any charges of heresy based on Briggs's address would cause a profound disturbance within the Church. The majority report was adopted by a vote of 44 to 30.

On May 17, the moderator of the New York Presbytery named a committee of five "to arrange and prepare the necessary proceedings appropriate in the case of Professor Briggs." Two days later, Union's Board of Directors formally affirmed their confidence in and support for Briggs.

PART II

When the General Assembly of 1891 convened in Detroit on 21 May 1891, Princeton influence was immediately apparent in the election of Professor William Henry Green as moderator. The Committee on Theological Seminaries, chaired by Francis L. Patton, insisted that the Assembly held the right to veto Briggs's appointment to the Edward Robinson chair.

Union's Board insisted that Briggs's transfer to the new chair did not constitute an election to the faculty. When Briggs had been elected to Union's faculty years before, the Assembly had not disapproved his election.

Nevertheless, Chairman Patton argued passionately that the Assembly should veto Briggs's transfer without any delay: "Now, then, you have the right to veto, and if you veto, you must veto now." The Assembly adopted the Committee's recommendation by a vote of 447 to 60. Union's Board deeply resented this action. On June 4, the Board voted 22 to 2 not to heed the Assembly's veto of Briggs's transfer.

On 5 October 1891 the New York Presbytery's Committee charged with preparing the case against Briggs returned two charges of heresy: (1)

with teaching doctrines that conflict irreconcilably with and are contrary to the cardinal doctrines taught in the Holy Scriptures and contained in the Standards of the Presbyterian Church, that the Scriptures of the Old and New Testaments are the only infallible rule of faith and practice; (2) with teaching a doctrine of the character, state, and sanctification of believers after death, which irreconcilably conflicts with and is contrary to the Holy Scriptures and the Standards of the Presbyterian Church.

These charges were answered by Briggs when the Presbytery convened in the Scotch Presbyterian Church on 4 November 1891. In his response, Briggs relied extensively upon criteria set forth by the General Assembly of 1824 in the Craighead Case. Briggs argued that the first of the two charges both alleged more than one offense and failed to set forth the specific offense that was being alleged. The second charge also failed to specify exactly which doctrine of the Standards and Holy Scripture had been violated.

In the case of the second charge, before the Presbytery could condemn Briggs's position, the prosecution would have to prove that immediate sanctification at death is the cardinal doctrine of the Standards and the Scriptures and that this doctrine is in irreconcilable conflict with progressive sanctification.

At the conclusion of Briggs's response, the question of the status of the prosecuting committee was raised. Should the committee be declared only an organ of the Presbytery, then its existence would end with the dismissal of the charges. But should the committee be declared a representative of the Presbyterian Church and an original party in the case, then the committee's existence would continue entirely independent of the Presbytery that created it. As an original party, the committee could then appeal any unfavorable verdict to a higher court.

Following a heated discussion of this issue in the Presbytery, the moderator ruled that the committee had functioned as a prosecuting committee and should be formally declared an original party in the case. This ruling was immediately appealed, but the Presbytery narrowly sustained the moderator. The committee then gave notice to the Presbytery that should the charges be dismissed, the committee would appeal.

A motion to dismiss the charges against Briggs was presented to the Presbytery and adopted by a vote of 94 to 39. As they had promised, the prosecuting committee gave notice of an appeal to the Synod of New York.

Shortly after the General Assembly of 1892 convened in Portland, Oregon, its Judicial Committee submitted two reports pertaining to the appeal of the New York Presbytery's prosecuting committee. A majority report found the appeal in order, thus confirming the status of the committee as an original party in the case. The minority report recommended that the appellants be instructed to bring their appeal to the Synod of New York instead of bypassing that body.

In rebutting the position of the appellants, Briggs noted that only twice had the General Assembly ever recognized appeals that bypassed the Synod. In both instances, these appeals had been brought by defendants and not prosecutors. Only one of these was actually entertained by the General Assembly. Therefore, no precedent whatsoever existed for an appeal by the prosecution.

In the confusion that followed, the minority report was tabled 385 to 122. The majority report was then adopted, and proponents and opponents were heard, respectively, concerning the appeal. Before calling for a vote on 28 May 1892, the moderator ruled that should the vote be to sustain the appeal, the entire case would be remanded to the New York Presbytery for trial. The vote was to sustain the appeal 429 to 87.

PART III

On October 13, Union's Board adopted by 19 to 1 a resolution that (1) rescinded the Assembly's veto power over faculty appointments and (2) terminated a long-standing agreement between Presbyterian seminaries and the General Assembly known as the Compact of 1870. Union's grounds for terminating its commitment to the Compact was that its charter placed complete control of the seminary in the care of its directors. The right of veto power could not therefore be delegated to any other party.

On November 9, the Presbytery of New York assembled to consider the logistics of the forthcoming trial and to receive the amended charges and specifications of the prosecuting committee. The original two charges were now expanded to eight:

1. With teaching that the Reason is a fountain of divine authority which may and does savingly enlighten men, even such men as reject the Scriptures as the authoritative proclamation of the will of God and reject also the way of salvation through the mediation and sacrifice of the Son of God as revealed therein. . . .

2. With teaching that the Church is a fountain of divine authority which, apart from Holy Scripture, may and does savingly enlighten men. . . .

3. With teaching that errors have existed in the original text of the Holy Scripture, as it came from its authors. . . .

4. With teaching that many of the Old Testament predictions have been reversed by history, and that the great body of Messianic prediction has not been and cannot be fulfilled. . . .

5. With teaching that Moses is not the author of the Pentateuch. . . .

6. With teaching that Isaiah is not the author of half of the book that bears his name. . . .

7. With teaching that the processes of redemption extend to the world to come in the case of many who die in sin. . . .

8. With teaching that Sanctification is not complete at death. . . .

The trial began on November 28, with Briggs's evaluation of the amended charges before the court. Only the eighth charge was sufficient in form and legal effect. Of the remaining seven, he would waive objections to five, providing that a separate vote be taken on each alleged violation of doctrine. Charges four and seven should be dismissed forthwith since both charged Briggs with views that he had expressly denied.

Charge four was based on a misquotation of the inaugural address that anyone who had read the address would clearly recognize. As for charge seven, Briggs had specifically rejected any belief in a doctrine of future probation. He insisted that both of these charges be set aside. After lengthy debate, charges four and seven were dismissed. Briggs pleaded not guilty to the other six.

Following the prosecution's presentation, which began on December 5, the defense opened on December 13 with Briggs asserting this remarkable claim. Questions that the Confession of Faith had not addressed, Briggs contended, allowed a believer to hold a private opinion as an "extra confessional" view so long as that opinion could be supported by Holy Scripture or some human experience.

In addressing the first charge, Briggs declared that the Confession was deficient in its attention to the "reason." The reason was the human capacity to understand the Holy Spirit speaking through Scripture. The reason was a great fountain of divine authority, though not a rule of faith and practice. The reason was God's greatest gift to mankind—"the holy of holies of human nature."

As for the second charge, Briggs insisted that the Church was a fountain of divine authority, though not a rule of faith and practice. The Church had served to channel divine authority through its divinely appointed institutions.

The third charge had grown out of the Princeton doctrine of inspiration. Briggs cited frequently from church history in disparaging verbal inspiration and its logical conclusion, textual inerrancy. He insisted: "You cannot exact of me that I shall say there are no errors in Holy Scripture, for the reason that the Confession does not assert this and I am not bound to your views of consistency or inconsistency—but only to the Confession and to my own judgment" (*The Defence of Professor Briggs before the Presbytery*, 87).

The chairman of the prosecution committee had argued in his opening statement regarding Scripture: "God is the arranger of its clauses, the chooser of its terms, and the speller of its words so that the text in its letters, words, or clauses is just as divine as the thought" (96).

Citing chapter one, section eight of the Confession, Briggs insisted that the Scriptures are the final appeal in religious controversies but not in matters of science. Questions relating to the movement of the earth around the sun or the creation of the earth in six days of 24 hours lie beyond the parameters of Scripture, as the Confession acknowledged.

Charges five and six deal, respectively, with the Mosaic authorship of the Pentateuch and the authorship of the Book of Isaiah. Drawing from the full range of church history, Briggs contended that the church had never held that Moses was the author of the Pentateuch. One need only compare the literary styles, theologies, and historical situations depicted in the various chapters to recognize that the Book of Isaiah was compiled over several centuries and was not the work of one person.

Of the charges that Briggs faced, none proved more difficult to overcome than that of teaching that sanctification was not complete at death. Briggs held that at death the souls of believers entered the middle state in which each soul was made perfect in holiness over a period of time through progressive sanctification. The souls of believers were not made perfect in holiness immediately, in a moment of time, upon death.

Briggs had to reconcile his views with Question 86 in the larger Catechism, which reads as follows: "The communion in glory with Christ, which the members of the invisible church enjoy immediately after death, is in that their souls are then made perfect in holiness, and received into the highest heavens, where they behold the face of God in light and glory." Briggs insisted that "immediately after death" in this context referred to the entire state that extends from death to judgment. He acknowledged, however, that his views went beyond the formulation of the Confession. This extra confessional opinion to which he was entitled he considered in no way a violation of the Confession.

For Briggs, sanctification went far beyond simply being cleansed of sin. Progressive sanctification filled the middle state with progress in grace, knowledge, holiness, and all perfections. It also provided for the education of each soul. Briggs believed that the educational aspect of sanctification was indispensable for all believers.

The voting on the various charges occupied December 29 and 30. Briggs was acquitted on each charge by margins ranging from 73–49 to 67–61. The ministers in the Presbytery strongly resisted every charge. The elders, however, barely sustained three of the six charges and split their votes evenly on one other.

Despite an effort at reconciliation on the part of the committee that drafted the judgment, the prosecution committee filed notice of an appeal to the General Assembly of 1893.

On February 18 the *New York Sun* reported that Briggs and his friend Henry Preserved Smith* of Lane Seminary were planning to leave the Presbyterian Church to form a new church. Briggs had made a practice of refusing press interviews on such topics. Smith quickly issued a denial through the Associated Press. Given the appeal before the Assembly in three months, this rumor was, no doubt, extremely damaging to Briggs and his supporters.

PART IV

The intensity of the personal antagonism on the part of the prosecution committee reached its peak in their appeal to the General Assembly of 1893 and largely obscured the theological issues in question.

The General Assembly convened on May 18 in Washington's New York Avenue Presbyterian Church. Two reports were presented by the Judicial Committee on May 23. The majority report recommended that "the appeal from the decision and final judgment of the Presbytery of New York in the case of Professor Charles H. Briggs, D.D., is hereby entertained and it is ordered that the case proceed to trial" (*The Case against Professor Briggs*, Part III, 128).

The minority report noted that this recommendation in the majority report prejudiced the case before the Assembly at a time when the parties had not been heard. Despite this objection, the case was opened the following afternoon in a sanctuary that quickly assumed the atmosphere of a courtroom.

Following the prosecuting committee's opening statement citing a disclaimer in the verdict of acquittal of any approval of the critical or theological views in the inaugural address as a lingering source of dissension within the New York Presbytery and thus a ground of their appeal, Briggs reminded the Assembly that a complaint was then before the Synod of New York pertaining to the status of the prosecution committee. He insisted that the complaint before the Synod took precedence over the appeal currently before the Assembly. Until the Synod should make its decision, the Assembly had no jurisdiction over the case.

In its closing statement, the prosecution pointed out that the only thing these proceedings were based on was the inaugural address. According to one minister who was present at every session, not one copy of that address was to be found in the Assembly. One commissioner requested that copies be brought in, but the request was ignored.

Following a lengthy period of discussion, a resolution was introduced on the floor of the Assembly seeking to have the appeal entertained and the case brought to trial. An effort to refer the appeal to the Synod of New York was tabled. The resolution was adopted by a margin of 405 to 145. The majority report was adopted, and preparations were begun to bring the case to trial.

Briggs was thoroughly discouraged by this action. Only the persuasive efforts of his strongest supporters prevented his withdrawal from the Presbyterian Church. The president of Union's Board penned these words to him: "The interests of the Seminary and the Presbyterian Church and the cause of truth require you to remain in the Church and stand fast—unless like Luther, you are driven on" ("Ninth Day," 54).

When the trial began on May 29, the prosecuting committee offered the following five grounds as the basis for its appeal: irregularity in the proceedings of said Presbytery of New York; receiving improper testimony; declining to receive important testimony; manifestation of prejudice in the conduct of the case; mistake or injustice in the decision. Thirty-four specifications were listed in support of these allegations.

Characteristic of the prosecution's case was the rationale dealing with the second specification under the fifth ground of the appeal. The prosecution argued that the court had "already substantially determined" that if Briggs had taught the doctrine with which he stood accused, he was guilty as charged. Since the allegations were proved by exerpts from the inaugural address that were not denied or retracted by the defendant, the proof was complete. The verdict should have been "guilty." Only if Briggs had produced evidence to show that he had not made such statements as were contained in the exerpts should he have been "acquitted." The only meaning that could be attributed to Briggs's words was that which the prosecuting committee attributed to them.

Concerning the fifth charge, the prosecution argued passionately for the Mosaic authorship of the Pentateuch: "If this claim be not true, then the Pentateuch is neither genuine nor authentic, and it must be untrustworthy. If the Pentateuch's claim of Mosaic authorship be false, and the work originated piece by piece during the centuries after the death of Moses, the document as it has come to us is a fraud, and no dependence can be placed upon it" (*One Hundred and Fifth General Assembly*, The Argument of Joseph J. Lampe, D.D., 54).

The prosecution then turned to the fourth and seventh of the amended charges that the New York Presbytery had rejected during Briggs's trial. Briggs immediately challenged the prosecution's right to resurrect these charges. The moderator ruled that the prosecution could proceed. This ruling was appealed but sustained. With the discussion of these two charges, the prosecution concluded its case.

In the course of his defense, Briggs denied the validity of both rejected charges. Of charge seven, Briggs insisted that his doctrine of redemption after death had only to do with believers "who enter the future life as born again under the influence of the Holy Spirit" (*The Case against Professor Briggs*, Part III, 147–148).

In refuting the fourth charge, Briggs read from his book *Messianic Prophecy* a passage in which he opposed the very views that the prosecution had attributed to him. As Briggs reviewed the charges against him, one commissioner asked for a recess, noting that a number of the commissioners seated near him were fast asleep. The request was ignored and Briggs continued.

The presentation of the case and the ensuing discussion of its merits on the floor of the Assembly concluded late in the evening of May 31. When the vote was taken, 383 commissioners favored sustaining the appeal in its entirety or in part; 116 voted in opposition.

The following morning a Committee of Judgment was appointed. When this committee interviewed Briggs, he refused to retract any of his views he had expressed before the Assembly. The committee's report cited the Presbytery of New York for having "erred in striking out said amended charges four and seven" (McCook, *The Appeal in the Briggs Heresy Case*, 376).

The committee recommended that the General Assembly "suspend Charles A. Briggs, the said Appellee, from the office of a minister in the Presbyterian Church in the United States of America, until such time as he shall give satisfactory evidence of repentance to the General Assembly. . . , for the violation by him of the said ordination now as herein and heretofore found" (377). The recommendation was adopted by voice vote.

The Assembly also adopted a report pertaining to Union Seminary that deplored Union's action in retaining Briggs on the faculty after the Assembly had disapproved his appointment as well as Union's unilateral abrogation of the compact of 1870. The Assembly disavowed all responsibility for the teaching of Union's faculty and declined to receive any further reports from that seminary until satisfactory relations were established (Prentiss, *Union Theological Seminary*, 291–292).

Perhaps during the course of that day, Briggs remembered the words written to him by his uncle Marvin Briggs in the early days of the Assembly: "Let the mocking be all done by the chief priests and scribes of the Washington Assembly. They will stone you if they can; But their children will build your sepulchre" (*Briggs Transcript*, IX, 3, #4821, 20 May 1893).

From the vantage point of later years, Briggs remained convinced that his struggle had been engendered by the revision controversy. He wrote: "[T]he Presbyterian Church was deliberately thrown into panic about the Bible in order to defeat the revision movement and to discredit Union Seminary.—Circumstances made me the convenient target on which to concentrate the attack. In all respects this conspiracy was successful. The revision movement was defeated; Union Seminary was discredited; and I was suspended from the ministry of the Presbyterian Church" (Prentiss, *Union Theological Seminary*, 333).

Following this ordeal, Briggs remained undaunted in the performance of his ministry. He was received into the priesthood of the Episcopal Church in 1899. As the first non-Presbyterian member of the Union faculty, his energies were increasingly devoted to the pursuit of Christian unity. The heresy trials had done more in two years to spread Briggs's views on higher criticism than he could have accomplished in a lifetime. Undoubtedly, much of the ecumenical concern that has remained the hallmark of Union Seminary can be traced to his influence.

In the wake of Briggs's death on 8 June 1913, Henry Preserved Smith, then librarian at Union, offered this observation concerning Briggs's ordeal in the Presbyterian Church: "It would hardly be too much to say that judged by the historic faith of the Church, Dr. Briggs was the last of the line of orthodox theologians. That the conservative party has not realized what a loss their church suffered is one of the strangest facts of our time" (Smith, "Charles Augustus Briggs," 502).

BIBLIOGRAPHY

Briggs, Charles Augustus. *Authority of Holy Scripture: An Inaugural Address*. New York: Charles Scribner's Sons, 1891.

———. "The General Assembly of the Presbyterian Church in the United States of America." *Presbyterian Review* 10 (October 1889).

Briggs, Emilie Grace. *Briggs Transcript*. Vols. 1–12. Housed in the library of Union Theological Seminary in New York.

The Defence of Professor Briggs before the General Assembly. The Case against Professor Briggs. Part III. New York: Scribner, 1893.

The Defence of Professor Briggs before the Presbytery of New York, December 13, 14, 15 and 19, 1892. New York: Charles Scribner's Sons, 1893.

Handy, Robert. *A History of Union Theological Seminary in New York*. New York: Columbia University Press, 1987.

Hodge, A. A. "Inspiration." *Presbyterian Review* 2 (April 1891): 225–260.

McCook, John J. *The Appeal in the Briggs Heresy Case*. New York: John C. Rankin Co., 1893.

"Ninth Day." *Tribune Monthly* 5 (May 1893): 54.

One Hundred and Fifth General Assembly. Record of the Case: From the Minutes of the Presbytery of New York, 1893.

Prentiss, G. L. *Union Theological Seminary, Its Design and Another Decade of Its History*. Asbury Park, NJ: M. W. & C. Pennypacker, 1899.

Presbyterian Review. Vols. 1–5, New York: Randolph; Vol. 6, New York: Presbyterian Review Association; Vols. 7–10, New York: Scribner, 1880–1889.

Rogers, Max G. "Charles Augustus Briggs: Heresy at Union." In *American Religious Heretics*, edited by George H. Shriver. Nashville: Abingdon Press, 1966.

Smith, Henry Preserved. "Charles Augustus Briggs." *American Journal of Theology* 17, no. 4 (October 1913).

Max Gray Rogers

Robert C. Briggs
(1915–)

Southeastern Baptist Theological Seminary,* a Southern Baptist Seminary, located at Wake Forest, North Carolina, aggressively sought to avoid an official "heresy trial" in the 1960s and was successful. The seminary was not quite ten years old when Robert C. Briggs joined the faculty in 1957 to become professor in New Testament studies. Within two years, tensions began to arise regarding the theological assumptions for New Testament research and teaching.

During the 1958–1959 academic year, some students arranged for a series of faculty-student discussions in which faculty members would respond to questions following a short statement. During the discussion following Briggs's presentation, Dr. Edward A. McDowell and other members of the New Testament faculty took sharp issue with some of the eschatological views of Briggs.

Soon afterward, similar reactions surfaced in a faculty discussion group in which the New Testament faculty reported on contemporary trends in New Testament scholarship. Briggs, reflecting later on the series of events, said, "I was aware of various attitudes toward my approach to the New Testament, but I assumed that such differences were evidence of a healthy environment in which I was to do my work" ("Personal Statement"). While it is not clear whether the administration or Board of Trustees were concerned about the differences of opinion about New Testament interpretation, the Trustees did instruct the president and dean of the faculty in February 1959 "to bring to the attention of the Board of Trustees any situation where a faculty member's performance was not satisfactory." The Trustees indicated that this statement was initiated to avoid abuses in automatic promotion. No evidence of controversy was noted in the president's report to the Board in February 1960 nor in the faculty's report at the same time. There is a vague statement in the minutes of the Board from the Instruction Committee that "one consideration is at present being processed."

Late in 1960 President Sydnor Stealey did indicate in a "Report to the Faculty" that he perceived a critical situation developing within the faculty concerning theology and teaching methods that could have serious implications for the seminary's relation with the Southern Baptist Convention. He reported to the faculty that he had called a meeting in his office of the faculty in New Testament studies along with other faculty members concerned with the teaching of particular theological positions. This meeting was followed by interviews with specific faculty members during which the conversations centered on the "resurrection of Jesus, the authority of the Bible, and the incarnation or the deity of Jesus" (Stealey, "Report to the Faculty," 12 December 1960).

In addition to Briggs, the other two professors under review were William C. Strickland and Harold H. Oliver. All three were invited individually to the meeting, not knowing that others would be present and that serious questions would be raised about the content of their teaching. Briggs remembered that the president specifically confirmed that the purpose of the meeting was to examine positions expounded by the three New Testament faculty members. Briggs also reported that he had refused to be interrogated by a small group of faculty members without due process and the protections afforded under academic freedom.

What followed was a series of events designed to force a response to the allegations that the president saw as "the application of radical Existentialism and so-called Bultmanianism." One unidentified professor was concerned that " 'they' use our terms but give them non-Christian meaning" (Stealey, "Report to the Faculty," 12 December 1960). An additional criticism was that such theology was over the heads of most of the students.

There was a subtext, at least in the initial period of the controversy. In the 12 December 1960 president's "Report to the Faculty," Stealey said that "some feel social groups are in danger of becoming theological groups. Motives have been attributed to men who deny such motives." Briggs also indicated that some of his opponents felt that those who played "Rook" at the president's home, which included Briggs and Strickland, discussed and influenced faculty policy ("Personal Statement"; Interviews).

In a "Report to the Faculty" of January 1961, the president praised the faculty for their recent voluntary self-examination but lamented that "we sometimes value scholarship as an end in itself rather than as an instrument for better teaching." He quickly added that he was "at this time quite unwilling to charge any colleague with heretical teachings" but did see dangers in some of the theological positions ("Report to the Faculty," 27 January 1961). He urged fairness in the consideration of divergent points of view, suggesting that theories should be discussed only as theories. In the president's "Report to the Board of Trustees" in February 1961, he reiterated these statements and pledged to respect the diversity of views. The "Report of the Faculty" to the Board of Trustees of the same date affirms commitment to the denomination and allegiance to the Abstract of Principles, which every member of the faculty had to sign upon election to the faculty. This report further urged that "if further study and reflection should ever destroy the adherence of any member of this body to the doctrinal standard of the school, he would make the fact known to the administration and ask to be relieved of his responsibility as a member of the faculty."

Briggs had wanted the discussion to remain with the seminary faculty, but it obviously had gone beyond that point. In fact, the president informed the faculty in April 1961 that no progress had been made in resolving the differences and that an impasse had been reached. He felt that regard for persons would take precedence over whatever ideas they expressed. "None should object to having his ideas examined, nor should we accept or reject *men* instead of ideas. . . . Attitudes of academic imperialism are certain to break fellowship." The president despaired of reaching a solution through his office, so he officially notified the faculty that he was asking the president of the Board of Trustees to become involved and give counsel. In the May meeting of 1961, the Board instructed the administration to try again to work for a harmonious resolution of the crisis.

The Board designated a Committee of Four (president, dean, and two representatives of the Board of Trustees) to meet with all the available faculty members in early summer to determine if their teachings were in accordance with the Articles of Faith and if any of them were "unable to accept any colleague as a Christian teacher or unwilling to cooperate with him in fraternal spirit and without captious criticism in the life and work of the Seminary" ("Report to the Faculty," 29 May 1961).

At the conclusion of these conferences, procedures were established in hopes of resolving the issues:

> 1. The one seeing the need should go first to the person or persons involved and strive person to person for understanding. 2. If such attempts should fail, write out your version of the matter and give it to the Dean or the President with the understanding that he will see that the party or parties involved will be given a copy of your paper and will be given time to prepare an answer to be given in your presence and that of the Dean or President or both. 3. If settlement cannot be reached by such conferences, any one involved may appeal to the President to present the matter to the Board of Trustees for final decision. In this way responsible action can be assured and dangerous procedures avoided. ("Report to the Faculty on Conferences," 21 June 1961)

The Committee of Four specifically directed the president to ask Briggs, Strickland, and Oliver to prepare a response to the following questions:

> What do you think about the nature of the Biblical revelation and the historical significance of the New Testament? Do you think and teach that demythologizing is a valid methodology of New Testament study? How do you define myth as you apply the term to the New Testament literature? Do you find mythological elements in the synoptic gospels? If so, list examples. Set forth precisely and in some detail what you believe and teach about the person and purpose of Jesus, the atonement, the resurrection of Jesus, the relation of Jesus Christ to the church, and eschatology. This is an opportunity for each one involved to present in his own way, and after careful consideration, the methodology used and some crucial points in New Testament theology.

After examining the three papers the Committee of Four agreed not to make any recommendation to the Board of Trustees at that time. Either evidence must have been lacking for heretical charges, there was reluctance to stir further denominational criticism of teaching at the seminary, or the seminary wanted to avoid charges of violation of academic freedom and due process. The seminary seemed to be trying to avoid being its own worst enemy.

Reports of the faculty to the Board attest to loyalty to the seminary and the denomination, and the only reference to the crisis was a brief statement unanimously approved by the faculty on 18 May 1961: "We recognize that we have problems of such depth, complexity, and gravity that their solution will require the cooperation of the Faculty, the Administration, and the Trustees. We assure the Trustees through our President that we shall cooperate with them in the search for a solution of the problems." No elaboration of the statement was included in the report, nor were there any comments by faculty members directly involved in the controversy.

By the time the Board of Trustees met in February 1962, additional guidelines were established that the Board approved. The Board agreed to "warn and require" Briggs, Strickland, and Oliver to reexamine their teaching in the context of the Abstract of Principles and the purpose of the seminary. They were also instructed to "state and discuss the basic presuppositions which they bring to the exegesis and interpretation of the New Testament with the faculty, in groups planned by the President and Dean of the Faculty and in a spirit of trust and professional regard for the colleagues" (Minutes of the Board, 15 February 1962). In addition, the three professors were to be reviewed annually for three years, and the results were to be reported to the Trustees. A news release by the Board of Trustees to the Baptist Press on 15 February 1962 dealt with doctrinal problems among the faulty and indicated that no "final charge was made against any member of the instructional staff."

Briggs did report to the faculty indicating that he "accepted historical-critical methodology as an indispensable tool for New Testament interpretation and was prepared to deal with the implication of that method in terms of the form and content of New Testament theology." He reported that no questions were raised by colleagues at that meeting.

President Stealey resigned his office on 31 July 1963 to be succeeded by Olin T. Binkley, who had been dean of the faculty. Briggs was granted sabbatical leave for the academic year 1963–1964 for study in New Testament at the Universities of Tübingen and Marburg. Professor Oliver also was on sabbatical leave during 1963–1964, studying at the University of Tübingen under D. Ernst Käsemann.

Each of the three men under scrutiny reported annually to the Board, declaring their belief that their teaching was in harmony with the purpose and content of the Abstract of Principles. President Binkley suggested to the Board in February 1964 that the process be brought to a close within one year after the Committee of Four consulted with the three men. All of this took place while the seminary was undergoing scrutiny from the Southern Baptist Convention concerning its interpretation of the nature of the Bible and its relationship to theological education. The Board concluded that the expectations of the denomination and the Abstract of Principles were in harmony. Yet the internal theological disagreement hung like a cloud over the seminary.

When Briggs returned from his sabbatical leave, he learned that the course in New Testament theology that he had regularly taught had been assigned to a recently hired New Testament professor. In ensuing conversations, the president indicated to Briggs that it was a mistake not to discuss his theological position with the faculty. Briggs emphasized that it was a matter of academic principle not to answer to a select group of professors when he in fact had not been charged with any heretical teachings. Trustees interpreted this refusal to participate in a "hearing" with other faculty members as a "pact of silence" made by the three professors in question "under the leadership of Dr. Briggs," thereby leading to faculty disunity. Again, it was noted that during the process of inquiry, no formal charges had been brought for investigation (Minutes of the Board, 17 December 1964).

Events at the end of 1964, although differently interpreted by the parties involved, began to bring the period of "unofficial heretical teaching" to an end. Briggs remembers making to the president an "offhand remark that I would have to decide whether or not I would be willing to continue my work at Southeastern." In response, the president asked if a full year's salary plus benefits would be satisfactory. After a discussion several weeks later, two year's salary was agreed upon, pending Trustee approval. Briggs remembers President Binkley taking the initiative to terminate his employment, while the president steadfastly maintained that Briggs arranged the interview in which he initiated discussion about the terms for resignation. The Board of Trustees approved the terms of resignation, ending Briggs's association with the seminary on 1 January 1965. Professor Oliver resigned effective 31 August 1965 to join the faculty of Boston University. Professor Strickland was approved by the Board after his third review to continue teaching. He resigned, however, at the conclusion of the spring semester, 1966, to join the faculty of Appalachian State University. Early in 1965, Briggs received an appointment to the faculty at Vanderbilt University and later to the faculty of the Interdenominational Theological Center in Atlanta, where he remained until his retirement.

The Alumni had been informed of the status of events in a letter of 4 January 1965 in which it was stated that no charges of heretical teachings had ever been made and that no resignations were forced by the administration or Trustees. The Student Coordinating Council, as elected representatives of the student body, formally registered their dismay at the loss of "able and dedicated scholars" and deplored the "failure, on the part of members of our faculty, to respect the integrity of their colleagues which is both a breach of personal trust and denial of the doctrine of the priesthood of all believers." The students further stated that the long impasse was aggravated by a lack of a stated procedure by which differences among faculty members could be resolved in an expedient manner.

While the controversy at Southeastern Baptist Seminary, 1959–1964, revolved around questions of New Testament interpretation, particularly the problem of history in the Gospels, the fundamental issue was the nature of religious authority, which had vexed Southern Baptists for many years. Was the basis for religious authority found outside of faith or within faith? It was Briggs's belief that his opponents, while accepting the claims of historical-critical research, refused to deal with the implications of such investigation.

Traditional theological interpretations of the New Testament, within the mainstream of Southern Baptist thought, defended by some of the established members of the faculty, were threatened by the younger European-influenced members of the New Testament faculty who believed existential theology was the key to understanding religious truth. This polarization made it impossible for either side to agree that a particular theological position is not necessarily the only one that is intellectually respectable. Whatever the personal motives or theological positions, the course of academic freedom was dealt a crippling blow at the seminary from which it would not finally recover.

BIBLIOGRAPHY

Briggs, Robert C. *Interpreting the Gospels*. Nashville: Abingdon Press, 1969.
————. "Personal Statement," 18 July 1983.
Interviews with Robert C. Briggs, Denton Coker, Harold Oliver, and William Strickland, February 1996.
Minutes of the Board of Trustees and Minutes of the Executive Committee, Southern Baptist Theological Seminary, 1959–1965.
News Release by the Board of Trustees, 15 February 1962.
"Report of the Faculty" to the Board of Trustees, 1961–1962.
Stealey, Sydnor. "Report to the Faculty" and "Report to the Board of Trustees," 1960–1962.

Coleman C. Markham

Fawn McKay Brodie
(1915–1981)

One of the most famous twentieth-century heretics to emerge out of the Mormon Church (officially known as the Church of Jesus Christ of Latter-day Saints) was Fawn McKay Brodie. She was a nationally renowned author by virtue of her controversial biographies, including *Thomas Jefferson: An Intimate History* (1974) and *Richard Nixon: The Shaping of His Character* (1981). These two works followed earlier biographies written on Thaddeus Stevens, a congressional leader of Radical Reconstruction following the Civil War, *Thaddeus Stevens, Scourge of the South* (1959), and on Richard Francis Burton, a nineteenth-century British explorer and author, *The Devil Drives: A Life of Sir Richard Burton* (1967).

But it was Brodie's first biography, *No Man Knows My History: The Life of Joseph Smith* (1945), that resulted in her excommunication from the Mormon Church at a heresy trial held at Cambridge, Massachusetts, in May 1946. Ironically, Brodie, herself, was not present at the trial that severed her 22-year membership in the Church of Jesus Christ of Latter-day Saints. Church officials took issue with Brodie's assertion that Joseph Smith, the founder of Mormonism, was not a divinely inspired prophet, as taught in Mormon doctrine, but rather a conscious fraud who in developing essential Mormon beliefs and practices was primarily influenced by ideas and forces within nineteenth-century American society.

In many ways, Fawn M. Brodie seemed most unlikely to become a Mormon heretic. Born on 15 September 1915 in Ogden, Utah, Fawn McKay came from patrician Mormon stock. Her paternal grandfather, David McKay, helped found Huntsville, the small Utah farming community ten miles east of Ogden, where she grew up. Her father, Thomas E. McKay, a respected church leader, served as president of the Swiss-German Mission, president of the Ogden Stake (diocese), and assistant to the Quorum of the Twelve, the Mormon Church ruling elite. Politically active, he had been president of the Utah State Senate and later state public utilities commissioner. Fawn's uncle, David O. McKay, was a member of the Quorum of the Twelve, and her maternal grandfather, George H. Brimhall, served as president of Brigham Young University from 1904 to 1921.

Fawn's formative years and upbringing appeared ideal. She fondly recalled her youth in Huntsville as "an idyllic childhood" and the family farmhouse "a great place to grow up in." The larger Huntsville community was a place she "loved madly" (Brodie, "Biography," 2). Throughout childhood, Fawn was both obedient and deeply religious. She asserted the virtues of obedience in her first published work, a poem entitled "Just a Minute, Mother," written when she was just ten and printed in *The Juvenile Instructor*, a Mormon Church periodical for children:

> "Just a minute, mother,"
> Is heard in all child homes,
> From the cottage of the peasants,
> To the castles with great domes
>
> If mother tried to count,
> The "just a minutes" of each day,
> We'd find that hours and hours
> Slip uselessly away.
>
> Let's drop our "just a minutes,"
> And make our mothers smile,
> And in this time we've wasted
> Do something that's worthwhile.

Within her Mormon religion, Fawn was active both spiritually and socially. She taught a Sunday school class and gave poetry readings as a member of the Huntsville Ward (congregation). In adolescence, her recreation centered around the Huntsville Ward's youth group, "the Builders Club" (Bringhurst, "Fawn McKay Brodie: Dissident Historian and Quintessential Critic of Mormondom," 279–281). Fawn's religiosity appeared strong into her teenage years. She later recalled: "I was devout until I went to the University of Utah" (Brodie, "Biography," 2).

There were, however, indications of Fawn's dissent long before her departure from Huntsville to attend the University of Utah in Salt Lake City. These stemmed from certain "inner conflicts" relating to her behavior and attitudes as well as from "external conflicts" involving her family and environment. Inner conflicts arose from Fawn's superior intelligence combined, paradoxically, with inferiority she felt because of her physical appearance. She demonstrated her exceptional intelligence as early as age three through her ability to memorize lengthy pieces of poetry. By age four, Fawn was reading fourth-grade-level books with ease, and after being formally enrolled in school at age six, she was given an IQ test. She went "over the top score." The principal promptly advanced the bright child from first to third grade and subsequently moved her up two more grades. She ultimately graduated from high school at age fourteen. Fawn's precocity, however, had a price. Because she was three to four years younger than most of her classmates, she was socially insecure and reticent.

Fawn was also extremely sensitive about her physical appearance. Despite being strikingly attractive to all who knew her, Fawn was quite tall (particularly for a female)—five feet ten inches, which she reached by adolescence. Fawn's height combined with her extreme intelligence and classic beauty contrasted with the norm expected in her patriarchal Mormon environment—wherein the typical Mormon female was expected to be of average intelligence and not too tall, certainly not taller or more intelligent than the males around her.

Also contributing to Fawn's dissent were certain tensions within her immediate family, much of it focusing on the differing religious views of her parents. Although Fawn characterized both her mother and father as "devout Mormons," each differed, significantly, in degree of religious commitment. Fawn's mother, to whom she was particularly close, was "a quiet heretic" whose heresy, according to Fawn's later recollections "mostly took the form of encouraging me to be on my own." Whereas Fawn's father, to whom she was more distant, was "very devout." "We both found it difficult to communicate" on religion or on "most other" topics, she later recalled. This "made for family difficulties." Such tensions, moreover, made for an extremely repressed family environment, particularly stifling for the bright, precocious, always curious adolescent (Bringhurst, "Fawn Brodie and Her Quest for Independence," 82–83).

As she commenced studies at the University of Utah in 1932, Fawn began moving away from her basic Mormon beliefs. This process was aided by various courses that she took in psychology, philosophy, and English (her major subject), wherein the young college student was encouraged by her professors to critically examine previously unquestioned beliefs and assumptions. Fawn also experienced shock when she first encountered a vast body of historical literature in the university library presenting the Mormons in a critical, sometimes hostile light. By the time Fawn graduated from the University of Utah in 1934 with her degree in English, she experienced "a quiet kind of moving out . . . of the parochialism of the Mormon community" and away from a belief that Salt Lake City "was the center of the universe as I had been taught as a child" (Brodie, "Biography," 1–4).

Pulling Fawn further away from her Mormon roots literally and intellectually was her departure from Utah in 1935 to pursue graduate studies at the University of Chicago. Shortly after arriving, she lapsed into complete inactivity relative to the Mormon Church. As she vividly recalled: "The confining aspects of the Mormon religion dropped off within a few weeks. . . . It was like taking off a hot coat in the summertime. The sense of liberation I had at the University of Chicago was enormously exhilarating. I felt very quickly that I could never go back to the old life [of Mormonism] and I never did" (Brodie, "Biography," 1–4). Further underscoring Fawn's break with Mormonism was her marriage in August 1936 to Bernard Brodie, a fellow graduate student and non-Mormon, who came from a Latvian-Jewish immigrant background.

Shortly after receiving her master's degree in English in 1936, Fawn began serious research into Mormon history. Her initial findings resulted in a highly critical article entitled "Mormon 'Security' " published in the *Nation* magazine in 1937. This article, representing Brodie's first open criticism of the Mormon Church, questioned the effectiveness of the Mormon Church welfare system—a highly respected program set up to combat the adverse effects of the Great Depression and one praised by both Mormon and non-Mormon alike.

From 1938 to 1945, Brodie's dissent became even stronger as she researched and wrote her biography of Joseph Smith. Work on the biography became almost an obsession, despite numerous distractions. These included having to devote significant time and energy to her role as a wife to husband Bernard and mother to young son Richard, born in 1942. Bernard, meanwhile, completed his own graduate studies at the University of Chicago, receiving a doctorate in international relations in 1940. He then sought a suitable academic position, which necessitated numerous moves for the Brodies during the period 1940–1945: first to Princeton, New Jersey, in 1940; then to Dartmouth in Hanover, New Hampshire, in 1941; and in 1942 on to Washington, D.C., following the outbreak of World War II, where Bernard served as an officer in U.S. Naval Intelligence. By the summer of 1945, as the war was winding down, the Brodies returned to New England, settling in New Haven, Connecticut, where Bernard accepted a position in the Institute of International Relations at Yale University.

Fawn, meanwhile, pushed ahead with work on the Joseph Smith biography, which she characterized as "a rather compulsive thing. I had to. . . . I wanted to answer a lot of questions" concerning Joseph Smith and Mormon origins. Brodie was also motivated by a sense of missionary zeal in that "she wanted to give other young doubting Mormons a chance to see the evidence" she believed proved the fraudulent nature of Mormon origins (Brodie, "Biography," 6, 10). Brodie was also motivated by subtle but deep-seated psychological factors. She characterized the writing of the biography as "a desperate effort to come to terms with my childhood" (Bringhurst, "Fawn McKay Brodie: Dissident Historian and Quintessential Critic of Mormondom," 285).

As Brodie worked on the biography, she was inspired and influenced by a diverse group of individuals known collectively as "Mormondom's lost generation." These individuals, like Brodie, had been brought up in Utah at the center of Mormon power and influence and came of age during the early decades of the twentieth century. They were well educated and expressed varying degrees of skepticism relative to Mormon beliefs and doctrines. Like Brodie, moreover, they were generally aspiring or published writers. This so-called lost generation included such nationally published writers as Vardis Fisher, Paul Bailey, Maurine Whipple, Virginia Sorenson, and Samuel W. Taylor, along with two notable non-Mormons with Utah roots, Bernard DeVoto and Wallace Stegner. One member of this lost generation, Dale L. Morgan, provided Brodie with significant help. Morgan, a western writer of minor renown, assumed the role of virtual mentor to the fledgling author. He aided Brodie in her research and critiqued early drafts of her manuscript (Bringhurst, "Fawn M. Brodie, 'Mormondom's Lost Generation,' and *No Man Knows My History*," 11–20).

Finally, in 1945, Brodie completed *No Man Knows My History*. Its publication in November of that year generated a variety of reactions, ranging from applause to attack. Applause came mainly from writers and commentators based outside of Utah. These were by and large non-Mormons, based mainly on the East Coast, where Brodie's biography had been published. The book was assailed by spokesmen from within the Church of Jesus Christ of Latter-day Saints (Bringhurst, "Applause, Attack, and Ambivalence—Varied Responses to Fawn M. Brodie's *No Man Knows My History*," 46–63).

The most direct Mormon assault on Brodie came with the author's excommunication in June 1946, some six months after the biography's publication. Brodie's own uncle, David O. McKay, because of his status as a high-ranking church official, played a leading role, albeit indirect, in the excommunication of his niece. It appears that McKay "initiated a resolution" calling for Brodie's excommunication in the fall of 1945, immediately after the book's publication. "But the matter was tabled on the grounds that it would make a martyr out of her" (Bringhurst, "Applause, Attack and Ambivalence—Varied Responses to Fawn M. Brodie's *No Man Knows My History*," 54).

By May 1946, however, such official reticence disappeared. Brodie's book had been reviewed in various national publications, often favorably, thus attracting widespread attention and comment, much to the dismay of Mormon leaders. Church officials were apparently also prompted by a subsequent article written by Brodie and published in *American Mercury* in April 1946. Entitled "Polygamy Shocks the Mormons," Brodie's article condemned the Mormon Church for alleged persecutions—specifically, its role in the arrest, conviction, and imprisonment, some two years earlier, of a group of so-called Mormon fundamentalists. These "fundamentalists" were part of a schismatic Mormon group that actively advocated and practiced polygamy, contrary to current teachings of the much-larger Mormon Church, which had officially abandoned plural marriage in 1890 (Brodie, "Polygamy Shocks the Mormons," 399–405).

Although Brodie had long since ceased all activity with the Mormon Church, she was still officially listed on the membership rolls of the New England Mission, headquartered in Cambridge, Massachusetts. The formal process of excommunication began on 25 May 1946. On that date, two Mormon missionaries arrived at the Brodie home in New Haven, Connecticut, and presented Fawn a summons ordering her to appear before a Church Mission court in Cambridge, scheduled for 1 June 1946.

That Brodie was directed to a church court in Cambridge and not summoned directly to church headquarters in Salt Lake City might seem puzzling, given compelling evidence that orders to excommunicate her originated at the highest levels of the Mormon Church. But the handling of Brodie's excommunication within the confines of the New England Mission was in keeping with long-established church practice that disciplinary actions involving individual members were to be handled by church authorities on the local level.

In the summons, itself, signed by Mission President William H. Reeder, Brodie was charged with "apostasy" wherein:

> That in a book recently published by you, you assert matters as truths which deny the divine origin of the Book of Mormon, the restoration of the Priesthood and of Christ's Church through the instrumentality of the Prophet Joseph Smith, contrary to the beliefs, doctrines, and teachings of the Church. (Bringhurst, "Fawn Brodie and Her Quest for Independence," 79)

Brodie, herself, in response to this summons "politely" informed church authorities that she would "not be present" at the church court to be held the following week. According to her later recollections, "I simply told them, or wrote a letter telling them, that I would not go because, after all, I was a heretic" (Brodie, "Biography," 4). A major factor in Brodie's decision was that she was in the crucial final stages of pregnancy, expecting her second child in less than two weeks. Attendance would have required Brodie to endure a one-day automobile journey from New Haven to Cambridge, a particularly risky undertaking for the expectant mother, who had a history of difficulty in carrying a baby to term. She had suffered a miscarriage since the 1942 birth of her first child.

The church court went ahead in Brodie's absence, directed by President

Reeder. It included nine other individuals, most of whom where young male missionaries, temporarily engaged in church work in the New England region. The proceedings, according to one eyewitness, were "very brief," concluding in "a manner of minutes." President Reeder, "after considering the evidence presented . . . declared that in his opinion 'Fawn McKay Brodie, by the statements in her book, was guilty of teaching false doctrines which denies the divine institution of the Church and its fundamental beliefs respecting the mission of the Prophet Joseph Smith, and that it was his [Reeder's] judgement that she should be excommunicated from the Church.' " All present and constituting the church court concurred with Reeder's opinion and Brodie "was declared excommunicated." Shortly thereafter, Reeder drafted a letter to Brodie officially notifying her of that fact (Bringhurst, *Fawn M. Brodie: From Devout Mormon to Controversial Psychobiographer*).

Brodie's initial reaction to her excommunication was shock, despite indications, beforehand, that such drastic action was imminent. It "caught me completely off guard and upset me a good deal more than I would care to have the [Mormon] authorities know," Brodie confessed to a close friend. "I was emotionally so vulnerable," she continued, because the excommunication, itself, "symbolized so dramatically the fact that my bridges are irrevocably burned." According to another account, Brodie came to one close family member "in tears, and . . . could hardly be comforted because she was so disrupted to be disfellowshipped" (Bringhurst, "Fawn Brodie and Her Quest for Independence," 90). Such reactions are not surprising, given the close-knit nature of the Latter-day Saint religion and Mormonism's characteristic as a distinctive subculture providing its members a sense of "quasi-ethnicity." Excommunication literally meant expulsion from that distinctive community.

Brodie coped with her sense of loss in several ways. On an immediate level, Fawn continued to maintain close contact and interaction with her immediate family—specifically, her father, mother, three sisters, and brother, all of whom remained within the Mormon Church, maintaining varying degrees of religious commitment. All members of her immediate family, in fact, strongly supported Fawn through her ordeal of excommunication.

Also Fawn, despite her loss of church membership, continued to embrace certain values and patterns of behavior emphasized as norms within the Mormon community. For example, developing and maintaining strong family bonds were important to her. Fawn and Bernard, despite what one son described as "not an easy marriage," remained together for 42 years until Bernard's death from cancer in 1978. Fawn's desire to forge strong family bonds was also evident in the way she related to her children. Although she enjoyed and needed the stimulation of research and writing, Fawn was strongly sensitive to and enthusiastically embraced her role as a mother to her three children: oldest son Richard; Bruce, who was born in 1946, immediately after her excommunication; and Pamela, who came along four years later in 1950, shortly before the Brodies moved to Pacific Palisades, California. Fawn asserted on more than one occasion that being a mother gave her much greater satisfaction than writing. "Children are more rewarding than books," she declared. Unlike children, once a book is finished, it is the deadest thing in the world" (Brodie, "Biography," 47–48).

Brodie also shared the Mormon emphasis on community involvement. "A political activist" she was, in the words of one observer, "more liberal and far more closely identified with student causes than her political scientist husband." She was particularly concerned with ecology or preserving the natural environment as reflected in her involvement during the 1960s in a crusade to protect the Santa Monica Mountains, near her Pacific Palisades home, from real estate development. Brodie also proclaimed the Mormon "work ethic . . . one that I greatly admire." Judging from her five major books, her tenure as a history professor at the University of California, Los Angeles, along with ever-present family responsibilities, it was one to which she strongly subscribed. Brodie attributed her habit of working "extremely hard" to "some kind of mad, inner compulsion which has to do with God knows what" (Brodie, "Biography," 47–48).

Brodie, moreover, continued to write and comment on various aspects of Mormon life and culture, even though her four subsequent book-length biographies dealt with non-Mormon subjects. She was particularly interested in controversial topics. She wrote an essay examining the role and place of intellectuals or so-called new writers within Mormonism, which was published in *Frontier Magazine* in 1952 (Brodie, "New Writers and Mormonism"). Brodie was also highly critical of the now-defunct Mormon practice of excluding blacks from the church's lay priesthood, expressing her opposition in public forum and in print. Ultimately, the offensive Mormon practice was discontinued in 1978 (Bringhurst, "Fawn M. Brodie as a Critic of Mormonism's Policy toward Blacks").

By the 1970s, Brodie became interested in the issue of women relative to their past and present status in Mormonism. This issue came to a head in 1979 with the excommunication of Sonia Johnson* in the wake of the latter's militant support of the equal rights amendment (ERA). Johnson's pro-ERA position stood in direct opposition to the official Mormon position against ERA. Johnson's excommunication received as much publicity in the national media as Brodie's own some 30 years earlier. Indeed, in a short encounter, Brodie reportedly told the recently excommunicated Johnson: "I think you [have] usurped my place as the leading female Judas Iscariot" within Mormondom (Bringhurst, "Fawn McKay Brodie: Dissident Historian and Quintessential Critic of Mormondom," 295).

In addition to such behavior and attitudes, Brodie retained certain emotional ties to her long-discarded Mormon faith. This was evident in an encounter between Brodie and her younger brother, Thomas B. McKay, in late December 1980. McKay was visiting Brodie, who was gravely ill in St. Johns Hospital in Santa Monica. According to Brodie's own account, "I was very glad to see [Thomas] and asked him for a blessing—as my father had communicated blessings over the years as a kind of family patriarch. This blessing he gave me, and I told him I was grateful, saying he had said what I wanted him to say." Brodie's account reveals lingering inner conflict: "My delight in asking for an opportunity for a blessing at that moment indicated simply the intensity of an old hunger." But then she carefully added: "Any exaggeration about my requests for a blessing meaning that I was asking to be taken back into the [Mormon] Church at that moment I strictly repudiate and would for all time" (Bringhurst, "Fawn Brodie and Her Quest for Independence," 92).

On 10 January 1981, Fawn Brodie died of cancer at the age of 65. In accordance with her wishes, her body was cremated and the ashes scattered over the Santa Monica mountains she loved near Pacific Palisades where she had spent the last 30 years of her life.

In summary, Fawn McKay Brodie was never able to free herself completely from Mormonism, despite having written *No Man Knows My History*, which prompted her excommunication, gaining for her a reputation as Mormondom's most famous twentieth-century heretic. Brodie, herself, seemed to recognize this fact, confessing to her brother Thomas B. McKay "that once you're a Mormon you can never escape it" (Bringhurst, "Fawn Brodie and Her Quest for Independence," 93).

BIBLIOGRAPHY

Bringhurst, Newell G. "Applause, Attack, and Ambivalence—Varied Responses to Fawn M. Brodie's *No Man Knows My History*." *Utah Historical Quarterly* 57, no. 1 (winter 1989): 46–63.

———. "Fawn Brodie and Her Quest for Independence." *Dialogue: A Journal of Mormon Thought* 22, no. 2 (summer 1989): 79–95.

———. "Fawn M. Brodie as a Critic of Mormonism's Policy toward Blacks: A Historiographical Reassessment." *John Whitmer Historical Association Journal* 11 (1991): 34–46.

———. *Fawn M. Brodie: From Devout Mormon to Controversial Psychobiographer*. Forthcoming.

———. "Fawn M. Brodie, 'Mormondom's Lost Generation,' and *No Man Knows My History*." *Journal of Mormon History* 16 (1990): 11–23.

———. "Fawn McKay Brodie: Dissident Historian and Quintessential Critic of Mormondom." In *Differing Visions: Dissenters in Mormon History*, edited by Roger D. Launius and Linda Thatcher. Urbana: University of Illinois Press, 1994.

Brodie, Fawn M. "Biography of Fawn McKay Brodie." Oral history interview conducted by Shirley E. Stephenson, 30 November 1975. Original in Oral History Collection, Fullerton State University, Fullerton, CA.

———. "Mormon 'Security.'" *Nation*, 12 February 1937, 182–183, 196. Published under pseudonym "Martha Emery."

———. "New Writers and Mormonism." *Frontier Magazine* 6 (December 1952): 17–19.

———. *No Man Knows My History: The Life of Joseph Smith, the Mormon Prophet.* New York: Alfred A. Knopf, 1945.

———. "Polygamy Shocks the Mormons." *American Mercury* 62 (April 1946): 399–405.

Newell G. Bringhurst

Horace Bushnell
(1802–1876)

BACKGROUND

Known as the "Father of Modern Liberalism" and the "American Schleiermacher," Horace Bushnell has been regarded as one of the most controversial and influential theologians in American religious history. The
Dictionary of American Religious Biography ranks him with Jonathan Edwards and Reinhold Niebuhr as one of the three foremost Protestant theologians in American history (*DARB*, 90).

Bushnell ministered and wrote at a time when many Congregational ministers lamented an alarming deterioration of orthodoxy. There were three
notable controversies in New England Theology that provided the background to Bushnell's theological writings and the furor they raised. In the
early years of the nineteenth century, Massachusetts Congregationalists
found themselves polarized into liberal and conservative factions. Harvard
College had gone to the liberals, prompting conservatives to establish the
alternative theological school at Andover, while a significant number on
the Left formed a new denomination, the Unitarian Church.

Second, Congregationalists in Connecticut were sharply divided over differing views of Calvinism. Nathaniel William Taylor and others developed
a more liberal form of Calvinism at Yale, and conservatives sought to maintain Calvinist orthodoxy at another alternative theological institution, this
time at Hartford.

Finally, within the Unitarian camp, radicals had developed Transcenden-
talism under the inspiration of Ralph Waldo Emerson and Theodore Parker. Whether or not they were justified, conservatives feared that Horace
Bushnell's theological speculations threatened to deal the knockout blow

to an already reeling New England Theology. Their suspicions grew within an atmosphere of change and controversy.

In a number of ways, Bushnell came by his innovative and creative propensities naturally. Two women were highly influential in his early development, his mother and his fraternal grandmother. Young Horace saw his grandmother, Molly (Ensign) Bushnell, only twice—once as a 6-year-old and later when he was 12 or 13—but she made a powerful impression on him. As he recalled many years later, "Somehow she has been always with me, and upon me, felt as a silent, subtly-operative presence of good" (quoted in Cheney, *Life and Letters*, 26). For many years, Molly had been a member of a Calvinist congregation, her grandson noted, "but had been so dreadfully swamped in getting her experience through the five-point subtleties that she nearly went distracted" (quoted in Cheney, *Life and Letters*, 24–25). Her theological relief came through transferring her membership to the Methodist Church.

Horace's mother also exerted a strong shaping influence on her son and his pattern of theological thinking. She was a gracious woman whom Horace recalled "never did an inconsiderate, imprudent, or any way excessive thing that required to be afterwards mended" (quoted in Cheney, *Life and Letters*, 28). Horace's mother had dedicated her son to the ministry and dealt gently with him during his years of questioning and theological doubt, ultimately winning him back to ministerial preparation. Horace remembered her gently nurturing relationship with her children.

> Other women are motherly enough, tender, self-sacrificing, faithful; but what I owe to her, I owe to her wonderful insight and discretion. By pushing with too much argument; by words of upbraiding and blame; by a teasing, over-afflicted manner; or by requiring me to stand to my engagements, she could have easily thrown me out of range and kept me fatally back from self-recovery. (Quoted in Cheney, *Life and Letters*, 33–34)

Horace matriculated at Yale College in 1823 and, upon graduation in 1827, became a tutor there while continuing studies in law. He had intended to study for the ministry but changed his course because of religious doubts. As he came to understand those doubts later, he attributed them to his overly rationalistic approach to the faith.

> My very difficulty was that I was too thoughtful, substituting thought for everything else, and expecting so intently to dig out a religion by my head that I was pushing it all the while practically away. Unbelief, in fact, had come to be my element. (Quoted in Cheney, *Life and Letters*, 32)

His daughter and biographer Mary Bushnell Cheney believed that his move away from rationalistic logic revealed his intellectual and spiritual maturity: "As he grew older, he abandoned formal logic, in which he was a youthful adept, as childish, just as some other men, maturing, throw away their poetry and sentiment" (Cheney, *Life and Letters*, 20).

From the perspective of some of his later critiques, his return to faith came about in an unlikely fashion—his daughter compared the change to the transformation of Saul of Tarsus into the apostle Paul. When religious revival broke out at Yale in 1831, Bushnell at first tried to remain aloof, but his duty toward his students to be a positive example and the melting of his doubts by the Holy Spirit led him to renewed faith. He recalled his words to his students.

> O men! what shall I do with these arrant doubts I have been nursing for years? When the preacher touches the Trinity and when logic shatters it all to pieces, I am all at the four winds. But I am glad I have a heart as well as a head. My heart wants the Father; my heart wants the Son; my heart wants the Holy Ghost—and one just as much as the other. My heart says the Bible has a Trinity for me, and I mean to hold by my heart. (Quoted in Cheney, *Life and Letters*, 56)

Bushnell captured the essence of his later theological work in a sermon entitled "On the Dissolving of Doubts."

> Now, this conversion, calling it by that name, as we properly should, may seem, in the apprehension of some, to be a conversion *for* the Gospel, and not *in* it or *by* it—a conversion by the want of truth more than by the power of truth. But that will be a judgment more superficial than the facts permit. No, it is exactly this: it is seeking first the kingdom of God and his righteousness—exactly that, and nothing less. (Quoted in Cheney, *Life and Letters*, 59)

Bushnell admonished the students:

> Never be in a hurry to believe; never try to conquer doubts against time. . . . One of the greatest talents in religious discovery is the finding how to hang up questions, and let them hang, without being at all anxious about them. . . . It will not hurt you, nor hurt the truth, if you should have some few questions left to be carried on with you when you go hence. (Quoted in Cheney, *Life and Letters*, 60)

The next autumn found Bushnell enrolled in Yale Divinity School. Though intrigued by Nathaniel William Taylor's "new divinity," Bushnell ultimately rejected Taylor's dialectical method and found himself increasingly drawn to the writings of Samuel Taylor Coleridge, especially the *Aids to Reflection.* That book, he said, opened to him "a whole other world somewhere overhead, a range of realities in a higher tier" (*Dictionary of American Biography* [*DAB*], 351). Near the end of his life, he acknowledged that he owed more to that book than any other except the Bible.

Bushnell was ordained on 22 May 1833 as pastor of the North Church of Hartford, Connecticut, a call he would hold until 1861 when he found it necessary to resign due to ill health. Later that year, Bushnell married his lifelong companion Mary Apthorp.

EARLY MINISTRY

Bushnell has been described as a "Preachers' Preacher." John Mulder calls Bushnell "[p]erhaps the last in a long line of American theologians who wrote theology from the parish rather than from an academic setting" (Introduction to Bushnell, *Christian Nurture*, viii). His theology was that of an effective, imaginative preacher rather than an ivory tower scholar. He was a poet and a mystic whose theology was more art than science. According to Mulder, Bushnell insisted that "Christianity is known primarily through intuition, not by reason or logic, and that its basic appeal is to the heart and the spirit" (Introduction to Bushnell, *Christian Nurture*, xv).

Bushnell's early ministry took place in the midst of the fierce Old School–New School debate among New England theologians. The North Church congregation was also divided over the issue. In the debate, however, Bushnell sided with neither group. Not only did he abhor their uncharitable spirits, but he believed both erred in their use of dialectical method.

His approach was that of freedom of thought in the midst of what he viewed as the strict legalism and rational rigidity that characterized Christianity in New England. Neither did he have much sympathy for revivalism, regularly sweeping the region. "What we complain of and resist is the artificial firework, the extraordinary combined jump and stir, supposed to be requisite when anything is to be done" (quoted in Cheney, *Life and Letters*, 83).

Another target for his barbs was the Roman Catholic Church. During a trip to Europe in 1845, hoping to recover his health, Bushnell visited Rome and was appalled by much that he witnessed. In characteristically bold action, he penned a *Letter to His Holiness, Pope Gregory XVI* that urged the pope to recognize and correct the many abuses the New Englander had seen. In what was not to be the last controversy with those in power, the Church placed Bushnell's letter, published in London, on the *Index Expurgatorius.*

In 1848, Bushnell's ministry and theology were transformed by a profound mystical experience he later called a "spiritual birthday" like those experienced by Augustine, Luther, and Wesley. He had noted a change beginning within him as early as five years before after the death of his son, and the experience in 1848 completed his transformation to belief in a "higher, fuller life that can be lived, and set myself to attain it" (quoted in Cheney, *Life and Letters*, 192). His daughter described the experience in her biography of her father.

> On an early morning of February, his wife awoke, to hear that the light they had waited for, more than they that watch for the morning, had risen indeed. She asked, "What have you seen?" He replied, "The gospel." It came to him at last, after all his thought and study, not as something reasoned out, but as an inspiration,—a revelation from the mind of God himself. (Cheney, *Life and Letters*, 192)

Many years later, Bushnell reflected back on the experience and its impact on his life.

> I seemed to pass a boundary. I had never been very legal in my Christian life, but now I passed from those partial seeings, glimpses and doubts, into a clearer knowledge of God and into his inspirations, which I have never wholly lost. The change was into faith,—a sense of the freeness of God and the ease of approach to him. (Quoted in Cheney, *Life and Letters*, 192)

The transformation of his basic understanding of theology was completed by the experience, and that understanding provided the basis for his book *God in Christ* and much of the controversy that would surround the rest of his career. Bushnell continues,

> Christian faith is the faith of a transaction. It is not the committing of one's thought in assent to any proposition, but the trusting of one's being to *a being*, there to be rested, kept, guided, moulded, governed, and possessed forever. . . . It gives you God, fills you with God in immediate, experimental knowledge, puts you in possession of all there is in him, and allows you to be invested with his character itself. (Quoted in Cheney, *Life and Letters*, 193)

H. Shelton Smith describes the idea that Christ "radically transforms the sinfully deformed creature" as "the keynote of Bushnell's preaching" and "the creative center of his theology" (Smith, *Horace Bushnell*, 25–26).

Throughout his career at North Congregational Church, Bushnell's congregation held their pastor in very high esteem, though some of the more conservative members felt some unease about their pastor's theological innovations. According to Smith, however, in the end the members' only complaint against him was that he "preached Christ too much." In reply, Bushnell said, "I cannot think [this] is a fault to be repented of, for Christ is all and beside him there is no gospel to be preached or received." Smith concludes that Christ was the "magnetic center" of Bushnell's thought and ministry (quoted in Smith, *Horace Bushnell*, 26).

For the rest of his life, Bushnell was convinced that true knowledge of God came only through an inward experience of God's infinite spirit and person. He hoped to lead others to such an immediate discovery of God that transcended both the limits of language and rational reflection.

Bushnell resigned as pastor of North Church in April 1861 after a number of months leave of absence for health reasons. He died on 17 February 1876.

SELECTED THEOLOGICAL WRITINGS AND CONTROVERSIES

With his earliest published works, Bushnell created controversy. His first book, *A Discourse on Christian Nurture*, first published in 1847, with a final revision in 1861, stirred such opposition that the publisher suspended sale of the book without even consulting the author. The publisher, the Massachusetts Sabbath-School Society, had some qualms about the book prior to its publication and asked Bushnell for some modifications of language, which he willingly provided. When the Society "suppressed the book," as Bushnell put it, he republished it himself with an "Argument" that attempted to prove that his ideas were not new but were, in fact, a return to "an older and more genuine form of orthodoxy" (Cheney, *Life and Letters*, 180).

Bushnell's view of the Christian nurture of children was clearly influenced by his own childhood experience under the gentle care of his mother and by Romanticism's emphasis on the education and nurture of children. His argument in *Christian Nurture* rests on three basic propositions: the organic character of the family, nature (in this case, the family) as an avenue of God's grace, and a theology of baptism that emphasized the covenant nature of the relationship of the family with God.

Much of the controversy to come swirled around Bushnell's conception of the uses and limits of language. In many respects, his theory of language was the foundation upon which he built the rest of his theology. According to Frederick Kirschenmann, "It was this new view of language which Bushnell fostered that distinguished him from his contemporaries, but it also made it impossible for his contemporaries [friends and foes alike], steeped in the old mental habits, to understand him" (Kirschenmann, "Horace Bushnell," 69).

Rather than viewing words as the building blocks of a logical system of theology, as theologians such as Hodge were prone to do, Bushnell insisted, rather, that words were "inexact representations of thought, mere types or analogies," at best "only proximate expressions of the thoughts named" (quoted in Cheney, *Life and Letters*, 204). Thus, the kind of precise systematic arrangement of the facts of Scripture that Hodge and others attempted was not only impossible, Bushnell insisted, but fraught with misrepresentation. Against his opponents who used words as precise instruments to express unequivocal distinctions in thought, Bushnell used language, "not as the logicians, but as the common people and the poets have always done, as suggestive of truth, as a symbol of thought" (*DAB*, 353). This approach, which lay at the heart of the conflicts surrounding Bushnell's theological writings, anticipated one of the major theological debates of the twentieth century about the nature of theological language.

More serious opposition came with the publication in 1849 of *God in Christ: Three Discourses*. Severe reviews poured in from theologians and ministers, including Princeton's Charles Hodge. Hodge's lengthy diatribe in the *Biblical Repertory and Princeton Review* accused Bushnell of assaulting the doctrines of the Trinity, the Incarnation, and the Atonement. In Hodge's view, Bushnell rejected doctrinal formulations that had been decided long ago within the church and were therefore no longer subject to speculation. Bushnell was clearly out of his depth, according to Hodge.

"Dr. Bushnell has undertaken a task for which he is entirely incompetent," Hodge charged, and as a result, "We think the book a failure." Not only that, "It is evident Dr. Bushnell does not fully understand himself" (Hodge, "Review of Bushnell's Discourses," 259–260, 262, 298).

Hodge accused Bushnell of reviving ancient heresies such as Apollinarianism, Sabellianism, and Eutycheanism, as well as drawing on the modern "heresies" of Friedrich Schleiermacher.

In all of these areas, however, Bushnell refused to grant that this theology was novel, much less heretical. He appealed to ancient authorities as well as to Scripture. He measured his ideas against the ancient thinkers and insisted that his theology was actually a return to an orthodoxy older than the "orthodoxy" defended by his accusers.

According to Hodge, Bushnell's false ideas grew out of a curious mixture of rationalism and mysticism. The main problem, according to Hodge, was that Bushnell was not consistent in his application of either reason or mysticism.

> But if rationalism is Dr. Bushnell's sword, mysticism is his shield. So long as he is attacking, no man makes more of the "constructive logic"; but as soon as the logic is brought to bear against himself, he turns saint, and is wrapt in contemplation. (Hodge, "Review of Bushnell's Discourses," 173)

Bushnell's view of the Atonement contrasted with many of his contemporaries who have been described as "dialectical rationalists." Bushnell explicitly rejected the traditional idea that the work of Christ effected a change in God's attitude toward humanity. God always had reached out in love and mercy toward sinners. The change took place in the hearts of people, who came to know and receive God's love.

Bushnell also departed from New England ways in his approach to the doctrine of the Trinity. He rejected rationalistic speculation as the way to know God as Trinity, insisting rather that the foundation for Trinitarian theology lay in the human experience of God. Rationalistic speculation beyond that experience was pointless and bound to error.

What made Bushnell's "heresies" so insidious in Hodge's eyes was that they came from within the household of faith.

> Let sceptics and philosophers teach what they please, or what they dare, but it is surely time to have some certain ground in Christianity, and to put the brand of universal reprobation on the hypocritical and wicked device of preaching infidelity in a cassock. (Hodge, "Review of Bushnell's Discourses," 298)

Disturbing as these attacks in print were to Bushnell, even more troubling were efforts by fellow ministers to bring him to trial for his "heretical" ideas in *God in Christ*. The problem they faced in their effort to bring Bushnell to a formal trial—and ultimately his defense against such an action—was the political structure of the Congregational Churches. While the fellowship of the Congregational Churches had been formed for conference and mutual support, it did not, in the final analysis, have adequate mechanisms to deal with ministers who appeared to be outside the pale of orthodoxy.

Hodge meticulously traced the events of Bushnell's controversy and lamented, "It is thus virtually decided that the General Association cannot properly take any measures to purge itself from any heresy, when avowed by any minister in its connection, and shielded by his Association" (Hodge, "Conflicts," 629).

A group of conservative ministers brought charges against Bushnell's *God in Christ* to the Hartford Central Association. A committee of five ministers evaluated the book with three reporting that "the errors of the book were not fundamental," while the minority of two members believed that "the errors were fundamental" (Cheney, *Life and Letters*, 225–226). The membership of the Association discussed the committee's report, heard Bushnell's own defense, and ultimately voted with the majority of the committee, with only three dissenting votes. Bushnell later quipped, "The conclusion being, with only two or three dissenting voices, that, though I am a frightful being, I am nevertheless substantially orthodox" (quoted in Cheney, *Life and Letters*, 227).

Bushnell's daughter and biographer recalled the anxiety of that day.

> I distinctly recall the solemn day when he was on trial before his own
> Association in Hartford. Two or three of his brother-ministers dined
> with him before going to the final and decisive meeting of the after-
> noon. All were grave, and full of the morning's debate. My father wore
> a look of deep emotion and anxiety new to me. . . . He never spoke
> bitterly of his opponents, but he had no conscientious scruples about
> a little harmless raillery. (Cheney, *Life and Letters*, 465)

Bushnell's ordeal, however, was far from over.

Responding to his critics in 1851, Bushnell published *Christ in Theology*,
which clarified a number of his positions. Within a few months, Hodge
again entered the fray with an article evaluating "Recent Doctrinal and
Ecclesiastical Conflicts in Connecticut." Hodge's concern was that his own
Presbyterian denomination was so closely allied with Bushnell's Congregationalism that damage to the one was, of necessity, harm to the other.
Despite the Hartford Central Association's decision not to pursue further
action against Bushnell, Hodge believed that the matter should not rest
there, nor had it. Heresy was heresy, and it must be fought. According to
Hodge, "Measures have been pursued with a constancy, fidelity, and sacrifice, seldom equalled, to procure by these circuitous, and therefore labo-
rious, processes, the removal of the heresy from connection with that body"
(Hodge, "Conflicts," 608). But Bushnell and his books remained.

The Fairfield West Association had asked Hartford Central to reconsider,
but Hartford had refused. Fairfield West then published a remonstrance
with a request that all District Associations in Connecticut meet and consider the subject. Some Associations agreed with Fairfield West, and ultimately together they lodged a formal complaint against the action—or
failure to act—of the Hartford Central Association, signed by 52 ministers
and presented to the General Association.

The General Association meeting at Litchfield brought matters to a head.
Bushnell's daughter and biographer recorded the events.

> At Litchfield, then, the first concerted attack was made. "Fairfield
> West" were in the front, but stronger and more influential forces were
> arrayed behind them. The defeated minority of the Hartford Central
> Association had not been idle; the hitherto privately active hostility of
> the Seminary of East Windsor was now openly avowed, and the sus-
> picion of a dangerous tendency in his writings, long smouldering in the
> Theological School at New Haven, had been fanned into flame by in-
> fluences from within and without. (Cheney, *Life and Letters*, 235)

Bushnell addressed the General Association and argued that the verdict
of the Hartford Central Association was final and that there should no
longer be any question about procedures against him. The meeting unanimously accepted a vaguely worded resolution that noted the duty of all

Associations to consider any remonstrance brought by another Association, and if the former declined to reverse the original decision, they should at least endeavor "to satisfy the complaining association in respect to their proceedings so complained of" (quoted in Cheney, *Life and Letters*, 237).

As a gesture to those who brought charges against Bushnell, the General Association reaffirmed the Westminster Catechism as the standard for orthodoxy among the Congregationalists and noted that any departure from the Catechism would be regarded as heresy. But the General Association refused to reverse the decision of the Hartford Central Association.

Bushnell recalled that the "meeting in Litchfield was the most beautiful scene to me that I ever saw. . . . It began like an *auto da fé*, and ended like an embrace of good-will and charity" (quoted in Cheney, *Life and Letters*, 241).

Still, however, the storm had only temporarily blown over.

The Fairfield West Association sent Hartford Central another letter of remonstrance, and once again, in May 1851, Hartford refused to reconsider its position concerning Bushnell. Ministers from Fairfield West moved ahead and, producing "heretical" extracts from *Christ in Theology*, brought the issue to the General Association meeting in Danbury in June 1852.

Again, a committee appointed by the General Association admitted that that body had no jurisdiction over the Hartford Central Association's decision about Bushnell but that if three members of Bushnell's congregation could be found who would bring charges of heresy against their pastor, he could be brought to trial. Bushnell's biographer reported that "for years industrious attempts had been made to find three such persons, but not one of them had been discovered" (Cheney, *Life and Letters*, 260). Neither were they found on this occasion. By this time, however, the congregation had become disgusted with the maneuverings of the Associations, and whether to protect their pastor from a possible heresy trial or to protest actions already taken against him, the congregation voted to leave the Consociation, thus removing their pastor from its jurisdiction. Hodge referred to that action as a clear evasion of responsibility, for when a trial appeared to be imminent, "he and his church fled from its jurisdiction. These things speak for themselves" (Hodge, "Conflicts," 614).

Opponents even considered forming a new Association that would be called the "Hartford Fourth Association," consisting exclusively of pastors and churches known to be anti-Bushnell. Fortunately for Bushnell, such a step was not taken.

In June 1853, the General Association met at Waterbury "where was re-enacted the yearly drama of assault and defense in the Bushnell case" (Cheney, *Life and Letters*, 305). A reporter for the *Religious Herald* quipped, " 'The weather has been unprecedentedly warm, so that it is coming to be believed that, as the cool Quakers always brought rain by their yearly meetings, so the warm, contentious, heresy-debating Connecticut Association is destined to attract and concentrate the sun's hottest rays' " (quoted in Cheney, *Life and Letters*, 306).

Finally, at the New Haven meeting of the General Association in July 1854, Bushnell faced his last formal confrontation with the Congregational structures of authority. At that meeting, Bushnell summed up the history of charges against himself and delivered his final diatribe against the injustices he had been forced to endure.

> A general assault, like the winds from the four quarters of heaven, was made upon my doctrine as a deadly and appalling heresy, and an inquiry was immediately, and very properly, instituted by my brethren, to find whether such allegations were true. After nearly half a year of careful deliberation, prepared and led by a committee comprising names as generally known and as highly respected as any in the American churches, my Association, fully advertised of their responsibility by the clamorous impeachment raised in every quarter, came to a final vote, seventeen to three, that, while my views were not accepted by the body, there was yet discovered in them no such evidence of heresy as would justify any further process. (Quoted in Cheney, *Life and Letters*, 284)

Bushnell continued,

> This, according to our system, was the finality of the case; there was no other method of instituting proceedings against me. Then came the 'Fairfield West' Association to mine in a bitter complaint. . . .
>
> You, [the General Association] in fact, allowed your body every year to be used as an instrument in their unlawful agitations. . . .
> And so, under manifold twistings of semblance and compromise, you have continued unto this day, taking no decided attitude, and standing for no principles of order. . . . The consequence, accordingly, has been,—I hope you will understand how much I mean when I say it,— that I have had this body, which ought to have been my protector, together with the Fairfield Association, on my back for the last five years. And you had no right to be there! While I have been bearing you thus in silence, with none but God and the truth to sustain my integrity, you have allowed this body, by so many agitations, to do all it could to break down my character as a minister and blast the public confidence in me. (Quoted in Cheney, *Life and Letters*, 343)

Again, the General Association refused to act, and the curtain went down on the drama of efforts to bring formal action against Horace Bushnell.

CONCLUDING REFLECTIONS

Although Bushnell was never formally condemned for heresy, accusations followed him throughout his career. He constantly stretched the boundaries of New England Congregational orthodoxy and infuriated his opponents by refusing to adopt either their statements of doctrine or their theological methods. Because of his deep piety and the loyalty of his congregation and his friends and associates in the Hartford Central Association, he avoided formal condemnation and potential discipline. He won those battles. And in retrospect, he "won" the larger war if judged by the influence of his ideas. His status as one of the most creative theological minds in American religious history and the relevance of his concerns remain while many of his opponents' ideas have settled into the dust of their historical period.

SELECTED BIBLIOGRAPHY

Adamson, William R. *Bushnell Rediscovered*. Philadelphia: United Church Press, 1966.

Bushnell, Horace. *Christian Nurture*. Introduction by John M. Mulder. Grand Rapids, MI: Baker Book House, 1979. Reprint of 1861 edition.

————. *Christ in Theology*. Hartford: Brown and Parsons, 1851.

————. *God in Christ: Three Discourses*. Hartford: Brown and Parsons, 1849.

Cheney, Mary Bushnell. *Life and Letters of Horace Bushnell*. New York: Harper and Brothers, 1880.

Cherry, Conrad, ed. *Horace Bushnell, Sermons*. Sources of American Spirituality. New York: Paulist Press, 1985.

Cross, Barbara M. *Horace Bushnell: Minister to a Changing America*. Chicago: University of Chicago Press, 1958.

Dictionary of American Biography. S.v. Bushnell, Horace. New York: Charles Scribner's Sons, 1929.

Dictionary of American Religious Biography. S.v. Bushnell, Horace. Edited by Henry Warner Bowden. 2nd ed. Westport, CT: Greenwood Press, 1993.

Duke, James O. *Horace Bushnell: On the Vitality of Biblical Language*. Chico, CA: Scholars Press, 1984.

Hodge, Charles. "Recent Doctrinal and Ecclesiastical Conflicts in Connecticut." *Biblical Repertory and Princeton Review* (October 1853): 598–637.

————. "Review of Bushnell's Discourses." *Biblical Repertory and Princeton Review* (April 1849): 259–298.

Kirschenmann, Frederick. "Horace Bushnell: Cells or Crustacea?" In *Reinterpretation in American Church History*, edited by Jerald C. Brauer. Chicago: University of Chicago Press, 1968. 67–90.

Munger, Theodore T. *Horace Bushnell: Preacher and Theologian*. Boston: Houghton Mifflin, 1899.

Smith, David L. *Symbolism and Growth: The Religious Thought of Horace Bushnell*. Chico, CA: Scholars Press, 1981.

Smith, H. Shelton. *Horace Bushnell*. A Library of Protestant Thought. New York: Oxford University Press, 1965.

Swift, David Everett. "Conservatism and Progressive Orthodoxy in 19th Century Congregationalism." *Church History* 16 (March 1947): 22–31.

Sydney E. Ahlstrom. "Theology in America: A Historical Survey." In *The Shaping of American Religion*, edited by James Ward Smith and A. Leland Jamison. Princeton: Princeton University Press, 1961. 232–321.

Stephen R. Graham

Theodore R. Clark
(1912–   )

Theodore Clark was associate professor of theology at New Orleans Baptist Theological Seminary when he was dismissed by the Board of Trustees of that institution. The announcement of his dismissal was made on 18 February 1960. The immediate cause of his dismissal was the publication late in 1959 of his book *Saved by His Life.*

Clark was an adult when he felt the call to become a minister. He attended New Orleans Baptist Theological Seminary (then Baptist Bible Institute) as a nondegree student and was encouraged by the faculty to pursue an undergraduate degree. He did this at Mississippi College and returned to the seminary, where he completed the basic theological degree and then a doctorate in New Testament. He became a member of the faculty in 1949, teaching biblical, historical, and theological subjects. As the faculty of the seminary grew, Clark was able to specialize in systematic theology. In 1956 he took a sabbatical leave and studied with Paul Tillich at Harvard.

Clark was an accomplished musician who used his musical skills to minister at various mission centers in New Orleans. He was a devoted parent. Friends who knew him tend to use phrases such as "the most Christian man I ever knew" and to say things such as, "He proved that a theologian could be humble." One of the trustees who voted to dismiss him said that he was especially "dangerous" because he was such a good man.

Clark was open and transparent as a person and as a teacher. One who attended most of his classes for three years said that he came to almost every class with a book he had just finished reading and talked about the book and its importance. A faculty colleague said that he gave no attention to the effect of his teaching but only to the truthfulness of it and that he was prepared to accept the consequences of telling the truth as he understood it.

Some of the Trustees seem to have felt that Clark intended *Saved by His Life* to be a controversial book, but this seems unlikely. Clark said that he was "confused and grieved in heart over the controversy that has arisen over my book," and it seems that he was genuinely surprised when the controversy developed.

He himself thought of the book as a meditation on salvation. The book begins with a long prayer written by the author, and it includes hymns that he also had written and that display his understanding of the theology of salvation. He was convinced that his book was true to the New Testament, and he seems to have felt that his faithfulness to the New Testament would ensure that his ideas would be greeted respectfully. He expressed the spirit in which he wrote the book in a letter of protest that he sent to the Trustees after his dismissal: "I am at a loss to understand the attitude which some are taking toward [the book]. It represents only my thinking and insights gained through years of studying Biblical systematic theology. I am not insisting that all agree with me."

He also seems to have been puzzled that the Trustees would dismiss him even if they vigorously disagreed with his theological views. He told a newspaper reporter: "Christians will always differ in their thinking concerning the truths of the Christian religion, but this difference should have no bearing upon the fellowship we all enjoy in Christ."

Given Clark's astonishment at the reaction to his book, it is natural to ask if other factors were at work in addition to his theological views. Clark had been employed at New Orleans during the presidency of Roland Q. Leavell (1946–1958), and he was dismissed during the presidency of Dr. H. Leo Eddleman (1959–1970). Some observers believe that Clark might not have been dismissed had Leavell still been president.

Moreover, the seminary had undergone at least four important changes in the years leading up to Clark's dismissal. In 1946, Helen Falls had begun teaching in the school of theology, one of the first women in America to teach in a graduate school of theology. Shortly thereafter, women students were admitted into the school of theology. Black students had been admitted to the seminary in the early 1950s, largely at the urging of faculty and students. The theology of a colleague of Clark's, Frank Stagg,* had been carefully investigated by the Trustees in April 1956 and exonerated. It seems that these factors set up a situation in which some Southern Baptist people and pastors began to feel uneasy about the seminary.

The Trustees' concerns about Clark antedated the publication of his book. When the Trustees dismissed Clark, they released a statement that said:

> In the light of problems with which the board has dealt over a period of years, it accepted unanimously the recommendation of a special committee that Dr. Theodore R. Clark be relieved of his status as an associate professor and teaching responsibilities as of March 12, 1960. His salary will be continued for 12 months, and the possible renewal of his relationship to the institution may be reviewed on or before the expiration of a five-year period. His recently published book is one of several instances in which the board had been confronted with questions as to limitations in the area of communication with students and hearers as well as content of lecture materials. ("Dr. Clark Fired from Seminary," 10)

Clark is remembered as a conscientious teacher who demanded a great deal of his students. There is nothing obscure about his book *Saved by His Life*. A reader of that book is likely to conclude that the criticism of Clark arose because he was quite clear rather than because he was obscure.

In response to the charge that he had difficulty in communicating, Clark said:

> So far as the matter of communications is concerned I feel this is a rather nebulous charge because there is no way of checking such a thing. Also, it should be understood that communication is a two-way street involving the communicator and the communicatee and that the full obligation of true com[munication in the] Christian fellowship cannot rest on the communicator [alone]. It is clear in the New Testament that Jesus himself had difficulty communicating his ideas to certain people. However, it is my conviction that the test of Christian fellowship cannot be based upon communication alone, for deeper than the level of verbal communication is the community in the Spirit of God which we share together in the living Christ. ("Dr. Clark Fired from Seminary," 10)

Clark made this comment concerning his dismissal: "I for one am convinced that rigid doctrinal tests and authoritative control of life and thought are, and always will be, inimical to our true Baptist heritage and principles, some of which are, as I understand them, complete soul freedom before God and responsibility to the spirit of truth alone in matters of doctrine and life" ("Dr. Clark Fired from Seminary," 10).

Several criticisms were offered of Clark's book at the time of his dismissal, although none appeared in the press statement issued by the Trustees.

Some people objected to the title. Accustomed to speaking of being saved by Christ's death, they thought the title inappropriate, perhaps not realizing that the title is a phrase of Paul's (Romans 5:10).

Some objected to the thesis of the book, which is that the church and its theologians have emphasized in their doctrine of salvation the death of Christ at the expense of the life of Christ. Throughout the book, Clark insists that his goal is to secure more emphasis upon the life of Christ rather than less upon Christ's death. However, some statements in the book support the idea that he was calling for the latter.

Closely related to this is the fact that Clark vigorously rejected the theology of some popular hymns about Christ's death. For example, he wrote: "It is my opinion that many of the hymns now used by Christians in worship are inadequate and misleading in theology, and therefore need to be revised or else excluded from Church hymnals. . . . A theology of the Cross will always be needed, but not one that will dominate and even distort other basic New Testament themes, as it has done in the past" (Clark, *Saved by His Life*, 65). In order to illustrate the fact that it is possible to have hymns that provide the balanced view that Clark favored, he offered some hymns that he himself had written.

Additionally, Clark mentioned in passing some other matters that caused concern. For example, in speaking of divine revelation, Clark emphasized God's personal, existential self-giving rather than the transmission of propositional truth (128, 129), and he mentioned that he believed in conditional immortality and that for God to preserve the life of lost persons eternally just so they could be punished would amount to torture (176).

Clark also expressed some ideas that played into the hands of those who opposed him. For example, he wrote: "Among numerous Christians there has appeared a kind of 'Jesusolatry,' a kind of 'Jesus cult' which, while ostensibly attempting to safeguard the truth of the Incarnation, actually distorts the Christian doctrine of Atonement and results in a sentimental and irrelevant 'Jesus' worship" (11). Clark meant that the results of the quest of the historical Jesus are not indispensable to Christian faith, but he was understood to mean that Christians are too devoted to Jesus.

In addition to his criticism of some popular hymns, he also criticized some popular preachers. He wrote about hearing "the preaching of a well-known pastor whose sermons consisted of a curious mixture of romanticism, ornate verbalism, moralism, puritanism, sensationalism, topped with an overbearing egoism and vanity" (143). On the following page, however, he added, "What has been said above concerning a 'well-known pastor' is not intended to be an attack on the person himself." Even sympathetic readers might agree that Clark's initial comment was intemperate.

The precise manner of Clark's dismissal is obscure. Clearly Clark was supported in his theology by at least some of the Trustees, yet the vote to dismiss him was unanimous. What could have happened is that even the Trustees who supported his theology became convinced that the charges of poor communication were substantive enough to warrant his dismissal. The names of persons on the special committee that investigated Clark were not disclosed. It is not known whether the committee or the entire Board ever met with Clark or whether the investigation was conducted without his being present and by means of communication through the president, H. Leo Eddleman. The dean, J. Hardee Kennedy, did not participate in the process.

Indeed, it is not clear whether, before the announcement was made that Clark had been dismissed, the faculty had been told that a committee was investigating Clark. Four years before Clark's dismissal, the Trustees had met to consider the dismissal of one of his colleagues, Frank Stagg; their decision not to dismiss Stagg may have reflected the fact that Stagg's colleagues expressed their support for him to the Trustees. It is possible that faculty members were not able to support Clark in advance of his dismissal because they were unaware that his work was under investigation. After the vote to dismiss him, it became clear that Clark had the active support of several of his colleagues on the faculty, though at least one of the faculty supported his dismissal. One faculty member, J. B. McMinn, who expressed his concerns about Clark's dismissal to the American Association of Theological Schools, learned in early May 1960 that he would not be teaching at the seminary in the coming year. Some students circulated a petition in support of Clark's reinstatement, but others supported his dismissal. The president indicated that he had received a great deal of mail criticizing Clark's book.

There are ironies in this story. For example, soon after the publication of *Saved by His Life*, President Eddleman arranged for an autograph party for Clark at the campus bookstore; a few months later, Eddleman informed Clark that the Trustees had dismissed him, in part because of ideas expressed in the book. Another irony concerned a party that friends and admirers of Clark planned in his honor and to celebrate the publication of his book. It was held at the Sheraton-Charles Hotel in New Orleans on the evening of 18 February 1960; as it turned out, that was the evening of the day that the Trustees voted to dismiss Clark. A third irony was that the dean, J. Hardee Kennedy, had written a realistic but generally approving review of Clark's book; it appeared in *Christianity Today* in March 1960, the last month that Clark taught at the seminary.

A gentleman to the end, Clark refused to criticize his critics. Now living in retirement, he indicates that he quickly moved on from his work in New Orleans to teaching at Pan American College in Edinburg, Texas, and that he prefers not to revisit the controversy of more than three decades ago.

BIBLIOGRAPHY

Alabama Baptist. 7 April 1960.
Baptist Message. 25 February 1960.
Christianity Today. 28 March 1960.
Clark, Theodore R. *Saved by His Life.* New York: Macmillan Co., 1959.

"Dr. Clark Fired from Seminary." *Times-Picayune* (New Orleans). 19 February 1960, Section 1, 10.

Richards, W. Wiley. *Winds of Doctrines*. Lanham, MD: University Press of America, 1991.

Fisher Humphreys

Concordia Theological Seminary (1969–1974)

From 1969 to 1974 the Lutheran Church–Missouri Synod conducted a series of investigations and adopted a number of resolutions designed to prove that the faculty of Concordia Seminary taught false doctrine. As a result of these actions, all but five Concordia faculty members left the school and established Seminex. The name *Seminex* referred to its founders' belief that Concordia Seminary-in-Exile would be a temporary expedient until the denomination resolved its theological crisis. In 1977, the school took the name Christ's Seminary–Seminex to indicate its more permanent status. In the long run, however, Seminex was temporary. In 1983 the remaining faculty dispersed and moved to the Lutheran School of Theology in Chicago, Pacific Lutheran Theological Seminary, and Wartberg Theological Seminary. Four years later (1987), after the creation of the Evangelical Lutheran Church of America, the school officially ceased to exist as an educational institution.

A TALE OF TWO LEADERS

The Concordia controversy involved many people at various levels of the Missouri Synod. Yet two individuals, John H. Tietjen* and Jacob A. O. Preus, came to symbolize the determination of their respective parties. Tietjen represented Missouri's moderates and easterners, while Preus represented the more conservative midwestern core.

A special panel of electors chose John H. Tietjen as president of Concordia Seminary in 1969. A graduate of Concordia and Union Seminary (New York), Tietjen spent his early ministry in churches in the East. Significantly, Tietjen was a member of the "English" District, the only district in Missouri that was not confined to a specific geographic area. His book *Which Way to Lutheran Unity: A History of Efforts to Unite the Lutherans of America* (1966) was part of the larger ecumenical trend among American Lutherans. The ethnic boundaries that separated Lutherans into competing synods weakened after World War II as many third- and fourth-generation persons lost their ethnic identity. In 1960, the American Lutheran Church united the older American Lutheran Church with a number of Scandinavian synods and councils. Two years later (1962), the Lutheran Church in America brought together many smaller ethnic bodies with the United Lutheran Church. Tietjen's book argued that the time had come to take the next step by considering the merger of these larger bodies with the Missouri Synod.

Preus was almost Tietjen's opposite. His father Jacob served as governor of Minnesota and accumulated a considerable personal fortune selling insurance to Lutheran clergy. Preus went to his father's alma mater, Luther College, and attended Luther Theological Seminary, a school of the Evangelical Lutheran Church (Big Norwegians). While there, he clashed with George Aus, the theology professor, over the proper relationship between the doctrines of conversion and election. Several years after graduation, Preus elected to join the Evangelical Lutheran Synod (Little Norwegians), a church that refused the 1917 merger of Norwegian synods because of the new denomination's supposed doctrinal laxity. Shortly after graduation from seminary, Preus earned his Doctor of Philosophy degree in classics from the University of Minnesota. Despite successes with the Evangelical Lutheran Synod, Preus found the denomination professionally confining. In 1958, he left the Little Norwegians for a position at the Springfield or Practical Seminary of the Lutheran Church–Missouri Synod. The founders of Missouri designed the Springfield school (now at Fort Wayne) to train pastors who could not meet the substantial academic requirements of Concordia at Saint Louis. The school's constituency was consequently older and often more conservative. Preus became president of the school in 1962 and during the next decade raised its academic and financial standards. In addition, Preus may have absorbed some of the Practical Seminary's distrust of the larger, more elite school in St. Louis.

POSTWAR RELIGION

The period following World War II was an exciting period for America's Protestant churches. The recently demobilized troops were as anxious consumers of religion as they were of automobiles, refrigerators, and suburban homes. Besides constructing numerous new church buildings, many congregations had to expand existing facilities to accommodate new worshippers. Denominational headquarters, long strapped by depression-era economies, flourished as well. The Missouri Synod, perhaps to its surprise, shared the general prosperity. The church dropped the word *German* from its official title during the war and, in 1947, proudly styled itself "The Lutheran Church—Missouri Synod."

The postwar religious boom accompanied a genuine American theological renaissance. The Christian Realism of the 1930s, associated with H. Richard and Reinhold Niebuhr, ripened into a neo-orthodoxy or neoliberalism that transformed American Christian thought. At least among American religious conservatives, the place where the new thought was most important was in biblical studies and their relationship to dogmatic theology. What the neo-orthodox did was to separate revelation from the words of Scripture. The text pointed to the work of God that the biblical text never completely encapsulated in human words. Hence, people could study the Bible with full historical and critical methods without compromising the integrity of its essential message. Further, this new hermeneutics permitted theologians to retain much traditional language about Christ, sin and salvation, and Creation.

Traditional Protestant theology (scholasticism) was linear and synthetic. The theologian collected the scriptural evidence, synthesized it into doctrines, and drew the necessary deductions and inferences from those teachings. In contrast, the neo-orthodox theological method was circular. For these thinkers, the system of doctrine was somewhat like the solar system with the doctrine of Christ (in Lutheran terms, the Gospel) at the center and other traditional loci (doctrinal statements) located either closer to that center or further from it. If a traditional belief was far from the core of faith, a theologian could disregard, ignore, or even quietly discard that dogma. Thus, neo-orthodox thinkers distinguished between ancient sagas such as Noah's ark and more weighty matters such as the Resurrection or the forgiveness of sins.

In 1945 an assembly of 44 Missouri Synod leaders, including a few Concordia (St. Louis) faculty members, met in Chicago to talk seriously about the theological problems of the Missouri Synod. At the conclusion of their conversations, they issued "A Statement." The document called for fundamental theological change in the denomination along more neo-orthodox lines and for increased attentions to the opportunities for Lutheran unity. While the Synod forced the 44 to withdraw their statement in 1947, there were new winds blowing. At the 1950 convention, some were already demanding the investigation of Concordia.

Behind the scenes, faculty members at Concordia, some of whom had studied at major graduate schools, began to experiment with the newer theology, including biblical criticism. In 1958, Concordia Professor Martin Scharlemann, a former military chaplain and biblical professor, published a series of attacks on the doctrine of biblical inerrancy. His work unleashed a violent protest, and Scharlemann officially withdrew the offending essays at the 1962 synodical convention. Ironically, this session of the convention declared a 1959 convention statement requiring synodical teachers to teach in accord with "A Brief Statement of Francis Piper" unconstitutional.

THE PARADOX OF THE 1960s

The same 1962 convention that received Scharlemann's apology for his biblical essays elected Oliver Harms as president of the Missouri Synod. A leading Lutheran administrator, Harms fit the optimism of the Kennedy years. He was optimistic about the future of the church and trusted people to do what was right. In 1965 when conservatives challenged him about the orthodoxy of the Concordia faculty, he accepted a somewhat noncommittal statement of faith as proof that all was well.

The high point of Harms's administration of the Synod came at the 1965 Detroit convention when the Synod adopted the "Mission Affirmations." American missiologists, inspired by the worldwide decline of European imperialism, began reexamining the theology of foreign missions at the end of the world war. Part of this reexamination was a separation between planting the Gospel and transplanting Western civilization. Increasingly, mainstream American boards chose to work through such agencies as the World Council of Churches and to seek strategies to work with churches in other lands. As soon as possible, most boards struggled to turn over control of churches abroad to indigenous Christians. While conservative, the "Mission Affirmations" followed a similar line of thought. They pledged the Synod to respect the faith of other people, to be humble in presenting the Gospel, and to recognize that the Missouri Synod sought to proclaim the Word of God as a confessional, not an exclusive, denomination. At the same convention, the delegates voted to allow women to vote at church meetings and took steps toward establishing table and pulpit fellowship with the American Lutheran Church.

CONSERVATIVES ORGANIZE

The 1965 Detroit meeting horrified many conservative Missourians. Conservatives had begun to organize before that meeting when they founded the Faith Forward—First Concerns Movement to try to influence the Harms administration. That year, the Lutheran Laymen's League turned to the Right when the group elected Robert Hirsch, a lawyer, as its president. This pressure from the Right led to some small, but important, victories at the 1967 New York convention, which inspired some conservatives to think that they might win the major offices. In 1967 the United Planning Council began to meet. The Council included among its members Waldo Werning, Edwin Weber, Ellis Nieting, Jacob A. O. Preus, and Karl Barth. The goal of the Council was to win control of the Synod, if possible, and, if not, to nudge the denomination to the Right. As part of its larger program, the United Planning Council apparently decided that conservatives should unite around the nomination of Jacob Preus at the 1969 convention.

Herman Otten, a fiery ecclesiastical muckraker, was never openly part of these more official conservative organizations. As a result of his attacks on professors at Concordia, that school refused to certify him for ministry. Nonetheless, the energetic Otten became pastor of a small congregation and established a biweekly newspaper, the *Lutheran News*. In 1968, this became the weekly *Christian News*. Historically, Otten's influence on the course of events is hard to determine. He was too much of a maverick to participate in the inner circle, and his newspaper writing was often too shrill for polite company. Nonetheless, more mainstream conservatives kept Otten informed of their plans, and the angry publisher did coordinate his trumpet blasts with the Right's overall strategy. At a minimum, Otten's angry journalism and exposés of Concordia professors kept the drums beating for something to be done about the heretics at the seminary. Even those who despised his writings suspected that the clouds of smoke rising from his articles hid a substantial fire.

The Missouri Synod's turn toward the Right paralleled similar shifts in other areas of American life. The year 1968 was pivotal. The angry riots that followed the assassination of Martin Luther King frightened many Americans. Further, Americans faced the tragedy at Mai Lay and increasing resistance to the Vietnam War on college campuses. Students at Columbia and San Francisco State went out on strike, and even Missouri's Concordia Seminary experienced a student "moratorium" in spring 1969. Abroad, Americans watched helplessly as the Soviet Union and its allies crushed the new Czechoslovak Republic under Alexander Dubcek. In November 1968, discontented Americans elected Richard M. Nixon as president of the United States.

VICTORY IN DENVER

Although the tide was running toward conservatism, Preus and his friends may not have understood the strength of their position or the effectiveness of their tactics. Longtime Preus observer James E. Adams believed that "the irony was that the UPC [United Planning Council] never expected victory with any certainty. A Denver meeting had been scheduled to plan what to do after Preus *wasn't* elected. Moreover, the UPC was hardly the sophisticated machine later fantasized" (Adams, *Preus of Missouri*, 137). While Adams may be right, the conservatives did use some very effective measures at the 1969 convention. Van drivers met delegates at the airport; activists distributed literature at the meeting; and floor managers, identified by their lapel pins, marshaled the proceedings. Preus's supporters were everywhere, talking to people about his candidacy.

Perhaps because such overt political action was untypical of American religious bodies, the Preus campaign appears to have caught the moderates by surprise. Continuing to believe that Harms was unbeatable, they tried to stay above the fray and refused to use the parliamentary powers that Harms possessed to delay the vote. Moreover, both Harms and his supporters studiously avoided anything that might suggest campaigning. In future elections, the moderates would not have either the parliamentary or psychological advantages of incumbency, and the conservatives would. In that sense, the first campaign was the crucial one; thereafter, all Preus had to do was not to lose.

THE CONTEST BEGINS

The conservatives elected Preus to do something about the seminary; the question was what. Preus had a number of alternatives ranging from formal heresy trials to the use of his executive power. Missouri's constitution charged the president with maintaining the doctrinal orthodoxy of the Synod's institutions. Moreover, Preus believed that the Synod itself was capable of establishing doctrinal statements that would be binding on its employees, providing that those statements did not conflict with Article II of the Synod's constitution. Article II established the Scriptures as "the written Word of God" and, hence, sole authority for teaching in the Synod, and pointed to the Lutheran Confessions as a "true and unadulterated statement and exposition of the Word of God" (cited in Danker, *No Room in the Brotherhood*, iv).

For Preus and his followers, the place where the Synod's confessional heritage was under attack was the doctrine of biblical inerrancy. Although this teaching had a long scholastic heritage, inerrancy became popular in the late nineteenth and early twentieth centuries when conservative Christians sought to negate higher criticism. After World War II, such neoevangelical theologians as Carl F. Henry and Bernard Ramm further adjusted the doctrine to contemporary conditions. The 1960 popularity of inerrancy language among Missouri Synod conservatives was another example of the denomination's Americanization.

THE FACT FINDING COMMITTEE

Preus's attack on the seminary came in two phases. In September 1970, Preus appointed a Fact Finding Committee to investigate allegations that Concordia's faculty taught false doctrine. The committee had five members: Paul W. Streufert, pastor from Rocky River, Ohio; Paul A. Zimmerman, president of a denominational college; Karl A. Barth, president of the South Wisconsin District; H. Armin Moellering, pastor from Palisades Park; and Elmer Foelber, staff of Concordia Publishing House. The taping of interviews with faculty members began in late December 1970 and continued until March 1971. The interviews were painful. Frederick Danker, professor of New Testament interpretation, left us a memoir of his experience with the committee (Danker, *No Room in the Brotherhood*, 48–69). His words record a conversation at cross-purposes. The committee's interest was primarily in the historicity of particular events mentioned in the Bible. In contrast, Danker was primarily concerned with the theological grounding that he had developed for his scholarship. Neither party's explanations satisfied the other! Similar comments could be made about the other interviews. The committee submitted its report to Preus in June 1971. In turn, Preus, following a resolution of the Milwaukee Convention, sent the report to Concordia's Board of Control for adjudication. Resolution 2–28 called for the Board to take appropriate action to commend or correct the faculty. The Board of Control began hearings on the substance of the charges in September 1971 and turned to the review of individual faculty members in December. The process would not be completed until 1973.

In the midst of this task, the reappointment of Dr. Arlis Ehlen, graduate of both the seminary and Harvard, came before the Board. Ehlen, an Old Testament instructor, was one of the rising stars on the faculty. When Ehlen's renewal was first considered in December 1971, the Board rejected the proposed contract, apparently because of Ehlen's views on the existence of angels and demons. Both Tietjen and Ehlen appealed the decision. As the Board discussion developed, Ehlen's views on the Exodus became the central concern. At one point, Preus introduced student notes into the discussion to demonstrate how far Ehlen was from Lutheran orthodoxy. After considerable debate, however, the Board granted Ehlen a one-year contract. The extension outraged Preus. He promptly wrote to Tietjen, demanding that Ehlen not be allowed to teach any courses where he might use historical-critical methods. Almost immediately, Tietjen refused. He wrote to Preus: "[I]t is not possible for Dr. Ehlen to teach any of his assigned courses at a seminary level of instruction, thus taking the text of the Holy Scriptures with utter seriousness, without using historical criticism" (Tietjen, *Memoirs in Exile*, 98).

AN APPEAL TO SYNOD

The second stage of Preus's attack on the seminary was an appeal to the Synod for authority to change the school. The first signs of this new phase occurred during the faculty interviews. In February 1972, Preus presented his "A Statement of Scriptural and Confessional Principles" to Concordia's Board of Control. Apparently, the Synod president intended the Board to use the statement's teachings as guidelines in the examination of individual professors. Preus organized the "Statement" around six doctrinal loci or topics: Christ as Savior and Lord, Law and Gospel, Mission of the Church,

Holy Scripture, Original Sin, and Confessional Subscription. In turn, Preus divided the various loci into propositions that the theologian should affirm and propositions that the theologian ought, consequently, to reject or deny. While not carefully worded or necessarily accurate, many of the rejected propositions were thinly disguised paraphrases of doctrines held by Concordia professors or attributed to them. Naturally, the faculty rejected the document as reflective of their position and the statement itself as inadequate to guide the Board in determining whether individuals held or did not hold unacceptable doctrines. A majority of the Board agreed. In its report to the Synod, the Board of Control stated that while its investigation was not yet complete, it "has found no false doctrine among the members of the seminary faculty."

Preus resolved to appeal this decision to the whole church. In September 1972 Preus released his *Report of the Synodical President to the Lutheran Church–Missouri Synod, in Compliance with Resolution 2–28 of the 49th Regular Convention of the Synod, Held at Milwaukee, July 9–16, 1971*. The report quickly became known as the "Blue Book" because of its cover's color. Neatly color coded, the Blue Book separated the committee's findings from the evidence that supposedly supported those findings. To protect the identity of individual faculty members, the Blue Book assigned a letter from the alphabet to each teacher before reporting the interview with that instructor. Although the report apparently contained some sloppy reporting of interviews and some distortions of faculty positions, its basic outline was clear. The majority of the faculty at Concordia held doctrines that, whether they were legally heretical or not, were opposed to the majority opinion in the Synod. Six specific areas of error were alleged: a false doctrine of the nature of Holy Scripture; a de facto denial of the doctrine of original sin by virtue of the denial of the events on which the teaching was based; a permissiveness toward false doctrine; a tendency to deny the value of the Law in Christian life; a conditional acceptance of the Lutheran Confessions; and a refusal to recognize the contemporary teaching authority of the Synod.

More important than the specific accusations was the place that the Blue Book assigned to Preus's "A Statement of Scriptural and Confessional Principles." The Blue Book made it clear that Preus believed that the Missouri Synod had the right to establish contemporary gauges of theological orthodoxy. The Blue Book also explicitly called on the Concordia faculty to desist from any teaching that called the doctrinal teachings of the church into question.

Tietjen replied immediately with his pamphlet *Fact-Finding or Fault Finding? An Analysis of the President J. A. O. Preus' Investigation of the Concordia Seminary*. Like Preus, Tietjen seems to have recognized that the 1973 New Orleans Convention would decide the issue. He had a copy of his response mailed to every clergy person in the denomination along with a personal letter detailing Tietjen's response to the crisis. With both Tietjen and Preus aiming toward a showdown in New Orleans, the Board of Control's April 1973 decision to commend each faculty member was anticlimatic. Everyone knew that events had changed the venue of the hearings.

THE END OF THE ROAD

The New Orleans Convention went entirely Preus's way. The delegates reelected Preus president, and his party secured majorities on the various boards and agencies that governed Missouri, including Concordia's Board of Control. Not surprisingly, the convention adopted Preus's "A Statement of Scriptural and Confessional Principles" as an expression of the Synod's position on contemporary doctrinal issues. Resolution 3–09 passed judgment on the majority of the Concordia faculty. Although the convention amended the resolution and placed the fate of individuals under the Board of Control, the convention intended the Board to clean house. A separate resolution, Resolution 3–12, dealt with the need to remove Tietjen as president of the seminary. In its final form, this resolution demanded that Tietjen "be dealt with in such manner as is permitted under applicable substantive and procedural provisions of the Handbook of the Synod."

Although New Orleans effectively ended moderate control of Concordia, Tietjen and the faculty fought through the fall to maintain their position at the school. The crucial Board of Control vote, originally scheduled for December, was delayed one month. This was due to the funeral of Arthur Carl Piepkorn, a senior faculty member who suffered a stroke just before the scheduled meeting. On 20 January 1974, the Board suspended Tietjen from office as president. The next day, the students declared a moratorium on classes, while the faculty declared that it considered itself suspended as well. At this point, the Board of Control and Acting President Martin Scharlemann set 17 February 1974 as the last day for the faculty to return to classes or have their salaries discontinued. Preparations to resume classes at another location went forward with haste as the faculty reached agreements with Eden Seminary and St. Louis University for classroom space and academic accreditation. Seminex negotiated an agreement with the Lutheran School of Theology in Chicago to allow Seminex graduates to receive a "Lutheran" degree shortly after the new school opened. Although faculty members missed one paycheck, the new Concordia Seminary-in-Exile established itself quickly.

Part of the reason for Seminex's success was that the school was part of a larger Missouri Synod schism. Evangelical Lutherans in Mission (ELIM), which was the core of the new denomination, was organized in August 1974. The ELIM did not formally become a denomination until 1976 when it reorganized as the Association of Evangelical Lutheran Churches. Before that, the organization was a convenient resting place for people as they moved toward new denominational affiliations. Thus, when the Board of Foreign Missions dismissed Martin Kretzmann, author of the Mission Affirmations, as secretary for planning, study, and research, the ELIM-sponsored Partners in Mission provided a place of temporary sanctuary. When the 1975 Anaheim Convention of the Missouri Synod declared membership in ELIM schismatic, the group transformed itself quickly into a new denomination, the Association of Evangelical Lutheran Churches. The members of the new body believed in cooperation and union with other Lutheran bodies and took an active role in the formation of the Evangelical Lutheran Church in America. Ironically, the leaders of this small splinter denomination may have had more influence on the larger course of Lutheran history than they would have had in a more moderate Missouri Synod.

BIBLIOGRAPHY

AAUP Bulletin (April 1975): 49–59.

Adams, James E. *Preus of Missouri and the Great Lutheran Civil War*. New York: Harper and Row, 1977.

Danker, Frederick. *No Room in the Brotherhood: The Preus-Otten Purge of Missouri*. St. Louis: Clayton Publishing, 1977.

Hillis, Bryan. *Can Two Walk Together Unless They Be Agreed: American Religious Schisms in the 1970s*. Brooklyn, NY: Carlson Publishing, 1990.

Marquart, Kurt E. *Anatomy of an Explosion: Missouri in Lutheran Perspective*. Fort Wayne, IN: Concordia Theological Seminary Press, 1977.

Rudnick, Milton L. *Fundamentalism and the Missouri Synod: A Historical Study of Their Interaction and Mutual Influence*. St. Louis: Concordia Publishing House, 1966.

Tietjen, John H. *Memoirs in Exile: Confessional Hope and Institutional Conflict*. Minneapolis: Fortress Press, 1990.

Glenn T. Miller

Algernon Sidney Crapsey
(1847–1927)

In contrast to other heresy trials in the late nineteenth and early twentieth centuries, such as those of Crawford Howell Toy,* Charles Augustus Briggs,* and Borden Parker Bowne,* the 1906 trial of Algernon S. Crapsey did not focus on biblical literalism but on faithfulness to the historic creeds of the church. One of only two heresy trials during this period in the Protestant Episcopal Church in the United States, Crapsey's provoked discussion of clerical authority and doctrinal interpretation but by no means resolved them.

Crapsey was born in Fairmount, Ohio, on 28 June 1847, the son of Jacob Tompkins Crapsey, a lawyer, and Rachel Morris. His maternal grandfather was Thomas Morris, abolitionist and U.S. senator from Ohio, "a seer and a prophet, a hero and a martyr," according to Crapsey in his autobiography *The Last of the Heretics* (2). Jacob Crapsey's declining legal practice forced Algernon at age 11 to leave school and seek employment in a dry goods store. During the Civil War, he served for four months as a private in the Ohio Infantry but was discharged when diagnosed as having a hypertrophied heart. He lived, despite doctors' predictions of his imminent death. In 1865 he moved to Washington, D.C. and worked in the Dead Letter Office for six months; from there he went to New York City and became a bookkeeper.

In New York he began attending Christ Episcopal Church and was strongly influenced by its Anglo-Catholic rector, Ferdinand Cartwright Ewer. He was baptized and confirmed and felt the call to preach. He studied at St. Stephen's (later Bard) College from 1867 to 1869 and graduated from General Theological Seminary in 1872. Crapsey's theological training was not extensive; in his autobiography he commented, "I do not think that there was ever an institution so inadequate to its purpose as this seminary when I was under its care" (*Last of the Heretics*, 85). He was ordained a priest of the Episcopal Church in 1873 and served on the staff of Trinity Church in Manhattan. In 1875 he married Adelaide Trowbridge; they had nine children.

In 1879 Crapsey accepted the pastorate of St. Andrew's Church in Rochester, New York. Under his leadership, the struggling congregation thrived. The church became the first free church in the city, as Crapsey refused to charge pew rental. He established the St. Andrew's Brotherhood, a mutual aid society, and the School of Practical Knowledge and Recreation, a training institute for kindergarten teachers. He helped to found an industrial school, supported mission efforts among African Americans, and was active in civic affairs. He was a member of the Fortnightly Club, a literary association; served as president of the Citizens Political Reform Association in the 1890s; and helped to found the City Club. He worked with Walter Rauschenbusch, a professor at Rochester Theological Seminary and the most prominent theologian of the Social Gospel. Crapsey and St. Andrew's became well known in Rochester and recognized throughout the Episcopal Church for their application of the Christian gospel to social issues. He was a beloved pastor, popular speaker, retreat leader, and writer.

Crapsey first clashed with Episcopal authorities in 1895. That year he disobeyed direct orders from the bishop not to fellowship with another denomination by preaching at Third Presbyterian Church in Rochester. This decision signaled his break from the Anglo-Catholic party within the church. In 1897 he published *A Voice in the Wilderness*, in which he argued for a separate diocese for Rochester, a move opposed by newly elected Bishop William D. Walker. In 1899, he wrote a tract entitled *The Disappointment of Jesus Christ* on the causes and remedies for church disunity. Although generally well received, the Rev. William R. Huntingdon, rector of Grace Church in New York, wrote Crapsey that his " 'waiver of creed-forms is a little too sweeping' " (*Last of the Heretics*, 223). Crapsey did not hesitate to challenge church authority and was more interested in moral and social issues than doctrine. Throughout his career, variously influenced by Darwin, Marx, and Ritschl, Crapsey, no systematic thinker, was not especially meticulous in expressing his theological views.

This lack of precision brought Crapsey under attack with the 1905 publication of *Religion and Politics*, based on a series of Sunday evening lectures given at St. Andrew's in 1904–1905 on the relationship between Christianity and the state. Crapsey acknowledged that the lectures had been hastily written and published as delivered, "as truly extempore as if I had spoken them without notes from the pulpit" (*Last of the Heretics*, 243). While most of the lectures were historical, one, entitled "The Present State of the Churches," contained the following passage:

> In the light of scientific research, the Founder of Christianity no longer
> stands apart from the common destiny of man in life and death, but
> He is in all things physical like as we are, born as we are born, dying
> as we die, and both in life and death in the keeping of that same Divine
> Power, that heavenly Fatherhood, which delivers us from the womb
> and carries us down to the grave. (*Religion and Politics*, 288–289)

This apparent denial of the doctrines of the virgin birth, bodily resurrection, and divinity of Jesus as contained in the Apostles' and Nicene Creeds provoked Crapsey's trial for heresy. After he refused to retract his views as requested by Bishop Walker, a diocesan committee of five was appointed to determine if there was sufficient evidence to present Crapsey for trial. On 11 November 1905, the committee reported its findings to the bishop: Two were in favor of presentment for trial; three were opposed. However, the committee was united in its condemnation of Crapsey's " 'intellectual vagaries,' " his " 'claiming to retain the spiritual reality for which Christianity stands while dismissing as indifferent the historical facts asserted in the Creeds' " (as quoted in Jansen, "Algernon Sidney Crapsey," 198).

The committee's condemnation of Crapsey without presentment for trial aroused a firestorm of controversy in the church. Denominational periodicals carried numerous articles on the " 'Rochester scandal' " (197). The reasons for Crapsey's subsequent presentment on 23 February 1906 after the first committee declined to do so are not clear. Bishop Walker may have initiated the action. He made no secret of his opposition to Crapsey's views; he believed in the literal truth of the creeds. The conservatism in the diocese of western New York may also have been a factor. Historian Hugh Jansen concluded that in the "strongly Anglo-Catholic context of the diocese at the time, Crapsey's vague and rather provocative comments on the creeds were unacceptable" (199).

Crapsey himself contributed to the furor by refusing to remain silent. In September 1905, he published "Honor among Clergymen" in which he defended the right of clergy to express their convictions free of episcopal interference. Clergy must base their beliefs solely on the Bible, especially the teachings of Jesus. This article may have contributed to his presentment, although it was not mentioned specifically in the charges. The simplest reason for Crapsey's presentment is that it became clear that the clamor would only be calmed by a trial.

According to the official account, new evidence of heresy necessitated presentment. Two charges were made against Crapsey. The first was that he " 'did openly, advisedly, publicly and privately utter, avow, declare, and teach doctrines contrary to those held and received by the Protestant Episcopal Church' " (*Arguments*, 3). The specific doctrines he was accused of denying included the deity of Jesus Christ, virgin birth, bodily resurrection, and the Trinity. Fifteen passages from *Religion and Politics* were cited as evidence, as well as a sermon from 31 December 1905. This sermon was the new evidence. The second charge was that Crapsey had violated his ordination vows by both his " 'public utterances' " and his conduct, that he was not " 'diligent to frame and fashion himself and his family according to the doctrine of Christ,' and to make himself and them, as much as in him lay, 'wholesome examples and patterns to the flock of Christ' " (*Arguments*, 5).

The trial began on 17 April 1906 in the parish house of St. James' Church in Batavia, New York. The lead prosecutor was John Lord O'Brian, a Buffalo attorney, while defense counsel was the Honorable James Breck Perkins, congressman from Rochester, and Edward M. Shepard, well-known New York lawyer. The court consisted of five clergymen appointed by the bishop, diocesan council, and the Standing Committee that had made the presentment. Although the bishop's and Standing Committee's positions on the case were clear, the court was canonically constituted. The defense's motion to adjourn until a new diocesan council and court were elected was denied. The defense was granted a week to prepare the case.

The court reconvened on April 25. The chief witness for the prosecution was the Rev. James Alexander, assistant rector of St. Andrew's and source of the new evidence against Crapsey, his notes of the December 31 sermon. Crapsey denied the heretical content of the sermon. During cross-examination, Alexander admitted that he had been denied a raise shortly before he recorded the sermon notes and that he hoped to succeed Crapsey, should he be convicted. Edward Shepard later commented that it would be " 'a sad day for the influence of the church in this community, if a man with the standards of life of Dr. Crapsey must be thrown out, and a man with the standards of life of Mr. Alexander shall stay in' " (as quoted in Jansen, "Algernon Sidney Crapsey," 207).

The defense presented its case on April 27. Crapsey was present but did not testify. His attorneys planned to call a number of prominent clergy and professors as expert witnesses and introduce scholarly publications as evidence to demonstrate that Crapsey's views were within the bounds of accepted belief in the Episcopal Church. The prosecution objected that individuals, regardless of academic or ecclesiastical credentials, had no right to testify on the creeds of the church because they were perspicacious and indisputable. Since creeds were uninterpretable, there was no need for expert witnesses to interpret them. The court agreed and prohibited the witnesses from testifying on doctrine. Crapsey was left with only character witnesses.

The trial concluded with lengthy closing statements by both sides. Included was a statement by Crapsey read by James Perkins, in which Crapsey affirmed his belief in the incarnation, Trinity, and resurrection, as well as the creeds as interpreted by the Bible. The court adjourned on April 28, with a verdict to be announced less than a month later. In the interim,

Crapsey continued to preach and lead worship. The verdict was delivered on May 15. By a margin of four to one, Crapsey was convicted of impugning and denying, in *Religion and Politics* and the December 31 sermon, the virgin birth, resurrection, Trinity, and deity of Jesus Christ. He was acquitted only of violating his ordination vows through his own and his family's conduct.

One member of the court, Francis Dunham, issued a dissenting opinion, declaring that Crapsey's error was in " 'presuming to define what God has not been pleased to reveal' " and "in interpreting the doctrines of the incarnation and resurrection 'in a manner not generally received by the Church, rather than in a denial and rejection of their truth and authority' " (*Arguments*, 8). Crapsey's sentence was that he be suspended from the ministry until he satisfied "the ecclesiastical authority of the diocese" of his orthodoxy (*Arguments*, 12). What constituted this ecclesiastical authority and how it might be satisfied was not clear.

Crapsey appealed the ruling to the Court of Review of the Second Department of the Protestant Episcopal Church, which oversaw dioceses in New York and New Jersey. The Court of Review heard Crapsey's appeal on 19 October 1906 in New York City. Shepard argued that the verdict should be overturned on two procedural grounds: that the lower court had no grounds to reject Crapsey's expert witnesses and that the ruling had not found that Crapsey denied church doctrine advisedly or intentionally. Therefore, he had not violated canon law as stipulated and was convicted of an offense for which he was not tried.

Shepard devoted most of his statement not to procedural issues but to arguing that the judgment to suspend Crapsey from the ministry was too harsh. He and Perkins eloquently argued for tolerance. Shepard asked the court:

> Can and will a church truly destined to a glorious career of catholicity thus discipline and dismiss a minister bountiful in good works for the church and with an unblemished career of nearly forty years in its service, for the sole reason that he does not hold or preach something never preached or mentioned by the Divine Founder of Christianity Himself or preached by any of His Apostles? (*Arguments*, 64–65)

Perkins declared, "It is the church which is on trial more than Dr. Crapsey," adding, "There are thousands of sincere churchmen and earnest thinkers who feel that if there is no room for Dr. Crapsey in the Episcopal Church, then there is no room for them" (*Arguments*, 172, 173).

For the prosecution, John O'Brian argued against the defense's objections that canonical procedures had been followed to the letter and that Crapsey's sentence was fair and appropriate. He queried:

> Are we going to listen to this cry of heresy trial, heresy trial, and fail
> to do our duty; or are we going to look straight in the face the fact
> that the Protestant Episcopal Church demands of man obedience, that
> he shall say that he believes the articles of faith as contained in the
> Apostles' Creed? (*Arguments*, 146)

O'Brian concluded that "if the church is to prevail against the gates of hell,
it must be the church of truth, not the church of double-faced sophistry
and casuistry" (*Arguments*, 150).

In a decision announced 20 November 1906, the Court of Review upheld
the lower court ruling. There had been no violation of judicial procedure;
the decision and sentence were within the bounds of canon law. The Court
declined to comment on doctrinal issues. It also refused to judge whether
or not the ruling was beneficial to the church, maintaining that it could
only enforce ecclesiastical legislation, not pass judgment on it. The Court
of Review declared that the church could not "permit doctrines which it
holds essential and fundamental to be impugned by those who minister at
her altars, however pure their motives or sincere their convictions" (*Arguments*, 201).

Crapsey felt he had no choice but to resign from the ministry. Less than
a week after the Court of Review's decision, he wrote Bishop Walker, requesting deposition. In this widely circulated, lengthy, and moving letter,
he stated that "a long, careful conscientious study of the Holy Scriptures
has compelled me to come to certain conclusions concerning the prenatal
history of Jesus which are not in physical accord with the letter of the
Creeds"; therefore, "If I am to hold the Creed at all I must give to certain,
if not all, of its articles a spiritual rather than a literally physical interpretation" (*Last of the Heretics*, 276).

As these views were not tolerated in the church, he said, he had opted
to leave it rather than lie. He declared he did not blame ecclesiastical authorities, and he urged the "hundreds of clergymen and thousands of laymen" who shared his views not to leave the church (*Last of the Heretics*,
278). He thanked his legal team, supporters, and the church itself. He departed, he said, "with the deepest gratitude for the opportunities of worship, of preaching and of service which have been the privileges of my
office" (*Last of the Heretics*, 278).

After his deposition and resignation from St. Andrew's, Crapsey remained in Rochester. While he did not join the ministry of another denomination, he remained interested in religious issues. He wrote several books
and lectured widely. He served as a delegate to the International Peace
Conference at The Hague in 1907 and in 1914 was appointed a New York
State parole officer. He exerted no direct influence in the Episcopal Church.
No other heresy trials, resignations in sympathy with his position, or re-

percussions in seminaries followed his exit. He died on 31 December 1927 in Rochester.

The main question raised by Algernon Crapsey's heresy trial is, Why Crapsey? When it was widely acknowledged that many in the Episcopal Church shared his interpretation of the creeds, why was he singled out? Crapsey claimed he "was condemned primarily not for theological, but for social, political, and economic heresy" (*Last of the Heretics*, ix). However, Crapsey's social views were not mentioned at any point during the investigation, trial, or appeal. Another possibility is that Bishop Walker had a grudge against Crapsey, who never concealed his hostility toward the bishop. However, after the diocesan court was appointed, Walker had little to do with the proceedings. It may be that rampant heterodoxy in the Episcopal Church necessitated a scapegoat, and Crapsey was unwittingly cast. The most plausible explanation is a combination of factors. Crapsey's defiance of ecclesiastical authority gained him little support among the church hierarchy. His imprecise expression of his views, refusal to nuance them when challenged, and confrontive personality all exposed him to heresy charges in a conservative diocese.

The underlying issue in the Crapsey case was not growing polarization between conservative and liberal theologies but ecclesiastical authority. Who has the right and responsibility to interpret church doctrines? By emphasizing the spiritual meaning of the creeds rather than their historical veracity, Crapsey tested the freedom of individual clergy to interpret the creeds against ecclesiastical authority to enforce one reading. For one who refused to be silent, that freedom was indeed narrow. Discussion of clerical freedom in the Episcopal Church did not end with the Crapsey case; it resurfaced in 1923 with discussion of a pastoral letter by the bishops urging adherence to the doctrine of a literal virgin birth. Yet by testing the limits and suffering the consequences, Crapsey opened the door for freer expression of divergent views.

To the end of his life, Crapsey was committed to beliefs that placed him at the outskirts of Christendom. In the final pages of *The Last of the Heretics*, he wrote:

> When I am asked in these days what my religion is, I hesitate and stumble, and men go away thinking that I have no religion. But I have a religion and if asked to give it a name I should say I am a Pantheistic Humanist, and if one were to ask, "What is a Pantheistic Humanist?" I should say one who believes in the divinity of a telegraph pole. . . . When I thought on these things I said if my Christ has in Him the divinity of a telegraph pole, then he is divine enough for me. (292–293)

SELECTED BIBLIOGRAPHY

*Arguments for Presenters and Defence of Reverend A. S. Crapsey before the Court
    of Review of the Protestant Episcopal Church upon His Appeal from the
    Judgment of the Court of the Diocese of Western New York*. New York:
    Thomas Whittaker, 1906.

Crapsey, Algernon S. *The Disappointment of Jesus Christ*. Rochester, NY: Printed
    and published by the author, 1899.

———. "Honor among Clergymen." *Outlook* 81 (2 September 1905): 25–29.

———. *The Last of the Heretics*. New York: Alfred A. Knopf, 1924.

———. *The Re-Birth of Religion*. New York: John Lane, 1907.

———. *Religion and Politics*. New York: Thomas Whittaker, 1905.

———. *A Voice in the Wilderness*. New York: James Potts, 1897.

Hughes, W. Dudley F. "Agreement on Fundamentals: Correspondence between Dr.
    Huntington and Dr. Manning on the Crapsey Case, 1906." *Historical Mag-
    azine of the Protestant Episcopal Church* 25, no. 3 (1956): 263–276.

Jansen, Hugh M., Jr. "Algernon Sidney Crapsey: Heresy at Rochester." In *American
    Religious Heretics*, edited by George H. Shriver. Nashville: Abingdon, 1966.
    188–224.

Swanton, Carolyn. "Dr. Algernon S. Crapsey, Religious Reformer." *Rochester His-
    tory* 42, no. 1 (1980): 1–24.

Evelyn A. Kirkley

Charles E. Curran
(1934–   )

The exchange between Charles Curran and Roman Catholic authorities at the Vatican and at the Catholic University of America over the issues of authority and dissent marks a departure from traditional church heresy trials. In the first place, the Curran trial was a civil procedure, initiated by Charles Curran against his employer, the Catholic University of America (CUA). In the second place, although his views had been the subject of strenuous debate among Catholic ecclesiastical authorities and theologians, the Vatican never charged Curran with heresy.

The Curran case introduced a novel claim in Catholic tradition, namely, that Catholic theologians have the right to publicly dissent from certain teachings of the noninfallible ordinary magisterium of the Catholic Church. Although opposition to Church teaching is an ancient practice, the claim of a right to public dissent arose only in response to the formal and juridical definitions of the teaching authority of the Church presented in the two modern ecumenical councils, Vatican I (1869–1870) and Vatican II (1962–1965), and in the Code of Canon Law, which was first published in 1917 and revised in 1983.

In addition to claiming the right to contest pronouncements that fall within the modern category of "the non-infallible universal magisterium," supporters of the premise of legitimate theological dissent specifically contend that such dissent could properly be made public. This issue became the most neuralgic point in the dispute. Over the centuries, the Church has developed elaborate juridical methods for managing "private" dissent (e.g., dissent confined to specialized theological journals or to the relationship between dissenting individuals and their religious superiors). But Charles Curran and his supporters took dissent public. Their methods included the use of the media, the organization of public protests, and a faculty and student strike at CUA that closed down the campus in 1967. They also strenuously insisted that administrators and trustees at CUA should be bound by the warrants for dissent provided by American practices of academic freedom and civil law. The struggle over the legitimacy of the practice of public dissent is therefore at the core of the Curran case.

ASSENT AND DISSENT

Ecclesiologist Francis A. Sullivan notes that under the rubric of Vatican I (1869–1870) an "assent of faith" is owed by Catholics to "all those things . . . that are contained in the word of God, whether written or handed down, and have been proposed by the Church, whether by solemn judgment or by its ordinary universal magisterium, as divinely revealed and to be believed as such." The same assent of faith is due to "revealed truths that have never been defined but which Catholic bishops throughout the world, together with the pope, consistently teach as definitively to be held with divine faith" (Sullivan, "Heresy," 610). Charles Curran has repeatedly agreed an assent of faith is owed to the revealed core of Christian belief, but he claims that there is a wide range of Church teaching that is not properly the subject of such unreserved assent and argues that this "noninfallible" teaching may become the proper focus of respectfully critical evaluation by Catholic theologians who believe their professional and pastoral responsibilities require them to participate in the development of understanding of the claims entailed.

Moral theologian Richard A. McCormick defines such dissent as "judgment of disagreement with an official teaching or practice" and supports Curran's claim that such dissent is a legitimate function of the Catholic theologian. McCormick also endorses the observation that the modern practice of elaborating the teaching authority of the Church in conciliar and canonical statements makes it possible (and necessary) to distinguish the "various levels of authoritative Church teaching and the appropriate response to them" (McCormick, "Dissent," 421).

Both Sullivan and McCormick accept the position expressed in Vatican I, namely: "When the Church, through the pope or the bishops with the pope, uses its fullest authority to propose a matter of revealed faith or morals, it acts infallibly. The proper response to such teaching is an act of faith." But infallible pronouncements are unusual. The bulk of Church teaching is composed of the authoritative but noninfallible pronouncements of the magisterium. All sides in this debate agree that this teaching of the noninfallible ("ordinary") magisterium should receive "the presumption of truth rooted in the fact that the pope and bishops have been commissioned to teach and enjoy the guidance of the Holy Spirit in fulfilling this commission" (McCormick, "Dissent").

McCormick suggests, however, that "the strength of this presumption can vary considerably since there is a broad range of subjects that can be proposed authoritatively and their status can vary. Some enjoy greater certainty than others." By way of example, he argues that "universal moral principles are proposed more authoritatively than their applications." A greater degree of certainty attaches to the maxim that the good should be done, for instance, than to the prescriptions for the application of that principle.

This question of the strength of the "presumption of truth" in any teaching becomes the pivotal issue in the argument over public dissent. The Code of Canon Law defines the proper response to authoritative noninfallible teaching as *obsequium religiosum* (1983, #751). The meaning of *obsequium* is contested between those who see it as a call for religious "submission" to authority and those who translate it more softly as a necessary "respect" for the magisterium. McCormick argues that the understanding of this term was significantly developed during Vatican II, when the Council implicitly and explicitly admitted that the noninfallible teaching authority of the Church had indeed made errors in the past. As a result, "many theologians began to understand the proper response to authoritative but noninfallible teaching as a kind of docility of mind and will that did not exclude a critical component and the possibility of dissent" (McCormick, "Dissent"). An important personnel change accompanied this newly emerging understanding of the role of the theologian. For the first time, lay Catholic women and men were earning advanced degrees in theology and teaching in institutions of higher education, both Catholic and secular. The effort to maintain a traditional understanding of *obsequium religiosum*, which had formerly touched only the clergy, was greatly complicated by the presence of these new theologians in the ranks.

The problematic nature of these developments became vividly apparent when Pope Paul VI published the encyclical *Humanae vitae* (1968), reaffirming the magisterium's traditional opposition to all forms of artificial contraception. Many Catholics, including both theologians and priests, could not accept the central assertion of *Humanae vitae* that every contraceptive act was intrinsically immoral. The sustained and very public reaction to the encyclical's conclusions on artificial contraception became inseparably bound up with the developing controversy on theological dissent.

The bishops of the United States responded to the crisis with the pastoral letter "Human Life in Our Day," upholding the authority of the papal teaching. But the statement also implied that public dissent might be a legitimate aspect of the theologian's role in the Church. In fact, the bishops conceded that dissent was "in order" [only] if "the reasons are serious and well-founded, if the manner of dissent does not question or impugn the teaching authority of the Church and is such as not to give scandal" (Nolan, *Pastoral Letters*, 174). Theologians supporting Charles Curran claimed to find a warrant for "licit dissent" in this document.

THE TRIALS OF CHARLES CURRAN

The chief episodes in the Curran case took place between 1967 and 1987. In these years, American identity and practice were dramatically challenged inter alia by the Vietnam War, *Roe v. Wade*, and the economic gospel of Ronald Reagan. For American Catholics, these general dislocations were accompanied by transformations in the Church that fundamentally altered their lives. The religious identity and practice of millions of them were irrevocably changed by Vatican II and by the 1968 encyclical on birth control.

Charles Curran was one of those Catholics. Curran received his graduate training in moral theology in Rome during the 1950s, studying particularly with renowned moralist Bernard Haring. Ordained a priest for the diocese of Rochester, New York, in 1958, Curran came to the papally chartered school of theology at Catholic University of America in 1965, where he taught both seminarians and lay students. The Catholic University of America, which was approaching its centenary when Curran initiated his 1987 lawsuit, was founded by the bishops of the United States to provide graduate education for the American clergy. Over the years, programs for graduate and undergraduate lay men and women were added to the curriculum, but the university remained in a special way "the bishops' school" and depended heavily on diocesan and religious support. It has retained its original juridical identity as both an independent, civilly incorporated entity and a papally chartered institution, subject to canon law and to special Vatican oversight. The latter requires that faculty members in the faculties of theology, philosophy, and canon law receive special permission to teach from Church authorities.

The first episode in the Curran case took place in 1967—after the conclusion of the Vatican Council but before the publication of *Humanae vitae*. During the 1966–1967 school year, Curran won approval for promotion to the rank of associate professor from his colleagues in the School of Theology (now the Department of Theology in the School of Religion) and from the university's Academic Senate. However, these recommendations were disregarded by CUA's Board of Trustees, who voted not to renew Curran's contract. Although it gave no reasons for its decision, Curran's views on moral issues and particularly on artificial contraception were clearly causing alarm among the bishops who composed the Board.

The action of the Board was not popular on campus. A public rally and strike by faculty and students shut down the campus and brought in the national media. One week later, the Board reversed itself and granted Curran a new contract with the status of associate professor. (In 1971, Curran was promoted to full or "ordinary" professor and granted tenure at the university.)

A year later, Curran was again the center of dispute. This second episode came in response to the publication of *Humanae vitae* on 29 July 1968. Curran and colleagues at CUA responded immediately, organizing a press conference and issuing a written protest against the absolute ban on artificial contraception. In it they identified "the possibility of dissent from such noninfallible teaching" and insisted that "as Roman Catholic theologians, conscious of our duties and our limitations, we conclude that spouses may responsibly decide according to their conscience that artificial contraception in some circumstances is permissible and indeed necessary to preserve and foster the values and sacredness of marriage" (Curran, *Faithful Dissent*, 17–19). Six hundred Catholics "qualified in the sacred sciences" subsequently signed this statement, including 20 professors from CUA. Many of the signers were members of religious orders.

This action put the issue of legitimate dissent from authoritative Church teaching by theologians squarely on the public table. The protest was welcomed by many ordinary Catholics who had struggled in the past, oftentimes heroically, to accept the Church's prohibition. Others, including many members of the hierarchy, were scandalized by this public action. The issue of contraception became the context for the question of legitimate dissent. And one new principle, this one drawn from American practice, soon appeared in the struggle when the claim of a right to public dissent became indissolubly wedded to the issue of academic freedom in the Catholic university setting.

The CUA Board of Trustees initiated an inquiry to establish whether the CUA signatories had violated their professional responsibilities as Catholic theologians. Standing academic procedures at CUA called for peer review, and the Board submitted the case to a committee of CUA faculty. Curran and his associates availed themselves of legal counsel from the law firm of Cravath, Swaine and Moore of New York, and the faculty committee ultimately exonerated the dissenters of all charges of professional misconduct. The Board received the report and took no further action against the members of the School of Theology. Curran and his supporters were convinced that this outcome had "established the principle of university autonomy and academic freedom at Catholic University and for all Catholic higher education in the United States" (Curran, *Faithful Dissent*, 19).

Through the decade of the 1970s, Curran kept up a demanding professional schedule at CUA and extended his influence off campus through his writings and through hundreds of lectures and workshops. His professional interests shifted from sexual ethics to social ethics during the decade, but his views on sexual moral questions, including contraception, divorce, sterilization, and masturbation, continued to fuel his popularity and to excite controversy.

In 1979 the simmering objections to his approach surfaced decisively when Curran was informed that his writings were under investigation by the Vatican Congregation for the Doctrine of the Faith (CDF). After several exchanges with Curran over the next seven years, the CDF determined that he should be declared "unsuitable and ineligible" to teach as a moral theologian at CUA. The university's Board of Trustees subsequently voted to implement the Vatican judgment and barred Curran from teaching in the Department of Theology or as a Catholic theologian anywhere in the university.

Curran firmly believed that his efforts to promote academic freedom at CUA in 1967–1969 and his subsequent receipt of tenure in the School of Theology should have protected him from this outcome. Although he acknowledged Rome's right to review and criticize his writings, Curran argued that the CUA was an independent corporation under American civil law and that it had guaranteed him the freedom to research and teach short of manifest incompetency. But CUA was a special case in American Catholic higher education. The pontifical standing of the faculties of theology, philosophy, and canon law, and the corresponding requirement that faculty members receive a special license or "canonical mission," was confirmed by Rome in the university constitution of 1937 and reintroduced in its Canonical Statutes of 1981. Although Curran and his attorneys argued that the canonical mission had fallen into disuse in the interim between 1937 and 1981, university administrators denied that was the case and claimed that the *missio* was always an implicit part of the contract with faculty in the pontifical schools.

Curran took the university to court, claiming that CUA had violated his academic freedom and his faculty contract. His complaint failed to find support in the judgment of the Superior Court of the District of Columbia. Judge Frederick Weisberg deliberately avoided reviewing First Amendment issues of free speech and free exercise. Construing the issue with the careful confines of contract law, and agreeing with the defense that the civil court could not touch the requirements of canon law that somehow governed CUA, Weisberg found that Curran's tenure contract had not been unduly abrogated when the university's Board of Trustees acted on the Vatican's injunction and prohibited Curran from teaching moral theology at CUA. The judge concluded that the "plaintiff's evidence describes the University he wanted to work for, maybe even the one he thought he was working for, but not the one with which he contracted" (Weisberg, Opinion and Order, 33).

CONTRACEPTION AND CATHOLIC COLLEGES

L'affaire Curran, as Richard McCormick has called this lengthy episode, focuses attention on two of the most important cultural pulse points in the Catholic community in the United States. One is the widespread and continuing dissent from the authoritative teaching against artificial contraception in *Humanae vitae*. The other is the growing tension surrounding the relationship between Church authority and American Catholic colleges and universities. Each of these issues has deep and complex roots.

Contraception became a public problem for Catholic Church authority in the United States before World War I, when Margaret Higgins Sanger began to defy both civil and Church law to promote what she christened the "birth control" movement. Her first copies of *The Birth Control Review* hit the streets of New York City in 1914 and were quickly confiscated by authorities, while Sanger fled to England to avoid prosecution under the federal Comstock laws. But her initial act of public defiance began a process that resulted in the legalization of contraception and a revolution in both private and public American life. Initially constructed as a means to relieve the hardships of the poor, the birth control campaign quickly built support among more genteel patrons. It also drew powerful opposition from law enforcement officials, the medical profession, and the Catholic Church.

By 1935 the economic depression eroded the strength of legal and medical objections, leaving the Catholic clerical and lay leadership lonely but still adamant in their opposition to the practice. Their reasons were clear. Apologies for contraception challenged the foundations of traditional natural law arguments, and the use of birth control promised to radically alter the established practices of family life. On both theoretical and practical levels, therefore, birth control threatened the survival of the traditional foundations of the Catholic subculture in the United States. With so much at stake, most Catholics dutifully bore the burden of the Church's proscription.

The dramatic withdrawal of support for the Church's position in the wake of the publication of *Humanae vitae* in 1968 was consequently of singular concern to Church identity and authority. It brought challenges to the traditional teaching on the role of natural law in moral discernment and by extension the teaching authority of the magisterium based on traditional natural law claims. Equally as troublesome have been the dramatic shifts in sexual practices and family life that reproductive control has brought in its wake. The family is a foundational element in modern Catholic social teaching, where it acts as the basic unit of society and the warrant for both the rights claims of individuals and the authority of the state. From the deliberate limitation of offspring to the explosion of women in the workforce (and corollary challenges by women to traditional male roles in the Church), the changes are of such magnitude that the family cannot easily serve in its established role as a foundation for the social teachings and social relationships of the Church. Dissent from authoritative teaching on artificial contraception, therefore, tends to call into question basic elements of the dogmatic and social teaching of the Church.

Charles Curran's case also serves to focus the growing controversy over the relationship of Catholic colleges and universities to Church authorities.

Catholic colleges and universities are leading edges in the encounter between Catholic tradition and modernity. Competent academic work customarily requires both an exposure to contents of disciplinary traditions and the development of critical intellect and judgment about those traditions. In the wake of Vatican II, the review of Catholic traditions of authority and practice was inevitable. The independence of colleges and universities under civil law seemed to provide guarantees for faculty claims of academic freedom commensurate with those in non-Catholic institutions. The desire to compete academically with the best of those institutions pushed the critical research agenda in Catholic schools.

Sister Alice Gallin, past president of the Association of Catholic Colleges and Universities, has tracked the exchanges between the Vatican and U.S. Catholic academic leaders over statutes governing colleges and universities for the Revised Code of Canon Law (1983). At the core of the controversy is Canon #812, which stipulates, "It is necessary that those who teach *theological disciplines* in any institute of higher studies have a *mandate* from the competent ecclesiastical authority" (Gallin, *American Catholic Higher Education*, 173–174). This canon in effect extends the requirement of a canonical mission to all Catholic colleges and universities in the country, and according to Gallin, it has raised "a storm of opposition in North America" from both university administrators and theologians.

Objections to Canon #812 echo the arguments in the Curran case: Extended ecclesiastical control will have "a chilling effect" on theological investigation, it is a "violation of the legitimate autonomy" of educational institutions and could jeopardize government financial assistance, and its purpose of welding colleges and universities more tightly to the pastoral mission and identity of the Church can be better achieved by "the judgment of peers and by conscientious administrators" (184–185).

The Code must be implemented by the action of national hierarchies. Proposals to this effect have been under consideration by the American bishops since 1983. The current form of the implementation has been heavily influenced from two sources: the publication of Pope John Paul II's views on the matter in the apostolic constitution, *Ex corde ecclesia* (1990), and the assiduous efforts of American Catholic higher education professionals and canonists to find a formulation that will accommodate Rome's concern to bolster the official connection between the magisterium and those colleges and universities that stand in the Catholic tradition without destroying the special character of these American institutions. As this process goes forward, the case of Charles Curran reappears on a much larger stage, and the stakes are exponentially higher.

BIBLIOGRAPHY

"Academic Freedom and Tenure: The Catholic University of America." *Academe: Bulletin of the AAUP* 75 (September–October 1989): 27–38.

Curran, Charles E. *Catholic Higher Education, Theology and Academic Freedom.* Notre Dame: University of Notre Dame, 1990, chap. 6.

———. *Faithful Dissent.* New York: Sheed and Ward, 1986.

Curran, Charles E., Robert E. Hunt, John F. Hunt, and Terrence R. Connelly. *Dissent in and for the Church: Theologians and Humanae vitae.* New York: Sheed and Ward, 1969.

Curran, Charles E., and Richard A. McCormick. *Readings in Moral Theology No. 6: Dissent in the Church.* New York: Paulist Press, 1988.

Gallin, Alice, ed. *American Catholic Higher Education: Essential Documents, 1967–1990.* Notre Dame: University of Notre Dame Press, 1992.

Hunt, John F., Terrence R. Connelly, Charles E. Curran, Robert E. Hunt, and Robert K. Webb. *The Responsibility of Dissent: The Church and Academic Freedom.* New York: Sheed and Ward, 1969.

May, William W., ed. *Vatican Authority and American Catholic Dissent: The Curran Case and Its Consequences.* New York: Crossroad, 1987.

McCormick, Richard. "Dissent." In *The Encyclopedia of Catholicism,* edited by Richard McBrien. San Francisco: HarperCollins, 1995.

Nolan, Hugh J., ed. *Pastoral Letters of the United States Catholic Bishops, III, 1962–1974.* Washington, D.C.: National Conference of Catholic Bishops, 1983.

Nuesse, C. Joseph. *The Catholic University of America: A Centennial History.* Washington, D.C.: Catholic University of America Press, 1990.

Orsy, Ladislas. "Bishops and Universities: Dominion or Communion?" *America,* 20 November 1993.

Sullivan, Francis. "Heresy." In *The Encyclopedia of Catholicism,* edited by Richard McBrien. San Francisco: HarperCollins, 1995.

———. *Magisterium: Teaching Authority in the Catholic Church.* New York: Paulist Press, 1983.

Weisberg, (Judge) Frederick H. Opinion and Order. *Curran v. Catholic University,* Civil Action No. 1562–87, 28 February 1989.

Elizabeth McKeown

Mary Dyer
(c. 1615–1660)

Months before the first Quakers appeared in Massachusetts, the Puritan magistrates had learned of their coming. These new sectarians were considered religious fanatics and political anarchists, determined to overthrow orthodoxy, government, and order. So anxious were the magistrates that upon their arrival in 1656 Anne Austin and Mary Fisher, the first Quakers to land within Massachusetts' jurisdiction, were immediately imprisoned. The following year a Quaker widow coming to collect debts owed her dead husband was led to prison, her dower rights denied. Her self-identification as Quaker so threatened the colony that her very presence, even for reasons of business, could not be tolerated. Still the Quakers came; still the colony forbade them. Countless Quakers were beaten and imprisoned, a few maimed, and several were escorted to the border, whipped at the cart's tail. Punishment of Quakers grew so harsh that in 1662 King Charles II, himself no friend of Friends, interfered. During the height of the persecutions in 1659 and 1660, four Quakers were hanged. Among the four, and the only woman to be executed, was Mary Dyer.

Mary Dyer immigrated to Massachusetts with her husband William during the 1630s, part of that "great migration" fleeing intensifying persecutions and seeking a new kingdom of God. She arrived in Boston in 1635 and soon became tied up with Anne Hutchinson* and her coterie. The Hutchinsonians, comprising a fairly large segment of Boston's population, were staunch Calvinist Puritans who believed that a person's salvation depended entirely upon the extension of divine grace from a merciful but unfathomable deity. They distrusted many of the clerics who preached that believers should try to prepare themselves to receive this divine grace, hearing in such preparation the promise that one could achieve salvation.

Hutchinsonians denounced preparationism and emphasized the free, arbitrary, and unmerited nature of God's grace. Had they held their opinions silently, or even within the privacy of their own homes, the state and the church may have left them undisturbed. However, they brought a crisis through their public praise of minister John Cotton and denunciation of many clerics, including Boston pastor John Wilson. William Dyer became deeply involved with the Hutchinsonians' unsuccessful attempts to challenge, first, the ministry of Wilson and, second, the government's efforts to suppress Hutchinson's brother-in-law John Wheelwright, a cleric who spoke aggressively against the established church power. The government found that Dyer's open and public involvement in the Hutchinsonian cause merited disarming and disfranchisement. The family's commitment to the Hutchinsonians was such that rather than seek rapprochement with the colonial government, as did many, they joined Hutchinson in Rhode Island.

Perhaps the most memorable connection between Hutchinson and Dyer was that within two years both suffered childbirth tragedies interpreted by New England leaders as special providences. The severely deformed child born to Dyer was seen as divine condemnation that required publication. Similarly, after her banishment to Rhode Island, Hutchinson was said to have given birth to some 30 monsters. Like Dyer's tragedy, Hutchinson's suffering was seen as a judgment: "God himself was pleased to step in . . . as clearly as if he had pointed with his finger, in causing the two fomenting women in the time of the height of the Opinions to produce out of their wombs, as before they had out of their brains, such monstrous births as no Chronicle (I think) hardly ever recorded" (Thomas Weld, preface to Winthrop, *Short Story*, 214).

While such tragic parallels are indeed memorable, they add little to an understanding about the strong friendship between Hutchinson and Dyer. Twenty years younger, Dyer might well have looked toward Hutchinson as a mentor and leader. After she had been tried and banished in November 1637, Hutchinson remained in the colony, under the guardianship of a hostile cleric, until the following spring; the pregnant Dyer also wintered there. When, in March, Hutchinson was tried by the church and excommunicated, she was, as she left the meeting house, accompanied by Mary Dyer. Long after William Hutchinson had died and Anne had moved with her children to Long Island (only to be killed in an Indian uprising in 1643), the Dyers and the Hutchinsons maintained their connection. Among the clearest signs of this familial relationship was the marriage of Mary's son Samuel to Ann Hutchinson, daughter of Edward and Catherine Hutchinson and granddaughter of Anne and William.

It is easy to see Mary Dyer as the spiritual daughter of Hutchinson. Hutchinson remained an outspoken, unwavering critic of the New England church and its clergy, proclaiming her faith and defending her right to hold and make public her beliefs. So, too, 20 years later Dyer would stand by her own beliefs, attack the abuses of the civil government, and defy the magistrates, risking not only banishment and excommunication but death itself. While Hutchinson, during her trial, appeared an intellectual master of biblical exegesis, her challenge remained centered in the freeness of God's grace, the inability of human endeavor to elicit divine response, and a spirituality that enjoyed direct, mystical communion with God. Hutchinson herself claimed to have received direct revelations from the Holy Spirit. Dyer, headquartered within the Quaker movement, also assured New England magistrates of the spiritual power of women. Like Hutchinson, she realized strength through a mystical spirituality, and she testified with the conviction that the spirit spoke to her.

After her departure in 1638, Massachusetts heard little of Dyer until 1657, when she landed at Boston on her way to Newport. In 1652 she had accompanied William to visit England. When William returned to Rhode Island, she remained and joined the Quaker movement, not surprising in light of her spiritual history. Many of the characteristics of the early movement were likely to attract a Hutchinsonian: their openness to the Holy Spirit, or the inner light; their rejection of education, birth, or wealth as the basis of personal authority; the sharing of power among all members of the movement, male and female, particularly the power of public speech. In fact, many Hutchinsonians would later find themselves among the Quakers, including William Coddington, Katherine Marbury (Hutchinson's sister), and Dyer. She might also have been attracted by the adventurous, missionary zeal of the early Friends, men and especially women who heard a call to travel around the world, bringing the message of the inner light.

Out of the heady climate of the Commonwealth, Dyer, in 1657, sailed for Rhode Island by way of Boston. The anxiety of the Massachusetts magistrates was such that even though she was merely on her way to Newport, she was arrested and imprisoned upon landing, only to be released later to go to her husband at Newport. The following year she traveled as a Quaker itinerant to New Haven colony and was expelled. In September 1659, she returned to Boston, visiting Friends in prison, and was banished, upon threat of execution. She returned again in October and was sentenced to death, reprieved at the last moment from the scaffold. Unwilling to accept a reprieve while her colleagues suffered, she returned to Boston in May 1660, and this time was hanged.

Apart from her witness against New England, Dyer wrote very little about her spiritual experiences and almost nothing about her stay in England or her decision to join the Quakers. Nevertheless, the nature and intensity of her New England activism indicate that the public passion of the early Quakers may have held great appeal for her. While later Quakers have been portrayed, accurately, as a sober, perfectionist people who asked simply to pursue their own spiritual journeys and temporal cares in peace, that first generation was turned outward, striving to convert the world through spirit-inspired testimony against hypocrisy, priestcraft, and intolerance. Quakers would always stand against false, artificial hierarchies, paid ministers, and a state religion that disfranchised other religious communities, but in this founding moment, they were vibrantly outspoken and aggressively demonstrative. They protested publicly, refused to pay tithes, heckled pastors during services, and processed (sometimes naked) through streets and into churches. The early decades represented an era of persecutions and testifying against such persecutions. Mary Dyer was part of this movement, and her commitment and devotion to this culture of dramatic nonconformity must be accepted and understood before scholars can begin to comprehend the choices she made.

While these years of Quaker itinerancy were extraordinarily difficult for a magistracy intent upon the maintenance of orthodoxy, this was not the first time that decisive political and judicial actions were required to constrain the religious wanderings of the colony's residents. The 1630s battles with the Salem Separatists, Roger Williams,* and Anne Hutchinson were followed by a multitude of disputes with communities and individuals. Baptists, rejecting infant baptism and refusing to bring their children to the sacrament, numbered such luminaries as Henry Dunster, president of Harvard College, and Lady Deborah Moody. Dissidents also included such ordinary women as the prophesying Sarah Keayne or the obstreperous Mary Oliver, as well as eccentric towns like the congregants of Malden who insisted upon calling the suspect Marmaduke Matthews as their minister. Problems were often easily resolved. Williams and Hutchinson were banished and stayed banished; their disciples either followed or remained silenced. Dunster stepped down from his post; Moody voluntarily left. The General Court brought Malden into line, while the church disciplined Keayne and Oliver, and when Oliver continued to speak out, she, too, was banished.

By the 1650s, heterodoxy flourished in England as well. Parliament had rebelled and overthrown King Charles I, executed him for treason in 1649, and established the Commonwealth government under the leadership of Oliver Cromwell as Lord Protector. As Puritan dissenters struggled to construct a new church along more reformed lines, a multitude of sectaries arose, including the old Separatist community, the Brownists; Baptists; millennialists like the Fifth Monarchists who awaited momentarily the reign of Christ; and politically radical sectaries like the Ranters. All were tolerated, provided they supported the Commonwealth. Although few sectaries advocated such political radicalism as the Levellers' opposition to civil rank and class, most were religiously radical in that they promoted the authority of the community, often the individual, and rejected such arbitrary, artificial boundaries as gender and class. Among the more radical, vocal communities arose a band of male and female Seekers who sought guidance in the voice of the Holy Spirit. Under the leadership of George Fox, a number of small societies of "Friends" appeared and established connections through correspondence and the travel of gifted itinerant preachers. The organization attracted large numbers of the disfranchised, including women, and a vast network of house communities was established and stabilized as Quakers developed strategies for building congregations, resisting persecution, and maintaining communal integrity. Within ten years of the restoration of Charles II to the throne, this society proved one of the few sectaries that survived intact.

Like New England Puritans, the Quakers were descendants of earlier dissenters who had challenged the Anglican commitment to hierarchical order and ritual formality. Quakers agreed with New Englanders in their fight against formal ritual, their stand against bishops, and their belief that primary spiritual authority was lodged in the congregation, but New England's dedication to political and social order was anathema to a people who challenged the very categories that constructed that order. They affirmed that each person heard the voice of the spirit and was required to follow the direction of his or her "inner light," and they denied that the state had any right to interfere with one's spiritual journey. In key ways, Quakers posed a serious threat to New England society. Politically, they denied the right of government to interfere with religion or worship, supporting separation of church and state. Socially, Quakers rejected hierarchy in all forms, affirming that the equality of souls before God countermanded artificial hierarchies of wealth and birth. Theologically, Quakers carried this equality into spirituality, rejecting an elevated role for an educated clergy, asserting that divine revelation beyond Scripture has continued to the present day and claiming that all believers had access to that revelation.

Between 1656 and 1666, several dozen Quakers came to Massachusetts, initially seeking converts. Although the magistrates moved with extraordinary speed to apprehend Anne Austin and Mary Fisher and to confiscate and destroy their books, they knew that they were acting upon the presumption of disorderly intent rather than upon any violation of the law. Thus, in the wake of the Quakers' appearance, with fears that more might follow, the General Court, in October 1656, passed a series of laws designed to eliminate the Quaker threat and then published these laws in broadside form. Any ship captain who knowingly brought a Quaker would be fined £100 and be required to return him or her to the port of embarkation. Those possessing Quaker books or writings would be fined £5 per item. Moreover, any Quaker arriving from outside the colony was to be "committed to the house of correction and at their entrance to be severely whipped, and by the master thereof be kept constantly to work, and none suffered to converse or speak with them during the time of their imprisonment." Anyone defending Quaker opinions was fined 40s, if they persisted, £4, and still continuing, he or she would be imprisoned until they could be banished. Such restrictions seem quite severe for people who had yet to challenge the peace, but a final order indicates the reason for this intensity. Whosoever "shall revile the office or person of magistrates or ministers, as is usual with the Quakers . . . shall be severely whipped, or pay the sum of five pounds" (Shurtleff, *Records*, 4: 277–278).

The following year, the year that Mary Dyer was initially imprisoned as a Quaker and later released to her husband, the magistrates raised the stakes. Every male Quaker who, once banished, returned would, for the first offense, have one ear cut off, for the second, his other ear. Every female Quaker who returned after banishment was to be severely whipped. Both would be imprisoned until they could be sent out, and if they returned, their tongue would be bored with a hot iron. Only one step remained, and in the face of a continued Quaker presence, that was taken the following October. If convicted of returning yet a fourth time, he or she would be executed (Shurtleff, *Records*, 4: 308–309, 345–346).

Amidst the rising intensity of Quaker witness and magisterial severity, Mary Dyer joined William Robinson and Marmaduke Stephenson in challenging the capital law. In September 1659, all three had been banished, but while Dyer returned home to Newport, Robinson and Stephenson had traveled north to cultivate the embryo communities, in Salem, New Hampshire, and Maine. When the two men returned south, they decided to test the law and so returned to Boston with a group of local Quakers who publicly proclaimed their support by accompanying the banished. Stephenson, Robinson, and their companions were all imprisoned by the authorities; the prisoners were soon joined by Dyer, who felt called to unite herself to this cause. On October 18 all three were tried and sentenced to death: They would be taken from the jail to the Boston Common, escorted by 100 armed soldiers, and there hanged (Shurtleff, *Records*, 4: 383).

At this same session, the court, in response to a petition from her son, decided to reprieve Dyer, although it is unclear how soon this was known to her. After she had left the court, they ordered that she join her compatriots on the gallows, with a rope about her neck, until the men were executed, but the Quaker account reflects a more dramatic theater. George Bishop claimed that she was not told of her reprieve until after the execution of Robinson and Stephenson. Peter Pearson wrote that after the two men had been hanged, Dyer "stepped up the Ladder and had her Coats tied about her feet, and the Rope put about her neck with her face covered, and as the Hangman was ready to turn her off, they cried out stop, for she was reprieved." Dyer, unwilling to recognize the magistrates' authority, "stood still, saying, she was there willing to suffer as her Brethren did: unless they would null their wicked Law, she had no freedom to accept their reprieve." Nevertheless, she was pulled down from the gallows by force and carried out of Boston and on to Rhode Island (Bishop, *New England Judged*, 134–135; letter of Peter Pearson, 6 December 1659, printed in Stephenson, *Call from Death to Life*, 32).

Quaker hagiographer George Bishop would describe Mary Dyer as "a Comely Grave woman, and of a goodly Personage, and one of a good Report, having an Husband of an Estate, fearing the Lord, and a Mother of Children" (*New England Judged*, 157). The Massachusetts' magisterium never, in the 1630s or 1650s, found her grave, or comely, or good. She not only returned after banishment, but she publicly denounced them for brutality and injustice. Bishop noted that when she entered Boston, she was set upon a horse and cried out, "Woe be unto you for Humphrey Norton's sake! Woe be unto you, because of the Cruelty done to him!" (Bishop, *New England Judged*, 205. Norton had had one ear cropped). When reprieved the first time, both Quaker and Puritan accounts agree that she refused to descend the ladder and had to be physically removed. The following May, she "rebelliously, after the sentence of death [was] past against her, returned into this jurisdiction." When questioned, she proclaimed herself a witness against their laws (Shurtleff, *Records* 4: 419). "I came in Obedience to the Will of God to the last General Court, desiring you to Repeal your unrighteous Laws of Banishment upon pain of Death; and that same is my work now, and earnest Request, because ye refused before to grant my Request, although I told you, That if ye refused to Repeal them, the Lord will send others of his Servants to Witness against them." When asked if she were a prophet, she said, "She spake the words that the Lord spake in her; and now the thing is come to pass" ([Burrough], *Declaration*, 28). The court sentenced her to be hanged on the first of June.

Dyer maintained her stance until the end. She was escorted to the place of execution by a band of soldiers, her speech overwhelmed by beating drums. On the scaffold, one leader proclaimed that she had brought the punishment upon herself: She reaffirmed her call to testify against unrighteousness. Some promised her life if she would return to Rhode Island; she said that she must follow the will of God, even unto death. When Pastor Wilson urged her to repent "and be not so deluded and carried away by the deceit of the Devil," she denied any need for repentance. At last, some asked her if she had said that "she had been in Paradise. And she answered, Yea, I have been in Paradise several days. And the more she spake of her Eternal Happiness, that's out of mind. And so sweetly and cheerfully in the Lord she finished her Testimony, and dyed a faithful Martyr of Jesus Christ" ([Burrough], *Declaration*, 29–30).

Although Dyer is rarely heard in the records, and never outside the context of her trials and execution, at those moments her voice spoke as a Quaker, loud in condemnation of the colony's attempts to silence, through intimidation and violence, the word of God's spirit revealed in the voices of Quakers. When sentenced to death in October 1659, Dyer wrote to the General Court on behalf of "that holy people and seed which the lord hath blessed forever, called by the children of darkness (cursed Quakers) for whose cause the lord is rising to plead with all such as shall touch his anointed or do his prophets any harm." Like all Quaker itinerants, Dyer demanded the repeal of unjust laws and expressed her certainty that if the magistrates would only listen to the voice of the spirit within, they would be so moved. "Take you counsel, search with the light of Christ in you, and it will shew you of answers as it hath done me and many more who hath been disobedient and deceived as you now are. . . . [Y]ou will not repent that you were kept from Shedding blood though it were by a woman" (Dyer, Petition to the General Court, 1659). For Dyer, her returns to the Bay colony in October 1659 and May 1660 were expressive testimonies against the injustice of Massachusetts' law, mandated by the holy spirit's voice within her.

It is impossible to disentangle Mary Dyer's tragedy from the Quaker persecutions of the surrounding years. Dyer was initially arrested during the first moments of the persecutions, after the magistrates had nominated the Quakers as serious disturbers of the peace. The government would soon construct restrictions and procedures that it believed, wrongly, would restore social order by silencing or excising the Quakers. Dyer stood among the many English and New England Quakers who could be neither silenced nor removed, who deliberately returned to Massachusetts to challenge the law and, by extension, the social order itself. Like others who suffered anti-Quaker brutality, Dyer was initially imprisoned and banished; when she returned, she was whipped and imprisoned again. Her confrontations reached their climax amidst the height of anti-Quaker fervor; she was neither the first nor the last to be executed.

In the October 1658 session, an exasperated General Court justified its increasingly severe laws as necessary to control a tumultuous people who displayed no respect for government and law. They "have published and maintained many dangerous and horrid tenets, and do take upon them to change and alter the received laudable customs of our nation in giving civil respect to equals or reverence to superiors, whose actions tend to undermine the authority of civil authority." Taking advantage of those disaffected from government and order, they "insinuat[ed] themselves into the minds of the simpler" and "infected and seduced" the inhabitants (Shurtleff, *Records*, 4: 345–346).

The magistrates' tone alternated among confusion, frustration, and outrage. The problem was partly the Quakers: Puritan leaders could not understand and, thus, could not successfully address a people whose apparently extreme disrespect, or delusion, led them to risk torture and death. "Notwithstanding all former laws made (upon experience of their arrogant, bold obtrusions to disseminate their principles amongst us) prohibiting their coming into this jurisdiction, they have not been deterred from their impetuous attempts to undermine our peace and hasten our ruin" (Shurtleff, *Records*, 4: 346). However, the roots of the crisis also lay in the magistrates. Their rigid, unwavering commitment to a political hierarchy ruled by themselves, accompanied by an intense fear of any who failed to value order or reverence their status, rendered them unable to tolerate any Quaker presence in public, private, or even printed space. Granting the Quakers speech would work to undermine their authority, yet the execution of four Quakers, including one woman, and the criticism generated, revealed the limitations of their vision and the ultimate failure of their policy.

It is also impossible to understand the tragedy of Mary Dyer apart from the female Puritan community of the early seventeenth century. She is one of several women of extraordinary personal authority, women with strength and power lodged in private spirituality but expressed and demonstrated upon the public stage. Such women, and the men who supported them, threatened the base of the patriarchal social order because they were women acting out their power in the public world of religion and the state. When only in her twenties she became a disciple of Anne Hutchinson, a woman who preached and proclaimed her right to a public voice out of the inspiration and authority of the Holy Spirit: a woman who was silenced, excommunicated, and banished because she threatened the primary gender base of the patriarchal order. Despite the hardship it must have involved for a young family, the Dyers followed the Hutchinsons to Rhode Island and slowly rebuilt their lives. Twenty years later, she extended a visit to England, apparently to spend time within a community that centered its spirituality in the voice of the spirit as it spoke to each and every person, regardless of education, rank, or gender. Out of this strength, Dyer returned to Massachusetts to confront the authority that had banished her twenty years before. While the Hutchinsonians may have disturbed the peace of the Bay colony, the Quakers promised a world turned upside down: a world of strong women, uneducated preachers, charismatic laborers, and men who respected the equality of the disfranchised. Dyer represented the most adamant, most prominent symbol of that promise in New England. Unlike Hutchinson, who left to pursue her vision alone and in peace, Dyer pursued her vision in community through confrontation, gathering her power through the voice of the Holy Spirit. She died in her battle, but her death brought final victory for her principles. Mary Dyer's martyrdom has remained one of the strongest indictments of Puritan intolerance and the failure of their hierarchical imperative.

BIBLIOGRAPHY

Bishop, George. *New England Judged, by the Spirit of the Lord*. In Two Parts. 1661, 1667; London: T. Sowle, 1703.

[Burrough, Edward]. *A Declaration of the Sad and Great Persecution and Martyrdom of the People of God, Called Quakers, in New England*. London: for Robert Wilson, [1660].

Chu, Jonathan M. *Neighbors, Friends, or Madmen: The Puritan Adjustment to Quakerism in Seventeenth-Century Massachusetts*. Westport, CT: Greenwood Press, 1985.

Dyer, Mary. Petition to the General Court of Massachusetts Bay, 26 October 1659. Massachusetts State Archives.

Jones, Rufus M. *The Quakers in the American Colonies*. 1911. Reprint, New York: Norton, 1966.

Mack, Phyllis. *Visionary Women: Ecstatic Prophecy in Seventeenth-Century England*. Berkeley: University of California Press, 1992.

Mary Dyer, Quaker. Two letters of William Dyer of Rhode Island, 1659–1660. Facsimile and transcripts. Cambridge, MA: University Press, n.d.

Norton, John. *The Heart of New England Rent*. Boston, 1658.

Pestana, Carla Gardina. *Quakers and Baptists in Colonial Massachusetts*. New York: Cambridge University Press, 1991.

Robinson, William, and Marmaduke Stephenson. Address to the Magistrates in Boston, 1659. In *Proceedings of MHS* 42 (1909): 359–363.

Rogers, Horatio. *Mary Dyer of Rhode Island: The Quaker Martyr That Was Hanged on Boston Common*. Providence, RI: Preston and Rounds, 1896.

Shurtleff, Nathaniel G. *Records of the Governor and Company of the Massachusetts Bay in New England*. 5 vols. Boston: William White, 1853.

Stephenson, Marmaduke. *A Call from Death to Life*. London: for Thomas Simmons, 1660.

Winthrop, John. *A Short Story of the Rise, Reign, and Ruine of the Antinomians, Familists & Libertines*. 1644. In Hall, David D. *The Antinomian Controversy, 1636–1638: A Documentary History*. Middletown: Wesleyan University Press, 1968. 201–310.

Worrall, Arthur. *Quakers in the Colonial Northeast*. Hanover, NH: University Press of New England, 1980.

Marilyn J. Westerkamp

Ralph H. Elliott
(1925–   )

The chairman of the Special Trustee Committee spoke briefly to Ralph Elliott, subject of its investigation. Turning away in tears, the accused professor told three faculty members sitting with him he was allowed no counsel or company. Alone until midnight, having heard no further word, he left the empty hotel lobby.

The next morning he and his wife told their two daughters, aged eight and ten, they would be moving because the seminary wanted their father to do something he could not do. The Trustees of Midwestern Baptist Theological Seminary formally dismissed 37-year-old Ralph H. Elliott from their faculty six days later, on 25 October 1962.

THE BACKGROUND

Heresy charges against Ralph Elliott continued a long-standing conflict rising in the gap between what most Southern Baptists believed and what contemporary critical tools in the hands of Baptist seminary professors suggested. Twice in the nineteenth century professors at Louisville's Southern Baptist Theological Seminary had been forced out in the name of institutional survival: Crawford Howell Toy* in 1878 and William Heth Whitsitt* in 1899. These tremors were forerunners of greater shocks to come.

In the 1950s at Southern Seminary a group of reformers championed internationally popular critical methods. Unhappily for this scholarly guild, its ecclesiastical vision was not parallel at all points with the larger Baptist constituency, with a portion of its fellow faculty in practical theology, or with its young president. Not all the differences were theological, but the results—13 simultaneous forced resignations in 1958—slowed dramatically the progress of critical studies for a season. Ralph Elliott, a fledgling Old Testament professor at Southern, missed the " '58 Massacre" by moving to Midwestern a few months before it happened.

The Elliott controversy was also part of a larger pattern of 1960s religious turmoil. Alongside an article on Elliott, *Time* magazine ran "Crisis in Immutability," examining the Vatican II debate as to whether expressions of faith must remain unchanged across all times and cultures (58).

Elliott's own Southern Baptist Convention (SBC), a denomination founded on southern regionalism, was shifting upon its foundations. It experienced a move westward numerically and geographically after World War II. In 1962, nine postwar and mostly western state conventions combined had fewer members and gave less money to the SBC than their elder partner North Carolina, but they held an 18 to 2 edge on the national convention's powerful nominating committee. Midwestern Seminary, Elliott's institution, was founded to provide Southern Baptist theological education in a non-southern region.

Elliott, from Danville, Virginia, graduated from Carson-Newman, a Tennessee Baptist college. Taking the B.D. and Th.D. at Southern Seminary, he immediately joined its faculty ranks. In 1958 he was named the first faculty member of Midwestern Baptist Theological Seminary in Kansas City, Missouri.

Chauncey Daley, editor of the Kentucky Baptist *Western Recorder*, placed Elliott correctly on the theological spectrum: quite conservative in the larger world of biblical scholarship, a moderate in SBC academic ranks, and quite liberal in comparison to the traditional viewpoints preached from most SBC pulpits and held in most SBC pews. Of the Midwestern Trustees, Daley wrote:

> They must know by now that Elliott is not a glaring example of heresy among a host of safely orthodox teachers in our seminaries. If he is a heretic, then he is one of many and indeed is not at the head of the line. (Daley, "Decision," 4–5)

Elliott's singularity was not his extreme views but his straightforward honesty in writing down for publication what he believed. He believed the Old Testament was more clearly understood as symbol than science, best interpreted as theological rather than objective history. He arrived at this conclusion by historical-critical methodology learned at Southern Seminary.

THE FIRST TRIAL

Ralph Elliott was tried twice. Accusations leading to his first trial for heresy began as early as January 1960 with complaints of "liberalism" against him and three other professors by Pastor Mack Douglas of the influential Tower Grove Baptist Church in St. Louis, Missouri.

The Book and Its Critics

Elliott became the focus of the controversy upon publication of *The Message of Genesis: A Theological Interpretation* by the Southern Baptist Sunday School Board's Broadman Press in July 1961. Elliott wrote the manuscript before leaving Southern Seminary. It was a revision of his lecture notes. He credited his dissertation adviser Clyde Francisco with most of the insights popularized in the material.

The book was the first from Broadman to take into account critical tools in Bible study. It was a rather conservative attempt, released by its second publisher, Bethany Press, with faint praise: "While it is not a major scholarly work, we believe that it will fit the Bethany line without discredit." Elliott's title revealed his plan: to promote the *message* of Genesis, its theological and religious purpose. He wrote in the preface: "The present work is an effort to combine head and heart by using the sound achievements of modern scholarship to ferret out and to underscore the foundational theological and religious principles of the stories of Genesis" (vii). He emphasized the parabolic nature of Scripture: "In other words, one must come to the place that he sees the parabolic and symbolic nature of much of the Old Testament Scriptures. Genesis is to be understood in this light. It is not science" (Elliott, *Message*, 15).

Criticism came swiftly and in mass from those who took precritical approaches to Scripture. Their accusations centered mainly upon specific passages of the book in which Elliott questioned the face-value historicity of such matters as the age of Methuselah, the fate of Lot's wife, and the actual number of hours in the seven days of Creation. They believed Elliott's symbolic approach to stories such as Noah's ark or the tower of Babel was a denial of the supernatural, undermining the Bible's authority and dependability.

The most influential critic was K. Owen White, pastor of First Baptist Church in Houston. He sent an article based on 2 Kings 4:40, "Death in the Pot," to all Baptist state papers and many other denominational leaders on 26 October 1961. He quoted without explanation or context passages from Elliott's book, calling them "liberalism, pure and simple." Response to White's article eventuated in his election to the presidency of the SBC in 1963. In 1961 it spread the Elliott controversy convention wide.

Exoneration

The flood of criticism raised against one professor and his book threatened to overflow into the halls of the seminary, the offices of the denomination's publishing house, and beyond. An investigating committee of seven Midwestern Trustees appointed by their Executive Committee met 30 November and 1 December 1961 to consider the heresy charges against Elliott. It spent one day with the professor and the next with 25 to 35 pastors from Kansas and Missouri. Its report supported the validity of the theological approach taken in *The Message of Genesis* and advocated it for Midwestern generally, concluding: "We take pride in the scholarship, theological and denominational soundness, and evangelistic witness of the institution." The full-board on 28–29 December 1961 considered the matter and, by a vote of 14 to 7, adopted a resolution that stated whereas Elliott's beliefs and doctrinal position had been investigated,

> BE IT THEREFORE RESOLVED that while there are members of the board of trustees who are in disagreement with some of the interpretations presented by Dr. Elliott in his book, we do affirm our confidence in him as a consecrated Christian, a promising scholar and teacher, a loyal servant of Southern Baptists, and a dedicated and warmly evangelistic preacher of the Gospel.

As the seminary had defended its professor, likewise in January of 1962, the Sunday School Board defended its decision to publish his book. In a position paper, the Board noted the book was representative of "a segment of Southern Baptist life and thought" and also noted it was a stated policy objective of Broadman to be "representative of Southern Baptist life and thought." Ralph Elliott's first trial for doctrinal heresy ended with his full exoneration by the adjudicatory body responsible for his teaching. Soon after that, his book's publication was defended as appropriate to his denominational press's mission.

SECOND TRIAL AND DISMISSAL

The catalyst for events leading to Elliott's second trial and dismissal was uninterrupted and continuous complaint similar to that analyzed and dismissed by his Trustees. The denunciations from precritical literalists, labeled "conservatives" in the debates of the time, continued unabated and took on ever more shrill, emotive tones. Kansas City police suspected a link between pastor Ralph E. Powell's radio address calling for a cross to be erected for Elliott and an explosive device that partially demolished the front door of the professor's home.

Oklahoma City Caucus

The conflict reached critical mass 8–9 March 1962. A caucus of laypersons, denominational servants, and pastors from several states met in

Oklahoma City to devise a strategy in the face of what they considered the disappointing action of the majority of Midwestern Trustees. *The Message of Genesis*, Professor Elliott, and Midwestern Seminary became the focal points of a general dissatisfaction with the direction of Southern Baptist theological education. The critics agreed on a twofold strategy: spread the word about liberalism at Midwestern and secure the election of a majority of Trustees at that institution sympathetic with their theological agenda.

San Francisco Convention

From March to June 1962, the Elliott or "Genesis" controversy appeared repeatedly in public and private, press and pulpit, throughout Southern Baptist circles. At the Southern Baptist Convention in San Francisco, 3–5 June 1962, a caucus of about 100 of Elliott's critics, presided over by Ross Edwards, Midwestern Seminary Trustee and pastor of the Swope Park Baptist Church, Kansas City, Missouri, met at a hotel.

They came divided over whether to focus their attack on banning Elliott's book or on the broader front of biblical authority tied to historical accuracy. *The Message of Genesis* was not widely distributed, having sold only 3,600 copies by then. Some allied against Elliott wanted him and his book gone but were determined not to be labeled book banners. Thus, the less specific course was taken. K. Owen White led in drafting a statement to be presented at the convention.

Two motions from the caucus found their way to the floor of the convention on Wednesday. White's represented the majority of the critics. It was a broadside against any theological method that presented the Bible as authoritative apart from "historical accuracy" and mentioned neither Elliott nor his book. The second motion, presented by Ralph E. Powell, represented the caucus's minority. It was specific, instructing the Sunday School Board to cease publication, printing, and sales of *The Message of Genesis*.

Both were considered on Thursday. White's motion passed by a large majority. It stated:

> That we express our abiding and unchanging objection to the dissemination of theological views in any of our seminaries which would undermine such faith in the historical accuracy and doctrinal integrity of the Bible, and that we courteously request the trustees and administrative officers of our institutions and other agencies to take such steps as shall be necessary to remedy at once those situations where such views now threaten our historic position.

Powell withdrew his motion to ban the book after Earl Harding, executive director of the Missouri state convention, stepped to the platform and requested him to do so. A second motion to ban the book was offered and also defeated.

As the convention ended, the Midwestern Board of Trustees began preparations for responding to White's motion. It was not the same Board that had cleared Professor Elliott the year before. The change in the makeup of Midwestern's Trustees happened quietly. Twelve vacancies were filled at San Francisco. Four of 6 Trustees eligible for reappointment were replaced. Letters to Sally Rice, a student at Duke University, from 3 of the 4 displaced Trustees confirm they were denied reappointment because they had voted the year before to affirm Elliott's methodology (Gragg, private correspondence). Nine of the 12 eventually voted for Elliott's dismissal in a final ballot of 22 to 7. A two-thirds majority was necessary. Duke McCall, president of Southern Seminary in July 1962, wrote that the SBC "went over the brink" in replacing Trustees who had voted wrong on an issue at their Board meeting. Most Southern Baptists never even knew they had been near the edge.

The Second Trial

In July 1962 the Executive Committee of the Trustees at Midwestern called for a September meeting to respond to the White resolution. In a July letter to a friend, Elliott seemed resigned to having to seek another position. At the full Board meeting in September, no formal charges were filed, but a motion was made to instruct President Berquist to ask for Elliott's immediate resignation. The motion failed by one vote on a parliamentary procedure test ballot. A special investigative committee named to work out a compromise met with Elliott. No formal action was taken, but considerable common ground was reached, according to Elliott's handwritten notes.

On 17–18 October the investigative committee met again. On the second day, Elliott was asked to respond to an agenda prepared by the committee. After much discussion, the committee and the professor affirmed nine of ten points, the first of which was: "The particular method in using the Literary-Critical and Historical approach was mutually recognized as a valid approach to the Old Testament studies."

The tenth point concerned the impact of *The Message of Genesis* and its republication. By voting to take no action, the Sunday School Board the summer before had allowed an executive order against printing a second edition to remain in effect indefinitely. The Trustees and President Berquist requested that Elliott "volunteer" not to seek its republication. The author balked, thinking such an action would suggest he did not stand by the ideas in his writing. He requested and was given a few hours to reconsider. He consulted with three fellow faculty members—Morris Ashcraft, Roy Honeycutt, and Heber Peacock. They agreed with his initial reaction: such voluntarism would violate his basic freedom as a Baptist and a Christian to stand by the truth as he interpreted it. He knew his wife Virginia understood and was willing to accept the consequences when she advised: "Ralph, if you go down there and sell your soul, don't come home" (Elliott, "Safeguarding," 2).

Returning to the committee, Elliott reported his refusal. Chairman Malcolm Knight asked Elliott if he would agree to forego seeking republication if requested to do so by the full Board. Elliott believed as an employee following the instructions of his employer he could do so and keep his integrity. He agreed. The committee went into executive session to consider the matter, but as Elliott left, he heard Trustee Earl Harding say he did not want the responsibility of banning the book. Elliott went back to the lobby where his three friends were waiting for him. Soon Chairman Knight came out and demanded they leave. The committee gave no more communication that night.

Elliott was called without prior notice from a revival in Virginia to a special called meeting of the full Board of Trustees on 25–26 October. His offer to accede to the request of the Board was not considered, and he would not "volunteer" to do that which they would not instruct him to do. Around midnight of the first day, Ralph Elliott was dismissed by a vote of 22 to 7. No charges were presented. The Trustee press release noted Elliott's refusal to agree to not seek republication but did not mention his offer to do so if the Board would take responsibility for the action. It said he was fired for refusing "to come to a mutual relationship" with the administration and Trustees, dismissed not for his theological stance but for insubordination. Fellow Midwestern faculty member Morris Ashcraft in a private memo, probably quoting Midwestern professor Hugh Wamble, wrote:

> "[I]t is incredible that Elliott was dismissed for refusing to do what the Southern Baptist Convention had refused to do in June, the Sunday School Board had refused to do in July, and Midwestern's board of trustees had refused to do in September. They all refused to ban the book, but Elliott was dismissed because he refused to." (Gragg, private correspondence)

Ralph Elliott went on to a rich ministry as pastor and academic officer in American Baptist church life. Bethany Press republished his book, which remained in print for about 20 years, often stocked in Southern Baptist bookstores.

THE REST OF THE STORY

In December 1961, heresy charges against Ralph Elliott were dismissed; in October 1962, Professor Elliott was dismissed. In both cases, theological differences were at the root of the matter, but in the second, certain forces allied themselves with the theological critics to bring down a once-acquitted foe. The common assumptions of the alliance shed light on heresy trials in the history of the Southern Baptist Convention.

The first ally found by Elliott's theological foes was a group of Missouri Baptist power brokers who fought for control of his infant seminary. Central Seminary in Kansas City, Kansas, had served both American and Southern Baptists since 1901. The SBC agreed not to cooperate with an institution it did not control, forcing Central to choose. It chose American Baptists. This disenfranchised a number of SBC Missouri pastors connected with Central. They turned to the newly forming Midwestern, hoping to move into its structures in any capacity "from janitor to president" and shape it along the then-conservative lines of Central. These plans were aborted when President Millard Berquist took office. He signaled a different theological direction by the appointment of Elliott as first faculty member. Not one of the former Central Trustees was hired in any capacity. A few did become Trustees at Midwestern and were some of Elliott's most implacable opponents. Two, Ross Edwards and Earl Harding, were named leading agitators in a *Christian Century* editorial, "A Desecration of Liberty," 14 November 1962.

A second ally found by Elliott's theological foes was his own community of academics who participated in what Chauncey Daley called "a conspiracy of silence." The most notable hush came from Southern Seminary, perhaps from fear that it was vulnerable to similar attacks, perhaps because five of Midwestern's first faculty had been fired from Southern in 1958.

Individual professors also tended to undermine Elliott. Joseph McClain served briefly on Midwestern's New Testament faculty. He actively contested the use of critical methodology and, according to Elliott, after departure from the campus continued to initiate charges against Elliott, organizing opposition in Oklahoma and Kansas as well as Missouri. Elliott's critics interpreted Clyde Francisco's spoken and written words in opposition to Francisco's friend and former student. In private communications, Francisco regretted such usage, but publicly he let it stand, adding much to Elliott's professional and personal hurt.

Denominational damage control provided a third partner in the coalition against Elliott. After the Oklahoma City Caucus, the national leadership's strategy was to stay below the fray by avoiding identification with either his supporters or his detractors. James Sullivan, executive secretary-treasurer of the Sunday School Board in April of 1962 quietly used "executive privilege" to halt reissue of *The Message of Genesis* without his personal consent. On Wednesday at the San Francisco SBC, according to Herschel Hobbs, pastor and president of the 1962 convention, he and Sullivan, along with Earl Harding and Ralph E. Powell, met. They agreed to keep the book from future publication if Powell would withdraw his motion to have it banned. Powell got the book suppressed; Harding publicly appeared in opposition to book banning while tightening the noose on Elliott and Midwestern through the White resolution and an altered Trustee Board; Sullivan and Hobbs kept peace at a price; Elliott paid the price. In July, Sullivan denied in writing to Elliott such a deal took place.

One month after the convention, the Sunday School Board voted to follow a Sullivan recommendation presented along with others regarding *The Message of Genesis*. Sullivan suggested:

> Simply let the matter pass without taking any sort of action. In this event, the book will simply cease to be current. Since it is the feeling of the executive secretary that the title should not be reprinted by administrative decision, the book would neither be continued, nor banned, if the board takes no action. It would just not be in stock. Little or no publicity would or should be given if this route is taken. (Cited in Elliott, *The "Genesis" Controversy*, 110)

The Board's official action was to take no action, effectively banning the book without taking responsibility for doing so.

In July and August 1962, Herschel Hobbs actively lobbied members of the Board of Trustees, Ralph Elliott, and Millard Berquist to do what was necessary to settle the controversy. President Berquist eventually came to believe the only way to save the seminary was to sacrifice Elliott. Elliott and other members of the faculty suspected this perspective came from Hobbs. After the dismissal, Hobbs defended the action, saying the issue was not theological but "one of school administration or of whose will would prevail." " 'He (Elliott) made his choice,' he said. 'They had to make theirs' " (Willingham, "Baptist," I).

Seminary personnel, ecclesiastical power brokers, and denominational damage controllers combined with theological idealists on the Right to dispatch an already weakened Elliott. Apart from their differences, the first three shared a common assumption in theological controversy: Disjunction of private belief and public expression were necessary for institutional survival. Specifically, what was said in the classroom should be separated from what was said in public to avoid the friction created by the gap between the pew and the lectern. Elliott, after Baptist historian Glenn Hinson, called this "doublespeak."

It figured in the breakup of his friendship with Francisco, who told Elliott he needed to learn to communicate better to the laity. Elliott insisted his problem was just that—he communicated too clearly what he really believed. Ross Edwards, appealing to doublespeak after the firing, wrote of Elliott:

> I wanted in the worst way to save him. As long as it is a matter between a professor and his student what he says, that is one thing. But when

he puts his beliefs in writing where everybody can read them—as in
The Message of Genesis—that's another thing. (*Kansas City Star*, 3
March 1963)

Hobbs and Sullivan and Harding were willing to make private deals to ban
the book, believing this would prevent greater suppression of freedom of
thought.

Even those responsible for finding and teaching theological truths also
were guided by the supposition that compromise of principle in public is
necessary to preserve integrity in private—here, the classroom. Believing
essentials were preserved by Elliott's dismissal, President Berquist wrote to
the remaining faculty: "Through it all we have remained as it were 'a little
colony of Heaven,' undergirding each other with our prayers and understanding. . . . For the sake of the cause for which we are giving our lives
let us hold fast to that which we have achieved" (Gragg, private correspondence). Elliott believed this evasion decisive, writing in 1992, "Had
the seminaries joined together in candid and honest statement as allies, I
very much believe it would have laid the matter to rest" (*"Genesis" Controversy*, 19).

Only a handful of seminary professors—Alan Gragg, Morris Ashcraft,
Hugh Wamble, and Heber Peacock at Midwestern; John Steely and George
Shriver at Southeastern Seminary; and a few others—expressed themselves
plainly on the side of Elliott in print. Peacock relinquished his faculty position in February 1963, writing in his resignation letter: "I must refuse to
proclaim my theological and biblical understanding only in private." The
leadership whose complicity ultimately undid Midwestern's experiment embraced a venerable SBC educational principle, stretching back to Toy: Public disobedience to the *magisterium* is as unacceptable as doctrinal heresy,
and the teaching office must accommodate the most highly offended segment of the community at any given time.

Not a too-high regard for doctrine among the laity but a too-low esteem
for it among the theologically trained proved most damaging for Ralph
Elliott and his *Message*. Elliott was tried and acquitted of heresy. Then he
was fired for refusing to voluntarily suppress the beliefs that had been officially vindicated. Some who contributed to his dismissal shared those beliefs along with a desire to preserve them in the classroom but valued
institutional control above the believer's freedom to hold them openly.
Three decades later, most of them and their progeny had also been forced
from their posts by those who demanded theological principles—albeit very
different from Elliott's—be affirmed, inside and outside the classroom.

SELECTED BIBLIOGRAPHY

"Crisis in Immutability." *Time*, 9 November 1962, 58.
Daly, Chauncey. "A Decision of Destiny." *Western Recorder*, 27 September 1962,
    4–5.

"A Desecration of Liberty." *Christian Century*, 14 November 1962.

"An End to Seminary Unrest Seen with Adoption of Professor Policy," *Kansas City Star*, 3 March 1963, 1.

Elliott, Ralph H. *The "Genesis" Controversy and Continuity in Southern Baptist Chaos: A Eulogy for a Great Tradition.* Macon, GA: Mercer University Press, 1992.

————. *The Message of Genesis: A Theological Interpretation.* Nashville: Broadman Press, 1961.

————. "Safeguarding Baptist Freedoms." *Whitsitt Journal* 1 (July 1994): 2–5.

Gragg, Alan. Private correspondence file. Brewton-Parker College, Mt. Vernon, GA.

Willingham, Edmund. "Baptists, Leader Differ on Elliott." *Nashville Tennessean*, 29 November 1962, 1.

William Loyd Allen

George Burman Foster
(1858–1918)

George Burman Foster was one of the great pioneers in shaping that particular brand of liberal theology that characterized the Divinity School of the University of Chicago in the early years of the twentieth century. He was a major influence on Shailer Mathews and Gerald Birney Smith, both of whom succeeded him in the Department of Theology at that institution. Moreover, Foster's writings aroused vehement opposition among several traditionally conservative American Christian denominations. From 1901 to 1910, he was the center of a storm of religious controversy that attracted nationwide attention and had profound effects on both northern and southern Baptists.

Foster was born at Alderson, West Virginia, on 2 April 1858. He spent three years at Shelton College but completed his collegiate training at West Virginia University, earning the A.B. degree in 1883 and the A.M. degree in 1884. He was ordained to the Baptist ministry in 1879. In 1884 he married Mary Lyon, daughter of one of his professors at West Virginia University. That same year, he enrolled in Rochester Theological Seminary. Graduating from there in 1887, he became pastor of the First Baptist Church of Saratoga Springs, New York, where he remained until 1891. With strong urging by the authorities of McMaster University, Toronto, Canada, Foster spent the academic year 1891–1892 in Germany, studying at the Universities of Göttingen and Berlin. Upon his return, he became professor of philosophy at McMaster, remaining there until 1895. Denison University awarded him an honorary doctorate in 1892. After repeated urgent invitations by President W. R. Harper of the University of Chicago, Foster finally accepted the post of assistant professor of systematic theology in the Divinity School at Chicago in 1895; and he was promoted to the rank of professor in 1897. During a time of vigorous agitation to have President Harper dismiss Foster from the university, Harper secured in 1905 Foster's acquiescence in transferring him from a professorship of systematic theology in the Divinity School to one in the philosophy of religion in the Department of Comparative Religion. However, most of Foster's students continued to be from the Divinity School; and despite continuous cries for his dismissal, he retained his professorship in the faculty of Arts and Literature until his death on 22 December 1918 at the height of the influenza epidemic.

From early childhood, Foster suffered from unusual privations in his family life. His mother died when he was five, and he stayed with grandparents while his father fought in the Civil War. Foster's own wife, Mary, seems to have had several nervous disorders, and calamity eventually overtook all five of their children. One son and one daughter were mentally incapacitated. The other daughter died shortly before her wedding. The oldest son, Raymond, drowned in a resort lake at age 16, and the other son, Harrison, died of pneumonia in a Texas army camp in February 1918. For many years, illnesses, deaths, and heavy financial burdens cast dark shadows of grief over the Foster household.

Regarding his theological beliefs, it is apparent that by 1895 Foster had already abandoned any version of orthodox Christian theology that remotely resembled that of his seminary theology professor, A. H. Strong. Indeed, by 1909, he had abandoned belief in all distinctively Christian theology. He felt that the orthodox interpretation of Christianity had been so thoroughly uprooted that he had difficulty understanding how it could be a live option for anyone. Moreover, he came to regard such liberal theologies as Ritschlianism that rested on belief in special Christian revelation as being attenuated remnants of strict orthodoxy and, therefore, as equally untenable. Consequently, he held that faith was in grave crisis:

> Today we are hearing much of the return of faith. Personally, I am unable to see any such *return*—there may indeed be signs of the birth of a *new* faith, but no return. In my opinion Christianity is in the most grievous crisis of its history. I do not refer to controversy in newspapers and on the street, but to the quiet, bitter battle which serious men are fighting out in their own souls.
>
> It may be objected that the old churches were never so powerful and active as today, never engaged so much in labors of love. But the question is whether all this is the blush of health or the last flush of fever on the cheeks of the dying—whether its glory is the glory of her springtime or of her autumn. . . . It is the dying of the old faith which western Christendom is experiencing. (Foster, "Concerning the Religious Basis of Ethics," 219)

Though he often spoke of belief in God, such belief was not an essential constituent of the basic humanism of his later maturity. In his later writings,

"God" often designates simply the ideal-achieving aspects of the cosmic evolutionary process. Although there has been some debate as to whether Foster ever completely abandoned Christian theism, the following excerpt from his last published statement before his death seems to be decisive on this point: "I, myself, think that we are witnessing the passing of theistic supernaturalism. Mankind is outgrowing theism in a gentle and steady way. Theism now has no clear meaning" ("Professor George B. Foster on Dr. Ames' New Book," 17).

With both Christian orthodoxy and liberalism behind him, Foster set out to combat an apparently all-engulfing tide of surging materialism, and he seems to have felt that all religious persons, especially Christians, would appreciate his efforts to salvage a minimal religious faith in a situation of grave intellectual and moral crisis. However, the dissolution of orthodox Christianity appeared so clear and certain to him that he seems not to have realized that many orthodox Christians did not share his belief that their faith had been abrogated. Consequently, many such Christians resented rather than appreciated his efforts.

As would be expected, Foster's theological outlook relative to orthodoxy provoked widespread and vigorous protest by conservative clergymen in this country. Foster himself was aware that while the dissolution of "authority-religion" might have taken place in principle, in actual fact such orthodoxy still remained entrenched in many denominations throughout the country. This realization was eventually fully confirmed to Foster, for his speeches, sermons, and books aroused an avalanche of criticism that attracted nationwide attention for several years. The fact that the University of Chicago had arisen under Baptist auspices and that Foster retained life-long membership in Chicago's Hyde Park Baptist Church naturally made the controversy most acute among the Baptists of the Chicago area.

The publication of Foster's largest and best book, *The Finality of the Christian Religion*, early in 1906 fanned into flames the controversy that already had been smouldering for some time. Lines of debate were soon clearly drawn. Some ministers fully approved of Foster's positions, while others condemned them as heretical and agnostic. The Reverend J. R. Straton, pastor of Chicago's Second Baptist Church, announced that his Sunday morning sermon would call for Foster's resignation from his position with the university, but two days later, Professor Charles R. Henderson, chaplain of the university, announced that Foster definitely would be kept as a professor. Henderson stated that the matter had already been settled sometime before when the Trustees discussed the question of Foster's dismissal, reporting that President Harper desired that Foster be retained and that the university should continue to stand for freedom of thought.

One week later, the *Chicago Daily Tribune* carried a front-page report of the heated debate concerning Foster and his book at the Baptist Ministers' Conference on the previous day. The Chicago Presbyterian paper,

The Interior, reassuringly declared that there was no cause "to have hydrophobia" over Foster's book but suggested that it would be better for him to reserve his "Ritschlianism" for the few desperate cases of skepticism like his own (37 [15 February 1906]:202). *The Standard*, the Chicago Baptist weekly, expressed itself editorially to the effect that though many of Foster's ideas were probably destructive of the fundamentals of the faith, the publication of the book "should not be an occasion for losing one's head" ("The Foster Incident," 4). Its pleas for dispassionate discussion and its warnings that expressions of disapproval must not be made in such a spirit as to do irreparable harm are good indications that the debate had already become acrimonious.

Nevertheless, the controversy grew apace, and two weeks after its plea for restraint, *The Standard* carried a report that the Baptist Ministers' Conference had split sharply over the issue. By a vote of 48 to 22, it had adopted the following resolution:

> WHEREAS, a member of this conference has issued from the University of Chicago Press a book entitled "The Finality of the Christian Religion." *Resolved*, That we as a conference declare it to be our resolute conviction that the views set forth in this book are contrary to scripture, and that its teaching and tendency are subversive of the vital and essential truths of the Christian faith. ("Ministers' Meeting," *The Standard* 53 [10 March 1906]:17)

Immediately following the meeting of the conference, the dissenting minority drew up a protest repudiating the resolution on the grounds that it tended to throttle free speech and to make the conference "an inquisitorial body." This protest was signed by such notable figures as Shailer Mathews, T. W. Goodspeed, T. G. Soares, Gerald B. Smith, and Ernest D. Burton. In the next issue, *The Standard* published its adversely critical review of Foster's book, which concluded that although Foster had presented "religion" in its closing chapters, it would be a misnomer to call this religion "Christian" (De Blois, "A Protest," 15).

Moreover, the verdict of *The Churchman*, the Protestant Episcopal journal of New York, was not more favorable: "Professor Foster's Christian finality not only lacks hands and feet, it lacks a backbone, to say nothing of its head" (quoted in "Replies to Professor Foster," 574). On 24 March 1906, *The Standard* carried Foster's repudiation of its review of his book. He said that *The Standard*'s review was similar to all those that had appeared in Baptist papers: "No one of them has said anything . . . which does not come under the head of misrepresentation, calumny, or ridicule—the hoary arguments which . . . have ever been the stock in trade of the champions of the orthodox system of thought" (Myers, "About That Protest," 14f). Some weeks later, F. J. Gurney declared that the resolution of the Ministers' Conference was especially lamentable because it had been made in great haste and without proper forethought. It appeared that fewer than a dozen of the ministers who condemned Foster's *Finality* had read it and that the rest had relied upon the brief extracts and sensational characterizations of the daily newspapers. In fact, Gurney largely placed the blame for the whole affair on the misinformed and sensationalistic reporting of the daily papers that he felt had greatly heightened the intensity and ferocity of the controversy (Gurney, "The Foster Matter," 13).

By the summer of 1906, the Foster controversy had subsided. However, it revived with even greater fury in the spring and summer of 1909 as a consequence of the publication in April of the most radical of Foster's works, *The Function of Religion in Man's Struggle for Existence*. The *Chicago Daily Tribune* printed a story about some phase of the controversy on 20 different days during the month of June in that year! The theological faculty of the University of Chicago voiced general approval of Foster's new book, but someone reported that the next meeting of the Ministers' Conference would seek his dismissal from the Baptist ministry, the Baptist Church, and the University of Chicago. Foster replied with the avowal that he was still "a typical, loyal, old-fashioned Baptist" and defended his practice of preaching in a Unitarian Church on the grounds that he would preach anywhere he was invited. In a Sunday morning sermon at Mandel Hall of the university, he denounced "the veiled, covert, subterranean warfare which is carried on by Protestant orthodoxy against free science" (*Chicago Sunday Tribune*, 13 June 1909, pt. 2, 8). He also released to the press an interesting statement of his position:

> According to the historic position, I am a true Baptist. There is no creed subscription in the Baptist church, the reason being that we have no formal creed. We have no formal creed because Baptists hold to the right of private interpretation of the Scripture, freedom of thought and speech, and the privilege of every man to hold communion with God without the mediation of a priest. This is the kernel of the Baptist position and this I hold with all my heart. (*Chicago Daily Tribune*, 14 June 1909, 1f)

Foster repeated his claim to be a "true Baptist" several times during the year 1909, and in view of the patent fact that he had by that time completely abandoned orthodox Christianity, this avowal would at first sight seem to suggest disingenuousness on his part. This problem can probably only be resolved by giving full weight to his repeated assertions that the stress upon absolute human freedom and the autonomy of the human soul constitutes the essential feature of "the historic Baptist position." Although this conception of historic Baptist thought probably is a bit one-sided, nevertheless, it is a good indication of Foster's own theological position at the time and seems to be the only way to explain his claim still to be an old-fashioned Baptist that is consistent with his own veracity.

The Standard for June 19 observed that there appeared to be two different Professor George B. Fosters, one being an eminent scholar, splendid preacher, and delightful companion, and the other being a hard-to-understand iconoclast, but it renewed its plea for moderation and suggested that his own church, and not the Ministers' Conference, should take disciplinary action if any were necessary. However, the same issue reported a heated session of the Ministers' Conference, with ministers being present from as far away as Canada and South Dakota. After three hours of debate and the consideration of numerous resolutions, it had finally agreed upon a resolution affirming belief in the deity of Jesus Christ and repudiating "any utterance to the contrary, whether preached by Professor Foster or any other" ("Ministers' Meeting," 21).

Moreover, this was not the end of the matter, because the same conference, one week later, voted overwhelmingly to expel Foster from its membership, "after four hours of wrangling which older members of the conference characterized as 'the most disgraceful affair in the history of the church' " (*Chicago Daily Tribune*, 22 June 1909, 1). However, after his expulsion, Foster insisted that he cherished no ill will against the conference and expressed the hope that it would have peace since he had been put out of the way. *The Standard* labeled the action of the ministers as most unfortunate, and one month later, as the controversy still raged, it announced its decision not to publish any further editorials, letters, or statements on the subject. Averring that the whole affair had "already created bitterness and aroused enmities which will never be removed," it declared its refusal to add any further fuel to the fires of heated discussion and expressed the wish that the daily papers would follow suit ("Fostering Peace," 4).

Other than his expulsion from the Baptist Ministers' Conference, the controversy resulted in no formal action against Foster. He did not surrender his papers of ordination to the Baptist ministry, and he retained his teaching post at the University of Chicago and his membership in the Hyde Park Baptist Church until his death. However, the furor did serve greatly to increase the knowledge and sale of Foster's books and thus to disseminate his ideas further than would have otherwise been the case. It also seems to have eventuated in a tendency to confirm the religious conservatives and liberals in their respective positions and to clarify some of the issues between them. The publication of Foster's *The Finality of the Christian Religion* was a major causative factor in the organization in 1907 of the Illinois Baptist State Association at Pinckneyville. Initially composed of 226 churches, it later united with the Southern Baptist Convention. Moreover, in order to offset the liberal influence of the Divinity School of the University of Chicago, Illinois Baptists founded Northern Baptist Theological Seminary at Chicago in 1913 for the training of a more conservative ministry. The religious journals of such traditionally orthodox groups as the Baptist, Presbyterian, and Episcopal denominations united in rejecting Foster's theology, the chief differences among them being the degree of exacerbation or of magnanimity with which they treated Foster. A Roman Catholic journal saw in the whole episode manifest evidence of the futility of the Protestant appeal to private judgment in the interpretation of the Bible and the conduct of Christian life. However, there can be no doubt that religious liberalism among many denominations received a strong thrust forward by the controversy, and the historically liberal religious groups welcomed Foster from the start as a fellow helper of the truth.

SELECTED BIBLIOGRAPHY

Books by Foster

Foster, George Burman. *Christianity in Its Modern Expression*. Edited by Douglas Clyde Macintosh. New York: Macmillan Company, 1921.

———. *The Finality of the Christian Religion*. 2nd ed. Chicago: University of Chicago Press, 1909. (The Decennial Publications of the University of Chicago. The first edition was published in 1906.)

———. *Friedrich Nietzsche*. Edited by Curtis W. Reese, with an Introduction by A. Eustace Haydon. New York: Macmillan Company, 1931.

———. *The Function of Religion in Man's Struggle for Existence*. Chicago: University of Chicago Press, 1909.

Materials Relating to the Foster Controversy

Articles in the Chicago Daily Tribune

10 February 1906, 9.
13 February 1906, 14.
20 February 1906, 1.
1 June 1909, 5.
8 June 1909, 6.
9 June 1909, 16.
10 June 1909, 5.
12 June 1909, 11.
14 June 1909, 1f.
15 June 1909, 3.
17 June 1909, 7.
18 June 1909, 2.
19 June 1909, 8.
21 June 1909, 2.
22 June 1909, 1f.
24 June 1909, 3.
25 June 1909, 1.
28 June 1909, 6.

29 June 1909, 6.
30 June 1909, 3.

Articles in the Chicago Sunday Tribune

11 February 1906, pt. 1, 7.
6 June 1909, pt. 1, 3.
13 June 1909, pt. 2, 8.
20 June 1909, pt. 1, 5.

Articles in The Standard

"The Case of Professor Foster." 56 (19 June 1909): 4.
De Blois, Austin K. "A Protest and a Protest." 53 (17 March 1906): 13.
"Editorial." 56 (26 June 1909): 4.
"The Foster Incident." 53 (24 February 1906): 4.
"Fostering Peace." 56 (24 July 1909): 4.
Gurney, F. J. "The Foster Matter—Per Contra." 53 (14 April 1906): 13.
Maclaurin, Donald D. "Some Foster Correspondence." 56 (3 July 1901): 15.
Mears, Lyman R. "Freedom of Speech." 53 (28 April 1906): 12.
"Ministers' Meeting." 53 (10 March 1906): 17f.
"Ministers' Meeting." 56 (19 June 1909): 21.
"A Modern Mind." "The Genesis of Prof. Foster's Book." 53 (21 April 1906): 9f.
Myers, Johnston. "About That Protest." 53 (24 March 1906): 14.
Parsons, F. W. "An Orthodox Defender of Dr. Foster's Book." 53 (13 April 1906): 14f.
Spaulding, C. D. "Dr. Foster's Book and Young Men." 53 (28 April 1906): 12.
Straton, John R. "The Foster Matter Again." 53 (28 April 1906): 12.

Articles in Other Periodicals

Arnold, Harvey. "The Death of God—'06: George Burman Foster and the Impact of Modernity." *Foundations: A Baptist Journal of History and Theology* 10 (October–December 1967): 331–353.
"The Battle of the Jargons." *The Outlook* 92 (3 July 1909): 530.
"Disturbing Scholarship in the American Church." *Current Literature* 40 (April 1906): 427–429.
"Editorial." *The Interior* 37 (15 February 1906): 202.
"Editorial." *The Interior* 37 (5 April 1906): 402.
Foster, George Burman. "Concerning the Religious Basis of Ethics." *American Journal of Theology* 12 (April 1908): 211–230.
———. "Professor George B. Foster on Dr. Ames' New Book." *The Christian Century* 35 (24 October 1918): 17–18.
"The Latest Heretic—George Burman Foster." *Current Literature* 47 (August 1909): 174–177.
"Replies to Professor Foster." *Literary Digest* 32 (14 April 1906): 573–574.
Towne, Edgar. "A 'Single Minded' Theologian: George Burman Foster at Chicago." *Foundations* 20 (January–March 1977): 36–59; (April–June 1977): 163–180.

Alan Gragg

William S. Godbe
(1833–1902)
and Elias Lacy Thomas Harrison
(1830–1900)

Since its founding in 1830, the Church of Jesus Christ of Latter-day Saints (the LDS or Mormon Church) has held many church trials that have helped to define its official doctrine. The 1869 ecclesiastical trial of William S. Godbe and Elias Lacy Thomas Harrison did exactly that, defining Mormon orthodoxy during the mid-nineteenth-century leadership of Brigham Young. But this unusual trial did more: It was one of the few times that LDS leaders and able opponents tried to sort out the issues of belief and dissent that have long troubled other Christian churches. What are the proper ways of knowing truth—personal revelation or a reliance upon church authority? What are the limits to dissent in a Kingdom of God? Can the divine and human voice in a church leader be sorted out? To these institutional questions, there was an immediate personal concern about Godbe and Harrison. Were they faithful church members whose only guilt lay in expressing a nonconforming viewpoint?

The Godbe-Harrison trial did a better job of raising these questions than in answering them. Participants thought and spoke on their feet; no formal arguments were made. Moreover, the minutes were not a stenographic report and sometimes were uneven. Yet the trial clerk managed a remarkable feat of producing a 41-page, single-spaced, detailed summary of the nearly all-day proceeding. Previously unexamined at length by historians, this document provides a fascinating window into nineteenth-century Mormonism.

At first Godbe and Harrison were among Zion's most eager converts. Both had British origins. Early records describe Godbe's London-based father, Samuel, as a "professor of music" who catered to an upper-class clientele that apparently included the royal household. In fact, Queen Victoria recognized Samuel by making him the conductor of her Royal Orchestra. In turn, William's maternal grandfather was a court violinist, conducted a dance salon in Soho, and assisted the queen with her dancing graces. However, by the time of William's adolescence, the Godbe family had fallen on hard times. Samuel had died early, and young William had gone to sea. While still pursuing this profession, William had found Mormonism. In 1850, while loading a ship on the docks of Hull, the teenager heard a Mormon itinerant missionary preach about a new American religious prophet named Joseph Smith. The preacher told of the "restoration" of the ancient Gospel of Christ and of a "Latter-day Saint" Zion that Smith's successor, Brigham Young, had set up in the American frontier West. The impressionable Godbe, not yet 17 years old, was soon baptized.

Harrison was also a young British convert, born at the village of Barking in Essex. He first heard of Mormonism while employed at a London architectural firm, where he had begun work at the age of 14. Harrison, like Godbe, was drawn to the Mormon claim that ancient Christianity had been restored and that the new religion was more than a lifeless communion of rented pews and formal liturgy. Harrison wanted a religion that united reasoned argument and the spiritual gifts, and he believed that Mormonism answered his quest. He abandoned his architectural study and began a decade of Mormon missionary service in Great Britain.

Eventually, both Godbe and Harrison immigrated to America to play a role in the Mormon Zion then being built in Utah. Godbe's rise was spectacular. Arriving in Utah without money or friends, Godbe soon established Utah's first drugstore, which proved an immediate success. He was soon one of the territory's wealthiest men. He was also active in religious matters. He became a "bishop's counselor" in Salt Lake City's Thirteenth Ward bishopric, one of Mormonism's leading congregations. He also occasionally joined President Young when the church leader toured outlying congregations, spoke from the city's main Temple Square pulpit, and as a further measure of his Mormonism, practiced polygamy: He had four wives and fathered 20 children. And he found time for community service. He served as a neighborhood school trustee and, at Young's nomination, became a Salt Lake City councilman. More than having Young's favor, Godbe had ability and restless energy.

Harrison's Utah activities also revealed a man of talent. Drawing on his earlier architectural training, he helped design several of Salt Lake City's most prominent buildings, including the Salt Lake Theatre and Godbe's imposing Exchange Building. Harrison gave popular lectures, helped to establish a library and reading room, took charge of displays at the territorial "State Fair," and advocated a "Deseret Academy of Arts" with an ambitious aim to create a school, library, and museum of art and design for Utah's young men and women. A writer of considerable skill, Harrison offered to write or edit personal and family history for clients. He received more notoriety as editor of the Intermountain West's first literary magazine, *Peep O'Day*, and its successor, the *Utah Magazine*.

In the mid-1860s, Godbe and Harrison began a close friendship. To most people, the new relationship seemed unusual. Godbe, then a promising member of the LDS establishment, was associating with someone who had a growing reputation for being a skeptic. Godbe explained his association by saying that he was attempting to reclaim Harrison. In point of fact, both men were reexamining their Mormon faith, Harrison publicly and Godbe more privately.

The issue that seemed most troubling to Godbe and Harrison was Brigham Young's Zion—the Mormon leader's blueprint for an ideal society. Young wanted a society that was devout, practical, and agricultural. He valued cooperation, order, authority, and hierarchy, and without any kind of apology, he merged and controlled Utah's church and state functions. As the transcontinental railroad stretched to Utah in the late 1860s, Young took bold steps to buttress his order. He began a boycott against Utah's merchants, whose huge profits were draining the territory of its capital. More to the point, these businessmen seemed too secular and individualistic. To meet their threat, Young unveiled a plan of church-controlled, cooperative merchandising called Zion's Cooperative Mercantile Institution (ZCMI).

To Godbe and Harrison, Young's social vision and the establishment of ZCMI were hopelessly antiquated. The two men were well read and au courant to the laissez-faire currents of the Gilded Age. They also reflected their British origins, which had featured the yeasty intellectualism of lyceums, mechanics institutes, reading rooms, pamphleteering, debates, crusades, and the penny press. In short, Godbe and Harrison wanted a society more in keeping with the times: more individualistic and pluralistic, more freewheeling, and with less power placed in the person of a single man.

Whatever their doubts and questions, Godbe and Harrison felt the tug of their long religious experience: They had been Mormon supporters for too many years to abandon their faith easily. Hoping to resolve their spiritual and intellectual doubts, the two men took an unusual step—at least from today's perspective. In the autumn of 1868, they traveled to New York City where they apparently consulted the renowned spiritualistic medium Charles Foster. Foster had a very uneven personal reputation, but this did not prevent many prominent people from seeking his services. His European clientele included the duke of Wellington, Lord Palmerston, Robert Browning, Lord Tennyson, and John Stuart Mill; in the United States, Foster had assisted on occasion such diverse figures as U.S. Presidents Abraham Lincoln and Andrew Johnson and writers Bayard Taylor and Walt Whitman.

Nineteenth-century spiritualism had much to offer these two troubled Mormons. For one thing, spiritualism and Mormonism had several parallels that at least superficially aided a transfer of faith: Both spiritualism and Mormonism rejected traditional Christianity, yet both accepted spiritual phenomena and the idea of a progressive and rational universe. Also important to Godbe and Harrison, spiritualism (at least to its disciples) had the appeal of cutting-edge, radical thought. It seemed almost a perfect salve to the spiritually troubled Godbe and Harrison.

Over a three-week period, Godbe and Harrison enjoyed a series of two-hour séances, by "appointment," which they came to regard as a personal epiphany. Their most frequent spirit visitor was the recently deceased Heber C. Kimball, Young's counselor, whom Harrison deeply admired. Also appearing were Joseph Smith, Solomon, Jesus, the early apostles Peter, James, and John, and German naturalist Alexander Humboldt. Each of these spirits had a similar message, implicit or explicit: Godbe and Harrison should return to Utah and reform Mormonism with "higher truths." But the two men should remain in Mormonism as long as possible in order to sow "such advanced truths as would elevate the people and prepare them for the changes at hand" (*Mormon Tribune*, 8 January 1870; Godbe and Harrison, "Manifesto," 407).

Godbe and Harrison returned to Salt Lake City with a renewed sense of mission. To complete the task given them, they greatly improved and expanded *Utah Magazine*, which became the vehicle for their views. These were at first expressed cautiously and subtly, but momentum built. By October 1869, the writers of *Utah Magazine* argued that Utah's future lay with the development of her mineral resources and putting the territory into the American mainstream—a direct challenge to Young's agricultural and exclusionist policies. If the editorial was tepid by modern standards, in Zion's carefully controlled atmosphere its meaning was unmistakable: It was meant—and was seen—as a direct challenge to Young's leadership.

Young's first reaction was anger. During a public meeting of Salt Lake City's church leaders, Young denounced Godbe, Harrison, and several of their friends and temporarily suspended these men from church membership. However, during the following days, the church leader seemed to have second thoughts. Apparently hoping to avoid an open break, Young delegated a committee to visit Godbe and Harrison and, at a meeting called to investigate the *Utah Magazine* and its writers, downplayed both the recent article and any possible personal disloyalty. These overtures, however, were not reciprocated. At a second public meeting—this one before 900 elders held at the Salt Lake Tabernacle—Harrison openly and angrily attacked Young. The verbal assault closed the door to compromise.

When the church trial of Godbe and Harrison was convened on Monday, 25 October 1869, at the Council Chamber of the City Hall (a venue that showed how easy the spiritual mixed with the civil in pioneer Utah), the public did not understand the depth of the two men's alienation. Godbe and Harrison had not mentioned, even to friends, the details of their New

York City experience. Nor had they revealed how far their religious questioning had taken them. The two were in the process of abandoning such beliefs as the Bible as canon, the value of religious sacraments, and even the Christian Atonement. However, nothing was publicly said about these things. Instead, their reform message centered on what they perceived as the excesses of Young's personal policy and on his social vision—precisely where LDS public opinion seemed most uncertain.

Young wanted no hint of secrecy at the trial. The city's bishops, bishops' counselors, and some of the church's neighborhood teachers crowded the interior of the City Hall, along with a half-dozen friends of Godbe and Harrison, who were given passes. Young went further. He apparently was willing to allow Godbe to choose his own jury. Did "Brother William" want to be tried by a congregation of the Saints, by High Priests, or by some of the church's General Authorities? Young's options were meant to signal openness and confidence. If a trial had to be held, he wanted to shape public opinion.

With no word from Godbe about the composition of the jury, church authorities finally decided to put the matter before the 12-man Salt Lake Stake High Council, with Stake President George B. Wallace conducting and Elder George Q. Cannon of the Quorum of the Twelve Apostles prosecuting. Leading General Authorities Orson Pratt, Wilford Woodruff, George A. Smith, and even President Young himself testified for the prosecution. For their defense, Harrison and Godbe had only themselves.

Despite its legal trappings (the case had "plaintiffs" and "defendants" and was called "George Q. Cannon vs. William S. Godbe and E.L.T. Harrison"), the trial was not a formal, adversarial hearing in the tradition of Anglo-Saxon law. Church canon allowed defendants to face their accusers, permitted witnesses, and had the unique rule of requiring an arbitrarily selected number of the councilors to speak on behalf of both the prosecution and defense—that "equity and justice" might be secured and "insult and injustice" avoided. Cases not deemed "difficult" required only two councilors, and more difficult ones used four or even six. "Cannon vs. Godbe and Harrison" had four.

Cannon led off. As a preliminary step, he listed the various offending articles that the *Utah Magazine* had published, which he claimed had undermined the policies and influence of church authorities. He then called for the testimonies of the teachers and apostles who had visited Harrison and Godbe a week earlier. These men all agreed that the two were in the "dark," with Harrison especially bearing a hostile spirit. Finally, Cannon concluded the opening phase of the proceeding by reading lengthy extracts from the *Utah Magazine*, which he labeled "sophistries mixed with truth."

Godbe next spoke. He was a compelling speaker, not so much because of the flow of his words but because of his sincerity. The merchant immediately signaled that he did not intend to retreat. The sentiments of the

Utah Magazine were his views, he admitted, but this admission, he insisted, could not be taken as evidence of apostasy. He had always believed in openness and discussion—from the moment of his conversion in England. "Hence I have not apostatized. I stand . . . on this same [principle] today," he said (for this and subsequent quotations from the trial, see "High Council Minutes").

By making the claim, Godbe framed one of the main questions before the court—and tried to move the discussion onto the appealing high ground of principle. Like Young, Godbe wanted to control public opinion. Could members openly disagree with church leaders and still be fellowshipped, he was asking? While acknowledging that any disagreement must be respectful, he claimed that the *Utah Magazine* had always tried to have such a spirit. And if Cannon regarded the magazine's views as "sophistries," he and Harrison thought otherwise. What was the magazine's danger? If its ideas had no merit, they would simply fall to the wayside. On the other hand, if the magazine's arguments were true, it served to combat error and helped the Mormon Kingdom.

Godbe also introduced an epistemological theme. He knew of "no higher test" for religious truth than the "light of Deity" within him. Using this light and the guide of human judgment, men and women could decide all issues for themselves and not rely on others to think for them.

Godbe complained of the compulsion implicit in Young's antimerchant policy: He complained that the people were watched in their trading habits and intimidation was used to ensure "correct" behavior. The prevailing climate in Utah, Godbe claimed, had driven many "good men" to "evasion and dissimulation."

In making his defense, Godbe repeatedly raised the question of personal accountability. "I do not claim that it is fit or necessary in my case that I should see the thing [proposed] from the beginning—that [I] should see the tall ladder that reaches into eternity, but it is necessary according to my understanding that I should know sufficient of a measure to feel that it was not wrong." Even here, Godbe said, he was willing to yield some ground. He claimed to value the ideal of community unity, which would be lost, he recognized, if the tenet of individual accountability were carried too far. However, he did not say how individualism and social cohesion, usually natural enemies, were to be reconciled.

Godbe concluded with a statement that put his protest in the most favorable light. "If I be severed from this church I do so against my solemn protest," he concluded. "We have been taught over and over again that the great fountain [of personal revelation] is within our reach and we can draw from its source light sufficient to lead and guide us from day to day. I have sought these with all the sincerity of my soul."

Now it was Harrison's turn. He repeatedly spoke of the importance of conscience and individualism, but the issue that most concerned him was

President Young's use of priesthood authority, which he called the doctrine of "infallibility." President Young wanted his complete obedience, Harrison complained. But he, Elias, could render compliance only with conditions. "I do not believe in the principle of implicit obedience, unconditional obedience, without the judgment being convinced," he argued. "Hence I see no good effect to result from it." It would be a "curious Zion," Harrison said, if it were built on a foundation of a forced belief in an incorrect policy.

For Harrison, authority in matters of faith had little role. People bowed to Jesus because of the superiority of his teaching, and Harrison vowed to accept even a child's tutoring if the ideas expressed were lofty enough—but never to a man simply because he presided. Such "unquestioning obedience," Harrison argued, failed to disentangle the "man" and "God" within the teaching of church leaders. In the case of Young's public ministry, only a disciple's personal judgment could separate God's voice from man's voice, aided by such respectful public discussion as recently provided by *Utah Magazine*.

Before taking his seat, Harrison placed in the trial's record a formal, eight-paragraph "Manifesto," which summarized the arguments of the two dissenters. Dated two days earlier, it had been prepared for delivery during the meeting at which Harrison had dramatically challenged Young. Not used on that occasion, Godbe and Harrison now placed the document before the Mormon public. It revealed that the comments of the two men at the trial were anything but impromptu. Their trial comments closely paralleled those of the "Manifesto." (The statement, dated 23 October 1869, was later published as a notice in *Utah Magazine* 3 [30 October 1869]: 407.)

Perhaps never in Mormon history had such an antinomian strain been argued so persuasively in a public forum, and certainly never so dramatically. Cannon, attempting to regain the prosecution's momentum, again revived the testimony of the block teachers and the inimical *Utah Magazine*'s passages. For Cannon, a "free press" and "free language" were "catchwords of the devil and those who are influenced by him." And picking up hints of the New York revelation in the words of the two men (during his testimony, Godbe had gratuitously denied any allegiance to spiritualism), Cannon wondered if some of the rumors being heard around town might be true. Were the two men "sustained by some [spiritualist] power we know nothing about?" Cannon wondered, and were they preaching a "new Gospel"?

However, the bulk of Cannon's rebuttal had to do with loyalty to the church as an institution. While Harrison and Godbe might make pretensions of church devotion and be honest as individuals, Cannon argued that their acts challenged "the progress and advancement of the Kingdom of God." Therefore, "we object to these brethren because they fight against the work of God."

Other church leaders followed Cannon, including Young's new counselor, George A. Smith, whose statements introduced to the trial a harshness that previously had been lacking. Smith denounced the "conceit" of Godbe and Harrison and suggested that they conspired to destroy Young and the church. When Smith was done, President Young rose to address the court. His position at the end of the trial was fitting—in pioneer Utah he usually had the last word. He was in no hurry. "There is so much to say upon this subject," he began—and he proved his point by continuing for over an hour. Almost a third of the trial minutes pages record Young's remarks.

There was none of Smith's blunt talk. Even Godbe and Harrison later said that Young spoke respectfully. As a matter of fact, he scarcely mentioned either of the dissidents. He was interested in ideas and principles.

Godbe and Harrison had reified the "liberty" of individuals. Young countered by suggesting the importance of "truth," and he pursued the idea doggedly:

> Where is our liberty? In truth. Where is our freedom? In truth, in the truth of God, in truth no matter where it is found. Where is our strength? In truth. Where is our power and our wisdom? In truth. It is truth that we want. It is truth that exalts us. It is truth that makes us free. It is truth that will bring us into the celestial kingdom, and nothing else.

These words became Young's text. All that followed in his discourse were explanations and emanations.

For Young, "truth" required order, discipline, and obedience. He could not imagine church members determining their own policy and teaching. "What confusion, what discord, what discontent, what hatred would soon creep into the bosom of individuals one against the other." Young likened the church to a family. Each man or woman might receive God's guidance according to their position in the Kingdom, but no more. Hierarchical revelation led to hierarchical authority. Could you imagine children telling their mother that they did not have to make their bed, Young asked?

Young understood that the Godbeite rejection of church authority was aimed at him and defended his stewardship, even when his decisions seemed to be erroneous. To Godbe's complaints of having invested in some of Young's projects and lost money, the church leader had a pointed question: Where did Godbe—his old protégé—get his dollars? According to Young, it was his policies and his help that had made the merchant wealthy.

President Young toiled at length to put down Harrison's claims for individualism and personal choice within the Kingdom. One argument focused on Christian conduct. True disciples, Young argued, traded self-interest (hitherto "the main spring in the world's progress") for helping others. True Saints therefore suppressed "individuality" for the corporate good. For Young, this selflessness—and the Godly obedience that accompanied it—was the only way the individual essence of men and women could be retained. To support his view, Young referred to the peculiarly Mormon idea that "righteousness" enlarged the noncreated "spirit" of men and women (their "intelligence" or "truth"). On the other hand, great sins, if not abandoned, could bring a loss of all contact with deity and subsequently, over the eon of postmortal life, the diminution of a person's elemental spirit—to the point of extinguishing a soul's existence.

At last concluding, the church leader left no doubt about the dissenters' right to publish their *Utah Magazine*—but not as members of the church. "You have the right to believe as you please," Young told the two dissenters, "but we have the same liberty to go the road the Lord wishes us." From the start of the trial, the verdict was probably predetermined, and at the end of the long day, President Wallace pronounced it: Godbe and Harrison were cut off from the Church of Jesus Christ of Latter-day Saints and were handed over to "the buffetings of Satan."

The spirit and equity of the hearing lay in the eye of the beholder. But T.B.H. Stenhouse, a friend of Godbe and Harrison, probably made a reasonable judgment: "The trial was as fairly conducted as these things ever are," Stenhouse later wrote (*Rocky Mountain Saints*, 64). In fact, both sides had kept intemperate remarks to a minimum. Nor could there be much doubt about the correctness of the verdict. On issues expressed and unexpressed, Godbe and Harrison clearly no longer sustained a traditional Mormon viewpoint.

The trial of Godbe and Harrison had partly been about Young's temporal policy. His antimerchant boycott and the establishment of ZCMI were important to Godbe and Harrison's dissent, and during the trial, Brigham Young's homogeneous and unified Zion was discussed. Incidentally, on these issues, the two dissenters would be proven correct: Twentieth-century Mormonism would abandon much of Young's quest for a communal and separate society.

Yet most of the trial was devoted to larger religious issues, such as religious knowing, the limits of religious dissent, and the fallibility of religious leaders. These were (and are) difficult questions, whose timelessness made the trial of Godbe and Harrison transcend its own time and circumstance. Godbe, Harrison, Cannon, and Young were grappling with issues that will always challenge disciples, whether Mormons or members of another branch of institutional religion. They have hardly been resolved 120 years later.

For those living at the time, the trial had its own meaning. For Elder Wilford Woodruff, a Mormon leader who testified during the trial, it was a matter of routine; he left the City Hall chamber to prune his grapevines, unaware of the metaphor. For President Young, he left the city the following day for one of his tours of the settlements. Once more, he wished to convey the image of business as usual. And for Godbe and Harrison, they were forever changed by the trial. The proceeding had moved their dissent from the shadows of hesitancy and secrecy into a position to fulfill the logic of its beginnings. During the next several years, the two men openly proclaimed a modified spiritualism and challenged the church leadership with a rival church, a rival newspaper, a rival assembly hall, and even a rival political party, which they helped to organize.

And finally, the trial affected the men and women of Utah. It made them choose sides. Would they accept or reject the arguments of Godbe and Harrison? Or would they defend Mormonism? In point of fact, when given a choice between the unfamiliar and skeptical teachings of spiritualism, most Utahans elected—to use a popular motto at the time—to continue to sail "on the good ship Zion."

BIBLIOGRAPHY

Godbe, William S. and E.L.T. Harrison, "Manifesto," *Utah Magazine* 3 (30 October 1869): 407.

"High Council Minutes," Salt Lake Stake, 25 October 1869, Historical Record Book, Library—Archives of the Church of Jesus Christ of Latter-day Saints, Salt Lake City, UT.

Mormon Tribune [Salt Lake City], 1869–1870.

Palmer, Grant H. "The Godbeite Movement: A Dissent against Temporal Control." Master's thesis, Brigham Young University, 1968.

Stenhause, T.B.H. *Rocky Mountain Saints*. New York: D. Appleton and Company, 1873.

Utah Magazine [Salt Lake City], 1869.

Walker, Ronald W. "The Commencement of the Godbeite Revolt: Another View." *Utah Historical Quarterly* 42 (summer 1974): 216–244.

———. "When the Spirits Did Abound: Nineteenth Century Utah's Encounter with Free Thought Radicalism." *Utah Historical Quarterly* 50 (fall 1982): 304–324.

Ronald W. Walker

Luther A. Gotwald
(1833–1900)

North American Lutherans were beset by several theological controversies in the nineteenth century. Already divided by language differences based on country of origin, by geography, and by the timing of migrations to the United States and Canada, the denomination was further fragmented by these controversies. Of fundamental importance was the controversy over the place, if any, that the sixteenth-century Lutheran confessions should hold in the life of the contemporary church. Some argued that the church should accept these confessions (or, at least, the Augsburg Confession of 1530), interpreted in a literal sense, as binding on all Lutherans of all times and places. Others virtually ignored the historic confessions, taking their theological cues from contemporary movements such as pietism, revivalism, or rationalism. Still others proposed a modified allegiance to the confessions that would recognize their historic importance but allow for modified interpretations of their doctrines.

Much of the controversy over the Lutheran confessions in the first half of the nineteenth century swirled around Gettysburg Seminary. Founded in 1826 by the General Synod of the Evangelical Lutheran Church, the leader of this seminary in its early years was its first professor of theology, Samuel Simon Schmucker. Grounding his position in older Lutheran pietism as well as in newer notions of what constituted evangelical Christianity, Schmucker favored a modified allegiance to the confessions; at his inauguration to the Gettysburg professorship, he said: "I believe the Augsburg Confession and the Catechisms of Luther to be a summary and just exhibition of the fundamental doctrines of the Word of God." That statement did not prevent him from disbelieving some things taught in those documents. He was especially critical of the traditional Lutheran understandings of baptismal regeneration and of the real presence of Christ in the Lord's Supper, claiming that these were "nonfundamental" teachings. At the same time, he lauded several American Protestant developments with strong theological overtones—especially the "New Measures" revivals popularized by Charles Grandison Finney—and encouraged German-American Lutherans to adopt the use of the English language as quickly as possible.

Schmucker's critics were numerous. On the one hand, there were those who objected to any form of confessional subscription; they insisted on the right of each individual to interpret the Bible and the Christian tradition for himself. On the other, an increasingly vocal confessional party asserted itself; these traditionalists, led initially by David Henkel of North Carolina, insisted that one was not entitled to the name "Lutheran" unless he embraced the historic teachings of the church in their literal sense. This party grew steadily during the 1820s and 1830s, receiving encouragement also from renewed immigration from Germany. Many of the new immigrants were self-conscious "Old Lutherans" who had been fighting the battle against confessional indifference in Germany and who brought their confessional militancy with them to the organizations that they founded in the American Midwest, the best known of which was the Missouri Synod. They were also generally opposed to American revivalism and to too-rapid acculturation, encouraging the immigrants to continue to speak their native languages and to follow the customs of their mother countries.

In the midst of the controversies between proponents of what Schmucker called "American Lutheranism" and a variety of native-born and immigrant confessionalists, a number of schisms and institutional realignments took place. In Ohio, the Lutheran community split down the middle over these issues in 1840. The confessionalist, antirevival, pro-German party retained control of the old Ohio Synod and its seminary at Columbus. The "American Lutheran" party soon founded three synods, in the eastern, southwestern, and northwestern areas of the state. These synods were the primary sources of support for a new literary and theological institution that was founded at Springfield in 1845—Wittenberg College.

Wittenberg was strongly American Lutheran from its beginning; its professors took a doctrinal oath that declared that "the doctrines of God's Word are set forth in a manner substantially correct in the Augsburg Confession." The first professor of theology and president of the fledgling college was Ezra Keller, who had experienced conversion in a revival and had been a devoted student of Schmucker at Gettysburg. He understood "substantially correct" to allow for selective modifications of the old confession. When he died in 1848, his successor was Samuel Sprecher, who not only held similar ideas but was a brother-in-law of S. S. Schmucker. Sprecher taught theology according to the American Lutheran pattern at Wittenberg until 1884. In some ways, Wittenberg became more of a center of the American Lutheran movement than Gettysburg itself. When, in 1855,

Schmucker produced a "Definite Synodical Platform," which embodied his doctrinal views and which he asked the synods of the General Synod to endorse formally, only three small midwestern synods influenced by Sprecher responded positively. Other synods objected to the "Platform" either because it would restrict their liberty or because they had come under the control of confessionalists. Indeed, Schmucker's views were increasingly challenged at Gettysburg Seminary itself. As the faculty had grown, the Board of Directors had appointed teachers whose views were closer to those of historic Lutheranism than were those of Schmucker, resulting in a diversity of theological positions on the faculty. (Even the introduction of more traditional Lutheranism at Gettysburg did not prevent the establishment of a rival confessional seminary, however; it opened its doors at Philadelphia in 1864.) Only at Wittenberg did American Lutheranism reign unchallenged for almost four decades, during which several hundred graduates passed into the ministry of the Lutheran churches in Ohio and beyond.

After the retirement of Samuel Sprecher in 1884, even Wittenberg began to change significantly in its theological teaching. Under the leadership of President Samuel Ort, the well-known confessionalist James W. Richard was appointed to the faculty in 1885. Richard was a leader in the successful movement to make the General Synod explicitly confessional, thereby repudiating the American Lutheranism that had earlier emanated from Gettysburg and was still taught at Wittenberg as late as the early 1880s. In 1864, in the context of the opening of the Philadelphia Seminary, the General Synod had declared that the Augsburg Confession is "a correct exhibition of the fundamental doctrines of the divine Word, and of the faith of our Church as founded upon that Word." While that was not unambiguous language, and the American Lutherans continued to express their views freely, the tide had clearly turned in the favor of a more traditional confessional subscription. Not until 1895 would the General Synod declare that the "unaltered Augsburg Confession" was "throughout in perfect consistence" with the Word of God. But in the meantime, most theologians in the General Synod taught and practiced a positive confessionalism that focused on the Augsburg Confession and Luther's catechisms, while treating the rest of the documents in the Book of Concord (1580) as having only secondary importance; this distinction separated General Synod confessionalism both from that of "Old Lutherans" in several conservative midwestern synods and from that of the rival General Council, founded in 1867 by the same leaders who had established the Philadelphia Seminary. The General Council affirmed that all of the confessions in the Book of Concord are binding on contemporary Lutheranism and "must be accepted in every statement of doctrine, in their own true, native, original, and only sense."

Richard's appointment caused a stir among Wittenberg's constituency, many of whom were still committed to American Lutheranism. By 1886 the *Lutheran Evangelist*, privately published at Springfield by several of Sprecher's former students and allies, was openly critical of Ort and Richard; Ort had in fact been its editor for a while but was now forced out of that position by the owners of the paper. Richard himself was not a target of the *Evangelist* or other critics of the new tendencies at Wittenberg for very long, however, for he left the college in 1888 to accept an appointment at Gettysburg Seminary.

The Wittenberg Board of Directors chose not one but two professors to replace Richard. In 1889, Samuel F. Breckenridge was made professor of exegetical theology, and Luther A. Gotwald was appointed professor of practical theology. At his inauguration, Gotwald proclaimed that the training of Lutheran pastors "should be distinctly and positively Lutheran, both in doctrine and ritual." Not long afterward, President Samuel Ort told the Wittenberg public that the college no longer taught theology "according to the statements of the Definite Platform, [which] was the way of theological teaching thirty years ago."

The forthright confessionalism of Ort, Breckenridge, and Gotwald was heartening to some but dismaying to others. By 1890, highly emotional criticisms of "The New Wittenberg" (a public relations phrase often used by President Ort) was a regular feature not only in the *Lutheran Evangelist* but in other church papers as well. The new administration and theological faculty were said to have forsaken the traditions of their ancestors in favor of an emphasis on historic liturgy and confession that would exclude "reason, reflection, [and] self-determination" and so lay "the foundations of despotism." To counter this barrage of criticism, the confessional party established its own paper, *The Lutheran World*, at Cincinnati in 1892.

Criticism of The New Wittenberg was especially intense at First Lutheran Church in Dayton, Ohio. This congregation had a long history of promoting American Lutheranism; it was especially opposed to the use of a liturgical service, which it considered to go hand in glove with strict confessionalism. In the 1890s, these views were reiterated both by a leading layman in the congregation, Alexander Gebhart, and by the pastor, Ernest E. Baker, a recent Wittenberg graduate. Because of the prominence of First Church, both were serving as representatives of the Miami Synod on the Wittenberg Board of Directors, where they had become fierce critics of the theological direction in which Samuel Ort was taking the school. Ironically, Luther Gotwald had for a time been pastor of this congregation (1865–1868); he remembered this brief pastorate as one of great difficulty, not least of all because he had publicly differed with Samuel Sprecher about some matters. In a further irony in light of later developments, Gotwald had even named one of his sons Frederick Gebhart Gotwald in honor of Alexander's father, who had been one of the founders of the congregation.

By 1892, Alexander Gebhart and Ernest Baker had determined to do something drastic to stem the tide of confessionalism and liturgical conformity at Wittenberg. Furthermore, they had decided to make Luther Gotwald the target of their action. Why this was so is not clear. Perhaps it was because of animosity on the part of Alexander Gebhart going back to Gotwald's pastorate at First Church. Perhaps it was because President Samuel Ort was personally very popular with the Wittenberg constituency, which militated against a direct attack on him. Certainly, Luther Gotwald had never shied from expressing himself freely about his theological positions, so there was plenty of ammunition if charges were to be brought.

Luther Gotwald was formally accused of false teaching on 9 February 1893 in a communication to the Wittenberg Board of Directors from Alexander Gebhart, Joseph Gebhart (Alexander's cousin, also a member of the Board), and Pastor Ernest E. Baker. Seven charges were leveled against Gotwald, the first and seventh of which expressed the essence of the complaint:

> *First*. His Dominant Attitude has been that of opposition to the Type of Lutheranism that dictated the establishment of Wittenberg College, that animated its founders in undertaking it, and in whose interest the original trust was created.
> *Seventh*. His continued occupancy of a Professorship . . . is in violation of the Charter and Constitution of Wittenberg College in this— Specification one. His teaching operates to defeat the original object for which the trust was created, namely . . . to educate ministers of the gospel for our churches in accordance with the Evangelical Type of Lutheranism historically characteristic of the General Synod, and distinct from the sacramental and exclusive Type which . . . set itself against the General Synod. . . . Specification two. His teaching as Professor operates to divert the institution, and the moneys given it . . . to the use of the sacramental and exclusive Type of Lutheranism. . . . Specification three. His retention . . . operates to discourage and in many instances to destroy the willingness of our people to give moneys for the building and endowment of any institution . . . if it may be diverted from its original object with the consent of the very Board of Directors to whom, by Charter and Constitution, it was committed to be sacredly kept in obedience to the original trust. (*Trial of L. A. Gotwald*, 3–6)

The nub of the matter from the complainants' point of view was that Gotwald taught a type of Lutheranism out of harmony with that of S. S. Schmucker, Ezra Keller, and Samuel Sprecher and that by so doing he had violated the very premise on which the college had been founded. In the early years, Wittenberg had proudly proclaimed itself "the revival college"; now, under the leadership of Ort, Breckenridge, and Gotwald, it was alleged to have repudiated that heritage, substituting a spiritually impotent confessionalism closely linked to liturgical conformity for the vibrant "Evangelical Type of Lutheranism."

The Board of Directors was distressed at having to deal with these charges. Many members of the Board clearly favored the increasing confessionalism of the General Synod and of the college, and other members seemed to want to avoid the unfavorable publicity that would certainly attend a "heresy trial." Nevertheless, a special meeting of the Board of Directors was called for 4 April 1893 to deal with the matter. Gotwald, his accusers, and the Board all employed legal counsel in preparation for this meeting, which lasted for two days.

The "Trial of L. A. Gotwald" proved to be a rather curious affair. The Board of Directors proceeded cautiously, adopting special bylaws for the occasion and employing a stenographer to make an official transcript. There were frequent interruptions for consultation with the counsel to the college. With no precedents to guide it, the Board became in effect judge, prosecutor, and jury. As judge, it controlled the process. As prosecutor, it decided that the original charges were too vague. It asked the complainants to amend the charges; when they would not, the Board itself made the charges "more specific," largely by citing instances when Gotwald had publicly stated his theological, confessional, and liturgical views. Its most controversial decision was that it dropped the three "specifications" entirely from the seventh charge; at that, the Gebharts and Baker refused to participate any more in the proceedings. Ernest Baker told the Board that "we came here prepared to enter upon the trial upon the charges we have preferred. We are not prepared to enter upon a trial upon charges to be formulated by counsel for the defense or upon charges to be formulated by the board" (*Testimony and Trial*, 231).

The trial proceeded, nonetheless, with the Gebharts and Baker in the role of spectators. Two members of the Board were appointed to present charges of misfeasance in office. Theirs was a halfhearted performance, since they obviously did not believe in the merits of the charges. After the presentation of the charges, Gotwald presented his own spirited defense. He asserted that his views were in perfect consonance with those of the General Synod, as that body now existed. He claimed that the General Synod had a perfect right to clarify and strengthen its confessional position and that Wittenberg College was right to follow the Synod in this direction. He objected to the charge that he taught "the Type of Lutheranism of the General Council," noting that the Council gave equal weight to all of the Lutheran confessions, while he, like the General Synod, held only the Augsburg Confession and the catechisms of Luther to be normative. There was no rebuttal to Gotwald's testimony, since the complainants continued to refuse to participate in the trial in any way.

At the conclusion of two days of testimony, the Wittenberg Board of Directors voted 25 to 0, with 3 abstentions (the Gebharts and Baker), to

exonerate Gotwald of all charges. With this conclusion, the Board undoubtedly hoped the matter would be laid to rest and that the church
press—especially the *Lutheran Evangelist*—would find something else with
which to fill its columns. It was clear that The New Wittenberg had solid
support, at least in the Board of Directors.

Luther Gotwald was not so ready to lay the matter to rest, however. He
felt that he had been severely wronged and that Wittenberg's public needed
to have a complete account of his vindication. Later that same year, he
published *Trial of L. A. Gotwald, D.D., Professor of Practical Theology
in Wittenberg Theological Seminary, Springfield, Ohio . . . upon Charges
of Disloyalty to the Doctrinal Basis of Said Theological Seminary*. In this
volume, he printed various documents connected with the trial, to which
he appended a lengthy essay entitled "Lutheran Confessionalism in the
General Synod: A Reply to the Charges of My Assailants." In his essay, he
reviewed the larger controversy, criticized his opponents for standing on
the discredited "Definite Platform," and insisted that confessionalism and
true Christian piety are not enemies, as the American Lutherans often
charged. Indeed, in the course of the controversy leading up to Gotwald's
trial, Samuel Sprecher himself—now living in retirement in California—
had acknowledged that he no longer believed that piety and confessional
fidelity were necessarily incompatible, although he by no means became a
confessionalist.

The trial of Luther A. Gotwald was one of the last gasps of the American
Lutheranism formulated by S. S. Schmucker, Ezra Keller, Samuel Sprecher,
and others, although the issues at stake—confessional subscription, liturgical practice, acculturation of immigrants, revivalism, and others—would
continue to be important ones for North American Lutherans for many
years to come. Gotwald himself remarked on the irony involved in the
charges that had been brought against him:

> Not with incompetency, not with unfaithfulness, not with immorality,
> not with heresy, am I charged, but with an excess, forsooth, of Lu-
> theranism. . . . In other denominations men, in our day, are being called
> to account on the charge of disloyalty to their denominational confes-
> sion—I for loyalty to mine; they, for holding and teaching too little of
> the faith of their church—I, for holding and teaching too much of the
> faith of mine. (*Trial of L. A. Gotwald*, 67–68)

While that was indeed a unique characteristic of this trial, it was perfectly
understandable in the light of the history of North American Lutheranism
in the nineteenth century. Nor did the triumph of confessionalism in the
General Synod and at Wittenberg College mean that the older pietism that
had fueled the American Lutheran movement was dead and gone. Gotwald
himself insisted that "the high type of earnest spiritual life, or experimental

piety" that had marked the early Wittenberg "pervades and dominates her today. . . . [O]ur piety is 'Pietistic Lutheranism' of the Spener, Francke, Arndt, Muhlenberg type" (*Trial of L. A. Gotwald*, 157). In fact, the Gotwald trial tended to obscure the real differences that continued to exist in the 1890s between the confessionalists of the General Synod and those of other Lutheran synods. Those differences would continue to surface after the General Synod and the General Council were reunited in the United Lutheran Church in America (1917) and have continued to affect the subsequent history of North American Lutheranism.

BIBLIOGRAPHY

Allbeck, Willard D. *A Century of Lutherans in Ohio*. Yellow Springs, OH: Antioch Press, 1966.

———. *Theology at Wittenberg, 1845–1945*. Springfield, OH: Wittenberg Press, 1945.

Gotwald, Luther A. *Testimony and Trial—An Autobiography*. Edited by Luther A. Gotwald, Jr. Davidsville, PA: Editor, 1973.

———. *Trial of L. A. Gotwald, D.D., Professor of Practical Theology in Wittenberg Theological Seminary, Springfield, Ohio, April 4th and 5th, 1893, upon Charges of Disloyalty to the Doctrinal Basis of Said Theological Seminary*. Philadelphia: Lutheran Publication Society, 1893.

Gotwald, Luther A., Jr. *The Gotwald Trial Revisited*. Davidsville, PA: Author, 1992.

Huber, Donald L. *Educating Lutheran Pastors in Ohio, 1830–1980: A History of Trinity Lutheran Seminary and Its Predecessors*. Lewiston, NY: Edwin Mellen Press, 1989.

Donald L. Huber

Francis Hodur
(1866–1953)

Poles began to arrive in the New World shortly after the Civil War. Most were peasants who had no intention of settling permanently in the United States but saw America as "the land of opportunities for advancing in the Old Country" (Thomas and Znaniecki, *Polish Peasant*, 2: 1521–1524). By 1875, there were more than 200,000 Polish foreign-born in America, with 50 established parishes. By 1890, their numbers had increased to 800,000, with 132 churches, 126 priests, and 122 schools. Buffalo, Pittsburgh, Cleveland, Detroit, Chicago, and Milwaukee had emerged as important Polish centers. Wisconsin had the largest number of Polish settlements, but Chicago had the largest population (Kuzniewski, "Catholic Church," 401). St. Stanislaus Kostka, established in 1867 as Chicago's first Polish parish, grew to such an extent that, by 1899, it was reported to be the largest Catholic parish in the world, with more than 45,000 parishioners and 50 extant societies.

Polish immigration peaked during the prewar decades, as more than 100,000 Poles came to America each year between 1901 and 1914. They generally settled north of the Ohio River, and east of the Mississippi, to such an extent that Chicago became the capital of these new communities, with 250,000 Polish residents by 1905 and 4,000,000 by 1910. In the Midwest, Milwaukee and Detroit each numbered 100,000 Poles, with Cleveland and Toledo also having significant populations. In the East, New York City was the largest settlement, with 200,000 Polish Americans by 1920. Buffalo, Philadelphia, Baltimore, and Boston also had significant Polish communities (403).

This American Polonia (or, *Polonja Amerykanska*) was not a geographical entity but a loose collection of individual communities, scattered across the eastern and midwestern states (Kantowicz, *Polish-American Politics*, 10). The national parish was "the most important Polish-American institution" within these communities, for it recreated the narrower village life from which most Poles had come. Thomas and Znaniecki, authors of the classic *The Polish Peasant in the United States*, noted that the ethnic parish helped break down the anonymity of American life and provided a center for the organization and unification of the community (1: 41–42). The societies and organizations grouped around the parish helped to affirm and give an identity to each of its members. And the festivals and celebrations that sprang from each parish deepened their religious sense (Woods, *Hamtramck*, 178–179). At the heart of each parish was the pastor, who "embodied religion, language, and national culture in his own person" (Kantowicz, *Polish-American Politics*, 30–31). The most significant core of Polish priests came from the Congregation of the Resurrection (CR), who established a large network of Polish-American communities throughout the East and Midwest.

The reaction of Polish Americans to their priests was generally positive. Karol Wachtl in *Polonja w Ameryce* noted:

> To our forgotten, unknown settlements in America came the priest-countryman. He came like a missionary and taught us how to pray, how to read in Polish; he told us what a Pole is and who the Polish people are. . . . [T]hese priests, together with the people, founded our parishes, raised up our temples, built schools, orphanages, and hospitals, founded brotherhoods and other associations, introduced the idea of harmony and unity, organized mutual aid—in a word, created a community out of a disorderly multitude. (Quoted in Kuzniewski, "Catholic Church," 404)

But there were disagreements from the beginning. At Polonia, Wisconsin, parishioners angered by the pastor's insistence on moving the church made raucous by neighboring saloons, hollowed out sticks of wood and put them in the pastor's woodpile (Kuzniewski, *Faith*, 160). To counter this tendency, bishops like Chicago's Thomas Foley invited the Resurrectionists to build up the Polish-American community.

The greatest individual of this period was Vincent Barzynski, pastor of St. Stanislaus Kostka parish from 1874 to his death in 1899. He organized more than 40 parish societies, opened a parish bank, founded the first Polish high school in Chicago, and was the guiding spirit of the Polish Roman Catholic Union for almost two decades. Pastors like Barzynski were not interested in the liberation of Poland but advocated a policy of close allegiance to the Catholic hierarchy and gradual assimilation into American society. Through the pages of the paper *Dziennik Chicagoski*, the Resurrectionists preached a trinity of language, history, and religion, all of which were aimed at becoming effective American citizens. As *Dziennik Chicagoski* stated:

> Among the principles guiding us shall be . . . to regard highly the Constitution of the United States, as citizens of the country. We must participate actively in the public life of our country. . . . [S]pecifically, we Poles must not consider ourselves as visitors but as an integral part of this country. (15 December 1890, 2)

But the strength of the Resurrectionists bred an independence movement within American Polonia that would eventually lead to the establishment of the Polish National Catholic Church (PNCC), led by the charismatic Francis Hodur, in 1897. While the independent movement centered around such reforms as lay ownership of church property and combatting excess spending of pastors, they were in reality the first stirrings of a militant Polish ethnic reaction to the policies of Americanization as championed by the Resurrectionists and the Irish American Catholic hierarchy. Independents in Buffalo began their own parish after unsuccessfully challenging the alleged autocratic rule of Reverend Jan Pitass, the dean of all Polish Parishes in the Buffalo diocese (Parot, *Polish*, 109). When Catholics loyal to the diocese tried to gain control of St. Paul's Church in Omaha, the independent pastor shot two of the infiltrators. The most significant reaction occurred at St. Hedwig's in Chicago, where independents led by the Rev. Anthony Kozlowski formed the schismatic All Saints Parish in 1895 (Parot, *Polish*, 110–114). Kozlowski was later ordained bishop by the Old Catholic Bishops of Europe and called his new church the Polish Catholic Church. When Kozlowski died in 1907, his followers joined the Hodur's Polish National Catholic Church (Wrodlowski, *Origins*, 16–18).

The seeds of the Polish National Catholic Church began in Scranton, Pennsylvania, in 1896. The city itself had grown from 35,000 in 1870 to more than 100,000 in 1900. While the Irish and Germans formed the cultural elite of the city, Poles were "poor, of little culture, without language among foreigners, [and] they seemed to be doomed to annihilation" (*Straz*, 7 October 1905). In 1885, Sacred Heart Parish was established in South Scranton for the Polish of that city. When the first pastor, the Rev. Adolf Snigurski, left for missionary work in Texas in 1892, Bishop William O'Hara, 80 years of age at the time, appointed the Rev. Richard Aust as pastor. Aust was a German priest from Silesia, whose Polish was very poor and who seemed to favor the Germans at the center of the city. Tensions finally broke out at the end of August 1896, when Aust demanded additional money for enlarging the parish cemetery. A number of parishioners demanded that all collections go through a committee, chosen by a parish assembly, and not the pastor. When a group of rebels stood both inside and outside the church, opposing Aust's use of funds, Aust appealed to Bishop O'Hara for help.

On Sunday, 16 August 1896, Bishop O'Hara spoke to the people to try to dissuade them from their course of action. But O'Hara knew no Polish, and his ideas were either translated poorly or misunderstood by his audience. Whatever the case, Aust exacerbated the situation the following Sunday by threatening to excommunicate anyone who would resist his actions. A group of rebellious parishioners responded by setting up a committee that decided not to allow Aust to enter the church until he changed his mind about the people. O'Hara himself refused to compromise, turning down a request by the committee to put the control of parish finances into the hands of the parishioners. On 30 August 1896—a day that came to be known as Bloody Sunday—some 800 parishioners tried to block Aust's way. A score of policemen arrived to escort Aust into the church. In the ensuing fracas, 24 were arrested and several injured. O'Hara, frightened by the episode, suspended Aust from further services at Sacred Heart and sent the Rev. Francis Hodur "that there will not be any rioting at Sacred Heart Polish Church tomorrow. . . . [T]here will be no crowding in the back yard as there was last Sunday to prevent him from getting into the sacristry" (*Scranton Tribune* [a.k.a. *Scranton Republican*], 12 September 1896).

Aust never returned to Scranton, for on 23 September 1896, he was transferred to Hazleton, Pennsylvania. The Rev. Bronislaw Dembinski, young and inexperienced, became the new pastor. Concessions were made, but by this time, the independent faction wanted more. The *Scranton Republican* reported that "the result of the Polish meeting was unsatisfactory . . . and for that reason they refused to attend or pay dues as members of that church. . . . [A] movement is afoot to build an independent church with Father Hodur as pastor" (29 September 1896). On October 1, 787 members of Scared Heart decided to leave the old church and build a new one. Parishioners raised $6,000 to purchase three lots for St. Stanislaus Polish Roman Catholic Church. Bishop O'Hara approved and, on 14 March 1897, appointed the Rev. Francis Hodur as its first pastor (Wrodlowski, *Origins*, 28–29). This is generally accepted as the birth of the Polish National Catholic Church in America.

Francis Hodur was born in Zarki, Poland, on 2 April 1866, the son of an impoverished peasant couple. When he reached the age of 14, he enrolled at the nearby secondary school of St. Anne near Cracow. Life was difficult, as he had to walk 33 miles between Cracow and Poland just to attend class. He soon obtained room and board and quickly reached the head of his class. Adam Krzynznowski, a close friend of Hodur's in his youth, noted that "he [Hodur] was a man of great individuality . . . full of love for poetry and man—always ready to bear sacrifice. . . . [T]he Gospel and poetry were to him like those Biblical commandments by which a man should be led in his life" (Wiktor, *Strzecha*, 112). Hodur graduated at the head of his class and went on to study at the Polish Lyceum and the University of Cracow. But he never completed his studies for priesthood and left the seminary a year before his completion in 1893. The Rev. John Gallagher, in a centenary history of the Diocese of Scranton, noted that he "had been expelled . . . because of his persistent political activism" (222). But the reality may be that Hodur was more influenced by the activism of the Rev. Stanislaus Stojalowski, whose ideal was to raise the Polish people from spiritual and material poverty to human dignity. And even though Stojalowski would later reconcile with the Polish Catholic hierarchy, Hodur remained tied to his ideals (*Straz*, 16 April 1898).

Hodur decided to immigrate to the United States to complete his studies for the priesthood and, in 1893, arrived in New York. His arrival caught the attention of the Rev. Benvenuto Gramlewicz, who succeeded in attaching him to Bishop O'Hara's diocese in Scranton. Hodur completed his seminary training at St. Vincent Seminary in Beatty and was assigned to the mining regions of Lackawanna and Luzerne counties in eastern Pennsylvania. At Sacred Heart Parish in South Scranton, Hodur's peasant origins, as well as his familiarity with the ideals of Stanislaus Stojalowski, led him to sympathize deeply with his parishioners. Hodur became rector of Holy Trinity parish in nearby Nanticoke in 1895. Holy Trinity had emerged as a distinctly Polish parish after several disputes concerning parish management and ownership of church property. Diocesan records show that Hodur was greatly admired for his work in Nanticoke, had taken charge of the dissidents, and had established peace in that community (Gallagher, *Century of History*, 169).

When the dissidents at Sacred Heart Parish, in South Scranton, received approval for their own parish, Bishop O'Hara thought that Hodur would reconcile the dissenting elements to diocesan policy. But Hodur's militant ethnic reaction to the American bishop's overall Americanizing tendencies forced him to side once and for all with his Polish flock. On 14 March 1897, Hodur appeared before his parishioners and said:

> So we shall go without fear. The rights of the people are stronger and holier than the privileges of bishops and priests, so God almighty will be on our side. . . . [T]hey will condemn and persecute me, but I do not fear either excommunication or any other punishment. . . . [Y]our courage will be an example for other Polish settlers to follow, and just as to day admire the Apostles for their fearless bearing of the Cross of Christ . . . so will your names be mentioned with reverence by the Polish generations to come. (*Nowe Drogi*, 19)

Bishop O'Hara immediately suspended Hodur from his priestly duties, but Hodur attacked the bishops and those who claimed he had come to America only to make money. Hodur insisted that his sole desire was to defend the rights of his oppressed parishioners.

In the first edition of *Straz* ("The Guard"), which Hodur published as a weekly, he wrote:

> We are living in times when no one can quietly sit back and watch socio-religious and national (ethnic) movements growing. Those who would stand by with folded arms will be brushed aside either by those who go forward or by those who would force the wheel of progress backwards. . . . But, because a retrograde current brings slow death to ethnicity, all those who do not wish to see the demise of their ethnic community should take action in the name of progress. (17 April 1897)

In 1898 Hodur went to Rome to petition that Poles be allowed to form parishes on a strict nationality base. He was optimistic at first, because "there are many priests—including the Rev. Stojalowski—who trusted and believed that the 'idea of the National Church would triumph' " (*Straz*, 26 February 1898). The memorandum succinctly summarized the four basic objectives of Hodur and his movement: (1) that a Polish bishop be selected among the American episcopacy; (2) that Poles have control of all church properties; (3) that the Poles administer their own church property through a committee chosen by their own pastor; and (4) that the Poles have the right to choose their own pastor (*Straz*, 30 October 1897). Upon his return to Scranton, Hodur gave a detailed report of his trip to Rome and waited for a response.

But no favorable response was forthcoming. The American hierarchy was emboldened when they learned that Bishop Anthony Kozlowski, of the schismatic Chicago church, was excommunicated. They worried about the rapid expansion of the National Church, as it began to spread throughout northeastern Pennsylvania. Hodur himself patiently awaited his own excommunication. "Let them curse and swear," Hodur wrote in the *Straz*, "but we are sure that the howl of dogs won't reach the throne of heaven" (3 September 1898). O'Hara demanded that Hodur "submit himself to the Catholic Church. . . . I do not suppose you are a Russian spy, but surely your actions would be willingly paid for by Russia, for you are splitting the miserable Polish nation" (*Straz*, 1 October 1898).

The excommunication was formally issued on 22 October 1898. The *Scranton Tribune* reported that Hodur "commented no further than to say that it was not effective. . . . [H]e spoke at length and alluded to the figures in Church history who have been stigmatized as heretics and schismatics" (3 October 1898). A few days later, Hodur exclaimed, "What naive people the bishops are. They still think in terms of medieval times when at the beckon of a pope . . . the innocent hands of Hus and Savonarola were shackled. . . . [N]either mighty czars, nor the rich, nor popes can destroy the spirit of truth" (quoted in Wrodlowski, *Origins*, 63).

The parishioners themselves were more demonstrative than Hodur. Some rang church bells, others sang hymns, all hugged and kissed each other. At one parish, the demonstration became so rowdy that three parishioners were thrown in jail for 30 days. Hodur himself hoped for some reconciliation with Rome, but none was forthcoming. Looking back some 50 years later, he said: "It is easy to say 'break your links with Rome, leave the Roman Church'—but it is very difficult to do it. A religious man is like a tree which grows with all its roots in the earth, but if the tree is taken out of the earth and is not given proper soil to grown in—it dies" (*Rola Boza*, 22 October 1949, quoted in Wrodlowski, *Origins*, 69).

The definitive break with Rome came on 16 December 1900. "The parish assembly decided to break once and for all with the Irish and German bishops . . . to ask Father Hodur not to look to the Vatican any longer, but to teach the people in the spirit of the Polish Church" (*Nowe Drogi*). Hodur began to distance himself theologically as well; his interpretation of the Bible became more Protestant than Catholic, as "the people of Scranton . . . know only one Bishop—one Master,—Jesus Christ." Liturgically, the assembly decided to introduce services in the vernacular (Polish). While these changes brought charges of "protestantism" against St. Stanislaus and the affiliate churches, Hodur emphatically insisted that they were made solely to keep the true meaning of "catholicity" alive (Wrodlowski, *Origins*, 77–80). In 1904, Hodur issued a proclamation stating "the open protest of the Polish people against the unfavorable and dangerous relations with the Irish and German bishops has manifested itself in a National (ethnic) movement within the Church. . . . Polish people for themselves—that is the slogan of the new movement" (*Straz*, 9 July 1904). Hodur went on to state his disillusionment with Rome and his reluctant conclusion that the Polish Church would have to go it alone. "It is time we take the problems of our Church into our own hands," he said. "It is time to organize the Polish National Catholic Church in America" (quoted in Wrodlowski, *Origins*, 79–80).

To this end, Hodur convoked the First General Synod of the Polish National Catholic Church in 1907. An assembly of 147 clerical and lay delegates, representing approximately 20,000 applicants, went even further than the 1900 assembly. It repudiated the notion that the Roman Catholic Church was the sole exponent of Christian doctrine; it declared the dogma of papal infallibility as false and blasphemous. It ordered all Latin service books be translated into Polish. It urged cooperation with Protestant denominations. And finally, it designated Hodur as bishop-elect. But there were problems to overcome, as some national priests tried to undermine the efforts of Hodur and the reforms of the Synod. "Some renegades entered our ranks," he noted. "They betrayed their oath. . . . [I]t was a year of collusion and intrigues, a year of plotting hand in hand with foreign mitred prelates" (*Straz*, 16 September 1905).

The ethnic tensions that had given rise to the Polish National Catholic Church in Scranton had also been the basis for the schismatic All Saints Parish in Chicago. When its leader, Bishop Anthony Kozlowski, died in 1907, his followers joined the Scranton movement under Hodur. The Old Catholic Bishops of Europe then decided to consecrate Hodur as bishop. The ceremony—which was performed in Utrecht on 29 September 1907 by the Most Reverend Gerald Gul, archbishop of Utrecht and head of the Old Catholic Church; the Rt. Rev. Jacob Jan van Thiel, bishop of Haarlem; and the Rt. Rev. Nicholas Spit, bishop of Deventer—culminated what has been called the only significant schism of the Roman Catholic Church in America (Zawistowski, "Polish National Catholic Church," 423).

After his consecration, Hodur labored for half a century to promote and consolidate the growth of the PNCC from his Scranton headquarters. He founded the Polish National Union in 1908 to strengthen ties between the clergy and laity and worked vigorously to provide priests for a flock that had grown to 28,000 by 1923 (Parot, "Hodur," 305). When efforts to obtain recruits from the Roman Catholic clergy failed, he opened the Savonarola Seminary in Scranton to fill the ranks. Hodur also aligned himself with the Polish National Alliance, the Polish Falcons, and the Polish Workers' Party, all of whom nurtured a people with "a warm feeling for Poland" (quoted in Kantowicz, *Polish-American Politics*, 37).

Hodur's impact on the doctrinal development of the PNCC was also highly significant. Like the Orthodox churches, he based his Confession of Faith on the Bible and the tradition of the first seven ecumenical councils. In 1923, he drafted the Eleven Great Principles of the Polish National Catholic Church (Wrodlowski, *Origins*, 214–226). He anticipated many of the reforms of the Second Vatican Council as he developed his theology. He spoke of the Church as "the great sacrament" of Christ's presence in this world. He elevated the Word of God to the position of sacrament. He anticipated the practice of the early Church in viewing baptism and confirmation as part of the initiation rites of the early Church. He instituted two types of confession, one for children and one for youth; by stressing the communal nature of reconciliation, he anticipated many of the later reforms of the Catholic Church itself (Wrodlowski, *Origins*, 214–226).

Hodur attempted throughout his life to effect a reconciliation with Protestantism. In 1914 he carried out a union with Lithuanian Old Catholics. He encouraged closer ties with Slavic Lutherans. In 1946 he effected intercommunion with the Episcopal Church of England (which included union with the Protestant Episcopal Church of America). It was resolved that "the relationship between the Churches is one of intercommunion . . . [and] implies that each believes the other to hold firmly all the essentials of the Christian faith ("First Joint Intercommunion Conference," Albany, NY,

1947). Intercommunion with the Episcopal Church brought the PNCC into closer ecumenical activity with other Protestant churches, and in 1948, the PNCC joined the World Council of Churches (Parot, "Hodur," 305–306).

At the time of his death in 1953, the Polish National Catholic Church administered to the needs of more than a quarter million believers, with laity controlling property in excess of $14 million. Missionary work, begun in Poland in 1919, had 229 parishes and a theological seminary in Cracow by the same year. Hodur himself has been variously described as a Marxist revolutionary and a naive opportunist (305–306). The truth may lie somewhere in between. Hodur's own peasant origins as well as his contact with priests like Fr. Stojalowski seemed to have contributed to his deep ethnic sensitivities. In the light of Vatican II, Hodur's theological, sacramental, and liturgical changes seem almost prophetic.

BIBLIOGRAPHY

Andrews, Theodore. *The Polish National Catholic Church in America and Poland.* New York: Macmillan, 1953.

Gallagher, John P. *A Century of History, the Diocese of Scranton, 1868–1968.* Scranton, PA: n.p., 1968.

Kantowicz, Edward R. *Polish-American Politics in Chicago, 1888–1940.* Chicago: University of Chicago Press, 1975.

Kuzniewski, Anthony J. "The Catholic Church in the Life of the Polish Americans." In *Poles in America: Bicentennial Essays*, edited by Frank Mocha. Stevens Point, WI: Worzalla Publishing Co., 1978.

———. *Faith and Fatherland: The Polish Church War in Wisconsin, 1896–1918.* Notre Dame: University of Notre Dame Press, 1973.

Nowe Drogi. Scranton, PA. (Pamphlet).

Parot, Joseph. "Francis Hodur." *Dictionary of American Biography.* Supp. 5. 1951–1955. New York: Charles Scribner's Sons.

———. *Polish Catholics in Chicago, 1850–1920.* Dekalb, IL: Northern Illinois University Press, 1981.

Thomas, William I., and Florian Znaniecki. *The Polish Peasant in Europe and America*, 2 vols. 2nd ed. New York: Octagon Books, 1974.

Wiktor, Jan. *Strzecha w cieniu chmur.* Warsaw, 1964.

Woods, Arthur E. *Hamtramck.* New Haven: Yale University Press, 1955.

Wrodlowski, Stephen. *The Origins and Growth of the Polish National Catholic Church.* Scranton, PA: Polish National Catholic Church, 1974.

Zawistowski, Theodore L. "The Polish National Catholic Church: An Acceptable Alternative." In *Poles in America: Bicentennial Essays*, edited by Frank Mocha. Stevens Point, WI: Worzalla Publishing Co., 1978.

Stephen Shaw

Anne Hutchinson
(1591–1643)

Anne Hutchinson, gifted with an extraordinary mind, intense spiritual passion, and remarkable charisma, arrived in Massachusetts in 1634. Like many Puritans, she had fled the "degenerate" English nation seeking the kingdom of God. Upon arrival, Hutchinson and her husband William established themselves among the leadership of New England society. Scarcely three years later, she was judged the primary disturber of consensual order, leader of a large number of Bostonians who challenged the colony's political, social, and ideological foundations. Nurtured by Minister John Cotton and supported by most Boston Church members, she had captivated the majority of the city's social and economic leaders. As these mobilized to oppose the colony's clergy, founding governor John Winthrop mustered all his political skill and resources to oust the Hutchinsonians from government, establish the clerical hegemony, and engineer the defeat of Hutchinson herself.

Wife of a prominent merchant, Anne Hutchinson easily found a respectable position among Boston's women, a place reinforced by her gifts as healer and midwife. Moreover, this daughter of learned clergyman Francis Marbury had been carefully educated, and her scriptural knowledge and theological sophistication were greatly admired. At some point, it is not known precisely when, Hutchinson instituted private religious meetings for Boston's women. Commonplace among English Puritans, such gatherings were both devotional and educational, an opportunity for women to continue their scriptural study and spiritual explorations. The natural leader in this venue, Hutchinson quickly moved beyond explicating ministers' sermons to delivering her own. Soon women brought their husbands; these meetings became so successful that Hutchinson held two each week, one for women only and one for both women and men. Hutchinson's enemies estimated the general attendance at 60 to 80 persons; that is, most of the town had gathered around her hearth.

By spring 1636, word of aberrant theology reached the clergy. The primary issue was the relationship between human endeavor and salvation. The Calvinist doctrine of predestination as espoused by Puritans led to the obvious conclusion that salvation lay completely in the hands of God. An individual could have no responsibility for achieving salvation because he or she was powerless to effect it. Only faith in Christ could justify the innately depraved soul before God, and faith was impossible except through divine grace. And because God is omnipotent, Calvinists argued that once offered, divine grace could not be refused; grace was, in fact, irresistible, and the saint could no more fall from heaven than the sinner could escape hell. Once grace was offered and, perforce, accepted, confirmation of justification came in the sanctification of the believer's behavior. In other words, a believer's gracious standing manifested itself in the saint's daily conduct.

Given the unconditionality of Christ's gifts of grace and faith, the Hutchinsonians (with Cotton) stressed the futility of any human action and the passivity of the believer in an absolute dependence upon God. Most New England clerics, however, found such arguments dangerous—such attitudes would lead inevitably to heresy, irreligion, and anarchy. While granting the arbitrary and unconditional nature of God's actions, these ministers also understood the anxiety of believers desperate to discern some sign of their own salvation; thus, they emphasized the hope that lay in sanctification. Since behavior provided some evidence of justification, it was important to be able to recognize sanctified conduct. Lectures on behavior would also benefit all saints who, imperfect until their triumph at death, must strive toward the glory of God.

The most intriguing direction that this preaching took was the idea that the potential saint could prepare for God's grace. Still affirming that no human effort could affect God's ultimate action, ministers nevertheless encouraged believers to study Scripture, attend sermons, guard their conduct, and pray so that they would be ready when divine grace came. Such preparatory efforts might have kept believers from feeling powerless when in the face of divine majesty, but the Hutchinsonians found in preparationism hints of salvation through works. Just as the clergy had labeled Hutchinsonians fanatical and antinomian, or anarchic, Hutchinson attacked the ministers for preaching a legalistic covenant of works.

Open conflict commenced in October 1636 with the arrival of John Wheelwright, Hutchinson's brother-in-law, a cleric in sympathy with Cotton and the Hutchinsonians. Although the clergy and Hutchinson had met privately to reconcile apparent differences, the Boston Church laity remained dissatisfied, challenging Pastor Wilson by voting to call Wheelwright as a third minister. By invoking a technicality, Winthrop derailed this effort, while Wilson further irritated his congregants with a polemical sermon decrying the divided condition of the churches and pointing to the rise of new, dangerous opinions. The General Court voted to hold a fast day to beg forgiveness and attempt to heal the breaches.

At Cotton's invitation, John Wheelwright preached the fast-day sermon, further exacerbating divisions. Wheelwright devoted much of his sermon to denying that sanctification could be seen as evidence of growing justification. He further asserted that God was absent from New England and implied that any one who disagreed with his vision of salvation was the Antichrist. So encouraged, Hutchinsonians took their struggle into outlying towns, disrupting sermons and publicly challenging the orthodoxy of preachers. They even refused to serve in the militia organized to assist Connecticut in its war against the Pequots because the militia's chaplain was the questionable John Wilson.

That March the colonial legislature, the General Court, considered the problems. Strong as the Hutchinsonians were, the movement was mostly confined to Boston, and most of the deputies, representing outlying towns, had wearied of the hectoring of the Hutchinsonians. The Court approved Wilson's speech and found Wheelwright guilty of sedition and contempt. A minority in the assembly protested, and the Boston Church petitioned on Wheelwright's behalf, but neither challenge was admitted. Also, in light of the chaos afflicting Boston, the Court moved the next meeting, including colony elections, to Newtown, effectively disfranchising Bostonians, who could ill afford the travel. Ignoring a petition presented on behalf of Wheelwright, Deputy Governor Winthrop and his party, now the majority, called for elections, and while Governor Vane and the Hutchinsonians refused to participate, the rest elected Winthrop governor, replaced two Hutchinsonian magistrates, and denied any office to Henry Vane.

Through the next six months, Winthrop worked to solidify his position and reconstruct social and religious hegemony. The General Court enacted a law that forbade any new person from staying in Massachusetts more than three weeks unless approved by the Court, thus barring Hutchinsonian immigrants from the colony. The Court also passed resolutions explicitly addressing the activities of Hutchinsonians: They condemned congregants' efforts to dispute doctrine with the preacher; restricted questions to information; and advised that such questions were rarely justified. Congregants were forbidden to forsake their churches for any difference of opinion that was not fundamental. Of greatest import, the Court banned Hutchinson's meetings, granting that while "women might meet (some few together) to pray and edify one another; yet such a set assembly, (as was then in practice at Boston,) where sixty or more did meet every week, and one woman (in a prophetical way, by resolving questions of doctrine, and expounding scripture) took upon her the whole exercise, was agreed to be disorderly, and without rule" (Winthrop, *Journal*, 1: 234).

The magistrates then called a clerical conference to address doctrinal errors, undoubtedly hoping to calm the dissent of Cotton, effect a theological consensus, and bring the laity to accept this orthodoxy. Whether or not Cotton and the ministers had worked out their differences, many of the errors named dealt explicitly with the relationship between sanctification and justification. Additionally, many errors addressed the nature of faith, spiritual assurances, and revelation, pointing up a hazardous undercurrent swirling amidst the challenges posed by the Hutchinsonians.

Having achieved a semblance of theological agreement, and having denied settlement to dangerous strangers (i.e., Hutchinsonian sympathizers), Winthrop needed to rid the colony of dangerous residents. Henry Vane gratifyingly left in disillusionment, as did several merchants and their families. Wheelwright, self-righteous and unrepentant, was banished, while leading Hutchinsonians were systematically disarmed, disfranchised, fined, and/or banished. Then, at last, Winthrop turned to the source of the dissension. On November 7, Mistress Hutchinson, "the breeder and nourisher of all these distempers . . . a woman of haughty and fierce carriage, of a nimble wit and active spirit," was brought to trial (Winthrop, *Short Story*, 262–263).

The trial lasted scarcely two days, yet during those two days the essence of the conflict became startlingly clear in the purposeful charges of the Court and Hutchinson's impressive self-defense. Unable to produce irrefutable evidence to support their accusations or scriptural evidence to support their position, the magistrates found themselves seeking help from the ministers who had enjoyed private, pastoral conversations with her. This, in turn, threatened to replace theological mire with legal, procedural disputes. Then, suddenly and unpredictably, Hutchinson told her own story, a story that would end in her banishment.

This incredible trial revealed Hutchinson in all her formidable intellectual prowess. For one and a half days she ran exegetical circles around her opponents. They quoted Scripture; she quoted back. They interpreted a verse against her; she responded with a second text and a valid interpretation. Winthrop first charged her with breaking the Fifth Commandment because she countenanced those who had signed a seditious petition on behalf of Wheelwright. She noted that she might entertain the petitioners as children of God without countenancing their sin. As a woman, Hutchinson had signed nothing, so the Court had no evidence against her. After a quick verbal thrust and parry, a frustrated Winthrop asserted that she did adhere to the petitioners, she did endeavor to promote their faction, and thus she dishonored the magistrates—her parents, breaking the Fifth Commandment. Furthermore, the Court did "not mean to discourse with those of your sex" ("Examination," 314).

Winthrop next turned to the equally dangerous subject of her private meetings. Scripture clearly forbade women to teach publicly, but, answered Hutchinson, her home was not public. She cited texts proclaiming the duty of elder women to instruct the younger; members of the Court retorted that she was known to instruct men. She responded that at the mixed meetings only men spoke, although she believed that if a man came to her, she was permitted to instruct him as Priscilla had guided Apollo. Yet again, Winthrop had no evidence with which to challenge Hutchinson's statements. When Winthrop refused to acknowledge that her biblical citations provided a guiding rule, she asked whether she must "shew my name written therein?" In a second display of authority, Winthrop announced that the meetings must end because he said so. "We are your judges, and not you ours and we must compel you to it." Hutchinson acquiesced. "If it please you by authority to put it down I will freely let you for I am subject to your authority" (Winthrop, *Short Story*, 269; "Examination," 316).

Nevertheless, this did not satisfy the magistrates. As Deputy Governor Dudley complained, three years before, the colony had been at peace, but from the moment Hutchinson landed, she was the fount of great disturbances. They wanted her gone, and to this end, Winthrop turned to her criticism of the clergy. When she compared the clergy unfavorably to Cotton, she undermined the colony's primary arbiters of divine authority. When she argued that the clergy did not preach the true pathway to salvation, she implied that they were, in fact, beneath the regard of the ordinary congregant. Obviously, such opinions had to be curtailed and condemned. Once again, though, Winthrop had to prove that Hutchinson had in fact delivered such opinions.

Magistratess had certainly heard some Hutchinsonians on this subject; Stephen Greensmyth had been fined £40 for asserting that all but three ministers taught a covenant of works. And the ministers had undoubtedly told Winthrop about some of Hutchinson's statements. Nevertheless, the magistrates had apparently never heard Hutchinson so speak, for they did not testify against her. Instead, Dudley and Winthrop opened a third potentially fruitless dialogue, accusing Hutchinson of making statements that she then denied. Finally, Hugh Peters, followed by other clergy, attempted to rescue the situation by reporting what Hutchinson had said at the conference held the previous December.

Here the Court appeared to approach higher ground, for several clergy were willing to give their accounts. Peters, who hoped that he and his fellow clerics "may not be thought to come as informers against the gentlewoman," proceeded to inform against her. He claimed that Hutchinson had described wide differences between most of the clergy and Cotton, that Cotton "preaches the covenant of grace and you the covenant of works." Hutchinson had discounted their spirituality, arguing that such preaching signified an absence of the spirit. Cleric after cleric rose and spoke to his own memory of her statements, and while some were relatively mild and hopeful and others almost vindictive, their testimonies overlapped in impressive corroboration. Hutchinson challenged these accounts, at one point asking Wilson for his notes of the conference ("Examination," 319–326; Winthrop, *Short Story*, 269–270).

The following morning, Hutchinson brilliantly redirected and enlivened the Court by demanding that clergymen testifying against her swear an oath. Already this evidence did not sit easily, for the conference had been private, and in testifying against her, the clergy were betraying a confidence. Now claiming that the ministers were both accusers and witnesses, she invoked standard legal procedure in order to reinforce her own denial of their accounts. She had refreshed her own memory with Wilson's notes and would call witnesses to support her own recollection. First, however, the original testimony must be taken upon oath, a position that many representatives supported. The obvious affront had its predictable effect, and Winthrop and Dudley ardently defended the sincerity of the ministers. Yet amidst the furor were sown seeds of doubt. The conference had occurred almost a year before, and as Simon Bradstreet, a clerical supporter, argued, "Mrs. Hutchinson, these are but circumstances and adjuncts to the cause, admit they should mistake you in your speeches you would make them to sin if you urge them to swear." Although Bradstreet implied that his concern grew out of the possibility of minor errors concerning peripheral matters, the specter of major memory errors appeared. Moreover, the clergy proved reluctant to swear, lending credence to Hutchinson's challenges ("Examination," 326–333; Winthrop, *Short Story*, 270).

Of three witnesses called in her behalf, John Coggeshall was frightened into silence by Peters, and Church Elder Thomas Leverett proved able to utter only three sentences before he was challenged by Winthrop. But the third witness delivered his troublesome testimony in full. John Cotton had not wanted to testify, but his memory of the conference agreed with Hutchinson's. He regretted that he and his colleagues were compared, but he did recall mild disagreements concerning the covenant of grace and the seal of the spirit, and, he gently reminded them, he had supported Hutchinson's position. Moreover, the difference was not then "so ill taken as it is [now]." Finally, he declared that she did not say they were under a covenant of works, nor that they did preach a covenant of works. Despite further challenges, questions, and objections, Cotton did not countermand his testimony ("Examination," 332–337).

Hutchinson chose this moment to proclaim her vision. Turning to her own spiritual conversion, Hutchinson recounted her early religious doubts, her ultimate dependence upon God, and God's response to her pleas. She had become "more choice" in selecting a minister, for God had led her to distinguish the voices of truth ("Examination," 336–337).

Mr. Nowell: How do you know that that was the spirit?

Mrs. H.: How did Abraham know that it was God that bid him offer his son, being a breach of the sixth commandment?

Dep. Gov.: By an immediate voice.

Mrs. H.: So to me by an immediate revelation.

Dep. Gov.: How! an immediate revelation.

Mrs. H.: By the voice of his own spirit to my soul.

Hutchinson compared herself to the prophet Daniel. As God had delivered Daniel from the lion's den, so had God promised that he would protect and deliver her from her adversaries. Pouncing upon her testimony, the accusers pursued this question of revelation. They believed that any claim to a miraculous deliverance was blasphemy, for the age of miracles had long past. By the end of the proceedings, the overwhelming majority of the Court would agree with Winthrop's disingenuous conclusion: "Pass by all that hath been said formerly and her own speeches have been ground enough for us to proceed upon" ("Examination," 345).

Yet if she really had condemned herself, why did the examination continue? After she had proclaimed her revelations, new indictments began, and witnesses testified to previous prophetic declarations. Nevertheless, the weight and character of these testimonies precipitated not immediate censure but a prolonged debate upon the nature of revelation itself. Perhaps the equation of revelation with blasphemy was neither automatic nor obvious. When asked to denounce Hutchinson, Cotton refused, presenting, instead, an abstract discourse upon the two sorts of revelation: miraculous and providential. While an expectation of the miraculous would represent a delusion, any soul might have a justifiable faith in special providence. Hutchinson reiterated throughout her conviction in a special providence, while her opponents accused her of prophesying the miraculous. As many became angry and confused at Cotton's discourse, Winthrop closed the debate, "Mr. Cotton is not called to answer to any thing," yet he could not silence everyone. As William Coddington said, "[T]he spirit of God witnesses with our spirits, and there is no truth in scripture but God bears witness to it by his spirit." Winthrop may have gloated over Hutchinson's self-destruction, but the trial was not over. Court delegates returned to the earlier charges and the lack of sworn testimony or substantial evidence. In the end, three clergymen testified, under oath; she was then convicted and banished ("Examination," 338–345; cit. 343, 345).

While most scholars have judged her declarations as weakness, one might as easily see this as a moment of strength. Hutchinson seemed to revel in her prophetic moment as the Court stood riveted upon her words. The magistrates and the clergy wanted, needed, for these revelations to be discounted, and several witnesses spoke critically of her previous invocations of revelations. The accusers tried to rally Cotton against her, but he would not follow. I suspect that rather than provide the evidence against her, the power gathered in her speech frightened Winthrop, warning him of just how necessary it was to remove her. He unwittingly revealed this anxiety in his own account:

> Mistris *Hutchinson* having thus freely and fully discovered her selfe, the Court . . . did observe a speciall providence of God, that . . . her owne mouth should deliver her into the power of the Court, as guilty of that which all suspected her for, but were not furnished with proofe sufficient to proceed against her, for here she hath manifested, that her opinions and practise have been the cause of al our disturbances, & that she walked by such a rule as cannot stand with the peace of any State. (Winthrop, *Short Story*, 274)

Long suspected of spiritual charisma grounded in her prophetic revelations, Hutchinson undermined the authority of secular and sacred officers. At last she had openly asserted that power, for which her opponents were profoundly grateful, but they remained unable to convince Cotton or all Court members that her claims were blasphemous. Winthrop and the clergy returned to charges of sedition, winning her banishment with the acquiescence of all but three participants.

Because she was sentenced at the beginning of winter, the Court extended a questionable mercy in permitting Hutchinson to remain in the colony until spring but demanded that she reside in the home of an unsympathetic cleric. While many of her followers, including her husband, moved on to their new home, Hutchinson became the unhappy focus of extensive clerical counsel. Supposedly interested in her repentance and ultimate salvation, the clergy began an emotional and intellectual barrage that explored a range of theological questions and dicta that had been raised in neither of the 1636 conferences nor in her examination before the General Court. All of this material was brought forward to her final examinations before the church.

On 15 March 1638, the Church of Boston, depleted by the emigration, voluntary and otherwise, of its many Hutchinsonian members, heard charges against Hutchinson. The investigation focused on her beliefs concerning the immortality of the soul, the resurrection of the body, and the union of the individual spirit to Christ. None of these questions had been raised the previous November, as Hutchinson insistently noted, but they became the center of this examination. In the record, Hutchinson seems a neophyte, working out her beliefs with pastors, but in a public forum determined to condemn her. The preliminary church trial ended predictably in the membership's dissatisfaction with her responses and a sentence of admonition. Interestingly, the elders requested that Cotton deliver the verbal chastisement as the pastor who commanded Hutchinson's highest regard and might therefore have the greatest impact. Unspoken but of greater import would be the effect of Cotton's denunciation upon the congregation. As the instrument of clergy and elders, Cotton's alignment with their position was fixed.

Throughout the church trial, the sexualized language of the accusers reflected a central subtext. In his own account, Winthrop argued that as a midwife and healer Hutchinson took advantage of women during childbirth or illness and "insinuated" herself into their hearts. Having seduced women, she then looked toward these women as fellow seductresses who would ensnare their own husbands (Winthrop, *Short Story*, 262–263; Weld, Preface to *Short Story*, 205–206). During the church trial itself, several congregants concluded that her views would lead people to promiscuity and chaos. One asked whether she held "that foule, groce, filthye and abhominable opinion held by Familists, *of the Communitie of Weomen*," for it was commonly believed that Familists practiced free love. Cotton assured her that from just one of her opinions—her denial of the resurrection of the body (a new accusation raised at the church trial)—"all promiscuus and filthie cominge togeather of men and Woemen without Distinction or Relation of Marriage, will necessarily follow . . . more dayngerous Evells and filthie Unclenes . . . than you doe not Imagine or conceave." He also questioned her marital life: "And though I have not herd, nayther do I thinke, you have bine unfaythfull to your Husband . . . *yet that will follow upon it*" ("Report of the Trial," 362, 372).

The following week, having seriously reconsidered the theological questions, Hutchinson seemed to acknowledge her errors. Trying to clarify her expressions and remove any doubts regarding her beliefs, Hutchinson admitted that she may have uttered dangerous words and extravagant phrases open to the misconstruction that the church placed upon them. However, she declared, she had never believed such heresies; her expressions were in error but not her judgment. Still, she accepted responsibility for her errors and admitted she had slighted the ministers. Despite this promising start, the caliber and sincerity of her repentance were challenged. Noting that she repented only those errors discovered after November and left untouched those doctrines raised at her state trial, Thomas Dudley declared that repentance was not in her countenance. Finding her remorse insincere, the congregation had no problem reaching judgment. The theological issues were murky, her continued adherence to her revelations was troubling, but, happily, Hutchinson's insincerity made her a liar. Because she had troubled the church with her errors, upheld her revelations, and had "made a Lye," she was excommunicated.

Upon leaving Boston, Hutchinson joined family and followers in Newport, Rhode Island. During her time there, Hutchinson experienced a disastrous "pregnancy," possibly the growth and expulsion of a tumor.

Winthrop would later describe this as the birth of some 30 monsters, representative of the 30 or more heretical beliefs she had promulgated. After her husband's death in 1640, Hutchinson and her seven youngest children moved to Long Island, where, in 1643, all but the youngest child were killed during an Indian uprising.

In their response to Hutchinson, the sacred and civil authority utilized state and church courts to rid the colony of her person and to discredit her intellect, integrity, and spirituality. Criticisms of her private meetings, of women teaching men, of her "haughty" carriage indicate the centrality of gender to the leadership's concerns. Winthrop was forced to engage a woman who refused to accept a subordinate position passively; refused to limit herself to the role of wife, housekeeper, and mother; and refused to remain silent. In proclaiming her right to teach others, in essence to speak, Hutchinson challenged the assumptions of the social order. The personal political battles did challenge Winthrop's power and the society's stability, while the theological disagreements did undermine efforts toward religious unity. But the activism of Hutchinson, buttressed as it was by extraordinary spiritual charisma, represented a female power that threatened to overturn the most basic inequality structuring the social order. For Winthrop, the extraordinary means he used to defeat Hutchinson were justified. Hutchinson's violent death and her birthing of 30 monsters were signs that could be (and were) read by Winthrop, and his cohort, as divine vindication, a reaffirmation of Winthrop as righteous magistrate and the patriarchal order as divinely countenanced. The tragedy of Hutchinson's last five years stood as the voice of God.

BIBLIOGRAPHY

Barker-Benfield, Ben. "Anne Hutchinson and the Puritan Attitude toward Women." *Feminist Studies* 1 (1972): 65–96.

Battis, Emery. *Saints and Sectaries: Anne Hutchinson and the Antinomian Controversy in the Massachusetts Bay Colony.* Chapel Hill: University of North Carolina Press, 1962.

Caldwell, Patricia. "The Antinomian Language Controversy." *Harvard Theological Review* 69 (1976): 345–367.

Erikson, Kai T. *Wayward Puritans: A Study in the Sociology of Deviance.* New York: John Wiley & Sons, 1966. 33–107.

"The Examination of Mrs. Anne Hutchinson at the Court at Newtown," 1637. In Hall, David D. ed. *The Antinomian Controversy, 1636–1638: A Documentary History.* Middletown, CT: Wesleyan University Press, 1968. 311–349.

Foster, Stephen. "New England and the Challenge of Heresy, 1630–1660: The Puritan Crisis in Transatlantic Perspective." *William and Mary Quarterly* 38 (1981): 624–660.

Hall, David D., ed. *The Antinomian Controversy, 1636–1638: A Documentary History.* Middletown, CT: Wesleyan University Press, 1968.

Koehler, Lyle. "The Case of the American Jezebels: Anne Hutchinson and Female Agitation during the Years of the Antinomian Turmoil, 1636–1640." *William and Mary Quarterly* 31 (1974): 55–78.

Lang, Amy Shrager. *Prophetic Woman: Anne Hutchinson and the Problem of Dissent in the Literature of New England*. Berkeley: University of California Press, 1987.

Miller, Perry. *The New England Mind: From Colony to Province*. Cambridge: Harvard University Press, 1956. 59–81.

Morgan, Edmund S. *The Puritan Dilemma: The Story of John Winthrop*. Boston: Little, Brown, 1958. 134–154.

Pettit, Norman. *The Heart Prepared: Grace and Conversion in Puritan Spiritual Life*. New Haven: Yale University Press, 1966. 125–157.

"A Report of the Trial of Mrs. Anne Hutchinson before the Church in Boston," 1638. In Hall, David D., ed. *The Antinomian Controversy, 1636–1638: A Documentary History*. Middletown, CT: Wesleyan University Press, 1968. 349–388.

Rutman, Darrett B. *Winthrop's Boston: Portrait of a Puritan, 1630–1649*. New York: Norton, 1965. 135–163.

Williams, Selma R. *Divine Rebel: The Life of Anne Marbury Hutchinson*. New York: Holt, Rinehart and Winston, 1981.

Winthrop, John. *A Short Story of the Rise, Reign, and Ruine of the Antinomians, Familists & Libertines*. With a Preface by Thomas Weld. London, 1644. In Hall, David D., ed. *The Antinomian Controversy, 1636–1638: A Documentary History*. Middletown, CT: Wesleyan University Press, 1968. 199–310.

———. *Winthrop's Journal "History of New England" 1630–1649*. Edited by James Kendall Hosmer. 2 vols. New York: Barnes & Noble, 1908.

Marilyn J. Westerkamp

Sonia Johnson
(1936–)

Sonia Harris Johnson, housewife, mother of four, and church organist, was known to few outside her family and close friends until she drew major media attention in November 1979 after receiving a summons to court in the Church of Jesus Christ of Latter-day Saints (Mormon). She was officially excommunicated from the church on 5 December 1979.

The fifth-generation Mormon was a leader in exposing the church's covert politics against the proposed equal rights amendment (ERA). However, this was not mentioned in the letter of summons and subsequent trial.

She was one of the founders and chief movers behind the small Mormons for ERA organization. She formed the organization with longtime friend Hazel Rigby, Maida Withers, and Teddie Wood in 1978 after the Mormon Church began to organize behind closed doors to defeat the proposed Twenty-seventh Amendment to the U.S. Constitution.

Sonia was born in 1936 in Malad, Idaho.

> The February night in 1936 when the doctor nearly let my mother bleed to death after my birth, Mom and Dad had driven the nearly snow-blocked roads to the small town hospital in Malad, Idaho. At that time, they were living in Washakie, a Shoshone Indian reservation just over the state line in Utah. They were school teachers there grateful to the Lord to be working for the government during the depression, teaching and feeding the "Lamanites," as Indians are called by Mormons. Dad was collecting Shoshone Indian legends for his masters thesis, while Mom did most of the teaching as well as preparing the daily lunch the school was required by law to give the Indian youngsters. Two children had already preceded me into the family: Joyce, aged nine, and Paul, four. (Johnson, *From Housewife to Heretic*, 66)

Soon after her birth, the family moved to Ferron, Utah. From there, they moved to Preston, Idaho, when she was 3. Her father taught high school seminary for the Mormon Church. Mormon high school students study church history and the Scriptures in seminary. In the summer of 1948 when she was 12, the family moved to Logan, Utah. By this time, the Harris children numbered five.

Soon after, she became organist for the junior Sunday school in the Logan First Ward and kept that position for years. A Mormon ward is roughly equivalent to a parish in other churches.

In the summer of 1958, while a student at Utah State University, she began dating classmate Richard Johnson, a stormy-looking "Eastern" from Wisconsin. Her summer school roommate told her she was going to marry "that guy," and the response from Sonia Harris was, "Don't be ridiculous, he's not even a member of the church" (2).

By October, Rick had seen the missionaries and was baptized in November. They thought of marrying in December, "but besides my wanting a temple marriage—one in which we would be married for eternity as well as for our lifetimes, and which would not be possible until he had been a member of the church for at least a year—we weren't getting along well all of the time" (28).

The romance was on and off for the next few months. They decided to marry in August 1959. They were married by Bishop Heber Sharp, one of their psychology professors, on 21 August 1959, at her parents' home in Logan.

Rick finished his master's degree, and in February 1960, Sonia, Rick, and her 15-year-old brother, Mark, went to western Samoa to teach for the church. "Rick taught math, I taught English, and Mark—whom we affectionately called 'Pubert' because he was in the throes of adolescence—was in both our classes" (40).

After their return to Utah, eight months after their marriage, they went to the temple for eternity. "Years later, he told me casually one day, 'It's a good thing we didn't go to the temple when we were first married. I wasn't ready for it. I'd have left the church' " (41).

The Johnsons immediately went back to school. This time, they entered the University of Minnesota in Minneapolis. Rick began working on his Ph.D. in educational psychology. Sonia took graduate classes in the English Department. While at the University of Minnesota, they became friends with Hazel and Ron Rigby, both graduates of Brigham Young University, who were graduate students there also.

The Johnsons' first child, Eric, was born in July 1963. Rick finished his Ph.D. and accepted a teaching position at Rutgers University in New Brunswick, New Jersey. Sonia received her master's degree there and completed her Ed.D. dissertation hours before giving birth to her only daughter, Kari, in 1965.

The third child, Marc, was born in Palo Alto, California, in 1967 where she was teaching a night-school class. Rick was teaching at Stanford. The next few years, the family lived in Korea, then in Malaysia where Noel Harris was born.

> Then in Palo Alto, where we had returned from Malaysia in 1974, Rick began to chafe at his job; he was also finding other women attractive, he told me, and this worried him. So he found a job we could do together: going about the country for the U.S. Office of Education, teaching educators how to evaluate their Title I projects. We bought a motor home, put all the kids in it, and set off for the next year. Twenty-one bicentennial states, hundreds of hours of teaching our own children and of feelings of severe strain on our marriage later, we came to Virginia. On Kari's eleventh birthday, June 25, 1976, we bought the house in which the seeds of feminism, planted long ago in Logan and watered and cultivated along the way by various repressive church programs and edicts, finally sprouted. "Hello Virginia, Sterling Park Ward, ERA, feminism, and the new world!" (88)

After arriving in Virginia, she phoned Hazel and Ron Rigby, friends from the University of Minnesota graduate school days. They had kept in touch for 15 years but had not seen each other during that time. After her first phone conversation in 15 years with Hazel, she turned to Rick and said, "Something has happened to Hazel, she sounds shocking!" (89).

Sonia, then 42, had just spoken to her first feminist. Both her Mormon background and the fact they had spent almost ten years outside the country had kept her from learning much about the women's movement going on in the United States. She also knew little of anything about the proposed equal rights amendment. She did not know that Utah members of the conservative John Birch Society were fighting against the amendment in 1973. She didn't read the *Church News* editorial on 11 January 1975 opposing the amendment. She didn't read the January 14 article in the *Salt Lake Tribune* quoting a member of the Utah legislature saying, "It is my Church, and as a bishop, I'm not going to vote against its wishes" (*MERA News-letter*, February 1983, 5).

A month prior to moving to Sterling, Virginia, near Washington, D.C., the *Washington Evening Star* printed a page-one interview with then–General Relief Society President Barbara Smith, "A Mormon Tells Why She Opposes ERA."

In the fall of 1976, a few months after the Johnsons moved to Virginia, the small band of Mormons for ERA marched in their first parade. In Alexandria, Virginia, they and their children joined the parade to commemorate early women's suffrage.

In 1977, Mormon Church activity against the ERA began to intensify.

Jan. 8: Apostle Boyd K. Packer spoke at a rally in Pocatello, Idaho, to rescind ERA. He was on the platform and also attended a press conference with Allen Larsen, Speaker of the Idaho House of Representatives and also a Mormon Stake President. ERA was rescinded a few days later by a simple majority. ERA had originally passed in the Idaho legislature with a ⅔ majority.

Jan. 15: Relief Society President Barbara Smith gives anti-ERA speech in Coeur D'Alene, Idaho and strongly urges people to rescind ERA in Idaho.

Feb. 1: Utah Senator Jake Garn inserts anti-ERA speech of Apostle Boyd K. Packer into Congressional Record (S. 1980–19882). Packer's speech was given in South Carolina.

March–April: Florida Mormons lobbied heavily in Tallahassee against ERA.

April 24: Oakton Virginia Stake President Clifford Cummings gave anti-ERA speech in Sterling Park, Va. Ward fireside.

June 4: Relief Society President Barbara Smith gives anti-ERA speech in Newport Beach, Ca. She is on platform with Phyllis Schlafly and she praises Schlafly.

June 24: Approximately 14,000 Mormon women and men crowd the International Women's Year Conference in Salt Lake City. They vote down all proposals including ERA and world peace.

July 9: IWY conference in Hawaii was taken over by anti-ERA Mormons. Anti-ERA slate was elected to national meeting in Houston. Hawaii was the first state to ratify ERA. Hawaii also has a state ERA.

July 8–10: Mormons attempt to take over IWY in Ellensburg, Washington. Mormon men with walkie-talkies instructed the women on meetings to attend and how to vote. Mormons are two percent of Washington state population.

Nov. 4: BYU Professor Stan Taylor gives anti-ERA speech at Oakton Va. Stake Center. (*MERA Newsletter*, February 1983, 5)

By August of 1977, some of this church anti-ERA information was known to the small group of Mormon ERA activists in Virginia. They later learned more of it when Sonia exploded into the headlines because other people began calling and writing from all over the country. They, with their husbands and children, formed a small group and marched down Pennsylvania Avenue under the name "Mormons for the ERA" in the women's equality day parade.

By January 1978, the small loose group of Mormons for ERA decided to actually form an organization, and Sonia was chosen president. She had a part-time teaching job but was basically a homemaker, while the others, Hazel, mother of one, Maida, mother of four, and Teddie, mother of two, were working full-time and raising children. Teddie was divorced, but the others were married.

On 26 May 1978, freshman Utah Senator Orrin Hatch inserted the official Mormon position against ERA and the extension into the *Congressional Record* (S. 8441–8442). Senator Hatch went on to insert the statement of the First Presidency of the Church of Jesus Christ of Latter-day Saints opposing ratification of the equal rights amendment issued 22 October 1976.

> From its beginnings, The Church of Jesus Christ of Latter-day Saints has affirmed the exalted role of woman in our society.
>
> In 1842, when women's organizations were little known, the Prophet Joseph Smith established the women's organization of the Church, the Relief Society, as a companion body of the Priesthood. The Relief Society continues to function today as a vibrant world-wide organization aimed at strengthening motherhood and broadening women's learning and involvement in religious, compassionate, cultural, educational, and community pursuits.
>
> In Utah, where our Church is headquartered, women received the right to vote in 1870, fifty years before the Nineteenth Amendment to the Constitution granted the right nationally.
>
> There have been injustices to women before the law and in society generally. These we deplore.
>
> There are additional rights to which women are entitled.
>
> However, we firmly believe that the Equal Rights Amendment is not the answer.
>
> While the motives of its supporters may be praiseworthy, ERA as a blanket attempt to help women could indeed bring them far more restraints and repressions. We fear it will even stifle many God-given feminine instincts.
>
> It would strike at the family, humankind's basic institution. ERA would bring ambiguity and possibly invite extensive litigation.
>
> Passage of ERA, some legal authorities contend, could nullify many accumulated benefits to woman in present statutes.
>
> We recognize men and women as equally important before the Lord, but with differences biologically, emotionally, and in other ways.
>
> ERA, we believe, does not recognize these differences. There are better means for giving women and men the rights they deserve. ("Opposition to ERA Time Extension," 15666–15667)

Prior to this point, the small group of Mormons for ERA had sat around at their potluck suppers and talked on the phone, grumbling about the church statement against ERA, but they had done little outside of personal support and some marches for the proposed amendment.

In June 1978, Washington, D.C. area public communications director Dale Ensign concluded a regional meeting by giving out the names of the members of Congress who were on the fence about the ERA extension. He encouraged everyone in the room to contact these members of Congress and lobby against the extension (*MERA Newsletter*, February 1983, 5).

When Sonia learned of this meeting, she went into action. She and the others decided it was time to do something. The first letter was sent to Congress. The organization didn't even have a letterhead. Twenty names were on the letter of supporters all over the country. They didn't have time to send it around to get signatures, so the names were typed.

The small group again marched in the ERA extension parade in July 1978.

> In July of 1978, the year I was converted heart and soul to the Equal Rights Amendment, we marched, one hundred thousand of us, for an extension of time to ratify it, seven years having proved too little time for such a revolutionary concept as legal equality to be properly understood by the country. Knowing that time limits imposed by Congress upon amendments are arbitrarily chosen and not constitutionally mandated, we felt confident that an extension would not violate our basic American document. On the hottest day of that summer, about twenty of us marched under the Mormons for ERA banner—and no one who ever saw that banner ever forgot it. (Johnson, *From Housewife to Heretic*, 121)

The extension passed the U.S. House of Representatives and was in the hands of Senator Birch Bayh (D–Indiana). As chair of the Senate Subcommittee on Constitutional Rights, he asked his staff to put together a religious panel for a series of hearings he was holding on the ERA extension. One of the senator's staffers remembered seeing the banner in the parade and began making phone calls.

Sonia agreed to testify and spend the next week praying and preparing for the five-minute testimony. On the panel with her were Joan Martin, a black Presbyterian minister from New York, representing the National Council of Churches and the Religious Committee for the ERA, Judith Hertz, representing the National Federation of Jewish Temple Sisterhoods, and Father William Callahan, a Catholic priest.

Because she had only recently become political, she was unaware that Senator Hatch was a member of this subcommittee and would question her after her testimony. Being alerted to the agenda, the senator and his staff notified other Mormons in the Washington area who opposed the proposed amendment, and many were in the hearing room.

Reporters in the hearing room woke up when the senator began questioning Johnson. "He began innocuously enough. You couldn't have foreseen that he was about to found Mormons for ERA on a national scale. In my journal, I have it recorded like this: 'It is implied by your testimony that you're more intelligent than other Mormon women, and that if they were all as intelligent as you, they would all support the Equal Rights Amendment.' And then he banged his fist on the table in angry emphasis and shouted, 'Now that's an insult to my wife!' " (135).

United Press International (UPI) reporter Cheryl Arvidson reported in articles that appeared all over the country on 5 August 1978, including the *Washington Post* and *Salt Lake Tribune*, that

> Sen. Orrin Hatch, R–Utah, a member of the Church of Jesus Christ of Latter-day Saints, clashed Friday with a woman of that faith who claimed a substantial number of female members are opposing the church's mandated opposition to the Equal Rights Amendment.
>
> She questioned how Mormon leaders, in their official statement opposing the ERA, can talk about the "exalted role of woman in our society" and yet follow policies in the church that push women into secondary positions.
>
> "Where equality does not even pertain, the word 'exalted' is a mockery," she said. "One wonders if the leaders of the church would gladly exchange their sex and become so exalted." (UPI, 5 August 1978)

Johnson was asked by Subcommittee chairman Senator Birch Bayh "whether she expected difficulty within the Mormon church because of her strong statements on behalf of the ERA." "I hope there won't be," she replied. "So do I," Bayh said (UPI, 4 August 1979).

Teddie Wood sent Johnson's testimony with an affidavit from Hazel Rigby to all the General Authorities of the church. "In her statement, Hazel recounted how the Mormon anti-ERA women who besieged me afterward felt I should not have made 'it' a Mormon issue, and how I replied that the church had made it a Mormon issue by choosing to publish their opposition widely, in the Congressional Record, for example" (Johnson, *From Housewife to Heretic*, 137).

"In the Salt Lake Tribune of August 19, ten Mormon women signed their names to this letter: 'Sen. Orrin Hatch is wrong in assuming that only 1/10th of 1 percent of Mormon women support ERA. The names listed below belong to a segment of Mormon women that are not afraid to sign their names in the support of the Equal Rights Amendment. We urge other LDS [Latter-day Saint] women who share our views to step forward and do the same' " (143).

The hearing brought unexpected publicity, and Sonia began to receive mail from other pro-ERA Mormons around the country, and the small group started expanding. "Mormons all over the country who had been suffering under the conviction that they were the only members of the church who support the ERA (which says volumes about how little one dares communicate with others in the church on this issue) had read one of the wire stories about Hatch and me, had thought, with boundless relief, 'Now there are two of us!' " (151).

During the fall of 1978, the church stepped up its political activities against the proposed amendment. The church officially organized against it in Virginia on November 8. "Gordon Hinckley, one of the twelve apostles and head of the Special Affairs Committee, which is the political action arm of the church, instructed two regional representatives in the Washington DC, area, Julian Lowe and Don Ladd, to organize the Mormon women there into an anti-ERA lobbying coalition" (164).

During the initial organization meeting November 8, to which all women in the Oakton Stake were invited to attend, "Dapper little Bob Beers, Mormon political action coordinator in Virginia for Schlafly's Stop ERA, contributed this gem: 'If you go to your state senator and say that he should be against the Equal Rights Amendment because the prophet is against it, you are going to get nowhere. That may be why we are against it, but when you are trying to convince a legislator to do something, you better talk his language, not yours' " (166).

After the LDS Citizens Coalition organizational meeting, Sonia, Hazel, and Maida met with Regional Representative Lowe. "We urged him to be aboveboard about the whole thing, to send out a press release right away announcing the formation of the coalition and informing the public that it was a church-sponsored, church-organized, church-financed, and church-directed political action committee" (171).

"At our meeting with Julian Lowe at his home, when we urged him to keep the church honest by informing Virginians of its political organization and activities, he let us know that the church was not going to make this activity public through press releases or in any other manner. It was at that point that we told him, portentously as it turned out, 'President Lowe, if you don't tell, we will' " (174).

The LDS Citizens Coalition was organized, and Beverly Campbell, a professional public relations woman, was selected to chair it by the male leaders. The coalition printed brochures, printed "concerns sheets," held meetings, had petitions signed, and lobbied in Richmond—activities of typical lobbying organizations. However, when the deadline arrived for lobbying groups to report to the secretary of the Commonwealth of Virginia lobbying expenses, if they exceeded $100, for the recently concluded session of the Virginia General Assembly, the LDS Citizens Coalition did not file a report.

Washington Star staff writer Marcia Ruth Fram wrote on 6 March 1979 that "the Virginia LDS (Latter-day Saints) Citizens Coalition failed to register as a lobbying group but engaged in substantial lobbying efforts." The coalition spent $3,500 in its efforts to defeat ERA in Virginia but claimed only $88.60 went for "material presented directly to legislators."

On March 15, Fram reported that the group had agreed to register with the state as lobbyists.

> According to Campbell, the coalition was financed by contributions from individual citizens sent to an organization called Families Are Concerned Today (FACT), in Potomac, Md.
>
> Ronald H. Thomas, a certified public accountant, said Julian C. Lowe, regional representative of the Church of Jesus Christ of Latter-day Saints (Mormon) in the Washington metropolitan area, asked him to establish the FACT bank account.
>
> Lowe said he asked Thomas to do this because otherwise "it would look like it was a church thing—which it is not. It is church people," he said, "but it's not the church."
>
> Former Oakton Virginia Stake (diocese) President Clifford Cummings said FACT was established "to make absolutely certain no church money was involved."

Sonia wrote:

> As a group and individually, we had been trying for a long time to get the president of the church to agree to meet with us, and had been repeatedly rebuffed. After I had accumulated a hundred or so pro-ERA Mormon letters heavy with pain and need, I wrote to him again, offering to bring them to him personally because I knew he needed to read them. I knew that since his mail was extensive he might not be able to read all of it, and therefore might have little idea of the extent of the anguish. I wanted to ask him outright whether he knew what was in the hearts of the women of the church. I wanted to ask him outright whether he had a revelation from God on this subject, and if so, to plead with him to make his revelation or lack thereof public. But his male secretary, Francis Gibbons, my pen pal in the president's office, wrote back:
>
> "President Kimball regrets that he will be unable to meet with you as suggested. He also asked me to say that he is conscious of the needs of the sisters of the church, and with the aid of the priesthood, and the Relief Society, and under the direction of the Lord, is endeavoring to fill these needs." (Johnson, *From Housewife to Heretic*, 154)

In the early summer of 1979 she received a call from the president of the small Kalispell, Montana, NOW chapter. She told her how the Mormons had nearly gotten recession through the previous session of the Montana legislature and asked her to visit Kalispell and "tell them what to do about their Mormons" (191). Because Rick was in Liberia, her mother came to Virginia to stay with the children while she went to Montana. "I delivered the most innocuous speech of my career, especially considering that the subject was Mormons in politics. Fortuitously (and you can say it's a coincidence if you wish) NOW had that speech videotaped, giving me permanent proof that one of the newspaper quotes contributing to my excommunication was in error" (192). The next day she picked up a newspaper in the hotel lobby and "read what I was supposed to have said in my speech the day before: 'Don't let Mormon missionaries into your home' " (192).

A few days after she returned from Montana, she and Hazel drove to New York City, where she delivered a speech entitled "Patriarchal Panic: Sexual Politics in the Mormon Church." She was on a panel entitled "Some Reflections on Women, Religion, and Mental Health" at the American Psychological Association's annual meeting. The speech basically said, "[I]n short, as you sow, so shall you reap" (193).

During this period, the church began holding area conferences all over the United States. President Kimball was scheduled to attend the Washington, D.C. conference scheduled in the Capital Centre, at Largo, Maryland. In another attempt to see President Kimball, Sonia wrote to him for an appointment. Regional Representative Don Ladd phoned her with the news that President Kimball would not be able to see her (notes of Alice Pottmyer).

A few days prior to the conference, Kimball was hospitalized and was unable to attend the conference.

Sonia's profile began to grow before the media, and she received speaking offers all over the country. The speeches brought more media coverage.

Rick Johnson arrived home from Liberia in time to assist with the picketing. Upon his arrival home, he found reporters in the home. His earlier decision to go to Africa made Sonia unhappy:

> But by the winter of 1979, when Rick began talking about going off to Africa, I had become a feminist and was finding that I could not accommodate to his escapist tactics anymore. He was after all an adult. He had helped bring these children into the world. Now he could stick around, put his personal preferences aside for a while, and work up the courage to tackle the problems parents have to tackle. (210)

He moved to the room over the garage and asked Sonia for a divorce. He also admitted he had fallen in love with someone else. Sonia did not immediately tell her Utah family. By late October, she had signed "phony" divorce papers. Also in October, she spoke before another panel, this time at the University of Utah. Her speech, "Off Our Pedestals, or Chronicles of the Uppity Sisters," combines portions of letters from Mormon women across the United States. Low-key, humorous, moving, and less strident, Johnson's remarks seemed to disarm those who expected something far more militant.

The audiences who heard Johnson speak that Friday and Saturday heard her say the words—"savage misogyny"—that would later damn her in bishop's court. Interestingly enough, they elicited no response at the time and in the context in which they were spoken. Johnson began her remarks by describing a banner with a woman seated on a pedestal.

> This made me think of one of my favorite rejected slogans for our airplane banner tow: PEDESTALS ARE THE PITS. It's true, of course, pedestals are the pits. I wish there were time to talk at length about why the pedestal, as a symbol of women's immobilization and isolation in our male-centered society, more than any other symbol—the gilded cage, the doll's house—reveals our savage misogyny. Briefly, it is physically, intellectually, and spiritually cramped. It is precarious and a fall is dangerous, if not fatal. It maroons women and keeps us emotionally stranded from one another. And by placing us in the position customarily occupied by statues, reveals society's attempt to render us as conveniently non-human, mindless and will-less as they [statues]. (Sillitoe and Swenson, "A Moral Issue," 23, 24)

A part-time reporter for United Press International, Linda Thielke, filed her story on the speech, which dealt with how "hatred of women" was applied to the Mormon Church: " 'Pedestals are the pits,' said Ms. Johnson. 'It shows most vividly the savage misogeny [*sic*] in the Mormon Church' " (UPI, *Deseret News*, 27 October 1979).

This news clipping soon joined those from Montana and other places on her bishop's desk in Virginia. In early November, the bishop of the Sterling Park Ward, Jeffrey Willis, called her into his office to tell her "he was in the process of deciding whether or not to call me to trial" (Johnson, *From Housewife to Heretic*, 227).

As she was reading five-year-old Noly his bedtime story at 9 P.M. on November 14, a knock came on her door. The two counselors in the Sterling Park Ward bishopric handed her a summons to a church court on Saturday, November 17. She had no idea how these courts operated. No charges were mentioned in the letter of summons (227).

"When she received the original court summons, the news had been leaked to Salt Lake media (UPI and AP) through a series of phone calls initiated by Sheldon Rampton, a Princeton student who visits the Johnson home and was on hand when the summons was delivered" (Sillitoe and Swenson, "A Moral Issue," 31).

With three days to prepare her defense against unspecified accusations, "Johnson met with Willis the following evening and asked for written charges. He refused, but agreed to consider December 1 as a trial date, which would allow witnesses who had heard her speak in various parts of the country to testify in her behalf."

Friday evening, November 16, Willis came to the Johnson home with a changed mind; he set the court date for November 27 at 6:30 P.M. After he left, Johnson, on the advice of another bishop, called the stake president to request a stake court. (Women and young men under 19 years of age can be tried in bishop's court; Melchizedek Priesthood–hearing adult males must be tried in stake courts if excommunication is recommended by a bishop's court. A woman may request a stake court, which gives her a hearing before 15 men rather than 3.)

However, Willis returned to her home on Friday evening on the instructions of stake president Earl Roueche to ask Sonia for her temple recommend and to tell her the stake president was taking charge of her case and the trial was still scheduled for Saturday morning.

But at 10 P.M. Friday evening, Willis, who by day was a personnel officer in the Central Intelligence Agency, informed her that the trial would begin at 11 A.M. Saturday, giving her 13 hours to get a night's sleep and prepare her defense. (The Mormon Church is a lay church, and bishops, stake presidents, Sunday school teachers, and so on, all serve without pay and hold full-time jobs elsewhere.)

For five hours that Saturday, she was behind closed doors with the bishopric. She temporarily fought off efforts to excommunicate her.

> Today's session, instead of being a trial as had been planned, merely thrashed out a specific formulation of the issues on which she will be tried next month. At the end of the session [she] summarized these issues for the press in the form of questions:
> "Is she influencing people in the church to distrust the leadership?" "Am I just being purely political or am I attacking the church?" she paraphrased.
> "Is her ERA stand undermining the teachings of the president of the church, who Mormons believe receives his revelations directly from God?" (Hyer, *Washington Post*, 18 November 1979)

> Johnson herself was again waiting for a letter from her bishop—to confirm the December 1 trial date. Willis told one Utah witness who called to confirm plane reservations that he could not commit himself to the December 1 date as he was awaiting "further developments." On November 28, a letter arrived by regular mail confirming the December 1 date (three days hence) but changing the location from the ward chapel [in Sterling Park] to the Oakton Stake Center, the time to 8:30 p.m., and mentioning a new charge: apostasy. The letter further stated that "the court session will be strictly held to one hour and thirty minutes." (Hyer *Washington Post*, 18 November 1979)

More than 200 people, including approximately 40 Mormon supporters of the equal rights amendment, stood in 20-degree weather in the parking lot of the Oakton Stake Center with the news media while Sonia was "now informed that she was charged not only with hampering the church's worldwide missionary effort, but with damaging other church programs, including temple work, the welfare program, family home evening, genealogy, and family preparedness (food storage)." Witnesses were unprepared to assess Johnson's impact on this panoply of church programs.

The false doctrine charge remained but was not detailed.

> Witnesses said the charges were difficult to address according to the rules of the court. Witnesses may testify only from firsthand experience and information. Each had come prepared to deal with her or his own experience in hearing Johnson speak, observing the audience, and analyzing their own impressions. They could not speak to her influence on members and non-members nationwide, assess hindrance to worldwide programs, or address the charge of false doctrine when, in their experience, she has not been speaking in a religious context. In every case, the context was the Equal Rights Amendment, and that they could not mention.

After the "trial," Sonia went out to talk to the crowd waiting in the cold. She described the feeling of the trial as "unsatisfactory" (Sillitoe and Swenson, "A Moral Issue," 28).

> Jeffrey Willis emerged and read a prepared statement, complete with press copies: He said that there would be no decision immediately announced, the ERA had not been an issue, nor had any issue of immorality been raised or considered by the court. (When the church denied that the trial had anything to do with the ERA, rumors of sexual immorality spread cross-country because moral offenses are the most common reason for church courts.) Willis' denial was not entirely generous, claims Maida Withers, since Mormons for ERA was threatening a defamation of character suit. Willis was courteously received by the crowd until he denied that the trial was not connected with ERA. Then came boos of disbelief. He did not respond to questions. (Sillitoe and Swenson, "A Moral Issue," 28)

Because a decision had not been made Saturday night, Sonia was in the Sterling Park Ward Sunday morning participating in full view of the congregation as the ward organist.

On Wednesday, December 5, two men in the ward delivered a letter—the letter she had been waiting for.

For the first time, the charges (reduced to three and much more lucidly expressed than at the trial) were in writing: The verdict was excommunication.

"The charges read: 1. Have your actions influenced members and non-members to oppose church programs, i.e., the missionary program? [No mention of family preparedness, welfare, genealogy, etc.] 2. Have your actions and statements advocated diminished support of church leaders? 3. Have you presented false doctrine which would damage others spiritually?"

"The letter then presented its judgments on the charges. 'You testified that you believe and have publicly stated that our society, specifically including church leaders, has a savage misogyny; when, in fact, it is church doctrine that exaltation can be gained only through the love that results in the eternal bonding of man and woman.'"

Sonia had specifically given them the University of Utah speech where she was misquoted about savage misogyny so they could read it.

Sonia appealed the decision of Jeffrey Willis' bishop's court to the next level of jurisdiction, Stake President Earl Roueche of McLean, Virginia, and the appeal was denied. Contrary to explicit direction in Mormon Scripture, Roueche did not allow Sonia to be present or to testify at her appeal hearing. When another stake president was asked about the procedure, he confirmed that an error had been made and said, "Mrs. Johnson deserves a new high council trial." But the error was ignored. In her final appeal, to the highest level of the church, Sonia Johnson pinned her hopes for justice and mercy on Spencer W. Kimball, the 84-year-old prophet and church president, whom Mormons hold in great veneration. "I just want to get that appeal to President Kimball before the man dies," she said.

"The appeal did reach Spencer Kimball, and in June 1980 he and his counselors denied it" (Arrington, "One Woman," 33).

Stake President Roueche read Kimball's verdict to her. She was not allowed to see or keep a copy of the final verdict. However, because of learning Gregg Shorthand in high school, she made accurate notes.

"What do I have to do to get back into this church?" she asked Roueche after he read her the verdict. He told her the church's stand on ERA was inspired revelation from God and that, to show her repentance, she would have to oppose the ERA publicly.

"Why don't you say that to the press?" she countered.

"You'd like that, wouldn't you?" he answered angrily.

"Yes," she said. "I'd like it if you'd tell the truth."

After the excommunication, she made her divorce public. A few months later, Rick requested that his name be removed from the rolls of the Mormon Church—he was excommunicated at his request.

"I found out that on my own I can support these kids and do it in the style to which they had become accustomed." She was providing for her family by working for the cause closest to her heart: lecturing on equal rights for women.

"The children," she said, "are very proud of me. I think the period of mourning about the divorce, the period of mourning over my misery [over being ousted from the Mormon church] is largely over," she told *Wash-*

ington Post reporter Marjorie Hyer in a follow-up interview published on 29 December 1980.

Doubleday published her biography *From Housewife to Heretic* in 1981 to mixed reactions and reviews.

In 1987, the Crossing Press published *Going Out of Our Minds: The Metaphysics of Liberation.* In her chapter entitled "High Treason," she admits that three years after her divorce and excommunication she had become attracted to another woman, Susan.

Sonia sold the Sterling Park home and moved to Arlington, Virginia, where she shared a townhouse for several years with her children and Susan, also her business manager. While in Arlington, her son Marc finished high school, and Sonia continued her writing.

Sonia now lives on several acres near Estancia, New Mexico, in the Albuquerque area. She has established a women's center and writes and lectures. Her Wildfire Books company published *Wildfire: Igniting the She/Volution* in 1989 and her fourth book, *The Ship That Sailed into the Living Room: Sex and Intimacy Reconsidered*, in 1991.

Her autobiography continues in *The Ship*, where she discussed her mutiny over relationships. She calls it *"relation Ship,"* two words, when used as a noun, or *"relationShip,"* when used as a verb, adjective, or adverb. "It was during our fifth year together that I began to be aware that I was suffering on some deeper, less visible level than I'd noticed before, that I was in a subtler, more constant sort of pain than my usual having relationship problems discomfort," she reports in this book (*The Ship That Sailed*, 9).

In *The Ship*'s "About the Author," she says about herself:

> Dr. Johnson was excommunicated from the Mormon church in 1979 for uppityness, and she has been uppity ever since:
>
> In 1981, she was presented with the Playboy First Amendment Award and refused the $5,000 prize; in 1982, she fasted for 37 days for passage of the ERA; in 1984, she ran for the presidency of the United States as the nominee of the Citizens Party, the Consumer Party, and the Peace and Freedom Party.
>
> A nationally prominent speaker and author of three previous books, she is currently doing only what she wants to do in the mountains of New Mexico with other uppity women. (*The Ship That Sailed*, unnumbered)

BIBLIOGRAPHY

Arrington, Chris Ribgy. "One Woman against the Patriarchal Church." *Savvy* (New York City), October 1980.

Fram, Marcia Ruth. *Washington Star*, 6 March 1979.

———. *Washington Star*, 15 March 1979.

Hyer, Marjorie. *Washington Post*, 18 November 1979.

———. *Washington Post*, 29 December 1980.

Johnson, Sonia. *From Housewife to Heretic*. Garden City, NY: Doubleday & Company, 1981.

———. *The Ship That Sailed into the Living Room: Sex and Intimacy Reconsidered*. Estancia, NM: Wildfire Books, 1991.

MERA Newsletter (Mormons for ERA Newsletter). Arlington, VA.

"Opposition to ERA Time Extension." *Congressional Record*, Senate #S 8441–8442, Vol. 124, pt. 12, 26 May 1978, 15666–15667 (95th Cong., 2d sess.).

Sillitoe, Linda, and Paul Swenson. "A Moral Issue." *Utah Holiday* (Salt Lake City), January 1980.

Alice Allred Pottmyer

Walter Wynn Kenyon
(1948–)

The year 1974 was a tumultuous time for many Americans. Citizens lined up at the gas pumps during the Arab oil embargo and energy crisis, argued the pros and cons of impeaching President Richard Nixon, and watched the approval rate of the equal rights amendment stall just short of adoption. Scholars of religion panned the Living Bible and convened to debate Robert Bellah's essay on "civil religion." Presbyterians considered "term limits" for pastors, laid plans for the church-wide celebration of the American Bicentennial, and debated a proposal to reunite northern and southern Presbyterians for the first time since the Civil War. That year, an observant reader of the *Presbyterian Outlook* might have noted a roster of that year's Presbyterian seminary graduates listing Walter Wynn Kenyon as serving the Harmarville United Presbyterian Church of Pittsburgh, yet Kenyon would never be ordained to that position. In a decision hailed as a victory for women's rights and criticized as a defeat for the authority of the Bible and matters of individual conscience, the courts of the United Presbyterian Church (UPC) ruled that Kenyon's stance against women's ordination barred his own ordination. More than two decades later, Presbyterians continued to debate the case.

Kenyon grew up in a household steeped in the conservative tradition of the old United Presbyterian Church in North America (UPNA), heir to the Scottish Covenanters and Seceders who settled in upstate New York, western Pennsylvania, Ohio, and the Carolina piedmont. Kenyon's father graduated from the UPNA's Westminster College and from the denomination's only seminary, Pittsburgh-Xenia Theological Seminary. In 1944, the Allegheny Presbytery ordained the elder Kenyon as pastor of the Atlantic Avenue United Presbyterian Church in McKeesport. In 1948, he became pastor of the Deer Creek United Presbyterian Church, just north of Pittsburgh. That same year, Walter Wynn Kenyon was born, the third of ten children (and the first son) of Walter Russell Kenyon and Mary Lillian Gethin. The Deer Creek congregation thrived, growing to a high of 525 members in 1963, and its members watched young "Wynn" grow up in their manse until he left for Ohio's Marietta College.

By the time Kenyon followed in his father's footsteps to Pittsburgh Theological Seminary, the institution had changed dramatically. In 1954, Pittsburgh-Xenia opened its new ten-acre campus on Highland Avenue, not far from the University of Pittsburgh. After the UPNA merged with the Presbyterian Church (USA) to form the United Presbyterian Church (USA) in 1958, nearby Western Theological Seminary consolidated with Pittsburgh-Xenia Seminary in 1959 and moved onto its Highland Avenue campus a year later. The seminary was renamed Pittsburgh Theological Seminary, and a new library, chapel, dining room, dormitories, and apartments were soon built to accommodate the larger student body. The theological atmosphere of the seminary broadened when the new denomination adopted the neo-orthodox "Confession of 1967" as part of a new multiconfessional *Book of Confessions*. At the same time, the church relaxed its ordination vows, asking all newly ordained or installed deacons, elders, and ministers to be "instructed by the Confessions" and to "endorse" the government of the United Presbyterian Church (USA).

At Pittsburgh Seminary, Kenyon found a mentor in Professor John H. Gerstner, Jr., who would later describe Kenyon as "one of the ten best students I have had in my quarter-century of teaching." Gerstner had been ordained by the old UPNA and had served as professor of church history at Pittsburgh-Xenia since 1950. A graduate of the UPNA Westminster College, Westminster Theological Seminary (of the Orthodox Presbyterian Church), and Harvard University, Gerstner placed himself in the theological lineage of Jonathan Edwards, Charles Hodge, Benjamin B. Warfield, and J. Gresham Machen.* He opposed the Confession of 1967 as "anything but sound" and an "indelible blemish on the escutcheon of the church" (Gerstner, "Church Historian," 243–246). Kenyon shared many of Gerstner's beliefs, including his conviction that an inerrant view of the Bible taught the "subordination" of women, thereby precluding their ordination as elders or ministers.

Kenyon and Gerstner were not alone in opposing the ordination of women. The UPNA ordained women as deacons as early as 1906, but it continued to deny ordination to women as elders or ministers at the time of its 1958 merger. The issue threatened to block that merger until denominational executives gave private assurances that no congregation would be compelled to accept women ministers or elders. Even the less conservative Presbyterian Church (USA) showed only reluctant support for women's ordination, although it had ordained women as elders and deacons since

1930 and as ministers since 1956. By 1974, women in the United Presbyterian Church (USA) comprised only 189 of 13,810 ministers and 26,951 out of 91,000 elders, and 1,712 of 8,729 congregations—including the Deer Creek church where Kenyon grew up—did not have a single female elder serving on its Session.

Early in Kenyon's seminary career, the Deer Creek Session—the council of elders who governed the church—met with him and endorsed his plans to enter the ministry. With their backing, Kenyon appeared before the ministers and elders of Pittsburgh Presbytery to testify to his sense of call. Satisfied, the Presbytery formally and ceremoniously enrolled him as a "candidate" for ordination, vowing to "provide a continuing, kindly, and sympathetic interest" in him, entrusting their Committee on Candidates and Credentials with the guidance for his course of study and the oversight of his service to the denomination.

With the Presbytery's consent, Kenyon began to serve part-time at the Harmarville United Presbyterian Church, a few towns to the northeast in the greater Pittsburgh area. The Harmarville Church had been a congregation of the UPNA before the 1958 merger, and it had no women on its Session. By 1974, its membership had declined to 57 members (23 men and 34 women), and its annual expenses of $19,181 exceeded its annual receipts by $3,812. It could no longer afford a full-time pastor, and Kenyon's father had agreed to preside as "moderator" of the Session, a role constitutionally reserved for ordained ministers. Young Kenyon served in a lay capacity for several years during his seminary training, extending his studies to accommodate his part-time work. Just a few months before Kenyon's graduation, the elders of the Harmarville congregation asked him to serve as its "stated supply," a temporary pastor serving on a year-by-year basis at the invitation of a local Session and with the approval of the Presbytery.

Kenyon sought the required approval of his Presbytery through its Committee on Candidates and Credentials. He had already graduated in December 1973, and he had passed the nationally administered written examinations on Presbyterian polity, theology, worship, and biblical exegesis, but he needed to meet one more time with the Committee and defend his personal statement of faith before the elders and ministers of the Presbytery. In accordance with its constitutionally mandated procedures, the Committee met with Kenyon on 14 February 1974 to determine his "readiness in all respects for ordination to the professional ministry," including the "acceptability" of his theology "within the confessional standards of the Church," his understanding of his ordination vows, and his commitment to the discipline of the United Presbyterian Church (*The Book of Order*, Form of Government XIX [49.025]). During the interview, one of the Committee members (who already knew something of Kenyon's views) pressed him about the ordination of women, asking point blank, "Would you ordain women who were elected to Session of the church?" (*Minutes, General Assembly of the UPCUSA*, 1975, Pt. I, 255).

Kenyon explained his views at length. Citing 1 Corinthians 14 and 1 Timothy 2:12, he disagreed with the Presbyterian practice of ordaining women elders and ministers. As a pastor, he would explain his beliefs to his congregation's nominating committee. If the congregation overrode his objections and persisted in electing a woman to the office of elder, he would refuse to participate in her ordination service, a service that would normally be held as part of the congregation's regular Sunday morning worship. As a matter of conscience, he would ask another minister to preside at her ordination. Kenyon made it clear that he would not block a woman's ordination, and he stated his willingness to work with women elders and ministers.

Following their interview, the Committee voted 10 to 5 against recommending Kenyon for ordination, based principally, but not solely, on his views about women's ordination. As the Committee later explained, he could hold his opinion privately and "not seek to advocate it from the pulpit or impose it upon his congregation," but his refusal to ordain women would be "an open insult to the congregation" and "a refusal to perform a lawful act which is ordinarily expected of pastors." When the Presbytery convened at Pittsburgh's First Presbyterian Church later that day, it uncharacteristically overruled the Committee's recommendation and allowed Kenyon to present his statement of faith. During lengthy questioning, he reiterated his stance against women's ordination but stated his willingness to affirm the required ordination vows, including the promise to endorse the church's government. After the Presbytery voted 144 to 133 to authorize his ordination, 55 commissioners crowded forward to "dissent," asking that the minutes list their names and note their disagreement with the vote.

The judicial processes of the United Presbyterian Church (USA) were soon set in motion. On 25 February 1974, the Rev. Jack Martin Maxwell, Th.D., a former homiletics instructor at Princeton Theological Seminary who served as pastor of the Presbyterian Church of Sewickley just outside of Pittsburgh, initiated a remedial case against Pittsburgh Presbytery by filing a formal complaint with clerk of the Synod of Pennsylvania–West Virginia. On March 6, Maxwell forestalled Kenyon's ordination until the settlement of the judicial case when he presented the Presbytery's stated clerk a "stay of execution," a petition signed by 155 members of the Presbytery. To defend its action in the approaching trial, Pittsburgh Presbytery appointed a five-person "Committee of Representation" consisting of Presbyterian elders and attorneys George Minsch and C. Bryson Schreiner; the Rev. Malcolm Alexander, Ph.D., pastor of the First Presbyterian Church of Carnegie and former faculty member of Pittsburgh-Xenia; the Rev.

Frank D. Moser, pastor of Monroeville's Bethel United Presbyterian Church; and Kenyon's mentor, John Gerstner.

In his complaint, Maxwell alleged that the Presbytery's consent to Kenyon's ordination violated Presbyterian constitutional law. By his avowed refusal to participate in the ordination of women, Maxwell argued, Kenyon opposed the established Presbyterian policy of ordaining both men and women, thus compromising his answer to the fifth ordination vow that asked, in part, "Do you endorse our Church's government, and will you honor its discipline?" When Pittsburgh Presbytery, nevertheless, approved Kenyon's ordination, he concluded, it effectively granted an illegal exception to the constitutional provisions for ordination, and its action should be rescinded.

In its defense, the Committee of Representation argued for the historical right of the Presbytery to determine the qualifications for ministerial ordination. Furthermore, they argued, the Adopting Act of 1729 allowed Presbyterian candidates for ordination to hold scruples about anything not deemed an "essential and necessary article of faith," and the ordination of women had never been considered an "essential" part of the Presbyterian tradition. Moreover, they noted, the first of the 1788 Preliminary Principles of Presbyterian government affirmed that "God alone is lord of the conscience," and Kenyon had merely sought to uphold that right of conscience. Finally, they cited the UPNA's 1925 provision that "forbearance in love" be exercised toward anyone "who may not be able fully to subscribe to the Standards of the Church, while they do not determinedly oppose them, but follow the things which make for peace and things wherewith one may edify another."

The trial convened at 10:00 A.M. on 19 April 1974 in the Camp Hill, Pennsylvania, offices of the Synod of Pennsylvania–West Virginia. Maxwell and Pittsburgh Presbytery's Committee of Representation made their successive arguments before 11 members of the Synod's Permanent Judicial Commission (PJC), the standing committee charged with hearing and deciding such cases on behalf of its "electing judiciary." The trial adjourned, and the PJC returned its judgment after almost two hours of private deliberation, voting six to four to sustain the complaint and overrule the decision to ordain Kenyon. By a vote of five to four, with one abstention, it upheld Martin's reasoning that the Pittsburgh Presbytery had granted an illegal exception to the constitutionally mandated ordination vow. Its decision called Pittsburgh Presbytery's actions "irregular" and "not prudent and equitable for the promotion of the mission and spiritual welfare of the Church." Because Kenyon held a position "in clear conflict with that of the Church," it found "his ordination and installation would operate to produce division among the membership of the Church." Kenyon's "opposition to a fundamental and constitutional position of the Church" put him "in irreconcilable conflict with Presbyterian polity, government and discipline."

Pittsburgh Presbytery appealed the decision to the highest court of the Presbyterian Church, the General Assembly Permanent Judicial Commission, which convened on 15 November 1974 in St. Louis, Missouri. The Commission heard arguments from both parties and considered a "friend of the court" brief from the Presbyterian-affiliated Organization of Church Employed Women, who argued in support of Maxwell that "discrimination against women within the United Presbyterian Church solely on the basis of their sex is forbidden by the Constitution of the Church." On November 18, with only three dissenting votes, the Commission upheld the Synod's reversal of the Presbytery's decision to ordain Kenyon. In support of its judgment that the power of a Presbytery "is not absolute" but "must be exercised in conformity with the Constitution," it cited a 1935 judicial opinion that "a presbytery should ever remember that it has entered into a solemn contract with the Presbyterian Church . . . to see that the constitutional requirements are fully complied with." Acknowledging the potential conflict of conscience and polity, it judged "that the decision to present oneself as a candidate for ordination is voluntary. A candidate who chooses not to subscribe to the polity of this church may be a more useful servant of our Lord in some other fellowship whose polity is in harmony with the candidate's conscience" (*Minutes, General Assembly of the UPCUSA,* 1974, Pt. II, 254–259).

Its decision found that Kenyon's views effectively compromised not one but four of the ordination vows, including vows to be "instructed by the Confessions," to be "guided by our Confessions," and to live "by following the Lord Jesus Christ, loving neighbors, and working for the reconciliation of the world." The vow calling for endorsement of the church's government was most significant, however:

> The United Presbyterian Church in the United States of America, in obedience to Jesus Christ, under the authority of Scripture, and guided by its confessions, has now developed its understanding of the equality of all people (both male and female) before God. It has expressed this understanding in the Book of Order with such clarity as to make the candidate's stated position a rejection of its government and discipline. Thus, the statement by itself would constitute a negative answer to Question 5 ["Do you endorse our Church's government, and will you honor its discipline? Will you be a friend among your comrades in ministry, working with them, subject to the ordering of God's word and Spirit?"].

The Judicial Commission concluded that the determining factor was neither the ordination of women, which had become the established polity of the

United Presbyterian Church (USA), nor the right of Presbyteries to ordain their ministers, which had always been constrained by constitutional provisions; nor the freedom of conscience, which could be alleviated by "passive withdrawal" to another denomination. Rather, the primary issue concerned a candidate's endorsement of Presbyterian polity. "There is no question," it concluded, "that refusal to ordain women on the basis of their sex is contrary to the Constitution."

The decision's implications reached far beyond Kenyon himself. When the Rev. Carl W. Bogue, Jr., pastor of Allenside Presbyterian Church of Akron, Ohio, asked for a ruling about the implications for other ordained officers, General Assembly Stated Clerk William P. Thompson advised that no officer would be removed from office. Henceforth, though, anyone taking the vows for the first time or retaking the vows, such as a pastor moving to another congregation or an elder or deacon assuming a new term of office, would have to "endorse" the Presbyterian policy of ordaining women. By "endorse," Thompson later explained, the ordination vow meant "to express approval of, publicly and definitely; to give support to; to sanction; to affirm." The PJC based its decision, Thompson concluded, "upon the premise that the issue before it was one of church government rather than of doctrine."

As word of the ruling spread, reactions were mixed. Some openly sympathized with Kenyon, including James A. Gittings, editor of the denominational magazine *A.D.*, who lamented, "The witness of a splendid young minister may be lost to pulpits of the United Presbyterian Church, and a son of the manse has been denied the place in which he has dreamed of serving" ("Ordination Denied," 58). Some gloated, such as Jeanne Welles, the author of a whimsical seven-stanza poem whose last verse concluded: "Candidate Kenyon is not awed. / Though unordained, he is not broken. / He listened for the word of God, / But She has spoken" ("Candidate Kenyon," 44). Many who agreed with the ruling took a middle ground, however, either expressing "shock and distress" at Gittings's sympathy or denouncing Welles's "poetry of ridicule" as a "cheap shot."

Some petitioned the General Assembly to change the church constitution or alter the judicial ruling. Seven such petitions ("overtures") came before the 1975 General Assembly, many of which were endorsed by several Presbyteries. Despite highly charged committee hearings at the General Assembly, the Plenary Session quickly voted down all seven overtures. Likewise, the 1977 General Assembly soundly defeated two proposals to alter the ordination questions to allow for greater freedom of conscience. The Presbyterian policy of ordaining women became further solidified when the 1979 General Assembly approved a proposal ("Overture L") that required all United Presbyterian Churches to elect women to their governing boards.

In the aftermath of the Kenyon decision, several pastors left the denomination to join the Presbyterian Church in America (PCA), often taking their congregations with them. Founded in part on its principled opposition to the ordination of women, the PCA split away from the southern Presbyterian Church in the United States (PCUS), beginning with 45,000 members in December 1973 and growing to 80,000 members in 370 churches a little over a year later. The Rev. Frank Moser, one of Kenyon's defenders on the Committee of Representation, and 25 families from Moser's church formed a new PCA congregation. Some predicted a mass "exodus" from the United Presbyterian Church, as church splits occurred in Akron, Ohio, and McKee's Rock and Plain Grove, Pennsylvania, and controversy arose among congregations in the Albany and Baltimore areas.

Kenyon's father was among those who left to join the Presbyterian Church in America. By transferring his ministerial affiliation to the PCA, the senior Kenyon effectively renounced the jurisdiction of the United Presbyterian Church (USA), and on 31 October 1975, Pittsburgh Presbytery removed the name of Walter R. Kenyon from its roll of ministers. He subsequently became the founding pastor of the Gospel Fellowship PCA, organized in nearby Gibsonia on 8 February 1976, with a total membership of 159. Many of Kenyon's supporters also left the denomination; between 1974 and 1976, the Deer Creek congregation declined from 347 to 157 members, and the Harmarville church dwindled from 57 to 35 members.

Kenyon himself pursued a career in academia. While he awaited the outcome of the trial, he continued to work part-time at Harmarville, simultaneously enrolling in advanced courses at Pittsburgh Seminary for a semester, and then at Duquesne University for a semester. He subsequently entered a doctoral program in the Department of Philosophy at the University of Miami. In 1981, he earned a Ph.D. for his 413-page dissertation "The Concept of God," which analyzed Anselm's understanding of God. He later became professor of Bible and philosophy at Belhaven College in Jackson, Mississippi.

One critic called the Kenyon decision an "offense to decency" that "might kill the union plan" with the more conservative, southern PCUS, which had followed a different course in two similar cases. In January 1975, Highlands Presbytery voted to ordain John A. Gess, whose views were similar to Kenyon's, and the Synod of the Virginias upheld that action in a July 1975 decision. Likewise, Atlanta Presbytery's 8 July 1975 decision to install the Rev. Thomas T. Ellis was upheld by the Synod of the Southeast and the PCUS General Assembly PJC, which ruled that Ellis's stated willingness to participate in ordaining women, despite his objections, constituted sufficient "approval" of Presbyterian polity. Before it was implemented in 1983, the "Plan for Reunion" incorporated written assurances that no PCUS congregation would have to accept women officers, and the proposed ordination vows adopted the changes turned down by the 1977 General Assembly of the United Presbyterian Church, thus eliminating the required "endorsement" of Presbyterian government.

The Kenyon case differs from most heresy trials in two significant ways. First, the case hinged not on Kenyon's views but on his actions. He was free to hold his beliefs privately, but his public actions had to comply with Presbyterian polity; he was not free to advocate his views or refuse to ordain women. Second, the case reflects a growing litigation against judicatories instead of individuals. Although Kenyon's statements were crucial in the case against Pittsburgh Presbytery, Kenyon himself was never prosecuted and was not even present at either trial. Likewise, judicial complaints challenged the decision of Highlands Presbytery to ordain John Gess and Atlanta Presbytery's reception of Thomas Ellis, yet neither Gess nor Ellis was the defendant. When the National Capital Union Presbytery enrolled the Rev. Mansfield M. Kaseman in 1979 despite questions about his christology, the Presbytery, and not Mr. Kaseman, was challenged in church court. In 1983 and again in 1984, several ministers filed a complaint against the Presbytery of San Gabriel for receiving noted theologian John Hick, whose theological views purportedly lay outside the bounds of the Reformed faith. After the Presbytery of Genesee Valley approved the call of the Rev. Jane Adams Spahr, who admitted to being a "self-affirming, practicing homosexual" in a long-term, committed relationship, a complaint was lodged against the Presbytery, but no charges were filed against Ms. Spahr.

Twenty years later, the Kenyon case has often been cited in discussions about homosexuality and Presbyterian ordination. In efforts to overturn the 1978 "definitive guidance" against ordaining "self-affirming, practicing homosexuals," many proposals have advocated a "local option" whereby the ordaining body would have the discretion to consider an individual's sexuality as one factor among many, arguing that views about homosexuality have never been considered an "essential and necessary" article of faith. Conservative opponents of such a local option cite the Kenyon case and its conclusion that the right to ordain "must be exercised in conformity with the Constitution." Kenyon's ordination and the ordination of gays and lesbians both hinged on actions declared unconstitutional by the courts of the Presbyterian Church. Ironically, liberal voices in the Presbyterian Church seek to broaden the same discretionary powers they had previously sought to constrain, while Kenyon's former supporters now argue to uphold the strict constitutional interpretation that had once denied Pittsburgh Presbytery the right to ordain Walter Wynn Kenyon.

BIBLIOGRAPHY

The Constitution of the United Presbyterian Church in the USA. Part II: *The Book of Order.* New York: Office of the General Assembly, 1973–1974. All quotes from the *Book of Order* are from this edition.

Gerstner, John H. "A Church Historian Warns: Presbyterians Are Demoting the Bible." *Christianity Today* 10 (3 December 1965): 243–246.

———. "Disturbing Decision: Candidate Denied Ordination." *Presbyterian Layman* 8, no. 1 (February 1975).

Gittings, James A. "Ordination Denied Opponent of Eldership for Women." *A.D.* 4, no. 3 (March 1975): 58.

McCarthy, David B. "The Emerging Importance of Presbyterian Polity." In *The Organizational Revolution: Presbyterians and American Denominationalism*, edited by Milton Coalter, John Mulder, and Louis Weeks. Louisville: Westminster John Knox Press, 1992. 279–306.

Minutes, General Assembly of the Presbyterian Church (U.S.A.), 1986, Part 1; 1993, Part 1.

Minutes, General Assembly of the United Presbyterian Church in the U.S.A., 1963, Part III; 1974, Part II; 1975, Part I; 1976, Part II.

Rogers, Jack. "The Kenyon Case." In *Women and Men in Ministry*, edited by Roberta Hestenes. Pasadena: Fuller Theological Seminary, 1985. 147–175.

Welles, Jeanne. "Candidate Kenyon . . ." *A.D.* 4 nos. 7–8 (July–August 1975): 44.

David B. McCarthy

Lane Theological Seminary
(1834)

In October 1834, 51 dissident, protesting heretical students of the recently established Lane Theological Seminary at Cincinnati, Ohio, reduced that academic community almost to nonexistence in an exodus by which they witnessed that they could no longer "continue [as] members of the Institution under existing circumstances." They left behind them but 2 seminarians in a theological department that had boasted 40, and only 5 scholars of the 60 formerly enrolled for the literary curriculum. Boldly, and with confidence, they proceeded to the suburbs where they established a free seminary in which they taught themselves. Sustained by confidence in the validity of their cause, and fed by the ravens, they persisted in a mode of life already labeled revolutionary by their critics while they discussed their next move. In due course, they accepted the hospitality of Oberlin, although not until the Trustees of the just-founded college met their specific demands concerning admission and administration policy. Then, and forever after, the expatriots of Cincinnati were referred to as the Lane Rebels—heretics with a cause.

Tension at the seminary had begun early in 1834 when Theodore Weld, the charismatic convert of Charles Finney, arrived at Cincinnati, firmly in the grip of concern for his black brothers, a passion that was to possess him to the end of his life. An avowed abolitionist, Weld committed himself to enlisting Lane students (many of whom were colonizationists and some even slaveholders) in the cause of abolition as the only and the Christian way of dealing with slavery. His strategy, after having brought several colleagues individually to his point of view, was to challenge the colonizationists to public examination of the issues.

The encounter—known subsequently as the Lane Debates—lasted for 18 evenings. Various students, including one former slave who had purchased his own freedom, spoke from personal observation and knowledge of the evil, with such telling effect that at the conclusion all except a small minority voted for immediate abolition. Meanwhile, the Lane students allied themselves so ardently with the cause of black freedom and education in Cincinnati, and associated so openly and sufficiently with the blacks of the city, as to bring down upon themselves accusations infinitely graver in the eyes of conservative Cincinnatians than that of merely prosecuting the abolitionist cause.

The president of the seminary, Lyman Beecher,* the great gun of Calvinism, newly arrived in the Queen City to assume the post at the theological school and also to accept the pastorate of a Presbyterian Church, became alarmed, and much of Cincinnati with him. Having already entertained misgivings regarding the debates because of the "divisive tendency, and the risk of exciting popular prejudice," he saw his early apprehensions justified by the impulsive actions of the students and the ill grace with which their efforts were received by a substantial segment of the Cincinnati population (Beecher, *Autobiography*, 2:324). The *Western Monthly Magazine* rebuked "embryo clergymen," who would have been better advised to "mind their own business and their books." Weld replied in the *Cincinnati Journal* that the attitudes and actions of the Lane students had resulted from "deliberate convictions of long, varied, and conscientious inquiry." In vain did Beecher—whose conciliatory eagerness to admit of peaceful coexistence for various attitudes toward slavery was already recorded in the pages of the *Spirit of the Pilgrims*—appeal to his "boys." He commended their humanitarian impulse but contended that they recklessly ignored money and help at hand by flaunting convention. Said he: "[I]f you will visit in colored families, and walk with them in the streets, you will be overwhelmed" (2:325). Even so, Beecher persisted in the naive hope that if more cautious Christians in Cincinnati did not "amplify the evil by too much alarm, impatience, and attempt at regulation, the evil would . . . subside and pass away." Nothing of the kind happened.

After the president and faculty left the city for the summer, the students who remained in the seminary lodgings continued their activity on behalf of the blacks with such zeal that certain of the Trustees, increasingly restive, decided to squelch both industry and inquiry of the students before trouble multiplied or crisis arose. The Executive Board of the Trustees met and not only recommended that the antislavery society be dissolved but, incredibly, demanded that students neither "hold general meetings among themselves," except for religious or academic purpose, "nor deliver public addresses, or lectures, at the seminary or elsewhere, in term time, other than those connected with ordinary religious exercises; nor make pubic addresses, or communications, to the students when assembled at their meals, or on other ordinary occasions, . . . without the approbation of the Faculty" (*A State-*

ment of the Reasons, 12). The rules were not binding upon Lane students, of course, without vote of the Trustees, an action not possible until autumn, but they were nevertheless published as a warning. When the official body did meet in the fall, the code was adopted in its entirety, save for two changes: the "item prohibiting private conversation among the students on the subject of slavery was omitted" (Mahan, *Autobiography*, 178), but the Prudential Committee was given power to dismiss students at its discretion.

Confrontation was inevitable. Students requested interpretation of the new regulations, and President Beecher, along with two faculty members, attempted unsuccessfully to respond. The dissident heretics deputized another postulant committee, and yet another, and after that, agreement seeming to them more remote than ever, they concluded realistically that further effort to bridge the widening chasm of misunderstanding was futile, and departed.

Although surface similarity invites easy comparison of the episode to phenomena of campus movements in the 1960s, the present contention is that the essential character of the Lane Rebels distinguishes them greatly from students of the so-called New Left of the 1960s and even reveals a dimension of the Lane revolt not completely apparent to the actors in the drama themselves.

In an impressive and often brilliant study, *The Conflict of Generations*, Lewis Feuer refers to the Lane revolt as the "only . . . episode in the pre-history of the American Civil War which partook of the characteristics of a students' movement" (322). Although much too honest and too percep-tive a scholar to class the Cincinnati chapter uncritically with leftist student movements, Feuer subsumes the story under the "question of rules of free-dom of speech and action." Careful to point out that the Lane students were "thoroughly atypical of the students in American colleges and uni-versities at the time," and even "exceptional among the American studen-try," Feuer still classifies them in the end with those activists who are motivated by that "back-to-the-people spirit, which is," he says, "the high calling of student movements" (322–323). Moreover, he believes that in certain of its manifestations "the uprising had all the traits of rejection of the old generation by the younger one" (323). Thus, Feuer, for all his qualifications, puts the nineteenth-century Lane Rebels (whom the Cincin-nati press taxed with "dreaming themselves into full-grown patriots, and setting seriously to work, to organize a wide-spread revolution") squarely in the company of radical students of the 1960s.

To take issue with Feuer, and those whose judgment he typifies, is in no way to derogate the significance of his work. Rather, reflection on his sen-timent furnishes convenient context for taking another look at a brief ep-isode of Americana that is forgotten by most and, when remembered, is too easily classified as Feuer himself does.

Let us consider the matter. There are parallels. Lane Rebels, uncertain of administrators before the exodus, and positively distrustful afterward, had expressed an early fear, even before the school began, that the "very fallible" Trustees might neglect to secure for professors only those "obligated to teach or starve." Hardly enrolled in the curriculum, they rejected one professor and informed Beecher that "they could not and would not attend his . . . obnoxious lectures any longer" (Beecher, *Autobiography*, 2: 322). Later, in actual exchanges over abolition they styled the official action "mean & despicable!" and eventually said baldly that President Beecher, in time a special object of their wrath, had played the role of turncoat and, moreover, had "blabbed the thing out so as to stir up . . . apprehension." The similarity between seminarians' contempt for Lyman Beecher's don't-rock-the-boat pleas and student denunciation of administrators at Berkeley and Columbia in the 1960s is too striking to require comment.

Additional identification between Lane activity and campus movements in the 1960s lies in the focus of moral outrage over wronged minorities. Moral indignation plainly brackets Lane Rebels and students of the New Left in the 1960s.

Motivated by righteous indignation toward identification with those to whom they ministered, Lane students aroused animosity and fear at the point of intercourse with blacks. The situation is clear in a letter from Theodore Weld to Arthur Tappan: "We have formed a large and efficient organization for elevating the colored people in Cincinnati," he reported to his benefactor, "have established a Lyceum among them, and lecture three or four evenings a week." Considering that most blacks in the city were still "in bondage," Weld prayed heaven to keep him "full of sympathy for suffering humanity" and added the realistic petition that he might continue to rejoice in the opportunity "to suffer" (Barnes and Durmond, *Letters of Theodore Dwight Weld*, 1:132–135). Unquestionably, he agreed with Beecher that the principle of "social intercourse according to character, irrespective of color" was as dangerous as it was just. The extent to which Lane students intermingled with blacks is obliquely illuminated by their careful and flat denial of the charges that they had promenaded with black women and had left their cards at the blacks' houses. At specific pain, they pointed out that their association with black women had been honorable and always with older, married women, whom they were at the time teaching. Whatever the explanation, the identification was admitted. Weld spent his time almost exclusively in their company, attending no social functions except theirs; and many of the other rebels found no better reason for remaining in Cincinnati than their projects with the black population there.

Another pronounced similarity between Lane Rebels and the radicals of the 1960s is insistence upon freedom of speech. In their published statement, the Lane students made it abundantly clear that they left school (or at least that they thought they had left the school) "*not* because the trustees and faculty claimed the right to exercise a supervision" nor because the administrators were largely colonizationists, nor because studies were "wearisome," or labor "drudgery" but because the authorities had "asserted the right to suspend free discussion" (*A Statement of the Reasons*, 26–27). Thus, Mario Savio, member of the steering committee of the Free Speech Movement at Berkeley, in an indictment accusing the bureaucracy of vast discrimination as the crowning evidence of the university's injustice, charged the administration with determination that "[s]peech with consequences, speech in the area of civil right, speech which some might regard as illegal must stop" (Lipset and Wolin, *The Berkeley Student Revolt*, 216–219).

Yet there is despair that separates the radicals of the 1960s from the Lane Rebels. Lane Rebels did not lose faith, even in the face of disaster. Said their leader: "Through evil report and good report, whether the storm beat in their faces or upon their backs, they will hold on their way. . . . [Y]ou have mistaken alike the cause, the age, and the men, if you think to intimidate by threats, or to silence by clamor, or shame by sneers, or put down by authority, or discourage by opposition, or appall by danger." They entertained "strong assurance that theirs was . . . the cause of God, and that God was . . . with them" (Barnes and Durmond, *Letters of Theodore Dwight Weld*, 1:145–146).

Again, as the Lane Rebels embraced the tradition passionately, the radicals of the 1960s renounced it bitterly, even rejecting the older liberalism and the social democrats. The Lane Rebels felt themselves a part of the past. They were hand in glove with the establishment. Arthur Tappan, the silk entrepreneur whose proprietary attitude toward society was confident enough, and whose established province secure enough, that he could require his employees to "board in respectable families, regularly attend church on the Sabbath, abstain from sinful amusements, and shun vicious companions" (Tappan, *The Life of Arthur Tappan*, 406–407), financed the rebels as enthusiastically as he had originally underwritten the founding of Lane Seminary. Directly after the dissidents' heretical departure, Tappan "immediately sent on five thousand dollars" for their pressing needs. The Trustees of the school who censured the rebels represented the solid business interest of Cincinnati, but so for that matter did those who came to the rescue of the rebellion. "A very wealthy individual, Mr. Ludlow, brother-in-law of . . . Chief Justice Chase, promptly vacated his ample residence, buildings and grounds, and gave them up for the occupancy of these students as long as occasion should require" (Mahan, *Autobiography*, 18). Affluent friends in the East authorized drafts and raised funds. Indeed, the Lane Rebels saw themselves also in continuity with the kingdom of heaven, with the tradition of martyrs and innocents who defied Torquemada, or suffered from decisions of the Venetian Council of Ten. Far from manifesting father-hate, which, in a Freudian analysis, supplies Oedipal reference for understanding student revolt, Lane Rebels (who did indeed distrust Lyman Beecher) doted on Asa Mahan, who qualified, at least psychologically, as father figure, and came close to worshipping Finney, who was almost old enough in years, and certainly hallowed enough, to merit their customary designation of "father."

Unlike the student rebels of the 1960s, the Lane Rebels lacked a sense of humor that allows one to laugh at oneself. They took themselves in deadly earnest. On occasion, they made crude or cruel fun of their opponents and defectors, accusing an unacceptable instructor of limiting his exercise to "journeying from his room to the backhouse" or judging a disagreeable student fit only to be "chief cook and bottle washer" (Barnes and Durmond, *Letters of Theodore Dwight Weld*, 1:82–83), while referring to themselves as God's servants, watched over by the special Providence they acknowledged.

More significantly, Lane Rebels were motivated by an almost exclusively altruistic passion, devoid, at least on the surface, of self-serving. "Woe be to us if we plead not the cause of the oppressed," they cried, the sincerity of the sentiment underscored by some who (before the exodus) left the seminary to teach the blacks of Cincinnati because, as they said, "these poor brethren and sisters MUST BE HELPED." "Soul!" demanded Weld. "Must I—ought I—can I—wait longer?" (1:173).

The Lane Rebels were not searching for a standard to which to pin their colors. They had the truth already, by revelation. Living in a cultural milieu that dictated an increasingly optimistic theological view of man, they were themselves far less conscious of a metamorphosis of doctrine than they were confident that truth was preserved in Holy Writ and outlined in the Westminster Confession. The dissidents from Lane believed not in man's future but in God's power. Actually, they saw themselves not as able but as agents of God. Their marching song was not "*We* shall overcome" but—if with less rhythm, certainly with more conviction—"The gates of hell shall not prevail." Their creed was oriented toward the transcendent.

So long as Lyman Beecher and the Trustees of Lane could confine the activity of the potential rebels and heretics to speculation and debate, they could contain the dissidents. The students' place in the community was real, though admittedly uncertain. The president of the seminary called them "a set of glorious good fellows, whom he . . . would not at a venture exchange for any others," but he admonished them to "be patient and take no course" (1:172–173). It was when the boys lost patience and acted, formed the antislavery society, and mixed openly with the blacks—it was then that Beecher called them he-goat men who butted everything that got in their way and then that they knew themselves cut off from the community of which they had fancied themselves members. Ostracism by men, though, if it came to that, was of little importance, because finally the Lane Rebels were oriented not toward men but toward God. It is not difficult to find apt quotations illustrating how they saw themselves bound to each other and to their work through their ties to eternity. "You must, you *will* more than ever," wrote Weld's father to his son after a crisis, "realize that you are not your own, and that you are bound by every tie to devote your time, your talents, your life, your all to the service of God" (1:76). Or, in another context, the acceptable sentiment is said thus: "If this school is not linked with the interest of the Redeemer's kingdom, I wish not to have it prospered" (1:90). Such sentiment is corroborative in understanding that for the Lane Rebels and heretics the matter was not, finally, that of free speech, nor even abolition, even though one of the rebels did insist that the heart of the matter was "prejudice against color." They were concerned for the black man because his plight was an affront to heaven. Slavery was a challenge for them to follow through in the Puritan attempt to order all things under God, and they were still Puritan enough that their activity was more reflective of a belief that man's chief end is to glorify God (which they could do by making his world reflect the divine community) than it was expressive of a desperate humanitarianism that could not be killed even though it could be frustrated. Lane Rebels could sustain a Manassas while they awaited a millennium in confidence.

Fifty years after the event, Huntington Lyman, whose name had led the list of those who signed the manifesto of Lane students, said of the designation "rebels" that "there was neither rebellion nor the shadow of rebellion in the event to which it points" (1:73). And he added that when the exodus occurred, there was no danger then that the phrase "would convey a calumny"; but, he added, "[T]he phrase survives while the events which environed and explained it are forgotten" (Ballantine, *The Oberlin Jubilee*, 60).

Asa Mahan said of the Lane Rebels that they went out not knowing whither they went. Perhaps so. But they felt that God knew, and that was sufficient. Oberlin became the promised land for these dissidents and rebellious heretics—a center of both abolitionism and revivalism.

BIBLIOGRAPHY

Ballantine, W. B., ed. *The Oberlin Jubilee, 1833–1883*. Oberlin: E. J. Goodrich, 1883.

Barnes, Gilbert H., and Dwight L. Durmond, eds. *Letters of Theodore Dwight Weld*. 2 vols. Gloucester: P. Smith, 1965.

Beecher, Charles, ed. *Autobiography, Correspondence, Etc. of Lyman Beecher*. 2 vols. New York: Harper and Bros., 1864.

Feuer, Lewis S. *The Conflict of Generations: The Character and Significance of Student Movements*. New York: Basic Books, 1969.

Lipset, Seymour M., and Sheldon S. Wolin, eds. *The Berkeley Student Revolt*. Garden City, NY: Anchor Books, 1965.

Mahan, Asa. *Autobiography*. London: T. Woolmer, 1882.

A Statement of the Reasons Which Induced the Students of Lane Theological Seminary to Dissolve Their Connection with That Institution. Cincinnati: n.p., 1834.

Tappan, Lewis. *The Life of Arthur Tappan*. New York: Hurd and Houghton, 1870.

Stuart C. Henry,
assisted by George H. Shriver

The Louisville Thirteen
(1958)

On 12 June 1958, upon recommendation of President Duke K. McCall, the Board of Trustees of the Southern Baptist Theological Seminary, Louisville, Kentucky, voted to dismiss 13 professors from the faculty of its School of Theology (it also had schools of church music and religious education). With some of the 55 Trustees being absent, the vote for dismissal was 32 affirmatives and 9 negatives.

Such an unprecedented wholesale firing of almost half of the entire faculty of the School of Theology of Southern Baptists' oldest and most scholarly seminary sent shock waves throughout the Southern Baptist Convention, America's largest Protestant body. Though appalled by the magnitude of this theological massacre, many Southern Baptists eventually accepted the devastating news on the grounds that the dismissed professors were guilty of gross doctrinal deviations or heresies. Nevertheless, this view was utterly groundless, for none of the official actions of the president or the Trustees ever charged the 13 professors with *any* doctrinal irregularities. Moreover, as every student knew, many of the remaining theology professors at the Seminary were just as "liberal" (or scholarly) as those who had been dismissed. However, after nearly 40 years since the firings, it now appears that the fired professors had been guilty of the gravest of "heresies" possible in the corporate life of the organizations of the Southern Baptist Convention in the last half of the twentieth century, for they had had the temerity to formally charge the president of their Seminary with misusing and abusing his enormous executive authority—and they never recanted their accusations.

The dismissals were startling for several reasons besides their devastating impact upon the professors' families and careers and upon the scholarly capabilities and reputation of the Seminary. One was that although all 13 had been assured by the Trustees at a meeting in Houston, Texas, on 23 May 1958 that any professor to be dismissed would be given a "full hearing," they were given no advance notice prior to the dismissal meeting that the president would recommend their dismissal, and they were not permitted to discuss their charges against him. A second striking fact is that 3 of the 13 were not even present at the meeting, 2 being on a trip to the Near East and 1 holding a revival meeting in Tennessee! A third arresting fact was that the president's recommendation provided that, except in unusual cases, the professors' salaries would only be paid until 31 July 1958, and this provision allowed no severance pay at all, for all professors had already earned salaries to that date by virtue of having taught the previous academic year. Another startling feature of the dismissals was their gratuitous nature, for the professors had written the Trustees less than a month before that they would resign if the Trustees did nothing specific to remedy the intolerable administrative situation.

Nevertheless, by far the most striking feature of the dismissal action was its inclusion of the president's recommendation that a special Trustee committee be authorized to *reinstate* to faculty status "one or more" of the dismissed professors who assured the committee they could "cooperate with the administration and serve in good conscience as a part of the faculty." This provision for possible reinstatement of all 13 clearly demonstrated the ambivalence of the president and Trustees about the wisdom and desirability of the entire dismissal proceeding. Only 1 of the professors, J. J. Owens, availed himself of this provision, being reinstated by the committee in early July 1958. The remaining 12 refused to meet with the committee, and as matters developed, their firings became permanent.

The names of the 13 professors, along with their faculty rank, home states, and year of joining the faculty, are as follows:

J. Morris Ashcraft, associate professor of archeology, Arkansas, 1955.

Thomas O. Hall, Jr., associate professor of Old Testament, North Carolina, 1956.

J. Estill Jones, associate professor of New Testament, Oklahoma, 1951.

John M. Lewis, associate professor of theology, Florida, 1956.

William L. Lumpkin, associate professor of church history, Virginia, 1954.

William H. Morton, professor of archeology, Missouri, 1948.

J. J. Owens, professor of Old Testament, Oklahoma, 1948.

Heber F. Peacock, Jr., associate professor of New Testament, Arizona, 1956.

Theron D. Price, professor of church history, Arkansas, 1948.

Guy H. Ranson, associate professor of ethics, Texas, 1952.

T. C. Smith, associate professor of New Testament, Louisiana, 1950.

Henry E. Turlington, associate professor of New Testament, Florida, 1949.

Hugh Wamble, associate professor of church history, Georgia, 1958.

On the day after the firings, the president was quoted as asserting that the crisis could have been avoided if the 13 had been willing to negotiate individually and not as a "power bloc." He also stated: "It is distressing to lose the services of these good men. They are competent men, whose continuing effective ministry I would do anything within my power to assist" ("Seminary Head," 1). The same newspaper article quoted the professors as follows:

> We have tried to uphold the Christian principles of human dignity and worth, personal freedom within the framework of Christian fellowship and Baptist institutions, personal responsibility in the light of Christian teaching, and mutual respect in working together. Only after many unsuccessful efforts with the administration to correct these problems in a way consistent with these principles did we refer the problems to the board of trustees. We had hoped for a reconciliation, but all efforts have been unsuccessful.

In December 1958, the American Association of Theological Schools (AATS) censured the administration and Trustees for the dismissal and indicated forcefully that they had one year to correct the injustices involved or face the loss of accreditation for the Seminary. Its report was severely critical of the administrative procedures involved in the dismissal and declared that it was a device intended to secure the discharge of 2 professors and the reinstatement of as many as possible of the remaining 11. Moreover, it also affirmed that "trustees and president are ultimately responsible for the conditions that have made possible the development of what they themselves call an 'intolerable situation' " ("Seminary's Dismissal," 1, 18). The AATS also requested the resignation of President McCall as one of its vice presidents and as a member of its accrediting commission. Understandably, the dismissed professors generally interpreted these steps by the AATS as vindications of the positions they had taken. However, most of them had taken other jobs by that time and had little desire or expectation of being reinstated to the Seminary faculty.

When it became clear that only 1 of the 13 would seek reinstatement to the faculty, the Trustees' Financial Board on 11 July 1958 took action to extend the salaries of the other 12 until 31 January 1959 or until they obtained employment elsewhere if they did so before that date. The action in December 1958 of the American Association of Theological Schools warned the Seminary that after one year it would note carefully if the Seminary had taken adequate steps "to repair the damage" to the dismissed professors. In January 1959, 3 of the 12—Lumpkin, Ranson, and Wamble—remained unemployed elsewhere; and apparently because of the concern of the American Association of Theological Schools, the Trustees voted in March 1959 to extend their salaries until 31 July 1959 unless they obtained employment prior to that date. Nevertheless, the AATS continued to prod the Seminary's Trustees and administration concerning the issue of repairing the financial damage to the professors, and in early 1961 the Seminary made payments to all 12 professors in varying amounts sufficient to bring the total paid each professor since dismissal to the equivalent of one year's salary.

Moreover, in an apparent further effort "to repair the damage" to the dismissed professors, in March 1959, the Seminary Trustees voted to rescind their action of 12 June 1958 that previously fired them and asked that the 12 then resign! As already indicated, most of them had by that time already taken permanent positions elsewhere, and it seems that they all then dutifully "resigned," although reportedly 1 or 2 never bothered with the formality. Thus ended one of the most bizarre "heresy trials" in the history of American religion.

What were the issues at stake in this conflict between some of the faculty and the president that resulted in such catastrophic personal and institutional consequences? In essence, they seem to have centered in a growing faculty disillusionment with some performances/practices of the president and his dismay at the sharpness and persistence of the professors' criticisms of him. However, the Seminary's faculty had not always been sharply critical of President McCall, who became the Seminary's seventh president in 1951. The annual reports of the faculty of the School of Theology given to the Trustees each March for the years 1952–1957 raise no discordant notes about the president and his administration. On the contrary, several of these reports are rather fulsome in their praise of him, referring to his "courageous and competent administrative leadership," to his "wise, tactful, and aggressive leadership," and to his "capable administrative direction."

However, the School of Theology's faculty report for March 1958 reflected a notable change in tone. Adopted by the entire school's faculty with only two dissenting votes over the objection of the president, it spoke of "low faculty morale" ("The Baptist Seminary's Troubles," 1). It indicated generally that there were concerns about the implementation of some recommendations of the Booz, Allen, and Hamilton management consultant firm; "administrative flexibility" regarding faculty additions, promotions, salaries, and tenure; and "unilateral" administrative action without full faculty consultation on matters of vital faculty significance. In response to this report, the Trustees took little action except to reaffirm their confidence in the president and to state that they planned no major changes regarding the administration.

Immediately after the March Trustee meeting, tensions between the faculty and president heightened greatly, with some professors being told that they must cease opposing the president's actions or else face swift termination. Faculty morale plummeted even more, and the president announced that the Trustee subcommittee on the School of Theology would return to the campus on April 28 in order to examine the situation further. Alarmed by what they regarded as ominous prospects for several professors, the 13 professors allied themselves into a group that prepared a written "Supplementary Report" (to the annual report given to the Trustees in March) and delivered it to the Trustee subcommittee when it convened on April 28.

The "Supplementary Report" affirmed that "accumulated evidence has brought us to the painful but inevitable conclusion that Dr. McCall, by word, act, and temperament, has lost our respect, confidence, and trust. We, therefore, appeal to the Trustees to help us resolve our difficulties" ("The Baptist Seminary's Troubles," 1). Beginning with a pledge of "full loyalty under God" to the Seminary and to the Baptist denomination, it stated that they had for many months witnessed alarming incidents and deplorable developments but had hesitated to voice their anxieties to others. After trying unsuccessfully to resolve their concerns by individual and group meetings with Dr. McCall, they had finally and reluctantly concluded that the Trustees should be made aware of the grave situation.

Stating that the president had declared that professors should "either cease challenging his decisions or leave," the "Report" continued as follows:

> Not one of us considers himself to be a "rebel," or a "warrior," momentarily or constantly, against the constituted authority, much less the denomination. But we understand these terms to place us in this dilemma: either surrender our minds and consciences to him, or be asked to resign. To do either of these, or by silence to acquiesce to them, is to be less than Christian men. If we consciously accept the first alternative, we reject our Christian freedom. If we quietly accept the second, we reject our responsibility as Christian stewards.
>
> For several years the Faculty has sought to work with Dr. McCall. Many of the faculty have found it increasingly difficult to do this. The principal reason for this difficulty is that in the President's mind "working with" him and "agreeing" with him are identical. This means there is an impossibility of responsible stewardship, except at the price of jeopardizing our positions. The fact that this meeting of the Theological Trustees is seated in special session is evidence enough of this.
>
> It is our considered judgment that the President's course of action is directed toward the objective of his inevitable and absolute control of the Seminary. ("The Baptist Seminary's Troubles," 1)

As supporting evidence for their pessimistic conclusions about the possibility of working with the president, the "Report" outlined four categories of concern: threats made against professors, pretensions of allowing faculty participation, "duplicity in method of operation," and misuse of published materials in *Broadman Comments*, a Sunday school lessons study guide. As an example of the first category, it stated that at the Pendennis Club on 3 February 1958 the president had told professors that "if anyone chooses to get in the [president's] way, he will get hurt"; and then it cites details of three different professors who had been told by the president that they must cease to disagree with him or else resign ("The Baptist Seminary's Troubles," 6).

Under the heading of pretensions of faculty participation, the "Report" detailed instances of the president's adding professors to the faculty or changing their teaching duties without allowing for the customary faculty involvement; but it dwelt heavily on the point that, in the pivotal matter of selecting a dean for the School of Theology, the president had first asked for faculty recommendations but then ignored those they gave and stated that he had decided that the faculty should not participate in the selection of a dean. The section on duplicity was very brief and mainly declared that the president had asserted both that he had spent years wresting power for himself from the Trustees and that they had thrust power upon him without his seeking it.

The "Report" also stressed the point that the president had twice misused or tried to misuse publishable materials prepared by professors. Once was when he stated that the centennial history of the Seminary, to be published in 1959, which had been researched and written by Professor William Mueller (not one of the 13), would be published in the name of McCall. However, it seems that Mueller (and other professors) had protested so vehemently that McCall finally gave in and said that it would be published in Mueller's name as the author. The other case involved published materials in the book *Broadman Comments for 1958*. Several professors (about 8) had agreed to prepare background notes on biblical passages for Dr. McCall to use as "starter materials" for his Sunday school lesson commentaries in the book. Although they accepted some pay for these services, the professors had understood that their materials would be completely reworked by the final author and not be published virtually unchanged, as proved to be the case. Some professors' materials were published practically verbatim under Dr. McCall's name and with no acknowledgment of the professors' role in preparing them. The "Report" suggested that the president's action in this case was "ethically wrong" and that for similar misuse of others' materials a student would be expelled from the Seminary ("The Baptist Seminary's Troubles," 6).

President McCall's replies to these grave charges to the Trustees (and eventually to the press) were that they were all prepared in anger and rebellion, some were false, others were distortions and misunderstandings, and others were contrary to his recollection. In any event, the Trustees in their meeting on May 23 in Houston voted to reaffirm their trust in Dr. McCall, declaring that he possessed "full administrative authority and responsibility" and that those "who find themselves in rebellion" against this policy should seek work elsewhere because continued disagreement could not be condoned. Consequently, the professors' situation looked extremely bleak.

Nevertheless, some further efforts at reconciliation were attempted but without success. The professors felt that the Trustees never fully heard *them* about their charges in the "Supplementary Report," but they offered to withdraw (and not press) the "Report." However, the president seems to have demanded its repudiation and their dissolution as a coalition or "power bloc," but the 13 steadfastly refused to make these two concessions. As a result, the president recommended their dismissals on June 12, declaring that they had been "swept into rebellion," had expressed contempt for the Trustees, and had breached the fellowship of the faculty and created "a disastrous division" within it. As stated at the outset, the Trustees approved this recommendation by a vote of 32 to 9 ("The Baptist Seminary's Troubles," 6).

In retrospect, it seems clear that the conflict between the president and the Louisville Thirteen was one of individual freedom and responsibility, on the one hand, and concentration of power in the hands of business executives of modern corporations, on the other. There can be no doubt that principles of big business enshrined in the Booz, Allen, and Hamilton management consultant firm's recommendations and embodied by President McCall won the battle. Ever since the 1958 conflict, freedom seems to have been on retreat among most institutions affiliated with the Southern Baptist Convention. Practically all of them have adopted the concept of a president or "executive director" as the "chief executive officer" with supreme administrative authority and often with exclusive official access to the governing board. Obviously, this trend does not comport well with traditional Baptist notions of individual soul competency and the "priesthood of all believers." Moreover, many may continue to ask whether Baptists who have contributed so much to the spirit of religious freedom in the modern era can maintain a school with freedom in it. Does "Baptist freedom" operate at all in the determination of policy in their colleges and seminaries, or is it an outmoded concept in this era of large, complex institutions? If it is now so outmoded as to be irrelevant except in the smallest groups, are there any effective safeguards against tyranny left? It seems unlikely.

SELECTED BIBLIOGRAPHY

"The Baptist Seminary's Troubles." *Courier-Journal* (Louisville), 22 June 1958, 1, 6.

Encyclopedia of Southern Baptists. Vol. 3 Supp. 1971. S.v. "Southern Baptist Theological Seminary," by Glenn Hinson.

Mueller, William A. *A History of Southern Baptist Theological Seminary.* Nashville: Broadman Press, 1959.

"Seminary Head Blames Bloc Action for Dismissal of 13 Professors." *Courier-Journal* (Louisville), 14 June 1958, 1.

"Seminary's Dismissal of 13 Teachers Censured." *Louisville Times*, 8 December 1958, 1.

Alan Gragg

J. Gresham Machen
(1881–1937)

A Princetonian scholar in the staunchly Calvinistic-Reformed tradition of Charles Hodge and Benjamin Warfield, by the mid-1920s J. Gresham Machen would be recognized as one of the leading opponents of modernism in America, especially within his own denomination, the Presbyterian Church in the USA (PCUSA). In conducting this war on modernism, he made many enemies, because of both *what* he said and *how* he said it, especially within the ecclesiastical hierarchy of the PCUSA, with serious repercussions for his work at Princeton Seminary and his standing within the church itself, eventually leading to his expulsion from the PCUSA and the formation of a new denomination.

The PCUSA had a history of divisiveness long before its clash with Machen. The 1837 split between the Old School and New School Assemblies involved a strict allegiance to the Westminster standards on the part of the former and an acceptance of the more liberal New Haven Theology on the part of the latter. Though both wings were reunited in 1870, the legacy of a more liberal theology would remain, surfacing in the ministry of Charles Augustus Briggs* of New York (who would be tried for heresy in 1893); in the 1903 revision of the Westminster Confession into a more broadly evangelical, less strictly Calvinistic creed; and especially in the ministry of Harry Emerson Fosdick, a Baptist, who became associate minister at First Presbyterian Church, New York City, in 1918. His famous sermon of 21 May 1922, "Shall the Fundamentalists Win?" (considered by Fosdick to be a plea for tolerance), contrasted the conservative and liberal views on such doctrines as the virgin birth, the inspiration of Scripture, the Atonement, and the second coming of Christ. Conservatives saw it as an open attack upon certain fundamental truths of the Bible, a challenge that simply could not go unanswered.

Machen had been at Princeton for 16 years at the time of Fosdick's sermon, building a solid reputation as a teacher and scholar. A native of Baltimore, Maryland, Machen earned degrees from Johns Hopkins (1901), Princeton University (1904), and Princeton Seminary (1905), with further study under several leading German theologians at Marburg and Göttingen in 1906. Despite the liberalizing changes occurring in the PCUSA from 1903 to 1922, Princeton Seminary had remained relatively unchanged in loyalty to Old School Calvinism and creedal Presbyterianism according to the original Westminster Confession. As he saw modernism gaining ground throughout the PCUSA, and with the emergence of Fosdick in such a prominent position and the national attention his viewpoint was receiving, Machen felt compelled to counter, and he did so in *Christianity and Liberalism* (1923), a book Walter Lippman described in *A Preface to Morals* (1929) as "admirable . . . for its acumen, for its saliency, and for its wit." To Lippman, Machen's book was "the best popular argument produced by either side" in the fundamentalist/modernist controversy (30). His main argument, and a most galling one to such modernists as Fosdick, was that liberalism/modernism was not a perversion of Christianity but another religion altogether, one that substituted the supernatural revelation of the Bible for a rationalistic naturalism based on human experience. To Machen, faith must be grounded in historical "facts," not "reflection," upon "something that happened," not something "deduced" or "discovered." "Christianity depends," he argued, "not upon a complex of ideas, but upon the narration of an event" (*Christianity and Liberalism*, 69). It has always been those "facts" that have made Christianity "Christian." To claim the Christian life apart from its dogma, as Fosdick and the modernists were attempting to do, Machen contended, was both hypocritical and unscientific.

Machen and the conservatives won this early round in the modernist/fundamentalist controversy, forcing the General Assembly of 1923 to issue a doctrinal Deliverance requiring adherence on the part of ordained PCUSA clergy to the five doctrines (originally affirmed by the Assembly in 1910) held essential to Christian belief: (1) the inerrancy of Scripture; (2) the virgin birth of Christ; (3) the substitutionary Atonement of Christ; (4) the bodily resurrection of Christ; and (5) the reality of miracles in the ministry of Jesus. A large group of PCUSA ministers, however, meeting at Auburn, New York, in December 1923, disputed the Deliverance and its findings, issuing their own document, known as the Auburn Affirmation. They contended that those "five doctrines" of the Deliverance were nonessential to the system of doctrine taught in the Bible and, rather, should be viewed only as "theories." Eventually, over 1,200 PCUSA ministers and elders would sign the Auburn Affirmation, sufficient reason, no doubt, for explaining why the General Assemblies in succeeding years never dealt with its signees or forced them to conform to the Deliverance of 1923. This was never acceptable to Machen, and he continued to wage war against the signers, especially so when they made their presence known both in his own Presbytery of New Brunswick and at Princeton.

Though he lost the battle for Princeton Seminary in 1929, Machen was not ready to give up the entire denomination to the liberals, especially the Board of Foreign Missions. Though several signers of the Auburn Affirmation were serving on the Board and holding key appointments within the heirarachy of the Board's Committees, most conservatives were still fairly confident in the overall state of Presbyterian missions during this period, until the publication by the Layman's Report of *Rethinking Missions* in 1932. This small book sought to create a new emphasis in missions work, one marked by tolerance and acceptance of other religions, not by the proclamation of Christian dogma alone. Machen responded with a 110-page pamphlet entitled "Modernism and the Board of Foreign Missions of the PCUSA," which he distributed widely at his own expense. Machen presented a case for historic missionary work and charged the Board with six counts of failing to uphold the orthodox tenets of the Presbyterian faith as expressed in the Confession and the original mission of the Board itself. Despite Machen's impassioned arguments against liberalism within the Board of Missions, the Presbytery rejected Machen's overture, as did the General Assembly on 25 May 1933. Immediately, Machen and other leaders in the PCUSA issued an announcement proclaiming the formation of the Independent Board for Presbyterian Foreign Missions designed "to promote truly Biblical and truly Presbyterian mission work" (Rian, *The Presbyterian Conflict*, 146).

Viewing the Independent Board as a direct threat to the PCUSA's own Board, the General Assembly of 1934 issued a Deliverance stating that all church members were required by the constitution of the PCUSA to support the missionary program of the church, just as they would take communion; if they supported any independent efforts at mission work, they would face the discipline of the church. Machen and those who supported the Independent Board refused to obey this Deliverance, declaring it unconstitutional, un-Christian, and unscriptural. The conservative Clarence Macartney wrote in the 19 July 1934 issue of *The Presbyterian* that this Deliverance "savors more of a papal bull than of the deliberations of the General Assembly of a free Protestant Church," predicting that it would "result in contention and bitterness in the ecclesiastical courts." His comments were most prescient. The Assembly directed local Presbyteries to take action against any who refused to sever ties with the Independent Board. Machen, of course, refused, and in a detailed statement of his position presented to the New Brunswick Presbytery, he declared, "I cannot, no matter what any human authority bids me to, support a propaganda that is contrary to the gospel of Christ; I cannot substitute a human authority for the authority of the Word of God, and I cannot regard support of the benevolences of the Church as a tax enforced by penalties, but must continue to regard them as a matter of free-will and a thing with regard to which a man is responsible to God alone" (488). This was not the answer the Deliverance required, and consequently, in December 1934 the New Brunswick Presbytery voted to press charges against Machen. A Judicial Commission was formed, with Dr. Cordie Culp as moderator and Rev. D. Wilson Hollinger as chair of the Prosecuting Committee. The trial was set for 14 February 1935.

Machen was represented by the Rev. H. MacAllister Griffiths (managing editor of *Christianity Today* and a founding member of the Independent Board), the Rev. Edwin H. Rian (later president of the Board of Trustees at Westminster Seminary and author of *The Presbyterian Conflict* [1940]), and the Rev. Charles J. Woodbridge (a former missionary for the PCUSA who became field director for the new Independent Board). Before any charges could be read, the defense initiated a series of challenges to the right of the New Brunswick Presbytery to commence any judicial action against Machen. First, Griffiths argued that the court was already predisposed against Machen by the very makeup of its members, some of whom were signers of the Auburn Affirmation and others who were involved in the reorganization of Princeton. They were essentially long-standing enemies of Machen, and Griffiths wanted all the current members of the court, including the moderator himself, removed from the Judicial Commission. The court only removed one member, but more important for Machen, the court denied him the opportunity to turn the trial away from an examination of his own Independent Board and toward a scrutiny of the doctrinal beliefs of his accusers. Griffiths argued that "in ruling out evidence of a doctrinal nature in this case before hearing it, they [the court] have denied to this defendant the constitutional right to object to any member for any reason that might show bias or other disqualification" (*Proceedings*, 82). This would prove an insurmountable barrier to Machen's defense strategy.

Failing to have the court disqualified for bias against the defendant, Griffiths next challenged the right of the court's jurisdiction in the entire matter. To Griffiths, the Presbytery of New Brunswick was completely out of order in pressing charges against Machen, for he was no longer a member of that Presbytery. On 5 March 1934, Machen had been received by the Presbytery of Philadelphia (the vote was 78 to 48) and proceeded to participate in the deliberations of the Presbytery on that very day. However, on 13 April 1934, a complaint was filed for a stay of Machen's reception into the Presbytery, signed by 44 members of the Presbytery (one third of those present at the March 5 meeting). Griffiths argued that since the original vote of March 5 constituted an official "action" of the Presbytery, the complaint that was filed could not "stay" that action; it could only "protest" that action. Otherwise, the minority would rule the majority in matters of democratic parliamentary procedure. The prosecution claimed that the New Brunswick Presbytery was never officially notified of Machen's reception by Philadelphia. Griffiths argued that this was merely a clerical error and was irrelevant as to whether Machen had been officially received at Philadelphia. Machen had been received by a vote of approval, which to Griffiths was sufficient ground for ending the trial on the basis of improper jurisdiction. The prosecution, however, disagreed, admitting that Machen had been received by Philadelphia but insisting he had not been "actually" received. According to the *Book of Discipline*, chapter 2, section 3, "A minister dismissed from a Presbytery shall be subject to its jurisdiction until he *actually* becomes a member of another Presbytery" (emphasis added). Since Machen, whether for clerical reasons or the issue of the stay, could not produce a valid certificate of membership in the Philadelphia Presbytery, he was held to be still under the jurisdiction of New Brunswick and hence subject to the court and its decision.

The defense next argued that the court be dissolved because of an earlier report issued on 25 September 1934 and approved by the New Brunswick Presbytery on 20 December 1934, citing Machen as "guilty" of various offenses against the church and his ordination vows. Mr. Hartmann of the prosecution thought this line of attack "altogether captious, technical and not upon the real merits of this case" (*Proceedings*, 207), to which Griffiths vehemently objected. The prosecution insisted the Presbytery had "passed no judgment" against Machen, nor was the court predisposed against him. The defense felt otherwise, but once again, they were overruled. Having failed in his efforts to have the members of the court disqualified, the jurisdiction of the court disallowed, and the court itself dissolved for reasons of pretrial bias, Griffiths now argued that the charges should be dropped because they were "insufficient and fatally defective" (*Proceedings*, 218), creating an illegitimate basis for the court's proceedings. As with the preceding attempts, so here the court overruled the defense and found the charges "sufficient and regular both in form and legal effect" (*Proceedings*, 241). Having rejected all the defense's motions for dismissal, the court finally presented the charges against Machen: "violation of his ordination vows," "disapproval of the government and discipline" of the PCUSA, "renouncing and disobeying the rules and lawful authority of the Church," "advocating rebellious defiance against the lawful authority of the Church," refusing "to sever his connection with the Independent Board for Presbyterian Foreign Missions," "not being zealous and faithful in maintaining the peace of the Church," rebelling "against his superiors in the Church in their lawful counsels," failing to keep "his lawful promises," and "refusing subjection to his brethren in the Lord" (Rian, *The Presby-*

terian Conflict, 175). Machen, of course, pled "not guilty" to all charges, *the only time* he spoke directly to the court throughout the entire trial.

The court, anticipating that Machen might use the proceedings to put its own members and the church on trial, introduced rules of argument (with no prior warning to the defense) that essentially denied Machen any opportunity to present the kind of case he desired. The court ruled that it would not allow "any further arguments or inferences based on the Auburn Affirmation," nor any "against the Board of Foreign Missions" or "the Princeton-Westminster Seminary controversy" (*Proceedings*, 268). It also ruled that it would not accept any arguments about the legality of the Assembly's 1934 Directive against the Independent Board and its supporters. The court defended its action by arguing that "it is one of the well established and fundamental principles of the Presbyterian system that a subordinate judicatory cannot sit in judgment upon the acts or deliverances of a superior judicatory, whether or not we think those acts or deliverances have been wise, equitable, and for the edification of the Church. So long as such acts and deliverances stand this Commission has no power but to obey" (268). The defense was outraged by this maneuver. To Machen, the Auburn Affirmation was material to the case, for he deemed it a heretical document. If he had made false charges against the Board of Foreign Missions, as he had been charged, then he ought to be allowed to show that what he had said was "not false, but true" (275). To be denied this opportunity, Griffiths argued, was "a violation of the constitutional rights of this defendent" (275), an exercise of tyranny on the part of the court, turning the entire proceedings into a travesty of justice. "It remains almost incredible," Ned Stonehouse wrote, "that a Presbyterian court should thus have flouted the most elementary principles of justice" (*Memoir*, 491). As the defense argued, "If God alone is Lord of the conscience, and if a man is not bound to obey the commandments of men contrary to the Word of God, then if a man is accused it is his constitutional right to plead before the courts of his church that the commandment is contrary to the Word of God, and his plea ought to be heard, because the constitution of his church gives him the right to disobey in such a case, for if the commandment is contrary to the Word of God he is no offender and should not be regarded as such" (*Proceedings*, 278–279). To remove Machen's right to question the legality of the Assembly's and the Board of Foreign Missions's actions was to eliminate "everything material to this case" and to prejudice "the rights of this defendant in all subsequent proceedings" (279). The defense was granted an exception, but the ruling stood.

The prosecution then proceeded to read the court's argument against Machen, beginning with a clear disclaimer as to any doctrinal basis for this trial. To the prosecution, this was purely an administrative affair. "We are *not*," prosecutor Hollinger insisted, "accusing him [Machen] of violating the doctrinal standards of our Church" (281). This was not "a contest between those popularly known as Modernists and Fundamentalists," he argued. The issue was that Machen had set himself above the directives of the Denomination. The Assembly of 1933 had voted its approval of the Board of Foreign Missions, but Machen would not accept that action and hence formed his own Independent Board. The General Assembly of 1934 then ruled that the formation of this new Board was "not only a usurpation of authority, but also a repudiation of the jurisdiction of the General Assembly," issuing a Directive requiring all members to "sever their connection with this Board." Refusal to do so would be "considered a disorderly and disloyal act on their part and subject them to the discipline of the Church" (286). The charges against Machen, Hollinger insisted, were not the result of doctrine but of "rebellion against the lawfully constituted authority of the Presbyterian Church in the U.S.A.," and as a result, Machen was "guilty of breaking his ordination vows" and "disturbing the peace of the Church" (287).

As the prosecution admitted certain documents concerning the Board of Foreign Missions, the defense tried once more to raise the doctrinal question, arguing that certain actions of the General Assembly placed "human authority" over "the Word of God" and that the Board of Foreign Missions was "furthering heretical propaganda" (302). For Machen to have complied with the Assembly's Directive and given full support to the Board of Foreign Missions would have made him "guilty of violating the ninth commandment," of "concealing the truth and undue silence in a just cause and of holding his peace when iniquity called for reproof," and of being "false to his ordination vow to study the purity of the church" (303–304). Once again, however, the court ruled that it would hear no evidence of this nature against the Assembly or the Board of Foreign Missions. Since this was the only hope the defense had of turning the trial toward the doctrinal issues that had been dividing the denomination for almost 15 years, Machen considered the trial a prejudged formality and advised his counsel to inform the court that "in view of the rulings of this Commission the defense has nothing further to say to this Commission" (310). They were not "resting" their case, Griffiths explained: "We cannot rest a case which we have not had an opportunity of presenting" (306). When the court clerk tried to clarify the defense's position ("In other words, to these six specific charges you offer no defense" [310]), Griffiths quickly pointed out that they *were* prepared to offer a defense but that the court would not allow them the opportunity to do so; hence, the defense had been silenced by the actions of the court, not by lack of evidence. The prosecution nevertheless insisted on presenting its evidence against Machen, whether the defendent responded or not, and they did so at the next session of the court.

When the trial convened again on 19 March 1935, the court expressed outrage over an article that had appeared in the New York *Times* on 9 March 1935 in which Machen had publicly attacked the proceedings of the court. Machen complained in his statement to the *Times* that "without allowing a word of evidence or argument, the commission simply announced that all consideration of the constitutionality of the action of the last General Assembly of the Presbyterian Church in the U.S.A. against the Independent Board for Presbyterian Foreign Missions would be debarred, and also all criticism of the doctrinal policy of the official Board of Foreign Missions of the Presbyterian Church in the U.S.A." (318). His case, he felt, had been prejudged without a hearing. "I am to be condemned on the ground that I have disobeyed a lawful order, but am not allowed to be heard when I offer to prove that the order is not lawful but unlawful. And I am to be condemned for making false assertions against the Board of Foreign Missions of the Presbyterian Church in the U.S.A., but am not allowed to be heard when I offer to prove that those assertions are not false but true. It is difficult to see how ruthless unfairness could go much further than that" (*Proceedings*, 319). The prosecution considered this behavior both unethical and illegal, but Machen and his defense team thought otherwise. The court clerk insisted the article be made a matter of record for the trial, which no doubt was exactly what Machen wanted.

Since Machen and his defense team had officially declared they had nothing further to say to the court, the prosecution proceeded to its closing argument. Its main point was this: Will the affairs of the church be conducted in a lawful manner or in a spirit of rebellion? To Hollinger, the issue was quite simple: You could protest lawfully or you could withdraw, but you could not choose to be divisive. Machen had refused to accept the Assembly's approval of the Board of Foreign Missions and had determined to thwart the efforts of the legitimate Board by forming his own illegitimate Independent Board. He thus became "guilty of the charge of disapproval, defiance and acts in contravention of the government and discipline of the Presbyterian Church in the U.S.A." (*Proceedings*, 373). Because he held the rulings and wishes of the Assembly in "contempt," Machen violated both his ordination pledge and the Word of God in his failure to submit to his superiors. Consequently, his actions disturbed the peace of the church, and for this he must be disciplined. Griffiths objected to the prosecution's "selective" quoting of the church's ordination pledge ("Do you promise to be zealous and faithful in maintaining the peace of the Church?"). Griffiths wanted the entire quotation read: "Do you promise to be zealous and faithful in maintaining the truths of the Gospel and the *purity* and peace of the church, which, *whatever persecution or opposition may arise unto you on that account?*" (384; emphasis added). To Machen, maintaining the "purity" of the church superseded maintaining "peace" if false doctrine were involved. To press for such "purity" was certain to be divisive and could even lead to persecution, but it was not to be overlooked, nor was the church to compromise its standards in order to accommodate false doctrine or illegal actions coming from any member, committee, or organization within the church. Thus, Machen's argument was that he was simply fulfilling his ordination vows and that it was the Assembly, the Board of Foreign Missions, and even this Judicatory Commission who were disturbing the peace of the church and violating the purity of its doctrinal standards.

This assertion, of course, the court would not entertain, and once again, the defense was overruled. The Assembly's Directive and the Board's actions merely violated Machen's ideas, not those of the Word of God, the prosecution countered. Machen had set himself up as supreme judge in these matters, and that could not be tolerated in a democratic institution. If "allowed to proceed unchecked," Hollinger argued, "there is no end to the disturbance which will ensue" (396). "Defiance of constituted authority" was the real matter of the trial and the issue before the court that day: "Shall a dissatisfied minority be permitted to set up an independent and defiant government within the borders of the Church to which they have pledged allegiance?" (397). Once again, Griffiths argued that Machen's "defiance of constituted authority" was based on fundamental doctrinal issues, but Hollinger again dismissed the claim.

> Doctrinal beliefs have nothing to do with this trial. The defense tried to throw what had the appearance of a smoke-screen to evade the real issues by bringing counter charges of a doctrinal character. The presbytery of New Brunswick, which is back of this trial, believes in the great fundamental doctrines of the Church as sincerely and loyally as does this defendant. It does not stand, however, for the divisive spirit which seems ever to follow in his wake. It believes in being loyal to the lawfully constituted courts and agencies of our Church, endeavoring to correct evils within lawful channels rather than to set up rebellious organizations in opposition. (398)

To Hollinger, the decision of the court was simple. It must condemn the rebellious spirit of a divisive minority and uphold the lawful submission and orderliness of the faithful majority. To no one's surprise, the court ruled on 29 March 1935 that J. Gresham Machen was guilty as charged on all six counts of insubordination and violation of his ordination vows, and was immediately "suspended from the exercise of his office as a minister in the Presbyterian Church in the United States of America, until he shall give satisfactory evidence of repentance" (*Minutes*, 25).

Reactions in the press were largely sympathetic to Machen, even by those who disagreed with his beliefs. Though admitting at times their dislike of his "intolerant" attitude, they could not accept the actions of the Presbyterian Church in condemning him either. The Rev. A. Z. Conrad of the Park Street Congregational Church in Boston commented in *Christianity Today* (June, 1935) "Not for a generation has anything so high-handed, so unjust, so utterly un-christian been witnessed as the trial of Dr. Gresham Machen" (cited in Rian, 186). Albert C. Dieffenbach, Unitarian writer for the Boston *Evening Transcript*, noted in an April 1935 column that the trial was "a dramatic situation, extraordinary for its utter reversal of the usual situation in a judicial doctrinal conflict. It amounts virtually to this: one man is declaring that, in administrative effect, his whole church has become heretical" (Stonehouse, *Memoir*, 491). Many agreed with Machen that the case was impossible to judge apart from any doctrinal considerations. As one writer asked in *Christianity Today*, "Is it not a doctrinal question to ask whether the authority of the General Assembly is superior to that of the Word of God?" (Stonehouse, *memoir*, 492).

Though expelled from the PCUSA, Machen was determined to preserve what he believed to be a truly Presbyterian Reformed Church in America, and so in 1936 he and several other like-minded conservatives (many of whom had been tried by the PCUSA as well) formed what would eventually become the Orthodox Presbyterian Church. But the new denomination struggled, both internally and externally, its first year, taking its toll upon Machen. He died inauspiciously of pneumonia in Bismarck, North Dakota, on 1 January 1937. Even H. L. Mencken, though no friend to fundamentalism, would recognize that Machen, in his relentless stress upon doctrine, had hit the central nerve of modernism. "The body of doctrine known as Modernism is completely incompatible, not only with anything rationally describable as Christianity, but also with anything deserving to pass as religion in general," Mencken wrote in January 1937 for the Baltimore *Evening Sun*. Machen "saw clearly that the only effects that could follow diluting and polluting Christianity in the modernist manner would be its complete abandonment and ruin," Mencken noted. "Either it was true or it was not true. If, as he believed, it was true, then there could be no compromise with persons who sought to whittle away its essential postulates, however respectable their motives" (Rian, *The Presbyterian Conflict*, 215).

Though never officially argued, the Auburn Affirmation provided one of the most important ironies in the Machen trial. The moderator, Cordie Culp, was a signer and, in so doing, had leveled a protest at what he and over 1,200 other Presbyterian ministers perceived as an attempt on the part of the 1923 General Assembly to go beyond the bounds of the Westminster Confession of Faith and violate an individual's liberty of thought by requiring "the submission of the mind or conscience to any human authority" (292). As the Confession states in chapter 20, section 2, "God alone is lord of the conscience and hath left it free from the doctrines and commandments of men which are in anything contrary to his Word, or beside it, in matters of faith or worship. So that to believe such doctrines, or to obey such commandments out of conscience, is to betray true liberty of conscience, is to destroy liberty of conscience, and reason also." The Auburn

Affirmation argued that to declare any doctrine "an essential doctrine" was "to amend the constitution of the church in an unconstitutional manner" (295). Thus, in pronouncing judgment upon the ideas expressed in Harry Fosdick's sermons, the church had acted unconstitutionally and, in effect, "condemned a Christian minister without using the method of conference, patience and love enjoined on us by Jesus Christ" (295). The signers of the Auburn Affirmation sought "for the preservation of the unity and freedom" (297) of the church, but it was a unity based upon ecclesiastical, not doctrinal, commitment. When Machen tried to use these same arguments concerning "freedom" and "unconstitutionality," however, they were not allowed, for Machen had gone beyond the realm of belief into action. The Auburn Affirmation, though a radical document to Machen, was nevertheless passive in its resistance to the Assembly. They simply refused to comply with a directive they disagreed with. Machen did the same, but he acted upon that disagreement by forming a counterorganization. To Machen, ecclesiastical "unity" could not come before doctrinal "purity." To the signers of the Auburn Affirmation, such purity was subsidiary to the overall unity of the church. Despite their rhetoric of "tolerance," however, when confronted by the arguments and actions of Machen, the Assembly of 1934, dominated by the liberalism of the Auburn Affirmation, reacted much the same way the Assembly of 1923, led by the conservatives, did in responding to Fosdick's modernism. Each was forced out, and neither with the best of hearings.

Machen's trial reveals another important aspect of the modernist/fundamentalist controversy, and that is the inevitable awareness among conservative evangelicals in the 1930s that the mainline denominations had been taken over by forces opposed to doctrinal purity and that actions from within would no longer work. Hence, the only alternative was to form "independent" movements and organizations that were free of ecclesiastical baggage and compromise. The Assembly's Directive against Machen's Independent Board presented conservatives with an "inevitable choice." As one writer for *Christianity Today* posited in July 1935, "If the old Board had by its policies forfeited its true Presbyterian spiritual heritage, then those who held without equivocation or compromise to the glorious faith once for all delivered unto the saints had no alternative but to establish their own agency" (Stonehouse, *Memoir*, 482). Since they could not break down the "walls of ecclesiastical bureaucracy," the writer continued, conservative evangelicals and fundamentalists would proceed to establish their own "independent" denominations, schools, and mission agencies, which they did in large numbers between 1925 and 1950. Each group, ironically, demonstrated their own brand of intolerance: The independent fundamentalists could broach no doctrinal variations; the denominational liberals could suffer no ecclesiastical countermovements. Both Fosdick and Machen would discover, unfortunately, that within this debate there would be no middle ground.

BIBLIOGRAPHY

Hart, Darryl G. *Defending the Faith, J. Gresham Machen and the Crisis of Conservative Protestantism in Modern America*. Grand Rapids, MI: Baker Books, 1995.

Lippman, Walter. *A Preface to Morals*. New York: Macmillan Co., 1929.

Loetscher, Lefferts A. *The Broadening Church: A Study of Theological Issues in the Presbyterian Church since 1869*. Philadelphia: University of Pennsylvania Press, 1954.

Longfield, Bradley J. *The Presbyterian Controversy: Fundamentalists, Modernists, and Moderates*. New York: Oxford University Press, 1991.

Machen, J. Gresham. *Christianity and Liberalism*. New York: Macmillan, 1923.

Marsden, George M. "J. Gresham Machen, History and Truth." *Westminster Theological Journal* 42 (1979): 157–175.

Minutes of the Special Judicial Commission of the Presbytery of New Brunswick. Trenton, NJ, 1935.

Proceedings of the Special Judicial Commission, New Brunswick Presbytery. Presbyterian Church in the United States of America vs. J. Gresham Machen. Trenton, NJ, 1935.

Rian, Edwin H. *The Presbyterian Conflict*. Grand Rapids, MI: William B. Eerdmans, 1940.

Roark, D. M. "J. Gresham Machen and His Desire to Maintain a Doctrinally True Presbyterian Church." Ph.D. diss., University of Iowa, 1963.

Russell, C. Allyn. "J. Gresham Machen, Scholarly Fundamentalist." *Journal of Presbyterian History* 51 (1973): 41–69.

Stonehouse, Ned B. *J. Gresham Machen, a Biographical Memoir*. Grand Rapids, MI: William B. Eerdmans, 1954.

Timothy David Whelan

Molly Marshall
(1949–   )

Molly Truman Marshall served from February 1984 through December 1994 as a member of the faculty of the Southern Baptist Theological Seminary. An associate professor of Christian theology at the Louisville, Kentucky, school, she was the first woman to teach theology at a seminary of the Southern Baptist Convention (SBC) and the only woman ever tenured to do so. Since 1995, she has been at Central Baptist Theological Seminary in Kansas City, Kansas, where she is now professor of theology, worship, and spiritual formation, with tenure (Marshall interviews, 1996). Central Seminary is affiliated with American Baptist Churches in the USA, not with the Southern Baptist Convention.

Although there was no heresy trial when Marshall left Southern in 1994, a trial was in the offing. It is questionable, as I will show here, whether such a trial could have been fair. For one thing, the outcome of that trial was known before the charges were even formulated.

CONTEXT: TWO PRESIDENTS

Professor Marshall's resignation from Southern Seminary at the age of 44 is incomprehensible apart from a 1979–1990 development within North American Protestantism that has been called both "the fundamentalist takeover" of the Southern Baptist Convention and "the conservative resurgence" in the SBC. I most often use the *takeover* terminology (James and Leazer, *The Takeover in the Southern Baptist Convention*; Hefley, *The Conservative Resurgence in the Southern Baptist Convention*).

So far as Southern Seminary's Board of Trustees is concerned, the "tipping point" came in April 1990. At that time extreme conservatives became a majority and took working control. Still serving as president, however, was Roy L. Honeycutt, a resourceful moderate. From 1986 on, having concluded that the takeover was probably inevitable, Honeycutt had pursued a strategy of reaching out to both sides (Honeycutt interview, 8 August 1996). Nor was it at all certain in the early 1990s that his strategy must fail: Some significant fraction of Southern's faculty might continue indefinitely to be moderates—though perhaps not Marshall, whose very existence as a former woman pastor was a provocation to fundamentalists.

In 1993, Honeycutt retired, however, and the Trustees elected 33-year-old R. Albert Mohler, Jr., to succeed him. In the mid-1980s Mohler had been active in moderate efforts to resist the takeover movement, very visibly so on the issue of women in the ministry. But since the late 1980s—and since being better instructed about what the New Testament teaches regarding women pastors, as he explains his switch on women pastors—Mohler had been a rising star in the ranks of the movement he had previously opposed (*Baptists Today*, 4 March 1993, 5; 15 April 1993, 15; Mohler interview, 13 August 1996).

Given this context, it might seem to be a foregone conclusion that a moderate evangelical feminist professor such as Marshall would have left Southern Seminary by 1994, especially since she had been a woman pastor and never repented of it. As a matter of fact, there were elements of "foregone conclusion" in her situation. By 1994, Marshall had decided that she would leave Southern of her own accord after a few years, although she had not made that decision public (Marshall interviews, 1996).

The unfolding events in the Marshall case were not experienced as foregone conclusions, however. Far from it.

THE "ULTIMATUM"

On Tuesday, 21 June 1994, out of the blue, Marshall was presented with what amounted to an ultimatum. It came from Mohler, who had been president since the previous August. The person fated to deliver the "Tuesday ultimatum," as I call it, was David Dockery, then the Seminary's vice president for academic administration. By all accounts, Dockery was not enthusiastic about the go-between role he had to play in this case.

And small wonder. In 1988, Dockery had been swept into one of the master strokes of Honeycutt's strategy of reaching out to both sides. The climactic events took place during the meeting of the Southern Trustees in April 1988. One of the issues to be decided at that meeting was whether Marshall, after four years on the faculty, would be granted tenure. On the eve of the meeting, conservative Trustees were confident they had 19 votes to deny Marshall tenure, 2 more than the number required. But before her case was considered, Honeycutt presented David Dockery to be elected to a faculty position in New Testament. Dockery is a believer in the inerrancy of the Bible and was at the time on the faculty of Criswell College; the president of that college was Paige Patterson—one of the three most visible leaders of the takeover movement. After Dockery was elected without dissent, Honeycutt made an impassioned plea. He asked the Trustees not to make it impossible for him to "reach out to both sides." He asked them not to "cut off one of my arms" (Honeycutt interview, 8 August 1996). In the end, the opposition to Marshall's tenure dwindled to a hard core of only 7 votes (Ammerman, *Baptist Battles*, 246–249).

One does not miss the irony. The Dockery who had been the means whereby one president was able to tenure Molly Marshall in 1988 must now, in 1994, be the means whereby another president would try to get rid of her.

According to the terms of the ultimatum Dockery delivered, if Marshall did not resign, Mohler would charge her with heresy—with teaching contrary to the Seminary's statement of faith (Marshall has consistently and vigorously denied that charge). If she were thus charged, Marshall would be tried by the Seminary's Board of Trustees in the fall; and if convicted, she would be removed from her classes in October—in midsemester—and any official connection she had with her graduate students would end at that point. Marshall was supervising seven doctoral students at the time, and—given other changes taking place at the Seminary, and without Marshall as their supervisor—most of these graduate students would have little chance of ever finishing their degrees (Marshall memo, 1994; Marshall interviews, 1995).

But if the embattled professor submitted her resignation by later that summer, she would be able to continue as a teaching member of the faculty through the upcoming semester, that is, until 31 December 1994. Further, she would receive a settlement, the terms of which have never been made public, though it "may have included an agreement for her salary and benefits to be provided though July 1996" (*Baptist Press*, 25 August 1994). And Marshall would be able to continue supervising her doctoral students for two and a half years, until 31 December 1996 (Marshall interviews, 1995).

CRITICIZED AND CLEARED

Although surprised by the ultimatum, Marshall knew that Mohler had questions about her views. Three months earlier, in the only direct contact she ever had with him in the outworking of this matter, Mohler had plied her with questions for an hour and a half regarding theological positions she had publicly espoused. But that March 16 meeting had been billed as a pastoral get-acquainted visit by the new president; and it was therefore a jolt—to Dockery, who was present, as well as to Marshall—when each of these two entered Mohler's office and saw that he had copies of Marshall's writings on his desk. Despite Mohler's questioning, however, nothing in that March 16 conversation indicated that dismissal proceedings were on the horizon. Marshall left the meeting with the understanding that there would be further conversations. The president would initiate them. For her part, she was invited to submit written clarifications of her views if she wished (Marshall letter, 1994).

To be sure, right through her 11 years on the faculty, Marshall had been accused of doctrinal deviations, time and again, by extreme conservatives in the SBC. But the Seminary's Board of Trustees or its Personnel Committee had cleared her on each occasion (*Associated Baptist Press*, 23 August 1994). The last such action had been in April 1992. Although the Trustees issued a warning at that point, it was a strange warning. They cautioned her not to teach views in the future that certain named persons *thought* she had taught—though the Trustees acknowledged that Marshall had not in fact espoused those views. And most important in this connection, in that same 1992 action the Trustees had brought to closure all charges against Marshall regarding things she had taught prior to that point in time (Honeycutt letters, 1992). Thus, any dismissal effort in 1994 would have had a perhaps insuperable legal hurdle to clear if it accused Marshall regarding things she had taught prior to April 1992. In Mohler's statements to the press in the summer of 1994, in fact, he said it was things Marshall had taught "during the last three years" that would provide the basis for his charges (*Baptist Press*, 25 August 1994).

ACTION CERTAIN: TIMING AND THE "SOFT MIDDLE"

Given all that, would the Trustees really dismiss her? They would indeed, Dockery told her on that Tuesday in June: "[T]hey have the votes already . . . and the will to dismiss [you]" (Dockery-Marshall exchange, 1994).

But why, one might ask, must Marshall be forced to a decision at just this time? Dockery explained that, at the just-concluded SBC meeting, a certain pastor, Jim Henry, had been elected SBC president. Because Henry had long been a prominent partisan of the takeover movement, his election would hardly seem surprising, especially in his own city. But Henry was less hard-line than the top leaders of the fundamentalist political machine, and in running, he had bucked them and defeated their man—the first time their choice had been defeated since 1978. Controlling the SBC presidency had been the key to the takeover from the outset, of course, and Henry's election was therefore troubling to the fundamentalist leaders. In fact, it was downright ominous, for Henry's candidacy had been backed publicly by a longtime leader of moderates, Russell Dilday, and for three months, this same Dilday had been a certified martyr-hero throughout much of the SBC. On 9 March 1994, after 16 years as a highly effective president of

Southwestern Seminary in Fort Worth, Dilday was fired abruptly, even brutally, after he turned down inducements worth $400,000 to quietly retire. Briefly thereafter, cracks appeared in the outer circle of fundamentalist leaders. Most of the prominent pastors aligned with the takeover remained silent. A few even criticized Dilday's firing. So much was this the case that Southwestern Trustees complained in public that they were getting no praise for doing something their leaders had urged them to do for 10 years, namely, to get rid of Dilday. Soon they got their pubic praise. But Jim Henry won anyway, 55 percent to 45 percent, and the Dilday factor made much or all of the difference (*Baptists Today*, 16 June 1994, 2; 14 July 1994, 1).

This situation was in Dockery's mind when he explained to Marshall on June 21 why she had to go: "The hardliners were unnerved by the election of [Jim Henry]; thus, they are in no frame of mind to allow another 'defeat.' " To this Dockery added, in words Marshall quotes verbatim, "They are afraid of a soft middle opening up in the SBC" (Dockery-Marshall exchange, 1994). Interestingly, Mohler has confirmed that Dockery made this "soft middle" statement: "I am aware that David said that, but I didn't say it to him" (Mohler interview, 13 August 1996).

On its face, this "soft middle explanation," says Mohler, was forced to remove Marshall by powerful fundamentalist leaders who could probably control who would be appearing on his Board of Trustees. That explanation would take much of the onus off Mohler for axing someone who had been his friend for years—not a close friend, to be sure, but certainly a friend. Thus, this version of the events would appeal to Dockery. But is it true?

Until insiders talk—and that could be decades—we must piece together an answer. Dockery would not get into the matter (Dockery interview, 7 August 1996). Mohler denied that the decision to oust Marshall was made out of fear of a soft middle (Mohler interview, 9 August 1996). For reasons to be explored, I believe we may take Mohler's denial at face value. Even on that basis, however, it remains possible, and I think it is the case, that the fear of a soft middle caused the timing of the move against Marshall.

And, in a very important sense, timing was everything. As we have seen, Marshall was already planning to leave Southern on her own after a few years.

Nevertheless, I find the "fear of a soft middle" rendering of events seriously lacking. It appears greatly to underestimate Mohler's role in the matter.

AN EARLY UNDERSTANDING TO OUST MARSHALL?

Dockery himself carries us a considerable distance toward a fuller account of events. Without dissenting from Marshall's summary of his soft middle remarks, Dockery nevertheless redescribes what he was trying to say as follows:

> I wanted to communicate to you that it was my understanding that the SBC '94 Convention in Orlando that elected Jim Henry as president would not change matters in any way at [Southern Seminary]. I wanted to suggest the possibility that indeed if any change did occur, it might heighten the concerns of some trustees. (Dockery memo, 1994)

At first glance, this looks like self-contradiction; in speaking of the soft middle, Dockery had said Henry's election caused the decision to oust Marshall, but now he says Henry's election means that something decided earlier—no doubt the decision that Marshall had to go—must now be carried out without delay.

The apparent self-contradiction disappears, however, if the soft middle fear only determined the timing, and the decision to oust Marshall had been set in concrete earlier.

I believe that is the case and that the decision dates from February 1993, when the Southern Trustees interviewed Mohler and two other candidates for the presidency of the institution (*Baptists Today*, 4 March 1994, 5). My evidence for that conclusion is a 40-page commentary that Mohler wrote on the Seminary's 1859 statement of faith and copyrighted in February 1993 (Mohler, *A Brief Affirmation*). Mohler supplied copies of his commentary to the Trustees during the interviewing process and said, according to a former Trustee, that his understanding of the Abstract was historically sound, that some recent interpretations of it had not been, and that his understanding would govern the life of the institution if he were elected president (Julian Pentecost interview, 15 September 1996).

The stand that Mohler thus took in his interviews meshed with the best-known concern of the takeover movement, namely, that the faculties in SBC seminaries were not being held accountable for teaching in accord with the statements of faith of those institutions. If the Southern Trustees were concerned about that, then Mohler's commentary on the Abstract would tell them in a flash that they had found their man.

Mohler gave his commentary on the Abstract a decidedly prosecutorial tone by the way he interleaved his own 40 pages with a half-dozen large-print, bristly pronouncements from former presidents and leaders at Southern Seminary. An example is the first of these half-dozen statements. In it the Seminary's founding president, J. P. Boyce, says the soon-to-be-founded Seminary should have a standard of belief. A teacher's "agreement with the standard should be exact," Boyce says. "No difference, however slight, no peculiar sentiments, however speculative, is here allowable" (Mohler, *A Brief Affirmation*, preface).

Late in his commentary, Mohler takes direct aim at Molly Marshall. He does not name her and does not need to do so. He takes the idea for which she was probably most infamous among leading SBC conservatives and cites it as an idea that the Southern Seminary Abstract, which is silent on the point, "effectively excludes." That idea, as Mohler phrases it, is the belief in "a post-mortem opportunity for saving faith" (39). This is a somewhat skewed oversimplification of something in the 1983 doctoral dissertation that Marshall wrote at Southern Seminary. Speaking of godly people who never encountered the Christian gospel, she suggests that, after death, "those who do not know [Christ] have the inevitable opportunity for clarification of or confrontation with him who has been the unknown object of their faith" (Marshall, "No Salvation," 270–272).

I conclude as follows: There was an understanding between Mohler and the Southern Seminary Trustees in February 1993 that if they would elect him president, he would, among other things, move with prompt and knowledgeable finesse against Molly Marshall, among others. Such an understanding would not need to have been spoken. In the circumstances, it would have been clear even if tacit.

Would the outcome of Marshall's case have been different if Mohler's runner-up for the Seminary presidency had gotten the job in 1993? The Trustee search committee interviewed this runner-up ahead of Mohler and was ready to nominate him to the full Board until they interviewed Mohler (Honeycutt interview, 8 August 1996). Did Mohler's emphatic readiness to use the Abstract to root out heresy make the difference?

ON WHAT CHARGES?

What would the charges against Marshall have been? They certainly would have had nothing to do with the quality of her teaching. She was recognized as one of the best at the Seminary, she had won a prestigious award and was about to learn she had won a second (Marshall interviews, 1995), and in announcing her resignation, the Seminary said she was "marvelously gifted" and commented upon "her ability to relate to colleagues and students" (*Baptist Press*, 23 August 1996).

Responding to Marshall's question about charges in June 1994, Dockery guessed that the charges would fall into two areas. The first was that she might be charged with failing to relate constructively to the SBC. But that area would have provided difficult legal footing (Stiver letter, 1995), and Mohler's public statements do nothing to confirm that charges would have developed in this area.

Dockery's second area, violations of the Abstract (Dockery memo, 1994), is the one Mohler's public comments confirm. The Seminary statement about Marshall's resignation says Mohler had conducted "a thorough review" of Marshall's publications and of transcripts of some of her oral presentations and that he had "determined that Professor Marshall's stated views were significantly outside the parameters of the Abstract of Principles in several areas" (*Baptist Press*, 25 August 1994).

Mohler would not say, then or later, what these several areas were. He said it would be inappropriate, inasmuch as it had been Marshall's choice to resign rather than to have her theology examined in a trial (Mohler interview, 13 August 1996).

Dockery's 1994 guesses as to what the charges might be pinpointed five topics, namely, what Marshall taught regarding (1) the Atonement; (2) salvation only in Christ, a question pertaining to her alleged espousal of "a post-mortem opportunity for saving faith," which I discuss above; (3) whether those once saved will persevere to the end, as most Baptists hold; (4) God, whether feminine language and concepts are appropriate; and (5) the authority of Scripture.

My own judgment is that only a tendentious interpretation of the Abstract of Principles would find Marshall in violation of it. And I may have interesting company. Marshall reports two answers from Dockery as to whether he thought she taught outside the Abstract: To her privately he said no; when asked in the presence of Southern faculty, he said, "I'm glad I don't have to answer that question" (Marshall interviews, 1995). Dockery would not discuss these matters with me, but judging from the way he understood his role at Southern Seminary—to support the faculty, to be loyal to the president—he must have felt he could not have said no in the second context without resigning forthwith (Dockery interview, 7 August 1996).

GENDER OR THEOLOGY?

Thus, the question: Was it what she taught or what she was, a woman, that brought about Marshall's separation from Southern? In a nice play on a word, she says she believes gender was the matrix issue, encompassing and pervading everything else (Marshall interviews, 1995). I agree, but I believe that claim only when it is qualified in three ways.

First, the problem she posed for the fundamentalized SBC was not just that she was a woman but that when she joined the faculty she was an ordained pastor of a rural church, that she remained such for another year, that she was afterward interim pastor of a sizable city church, and that she was therefore a compelling role model for something that is anathema to fundamentalists (Marshall interviews, 1995). Her time as a pastor coincided with a famous/infamous resolution adopted by the SBC in June 1984. That resolution argues that although the New Testament approves women in other ministerial roles, it "excludes women from pastoral leadership (1 Tim. 2:12) to preserve a submission that God requires [of women] because the man was first in creation and the woman was first in the Edenic fall (1 Tim. 2:13ff.)" (Shurden, *The Struggle for the Soul of the SBC*, xiii).

The second qualification is that whereas a tenured woman-pastor theology professor might conceivably have been ignored if she were suitably demure and retiring, Marshall was too outspoken, too colorful, too persuasive, and too biblically and theologically grounded to be ignored.

And third, we must be clear that we are talking about why the SBC establishment went after Marshall early and late and not about the grounds on which the Seminary would press charges. On precisely that legal issue, Mohler's disclaimer may pass muster. He said that gender had "absolutely nothing to do with this issue" (i.e., grounds for dismissal in a trial, so I read him) and that "the issue is not the gender of the professor, but the substance of what the professor teaches or advocates" (*Baptist Press*, 23 August 1994).

A LATE INITIATIVE

Despite all, Marshall was deeply attached to the school and had a strong sense of divine calling there—and one more thing: She had a persuasive colleague named Glen Stassen, a Christian ethicist. Stassen understands such commands as "turn the other cheek" and "go the second mile" as Jesus' summons to his disciples to be not passive but aggressive, very aggressive: They are summoned to undertake daring initiatives, sometimes vulnerable initiatives, in the effort to break through destructive deadlocks and open up new possibilities.

Accordingly, three days before her final deadline, and still struggling with her decision, Marshall wrote Mohler a four-page letter in which she took "an initiative in a new direction that can help us avoid the impasse and mutually destructive confrontation that would ensue" (Marshall letter, 1994). The letter was hand delivered to Mohler's office and posted at several locations around the Seminary. Since she did not know what the charges would be, Marshall said, she would in that letter take up the 20 articles of the Seminary's Abstract in turn, affirm her thorough agreement with each, and on the articles where Mohler had questioned her views in March, explain how her views fell within the parameters laid down by that article. She concluded by offering to discuss the letter with Mohler.

Mohler responded in a hand-delivered note of August 18. "In my judgment," he wrote, "it is in our best interests to continue the process now under way between the Seminary's attorney and your own attorney."

Asked later why he did not take Marshall up on her offer to talk—perhaps she might recant, it was suggested—Mohler replied that he saw nothing new in her letter, no reason to believe there was any change in her position (Mohler interview, 9 August 1996).

RESIGNATION

At 4:55 P.M. on Friday, 19 August 1994, with the Seminary lawyers waiting outside her own attorney's office, Marshall submitted her resignation. She has given four reasons why she resigned. (1) Given what Dockery said about the Trustees having the votes and the will to dismiss her, she did not believe she would receive a fair hearing. (2) She did not believe voices of dissent would be tolerated at Southern, and thus she had no future there. (3) If she proceeded to teach in the fall without having resigned, she would in mid-October have been "yanked out of" both a master's-level class and a doctoral seminar she would be teaching. (4) Most important, she wanted to rescue her seven doctoral students—to give them a chance to finish their degrees (Marshall interviews, 1995; *Baptists Today*, 8 September 1994, 17).

BIBLIOGRAPHY

Ammerman, Nancy Tatom. *Baptist Battles*. New Brunswick, NJ: Rutgers University Press, 1990.

Dockery, David. Memo to Molly Marshall, 30 June 1994.

Dockery-Marshall exchange. 1994. See Molly Truman Marshall, memo to David Dockery, 24 June 1994, and David Dockery's 30 June 1994 memo in response. In this exchange, we have "in stereo," as it were, what Dockery told Marshall in delivering the "ultimatum" on Tuesday, 21 June 1994. Marshall summarizes what Dockery said and Dockery confirms her, point by point.

Hefley, James C. *The Conservative Resurgence in the Southern Baptist Convention*. Hannibal, MO: Hannibal Books, 1991.

Honeycutt, Roy L. Letters to Molly Marshall, 5 February and 20 April 1992.

James, Rob [Robison B. James], and Gary Leazer, eds. *The Takeover in the Southern Baptist Convention: A Brief History*. 2nd ed. Decatur, GA: Baptists Today, 1994.

Marshall, Molly Truman. Interviews by telephone, 12, 14, and 23 August 1996.

———. Interviews in person, 6–7 June 1995. On this occasion, I was able to photocopy approximately 200 pages of documents from Professor Marshall's files before she began moving out of her seminary office in Louisville, KY.

———. Letter to R. Albert Mohler, Jr., 16 August 1994.

———. Memo to David Dockery, 24 June 1994.

———. *No Salvation outside the Church?" A Critical Inquiry*. NABPR Dissertation Series, no. 9. Lewiston, NY: Edwin Mellen Press, 1993.

Marshall-Green, Molly Truman. "No Salvation outside the Church?" Ph.D. diss., Southern Baptist Theological Seminary, 1983.

Mohler, R. Albert, Jr. *A Brief Affirmation and Interpretation of the Abstract of Principles of the Southern Baptist Theological Seminary*. Atlanta, GA, and Louisville, KY: Author, 1993.

Shurden, Walter B. *The Struggle for the Soul of the SBC*. Macon, GA: Mercer University Press, 1993.

Stiver, Dan R. Letter to Michael Gilligan, Association of Theological Schools, 23 January 1995. Professor Marshall has vouched for the accuracy of the many details in this five-page letter from the person serving as chair of the Southern Seminary Faculty Committee or Liaison [with the Trustees] Committee (Marshall interviews, 1996).

Robison B. James

William Clement McCune
(1821–1894)

"The hour is a momentous one," exclaimed the Reverend Thomas H. Skinner, bringing to a close the opening argument of the prosecution against the Reverend W. C. McCune. "Never before in all our history has there been such a disposition to put 'Union before Truth' as there is to-day" (*Process*, 169). As he put his argument before the Presbytery of Cincinnati, Skinner assumed truth lay in a strict interpretation and enforcement of the Westminster Confession of Faith (1642); therefore, all attempts at the external union of Christian believers on any other basis fell outside the bounds of "Truth."

McCune did not see matters from that perspective. Coming to Cincinnati to pastor the Lincoln Park Presbyterian Church in 1867, McCune's pastoral relationship with that church was dissolved by action of the Presbytery of Cincinnati in 1873 in order for him to pursue his work for the union of evangelical Christian churches. To that end, he became editor of *Unity*, a publication dedicated to the Christian Union movement, and a speaker on behalf of Christian Union. He attended conventions of the Christian Union movement, serving as a writer for pronouncements from the conventions. He pursued this course of action after regular discharge from his pastoral duties at Lincoln Park, with Presbytery fully aware of his intent to work full-time on behalf of Christian Union, a cause in which he fervently believed and which he believed had the sanction—indeed, the command—of the New Testament. Yet in March 1877, McCune found himself before the court of Presbytery, charged with disloyalty to the Presbyterian Church because of his opinions and actions on behalf of the Union movement.

The Presbyterian Reunion of 1869 serves as the backdrop to the McCune case. After three years of negotiations, the Old School Presbyterians, those who favored a strict Calvinistic orthodoxy, and the New School Presbyterians, those who favored loosening the hold of strict Calvinistic doctrine in order to participate in the work especially of revival, reunited. During the period of schism between the two schools—which lasted from 1838 to 1869—George Marsden points out the ways in which the New Schoolers moved back toward Calvinistic orthodoxy (Marsden, *Evangelical Mind*, esp. 228). The agreement that cemented the reunion of the two churches was the adoption, by the General Assemblies and constituent Presbyteries of each body, that the Westminster Confession of Faith "shall be sincerely received and adopted as containing the system of doctrine taught by and in the Holy Scriptures." The vote was unanimous in the Assembly of the New School and overwhelming (285–9) in the Old School (Marsden, *Evangelical Mind*, 224–225).

In Skinner's view, McCune stood in violation of the basis of reunion. Skinner accused McCune of subterfuge, voting in support of reunion, with the Westminster Confession as its basis, while at the same time operating under principles that undermined the Confession's authoritative position within the church. On this view, Skinner spearheaded the prosecution.

The Prosecuting Committee was appointed by Presbytery on 4 October 1876. This appointment followed on the heels of an April investigation in which a Committee of Inquiry looked into rumors concerning McCune's beliefs and actions. After two and a half months of preparation, the prosecution brought judicial action against McCune on 18 December 1876 (*Process*, 5; *Minutes*, 261).

One offense was claimed: that McCune was disloyal to the Presbyterian Church. The offense was prosecuted under two charges: McCune's beliefs and actions. Skinner presented the first charge:

> That the Rev. W. C. McCune, being a minister of the Presbyterian Church of the United States of America, and a member of the Presbytery of Cincinnati, has, for years past, in contravention of his vows of loyalty to the distinctive faith and order of the Presbyterian Church, as also in opposition to the terms of the doctrinal and ecclesiastical Basis of union adopted, unanimously, by the Presbytery of Cincinnati (O.S.), at Avondale, September 8, 1869, Mr. McCune being present and voting for the same, and adopted by the whole Presbyterian Church (O.S. and N.S.), and in joint convention November 12, 1869, declared as of binding force, openly proclaimed and persistently advocated doctrines, principles, and views, not only at war with the standards of the Presbyterian Church, but, if generally accepted, totally subversive of its constitution and of the very existence of the Presbyterian denomination itself. (*Process*, 9–10; *Minutes*, 261–262)

Eleven specifications followed charge number one; varying numbers of proofs attended the specifications. The prosecution sought to move from the specific to the general: Proofs would sustain the specifications, specifications would sustain the charges, and charges would sustain the offense.

The 11 specifications can be summarized as follows (see *Minutes*, 262–272; *Process*, 10–36):

1. *Law of organization.* On the basis of Romans 25:7 ("Receive ye one another, even as Christ received us to the glory of God"), all evangelical denominations should join in visible, external oneness and preparation should be made immediately to prepare for this union. No member or minister should be excluded from full fellowship unless proven to be unregenerate.

2. *Antidenomination.* Existing evangelical churches, including the Presbyterian Church, have no right to exist and are essentially sinful. Denominations have no right to enforce their "peculiar and distinctive creed as to doctrine and polity."

3. *Creeds.* The Bible is the only proper creed. "The enforcement of distinctive tenets [those not commonly held by all evangelical Christians] upon the official ministry [is] an oppression of conscience."

4. *Vows of ordination.* Ministers may change their views on the doctrine and polity they affirmed in their ordination vows.

5. *Plurality of official membership.* Evangelical ministers may belong to more than one denomination, even if the principles of those denominations are in conflict.

6. *Terms of ministerial fellowship.* An evangelical minister of an evangelical denomination has a right to pastor a Presbyterian Church and sit in Presbytery, with that minister's rights of private judgment and free speech protected.

7. *Infant church membership denied.* A church based on New Testament principles is composed solely of the regenerate; therefore, infant church membership "is to be repudiated as a High-Church theory."

8. *Admission of unbaptized persons.* The only criterion for admission into the church is credible evidence of faith in Christ. Therefore, even those who do not accept the necessity of water baptism may be admitted as members.

9. *Saving faith, What is it?* True faith ipso facto excludes all heresy.

10. *Time of advocating his views.* McCune has advocated his Christian Union views, openly and actively, for years, both before Presbytery and in the secular and religious press.

11. *Common fame.* In addition to the proofs presented before Presbytery, Mr. McCune's views are widely publicized in many newspapers; moreover, a Committee of Investigation was established in

April 1876 because of "certain rumors touching [McCune's] loyalty to the Presbyterian Church."

Skinner then presented the second charge, which, in the prosecution's
view, also sustained the general offense of "Disloyalty to the Presbyterian
Church."

> That the Rev. W. C. McCune, being a minister of the Presbyterian
> Church of the United States of America, and a member of the Presbytery
> of Cincinnati, has, in contravention of his vows of loyalty to the distinc-
> tive government and discipline of the Presbyterian Church, and for the
> publicly avowed purpose of carrying into practical effect the doctrines,
> principles, and views specified under Charge I, been instrumental in ad-
> vising, promoting, and encouraging the new anti-denominational asso-
> ciation of "Union Christian Churches of America"; and, also, the new
> anti-denominational organization at Linwood and Mount Lookout,
> founded on these doctrines, principles, and views, his course herein be-
> ing, if generally allowed, totally subversive of the Constitution of the
> Presbyterian Church, and of its very existence as a distinctive denomi-
> nation. (*Process*, 37–38; *Minutes*, 272–273)

The second charge was supported by two specifications (*Minutes*, 273–276;
Process, 38–44).

1. That McCune has, in years past, been an advocate for the "Union
   Christian Churches of America"; edited *Christian Unity*; lectured
   on Christian Union principles; issued an "Address to All the Christian Ministers and Churches in North America with a Basis of
   Union"; and encouraged others to join the association, send
   delegates to its conventions, and work for "the peculiar principles
   of organic union."
2. McCune organized the Christian Union Church at Linwood and Mt.
   Lookout in order to put into practice the principles of Christian
   Union. Furthermore, he became its pastor without proper leave or
   dismissal from Presbytery.

Such was the substance of the offense, charges, and specifications submitted to the Presbytery of Cincinnati by the prosecution on 18 December
1876. Proofs were cited, as were the standards of the church that the prosecution thought McCune's beliefs and actions violated. Presbytery accepted
the charges and specifications, and a judicial investigation began. A copy
of the charges and specifications was given to McCune. Presbytery then
adjourned for the year.

At its adjourned meeting of 2 January 1877, the Presbytery of Cincinnati
adopted an order of proceedings for the trial of McCune (*Minutes*, 279–

281). Presbytery decided that the trial would proceed as follows: (1) the moderator charge the court, (2) reading of the charges to the defendant, (3) call for defendant's plea, (4) prosecution's testimony, (5) defendant's testimony, (6) hear the prosecution, (7) hear the defendant, (8) hear the prosecution in a closing speech, (9) roll call of members for opinions, (10) take the vote on specifications, and (11) take the vote on the charges. McCune then requested a postponement of the trial until the first Monday in March due to the recent illnesses of himself and his family. His request was approved.

The Presbytery of Cincinnati met on Monday, 5 March 1877, to begin the trial, concluding its work on Tuesday, 27 March, having met most weekdays for three weeks. The moderator charged the court, and the two charges formulated to sustain the offense of disloyalty to the Presbyterian Church were read to McCune. Asked to enter a plea, McCune stated, "Not guilty." The trial began in earnest (*Minutes*, 284–285).

Over the course of the next four days, 5–8 March, the prosecution presented its testimony, reading the proofs it had cited previously when it had put the case before the court on 2 January. The proofs, 48 in all, were to support the 11 specifications of charge one and the two specifications of charge two (*Minutes*, 285–325; see also *Process*, 10–44). By and large, the proofs were textual evidence, drawn primarily (though not exclusively) from the writings of McCune. McCune "professed to admit the correctness of the quotations" (*Minutes*, 285). During the course of the prosecution's testimony, McCune objected five times. The very first proof, from *Christian Unity* (1873)—which stated the necessity, based on Romans 15:7, of organic Christian union—called forth an objection because it spoke of an offense over a year old (*Minutes*, 285). McCune objected to another proof because the editorial cited from *Christian Unity* was authored by someone else (*Minutes*, 304). A third proof assumed a living witness, but the proof rested on newspaper citations (*Minutes*, 311–312). These objections were sustained. A fourth objection, claiming a committee report did not meet the criteria of being a living witness, was not sustained. After the conclusion of the prosecution's testimony, McCune withdrew his exceptions to their testimony (*Minutes*, 328). Thus, the entire textual testimony presented by the prosecution stood as uncontested testimony as to the beliefs and actions of McCune.

The prosecution closed its testimony with the argument that, as the charges showed, McCune's beliefs and actions constituted disloyalty to the Presbyterian Church, for, according to the prosecution's reading of the proofs, McCune's views and actions stood in "contravention" to (1) his ministerial vows, (2) the doctrinal and ecclesiastical terms of the Basis of Union (the Westminster Confession) for the reunification of the Old School and New School Churches adopted by the Presbytery to which McCune belonged, (3) McCune's vote for the Basis, 8 September 1869, and (4) the

Basis of Union adopted by the whole Presbyterian Church, Old School, and New School (*Minutes*, 325–326). In other words, McCune swore in his ordination vows, according to the prosecution, to uphold the standards of the church, and that standard was—by vote of Presbytery, by McCune's own vote, and by vote of the entire church—the Westminster Confession of Faith. The entire gist of the proofs was that McCune no longer upheld the Westminster Confession in either thought or practice.

The testimony of the defense began on 8 March, running through 14 March (*Minutes*, 331–382). Much of the testimony relied on witnesses called by McCune; the driving concern of McCune was to bring out that he was not disloyal to the Presbyterian Church and that he had never spoken out against it. Many of the witnesses were ministerial colleagues of McCune, coming from a variety of denominations. Many had participated as members of the council that had installed him as pastor of the Union church at Linwood and Mt. Lookout.

Rev. E. Halley, a Congregational minister, testified as to the evangelical character of the basis of membership of the Linwood and Mt. Lookout church and that, at least from a Congregationalist point of view, its founding was not irregular. More important, Halley emphasized that the church was organized by the members, not McCune. When asked, "Do ministers or members organize churches in the congregational body?" Halley answered, "Members always" (*Minutes*, 333). This testimony contravened the prosecution's argument in charge two that McCune had organized the church. Moreover, Halley testified that he had never heard McCune argue that evangelical churches have no right to exist (*Minutes*, 343).

Another Congregational minister, B. C. Lee, testified. His testimony showed that the Presbyterians and Congregationalists were in correspondence and cooperated in the founding of churches where there were no evangelical churches. McCune questioned Lee specifically on how the polity in such churches was to be decided. It was left to the membership, Lee said. Thus, McCune established that the Congregationalist method by which he was appointed to the pulpit was in order with standing agreements between the Presbyterian and Congregationalist churches (*Minutes*, 347–348). By implication, there could be no disloyalty to the Presbyterian Church based on his actions.

O. A. Hills, a member of the Presbytery of Cincinnati, was called to testify. His testimony centered first on the Common Fame issue and then on doctrine. By and large, he denied that it was known by common fame that McCune was disloyal to the Presbyterian Church. He did not accept the prosecution's testimony as having established it (*Minutes*, 355). Furthermore, Hills seemed to allow a greater latitude in the interpretation of doctrine—a position that favored McCune—than did Skinner and his committee (*Minutes*, 355–357). Hills thought one could hold to the system of doctrine represented by the Westminster Confession of Faith without holding to every particular doctrine contained within the system.

Perhaps some of the most important testimony came from Baptist minister T. J. Melish. Melish had known McCune for over 20 years, and he was well acquainted with McCune's views on Christian Union. Besides establishing that Melish had never heard McCune express a hostile opinion toward the Presbyterian Church (*Minutes*, 358, 359), McCune led his witness into a discussion of the "Address to All the Churches" that accompanied the Basis of Union adopted by the Union Christian Churches of America. McCune had helped author the Basis, and he signed the Address written by Melish. This testimony addressed the prosecution's charge that McCune taught that the Presbyterian Church was essentially sinful and had no right to exist as a denomination. Melish's testimony clarified the phrase "essentially sinful":

> Ques.—Does the phrase, "essentially sinful" occur on the first page of that address? Ans.—It does. Ques.—Did you use the phrase, "essentially sinful" as applicable to a state of things, or as applicable to evangelical denominations? Ans.—It expressly says, a state of things. . . . Ques.—Did you mean to affirm by this phrase "essentially sinful" that evangelical denominations were essentially sinful? Ans.—Not at all. I referred to the state of things before mentioned. . . . Ques.—Did the accused sign this "Address" in the sense that "essentially sinful" applied to evangelical denominations? Ans.—I presume not. The document itself does not intimate that. (*Minutes*, 359)

Moreover, Melish contended, McCune's comments about the Presbyterian Church itself had always been "very kind and respectful and fraternal."

The final witnesses called were members of the Presbytery of Cincinnati. W. H. James, who had served on the Committee of Inquiry in 1876, testified that "Common Fame" did not accuse the defendant of disloyalty to the Presbyterian Church (*Minutes*, 362). J. J. Cortelyou testified that McCune's release from the Lincoln Park Presbyterian Church had been in order and that all knew to what work—that of Christian Union—he was being released (*Minutes*, 373–374). Rev. A. Ritchie, having heard McCune lecture on Christian Union, stated that he had never heard McCune say that the existence of evangelical denominations was sinful (*Minutes*, 374, 378).

Some of the strongest evidence for the defendant was textual—especially extracts from the preface of McCune's book *Organic Unity*. Though objected to by the prosecution, the material was allowed as evidence. The extract had clear ramifications for the case before Presbytery.

> This book is thoroughly loyal to the United Presbyterian Church. It seeks to promote her purity and to increase her power to extend Christs

[*sic*] kingdom. For this end it pleads that the doctrine of close communion, and all rigid, unscriptural terms of membership may be utterly abandoned. It simply proposes that the broad union doctrine of the Westminster Confession and of the New Testament, may be the higher law. . . . It raises no question concerning any statement in the Westminster Confession.

This paragraph (*Minutes*, 368) neatly captures the entire spirit of McCune's defense: He was loyal to the Presbyterian Church and to the Westminster Confession.

On 14 and 15 March, Thomas Skinner addressed the court on behalf of the prosecution; on 19 March, McCune delivered a final speech; and on 20 and 21 March, S. J. Thompson made a closing speech for the prosecution. On Wednesday, 21 March, the process of voting on the case began, as each member of Presbytery was called upon to vote upon the specifications and charges. Because of challenges and protests by the prosecution, the process was not completed until Friday, 23 March. Of the 13 total specifications, only 3 were sustained—that McCune denied infant church membership, that he believed unbaptized persons could be admitted into the membership of a church, and that he had held Christian Union views for a number of years. The Presbytery of Cincinnati voted not to sustain charge one (that McCune's beliefs made him disloyal to the Presbyterian Church) by a margin of 29 to 8; charge two (that McCune's actions constituted disloyalty to the Presbyterian Church) was not sustained by the same margin (*Minutes*, 400). Presbytery adjourned until Tuesday, 27 March, by which time an appointed committee of five would present a final minute for the trial.

The final minute prepared for the close of the trial (*Minutes*, 401–409; *Process*, 172–178) presented a balance between an exoneration of McCune's loyalty to the Presbyterian Church and a clear disagreement with some of the language he used to propagate Christian Union views. Under charge one, regarding disloyalty because of McCune's opinions, the final minute declared that common fame had not been established (specification 11) and that the length of time issue (specification 10) was not sustained "chiefly for the reason that the statute of limitations forbids the instituting of process in the case of any person for such protracted period 'unless it (the crime) shall have recently become flagrant' " (*Minutes*, 402–430; *Process*, 173).

The nine doctrinal issues were more complicated. Six specifications were declared not sustained, the final minute noted, because, by the defendant's own testimony, he did not hold the views attributed to him. Much of the prosecution's evidence and argument were inferential. And "though the [nine doctrinal] specifications disclose some things in language and expression which are to be deprecated, and some things which the Presbytery does not approve, there is not to be found in them, in the judgment of the Court, any support for the charge of disloyalty" (*Minutes*, 404; *Process*, *174*).

There were three specifications that were sustained: those relating to infant church membership, admission of nonbaptized persons into church fellowship, and the terms of ministerial fellowship. The final minute records that the Presbytery did not think McCune's doctrine of Organic Union was established by Scripture or warranted by the Westminster Confession of faith and that McCune had been led into extreme positions on these three specifications. And though Presbytery was adverse to these three items, in and of themselves they did not constitute disloyalty to the Presbyterian Church.

In regard to charge two, that McCune's actions constituted disloyalty to the Presbyterian Church, the vote of Presbytery not to sustain the two specifications (McCune's general work in Christian Union work—editorials, conventions, associations, and the like—and his specific involvement in the Linwood and Mt. Lookout church) was interpreted by the final minute in this way. In regard to specification one, the Presbytery simply did not see McCune's involvement in Christian Union activity as ipso facto disloyalty to the church, though this position did not constitute endorsement of McCune's work, for as the minute states, "the question whether such affiliations and co-operations were wise is very different from the question whether engaging in them is evidence of a spirit of disloyalty" (*Minutes*, 407; *Process*, 176).

In regard to specification two—McCune's work at Linwood and Mt. Lookout—the judgment was mixed. Although Presbytery voted not to sustain, there were reservations expressed by the final minute. While it was shown to the satisfaction of most Presbyters that McCune was not the originator of the church, as Skinner had claimed, his acceptance of pastoral office therein could be seen in no other light than as an irregularity. Rules were not followed. McCune should have consulted with Presbytery and followed appropriate process. Yet, the final minute noted, "we are obliged to temper our judgment with mercy in view of the fact that the rule has not heretofore been strictly enforced. Our own negligence so far condones the offense as to render it unjust in us to inflict censure on account of it in the case before us" (*Minutes*, 409; *Process*, 177).

McCune thus came through the trial with "his character and standing as a Presbyterian minister . . . unimpeached" (*Minutes*, 402; *Process*, 172). He received the Presbytery's commendation as a faithful minister of Jesus Christ. Yet as soon as the final minute was read to the Presbytery, McCune requested a letter of dismissal to the Miami Conference of Congregational Churches of the State of Ohio. His reasons for this request were threefold: He thought that the eight ministers who had voted to sustain the charges would not extend him fellowship as a Presbyterian minister; that he was unwilling to impose upon such men of conviction his presence when not wanted, which he thought would result in further disharmony; and that, in his words, "I would never feel secured against individual animadversions, nor yet against the possible authoritative admonitions of the Presbytery, in the advocacy of Christian Union which I think I clearly see in the Precepts and in the examples of the New Testament" (*Minutes*, 412). McCune was dismissed. The McCune trial in Cincinnati Presbytery thus came to an end.

Yet the McCune case continued. The prosecution appealed the decisions of the Presbytery to acquit McCune. In 1878, under the leadership of the General Assembly moderator, the conservative Francis L. Patton, the highest court of the church declared that the Presbytery of Cincinnati had erred. Skinner and the conservative element of the Presbytery were vindicated for the time being.

But if the case has a broader meaning than simply the machinations involved in a local heresy trial, it has to do with what the Presbyterian Church did, in fact, become. The actions of the Presbytery of Cincinnati, dominated by Old School and strict Calvinist concerns, showed a modicum of tolerance. Indeed, even to the end, in his letter requesting transfer, this was McCune's concern—to operate in an atmosphere of "unquestioned liberty" (*Minutes*, 411). Nothing, McCune claimed, should be enforced that was not essential, and that "every member should enjoy untrammeled the Protestant right of private judgment and of liberty of speech" (*Minutes*, 368–369). In this, he was able to claim the sanction of the Westminster Confession itself, which states that "God alone is Lord of the conscience, and hath left it free from the doctrines and commandments of men" (Article xx). Every Form of Government of the Presbyterian Church, since the first of 1788, has carried that article. McCune sought to use, thus, the Confession and the Form of Government to validate his right to liberty in the way he interpreted Scripture and the Westminster Confession. On this basis, the Presbytery allowed McCune the right to interpret both Scripture and the Confession, without agreeing to his interpretation.

Skinner, of course, opposed this perspective. In one of his most bald statements on the matter, he stated: "It is time the appeal to 'conscience,' 'liberty,' 'private judgment,' 'usage,' all perverted as it is, were hushed." Skinner, in his appeal of the McCune case, did, for a time, see private judgment as a standard suppressed. The strong conservative movement in the church toward strict adherence to Westminster prevailed. Yet, not in the long run.

In a major study of Presbyterianism in the twentieth century, it is revealing that the book on belief in twentieth-century Presbyterianism is called "The Confessional Mosaic." Skinner may have won the battle; what McCune represented, at least in terms of the doctrinal standards of the

Presbyterian Church—right of conscience, right of private judgment, right of interpretation—seems eventually to have won the war.

BIBLIOGRAPHY

Loetscher, Lefferts A. *The Broadening Church: A Study of Theological Issues in the Presbyterian Church since 1869.* Philadelphia: University of Pennsylvania Press, 1954. Esp. 15–17.

Marsden, George M. *The Evangelical Mind and the New School Presbyterian Experience.* New Haven: Yale University Press, 1970. Esp. chap. 11.

Minutes of the Presbytery of Cincinnati, 1877. Presbytery of Cincinnati Microfilm Records.

Nutt, Rick. *Contending for the Faith: The First Two Centuries of the Presbyterian Church in the Cincinnati Area.* Cincinnati: Presbytery of Cincinnati, 1991. Esp. 71–73.

The Process, Testimony and Opening Argument of the Prosecution, Vote and Final Minute, in the Judicial Trial of Rev. W. C. McCune by the Presbytery of Cincinnati, from March 5 to March 27, 1877. Cincinnati: Robert Clark and Co., Printers, 1877.

Thomas J. Davis

Arthur Cushman McGiffert
(1861–1933)

LIFE

Arthur Cushman (A. C.) McGiffert was born on 4 March 1861, the son of Presbyterian minister Rev. Joseph Nelson McGiffert and Harriet Whiting Cushman McGiffert. He received his A.B. degree from Western Reserve University in 1882 and graduated from Union Theological Seminary in New York three years later with his B.D. degree. At Union he became a student and close friend of Philip Schaff,* professor of church history there. Upon graduation, McGiffert went to Europe to pursue a Ph.D. in church history, which he received from the University of Marburg, Germany, in 1888. His studies had taken him to universities in Berlin, France, and Italy before he came under the most important influence of his academic life at Marburg, Adolf von Harnack.

McGiffert enjoyed an unusually intimate association with Professor Harnack at Marburg. Harnack invited the young scholar to rent a room near his own home, and the two strolled together nearly every day. When Harnack journeyed to Paris to work on Greek manuscripts in the Bibliotheque Nationale, he took McGiffert along (Rockwell, "In Memoriam," 105).

> The young American recounted his unusual good fortune in a letter to Schaff. I have been working hard here [Paris]. Harnack spent three weeks with me—living in the same hotel—and you may imagine that it was a rare treat for me. We were together all the time—worked in the library together, walked, took our meals together, etc., and I gained a great deal from the companionship. (McGiffert, Jr., "Scholar," 36)

Harnack nurtured in his student a modern approach to and a deep enthusiasm for editing and translating ancient documents. An important aspect of late-nineteenth-century liberal theological development involved the discovery of many hitherto unknown historical documents. Rather than the lifeless study of dusty tomes, "historical study took on the dimension of surprise." Historians such as Harnack, and later McGiffert himself, were at work constructing "a new past" (32). Throughout his career, McGiffert embodied a "striking combination of careful scholarship and liberal interpretations" (Bowden, *Dictionary of American Religious Biography [DARB]*, 272). Under Harnack's guidance, McGiffert completed his doctoral dissertation in 1888, an edition of an eighth-century Greek text called a "Dialogue between a Christian and a Jew."

Also from Harnack, McGiffert learned a zest for comprehensive delineation of the entire course of Christian thought. Thereafter, whatever the specific focus of his work, McGiffert would place it within a comprehensive view of the whole history of the church.

Returning to the United States, McGiffert was ordained by the Presbytery of Cleveland in 1888. He applied for a post at Princeton Theological Seminary at Schaff's urging, the elder historian noting that "a professorship there would be in every way desirable. The only objection is that it may possibly hamper you in your freedom of investigation. But the historian has the advantage over the teacher of doctrinal theology" (quoted in McGiffert, Jr., "Scholar," 38). Though McGiffert did not land the post at Princeton (something he must have looked back on with relief), the issue of academic freedom would become a crucial issue for the young church historian.

Later in 1888, McGiffert joined the faculty of Lane Theological Seminary* as an instructor of church history and remained in that position until 1893, the final three years as professor of church history. During that time, he produced a translation of Eusebius that was included in the *Select Library of Nicene and Post-Nicene Fathers*, edited by Schaff.

In 1893, Schaff retired from his professorship at Union, and his desire was fulfilled when the school named McGiffert to succeed him. As Schaff had put it earlier, "If I had the power I would at once appoint you as the successor in the chair which I must vacate in a very few years by resignation or death. I could not wish for you a better field of labor" (McGiffert, Jr., "Scholar," 40). McGiffert taught church history at Union through 1926 when he was named professor emeritus.

Schaff's high regard for his former student is revealed in his offer to allow McGiffert to complete his multivolume *Church History*. "As the finisher of my life work, you would naturally have a claim upon the editorship of new and revised editions of the whole as they may be needed after my death" (43).

Earlier McGiffert had been approached about the position of systematic theology at Union upon the retirement of Dr. W.G.T. Shedd, Jr. His initial response had been a prompt no, but upon reflection, he seriously considered this shift of disciplines in order to become part of the faculty of his alma mater. "I have thought of Union's attitude and have realized that liberty is to become increasingly its watchword" (40). Ultimately, however, the post went to someone else. Upon McGiffert's election as Washburn Professor of Church History, Union's President Thomas S. Hastings gave him complete freedom to choose his subject for the inaugural address. Hastings confirmed fully McGiffert's belief in Union's liberty. "I am proud and grateful that there is no disposition on the part of anyone in our faculty to meddle with any other in any way, or to use undue influence with reference to governing his actions." McGiffert must have rejoiced to hear that, despite recent turmoil at Union, "[y]ou will find when you have been with us a while that each Professor is allowed a beautiful liberty in almost all matters, and that we concede to one another in a very generous way" (45).

Vastly different opinions about the inaugural address, however, signaled tensions to come within the Presbyterian Church. Schaff noted that the address was "excellent." Princeton's B. B. Warfield thought otherwise, labeling it "historical rationalism." Warfield continued, "It is most excellent Quaker teaching, but it is a direct onslaught on the very basis of Reformed and, indeed, of the whole Protestant theology" (quoted in McGiffert, Jr., "Scholar," 45).

There was clearly a distinctive atmosphere at Union in which both students and faculty expected freedom to state opinions and disagreements. When champions of "orthodoxy" charged McGiffert with heresy a few years later, a Union student defended him, saying:

> His statements, along with those of every other Professor, are often called in question, and fearlessly criticized by the students. It is the spirit of Union, and who will deny that men reared in such an atmosphere are more robust Christians, and will make them stronger ministers, than the goody-goody fellows who are taught to sit open-mouthed before some dear old Professor and swallow all his precepts whole? . . . to suppose that the result of such operations can be inimical to the faith is to confess to a very feeble belief in the ultimate triumph of truth. (Quoted in McGiffert, Jr., "Scholar," 46)

Reactions to the inaugural address were mild, however, compared to the storm of protest raised by McGiffert's publication in 1897, *A History of Christianity in the Apostolic Age.* Much of the hostility against the book was due to the legacy of the controversy a few years earlier surrounding Union professor Charles Augustus Briggs.* *The Methodist Review* noted the "positive and constructive portions" of the book but lamented its "negative and destructive work" (Tigent, "Paulinism of the First Peter," and "Dr. McGiffert and the General Assembly," 435).

In that article—a dialogue between a Congregational layman, a Presbyterian minister, and a Baptist minister—the Presbyterian laments Mc-Giffert's "views so utterly subversive of the Christian faith and so inconsistent with the standards of his own Church, which he is solemnly sworn to maintain." He fears McGiffert's "dangerous book," with its "seductive arguments." The Baptist, on the other hand, notes the virtues of freedom for theological education (Terry, "McGiffert's Apostolic Age," 196, 201).

As a student, McGiffert had wrestled with orthodoxy. He noted both its constraints and its protections in a letter to Schaff.

> It's a hard problem, how much does one owe to orthodoxy? How much of a restraining power should it be upon him in his studies, and his search after truth? The absolute freedom of investigation which exists in Germany is so fascinating and seems abstractly considered the ideal condition. I chafe against any restraints which may be imposed by the preconceptions of American orthodoxy and yet on the other hand I feel a great safeguard which Germany lacks and perhaps the real cause of truth isn't best served after all—or truth itself best found by such perfect freedom of search after it. Freedom becomes so often only another name for bondage and that is still worse. (McGiffert, Jr., "Scholar," 34)

The book was just the beginning of McGiffert's prodigious literary output, which included ten books and around 40 articles. His work has been called "the most impressive body of modernist religious scholarship in his generation" (Bowden, *DARB*, 272). Throughout his career, McGiffert worked with the basic assumption that historical change makes all religious teachings relative because of changing contexts. He finally came to deny any continuing "essence" of Christian history, insisting that as conditions change, it is necessary to address new questions with full freedom to pursue new answers. With a statement that reveals thinking in advance of most American theologians, he concluded, "History shows us . . . that Christianity has not been one thing but many and often contradictory things—and this simply means that there is no such thing as Christianity in general—though there are many particular Christianities" (Bowden, "Liberal Theology," 75).

Henry Warner Bowden insists that the most important factor in Mc-Giffert's thinking was "his conviction, as a professional historian, that what we call Christianity 'lives and grows and therefore changes. . . . It cannot be embraced within the compass of a single formula. It has no unchangeable essence, no static form, by which we may test its every varying aspect' " (76).

Such assumptions did not challenge the heart of Christianity, however, because his own piety allowed him to insist that historical certainty was not, after all, the basis for the Christian faith. Instead, he believed that

religious assurance was independent of particular historical proofs. Mc-
Giffert was able to separate his piety from his historical objectivity. In
classes he urged students to pursue objective truth relentlessly, while he
revealed the warmth and depth of his religious life only in chapel talks,
sermons, and intimate gatherings. His son spoke of the father's piety, saying, "He could say almost without exaggeration that he prayed all the
time" (McGiffert, Jr., "Father's Faith," 7).

Subjective piety and objective scholarship began to grow away from each
other. "Whereas the religious thinker in him always confessed that persons
of every age had devoted themselves to the purpose of Jesus' life and teachings, the historical scholar found little basis for making such a statement"
(Bowden, "Liberal Theology," 74).

Other notable works from McGiffert's pen include: *The Problem of
Christian Creeds as Affected by Modern Thought* (1901), *The Apostles'
Creed: Its Origin, Its Purpose, and Its Historical Interpretation* (1902),
Martin Luther, the Man and His Work (1911, a popular biography), *Prot-
estant Thought before Kant* (1911), *The Rise of Modern Religious Ideas*
(1915), *The God of the Early Christians* (1924), and *History of Christian
Thought*, 2 vols. (1932–1933).

In 1917, McGiffert accepted an appointment to the presidency of Union
Theological Seminary, a post he held until his retirement in 1926. He became known as an excellent fund-raiser, collecting $4 million to help erase
a postwar debt, provide funds for new buildings, and secure retirement
allowances for the faculty. He was also known for encouraging educational
innovations, such as charging tuition fees, lengthening the seminary course
of study to four years, and implementing early developments in field education. He also encouraged educational collaboration with Columbia University, Union's neighboring institution since the Seminary moved to
Morningside Heights in 1910.

His efforts in theological education and his publications, which were
acclaimed on two continents, "sustained McGiffert's reputation as one of
the foremost religious luminaries in the first third of this century" (Bowden,
DARB, 273).

McGiffert was married from 1885 to 1887 to Eliza Isabelle King, with
whom he had one daughter, Elizabeth. In 1891, he married Gertrude
Huntington Boyce, who bore him two children, Arthur Cushman and Ka-
tharine Wolcott.

He died after a cerebral hemorrhage on 25 February 1933.

CONTEXT OF CONTROVERSY IN THE
PRESBYTERIAN CHURCH

When McGiffert's *A History of Christianity in the Apostolic Age* appeared in 1897, the storm of controversy it raised was nothing new within
the Presbyterian Church. In the years since the reunion of New School and

Old School Presbyterians in 1869, a number of new ideas had been challenged as beyond the scope of orthodoxy. Charges against Chicago Pastor David Swing* in 1874 and the William Clement McCune* case in the late 1870s had both served notice of controversies to come.

When many leading Presbyterians advocated revision of the Westminster Confession of Faith, the battle took another form. Despite the high hopes of some that the Presbyterian Church would be "modernized," conservatives prevented the necessary two-thirds vote to implement the changes in 1892.

McGiffert's own problems with the guardians of Presbyterian orthodoxy were intertwined with two other seminary professors whose views were attacked, Henry Preserved Smith* of Lane and Charles Augustus Briggs of Union. McGiffert was a colleague of Smith on the Lane faculty during Smith's difficulties, and he joined Briggs on the Union faculty just months after Briggs had left the Presbyterian Church.

Henry Preserved Smith, professor of Old Testament at Lane Seminary, published an article on Wellhausen in April 1882. A few months later the General Assembly issued a warning on "the introduction and prevalence of German mysticism and 'higher criticism,' and of philosophic speculation and so-called scientific evolution." It cautioned "all who give instruction in our Theological Seminaries, against inculcating any views, or adopting any methods, which may tend to unsettle faith in the doctrine of the divine origin and plenary inspiration of the Scriptures, held by our Church, or in our Presbyterian systems of doctrine" (quoted in Loetscher, *The Broadening Church*, 35).

Dr. Francis L. Patton of Princeton insisted that the biblical critic "is free to investigate, but he is not free to teach contrary to the Confession of Faith." Patton defined as contraconfessional "any opinion inconsistent with the inerrancy of Scripture" and "belief in the non-Mosaic authorship of the Pentateuch" (36–37).

In the fall of 1892, McGiffert became embroiled in the heresy trial of his senior colleague at Lane, Henry Preserved Smith, professor of Old Testament. McGiffert acted as counsel for the defense; he alone on the Lane faculty supported Smith. McGiffert had expressed his firmness of purpose to Briggs. "Whatever happens, I will stand by the liberal party. I do not believe in compromise, and do not intend to be compromised" (64).

Smith was brought to trial in the Presbytery of Cincinnati in November 1892. The Presbytery found him guilty, by a vote of 31 to 26, and on 13 December 1892 suspended him from the Presbyterian ministry (65). The General Assembly in 1894 rejected his appeal.

Later, when McGiffert was being considered as Schaff's replacement at Union, some conservative members of the Board of Directors raised questions about his fitness, since he was reported to have placed himself "decidedly on the side of Dr. Briggs." Schaff counseled his former student to "be as quiet as you can" (quoted in McGiffert, Jr., "Scholar," 41–42).

McGiffert was in no mood to compromise, however. "If my true position—truly represented—unfits me for a professorship in Union I shall of course be sorry but my position will remain the same" (43).

Charles Augustus Briggs of Union Seminary hoped to help the Presbyterian Church reject both non-Christian and "rationalistic" biblical criticism in favor of a moderate biblical criticism that would avoid both extremes of reactionary conservatism and radical skepticism. Instead, his hopes were dashed, in part because of the climate of controversy that had been building within the Presbyterian Church. In his inaugural address as professor of biblical theology, Briggs lashed out at opponents and, in turn, was attacked by critics across the denominational spectrum.

The Presbyterian General Assembly's Standing Committee on Theological Seminaries recommended that Briggs's election be vetoed. The Seminary stood behind his appointment, however, and ultimately separated itself from the Presbyterian denomination. The General Assembly responded by disavowing "all responsibility for the teaching of Union Seminary." Neither would the Assembly "receive any report from its Board until satisfactory relations are established" (Loetscher, *The Broadening Church*, 55).

McGiffert's support for Briggs was less for his specific ideas than for his "fearless statement of his positions," which "would clear the way for a larger liberty within our church." McGiffert admitted, "At some points Dr. B. is in error, but I believe that in his main positions he is within confessional lines and consequently that he ought not to be condemned or silenced. Against any attempt to condemn I would stand like flint; for I believe that we must have a reasonable degree of liberty and that we must insist upon it." Like others, McGiffert was compelled to admit, "I regret his [Briggs's] tone as much as anyone can" (McGiffert, Jr., "Scholar," 42).

Failing to reach Briggs through the Seminary, his critics next attempted to have him removed from the Presbyterian ministry. He was vindicated by the Presbytery of New York, but his opponents took the case to the General Assembly. The General Assembly sent it back to New York for action. New York formally acquitted Briggs, but the General Assembly decided on a retrial. Finally, the decision came down: "This General Assembly . . . does hereby suspend Charles A. Briggs, the said appellee, from the office of a minister in the Presbyterian Church in the United States of America, until such time as he shall give satisfactory evidence of repentance to the General Assembly of the Presbyterian Church in the United States of America" (Loetscher, *The Broadening Church*, 61). In 1898, Briggs entered the priesthood of the Protestant Episcopal Church.

Philip Schaff wrote to McGiffert, who was at that time contemplating a move to Union.

> Our Union seminary and in fact the whole Presbyterian Church is in a very critical position, as you know. We are in the midst of a theological revolution, and I fear in danger of a division, which I would most deeply deplore. I would much rather diminish than add to the number of sects of which we have already too many.
>
> These heresy trials will keep the Church in hot water for at least two years. . . . As historians we have good reason to be optimists as regards the final results. (Quoted in McGiffert, Jr., "Scholar," 44)

The searchers for heresy would soon sniff out error in McGiffert's own works.

MCGIFFERT ON TRIAL

Throughout his career, McGiffert had supported scholastic freedom. He had been Henry Preserved Smith's staunchest supporter, and he had steadfastly defended Briggs's right to explore critical questions.

With the publication of his *A History of Christianity in the Apostolic Age* in 1897, McGiffert raised his own storm of controversy. The Presbytery of Pittsburgh called the book a "flagrant and ominous scandal" (*Dictionary of American Biography* [DAB], 528). That Presbytery brought charges to the General Assembly in 1898, listing four key heresies. First, in a footnote McGiffert had expressed his doubt whether Jesus had intended to institute the Lord's Supper as a perpetual rite. Second, according to the Presbytery, the book implied that Christ was mistaken in some of his views. Third, McGiffert had denied that early Christians held substitutionary theories of the Atonement. Finally, at the heart of the matter was the charge that McGiffert had impugned the authority of Scripture. The New Testament, the charges read,

> is very irreverently handled, no special supernatural guidance is ascribed to its sacred writers, the genuineness of more than one-half of the books composing it is called in question; discordant and mutually contradictory teachings are declared to be contained in it and its authority as a divine rule of faith and practice is set aside. . . . [I]t is the most daring and thoroughgoing attack on the New Testament that has ever been made by an accredited teacher of the Presbyterian Church in America. (Quoted in Loetscher, *The Broadening Church*, 71)

The Assembly tried to strike a balance between condemnation of McGiffert's alleged errors yet avoiding formal heresy proceedings. The official wording of the Assembly's decision expresses this tension.

> The Assembly deplores the renewal of controversy occasioned by the publication of a book at this time when our recent divisions were

scarcely healed. It sympathizes with the widespread belief that the utterances of Dr. McGiffert are inconsistent with the teachings of Scripture as interpreted by the Presbyterian Church and by evangelical
churches. And the Assembly stamps with emphasis disapproval of all
utterances in the book called to its attention by the Presbytery of Pittsburgh not in accord with the standards of our Church. (Quoted in
Tigert, "Paulinism," 436)

Having expressed its frustration with McGiffert's progressive thinking,
the Assembly issued a warning and revealed the exhaustion of a denomination that had been involved in internecine warfare for decades.

But the Church needs peace, the union of all its forces, the cooperation
of all its members, a spirit of brotherhood, and mutual confidence, so
that it may address itself with intense zeal and no waste of energy to
its great, pressing, and practical work of saving the souls of men.
    The Assembly, therefore, in the spirit of kindness, counsels Dr.
McGiffert to reconsider the questionable views set forth in his book,
and if he cannot conform his views to the Standards of our Church,
then peaceably to withdraw from the Presbyterian ministry. (Quoted
in Tigert, "Paulinism," 436–437)

The General Assembly defended its balancing act by an appeal to a previous Assembly's decision, in 1835, that a minister's "views may be denounced by a court of the Church without placing the man on trial" (437).
McGiffert, convinced that his views were not heretical, chose neither to
modify them nor to leave the Presbyterian Church.

In March 1899, McGiffert published an article in the *New World* entitled
"The Study of Early Church History," which clearly showed that his views
had not changed.

The controversy was far from over since ten Presbyteries dissatisfied with
the 1898 General Assembly's action (or lack of action) called attention to
McGiffert's unchanged views at the next General Assembly. McGiffert had
prepared a statement that was read to the Assembly. His letter asserted that
"many of my positions, together with the spirit and purpose of my book
as a whole, have been seriously misapprehended" (quoted in Birch,
Charges, 44–45). He continued:

So far as my views are concerned, they have been and remain, as I
believe, in accord with the faith of the Presbyterian Church and evangelical Christendom in all vital and essential matters, and I, therefore,
cannot feel that it is my duty, or even my right . . . to withdraw from
the ministry of the Presbyterian Church. (Loetscher, *The Broadening
Church*, 72)

It is a sign of the strong desire of many to avoid another heresy trial that the reading of the letter was greeted with loud applause.

The 1899 General Assembly reaffirmed the earlier body's disapproval but also refused to act and referred the case to the New York Presbytery for resolution. While leaving the dirty work to New York, however, the General Assembly signaled its resolve to guard orthodoxy by adopting four "fundamental doctrines": the inerrancy of the Scriptures, the inerrancy of all statements made by Jesus Christ, the belief that the Lord's Supper was instituted by Christ himself, and the doctrine of justification by faith alone. The statement concluded, "This Assembly enjoins upon all Sessions and Presbyteries loyally to defend and protect these fundamental doctrines of this confessional Church" (72).

To adopt particular "fundamental doctrines" was consistent with a pattern that had developed in Presbyterian General Assemblies over the previous few years.

The New York Presbytery, forced to deal with the case, arranged for McGiffert to meet with a special committee of the Presbytery. In that meeting, he stated his beliefs on the four subjects that the Assembly had declared to be fundamental doctrines. He stated that Scripture is "the only infallible rule of faith and practice" as the Confession teaches but rejected the Assembly's definition of Scripture as inerrant. McGiffert affirmed his belief in the deity of Christ but insisted that this does not carry with it "absolute freedom from all liability to error, during his earthly existence" (quoted in Loetscher, *The Broadening Church*, 72–73).

Concerning the Lord's Supper, McGiffert affirmed that he received the sacrament "with the greatest joy and spiritual profit." He acknowledged that Christ had celebrated it with his disciples but that he doubted if the Lord had intended it as a ceremony to be permanently observed (quoted in Loetscher, *The Broadening Church*, 73).

On the fourth point, McGiffert insisted that he was unaware that he had ever said or written anything against the doctrine of justification by grace through faith.

After an extended discussion, the committee pronounced itself satisfied with McGiffert's statement and concluded the proceedings. The committee's statement condemned parts of McGiffert's book, such as his view that the Lord's Supper was not instituted by Christ, his opinion that Luke and Acts were not written by Luke, his uncertainty about the authorship of the fourth gospel and his assertion that some of the statements by Christ in it were invented by the author, and the view that Christ stressed not faith in himself but in his message.

Such ideas were "erroneous and seriously out of harmony with the facts of Holy Scripture as they have been interpreted by the Presbyterian Church" (quoted in Birch, *Charges*, 45). Despite these reservations and because most believed a heresy trial would do more harm than good, the New York Presbytery voted 77 to 39 not to bring McGiffert to trial.

While clearly McGiffert, his supporters, and even many who strongly disagreed with his views hoped that the action against him was at an end, that was not to be the case. Dr. George W. F. Birch, stated clerk of the Presbytery, who had served as chairman of the committee that prosecuted Briggs, emerged as an individual prosecutor and filed formal heresy charges (Loetscher, *The Broadening Church*, 73). In a highly detailed and meticulously argued 46-page diatribe, Birch quoted at length from McGiffert's *A History of Christianity in the Apostolic Age* and the historian's inaugural address published as "Primitive and Catholic Christianity." These stacked up unfavorably against Scripture and the Standards of the Presbyterian Church. Not only had McGiffert departed from the four fundamental doctrines, Birch charged, but he had violated his ordination vow, "that is, that he has not been zealous and faithful in maintaining the truths of the Gospel and the purity and peace of the Church" (Birch, *Charges*, 44).

When the New York Presbytery refused to prosecute Birch's charges, he appealed to the General Assembly of 1900. Having come so close to a peaceful resolution of the situation, McGiffert was faced with the most serious threat to himself and the unity of his denomination. Clearly, since McGiffert's views had been condemned by earlier General Assemblies— even though those bodies had refused to take action against him—any prolonged litigation would bring great harm to the church and probably result in action against him. The battle was lost.

In the interests of peace, in 1900 McGiffert quietly withdrew from the Presbyterian ministry and joined the Congregational Church, "[t]o save the Presbyterian Church which he loved dearly, from a great heresy trial" (Rockwell, "In Memoriam," 106).

Despite the lengthy controversy surrounding McGiffert and the change in his ordination, he retained his professorship at Union, became more celebrated and sought after as a teacher and scholar, and eventually led the Seminary as its president.

SELECTED BIBLIOGRAPHY

Birch, George W. F. *Charges and Specifications against the Rev. Arthur Cushman McGiffert, Ph.D., D.D., Presented in the Presbytery of New York, January 8, 1900*. N.p., n.d. A. C. McGiffert Materials. The Burke Library. Union Theological Seminary, New York.

Bowden, Henry Warner. *Dictionary of American Religious Biography*. Westport, CT: Greenwood Press, 1977.

———. "Liberal Theology and the Problem of Continuity in Church History: A. C. McGiffert as a Case Study." *Union Seminary Quarterly Review* 27 (winter 1972): 67–79.

————. "W.G.T. Shedd and A. C. McGiffert on the Development of Doctrine." *Journal of Presbyterian History* 49 (fall 1971): 246–265.

Dictionary of American Biography. New York: Charles Scribner's Sons, 1944.

Loetscher, Lefferts A. *The Broadening Church: A Study of Theological Issues in the Presbyterian Church since 1869.* Philadelphia: University of Philadelphia Press, 1954.

McGiffert, A. C., Jr. "The Making of an American Scholar: Biography in Letters." *Union Seminary Quarterly Review* 24 (fall 1968): 31–46.

————. "A Son Looks at His Father's Faith." *Chicago Theological Seminary Register* 25 (1935): 5–8.

Rockwell, William Walker. "In Memoriam: Arthur Cushman McGiffert, D.D., Ph.D., Ll.D." *Church History* 2 (1933): 105–106.

Terry, Milton S. "McGiffert's Apostolic Age: A Conversation." *Methodist Review* 82 (March 1900): 196–209.

Tigert, John James. "Paulinism of First Peter" and "Dr. McGiffert and the General Assembly." *Methodist Review* 47 (July–August 1898): 426–437.

Stephen R. Graham

Mercer Heresy Trial
(1939)

"HERESY CHARGE AT MERCER FAILS" screamed the headlines of the *Macon Evening News* of Macon, Georgia, for Friday, 31 March 1939. The small town southern newspaper recounted how 13 zealous Mercer University ministerial students, including one John M. Birch, whose namesake was later attached to the famous anti-Communist society in America, had precipitated the trial by charging four professors and a student laboratory assistant with heresy at the Baptist school.

Spurred on by local pastors, the students dramatically aired their sweeping complaints through nine legally sworn affidavits. Five of the affidavits focused on Professor John D. Freeman, beloved and oft-criticized chair of the Department of Christianity. The students aimed the rest of their legally registered protests against Professor Josiah Crudup, a physics teacher; Professors John D. Allen and W. T. Smalley, both English professors; and James Wallace, a biology laboratory assistant.

While the allegations took several forms, biblical and theological heterodoxy constituted the heart of the accusations. If one fixes attention, however, only on the theological dimensions of the 1939 trial, one may miss a major significance of the event for the history of Mercer University. More is at stake here than the alleged theological waywardness of five professors or the immature witch hunting of ministerial students. The 1939 trial was important because it set a course, as Kornegay demonstrated, for academic freedom, for control of the university, and for the nature of Christian education at the Georgia Baptist school.

Of course, the broader backdrop of the conflict stemmed from the nineteenth-century rise of biblical criticism and the intense conflict between science and religion. Nationally, the emergence of theological liberalism and the subsequent rise of fundamentalism as a reactionary force in American religious life lay behind the Mercer story. Denominationally, Southern Baptists experienced a fundamentalist assault in the mid-1920s, led by J. Frank Norris of Texas and C. P. Stealey of Oklahoma. Norris played a minor role in the Mercer story. Reacting to fundamentalism, the Southern Baptist Convention (SBC) adopted a confessional statement in 1925, marking the beginning of creedalism in the SBC. The SBC also adopted an anti-evolution statement in 1926, hoping to stave off further conflict. The Mercer 13 created their "Fellowship" around the SBC confessional statement and fiercely attacked the teaching of evolution.

Specifically at Mercer, behind the brassy student complaints in 1939 lay a century of uneasiness between Baptist higher education and the Baptist constituency of Georgia and 40 years of intense theological stress between progressivism and conservatism at Mercer. The 1939 heresy trial at Mercer University, a Georgia Baptist Convention–owned and –operated school in Macon, Georgia, mirrored and extended the national fundamentalist-liberal imbroglio, but it had roots that reached even further back into Mercer's history.

ANTECEDENTS TO THE 1939 MERCER HERESY TRIALS

Early Mercer History

From its founding in 1833 at Penfield, Georgia, by the Georgia Baptist Convention, Mercer University, like many denominational colleges in America, often found itself at the center of bitter controversy between elements among its sponsoring constituency, on the one hand, and its faculty and administration, on the other. Indeed, Jesse Mercer and Adiel Sherwood, the founders of Mercer University, encountered vigorous antieducational forces among Baptists in the early nineteenth century when they launched the school. Maybe even worse, however, than the original antieducational elements was the later paradoxical pro-educational but anti-intellectual spirit among Baptists. Baptists have a long and enviable pro-educational tradition, establishing colleges and universities all over the country and especially the South. Often beneath the surface of that pro-educational spirit, however, has been a fearful and reactionary anti-intellectualism.

Professor Joel Rufus Moseley

Throughout the nineteenth and early twentieth centuries, the Georgia Baptist Convention, through its established committees and university Trustees, scrutinized, even policed, the administrators and faculty working at Mercer. In 1894, for example, Professor Joel Rufus Moseley, a professor of history and modern philosophy, left the University of Chicago to teach at Mercer. Immensely popular with both students and faculty, Moseley made the mistake of leaving his Baptist Church to unite with the Christian Science movement. Under threat of dismissal by the Board of Trustees, Moseley voluntarily resigned in July 1900. Denominational deviancy, as defined by the Trustees, was intolerable. Faculty at Baptist Mercer were obviously expected to be Baptist.

The Four Professors in 1905

Five years later in 1905, a special committee of the Trustees investigated all faculty members whose appointments were due for renewal. As a result, four Mercer professors resigned under pressure. Professor B. D. Ragsdale, professor of Bible, failed to specify a reason for his resignation, but some suspected theological accusations as the source. Professor George H. Clarke, an English professor, ostensibly did not attend church often enough, and Professor Edmond Burnett, professor of history and philosophy, lacked "piety." W. C. Jones, a teaching fellow in English, resigned, protesting the pressure on his friend Clarke. These coerced resignations demonstrated that Trustees enforced self-determined religious standards for faculty members at Mercer in the early twentieth century. Moreover, faculty appeared to abide passively by such standards.

The Kilpatrick Case

W. H. Kilpatrick, who came to Mercer as a student in 1888, eventually became a math professor, vice president, and acting president. Because of Trustee opposition to some of his rumored beliefs, he resigned his vice presidency under pressure in 1905 and returned to his teaching role in the Math Department. Kilpatrick hoped his action would defuel opposition to his presence at Mercer, but he hoped in vain. In June 1906, a special committee appointed by the Board of Trustees investigated Kilpatrick's "heresies." The committee recommended that the popular professor and former administrator be allowed to appear before the Trustees to make a statement and respond to questions.

Specific charges against Kilpatrick are not reflected in official school documents, but apparently a small group of Trustees—as few as four—accused him of denying the virgin birth of Jesus and the full inspiration of the Bible. Moreover, they threatened to take the issue to the Georgia Baptist Convention if Kilpatrick did not sever his ties with Mercer. Urged by a friendly Trustee to resign, Kilpatrick did so. Later W. H. Kilpatrick became an internationally known authority on education at Columbia University. The Kilpatrick case at the turn of the twentieth century proved that just as

Trustees demanded their understanding of Baptist orthopraxy, as with Moseley, they also required theological orthodoxy, albeit of a math professor. Kilpatrick's resignation also indicated the power of the Georgia Baptist Convention to control the internal life of Mercer and the faculty pressure to conform or quietly exit.

Professor Henry Fox

The faculty pressure to conform, however, began to crack slightly during the fierce evolution controversies of the 1920s. The evolution issue at Mercer centered on Professor Henry Fox of Mercer's Biology Department. While his teaching of evolution doubtless stimulated the charges against Fox, his dismissal from the faculty in October 1924, a year before the Scopes trial in Tennessee, came because of theological, not scientific, beliefs (Thompson, *Tried as by Fire*, 79; Kornegay, "Changing Concepts," 41–42).

Fox proclaimed himself an agnostic regarding God's "objective existence," expressed doubt about the divinity of Christ, described the incarnation and Atonement as "speculative theological doctrines," dismissed as irrelevant the inspiration of the Bible, and questioned the virgin birth of Jesus. Small wonder that historian James J. Thompson, Jr., suggested that Southern Baptists had a few bona fide "modernists" during the science-religion conflict (*Tried as by Fire*, 79).

Told he must terminate his services in October of the 1924 school year, Fox, in uncharacteristic faculty fashion, refused and threatened a lawsuit. The Trustees blinked, paid him a year's salary, then declared his faculty position vacant. Fox, apparently happy with his financial settlement, withdrew his legal challenge but argued his case in the press. One interesting aspect of the Fox controversy was President Rufus Weaver's administrative management of the incident. He involved the Administrative Committee of the Georgia Baptist Convention as well as the Trustees of the university, indicating again the vigilant monitoring of Mercer by the sponsoring organization. By the time the 13 students lodged their protests in 1939, Mercer professors and administrators had garnered enormous experience in dealing with theological controversies.

THE 1939 HERESY TRIAL

After John Birch and his student collaborators filed their affidavits against the five professors, they dispatched letters to Baptist pastors across the state of Georgia, detailing their beliefs regarding the rampant heresies at Mercer University. The Baptist Pastor's Conference of Macon, meeting on 20 March 1939, passed a resolution agitating for a thorough investigation of the student charges. In part, the resolution said that it has come to our attention that certain charges, made in several affidavits, have been made concerning the character of teachings given in certain class rooms at Mercer University. We feel that, in justice to all concerned, a thorough investigation should be made into these charges by the Trustees of the University, and that such investigation should be made speedily because every day this report is spreading more widely among the Baptists of Georgia. ("Proceedings," 35)

In response to these developments and after several efforts to solve the problem privately, President Spright Dowell encouraged the Executive Committee of the Trustees to conduct a "hearing" on the issue. A special Trustee committee presided over the "Investigation," its official label, and closed the meeting to the public. The Trustees invited the accused professors, the accusing students, students who defended the professors, and all pastors who wanted to observe the proceedings in Roberts Chapel on 30 March. Acting as "counsel" for the students, three Baptist pastors placed alternately on the stand both students and professors for interrogation. Likewise, the professors had occasion to question the students and their pastor-advocates.

Lacking the official jurisprudence of the Scopes Monkey Trial almost 15 years earlier, the Mercer trial assumed an unmistakable courtroom atmosphere. One of the golden benefits of that courtroom milieu is a historian's delight. It is an 85-legal-size-page stenographic report by a court reporter, replete with descriptions that had little if anything to do with the testimony at issue (see "Proceedings").

Several times the chairman of the Trustee committee, attorney Fred R. Martin, implored the audience to refrain from cheering, laughing, demonstrating, and applauding ("Proceedings," 43, 50, 57). The faithful stenographer, a historian at heart, recorded it all. Rapierlike sarcasm, uncontrolled anger, rude interruptions, malicious innuendo, feigned courtesies, offensive insinuations, wily intimidations—all of these characterized the interrogations and responses. On one occasion, one of the pastor-lawyers for the students, who himself had taken the witness stand, broke down and sobbed. The stenographer recorded the tears for posterity.

Having begun at 11:00 A.M., the grueling trial adjourned at 9:15 P.M. with a break of only ten minutes (57). Two distinct groups dominated the day and the entire controversy: the accused (John Freeman and the other professors) and the accusers (John Birch and his student and pastor colleagues).

John D. Freeman: The Primary Target

While the trial included five professors at Mercer, it clearly centered on John D. Freeman. Fifty-seven of the 85 pages of the proceedings involved

Freeman; the other four professors merited only 28 pages among them. Ten days prior to the trial and in an effort to forestall such a public display, the executive committee of the Trustees appointed a committee of five Baptist ministers to make an investigation of the student complaints and recommend solutions to the Trustees.

Freeman's centrality in the controversy manifested itself in the committee's recommendation to the Executive Committee of the Trustees. Professor Freeman, said the committee of five ministers, should be requested to resign voluntarily from Mercer. If Freeman acquiesced, "the problem would be solved." If not, a public investigation of Freeman and the other professors should be made (see Dowell, "Heresy," 9–10). President Dowell, in obvious defense of Freeman, rejected such an approach, and the trial followed a few days later.

Who was this Professor John Dolliver Freeman around whom such a storm brewed? By the time President Rufus Weaver persuaded Freeman at age 63 to come to Mercer in 1927, Freeman was an internationally known Baptist. A Canadian by birth, he served as pastor of influential Baptist pulpits in Canada, England, and America. He wrote eight books, among them three novels, three compilations of sermons, one on the literature of the Bible, and one on the Twenty-third Psalm (Dowell, *Mercer*, 338).

At age 41, John Freeman, then a Canadian pastor, delivered a rousing keynote address on the Baptist commitment to individualism, soul liberty, and the Lordship of Christ at the first meeting of the Baptist World Alliance in London, England, in 1905. Being asked to give the sermon at this first international gathering of Baptists was a distinct honor. His address, "The Place of Baptists in the Christian Church," doubtless helped make Freeman prominent in Baptist circles throughout the world. It also underscored Freeman's commitment to freedom and his repudiation of tyranny of any kind. Speaking of Baptists and their major distinctives, Freeman said, "In our postulate of soul-liberty we affirm the right of every human being to exemption in matters of faith and conscience from all coercion or intimidation by any earthly authority whatsoever" (as quoted in Shurden, *The Life of Baptists*, 20).

As his writings suggest, Freeman was more a master of the pulpit than a scholarly academician. He nonetheless advocated progressive ideas rooted in the Baptist spirit of freedom. All sources, friendly and unfriendly to Freeman, agreed that his liberal ideas precipitated the 1939 trials. In his exposé of the Mercer situation to Georgia Baptist ministers, pastor A. C. Baker, Freeman's critic, said, "For nine years Ministerial students have been coming to me and to other pastors of this city asking that something be done about the teachings of Dr. Freeman. . . . Therefore, this is not a new thing at Mercer" (Baker, "Letter," 1). Freeman's friend and president, Spright Dowell, said, "[T]he attack was aimed primarily at Dr. Freeman" (Dowell, *Mercer*, 323). At one point during the trial and while on the stand,

Freeman himself said, "All that is here in these affidavits of these students is but a small dust in the balance, compared with what has been charged against me now for a good many years, here and there throughout the state, charges that I have taught the exact opposite of what I do teach" (39).

While Freeman personalized the 1939 Mercer trials, the controversy involved much more than one man's theological opinions. In his brief recounting of the controversy, President Spright Dowell pointed out that only a few years prior to the 1939 episode all Christianity professors were under attack:

> The present so-called heresy trouble at Mercer would seem to be the cumulation of influence at work for years. When I came to Mercer eleven years ago Rev. S. J. Baker of Macon, Rev. J.I.D. Miller of Camilla, and perhaps two or three others were critical and at times caustic about the teachings in the Department of Christianity and certain teachers, namely, Dr. Freeman, Dr. Harrison, and Dr. Poteat. (Dowell, "Heresy," 1)

Dowell goes on to say that "some five or six years ago the criticism became more or less open and direct," and the professors and their accusers met in the president's office to resolve the dispute. Each of the three professors wrote out a personal confession of faith regarding fundamental doctrinal issues and satisfied the accusers. With the exception of B. D. Ragsdale in the forced resignations of 1905, Christianity faculty members appear to be relatively unscathed in previous Mercer controversies. Beginning in the 1930s and as a result of the national fundamentalist-modernist debate, Christianity professors became increasingly the focal point of criticism.

Intradepartmental faculty rivalry between Freeman and Professor William Arnold Keel of the Christianity Department also contributed to the tensions at Mercer. A number of the fundamentalist ministerial students identified with Keel and against Freeman (see Dowell, "Heresy," 1–2; Baker, "Letter," 2). Pastor A. C. Baker also cited a lecture delivered by Shirley Jackson Case of the University of Chicago at Mercer on 22 February 1939 as an immediate causal factor in the 1939 trials. Speaking on "Science and Religion," Case, according to Baker, denied the miraculous, the Genesis account of Creation, the fall of humanity according to Genesis, and the idea that Eve was made out of the rib of Adam. As a result, said Baker, 50 percent of the ministerial students on the campus protested to President Dowell. When the president of the university failed to respond to a resolution of the students, said Baker, "some twenty students came to me for advice about the matter. I asked them to get me at least twelve affidavits carrying the statements of certain professors in the institution" (Baker, "Letter," 1–3).

Freeman's personal feistiness doubtless complicated the controversy. In describing Freeman's faculty differences with Professor Keel, President Dowell said, "Dr. Freeman through his long years of service and recognition had developed a somewhat critical attitude toward his fellow teachers and ministers" (Dowell, "Heresy," 1–2). One suspects Dowell understated. A former student of Freeman's testified at the trial that Freeman often ridiculed Georgia Baptist leaders, pastors, and their preaching in his classroom teaching (33–34). Reading the trial proceedings, one does not have to look long or hard to discover Freeman's testiness, short fuse, and sharp tongue. He was manifestly a Christian theologian who savored a bit of a fight. The old Baptist patriarch met something of his match, however, in fundamentalist ministerial students John M. Birch, Reid Lunsford, and the pastors who supported them.

John Birch and Colleagues: The Discontented Accusers

John Birch, a student scholar at Mercer, filed three affidavits against Freeman. Selected as a Mercer applicant for a Rhodes Scholarship, Birch often made the Dean's list. On one occasion prior to the trial when the "unholy 13," as they were dubbed by their student adversaries, visited President Dowell in his office, the ministerial students designated John Birch as their spokesman. President Dowell described Reid Lunsford as "the most active and bitter" of the students (Dowell, "Heresy," 7). Dowell also said in a letter to the editor of *The Christian Index*, the Georgia Baptist state paper, "It is generally accepted that Reid was the chief promoter of the trouble among the students and that his chief ally was C. K. Everett" (Dowell, "Letter to O. P. Gilbert," 1). While Lunsford may have been the most combative and volcanic of the students, John Birch stood out as their intellectual leader. Birch also appeared to have the cooler head (Dowell, "Heresy," 7). Confident and unshaken on the witness stand when peppered by Freeman's questions, Birch nonetheless manifested civility.

In the early part of the academic year 1938–1939, Birch, Lunsford, and other ministerial students formed the "Fellowship Group." Designed to study the Scriptures in conjunction with the articles of faith adopted by the Southern Baptist Convention in 1925, the Fellowship Group used their meetings to discredit Professor Freeman. Supported by local pastors, especially A. C. Baker of Tabernacle Baptist Church and J. Seaborn Winn of Cherokee Heights Baptist Church, the group eventually filed the affidavits that issued in the trial.

What specific charges did the 13 students and their pastor friends level at Freeman and the other four professors? Of the nine student affidavits, five incriminated John Freeman. John Birch, swearing to three of the depositions himself, accused Freeman of denying the existence of demons, the blood Atonement of Christ, and conversion from sin. According to two other students, Freeman denied the second coming of Christ and said that the Bible contained contradictions.

Following up on these publicly read charges, the "pastor-lawyers" pelted Freeman with accusations clothed as questions. Before his critics finished roasting Freeman, they had charged him with denying what they considered to be a long list of the fundamentals of the Baptist understanding of the Christian faith: the inspiration and infallibility of the Bible, the second coming of Christ, the resurrection of the body, hell, the Genesis account of Creation, and the belief that woman was made from the rib of Adam. They even made an issue out of the fact that Freeman had not been properly baptized. The last point referred to the fact that Freeman had been baptized by a Disciples of Christ minister and had never been baptized in a Baptist Church.

An issue not included in the affidavits, but which concerned the Trustees themselves greatly, was Freeman's use of liberal theologian William Newton Clarke's *An Outline of Christian Theology* as a textbook in one of Freeman's classes. At one point a former hostile student brought Clarke's book to the witness stand as a kind of "show and tell" ("Proceedings," 19ff.).

From the questions asked by the Trustee investigative committee at the trial and the amount of attention given to the Clarke book, one might conclude that the Trustees were trying to suggest that the textbook was the most serious issue of all (55, 56). However, they may have utilized the textbook issue as a distraction from some of what they considered the more serious issues leveled at Freeman. After all, Freeman discontinued use of the book a year or so before the trial. Also, Freeman publicly dissented from some of the book while agreeing with other portions of it.

In addition to the long litany of Freeman's theological heresies and his use of Clarke's textbook, critics hammered Freeman at the trial for damaging the faith and calling of his students. Indeed, the counselors for the students seemed more intent on proving that Freeman crippled the spirituality of the young than in proving Freeman's specific heresies. Pastor Winn, the chief interrogator for the students, asked witness John Birch if Birch's faith "in the Bible and Christ" would have been impaired had Birch subscribed to the teachings of Professor Freeman. Birch responded, "I most certainly think so" (8). A parade of antagonistic student witnesses testified against Freeman in like fashion (12, 16, 22, 33, 34). One former student, J. S. Hayes, when asked the consequences for his personal faith had he accepted Dr. Freeman's teachings, responded, "I would have had no faith at all, if I had accepted it" (33).

When Freeman got his opportunity to question the disgruntled students, he pursued this same line of questioning. Of John Birch, Freeman asked with language designed to reflect Freeman's warm piety,

> Do you feel, having attended my classes as you have, that the tendency
> of my teaching is to lessen the confidence of my students in the au-
> thority of the Bible and weaken their faith in the Lord Jesus Christ and
> tend to discourage them from entering the ministry to which they be-
> lieved they were called? Do you feel that you could say it has that
> tendency as a whole? (9)

"I do so feel," snapped Birch.

Pastor Grover C. Tyner pressed this issue on Freeman. "Do you consider
that you have been as careful as you knew how to keep these men in the
faith?" The seventy-four-year-old Baptist pastor and teacher responded,
"Yes sir, assuredly, as careful as I know how. It is my constant and un-
varying aim to strengthen in the Christian faith. God forbid that I should
at this stage of my life be the means of shaking or weakening or shadowing
[sic] the Christian faith of anyone" ("Proceedings," 42). A weak question
issued in a strong answer, giving Freeman a chance to reinforce what most
people believed—that he was a man of authentic Christian commitment.
John Birch's added insinuation that Freeman was not a Christian would
not have been heard with seriousness by most of the people in the courtroom, even Freeman's critics (8–9).

For his defense, Freeman maintained vigorously his love for and devotion
to the Bible as Holy Scripture. While obviously not a fundamentalist, Freeman disagreed with his accusers primarily on the theological interpretation
of the Bible, not upon the importance of the Bible itself. The "thirteen"
constituted a minority of ministerial students, and this helped Freeman's
cause. Moreover, student supporters gladly and zealously testified in behalf
of their beloved professor. Of the ten-hour trial, Freeman's interrogation
and defense absorbed half of that time.

Charges against the other four professors ranged from issues of theology
to science and even Baptist history. Some of the theological objections paralleled Freeman's teaching: denying the blood Atonement of Christ, denying
the existence of Adam, denying the necessity of the death of Christ for
human salvation, and denying that Christ is the only way to heaven.

Evolution remained a hot issue at Mercer. Reid Lunsford accused James
Wallace, the biology lab assistant, of saying that "five babies were born at
the Macon hospital, December, 1938, with tails and the doctor had to clip
them off." Wallace denied saying such but brought a human skeleton into
the trial room to demonstrate a lesson in human anatomy. English professor John D. Allen denied, according to three of the students, the Genesis
story of Creation.

Landmarkism, the nineteenth-century high ecclesiology of J. R. Graves,
maneuvered its way into the Mercer trials on two occasions. The first concerned the validity of Freeman's baptism. On the second occasion Reid
Lunsford lambasted physics professor Josiah Crudup for the audacity of

equating Baptists with Protestants. Moreover, Crudup denied, said Lunsford, that "Baptist churches have existed since Christ was on earth."

THE RESULTS OF THE 1939 TRIAL

The controversy contained both immediate and long-range consequences for Mercer University and for the people impacted. One may measure the results by pointing to the responses of the various groups and persons involved.

Action of Trustees

The six-member Trustee investigative committee presented a two-page report to the Executive Committee of the Board of Trustees the day after the trials. The Executive Committee quickly adopted it. The special committee began their report with a statement of the purpose of Mercer University as an institution for Christian education. And while pledging they "would not abridge the legitimate academic freedom of any professor," the committee warned:

> We recognize the right of any American to hold any views of a religious nature he may wish; but we respectfully submit and insist that in all intellectual and moral honesty any professor in Mercer University should resign and seek a more congenial field of labor should he ever feel that in his heart he cannot subscribe to and teach as far as it is his province things believed by the Baptists of Georgia to be vital to the Bible truths as they interpret them. ("Action of the Special Committee," 1)

The committee spelled out some of those necessary beliefs in a previous paragraph.

For the four professors other than Freeman, the committee responded with only a "word of caution." The committee told the professors to stick with their disciplines, to maintain Baptist orthodoxy, and to be sure and articulate their positions in the classroom lucidly. In light of the professors' explanations at the trial, the committee believed that no other action was necessary.

The next sentence in the Trustee report said, "As to Dr. John D. Freeman, against whom the major charges were made, this committee has given careful and prayerful attention." Pointing out that rumors about Freeman had persisted for years and that the professor "has made some mistakes" in textbook selection, the committee also gently reprimanded Freeman for failing to communicate his personal faith in the classroom.

"However," said the committee, "we are convinced of his personal faith

... and recommend that the charges be dismissed." They closed their report with a ringing affirmation of Freeman, saying, "For fifty years Dr. Freeman has been a Baptist preacher and teacher, a man greatly beloved, a leader among the Baptists of the world and one who through the years has been regarded as a conservative in his theology" (see "Action of the Special Committee," 2). On 5 June 1939 the entire Board of Mercer Trustees approved the action of the special investigating committee.

Reaction of Mercer Students

Upon leaving the trial the night of 30 March the "unholy 13" encountered an incensed group of their Mercer students. The irate students placarded the building with signs that read: "Lynch Saint Birch," "Wanted Dead, Reid Lunsford," "Witchcraft Trial Inside—Salem, Mass–Mercer University," and "Stay Out—Spanish Inquisition in Progress" (see Kornegay, "Changing Concepts," 67). In a letter to the editor of the Georgia Baptist newspaper five days after the trial, Reid Lunsford said, "The dents and scars on my car will testify if it was fun or murder that was behind the rocks and sticks hurled when I crashed through and over a blockade of timbers this lawless group had placed across a public street." He also accused President Dowell of failing to stop the student demonstrations or offering to protect him from "a mob of Mercer students" (Lunsford, "Letter to O. P. Gilbert").

Articles in the student newspaper, *The Mercer Cluster*, for 31 March and 7 April reflected student outrage at "the 13." The student editor referred to actions of the ministerial students as "crass, medieval bigotry." Students sided overwhelmingly with the accused faculty.

Continued Agitation by Fundamentalists

Neither the wrist slapping of the professors by the Trustees nor the near-riot of the student body quelled the determination of the 13. In a letter to the editor to be printed in the Georgia Baptist newspaper, the students claimed the Trustees and administration whitewashed a very serious situation at Mercer. When Mercer, according to pastor A. C. Baker, sought to denigrate the entire episode by identifying it with the radical fundamentalism of J. Frank Norris of Texas, Baker himself mailed a letter to 100 ministers, defending the 13 and attacking Freeman anew.

Despite Baker's denial of the Norris-Mercer connection, signs existed. Norris used his newspaper to describe the Mercer situation to his readers one week after the trial. "Hell Broke Loose in Georgia" Norris proclaimed in his headlines. Reacting with dismay at the professorial acquittals, Norris promised to go personally to Macon and retry the professors publicly in the city auditorium. With an obvious reference to the professors and the student uprising, Norris said, "We will try these modernistic infidels one night in the auditorium and you can serve notice on that bunch of hyenas that they will not break up that meeting either" (as cited in Kornegay, "Changing Concepts," 69). Understandably, the *Christian Century* magazine named Norris "the most belligerent fundamentalist now abroad in the land" (as cited in Thompson, *Tried as by Fire*, 143). Norris failed to show in Macon. Dowell speculated it was because he could only get 1 of the 13 complaining students and none of the three local ministers to appear. The identity of the 1 student is unknown, but John Birch later attended Norris's seminary in Ft. Worth.

Resignation of John D. Freeman

On 4 August 1939 after serving the Baptist denomination 50 years, Dr. John D. Freeman resigned his faculty position at Mercer. In the end, the fundamentalist students and their pastor associates got what they wanted: the removal of John D. Freeman from Mercer. Did Dowell support Freeman during the anxious months of the trial, only to find a way to remove him afterward so as to reduce future conflict? No records indicate that Dowell asked Freeman to resign. Freeman, after all, was 75 years old at the time; it was time to retire. President Spright Dowell's personal correspondence, however, is abundantly clear that friends and foes alike pressured him to replace Freeman. Dowell's letters also clearly indicate that he was searching for a new chair of the Christianity Department several months before Freeman's resignation.

If Dowell pressured Freeman into retirement, it did not appear to impact their friendship. Freeman had enormously warm words for Dowell in his letter of resignation (Dowell, *Mercer*, 326–327). The old professor said he was retiring from Mercer "with a heart full of gratitude and love." The Executive Committee of the Trustees accepted his resignation, adopted a resolution praising his "eminent life and work," and rewarded him with a pension of $100 per month, an uncharacteristic gesture (Kornegay, "Changing Concepts," 71). Freeman died three and one half years later on 18 February 1943 and was buried in the Mt. Zion Baptist Church cemetery, the church where he served as pastor during the last ten years of his life. President Spright Dowell delivered the eulogy at the funeral.

Tension over Governance within Mercer

Unquestionably, Dowell's handling of the 1939 trials enhanced the role of academic freedom for the future Mercer faculty. Whereas previous presidents may have sought to resolve such explosive issues through official committees of the Georgia Baptist Convention, Dowell kept the decision-making powers within the purview of the Board of Trustees. Unlike his successors, however, Dowell continued to involve Baptist ministers on an ad hoc basis in resolving theological issues. In terms of Mercer's academic freedom and independence, Dowell was a transitional president. More independent than his predecessors, he was less so than his successors. In the 1939 heresy trials, however, Dowell turned Mercer toward freedom.

While some administrators would have been daunted by the fundamentalist attack and may have sought to hire "safer" faculty in the future, Dowell's commitment to quality education was evident in his replacement of Freeman. The popular Solon B. Cousins of Virginia was his first choice. When Cousins declined, Dowell employed Hansford Johnson, a prominent pastor of Louisville, Kentucky.

The tension between Christian higher education and denominational dictates continues to the present at Mercer unresolved, as it does at most institutions of its kind. The heresy trial of 1939, however, probably facilitated rather than inhibited Mercer's independent spirit. The trial certainly did not appear to intimidate the educational process.

In a subsequent attack of fundamentalists on Mercer in 1987, President Kirby Godsey said that Mercer would not compromise on four issues: the governing authority of Trustees, academic freedom, the means by which Trustees are elected, and commitment to religious freedom (Hefley, *The Truth in Crisis*, 187). During the same controversy, President Godsey declared that no "war panel" committee, elected by the Georgia Baptist Convention, would investigate Mercer. "The control of Mercer is not negotiable," said Dowell's current successor (193).

BIBLIOGRAPHY

All letters and manuscripts cited may be found in the Mercer University Library, Special Collections, Macon, Georgia.

"Action of the Special Committee of the Board of Trustees Appointed by the Executive Committee to Investigate Charges Brought Against Four Faculty Members by Certain Ministerial Students." 31 March 1939.
Baker, A. C. "Letter to One Hundred Ministers," 18 May 1939.
Dowell, Spright. *A History of Mercer University, 1833–1953.* Atlanta: Foote and Davies Co., 1958.
———. "History of the Heresy Controversy." Appended to the Minutes of the Mercer University Board of Trustees at the request of President Dowell, 23 March 1939. Mercer University Library.
———. "Letter to O. P. Gilbert," 10 April 1939.
Fulgham, James H., Jr. "The Evolution of Fundamentalism at Mercer." Research Paper. 28 May 1956, Mercer University Library.
Hefley, James C. *The Truth in Crisis.* Vol. 3. Hannibal, MO: Hannibal Books, 1988.

Kornegay, George Henry, Jr. "Changing Concepts of the Christian University at Mercer." A Senior Honors Research paper, 1985, Mercer University Library.

Lunsford, Reid. "Letter to O. P. Gilbert," 4 April 1939.

"Proceedings of Investigation Conducted by the Executive Committee, Board of Trustees of Mercer University." 30 March 1939, Special Collections, Library, Mercer University.

Ragsdale, B. D. *Story of Georgia Baptists*. 3 vols. Atlanta: Foote and Davies Co., 1932, 1935.

Shurden, Walter B. *The Life of Baptists in the Life of the World*. Nashville: Broadman, 1985.

Thompson, James J., Jr. *Tried as by Fire*. Macon: Mercer University Press, 1982.

Walter B. Shurden

Hinckley Gilbert Thomas Mitchell
(1846–1920)

Hinckley Gilbert Thomas Mitchell was a clergyman, educator, theologian, and scholar of the Methodist Episcopal Church whose heresy trial in 1905 for "misteaching" (higher criticism) became the cause célebrè of the American Methodist connection.

Born in Lee, Oneida County, in upstate New York on 22 February 1846, the son of James and Sarah Mitchell, Hinckley was educated at Falley Seminary, Fulton, New York, 1867; Wesleyan University, Connecticut, A.B., 1873, A.M., 1876; and D.D., 1901. At Boston University School of Theology, he earned an S.T.B. in 1876; then at the University of Leipzig, Germany, he received his Ph.D. in 1879. Mt. Union College awarded him a D.D. in 1888. Married to Alice Stanford on 29 June 1880, his career included a pastorate of the Methodist Church in Bearytown (or Fayette) in 1879, within the Central New York Conference. From 1880 to 1883 he was instructor in Latin and Hebrew at Wesleyan University; professor of Hebrew and Old Testament exegesis at Boston University School of Theology, 1883 to 1905; and chair of Hebrew at Tufts College until his death on 19 May 1920.

Professionally, he served as director of the American School of Oriental Research in Jerusalem, 1901 to 1902; held membership in Alpha Delta Phi fraternity, the Twentieth Century Club, and the Harvard Club; and served as secretary of the Society of Biblical Literature and Exegesis and editor of its journal from 1882 to 1888. His publications include *Hebrew Lessons* (1885), *Amos-Essay in Exegesis* (1893), *Theology of the Old Testament* (translation, 1893), *Isaiah I–XII* (1897), *The World before Abraham* (1901), *Tales Told in Palestine* (with J. E. Hanamer, 1904), *Genesis* (1909), "Haggai and Zechariah" in *the International Commentary* (1912), and

Ethics of the Old Testament (1912). His dissertation "Final Construction in Biblical Hebrew" was reprinted in the *Journal of Biblical Literature and Exegesis* (1915). In addition, he contributed to the *Harvard Theological Review*, the *American Journal of Theology, Old Testament Semitic Studies*, and the *Journal of Biblical Literature*. He left an unfinished autobiographical work entitled *For the Benefit of My Creditors*, published posthumously in 1922.

Having studied at the University of Leipzig between 1876 and 1879, when the works of Abraham Kuenen, Judius Wellhausen, Edward Reves, Karl Heinrich Graf, Wilhelm Vatke, and others were revolutionizing biblical studies, it was natural that their works influenced Mitchell in his academic career. The method of research used by these European scholars was called "higher criticism." This meant that researchers used the inductive or scientific approach to research rather than the deductive based upon tradition or dogma. Hence, sources, authorship, history, language, and so on of the books of the Bible were investigated and analyzed. The purpose of this approach was to view biblical literature as it actually was and to evaluate it as such and not to impose or introduce a preconceived interpretation upon it. In this context, it was important to relate biblical literature to the ideas, experiences, peoples, environment, and culture of other countries.

In Germany, France, the Netherlands, and Great Britain, scholars trained in this method of critical analysis and comparative studies had examined the text of the Bible and then tested their findings with the use of other disciplines. For example, it was shown that the Bible was a compilation of a variety of writings collected over a period of a thousand years. Problems and contradictions found within the text did not square with the idea of an infallible record. That the language of the Bible did not originate out of a babble of tongues but was the creation of a gradual development became evident. That the Bible had not originated in the way many Christians thought, who accepted it as literal truth, was disturbing. To many this meant that the foundations of orthodox belief in the supernatural origin of the Holy Scriptures were being subverted.

Researchers in anthropology and comparative religions further dismantled preconceived notions about the distinctive origin of the Hebrew-Christian religion. Accounts of floods, virgin births, crucifixions, and atonements were found in the writings of other peoples. Many of the assumed unique features of Christianity were common to other religions. Elements of the Christian faith that had been accepted as of supernatural origin now appeared less so. While American scholars limited themselves to translating, synthesizing, interpreting, and popularizing the works of European authors, they did make this "new learning" known in the United States. In this regard, Philip Schaff* of Union Theological Seminary, through *A Commentary on the Holy Scriptures* (1865–1880), 25 volumes, played a central role. The *Religious Encyclopedia* (1882–1884), based on the studies of John P. Lange, relied on the "higher critical" studies of continental scholars. James Freeman Clarke's *Ten Great Religions* (1871) and Orello Cone's *Gospel Criticism and Historical Christianity* (1891) contributed to the transmission of higher criticism. Then in 1885, a revised King James Bible, a joint Anglo-American project, was published. But to many, these developments were interpreted to mean that the Bible was not revealed truth but rather a collection of wisdom writings or a series of ethical lessons for inspirational guidance.

Hinckley G. Mitchell was an integral part of this new learning and upon the assumption of his duties at Boston University School of Theology proceeded to incorporate it into his lectures and writings. Influenced by the work of Julius Wellhausen in his *Prolegomena to the History of Israel* (1885), but first published in 1878 as *History of Israel*, the traditional view that the Holy Scriptures were a gift of the Jewish community to the Christian Church was challenged. Instead, it was argued that the Mosaic history was not the starting point of the history of ancient Israel but of the history of Judaism. Parts of the Pentateuch and the Levitical Law were not written until after the fall of the kingdom of Judah (597 B.C.), and the Pentateuch as it presently existed was not viewed as authoritative until the time of the reformation of Ezra (458 B.C.). This meant that the Pentateuch was not given to Israel prior to the crossing of the Jordan (c. 1200 B.C.), but rather, the law grew from a Mosaic germ until the time of Israel's captivity (722 B.C.) in a foreign nation. Indeed, this documentary theory of how the Pentateuch was created was increasingly accepted on both sides of the Atlantic.

It was not exclusively the denial of the Mosaic authorship of the Pentateuch that brought Mitchell under suspicion and then attack at Boston but his assertions that the rest of the historical books of the Old Testament, except Nehemiah, were by anonymous authors. Because Jewish tradition for the Mosaic authorship of the Pentateuch had been uncritically accepted by the Christian Church for 15 centuries was no reason to apply the same tradition to other books. Mitchell contended that Amos must be regarded as one of the greatest prophets, since nearly all the later ones were to varying degrees influenced by him, including Isaiah and Jeremiah. This challenged preconceived ideas about who were major and/or minor prophets. When Mitchell pointed out that Jesus never claimed to be omniscient, and on at least one occasion (Mark 13:32) confessed his knowledge was limited, the added suspicion was raised that higher criticism was also eroding the role of Jesus. Critics of Mitchell claimed that his theology was rationalistic, diminished the authority of the Bible, tended toward Unitarianism, and could conceivably revolutionize Methodist beliefs. Of particular concern to his examiners was his use of the Darwinian theory of evolution to explain the story of the Fall. His interpretation, it was charged, implied that man had within himself the power of self-fulfillment and denied the need for redemption through the death and resurrection of Christ.

An early account of the conflict over Mitchell's views of biblical literature was printed in the *New York Times*, 5 April 1894. Mitchell addressed the forty-sixth annual session of the New York East Conference of the Methodist Episcopal Church on the topic "Profit and Loss: A Reckoning with Biblical Criticism" in which he endorsed to a great extent the advanced criticisms of the Old Testament. In respect to the Pentateuch, the role of Moses, and the Books of Isaiah, he asserted, critics have disclosed "the human element," but the Bible is still "able to convey a knowledge of God." When asked how he interpreted the Apostle Paul's statement "that all Scripture is inspired," he replied, "[I]nspiration does not imply infallibility." To the comment "[I]f the Bible is not all inerrant what parts are inerrant," he responded, "[T]hat is a question to be determined." It is evident from the question, comment, and answer period that this assembly of 375 clergy was divided, skeptical, and reserved in response to the lecture. When it came time to adjourn the session, a vote of thanks for Professor Mitchell's lecture was strenuously opposed but passed as a note of courtesy.

The next year, 1895, a group of 38 students of the Boston School of Theology addressed a petition to the Trustees of Boston University requesting an investigation into the teachings of the Department of Old Testament Exegesis of which Mitchell was chair. The charges were that his teaching leaned toward naturalism and Unitarianism rather than Methodist and Christian doctrine. He had allegedly made remarks that blurred a distinction between Unitarianism and Trinitarianism, which implied uncertainty about the deity of Jesus Christ. In short, his theology was unorthodox and un-Methodist. The Board of Trustees authorized an investigation. A committee of five, including Bishop Randolph S. Foster and President William F. Warren, listened to the students' presentation for five hours. Next they received Mitchell's views in writing. Subsequently, the students were advised that Professor Mitchell acknowledged himself in error as regard to his method of teaching and would make corrections. Mitchell's written statement was found satisfactory to the committee, and the case was closed.

In 1899, however, a second attack upon Mitchell's teaching was mounted from within the ranks of Boston University School of Theology. It was initiated by nine students, who individually prepared and signed their own statements and added a petition listing 15 specific charges. Of particular concern within the Department of Old Testament Exegesis were the views of Dr. H. G. Mitchell. The charges were similar if not identical to the ones in 1895 but with some additions. It was asserted that Mitchell taught "no prophet of the Old Testament knew anything about the person of Jesus Christ," he questioned "the existence of Noah and Isaac," he stated "the Sabbath is not of Divine origin," and he "[taught] the general positions of the Wellhausen school with reference to the Pentateuch to the exclusion of all others." To these charges Mitchell responded at length in writing, but this first exchange led to others that were eventually compiled, after a fashion, into a book entitled *Shall Methodism Remain Wesleyan in Type, and Evangelical?* edited by William W. Shenk, one of Mitchell's accusers.

An investigating committee was selected to hear the students' statements. Mitchell declined attending on the ground that the proceedings were not a trial. At the conclusion of the hearings, 3 April 1899, it was agreed that the materials presented were not to be published. But it was subsequently discovered that similar complaints had been raised in 1895. Although another investigation was launched based on this discovery, it did not prevent Professor Mitchell's renomination on 24 October 1899 to another five-year term. This sequence of events led Shenk and associates to charge "secret nomination" and to send copies of their materials against Mitchell to the Episcopal Board of the denomination. After another round of charge and countercharge, the Board of Trustees of Boston University met on 13 November 1899 and unanimously reelected Professor Mitchell, without discussion, "subject to the approval of the Bishops."

In the midst of this 1899 attack on Mitchell, President Warren, who had been elected president of Boston University in 1873 and served in that post until 1903, defended his institution against the misrepresentations inherent in these attacks on Mitchell. A graduate of Wesleyan University, who had studied at the Universities of Halle and Berlin, he was familiar with the new learning generated in Europe. His efforts to relate evangelical Christianity to the changed intellectual climate were acknowledged within the denomination. In an article entitled "Current Biblical Discussions—The Proper Attitude of Theological Faculties with Respect to Them," published in the *Methodist Review* (May–June 1899), he announced that "his own personal sympathies are, and always have been, with the conservatives in these discussions," but "scholarship with its findings may confirm the truths of the Bible as Methodists understand it." "The Spirit of truth," he wrote, should keep us "from closing the gate to any knowledge, is evermore striving to lead us into all truth."

In 1904, legislation by the General Conference of the Methodist Episcopal Church provided a basis for a third major attack on the teachings of H. G. Mitchell. New legislation stipulated that as a condition of employment in any school of theology in the Methodist Episcopal Church a professor must be confirmed by a majority vote of the bishops present and voting at any regular meeting of the school's Board. It added that when specific charges of misteaching were made in writing by responsible parties, members, or ministers of the church, the bishops were to appoint a committee from among themselves to investigate the charges. Their report, if adopted by the Board of Bishops, was to be transmitted to the Trustees of the theology school involved for appropriate action. It was the publication of Mitchell's book *The World before Abraham* (1901) that provided in documentary form charges of misteaching, and this time denominational legislation facilitated the cause of his opponents.

In this volume, Mitchell restated positions he had previously taken: "the Pentateuch, like all the rest of the historical books, except Nehemiah, is an anonymous production"; "laws were thus introduced and transmitted orally for centuries and finally incorporated into the Pentateuch by an exilic compiler"; "infallibility, a doctrine for which there is no example in the history of revelation"; and the Pentateuch is not the product of a single pen. Although this book is a model of scholarship in respect to research, sources cited, linguistic analysis, and narrative writing, it did not exempt the author from another major attack. A statement of Charges and Specifications, signed by four clergy and three laymen, was made in November 1904 and sent to the bishops of the Methodist Episcopal Church. In essence, the charge was that the teachings of Dr. Hinckley G. Mitchell, of Boston University School of Theology, were not in "agreement with our doctrinal standard." The charges were referred to a committee of seven bishops, of which Bishop Edward G. Andrews was chair.

The report of this committee stated, "[I]t appears on examination of the charges that they do not allege any instance of misteaching in Professor Mitchell's classes since May, 1900." All of the charges were based on his book *The World before Abraham*, published in 1901, and on an extract from a letter written by him to Dr. W. F. Warren, president of Boston University, under the date of December 1899. This committee report went to the Board of Bishops on 1 May 1905. The bishops' decision was forwarded to the Trustees of Boston University. Their pronouncement contained the statement that "some of the statements of Professor Mitchell concerning the historic character of the early chapters of the book of Genesis seem to us unwarranted and objectionable, and as having a tendency to invalidate the authority of other positions of Scriptures. We therefore think there is some ground of complaint on the head contained in the paper laid before us." This document was read to the Trustees on 11 May by Bishop Daniel A. Goodsell, who left the impression the Mitchell case was not closed. A Trustee Committee was then formed to examine Mitchell's fitness for the post to which he had again been elected. This committee respectfully requested the Board of Bishops to confirm the reappointment of Mitchell for a five-year term.

On 31 October 1905, the reply from the bishops read:

> [O]ur action of six months ago was equivalent to a refusal to confirm the election of Professor Mitchell, and that we have no reason to alter the conclusion reached, which was based upon the conviction that some of the statements (contained in his book) concerning the historic character of the book of Genesis seem to be unwarranted and objec-

tionable as having a tendency to invalidate the authority of other portions of the Scriptures. It is furthermore our opinion that we are not even at liberty to reopen the question of Professor Mitchell's confirmation under the law above cited. Unanimously adopted. (Mitchell, *For the Benefit of My Creditors*, 252)

In self-defense, Mitchell requested a trial by the Central New York Conference of which he was a member. Although the conference formed a committee to investigate, it declined to hold a trial upon hearing its committee's report. The conference did, however, pass a resolution of censure for teachings, which it believed were contrary to the Holy Scriptures and doctrinal standards of Methodism. The reason given for denying Mitchell a trial was that he no longer held the chair at Boston and now such a trial would cause a disturbance. Francis J. McConnell, a graduate of Boston University School of Theology 1897 and Ph.D. 1899, demanded a trial for Mitchell but was refused. But in 1908, the Judicial Committee of the General Conference held that the action of the Central New York Conference was illegal. Because its report reflected upon Mitchell's character, the conference should have granted his request or struck from the record references to his character. Although the Judicial Committee sustained the bishops' right to investigate reported erroneous teachings in Methodist seminaries, the Mitchell case did prompt the General Conference in 1908 "to relieve [the bishops] from the duty of investigating and reporting upon charges of misteaching in our theological schools." The formal approval of faculty appointments, however, was required until 1928.

While the explicit charge of "misteaching" was the issue that brought about Mitchell's nonconfirmation in 1905, there were implicit forces at work in American society that set the stage for his heresy trial. In the last quarter of the nineteenth century the validity of the Bible seemed in jeopardy due to the pronouncements of science as well as biblical scholarship. Darwinism had been finding acceptance not only in scientific circles but with the public as well. Herbert Spencer, Aldous Huxley, and John Fiske had made the case. Inherited beliefs were under attack, and labeling Darwinism "materialistic" or "atheistic" did not satisfy thoughtful people. Likewise, textual criticism of the Bible convinced many that not only the infallibility of the Bible but the foundations of Christianity were being destroyed. Several clergy, authors, and theologians tried to synthesize the new learning with evangelical beliefs. Washington Gladden in *Who Wrote The Bible?* (1891), *How Much Is Left of the Old Doctrine* (1899), and *A Modern Man's Theology* (1914), George Crock and J. F. Hurst's seven-volume *Biblical and Theological Library* (1877–1900), William N. Clarke's *Sixty Years with the Bible* (1909), and Charles Augustus Briggs's* *The Bible, the Church and the Reason* (1892) tried to relieve the uncertainty of conscientious doubt over these issues.

A second force at work was the changing role of education and especially so within American Methodism. The circuit-riding, frontier-approach, camp-meeting style of ministry was being questioned in certain quarters of the denomination by the 1820s. The realization was growing that a better-trained and -educated clergy was desirable to defend and explain the theological and doctrinal position of Methodism. A number of academies and colleges were sponsored by Methodists, among which were Wesleyan in Connecticut (1831) and Dickinson in Pennsylvania (1833). Theological seminaries were still institutions of suspected heresy, and the first two Methodist seminaries founded were named Biblical Institutes. The first, the Methodist General Biblical Institute (1847) organized in Concord, New Hampshire, was moved to Boston and chartered in 1869 as Boston University. The second was Garrett Biblical Institute, Evanston, Illinois (1854), later known as Garrett-Evangelical Theological Seminary. Although education in this period tended to be instrumental, it was advanced over the earlier period.

In the post–Civil War era, Methodism devoted more and more attention to education. Daniel D. Whedon, editor of *The Methodist Quarterly Review* from 1856 to 1884, made it a journal of superior merit for introducing religious knowledge of the newest and highest order. Then in 1888 when the editorship went to James W. Mendenhall, he turned the journal into a veritable fortress defying biblical criticism, new science, and agnosticism. It was not until 1892 that the General Conference put William V. Kelley at the helm and the journal was revived. At the same period that President Warren of Boston University was assembling a distinguished faculty including Alexander Graham Bell, Borden Parker Bowne,* Dallas Lore Sharpe, Henry C. Sheldon, and so on, the conservative ranks of the Methodist Episcopal Church through General Conference action required a doctrinal test for membership-subscription to the Articles of Religion—and professed loyalty to one's Methodist heritage became a rallying cry to those opposed to the new learning.

At this time when the northern wing of Methodism was experiencing serious internal tensions over the role of education, the attitude of the Methodist Episcopal Church, South, was expressed in the *New Orleans Christian Advocate* of 1882, which reported "the isms and heresies of the North cannot live and thrive in the South." Many Southern Methodists were suspicious of the new learning. When Bishop Holland N. McTyeire endeavored to secure a definitely trained ministry by establishing a central theological seminary in Nashville, Tennessee, in 1872, Bishop George F. Pierce announced his belief that "every dollar invested in a theological school" would prove damaging to Methodism. Hence, it was primarily through the generosity of Cornelius Vanderbilt and his family that the school was founded and McTyeire made president of the Board of Trustees. Even then in 1878, Alexander Winchell* was dismissed from Vanderbilt because of his views on evolution. It was against this background of social and cultural conflict expressed in specific and general terms that H. G. Mitchell had his career at Boston University School of Theology terminated. While several journals carried critical articles—for example, "The Case of Professor H. G. Mitchell"—the verdict of the Board of Bishops stood.

For Mitchell the period 1906 to 1908 was devoted to literary work, and in 1909 he traveled to Europe. Between 1907 and 1920 he contributed six articles to the *Journal of Biblical Literature*, and in 1909 his *Genesis* was published, followed by his contribution to the *International Commentary* and *Ethics of the Old Testament* (1912). Tufts College appointed him to the chair of Hebrew in 1910, to which New Testament was added in 1915. Here he remained until his death in 1920. In his autobiographical account of his experiences, entitled *For the Benefit of My Creditors* (1922), much verbatim material about the three attacks upon him is included. While his primary purpose is to express "gratitude" for those who were helpful and influential in shaping his life, he is respectful of his adversaries throughout his book. The impression that emerges from this book is that while Mitchell was deeply hurt by his ordeal, he did not indulge in self-pity or consider retaliation in any form. As a person, he managed to transcend the conflict and died a genuinely revered teacher, scholar, and Christian gentleman.

BIBLIOGRAPHY

Chiles, Robert E. *Theological Transition in American Methodism*. New York: Abingdon Press, 1965.

Harmon, Nolan B., gen. ed. *The Encyclopedia of World Methodism*. 2 vols. Nashville: United Methodist Publishing House, 1974.

Mitchell, H. G. *For the Benefit of My Creditors*. Boston: Beacon Press, 1922.

Shenk, William W., ed. *Shall Methodism Remain Wesleyan in Type, and Evangelical?* Omaha, NE: Douglas Printing Co., n.d.

Warren, W. F. "Current Biblical Discussions—The Proper Attitude of Theological Faculties with Respect to Them." *Methodist Review* (May–June 1899): 368–381.

Frederick V. Mills, Sr.

Dale Moody
(1915–1992)

ARTICLE XIII
PERSEVERANCE OF THE SAINTS

Those whom God hath accepted in the Beloved, and sanctified by His Spirit, will never totally nor finally fall away from the state of grace, but shall certainly persevere to the end; and though they may fall, through neglect and temptation, into sin, whereby they grieve the Spirit, impair their graces and comforts, bring reproach on the Church, and temporal judgments on themselves, yet they shall be renewed again unto repentance, and be kept by the power of God through faith unto salvation.

Abstract of Principles
Southern Baptist Theological Seminary, 1858

Dale Moody had been reared on the King James and Scofield Bibles, but in 1933, when he entered Baylor University at age 18 as a ministerial student, he began to study Greek. As he compared the two versions with the Greek text, he found discrepancies. He discovered A. T. Robertson's *Word Pictures in the New Testament*, a Greek grammatical commentary, and began to preach expository sermons based on his own translations and those of Robertson.

Finances forced Moody to leave Baylor before completing his degree. After two terms at Dallas Theological Seminary, Moody hitchhiked from Texas to Kentucky's Southern Baptist Seminary in order to study where Robertson had taught Greek. Moody financed his education by preaching and tutoring in Greek. In 1940 he returned to Baylor in order to complete requirements for a B.A., since Southern would not confer a degree until such requirements were met. During this period, Moody preached a series of expository sermons on Hebrews to the Calvary Baptist Church in Mexia, Texas, using Robertson's *Word Pictures* as his chief guide. His sermons drew crowds and were published in the *Mexia Daily News*. W. H. Sealey, a columnist for the paper, wrote a letter to John R. Sampey, president of Southern Seminary, protesting Moody's interpretation of Hebrews (Moody, draft of letter to Penrose St. Amant, 4). Moody discussed his views with Dr. Sampey, who said, "You will not go wrong following Robertson. I would trust him with my very soul" (4). Robertson, when discussing Hebrews 6:6, had written that "the present active infinitive of *anakainizo* . . . with *adunaton* bluntly denies the possibility of renewal for apostates from Christ" (*Word Pictures*, 5:375).

Shortly before the death of Dr. Sampey, Moody had a conversation with President Ellis Fuller, Sampey's successor. Sampey had called Fuller's attention to the Sealey letter and wanted to make sure Fuller knew about Moody's position concerning apostasy, should he offer him a faculty position. Fuller showed Moody the newspaper clipping and asked him if he had ever seen it, whereupon Moody related his conversation with Sampey.

"Fuller," he wrote later, was "warm in his recommendation that I continue to follow Robertson, but he expressed the hope that I would not go out of my way 'to disturb the boys' " (Moody, draft letter, 4). Moody stated that Fuller recommended him to the Trustees as a professor with "the full knowledge that I agreed with Robertson on Hebrews 6:4–6 and had reservations as to whether Article 13 in the Abstract of Principles contradicted this passage in Holy Scripture" (4).

Although the Abstract had been signed by every tenured faculty member since the Seminary's founding, Dr. W. O. Carver (professor, 1898–1943) suggested that certain changes might be made in the instrument, were it written in the 1950s (Mueller, *A History*, 32). William Mueller praised Boyce and Manly for excluding from the instrument matters of belief on which Southern Baptists were in disagreement (32). The exclusion of apostasy, however, caused Moody to struggle with the Abstract throughout his 36 years as a professor at Southern. Article 13 specifically refers to those who will be saved in the end. Moody wanted reference to those who did not persevere to the end, but renounced their faith (apostates), to be referred to as well. He feared that without such a reference, one might assume that a person could profess faith in Christ once, then ignore Christ's teachings or even renounce Christ but be assured of a final salvation.

Thus, in the early years of Moody's career, all the issues that erupted in 1961 and 1982 were present. Conflict between Article 13 and Articles 1 and 18 in the Abstract gnawed until 1962. At that time, he drafted a 14-page letter containing 48 points to Penrose St. Amant, then dean of the School of Theology, explaining how the conflict came into being (10). According to Moody (points indicated in parenthesis):

(10) . . . I discovered that Basil Manly Jr. took every statement in Article XIII from the Particular Baptist Confession of faith in 1677 known as the Second London Confession. In a study of that confession, I found the source of Dr. Manly's error.

(11) . . . [W]ith the three documents before us (Westminster Confession of Faith, 1647, Article 17, Second London Confession, 1677, Article 17, Abstract of Principle, April 30, 1858, Article 18) it is easy to see what has happened. When we compare the Second London Confession of 1677, Article 17, with the Westminster Confession of 1647, Article 17, we see the significance of this statement:

> "The Particular Baptists of London and vicinity determined therefore, to show their agreement with Presbyterians and Congregationalists by making the Westminster Confession the basis of a new confession of their own. A circular letter was sent to the Particular Baptist churches in England and Wales asking that representatives be sent to a general meeting in 1677. By the time this meeting was held, it appears that Elder William Collins of the Petty France Church in London had worked over the Westminster document, altering it as he saw fit" (W. L. Lumpkin, *Baptist Confessions of Faith.* Philadelphia: Judson Press, 1959, p. 236).

(18) It takes little reading to see how it was worked over: To part I, the Elder William Collins added: "and given the precious faith of his elect unto" and changed "can neither" to "will never." He tries to be more Calvinistic than the Presbyterians.

(21) The Elder William Collins obviously had Luke 22:32 ("when thou art converted") in mind, but used the language of Hebrews 6:6 in the positive when it is actually in the negative. This is the error of the Elder William Collins. This contradiction of Scripture we are unable to accept. How can any person harmonize the following statements: Second London Confession, 1677: "Yet they shall renew their repentance"; Scripture, Hebrews 6:6: "it is impossible to renew them again unto repentance" (RSV).

(26) Basil Manly Jr. made his mistake when he "abstracted" the error of Elder William Collins. Repetition does not make an error accurate. It may all sound like a small error, but it has been said that I have "challenged the Abstract of Principles" for calling attention to this error. I can accept the statement of perseverance in the New Hampshire Confession of Faith, especially the 1853 revision, but I am unable to accept a contradiction of Scripture, especially when I have demonstrated the source of this error. Scripture for me is supreme.

(28) The problem is much deeper than the contradiction of a biblical statement. It is also the contradiction of the teaching of repentance in Hebrews.

Moody continued to cite Baptist scholars who supported his teaching of apostasy, such as Theodore H. Robinson and Johannes Schneider. Their interpretations on apostasy, he said, were identical with that of John Calvin, "with the exception that these modern Baptists make no appeal to double predestination. Thank God" (Moody, draft letter).

In point 37, Moody declared himself to be bound to the Greek New Testament that he believed to be fully inspired of God. His constant appeal to the Greek text demonstrates his allegiance to academic standards and biblical conservatism. Moody was a scholar but a conservative scholar. Words were important to him—he called them the tools of his trade. Syntax and proper translation from Greek to English caused him to move from RSV (Revised Standard Version) to AS (American Standard) to the Jerusalem Bible when discussing a passage.

This letter had been prompted by a resolution passed in 1961 by the Oklahoma Pastor's Conference charging that Moody taught that it was possible for "a person once saved to be lost" (Honeycutt, Chronicle, 1). President Duke K. McCall referred the resolution to the Trustee subcommittee on the School of Theology. On 14 March 1962, they reported to the Board of Trustees: "A careful and thorough discussion with Dr. Moody led to a unanimous conclusion that Dr. Moody carefully interprets the Abstract of Principles in harmony with what seems to us to be the obvious intent and purpose of the framers of the Abstract of Principles" (1). The subcommittee and the Board of Trustees concluded that no further action should be taken by the Board.

McCall realized, however, that the charges could erupt into a major controversy within the Southern Baptist Convention (SBC) because he "knew Dr. Moody would defend himself in correspondence with anybody" (McCall, personal letter, August 28, 1995). A special sabbatical at Oxford University, Oxford, England, was arranged by Dr. McCall. During this time Moody earned a D. Phil. from Oxford, and according to McCall, when Moody returned to Southern "there was no vestige of controversy left" (McCall, personal letter, 28 August 1995).

In 1980, Moody turned 65—retirement age. The normal procedure at that time was for the Board of Trustees to determine, approximately 18 months before initiation of service, whether or not to elect a faculty member approaching retirement as senior professor. Southern had established this role to provide for the employment of an individual beyond retirement age. Consideration of Moody, however, had been deferred to 1980. One of the issues involved was the Abstract of Principles, more specifically Article 13 (Honeycutt, Chronicle, 2). The year 1979 was the year the fundamentalists elected Adrian Rogers as president of the SBC. Southern Baptist Seminary was becoming increasingly anxious about persistent concerns expressed by individuals within the SBC that it was controlled by "liberals." There had been a review of charges received against any faculty member, which, of course, would have included Moody. At the 3 December 1979 faculty meeting President McCall asked if anyone had a proposal for revision of any part of the Abstract of Principles because he or she found it impossible to teach "in accord with and not contrary to the present statement" (3). Moody was not present for the meeting but did submit substantial suggestions for improvements in the Abstract, should it be revised. McCall wrote a response to Moody, saying he believed this proposal would prove "helpful if a revision of the Abstract of Principles is undertaken in the future. It is the overwhelming sentiment of the faculty in their communications with me that no revision of the Abstract should be undertaken at this time" (3). Moody underscored "at this time" in his copy of the Chronicle by Honeycutt and again when McCall continued, "The trustees are not of a mind either to amend the Abstract of Principles at this time or to alter the freedom given to faculty members across the years in their interpretation of the document. They will not extend your teaching responsibility beyond normal retirement unless you teach in accordance with the Abstract of Principles as understood by men like Carver and Robertson" (3). A handwritten inscription by Moody notes by this paragraph, "My view has been and still is that of A. T. Robertson, as ch. 55 of *The Word of Truth* demonstrates."

McCall wrote that if Moody "continued to differ substantively with the Abstract of Principles . . . within the traditional freedom accorded faculty members . . . his teaching would be terminated at the current ('79–'80) academic/fiscal year" (3). Moody and McCall had a good working relationship. Both were men of integrity, loyal to Southern Seminary, Baptist beliefs, and academic freedom—yet it seemed that an impasse had been reached. McCall insisted that Article 13 could be interpreted in more than one way—that is, that it spoke only of those who did persevere to the end and that this had been the assumption of those who had signed the Abstract (McCall, personal letter, 11 February 1980). Moody wanted nothing to be assumed and sought explicitness. Among his many proposals for revision was the insertion of Hebrews 6:4–6 as a second paragraph to Article 13. McCall believed Moody was escalating the issue by making an 1858 document mean what the words would have meant had it been written in 1980. For his part, Moody was becoming increasingly fearful of "creeping creedalism" and of an insistence upon one interpretation of Article 13.

In 1980 McCall and Moody spent an afternoon debating the force of Hebrews 6:4–6 and its relations to the Abstract of Principles, but neither changed positions (McCall, personal letter, 28 August 1995). During that meeting, McCall produced a copy of the Abstract and asked Moody to sign it as a personal assurance that he would "teach in accordance with and not contrary to it this fall." Moody signed but added at the bottom of the copy, "[S]ee my letter of Feb. 8, 1980," in which he had presented suggestions that he believed "to be in harmony with the superb Article 1, which I assume takes precedence over all that follow" (Moody, personal letter, 8 February 1980). This notation, for Moody, was a declaration that anything in the Abstract contrary to Scripture was not binding, and since he had demonstrated that Article 13 was a misquotation of Scripture in his 1962 letter to St. Amant, his teaching of apostasy was correct and thus in keeping with and not contrary to the Abstract of Principles.

McCall was weeks away from his retirement when he received a letter from the Little Red River Baptist Association expressing concern about Moody's position on apostasy as printed in the book *The Word of Truth*. The Association wanted to know if Moody would finish his contract with the Seminary without a reprimand of his heresy. McCall responded, saying that he had not read Moody's book with "care and precision" (Moody, personal letter, 21 January 1982) and requested specifics from the Association. Moody wrote to the Association on 21 January 1982, explaining his position, requesting that they read chapter 55 in his book with the Scriptures, and asking for a written response to any of his interpretations they considered incorrect. He offered to come and discuss the matter with "the brethren."

A letter to McCall of 16 February 1982 from the Association asked when their position concerning Moody would be placed before the Academic Freedom and Tenure Committee and if representatives could attend the next meeting of the Board of Trustees (Honeycutt, Chronicle, 6). By this time, Honeycutt had become president of Southern Seminary. On 24 February he received a letter requesting that he respond to the questions of the 16 February letter (6). Honeycutt telephoned David Miller, director of missions, on 5 May, requesting time to study the issues. Miller mentioned "the possibility of 'Convention action' if Moody continued to teach" (6). On 26 August the Executive Committee of the Arkansas Baptist Convention moved that the Executive Board contact Honeycutt, requesting him to elicit a written clarification by Moody of his stance on apostasy and that it be published in the *Arkansas Baptist Newsmagazine* (6). Moody's response was to grant permission to publish chapter 55 of his book. In September and October, Honeycutt continued to correspond with Arkansas Baptists through a letter published in the *Arkansas Baptist Newsmagazine*. Honeycutt assured them of "Southern Seminary's commitment to the authority of Scripture and to the liberty of conscience as primary Baptist emphasis" and reaffirmed the centrality of the Abstract of Principles (8). In Moody's copy, he penned these words: "The real difficulty." Indeed, for Moody this was the difficulty. He insisted that the Abstract be judged by Scripture, yet he was being asked to adhere to a misquotation of Scripture. Honeycutt was bound to either uphold the Abstract or resign. Article 13 had been previously interpreted by some as a statement concerning only those who persevered. The Abstract had not been revised, and Honeycutt was bound to support it as written.

The officers of the Board of Trustees were forwarded all correspondence related to the Moody issue (9) prior to the 21 October meeting. On 20

October Moody responded in writing to a request from Honeycutt for clarification on passages cited in "charges made by David Miller" (Moody, personal letter, 20 October 1982). "Miller," he said, "seems always to think of salvation purely in the past tense. . . . [T]he New Testament often uses as a paradigm the Exodus from Egypt and entrance into the Land to describe salvation. . . . Hebrews, the most detailed new Testament writing on apostasy, elaborates the paradigm with utmost clarity."

Moody, the scholar, the teacher, the preacher, could not comprehend how any Baptist would be placing the nineteenth-century terms "security of the believer" and "eternal security" with the scriptural term "perseverance of the saints" (Moody, *The Word of Truth*, 362). Furthermore, Moody retorted, since the very word *apostenai* appeared in Hebrews, the resolution should be passed against the author of Hebrews (personal letter, 20 October, 2). Moody insisted upon arguing from the Greek New Testament, and for him, "there is a clear choice between the terms used in the New Testament and the clichés accumulated by Augustine, Calvin, John Owen, J. R. Graves and their followers who don't even bother to do their own study of the New Testament" (2).

Honeycutt asked Moody if he would stand behind him on the Abstract since he would use that in his response to the Arkansas critics. Moody refused. The Abstract had an error that had not been corrected, and he would not defend an error (Honeycutt, personal letter, 8 August 1995).

On 1 November, Honeycutt offered Moody several options. Moody could resign as a matter of conscience, or he could retire since he was 65. Otherwise, the president would be forced to "deal responsibly with overt faculty deviation from the Abstract of Principles of significant portions thereof" (Honeycutt, personal letter, 1 November 1982, 2). Should he resign, Honeycutt was still prepared to recommend the continuation of his full salary until 31 July 1983 and 50 percent salary for the 1983–1984 leave of absence approved by the Executive Committee of the Board of Trustees, allowing him to teach in Hong Kong (2).

That same day the North Pulaski Association of the Arkansas Baptist State Convention passed a resolution requesting that the Trustees of Southern Seminary consider termination of Moody from any and all responsibilities at any institution supported directly or indirectly by the SBC. Since the Trustees would not meet again until April 1983, the matter could have remained an issue between Honeycutt and Moody. Miller wrote to Moody in September and invited him to speak at the Arkansas Baptist State Pastor's Conference on 15 November. Moody replied that if his task was to "expound the Scripture before those who are willing to 'search the Scriptures,'" he would accept, but if the intent was to make "a resolution against me and the administration of Southern Seminary, as was done in Oklahoma City in 1961, then I must decline" (Moody, personal letter, 29 September 1982).

Miller scheduled Moody for 15 November, for the topic "Can a Saved Person Ever Be Lost?" On 11 November, at Honeycutt's urging, Moody agreed to decline the invitation. Then, however, between 11 November and 14 November Moody's students encouraged him to speak.

Anyone who knew Moody realized he thoroughly enjoyed a debate. Moreover, he believed that by logical exegesis of the Greek text he could convince the pastors that his teaching was biblical and correct. The issue, however, was more emotional than logical. Although Moody was roundly applauded at the end of his address, the Arkansas Baptist State Convention on 17 November passed a resolution requesting the Trustees of Southern Baptist Theological Seminary to consider the termination of Dale Moody for advocating apostasy as a true doctrine (Resolution No. 2 on Apostasy). The Resolution appeared in the Baptist press and in Baptist state papers. The "Moody Issue" became the subject of editorials and letters to the editor. Moody remained frustrated by the lack of exegetical debate. A lengthy interview appeared in the 27 November *Louisville Times*. "At the present time he is a professor in good standing," said Honeycutt, but Moody had been reminded that professors who could not support the Abstract had the option of resigning.

In the press, in Arkansas, and in Moody's mind, the issue was apostasy, but for Honeycutt and the Trustees, it was the Abstract of Principles. Moody believed Article 13 denied the possibility of apostasy: Honeycutt and McCall believed that it could speak of those who persevered to the end. Since Moody insisted he would not retire, some form of Trustee action now seemed mandatory.

On 21 November Honeycutt wrote a six-page report to the officers of the Board of Trustees. Moody read and agreed with the text, suggesting a few corrections. Honeycutt listed the following as areas in need of review: Miller's letter of protest of Moody's treatment of apostasy in *The Word of Truth*; the request for clarification by Moody concerning the perseverance of the saints by the Executive Committee of the Arkansas Baptist Convention; and Moody's preaching at the Pastors Conference in Arkansas. He traced Moody's problem with Article 13 since his student days. Finally, he recommended that any action taken at that time remain with the president.

Through December, Honeycutt and Moody discussed the issues; in March they discussed his contractual relationship with the Seminary (Honeycutt, personal letter, 17 March 1983). Moody had raised questions because he was scheduled to teach in Hong Kong and Asia during 1983–1984. For two years he had been on an annual contract with the title of senior professor, but in the third term he had been elected as professor of Christian theology, with no date of termination. Moody assumed he was now employed until 1985. The assumption caused a bitter reaction from Moody during the last months of his teaching. It was Honeycutt who had recommended Moody's election as professor because "it was my intention to move Dale to a somewhat more permanent position than an annual contract. I wanted to affirm Dale and set his position in at least a semi-permanent context" (Honeycutt, personal letter, 8 August 1995).

Regulations for contractual agreements for those over 65 had been in effect since 1961. With pressure mounting to bring the Moody issue before the June SBC meeting, the Academic Liaison Committee decided to recommend to the Board of Trustees that July 1984 be set as a termination date. Moody would remain as an employee in 1983–1984 since a leave of absence had been granted in October 1982.

"It is the judgment of the President that it is not in the best interest of the Seminary to offer Professor Moody a fourth teaching contract for the period 1984–1985" (Honeycutt, Statement of President Roy L. Honeycutt, 12 April 1983, 2).

Southern Seminary released the information on 13 April 1983 during the Trustees meeting. An official statement reaffirming the contractual nature of the Abstract of Principles, terming it a doctrinal consensus, was also adopted (*SBTS News*, 13 April 1983, 2).

After the Trustees' action, Moody kept a brave front, but the effect was devastating. In a telling letter to Honeycutt dated 19 April 1983 Moody wrote, "Southern Seminary has meant more to me than life since 1937 when I arrived as a student."

During my life with him I saw him cry once—when he told me he would not be allowed to teach in Hong Kong. There is great irony in the fact that the book he dedicated to Southern Seminary caused so much pain and discord. Until his death, he continued to write and teach about the danger of apostasy. In 1991, Smyth and Helwys published *Apostasy: A Study in the Epistle to the Hebrews and in Baptist History* by Dale Moody. Half an hour before his death, he gave me the three books he had with him— the poems of Robert Burns, the New Jerusalem Bible, and the third edition of the 1983 United Bible Society (UBS) Greek New Testament. Until the end, he was checking translations by Scripture.

BIBLIOGRAPHY

Arkansas Baptist Convention. Resolution No. 2 on Apostasy, 17 November 1982.
Honeycutt, Roy L. Personal letter, 1 November 1982.
———. Personal letter, 17 March 1983.
———. Personal letter, 8 August 1995.
———. Statement of President Roy L. Honeycutt, 12 April 1983.
———. Unpublished but privately circulated Chronicle, 9 December 1982.
Marty, Martin E., and R. Scott Appleby, eds. *Fundamentalisms Observed*. Chicago: University of Chicago, 1991.
McCall, Duke K. Personal letter, 11 February 1980.
———. Personal letter, 28 August 1995.

Moody, Dale. *Apostasy: A Study in the Epistle to the Hebrews and in Baptist History*. Macon, GA: Smyth and Helwys, 1991.

————. Draft Letter to Dean Penrose St. Amant, 1962.

————. Personal letter, 3 January 1962.

————. Personal letter, 8 February 1980.

————. Personal letter, 21 January 1982.

————. Personal letter, 29 September 1982.

————. Personal letter, 20 October 1982.

————. Personal letter, 19 April 1983.

————. *The Word of Truth*. Grand Rapids: William B. Eerdmans, 1981.

Mueller, William A. *A History of Southern Baptist Theological Seminary*. Nashville: Broadman Press, 1959.

Robertson, A. T. *Word Pictures in the New Testament*. 6 vols. Nashville: Broadman Press, 1932. Vol 5: *The Fourth Gospel, the Epistle to the Hebrews*.

SBTS News. 13 April 1983.

Reverend Sue Ellen Moody McDaniel

James A. Pike
(1913–1969)

James Albert Pike was born in Oklahoma City, Oklahoma, on 14 February 1913 to James Albert and Pearl Agatha Winsatt Pike. Pike's father died in 1915. Six years later he and his mother moved to Hollywood, California. They were active in the Roman Catholic Church, and James decided to study for the priesthood. In pursuit of this goal, he enrolled at a Jesuit school, the University of Santa Clara (Laughlin, "James A. Pike," 335).

It was at Santa Clara that young Pike's first challenges to institutional religion began to be felt and voiced. He was especially bothered by the church's position on birth control and papal infallibility. As a sophomore, he withdrew from the Roman Catholic Church and the university (Laughlin, "James A. Pike," 335; Stringfellow and Towne, *The Death*, 244–250). Upon later reflection, Pike referred to himself as "a thoroughgoing humanist agnostic" (quoted in Stringfellow and Towne, *The Death*, 244).

In 1933 Pike enrolled at the University of Southern California, where he earned an undergraduate degree, followed by a degree in law. In 1936 he was admitted to the California bar but soon left the state to enroll at Yale University, where he secured the doctor of sciences in law degree. He moved to Washington, D.C. in 1938 and rapidly ascended through its legal circles. He was a cofounder of a law firm and became an attorney with the Securities and Exchange Commission. Pike also married Jane Alvies, but the marriage was dissolved by divorce in 1940 (Laughlin, "James A. Pike," 335; Carey, "Life on the Boundary," 155; Stringfellow and Towne, *The Death*, 273–275).

Advancement within the legal profession continued when in 1940 Pike joined the faculty of George Washington Law School and became a member of the bar of the United States Supreme Court. His interest in religion was renewed, and he joined the Protestant Episcopal Church. As was true of most young men of that era, Pike's life was interrupted by World War II. He joined the navy and used his legal training first as a Naval Intelligence officer in Washington, D.C. and later as an attorney with the U.S. Maritime Commission and War Shipping Administration. His personal and religious life continued when in 1942 he married a former student, Esther Yanovsky, and became a postulant for the Episcopal priesthood (Laughlin, "James A. Pike," 335).

Near the end of the war, Pike's move into the profession of the clergy became clear. In 1944 he was ordained to the diaconate at St. John's Church in Washington, D.C. He then began studies at Virginia Theological Seminary while serving both as curate at St. John's and as chaplain to students at Georgetown University. A year later he moved to New York to study at Union Theological Seminary, where he thrived under the teaching of Paul Tillich and Reinhold Neibuhr. After his ordination to the priesthood in 1946, he began three years of service as rector of Christ Church in Poughkeepsie, New York. During the same time he served as chaplain to Episcopal students at Vassar College (Laughlin, "James A. Pike," 335; Stringfellow and Towne, The Death, 276–281).

Pike left Christ Church to enter the academic world as chair of the Department of Religion and chaplain at Columbia University. He returned to the clerical profession in 1952 when he became dean of the largest Episcopal Church in the country, the Cathedral of Saint John the Divine. Pike took the opportunity of his rapid rise in the Episcopal ministry to take dramatic steps in moving the church into the affairs of the world. He had the church's name changed to the Cathedral of New York. His sermons were topical and controversial and attracted large attendance. His dialogue sermons were very popular, as was the creative involvement of the Cathedral with the artistic community. He began a national television talk show where he and guests addressed the most current religious, social, and political issues (Laughlin, "James A. Pike," 336; Carey, "Life on the Boundary," 155–156; Stringfellow and Towne, The Death, 282–291).

Pike never shied away from controversy and in New York found the perfect foil for his progressive agenda in the person of the very conservative voice for Roman Catholicism, Francis Cardinal Spellman. Pike found in Spellman a useful antagonist against whom to promote a social crusade for the interests of the poor and outcast. Cynics, atheists, and those searching for faith were embraced by Pike and his ministry (Carey, "Life on the Boundary," 155–156).

Both the content of what he was saying and his "in your face" style bothered some Episcopal clergy. This antipathy was increased in 1953 when he refused an honorary doctor of divinity degree from the University of the South (Sewanee) because the school was segregated. Pike said publicly that he would not accept "a degree of white divinity" (quoted in

Laughlin, "James A. Pike," 336). This conflict came to have a long-term effect on Pike's problems within the Episcopal Church. Bishop Henry Louttit, a Trustee of Sewanee, was very angry about Pike's public condemnation of the school and later led the effort to have him tried for heresy (Stringfellow and Towne, *The Death*, 339).

Within the general public, Pike's popularity as a national religious leader continued to grow. In February 1958 *Reader's Digest* reprinted an article entitled "The Joyful Dean." In that same month, he was elected bishop coadjutor of California. The ailing incumbent bishop died in September 1959, and Pike was installed as bishop of California, a position he held for the next seven years. These were momentous years for the nation and for Pike, marked by success and conflict. He was able to combine roaring successes in all the ways ecclesiastical development is measured (growth in communicants and contributions) and in developing creative and effective social service ministries. For example, he raised $3 million for the completion of Grace Cathedral in San Francisco and simultaneously began a ministry to "street people." It was at this Cathedral that he invited Martin Luther King, Jr., to speak, ordained the first woman to the Episcopal ministry, and installed stained glass windows in honor of "secular saints" Albert Einstein, Thurgood Marshall, and John Glenn (Laughlin, "James A. Pike," 336; Stringfellow and Towne, *The Death*, 309–315).

THE TROUBLES BEGIN

Challenges to traditional Christian doctrines had been rather oblique in Pike's statements until the 21 December 1960 Christmas issue of the *Christian Century*, which included the thirteenth installment of the popular "How My Mind Has Changed" series. In the article, entitled "the Three Pronged Synthesis," reservations were expressed about the doctrines of the Trinity, virgin birth, and Christ as the only way to salvation. Pike proclaimed his own faith in a "big God" who "cannot be enclosed in a tabernacle or in a philosophical or theological concept." He said that he was driven by the conviction that these traditional doctrines did not do justice to God, who alone is final, while all else, including doctrine, is tentative. Pike confessed, "I don't believe as many things as I believed ten years ago, but I trust that what I do believe, I believe more deeply" (Pike, "The Three Pronged Synthesis," 1496–1500). This article and his responses to it led to his being officially charged with heresy three times. Three weeks after publication of the article, the more conservative journal, *Christianity Today*, contained an editorial criticizing Pike for having doubts (Laughlin, "James A. Pike," 336).

In Pike's defense, we see the influence of the two persons whose thought seemed to have been most formative for him. He frequently acknowledged his indebtedness to his friend Anglican Bishop John A. T. Robinson, whose book *Honest to God* had become a best-seller. Pike also appealed to Til-lich's concept of the symbolic nature of theological statements and the need to get beyond them to understand the deeper realities toward which they pointed. He felt that the changes of the modern world especially required a restatement of what was most important to the contemporary Christian. He advised the modern church to "travel light" with little doctrinal baggage (Carey, "Life on the Boundary," 156–157).

Parallel to the developing heresy charges was an increasingly troubled personal life for Pike. In 1964 he joined Alcoholics Anonymous, after 12 years of debilitating drinking. In 1966 his son, Jim, Jr., who had a long-standing problem with drugs, committed suicide with a rifle in a New York City hotel room. The next year, Maren Bergrud, a woman with whom he had an affair and whom he had supported with church funds, committed suicide with an overdose of sleeping pills. The matter was complicated by Pike's involvement in the suicide. Apparently, confused and embarrassed, he attempted to move her body and some of her clothes from his apartment to her apartment. This bungling effort was discovered by the police, and there was much embarrassing publicity. Soon, Esther, his wife of 25 years, secured a divorce. In all the publicity, it became known that his marriage had been troubled for some years by both his alcoholism and his infidelities. Finally, he moved out of the bishop's residence in San Francisco and lived the rest of his life "out of a suitcase." He was yet to endure in February 1968 the attempted suicide of his daughter Connie (Laughlin, "James A. Pike," 337; Carey, "Life on the Boundary," 157–158; Stringfellow and Towne, *The Death*, 56–62, 81–83, 147–149).

Pike began to claim that he had contact with his dead son "from beyond the grave." There were many séances, including one with well-known psy-chic Arthur Ford. It was later shown that Ford had used notes and faked the event. Pike also claimed to have communicated with Paul Tillich's spirit, which brought a sharp and indignant response from Hannah Tillich. His engagement with mediums from North America and England led to much bewilderment and embarrassment for many of his friends. He also began to interpret some of the traditional doctrines, especially the Resurrection, in light of these experiences. In 1968, he wrote about his séance experiences in the book *The Other Side* (Laughlin, "James A. Pike," 338; Stringfellow and Towne, *The Death*, 66–68).

Under the pressure of the negative publicity, Pike submitted his resig-nation as bishop of California in 1968 but retained his Episcopal status. He joined the Center for the Study of Democratic Institutions, a liberal think tank in Santa Barbara, California, where he studied, among other things, the Dead Sea Scrolls. He married Diane Kennedy, a former student who had assisted in the writing of *The Other Side*. The new bishop of California, C. Kilmer Meyers, announced that Pike had not secured per-mission to marry and banned him from all priestly functions, including preaching (Laughlin, "James A. Pike," 337–338; Stringfellow and Towne, *The Death*, 163–166).

Pike felt vindicated in much of his efforts when in 1969 the Episcopal Church called for a new openness in theological inquiry and made a commitment to social justice. With an air of optimism he revealed in the April 29 issue of *Look* magazine that he and his wife were leaving the institutional church and beginning "an unencumbered journey into an open future." Like the early Christians, they were going "to the wilderness" to organize a Foundation for Religious Transition for other like-minded "church alumni" (Laughlin, "James A. Pike," 337; Stringfellow and Towne, *The Death*, 165–166).

Later in 1969, Pike and his wife went to Israel to study the Essene communities of Jesus' day. During a poorly planned automobile trip into the Judean desert, they became lost. His wife was able to make her way to safety. A search party found Pike's body five days later. He was buried in Jaffa, Israel, on 8 September 1969 (Laughlin, "James A. Pike," 338).

THE CHARGES OF HERESY

There were three specific efforts by Pike's antagonists to bring formal charges of heresy against him. Those charges and the resulting procedures and debates contained a complex mix of issues ranging from doctrine to social ethics to personal lifestyle. Through it all, Pike staunchly defended what he had said and done.

In January 1961, the first serious effort to bring formal charges of heresy was made by a group of Georgia clergy. They asked Bishop Albert R. Stuart of Savannah to present charges of heresy against Pike on the basis of what he had written a month earlier in the *Christian Century* article on how his mind had changed. The accusations against Pike were that he did not believe "in the virgin birth of Our Lord, the doctrine of the Holy Trinity as stated by the church and the necessity of salvation through Jesus Christ alone." Stuart delayed in taking the charges to the House of Bishops, the only group that could try a bishop for heresy. He voiced a concern that was to become a theme in the upcoming debates when he said, "I don't know of any great good which can come of this matter" (Gray, "Bishop Pike Catches Attention at Richmond," 221). The mixed motives of the accusers and the promise of bad publicity led much of the leadership of the Episcopal Church to conclude that nothing good would come from a heresy trial.

Pike responded to the specific charges: "Both as a bishop and as a lawyer I can say safely that my comments in *The Christian Century* article are within the bounds of doctrinal orthodoxy as judged by such norms as the House of Bishops' recent pastoral letter on doctrine." He also went on the offensive against his accusers from the Deep South by suggesting that racial segregation was a more important heresy worth investigating. He concluded: "The Bible also reminds us that doing the truth is as important as saying the truth" (221).

The second set of formal charges against Pike came in July 1965 when a group of clergy from the diocese of Arizona petitioned the House of Bishops to challenge his faithfulness to the Christian religion and to his office as bishop. Their charges were twofold. First, they criticized Pike's "plan to ordain women to the sacred ministry of the church, [considering] such action at variance with apostolic custom, Anglican tradition and practical wisdom." Second, they charged that he

> has been false to the vows he took at ordination . . . has repudiated our Lord's Virgin Birth . . . has denied the doctrine of the Blessed Trinity and of the Incarnation as the church has received the same . . . [has denied] the empty tomb and the bodily Resurrection and Ascension. (*Christian Century*, 1 September 1965, 1051)

Pike's defense was vigorous as he rejected the charges as either false or grossly misleading. He acknowledged that he had rejected the formulations of doctrine "as couched in the late Greek philosophical concepts of the fourth and fifth centuries." He also claimed that he held on to the essential meaning of the doctrine of the virgin birth and other verbal structures of Christian tradition while rejecting the traditional formulations of those doctrines. Like others, the doctrine of the Holy Trinity was renounced as "outdated, incomprehensible, and inessential." In a positive claim he confessed, "I affirm of God all that has been affirmed of the Three Persons" and said that he believed in the Jesus Christ of the Nicene Creed as "God of God, Light of light, very God of very God" (1051).

In September 1965 the House of Bishops cleared Pike of all the heresy charges against him, but this did not end the controversy. His actions in recognizing Phyllis Edwards as a minister and listing her as a member of the diocesan clergy made him a target of a substantial segment of the more conservative element in the Episcopal clergy. The House of Bishops, while not naming Pike specifically, ruled that women could not be ordained and banned them from administering the sacraments (*Christian Century*, 6 October 1965, 1214).

The third attempt at heresy charges came in 1966 when Pike's longtime nemesis Bishop Henry I. Louttit of Florida led a group of bishops seeking to get the House of Bishops to pursue heresy charges. The claim was that Pike "had for the past several years held and taught publicly and advisedly . . . doctrine contrary to that held by this Church." Furthermore, "this teaching had confused, not to say bewildered, many of the faithful laity of the Church" and that it had become increasingly difficult to discipline the clergy "who see one of their right Reverend Fathers in God unwilling to discipline himself" (Stringfellow and Towne, *The Bishop Pike Affair*, 203).

In October 1966 the House of Bishops, meeting in Wheeling, West Virginia, attempted to head off heresy proceedings against Pike. Presiding Bishop John E. Hines and many others believed that great harm would come to the church if there were a heresy trial. The fear was that the church would be sharply divided along doctrinal lines. Hines appointed a committee to handle the case and hopefully reach some solution without a formal heresy trial. The committee was composed of both friends and detractors of Pike. Pike was not allowed to appear before the committee.

The committee produced a 1,200-word statement that was presented to the bishops at an October 1966 meeting. The statement declared Pike's utterances as "irresponsible." They said that "his writings and speaking on profound realities with which Christian faith and worship are concerned are too often marred by caricatures of precious symbols and at the worst, by cheap vulgarizations of great expressions of faith." They specifically focused on the "disparaging way" Pike treated the doctrine of the Trinity. They continued:

> Yet he knows well that a triune apprehension of the mystery of God's being and action is woven into the whole fabric of the creeds and prayers and hymnody of our Episcopal Church, as it is into the vows of loyalty taken by our clergy at their ordination. It is explicit in our membership in the World Council of Churches and in our consultations on church union with other major churches.

It is important to note how this line of argument rests primarily upon the desire to protect the institutional integrity of the church and avoids the substance of the doctrine of the Trinity. This institutional interest is further reflected in the committee's contention that Pike's statements did not deserve the "work and wounds" that a trial would involve (Pitts, "Pike Demands a Trial," 53).

The force of the statement was to criticize Pike and yet avoid a heresy trial. The floor debate on the statement was limited to one hour and tightly controlled. Clearly, the bishops wanted to end this conflict soon. Pike and Louttit were each allowed only ten minutes, and all theological arguments were ruled out of order. This ban on theological debate again shows the anxiety about theological division and the silent awareness that there were other bishops who held essentially the same theological position as did Pike. Near the end of the hour debate, there was some sentiment that Pike was being treated unfairly because each time he tried to deal with doctrine, he was ruled out of order. He finally claimed that "this House is not interested in theology, but only public relations." The debate was extended for another hour, but by a vote of 103 to 36 the bishops approved the committee's report. A minority of bishops signed a formal statement of dissent (54).

Pike's response was predictable. He demanded, under the rarely used Canon 56, that he be tried for heresy. He insisted on an opportunity to answer the charges against his theology and character. The proposed process was complicated and required that a committee of bishops decide if the charges constituted a canonical offense. If so, then a board of inquiry would determine if there was sufficient evidence to put Pike on trial. A trial could not occur before the September 1967 triennial convention. The tortuous and painful process continued.

Pike sensed that publicity of the dispute was to his advantage. He threatened a lawsuit to ensure that all stages of the investigation and the trial would be open to the public. He wanted to bring theologians from all over the world to testify. His public criticism now focused on the majority of the House of Bishops, whom he claimed had bungled the entire affair by the unfairness of their proceedings. Furthermore, he called attention to the bishops' avoidance of the theological issues. He said: "The House of Bishops never will discuss theology. But we don't talk about God in the House of Bishops. . . . Honesty in the church is the issue" (Hyer, "Bishop Pike and Advent in New York," 29).

Looking back on the episode to this point, it is now clear that there had been a series of serious blunders by all the parties involved. The House of Bishops was naive to think that it could, by avoiding a heresy trial, pacify Pike's enemies, silence the strong-willed Pike, and quiet the tumultuous forces surging through the Episcopal Church. It was a tragic mistake to try and avoid the theological issues in the belief that they would go away. Bishop Hines admitted a blunder he made. In 1965 Pike had prepared a six-page, single-spaced letter in response to meeting with and a request from seven of the eight provincial bishops. The letter was to be distributed by Hines to all the church's bishops and contained explanations of some of his theological statements and actions regarding the ordination of women. Hines's failure to distribute the letter to the bishops was not discovered by Pike until he arrived for the October 1966 meeting. All in all, there was much failed communication and fear-driven misperception (*Christian Century*, 21 December 1966, 1959–1960).

Dominated primarily by the passion of dread, the Episcopal Church marched toward the September 1967 showdown. One last attempt was made to avoid the perceived disaster. An 11-member Committee on Theological Freedom and Social Responsibility was formed, composed of bishops, laypersons, parish ministers, and theological professors. The committee was also supported by an advisory group composed of prestigious figures like John Courtney Murray and John A. T. Robinson. Furthermore, Pike served on the advisory committee and in this way was finally perceived as having his chance to speak. The committee's statement sought to achieve a meaningful balance among the church's responsibility to creedal faithfulness, ecclesiastical responsibility, and theological dissent. The search for this balance is reflected in some of the committee's statements.

> God makes men free. It does not behoove his church to try to hobble their minds or inhibit their search for new insights into truth. . . . While we affirm the right of every man to choose what he will believe without any kind of coercion whatever, we also assert the right of the church to maintain its distinctive identity and continuity as a community of faith centered around the historic revelation of God in Christ. . . . Although the church may feel that it must maintain a last-resort power to deal juridically with bishops or priests who publicly engage in persistent and flagrant contradiction of its essential witness, we strongly recommend that initiation of this process be made extremely difficult.

Pike indicated his willingness to withdraw his demands for a trial if the church's convention accepted this report. The convention did that, and the Episcopal Church was spared a heresy trial (*Christian Century*, 13 September 1967, 1147–1148).

CONCLUSION

The title of this story could be "The Trial That Never Was." With strenuous persistence the leadership of the Episcopal Church sought to and finally did avoid a heresy trial. The primary motivation seems to have been their desire to avoid a serious conflict about doctrine. It is remarkable to read the literature on this episode and discover how infrequent any frank discussion of doctrine occurs. Charges are hurled back and forth but there is no true engagement. There was the acknowledged fear that any such engagement would fracture the church. Also, there was the widespread opinion that the real animus against Pike was not doctrinal but rather both the content and style of Pike's prophetic stands on the volatile social issues of his day. Finally, when viewed within the wider context of the Episcopal Church, the conclusion has to be that Pike's doctrinal positions were not especially radical. An exception might be when near the end of his life Pike began to mix séances with Resurrection. For the most part, Pike affirmed far more than he rejected, and what he rejected tended to be the letter of the creeds while trying to hold on to their meaning. There may have been much less criticism of him, had he been a theological professor and not a bishop.

The consequences of the Pike affair seem to have been twofold. First, the Episcopal Church took a stand, at least formally, that allowed more room for doctrinal differences within its fellowship without the charge of heresy.

There seems to have been the recognition that there was more doctrinal diversity than had been acknowledged and therefore the church should avoid any rush to judgment on heresy charges. Indeed, the final committee report stated that it should be very difficult for anyone to file heresy charges. A second understanding that emerged from Pike's debate with his critics was the recognition of the importance of orthopraxy as well as orthodoxy. The church was forced to recognize the importance of faithfulness to God in practice as well as in creedal statements.

One cannot come away from a review of this case without recognizing the dominance of James Pike's persona in the story. Clearly, he was a very gifted person who was especially effective as a communicator and administrator. Through strength of intellect and personality, he was able to control almost every conversation or debate in which he became involved. It should also be recognized that he was not especially creative in any of his theological or ethical analyses, with the result that he faded quickly from public and scholarly view after his death.

The most troubling dimension of this study is the role that the dark side of Pike's personality plays in the story. His persistent philandering and the bizarre involvement in the occult near the end of his life beg for explanation. This can be read as consistent with Pike's rejection of strict rules and boundaries. It should also be recognized that much of this behavior also reflects a self-serving tendency that marked much of his activity. We are left, however, to square this behavior with the great effort he put in defense of those who had been rejected and oppressed by the insensitive institutions of church and society. Even here, we must note Pike's failure to exercise the same level of empathy in relating to conservative institutional leaders that he did in dealing with the cynic and nonbeliever. Finally, we must recognize this remarkable drama of flawed prophet and flawed church as a common story in our history.

ACKNOWLEDGMENT

Special thanks is due to John P. Andersen, Sr., my graduate assistant, for his research and editorial assistance in preparing this entry.

BIBLIOGRAPHY

Carey, John J. "Life on the Boundary: The Paradoxical Models of Tillich and Pike." *Duke Divinity School Review* 42 (fall 1977): 149–164.

Christian Century. "Bishop Lickfield Attacks Bishop Pike." 82 (6 October 1965), 1214.

———. "Episcopal Blunders." 83 (21 December 1966), 1559–1560.

———. "Episcopal Report May Preclude Pike Trial." 84 (13 September 1967), 1147–1148.

———. "Pike: Heretic or Iconoclast?" 82 (1 September 1965), 1051–1052.

Gray, William B. "Bishop Pike Catches Attention at Richmond." *Christian Century* 84 (15 February 1967), 221–222.

Hyer, Marjorie. "Bishop Pike and Advent in New York." *Christian Century* 84 (4 January 1967), 28–30.

Laughlin, Paul A. "James A. Pike." In *Twentieth Century Shapers of American Popular Religion*, edited by Charles L. Lippy. Westport, CT: Greenwood Press, 1989. 334–342.

Pike, James A. "The Three Pronged Synthesis." *The Christian Century* 77 (21 December 1960), 1496–1500.

Pike, James A., with Diane Kennedy. *The Other Side*. Garden City, New York: Doubleday, 1968.

Pitts, Edward H. "Pike Demands a Trial." *Christianity Today* 11 (11 November 1966) 53–54.

Stringfellow, William, and Anthony Towne. *The Bishop Pike Affair: Scandals of Conscience and Heresy, Relevance and Solemnity in the Contemporary Church*. New York: Harper and Row, 1967.

———. *The Death and Life of Bishop Pike*. Garden City, NY: Doubleday & Company, 1976.

Daniel B. McGee

Walter Righter
(1923–)

In May 1996, a Court for the Trial of a Bishop ruled by a vote of seven to one that no "core doctrine" of the church barred the ordination of a noncelibate homosexual to the ministry of the Episcopal Church. This decision concluded a complex judicial process, formally initiated more than a year earlier, that exhibited the fundamental divisions about authority and doctrine in a relatively small but historically influential religious community. Bishop Walter Righter, the retired bishop of Iowa, had been charged for violating his responsibilities on two counts: first, because he had signed a statement supporting the ordination of noncelibate homosexuals, who were deemed qualified by the appropriate church bodies, and second, for presiding on behalf of the bishop of Newark (New Jersey), John S. Spong, at the ordination of Barry Stopfel in September 1990.

In his January 1995 covering letter for the presentment (charge) to the presiding bishop of the Episcopal Church, Bishop William Wantland of the Diocese of Eau Claire (Wisconsin), writing on behalf of nine other bishops joining him in bringing the charge, made it clear that the presentment against Righter was intended to be the first of several such actions directed against bishops who had acted "contrary to the teaching of the Church" by ordaining noncelibate individuals, that is, those who engaged in sexual relations outside of marriage. Wantland explained that Righter was being targeted initially because his action in presiding at the Stopfel ordination was the "least recent such ordination" within the five-year statute of limitations imposed by church law. Thus, Wantland made it plain that this action would be the first of several such efforts to discipline bishops like Righter, who knowingly had ordained noncelibate homosexuals.

In the Episcopal Church, heresy is defined as "holding and teaching . . .

any doctrine contrary to that held by [the] Church." Only once in the history of the Episcopal Church has a bishop been convicted of heresy. In 1924, William Montgomery Brown, the retired bishop of Arkansas, was convicted of heresy for questioning the divinity of Jesus in a book about Christianity and communism. There have been other instances, however, most recently in 1966 in the matter of James A. Pike,* retired bishop of California, when preliminary proceedings have addressed the possibility of such action. Pike had questioned the meaning and the historicity of the virgin birth. In the Pike case, the possibility of a trial was eliminated by a vote in the House of Bishops to censure. There have also been a few cases involving priests, including Algernon Sidney Crapsey* in 1906. Overwhelmingly, however, the tendency in the Episcopal Church, a religious community known for tolerating diverse points of view, has been to avoid heresy proceedings.

The Episcopal Church in the United States counts approximately 3 million members. This membership is widely dispersed but is more concentrated on the East and West Coasts and in the major metropolitan areas of the country. Theologically and historically, the Episcopal Church is part of the Anglican Communion, a global association of independent religious communities that acknowledge a shared heritage of the Church of England. As such, the Episcopal Church has relied more on consensus and common liturgical practice than on hierarchical authority or an ordered summary of belief to maintain the integrity of the community. Anglican theology has frequently been compared to a three-legged stool supported by the appeal to Scripture, tradition, and reason. In this formulation, it is assumed that the appeal to Scripture and antiquity is necessary but not a sufficient standard and that the common reason and experience of the community provide an essential basis for ongoing discernment about the will of God.

The Righter case illustrates the difficulty of achieving consensus about issues that represent change or theological development in a tradition that has deemphasized confessional or dogmatic definitions of community. Within the Episcopal Church, as in many other mainline religious groups, a split has developed between a group that is self-consciously traditionalist and those of more liberal sensibility who have accommodated changes in liturgical patterns as well as the ordination of women. The Episcopal Church, which has always sheltered a range of theological and liturgical patterns, has been able to cope with that diversity within the context of a consensus about the centrality of worship, common prayer, and the importance of the episcopate, the unifying symbol of leadership and apostolicity.

The embrace of the secular world represented by the engagement of the liberal church with issues of civil rights, feminism, and the other "isms," including liberation theology in a framework that minimizes the traditional markers and symbols of the sacred community, has created a context in which personal values, particularly values about sexuality, seem less securely anchored. The fact that a bishop, one who, by virtue of office, embodies the apostolic tradition, had exercised a judgment in which traditional boundaries about sexuality were challenged made this a poignant paradigm about the theological and cultural quandary.

During the last third of the twentieth century, both church and culture have struggled with questions about human sexuality and relationships. Traditional constraints about marriage after divorce and, more generally, an increasing tolerance, if not acceptance, of sexual expression outside of marriage provide important background for this case. In addition, the decision taken by the church to ordain women represented a profound reorientation of assumptions about gender and ordination. In different ways, each of these developments represents a move away from a commitment to modes of thinking based on objectively definable boundaries to patterns of engagement emphasizing judgments and process. The result has been a distinctive capacity to mediate developments emanating from modern culture, including the challenges of the sexual revolution. Anglicanism had relatively little difficulty adjusting to evolution and to the results of literary and historical criticism of the Bible. It has been particularly receptive to the arts and, because of its liturgical character, has provided support for sustaining and innovating traditions of musical expression. In liturgy, music, and the arts, the Episcopal Church has also been forced to confront the reality of the convergence of gay and lesbian culture with important dimensions of Christian and, particularly, Anglican experience.

With respect to the question of homosexuality, two external developments have also been critical. First, the legacy of the civil rights movement has made discriminatory practices of any sort hard to defend. Second, the decisive shift in the view of homosexuality represented by the 1973 decision of the American Psychiatric Association no longer to classify it as a diagnosable condition—that is, not to consider homosexuality as a form of mental illness—contributed to a changed climate of scientific opinion about gay and lesbian experience. Finally, it is widely recognized, but only reluctantly acknowledged, that the Episcopal Church has for a long time ordained homosexuals on the unrealistic assumption that they would all remain celibate.

In response to these factors, a debate ensued to which the 1979 General Convention responded cautiously: "We believe it is not appropriate for this Church to ordain a practicing homosexual or any other person who is engaged in heterosexual relationships outside of marriage." Thus, the argument against ordination of "practicing" homosexuals was based on the view that marriage alone provided an appropriate context for sexual relations. In the same General Convention, the House of Bishops passed an additional resolution reinforcing the sense of the conveyed above that it was the "mind of this House [of Bishops]" that "pending further inquiry and study by the Church, no Bishop of this Church shall confer Holy Orders in violation of these principles" (*Journal of General Convention*, 1979, B-192). As a practical matter, a large number of bishops and their commissions on ministry responded with a "Don't ask, don't tell" policy.

The status of this resolution, which in its fundamental assertion has not been altered, would become an important issue in the Righter trial. The presenters would make the claim that this represented a doctrinal matter, for which the disciplinary power of the church should be used in the case of a violation. The respondent, Walter Righter, argued that this resolution, about which there had been and continued to be much disagreement, was at most a matter of discipline, the violation of which under the canons of the church could not lead to a heresy trial.

The trial of Walter Righter should be understood against the backdrop already sketched as well as the following circumstances: the liberal-conservative split in American society and culture around social values, a gap that frequently occurs within religious denominations as well as between denominations; the increasing acceptance of the concept of domestic partnership as a generic description of a significant emotional relationship to which partners—homosexual or heterosexual—make a long-term commitment; the essentially decentralized and voluntaristic polity that binds the dioceses of the Episcopal Church on the basis of consensus and not on the basis of doctrinal order; and the ways in which this "decentralism" works around matters of evaluating the qualifications of candidates for ministry. Finally, it should also be noted that the AIDS (acquired immunodeficiency syndrome) crisis of the late 1980s and 1990s has exercised enormous influence on discussions about sexuality. Fears and uncertainty about how the AIDS virus is transmitted have also made it difficult for candid exchanges of views to occur in a church that has a significant gay constituency. While concerns about AIDS were not formally treated in the presentment, they do comprise a significant part of the background for this discussion.

In the "Brief in Support of Presentment" against Walter Righter, four questions are put forward as underlying the charge of heresy:

> What is Doctrine?
> What specifically is the Doctrine of this Church concerning the ordination of homosexuals?
> What constitutes teaching Doctrine contrary to that of the Church?
> What constitutes an act in violation of ordination vows? ("A Memorandum Prepared by the Complaining Bishops," no pagination)

The conclusion to the "Brief" summarizes the response of the presenters to each of the above questions:

[D]octrine is the teaching of the Church as determined by the formularies of the Church, including declarations by the House of Bishops.

The teaching or doctrine of the Episcopal Church in regard to the ordination of homosexuals is that while it is permissible to ordain a person of homosexual orientation, it is not permissible to ordain a practicing homosexual. Further, no Bishop shall knowingly confer holy orders on a practicing homosexual.

Should any bishop preach or otherwise publicly proclaim that it is permissible and right to ordain practicing homosexuals, that teaching or doctrine would be directly contrary to the declared teaching of the Church, and would be a violation of Canon IV.1.1 (2), prohibiting teaching contrary to the doctrine of the Church.

[Finally], should that Bishop actually proceed to ordain a practicing homosexual, knowing the ordinand to be such, that act would be a violation of the Bishop's ordination vow to conform to the doctrine of the Church. ("A Memorandum Prepared by the Complaining Bishops," no pagination)

Only if the court were to accept the definition of doctrine set forth in the presentment would the recourse of discipline under the "heresy" canon have been possible. Those who represented Bishop Righter took on this question directly, asserting that the only "recognized sources" of doctrine in the Episcopal Church are Holy Scripture, the Apostles' Creed, the Nicene Creed, and the Book of Common Prayer. Since none of these "authorized formularies of the Church" addressed the specific issue of ordination of noncelibate homosexuals, they concluded that "[t]here is no DOCTRINE of the Episcopal Church on the issue of whether it is permissible or impermissible to ordain non-celibate homosexual persons" ("A Memorandum of the Decision of Trial Court," no pagination).

In its decision rendered in May 1996, the court, which consisted of eight bishops, one of the original number having been asked to step aside because he had also allowed a noncelibate homosexual to be ordained, essentially agreed with Righter's position. In so ruling, the court made it clear that it could not include what many had regarded as normative teaching about human sexuality among the core matters of faith and practice. Taking a more limited view, a kind of strict constructionism more frequently associated with conservative jurisprudence, the court made it clear that without a formal action by the General Convention of the church, there were no grounds for disciplining a bishop or any other person for violating their ecclesiastical responsibilities if they acted contrary to the resolutions of either the House of Bishops or the General Convention, a bicameral body consisting of the House of Clerical and Lay Deputies, and the House of Bishops.

The judgment of the court rested fundamentally on the view accepted by the majority of the bishops of the court that a fundamental distinction must under canon law be drawn between the doctrine of the church and the theology of the church. The bishops argued for a somewhat more inclusive view of core doctrine than Bishop Righter had proposed in response to the presentment. But they did not accept that the resolutions of the House of Bishops or of General Convention should under present arrangements count as doctrine, even as they expanded its content to include other propositions included in the early preaching and teaching of the Christian community.

The court did not endorse the ordination of practicing homosexuals, so that the reception and interpretation of this decision in some quarters as a "victory" for that position is technically without justification; there is a difference between saying that an action is licit and saying, as the court did, that there are no grounds for discipline. In essence, the court's ruling was constrained by the minimalist tendencies of canon law in the Episcopal Church. The question at best remains unsettled. Until the mind of the church can be clarified further, individual bishops and dioceses will exercise the discretion preserved for them through long-established practice.

For the Episcopal Church, this incident has called attention to the extent to which consensus binds its members together as voluntary community regulated by their willingness to accept its discipline even when it cannot be enforced. Put differently, this denomination is in the midst of a struggle concerning its identity and mission as the twentieth century draws to a close. The markers of community that differentiate this group from other kinds of human associations are boundaries that lack the objective power that the language and the patterns of traditional religious discourse have imputed to religious categories. While avoiding divisions about scripture and creeds, the Episcopal Church has tended to take other "markers" of community for granted, not markers that are easily objectified but markers nonetheless embedded in a consensus about common prayer, ministry, the essential reasonableness and accessibility of its theology, and its capacity to change and evolve as new truths are grasped and incorporated in human experience.

Issues of heresy tend to arise in human communities during times of uncertainty about community boundaries. The Righter case illustrates how divisive issues of change can be in the absence of a consolidating consensus about theology and sexuality. The Episcopal Church has been characterized by comprehension of different points of view and by a tolerance for diversity. Its boundaries have perforce been more evident in the language and the patterns of its religious practice. The decision of the bishop and the Diocese of Newark that a gay man living in a committed domestic partnership with another gay man was fully qualified to be ordained to the ministry of the Episcopal Church was a decision that extended the boundaries of theology and practice beyond what many in the church regarded as acceptable. For Bishop Righter and others, it was a considered judgment based on the duty to discern and empower the gifts of ministry for the good of the church and the glory of God. That decision and the church's struggle in its wake each in different ways represents the relationship between innovation and tradition in human communities. At such junctures the possibility of heresy will often lurk, because there will not be a consensus about the meanings, or the appropriateness, of change.

SELECTED BIBLIOGRAPHY

Avis, Paul. *Anglicanism and the Christian Church*. Minneapolis: Fortress Press, 1989.

Holmes, David L. *A Brief History of the Episcopal Church*. Valley Forge: Trinity Press International, 1993.

Journals of General Convention of the Protestant Episcopal Church. 1979, 1991.

"A Memorandum of the Decision of Trial Court," no pagination.

"A Memorandum Prepared by the Complaining Bishops," no pagination.

Pritchard, Robert. *A History of the Episcopal Church*. Harrisburg: Morehouse, 1991.

Stringfellow, William, and Anthony Towne. *The Bishop Pike Affair: Scandals of Conscience and Heresy, Relevance and Solemnity in the Contemporary Church*. New York: Harper and Row, 1967.

Sykes, Stephen W., ed. *Authority in the Anglican Communion*. Toronto: Anglican Book Centre, 1987.

Wuthnow, Robert. *The Restructuring of American Religion*. Princeton: Princeton University Press, 1988.

Eugene Y. Lowe, Jr.

Philip Schaff
(1819–1893)

One of the greatest church historians in the United States in the nineteenth century nearly had his career cut short by heresy trials. Philip Schaff's academic life in the United States actually opened and closed with heresy trials, the last not his own but that of a close colleague. Like bookends, these trials were at each end of a productive career that contributed so much to the achievement of academic freedom in the religious quest for truth. If the outcome of Schaff's trials of 1845–1846 had been different, his career in the United States might have been nipped in the bud, and by his own admission, Schaff would have returned to Europe.

Born in obscurity, poverty, and illegitimacy, Schaff's early years were spent in an orphanage in Chur, Switzerland. Without the benefit of immediate family during those formative years, he was forever reaching out for the family he never had. Throughout his life, there were numerous surrogate fathers and mothers, brothers and sisters. Perhaps this was the driving force behind his sociability and gemütlichkeit, for Philip Schaff never met a stranger.

Mountain stamina, dogged determination, and the financial support of Chur and a loan got him through the boy's academy in pietistic Württemberg and then the Gymnasium in nearby Stuttgart. From there this brilliant student made his way on to a multiple university experience in Tübingen, Halle, and Berlin. The list of scholars under whom he studied is a veritable theological Who's Who of the century, including the famous F. C. Baur and August Neander. Schaff was especially drawn to the historical methodology of Neander and to Baur's idea of historical development. In Berlin, he also began to nurture that explosive concept of "evangelical catholicism" around which so much of his later life and career would nucleate.

Schaff's eclectic style of blending the ideas of many scholars was already under way.

Within a short time of his completion of his university work, the wheel of destiny turned ever so slightly for this young scholar, and his line of movement was to the far West. He accepted an invitation to come to the United States to teach in the small, struggling seminary of the German Reformed Church in Mercersburg, Pennsylvania, and, in his own words, "never regretted it." This son of Romanticism and pietism, this product of the academically free German educational system, was off by way of six weeks of language orientation in England to a very restless "forties" in the United States.

Part of that restlessness would be Schaff's own heresy trials in 1845 and 1846. Many years later in New York City, his career would be ending on a similar note as he became a witness for the defense in the famous Charles Augustus Briggs* trials of 1891–1893. The contextuality of heresy in religious circles in the nineteenth century—and the twentieth as well, for that matter—is illustrated by Sidney Mead in his preface to that jewel of a book *The Lively Experiment*, where he said: "Their [the German] tendency to believe the worst about America was probably confirmed when Schaff was tried for heresy for expressing ideas in his Mercersburg Inaugural that had become a part of conventional learning among the German scholars."

Schaff began lecturing before candidates for the ministry in the fall of 1844. Only 25, he delivered the traditional inaugural address for a new professor on 25 October 1844 before the Eastern Synod of the German Reformed Church. Only one week earlier the Synod had listened to the conservative pastor from Philadelphia, Joseph F. Berg, as he condemned "innovators" and "new-measure men" who had forsaken what he called denominational landmarks that included the idea that the fathers of the Reformed faith were Waldensians and other persecuted groups of the Middle Ages. Only one week after his own address, Berg, ironically the man who signed Schaff's invitation to come to Mercersburg, was himself to hear one of these "new-measure" men—namely, Philip Schaff.

For his address, Schaff took the topic of "The Principle of Protestantism" and crammed into it virtually everything of importance he had been taught in Germany. He had no idea whatsoever that he was offending anybody with his ideas, but offend he did. He launched his career in acrimony by setting forth his commitment to the idea of organic development in the history of the church and by describing what he considered to be authentic Protestant, evangelically Catholic, ecclesiasticism. His theory of organic development with its attendant appreciation of medieval Catholicism simply would not be tolerated by the conservative Berg element in the German Reformed Church. To speak of the Reformation as developing quite naturally out of the medieval Catholic period and as a normal growth of the church was utter nonsense and heresy to those who held to the Waldensian view of the church. To them Schaff was merely playing into the hands of the papists and Puseyites and thus leading the Reformed Church astray.

As shadows lengthened and heads nodded, Schaff concluded his long address with a vision that would inform his entire career:

> May the Nineteenth Century, by a magnificent union consummate the ever memorable Reformation of the sixteenth. May the New World, enwombing the life spirit of almost every nation of the Old, prove the birth soil of this new era for the Church! As the distractions of Protestantism have been most painfully experienced here, so here also may the glorious work of bringing all the scattered members of Christ's body into true Catholic union be carried forward with the greatest zeal and soonest crowned with the great festival reconciliation, transmitting its blessings, in grateful love, to the world we honor and love as our general fatherland. (*The Principle of Protestantism*, 176)

The conservative, if not fundamentalist-before-its-time, element in the German Reformed Church with its mood of anti-Catholicism, antihistoricism, and "trial-of-blood" mentality would oppose the whole spirit of the address as well as its content and the much-expanded published version of the same title. Another irony is to be observed in the charges made against the inaugural as being Romanistic and Tractarian, for Schaff's theory of development legislates against both these positions and moves on to a higher development of the church. Schaff was already breaking ecumenical ground, and Berg and friends were obviously antiecumenical.

Joseph F. Berg led the charge for the heresy hunters as they attempted to discredit not only Schaff but also his sole colleague on the faculty, John W. Nevin. Sarcasm, bitterness, and diatribe marked the rhetoric of the conservatives. Probably the most colorful illustration of these invectives is given in a letter from Baltimore to *The Weekly Messenger*, news outlet of the German Reformed Church:

> Well, really Doctor, you have done remarkably well, considering your brief sojourn at Jericho, and the distance you have lived from "Oxford and Rome." You seem to have made rapid advances indeed, considering the time you have been journeying towards the celestial cities, and the difficulties you had to encounter on your way! And may we not hope that you will at length safely arrive at the seven hilled city, having passed a night at Oxford on your route, and then and there have the unspeakable joy of throwing yourself into the loving arms of Holy Mother!—enjoying to your heart's content her fond and affectionate caresses. She will no doubt be overjoyed to see an erring son restored to her embrace. (*The Weekly Messenger*, 11 (15 October 1845, 2096)

It is difficult to conceive that all these slurs were meant to describe Philip Schaff, pietist evangelical par excellence!

Fiery charge after fiery charge was directed at Schaff and Nevin until Nevin reacted with some sharply worded articles of his own in *The Weekly Messenger*. He described his attackers as "loveless, intolerant, harsh—a new incarnation in fact of the papacy itself." He referred to their "bastard zeal" and their "loud ecclesiastical libel." It is no wonder that in later years Nevin bore the brunt of the attack, for he answered his opponents in kind. Schaff's irenicism and mediational interests did not allow him to give public vitriolic answer to criticisms. Even in his private diaries, he found it hard to be judgmental on persons and positions.

Berg put the pressure on the Philadelphia Classis to give attention to the Mercersburg matter at its September 1845 meeting. A committee chaired by Berg examined Schaff's *The Principle of Protestantism*. The outcome of their examination was a foregone conclusion. Long resolutions drawn up by the committee were adopted by the Classis. In brief, the final resolution stated that all the central doctrines of the German Reformed Church were denied by Schaff's book and resolved that "the attention of Synod be called to the work in question." The technical intent of the resolutions was to put a book on trial, but the result was far more personal than dealing with an inanimate object.

If read in its entirety, *The Principle* was not out of keeping with the central doctrines of the church as described in the resolutions themselves. These heresy hunters were attempting to discredit a man and his ideas by means of false generalities and alleged defense of the faith ostensibly attacked by a heretic. In relation to the doctrines as defined, Schaff was no heretic, nor was his book heretical. Unfortunately, though, now the burden of proof was placed upon him and his friends. One lone voice in the Classis expressed disagreement with the attack on Schaff. One more resolution was adopted by the Classis illustrating its anti-Catholic mood and its major reason for attacking Schaff. It read as follows:

> Resolved, That in accordance with the general sentiment of the protestant Church we regard the *Papal System* as the great Apostasy under the Christian dispensation . . . and as such, is destined to utter and fearful destruction. ("Minutes of the Classis of Philadelphia, 1836–1868," no pagination)

This was a final blow by the Berg faction at Schaff's view of historical development.

The Synod met in York in mid-October and received the resolutions of complaint from the Philadelphia Classis. Actually, the Synod bypassed a constitutional technicality in even considering the charges made by the Classis since such complaints were supposed to come before the Board of

Visitors of the Seminary prior to the Synod's receipt of them. At the request of Nevin and Schaff, however, the case was opened before the entire Synod.

The Synod appointed a special committee consisting of one person from each Classis for the purpose of considering the charges against Schaff and his book. Upon completing its work, the committee brought back a number of resolutions that it urged the Synod of York to adopt. These resolutions exonerated Schaff, and a key sentence noted that "the Book [*Principle*] if fairly understood is well calculated to promote the true interests of religion, and entitles its author to the respect and affectionate regard of the protestant community" (*Acts and Proceedings of the Synod of York*, 1845, 80). The professors at the Seminary were then complimented, and Berg's faction was criticized for their failure to follow the proper procedures in this matter.

Minutes of the Synod spoke of "acrimonious discussion" that followed over a period of several days. Unfortunately, no records were kept, so one can only imagine the course the speeches on both sides took. If a court reporter had been present, the most interesting days of the trial would have been preserved for posterity. Only intelligent guesses can fill this gap in the record. There was much discussion and numerous speeches. We do know that Joseph Berg spoke for two hours in opposition to the report and that Nevin spoke for two hours in defense of the report. Philip Schaff defended himself and his ideas for four and one half hours. When the vote was finally taken, a large majority placed its stamp of approval on the entire report of the committee that, among other things, had criticized the action of the Philadelphia Classis as "characterized by an entire absence of consideration and forethought" (*Acts and Proceedings of the Synod of York*, 1845, 80).

Schaff and his book had been officially exonerated by this "church court." The opposition was far from being silenced, however, and in later years Schaff was completely correct in referring to his "second trial" for heresy. Heresy hunters never die; they just change their strategy. Since *The Principle* had been judged to be orthodox by the Synod, Berg and his friends simply sought out other writings by Schaff that might serve their purpose. They found them quickly.

When the Philadelphia Classis met in the fall of the following year, 1846, it angrily denounced the Synod's censure of their Classis and complimented Berg for his "firmness under the trying circumstances." New resolutions opposed Schaff's *The Principle* again as well as his most recent publication, *What Is Church History?* This is probably the only time in American religious history that a strictly historiographical volume has been attacked for heresy. This was the limit for a publish *and* perish syndrome. The Classis condemned anew the idea that the Roman Catholic Church be regarded as being in the mainstream of Christian history. The Classis' last resolution zeroed in on its new attack on Schaff. It read: "Resolved, That

Synod be requested to inquire into Dr. Schaff's views concerning the intermediate state; to ascertain whether he believes that death terminates the probation of all men, and closes to them the gospel offer of pardon" (*Minutes of the Classis of Philadelphia, 1836–1868*, no pagination). Heresy hunters had now landed on a highly speculative point in eschatology, and this time it appeared that a man would stand trial for heresy instead of a book.

The Berg group had done its homework. It had found passages it considered to be heretical on "the middle state" in a German work Schaff had published in Germany before ever even considering an invitation to the Mercersburg Seminary. The work was entitled *Die Sünde wider den Heiligen Geist* (The sin against the Holy Spirit)—a book about which Schaff had informed the committee that recruited him to come to Mercersburg and also requested that it never be published in the United States.

The events leading up to the second trial are even more interesting than the trial itself, especially in their revelation of the moral character or lack thereof of Schaff's opposition. It must also be noted that a proposed merger of the Dutch Reformed Church, a more conservative communion, and the German Reformed Church gave certain institutional vested interests additional reasons to investigate the Mercersburg professor. Berg had conservative friends in both denominations who were willing to try to give him more maneuvering room. Those opposed to the merger would welcome more ill feeling between the denominations.

In July 1846, *The Christian Intelligencer*, a Dutch Reformed news agency, published the Reverend J. C. Guldin's translation of selected extracts from Schaff's *Die Sünde*. The translation closed with Schaff's conclusion that for all persons "there is a middle state, which begins with death and continues to the final judgement."

Schaff in this work had speculated about a topic that was very popular in nineteenth-century theological circles: What happens to persons between their death and the final judgment in that out-of-time period (the "middle state"), especially those persons born at the wrong time and place who have no historical Jesus knowledge? Does "general revelation" "save" a person? Do these persons have a chance for salvation through some middle state opportunity? Schaff thought so. He was too gentle to consign millions of Chinese to hell just because they lived in China. Yet his middle state was not in any sense a Catholic "purgatory." He was simply giving these people who had never heard of Jesus the Christ an opportunity to respond in faith to the Christ event. His high Christology required this experience, and so his idea of a middle state provided this opportunity. Salvation, to Schaff, whether in this present life or in the middle state, depended on a positive faith response to the Christ event once it was presented. In the midst of his eschatological speculation, he retained a very high Christology. And after all, in the nineteenth century (as in the twentieth) it was quite normal for theological scholars to speculate on questions of ultimate destiny, general revelation, and God's mercy. To Berg and friends, however, the case was closed and there was little room for speculation or mercy—especially if all this involved Roman Catholics in any favorable way.

The next issue of *The Christian Intelligencer* carried an article thanking the translator for exposing the heresy of the professor and making negative remarks about any merger of the two denominations. The same paper was fair enough to print Schaff's answer to all this the very next week. Schaff pointed out that the translator's selections and motives were in error. He also observed that the translator had known of Schaff's request that the work never be reproduced in the United States and that it was rather unfair to use a work to discredit him that had been written in younger years and in a very different context. As cutting as the gentle Schaff could be, he urged that a more competent translator be used the next time. He closed with a mature commitment to his own responsibility in the matter:

> Whether, after all, my views of the Middle state, as held with more mature judgement at the present time, (and as I may yet lay them before the world, if God sees fit, in a new edition of the Essay in question,) would be found to accord with the theology of your correspondent, I, of course, am not able fully to say. My apprehension is, that they would not. But all this is of no particular account. I stand responsible for them, as already said, to my own Church; and this responsibility I am perfectly willing to meet at any moment. (*The Christian Intelligencer*, XVII, 23 July 1846, 6)

The Weekly Messenger also carried a copy of Schaff's letter to the Dutch Reformed paper.

Due to the resolutions of the Philadelphia Classis, the new charge was bound to be dealt with by the Synod of 1846 in Carlisle, Pennsylvania. The charges brought against his work in historiography were not even considered, and the question of his views on the middle state proceeded through proper channels. Schaff was interviewed privately on this subject by the Board of Visitors of the Seminary, and this report was then submitted to the Synod. In the interview, Schaff gave an honest and strongly Christological answer that affirmed general revelation as well as God's mercy. His views did not win the unqualified endorsement of the Board of Visitors, but it did report to the Synod that there was nothing in these views of such gravity that any special action should be taken by the Synod. The Board added in its report the comforting or political sentence that "the view has not been taught nor is it contemplated ever to be taught in the Theological Seminary" (*Acts and Proceedings of the Synod of Carlisle, 1846*, 42). The Synod adopted the Board's report but was reported to be in a "very nervous condition." An additional resolution by the Synod regarding Schaff's current view of the middle state carefully noted that "we nevertheless cannot endorse the reported modification of the view in question."

The Synod certainly expressed its nervousness by the added resolution, but it refused to fire or even censure one of its professors simply because his view on a single doctrine did not correspond exactly with that of the majority. Although not refusing to express disagreement with Schaff, it did refuse to express its belief in its own infallibility, a claim that would have stifled Schaff or any other theological professor who might teach in their Seminary. Thus, early in the history of the Seminary a precedent was set preserving the full freedom of the teacher to search for truth and then to express it in teaching and writing as one believes one has found it at that point in one's religious and academic pilgrimage.

Even though the Board stated that Schaff's views on the middle state were not being taught at the Seminary (a good public relations move), there is definite proof that Schaff in his classroom lectures was speculating about an intermediate state as late as the 1859–1860 academic year. The class notes of one of his students that term read as follows: "There here arises a serious question. May there not be an intermediate state for those who have never had the advantage of becoming Christian?" The notes continue with a detailed discussion of the question. By then Schaff was enjoying academic and religious freedom as a seasoned professor. After 1847, heresy trials in the German Reformed Church are events of the past.

Formally, Schaff's case was closed. Informally, the complaints continued for a season. At the very next year's Synod, Berg and his friends were still complaining that the professor's teaching and writing did not meet biblical standards, to say nothing of the creedal standards of the denomination. The Board of Visitors refused to hear them formally. Schaff's opponents had been effectively silenced in the Synod, but they would continue to make theological noise outside these formal meetings.

Berg found little sympathy for his continued attacks. With such diminishing support, he switched denominations, moving to the more conservative Dutch Reformed Church in 1852 and becoming a professor at Rutgers College.

On the count of "Romanizing," however, Schaff continued to be attacked, especially by certain persons in the Dutch Reformed Church. When Schaff's majestic *History of the Apostolic Church* appeared in 1854, a scathing review of it by a Rutgers professor, J. W. Proudfit, appeared in the *New Brunswick Review*. Proudfit closed his review with a sarcastic suggestion that if Schaff's book were used by seminaries as a text, some Jesuits should be employed to teach it! The most caustic attack on Schaff, however, came from J. J. Janeway in his *Antidote to the Poison of Popery in the Publication of Professor Schaff.*

Schaff was battle tried at Mercersburg, but after 1852, he enjoyed comparative theological peace as he busied himself with his lectures and writing as well as with the liturgical movement within the German Reformed Church. Synodical action at Carlisle was significant in the story of academic freedom in the German Reformed Church, for there was never another heresy trial within the denomination. The Synod did not refuse to express disagreement with some of Schaff's views, but it did refuse to express any pretension to its own infallibility by stifling Schaff or any other professor who might teach at Mercersburg. Early on in the history of this Seminary, a precedent was set preserving the full freedom of the teacher to search for truth and then to express it in teaching and writing. Schaff, Nevin, and others were left free in their academic and religious quest.

By 1863 Schaff was gone from Mercersburg, traveling and studying in Europe as well as getting settled in New York City. By 1870 he was teaching there in Union Theological Seminary and making a name for himself in national and international scholarly circles. If the heresy hunters of 1845–1846 had been successful, the American religious community would have lost to Germany its most formidable prophet of the ecumenical movement and the founder of the American Society of Church History (1888).

The bookend at the close of Schaff's career was another heresy trial, that of his colleague at Union, Charles Augustus Briggs. Through the Briggs trials of 1891–1893, Schaff stood firm as a supporter in presence and in print. Against conservative Presbyterianism, Schaff labeled the charges against Briggs as "one of the curiosities of American theological literature." Ironically, he saw one of the charges against Briggs coming full circle from 1846 as he defended Briggs and anyone else who speculated about the middle state. Schaff urged that theological scholarship not be stifled as he said: "Christian scholars who combine faith with learning and critical ability are rare and now more needed than ever, to disentangle the scriptures from traditional embarrassments, such as the theory of a literal inspiration or dictation" ("Other Heresy Trials and the Briggs Case," *The Forum* 12 (January 1892), 633). The true but now old pietist still knew that faith afraid to think is simply unbelief cloaked as piety. He wrote to one of his friends: "There is such a thing as Presbyterian popery, as well as Prelatical and Roman popery, and the first is the most inconsistent and unreasonable of the three. There must be elbow room for development and liberty of investigation, or we may as well shut up our seminaries (Cited in Shriver, *Philip Schaff*, 93).

One of the mottoes of Schaff's life was that oft-quoted ecumenical maxim: "In essentials, unity; in nonessentials, liberty; in all things, charity." There had been little unity and charity in the bookend experiences of his life—the heresy trials—but the end result was a great deal of liberty. The freedom of Christian scholars everywhere was thus championed in these heretical bookends of a great career. In this important way the legacy of Philip Schaff lives on in our present academic and religious pilgrimage.

BIBLIOGRAPHY

Acts and Proceedings of the Synod of York, 1845.

Acts and Proceedings of the Synod of Carlisle, 1846.

Bowden, Henry W. *Church History in the Age of Science*. Chapel Hill: University of North Carolina Press, 1971.

———, ed. *A Century of Church History*. Carbondale: Southern Illinois University Press, 1988.

Graham, Stephen R. *Cosmos in the Chaos*. Grand Rapids: William B. Eerdmans, 1995.

Mead, Sidney E. *The Lively Experiment*. New York: Harper and Row, 1963.

"Minutes of the Classis of Philadelphia, 1836–1868," handwritten, no pagination.

Nichols, James H. *Romanticism in American Theology*. Chicago: University of Chicago Press, 1961.

Penzel, Klaus. *Philip Schaff*. Macon, GA: Mercer University Press, 1991.

Schaff, Philip. *America*. New York: Scribner's, 1855.

———. *Germany*. New York: Sheldon, Blakeman and Co., 1857.

———. *History of the Apostolic Church*. New York: Scribner's, 1854.

———. *History of the Christian Church*. 8 vols. Grand Rapids: William B. Eerdmans, 1950.

———. "Other Heresy Trials and the Briggs Case." *The Forum* 12 (January 1892), 633.

———. *The Principle of Protestantism*. Chambersburg: Publication Office of the German Reformed Church, 1845.

———. *The Reunion of Christendom*. New York: Evangelical Alliance Office, 1893.

———. *What is Church History?* Philadelphia: J.B. Lippincott, 1846.

Shriver, George H. *Philip Schaff*. Macon, GA: Mercer University Press, 1987.

———, ed. *American Religious Heretics*. Nashville: Abingdon Press, 1966.

George H. Shriver

Paul D. Simmons
(1936–   )

Paul D. Simmons served as professor of Christian ethics at the Southern Baptist Seminary from 1970 through 1992. During that time, he had numerous administrative responsibilities including chairmanship of the Graduate Studies Committee and serving as acting dean of the School of Theology in 1983. He received a Ph.D. degree from Southern in 1970 and did postdoctoral studies at Princeton Theological Seminary (1976–1977) and Cambridge University (1983–1984). He is author of three books, several monographs, and over 50 articles in scholarly journals, especially in the area of bioethics. During his entire career at Southern, his excellent scholarly record has never been challenged by either the administration or the Trustees. Rather, he was attacked and finally removed from his teaching post for interpretations in the field of ethics that ran counter to political trends in the Southern Baptist Convention even though they were solidly grounded in thorough research and careful biblical exegesis. The "heresies" of which he was accused centered on interpretations related to ethical issues, not theological beliefs. He was attacked as being out of step with concepts recently styled and minted by Southern Baptist fundamentalists that focused on abortion, elective death, and homosexuality.

Simmons, like dozens of persons before him, signed the Abstract of Principles upon receiving tenure as professor in the Seminary. The Abstract is part of the "fundamental law" of the Seminary as outlined in the founding Charter. Professors are required "to teach in accordance with, and not contrary to" this statement of 20 traditional beliefs among Baptists as understood by the scholars who founded the Seminary in 1858. Departing from or openly challenging these principles is contractually regarded as "grounds for resignation or removal by the Trustees." The statements range from affirmations regarding the authority of Scripture to the final judgment. None deal with ethical matters such as those raised by complex issues in biomedicine.

Not once during his entire career was it demonstrated that Simmons deviated from his contractural obligations including Baptist principles outlined in the Abstract and others outlined in the Faculty-Staff Manual. Rather, Simmons's "crime" in the eyes of the Trustees and the administration was his failure to adjust his teaching of ethics to the radical shift toward inerrantist fundamentalist dogma and politics that gained ascendency in the Southern Baptist Convention in the mid-1980s. A newly minted policy agenda was insinuated, thereby establishing an unwritten agenda of expectations regarding beliefs and teachings. Those were more or less related to resolutions on social issues passed by the Convention in annual sessions. That agenda included a rigid stance against abortion for any reason other than to save the life of the mother, and an unrelenting attack on the Supreme Court's 1973 *Roe v. Wade* decision. Southern Baptist resolutions supported a Human Life Amendment to the U.S. Constitution that Simmons found entirely unsupportable on scriptural grounds and inconsistent with First Amendment protections.

Simmons, throughout his career at Southern, insisted on academic and individual integrity, believing that the Seminary's commitment to academic freedom for scholarly pursuits, within its contractual framework, was solid. But a new order was emerging for the school as the Convention structure became dominated by fundamentalists who were committed to a right-wing social agenda, an agenda that became a hallmark of the Reagan-Bush years.

In 1986, a visit to the Louisville campus by a subcommittee of the cynically labeled "Peace Committee" of the Convention signaled the descent of an iron curtain that would contradict and undermine hundreds of years of Baptist commitment to religious liberty and scriptural authority. What amounted to a rigid creed was to be imposed upon the teachers at the "mother" Seminary. Faced by a tide of right-wing extremism, the Seminary administration and Trustees were to face the implications of the genuine freedom of the Christian believer and fail in their stewardship. Trustee micromanagement was imposed on a docile administration that ultimately abandoned protection of its faculty.

Simmons was not the first to be attacked and removed from the Seminary. In 1879, Old Testament professor Crawford Howell Toy* was forced to resign; in 1901, President William Heth Whitsitt* was forced to take refuge at the University of Richmond; and in 1958, 13 established scholars (The Louisville Thirteen*) were fired by Trustees who supported the president's high-handed abuse of proper governance. Censured by the American Association of Theological Schools after the 1958 outrage, the Seminary had made a remarkable recovery. By 1970, Southern had begun to recover and was on the way to restoring its place as one of the outstanding seminaries in the United States.

The strangling effects of fundamentalism emerged in the Convention with the election of Adrian Rogers as president in 1980. A fanatic cadre of Southern Baptist politicians set out to control the denomination through its institutions. They succeeded within 10 years. The first Southern Seminary casualty was Professor Dale Moody,* a veteran of 40 years teaching at the school. President Roy L. Honeycutt, shortly after assuming the office, removed Moody from the faculty in 1983. Moody had become the target of attacks by David Miller, director of Missions in Arkansas, who, as a Trustee, would later play a central role in vilifying Paul Simmons.

By 1986 the fundamentalists were beginning to impose a theological straitjacket on all Convention agencies. They began to purge all thinking as intolerable. By 1990 fundamentalists dominated the Southern Board of Trustees. By 1992 they held a two-thirds majority, able to pass any restrictive measure they chose. Thus began an unrelenting attack on scholarship, theological reason, and Christian ethics, orchestrated to eliminate any taint of openness in thought and teaching. They succeeded in laying down a blanket of fear, indoctrination, and intimidation that engulfed the faculty to a degree so pernicious that by 1996 they had removed education from the Seminary's agenda altogether. Championing an unrelentingly rigid Calvinism and an authoritarian style, President Albert Mohler, who took office in 1993, insists that faculty members embrace the concepts of biblical inerrancy and infallibility, reject women as ministers, endorse the fundamentalist takeover of the Convention, and acquiesce in the extremist social agenda of the Christian Coalition. Mohler enforces conformity by a "gag" rule on all critical comments about the Convention and Trustee actions. He has instituted a policy that permits him to demote faculty a full rank without hearings or showing of cause.

Paul Simmons had become a target of fundamentalists by 1986. A gentle man and a dedicated Christian scholar, he never flinched in his commitment to an open search for truth. For that commitment he was set upon by a new breed of angry, self-righteous heresy hunters. In the struggle that ensued, his insistance upon the freedom of the believer to interpret the Bible in light of conscience witnessed to the best in the Baptist heritage.

Following the capture by a fundamentalist faction of the Southern Baptist Convention political machinery in the early 1980s, there was an effort to mollify the opposition. There were no concessions but a great deal of posturing by the new leadership. Part of the strategy was to create a "Peace Committee" to test the theological loyalty of persons in leadership positions in Southern Baptist institutions, including Seminary professors. With no credentials other than arrogance, the Committee, headed by Charles Fuller, undertook an "investigation" of Southern Baptist Seminary in 1986. A subcommittee chaired by Adrian Rogers scrutinized the writings and teachings of over a dozen faculty members. Simmons was on the list. Using the Abstract of Principles as a guide, Rogers and his colleagues found no substance to the charges against Simmons. He was, they thought, in accord with the Abstract. With the Peace Committee report in hand, the Seminary Trustees determined in that same year to accept the Committee report and not to revisit the charges.

But the radicals on the Board were increasing in number, and among them there was a continued attack upon certain targeted professors, regardless of previous Board action. An unrelenting attack was launched on Professors Simmons, Glenn Hinson, and Molly Marshall.* Hinson ultimately resigned to accept a position at the newly established Baptist Theological Seminary in Richmond, Virginia. The controversy and acrimonious attacks on him had serious adverse effects on his health. Marshall was attacked for supposedly teaching univeralism, though the real issue was the fact of a woman teaching theology. She managed to survive until August of 1993, when Mohler forced her termination.

As the official description of the spring Board meeting of 1987 makes clear, the Trustees were sharply divided on the future course of action in light of attacks on the Seminary faculty. While they overwhelmingly endorsed the 1986 statement approved by the six Seminary presidents and the Peace Committee, the Trustees also focused on perceived problems surrounding both Simmons and Glenn Hinson. In a 25 to 22 vote the Trustees rejected a motion disapproving of recent remarks by Hinson. This was the last time the Board demonstrated restraint. The wave of new, safe Trustees was becoming tidal in dimensions. At the same meeting the Trustees discussed the abortion issue and the call by some on the Board for the firing of Simmons. The Academic Personnel Committee took under advisement demands by several Trustees that Simmons be fired for statements made in a recent article in the *Indiana Baptist*, a state paper. The Committee recommended to the Board that while they were "not in unanimous accord with Dr. Simmons' position on abortion as reflected in the article (Missouri *Word and Way*, January 15, 1987), we do unanimously concur with President Honeycutt that there are no grounds for dismissal of Dr. Simmons." The full Board voted to add a sentence to the report that the Board "expressed its concern with Dr. Simmons' position and requests the President to encourage him to moderate his public involvement in this issue."

Simmons refused to accommodate his beliefs to the newly imposed dogmatism of politicized fundamentalists. He was given the option of (1) embracing the Convention's view regarding abortion (and other ethical issues); (2) remaining silent and refusing to criticize or teach contrary to the resolutions (of the Board); or (3) resigning. Simmons refused them all, choosing the historic Baptist commitment to the freedom of the believer-scholar to interpret the Bible in light of conscience.

Simmons did meet with Honeycutt and in a good-faith effort canceled a meeting on abortion rights in St. Louis and agreed to "moderate his public involvement." Even so, with Honeycutt's knowledge, Simmons determined that he should keep an engagement to speak in Washington at a meeting of Americans for Religious Liberty in May 1987. In no way was Simmons defying the Trustees when he made that appearance. Nevertheless, the speech ignited new attacks focused anew on Simmons's defense of what he regarded as "the genius of *Roe v. Wade*" that allowed all religious groups to teach as they believed about abortion but not to impose sectarian beliefs in law.

A determined core of Trustees attacked Simmons for his "insubordination," his biblical exegesis, and a booklet he wrote that was printed and distributed by the Religious Coalition for Abortion Rights. Dean G. Willis Bennett wrote to Honeycutt on 4 June 1987, stating, "In light of my conversation with Professor Simmons, I have every reason to believe that he will seek to be cooperative and responsible in his further performance as a professor. I shall continue to monitor these matters as necessary and will welcome receiving any communication you have regarding criticisms of him." Simmons recounts that "no one was more fully supportive of me either as a competent and responsible scholar or as a defender of abortion rights than was Dean (later Provost) Bennett."

This was a remarkable exchange. There is no evidence that the administrators had any quarrel with Simmons's scholarship or responsible performance of faculty and classroom duties. Neither faculty nor administrators argued against Simmons's long-held position on abortion. Appearances and political pressure became the issues. "You can believe it, but you can't say it" seemed to be their advice. Simmons's credentials as a highly respected scholar in Christian ethics were never in question. Nevertheless, the administration began a not-very-subtle pressure on him to be silent in class and off campus. Such restrictions would have meant the end of competent scholarship.

In 1989, Trustee Paul Stam criticized Simmons for a review of a book by Bishop John Shelby Spong, *Living in Sin*, which appeared in the Seminary's own publication, the *Review and Expositor* of winter 1989. Simmons had addressed the issues posed by Spong as a thoughtful scholar. Stam accused Simmons of agreeing with Spong. Trustee Alton Butler wrote to Paul Stam, assuring him that President Honeycutt would handle the matter, saying, "I certainly appreciate your stand for Christian morality and I believe we should always find ourselves on the right side of social issues." Butler gave a nuanced answer, avoiding explicitly siding with Stam. In June, Honeycutt asked Simmons for a "brief statement which I might quote in responding to critics" about the review. As the pressure mounted from dogmatic and determined Trustees in their harrassment of Simmons, he spent countless hours responding to critics.

In November 1989, student Clark Kirkbride wrote a letter accusing Simmons of saying that "Jesus was sexually active" in a course entitled "The Church and Sexuality." Kirkbride charged Simmons with saying that Jesus may have "engaged in homosexual activity." Simmons had made no such statement. Dean Larry McSwain interviewed every other student in the class and found no one who would corroborate Kirkbride's accusations. Simmons's own recording of the lecture showed conclusively that the charge was entirely fabricated. Simmons described in his lecture the different views that had been advanced over time. Simmons made clear his own view that "Jesus was a fully sexual human being who was celibate and single."

Kirkbride had copied his letter to 11 other recipients, 3 of whom were Trustees—Jim Bullock, John Hicks, and John Michaels. Those 3 signed on to Kirkbride's letter and distributed it to all Trustees and 8 other persons. That distribution took place *before* either the administration or Simmons knew of the accusation. Asked why that was done, Michaels, who paid for the distribution, said only that he "wanted trustees to be fully informed."

Responding to the letter, and based upon reports by Simmons and the dean, President Honeycutt wrote on 4 December 1989, "I am convinced Mr. Kirkbride's charges are inaccurate; indeed, they are contrived." He added that "there was no evidence to substantiate the student's charges" and characterized the letter as "libelous."

In January 1990 the Louisville *Courier Journal* ran the story under the heading "Probe Clears Baptist Professor of Student's Charges of Heresy" (Wolfe). This elicited a quick response from Honeycutt, who wrote to the reporter, "To use the word 'heresy' in any context creates images of theological deviation which is so far from reality at Southern Seminary as to prompt me to call in question your use of the term 'heresy' in your article. . . . Again, at no time did anyone in the student body, faculty, staff or Executive Committee of the trustees associate the Kirkbride issue with heresy." Perhaps not, but Kirkbride's letter contains the following: "I am fully aware that there are many professors at Southern that are very sound theologically and I praise God for them. . . . I believe that heresy rips at the seam of a fundamental heritage that we as Christians have built our faith upon" (Letter to Dr. Alshire).

Of course, the issue was about heresy, and the three Trustees who distributed the letter knew it and were attempting to create a climate in which the term would seem appropriate. Honeycutt had carefully omitted from his list those who saw it as a matter of heresy on the Board of Trustees. No president of a seminary wants to be caught in a heresy hunt. Honeycutt may have been understandably nervous about any appearance of a heresy hunt at the Seminary, but, by any other name, that is precisely what Honeycutt and the Trustees were about.

The stage was now set for the final solution. In 1990 Trustee Jerry Johnson produced a polemic against both Honeycutt and faculty members including Frank Tupper, Glenn Hinson, Marshall, and Simmons. His lengthy diatribe was published in the March–April 1990 *Southern Baptist Advocate* and was circulated even before Johnson took his seat on the Board. He accused Honeycutt of duplicity, saying, "[A]nyone would have to be blind as a mole to believe that Honeycutt believed the Bible." Simmons was attacked as a professor who "precipitated problems" and showed "denominational insensitivity." Johnson's "The Cover-up at Southern Seminary" was filled with falsehoods and half-truths. His main complaint against Simmons was his support for legalized abortion. That much was true, but the article contained, according to Simmons, four untruths and 13 misrepresentations.

Responding to Johnson, Simmons wrote the Board of Trustees:

> At stake in Johnson's attack on me is not my position about abortion. The issue is whether all points of view should be explored and whether each person has a right to engage in the discussion of an issue of importance to us all. . . . To attempt to coerce others into silence because they dissent from our point of view is to betray an intolerance that is unchristian and that denies the Baptist heritage of opposing any type of religious oppression of conscientious convictions. . . . Baptists were the original champions of democratic values because of their commitment to biblical principles such as soul competence and the priesthood of the believer. . . . The abortion debate may well be a test of the sincerity with which we hold the fundamental of our faith. ("Unpublished Response to Board of Trustees," 1990, n.p.)

The spring 1990 meeting of the Board of Trustees was dominated by the Johnson polemic and Simmons's position on abortion. A resolution by Trustee David Miller (who had attacked Dale Moody) against abortion was approved by the Board. It resolved, "That the Board of Trustees . . . respectfully request that all employees of this institution cease and desist from publicly espousing the right of a woman to have an abortion except where the physical life of the mother is in danger." It passed as well a motion expressing "disappointment, disapproval, and deep concern over the harm done this Seminary by the activities of Professor Paul Simmons relating to abortion and we request that the President personally communicate these concerns to Professor Simmons, and that his continued activities in this area may be considered sufficient grounds for dismissal" (Memo of Resolution by Board of Trustees, Spring, 1990).

The Trustees had also received a sabbatic report from Simmons in which he attempted to assuage Trustee anger. His letter indicated that he would do three things to "moderate his involvement in the abortion issue": (1) he would always make it clear that the position he espoused was his own and not that of the Seminary or the Convention; (2) he would avoid portraying those who disagreed with him in any inflammatory way; and (3) he would refuse interviews with the press on the subject of abortion.

On 4 September 1991 David Miller wrote to Honeycutt reminding him of the 1990 actions and claiming that Simmons had violated the Trustee resolutions. He asked for "a formal and official charge against Professor Simmons on the grounds of insubordination, and requested Simmons' dismissal from the employ" of the Seminary. Honeycutt turned to Seminary attorney Joseph Stopher for a legal opinion of Simmons's status in light of Trustee Miller's request. Stopher informed him that there were no grounds for dismissal. He continued by noting that Simmons was not in violation of his contractual obligations in any way. He repeated that opinion the following spring. A third opinion from a different law firm agreed with Stopher.

On 11 May 1992, Honeycutt sent a letter to the Trustee Committee on Academic Personnel concerning the Simmons affair. He recalled his report to that Committee in February 1992 rejecting Miller's call for dismissal because of the legal opinion received, because there were "inadequate grounds for dismissal charges," and because there was "no evidence for dismissal on the grounds of insubordination." The concluding paragraph, however, included Honeycutt's concession to Trustee pressure. He recommended that Trustees "implement a future course of action concerning Professor Simmons which would produce an agreement stabilizing relationships between Professor Simmons and concerned trustees, while avoiding charges of dismissal and the potential damages to the seminary attendant to the settlement of those charges through a formal seminary hearing and the probability of subsequent litigation in the courts." Honeycutt had simply abandoned Simmons and from that point would attempt to have Simmons removed by some mutually agreeable terms.

In July 1992, Honeycutt called Simmons to his office and explained his position that he concurred with the Trustee opinion that it was time for Simmons to go. He said he regretted the decision and hinted at the possibility of buying out Simmons's contract. But he made no explicit offer. Honeycutt appeared to want Simmons to give him a price. He refused to act on the Personnel Committee recommendation that a buyout be through age 65. Simmons responded by saying he simply was not for sale. The issues of academic integrity and stability of professors who had violated no part of their obligation to the Seminary were at stake.

Honeycutt's reluctance to act without specific direction from the full Board was political. He had the authority but may have feared retribution. Trustees Johnson and Miller were violently opposed to any severance pay. Johnson said, "President Boyce walked Crawford Toy to the train; Honeycutt wants to walk Simmons to the bank." Employing the names of Boyce and Toy to justify the destruction of Simmons's long and honored career of 23 years of service to the Seminary is unjustified.

The drama was nearly concluded. In his fall 1992 class on sexuality, Simmons showed a 15-minute videotape dealing with the ethics of rehabilitative therapy for spinal cord–injured persons. Members of the class had been informed for two weeks prior that the video was sexually explicit. Students were told that attendance was not required and that those who attended would be understood to be supportive of its use. Simmons wanted ministers to become part of a team of professionals to work with parishioners to restore hope and vitality—to recognize sexual function as a vital part of God's will for married people.

Four students wrote letters of complaint to the president. Provost McSwain proposed a list of sanctions on Simmons "to protect him from the trustees." That was a ruse. A week later the Trustees met in Atlanta, and nothing was mentioned about the tape. It was not the Trustees now but the administration that intended to exploit a groundless controversy to force Simmons's departure.

Simmons responded to the administrative action by saying that the "use of the video was not prudent given our political context; but academic decisions should not be driven by the negativism of the convention climate. The material was appropriate to the course, and certainly morally supportable by Christian ministers because of its redemptive and therapeutic uses" (Letter to Board of Trustees, Fall, 1992). Even though the video had been shown on the campus by others and it was academically appropriate, Simmons was victimized by it. The president proposed a letter of apology by Simmons, a letter of reprimand, and reassignment of teaching responsibilities. Feeling strongly that those punitive actions would amount to "enormous harm to me as a professional," Simmons asked that any sanctions be delayed until he and Honeycutt could talk. The president assured Simmons that no action would be taken until they had met upon Honeycutt's return from Atlanta. They agreed on a meeting to be held on 4 January 1993.

On Wednesday, 30 December the dean, provost, and president, persisting in their call for sanctions, met and agreed on penalties Simmons had already declared unacceptable, harsh, and vindictive. Simmons felt betrayed by Honeycutt. The provost informed Simmons on 31 December of the sanctions. In response, Simmons, finding no "access to a discussion that might alter the conditions of the Administrative sanctions against me," submitted his resignation through early retirement.

On 6 January 1993, Honeycutt wrote to the faculty that Simmons had "at his initiative . . . announced his early retirement" effective 31 December 1992. That was a lie. The initiative was taken by the school when it imposed sanctions unilaterally. Further, Honeycutt stated that formal grievances had been filed about the video when in fact the administration did not follow Board procedure. Finally, Honeycutt wrote that "before completing the review, however, Professor Simmons announced his retirement." That is patently false. The provost had told Simmons by phone about the sanctions.

Simmons was not intending to quit as a result of the heresy trial that was certainly coming in April 1993. He knew about it, and news of it appeared in an Associated Baptist Press release for 23 December 1992 carrying the headline "Southern Trustees Appear Headed for Heresy Hearings on Simmons" (Warner). It was Honeycutt's violation of proper procedure and failure to keep his promise to Simmons that brought on the retirement. He received no severance pay and a very small settlement.

As Simmons was pondering his options the Fifth Federal Circuit Court in New Orleans handed down an opinion that a church could fire a minister with no grounds required.

Roy Honeycutt went on to retire in 1993 with a generous financial settlement and a new $30,000 job as chancellor. His tenure was marked with a consistent policy of avoidance and containment. In 1983 newly elected President Honeycutt made a goodwill trip to Virginia to reassure Virginia Baptists about the Seminary's future. A conversation on that occasion at the First Baptist Church in Richmond between this writer and Honeycutt confirmed that he had no understanding of the cauldron he was entering at Louisville at a time when militant fundamentalists were already well on the way to total control of the Southern Baptist Convention and Southern Seminary. He spoke some peace-oriented platitudes and assured me that all would be well at our alma mater. Like the skipper of the *Valdez*, he was going to pour oil on the troubled waters. The cleanup has not begun. The disaster is obvious. Too bad Honeycutt failed to read Revelation 3:15–16.

Paul Simmons continues his bright career in Christian ethics from his home in Louisville, Kentucky. He acted in accord with the highest principles when he performed his task as a teacher of Christian ethics in spite of those who would demean and destroy him.

BIBLIOGRAPHY

Hasty, Stan. "Southern Baptist Ethicist Defends Abortion Rights." Baptist Press, release, 2 June 1987.

Johnson, Jerry. "The Cover-up at Southern Seminary." Distributed by the author in typed form, 1990. Also in the *Southern Baptist Advocate*, March–April 1990. See also letter to Paul Simmons from Robert Tenery, editor of the paper, dated 8 May 1990.

Knox, Marv. "Embattled Professor Takes Early Retirement." *Baptists Today*, 21 January 1993.

Letter to Bill Wolfe from President Honeycutt. 26 January 1990.

Letter to Dr. Alshire from Clark Kirkbride. 7 November 1989.

Letter to Jack Brymer, *Florida Baptist Witness*, from President Honeycutt. 16 February 1993.

Letter to Paul B. Stam from Alton Butler. 15 April 1989.

Letter to Paul Simmons from President Honeycutt. 11 May 1992.

Letter to President Honeycutt from David Miller. 4 September 1991.

Letter to Recipients of the Kirkbride letter from President Honeycutt. 4 December 1989.

Letter to "The Seminary Faculty" from President Honeycutt. 6 January 1993.

McCormick, Mark. "Some Students Say Departure of Simmons Chills Seminary." *Courier Journal*, 11 January 1993, 1.

Memo to Dean Bennett from Paul Simmons. "Response to Request from Peace Committee Sub-committee," 11 March 1986.

Memo of Resolution by Board of Trustees, Spring, 1990.

Memo to Paul Simmons from President Honeycutt. Review in *Review and Expositor*, 2 June 1989.

Memo to President Honeycutt from Dean Bennett. "Conference with Professor Simmons," 4 June 1987.

Memo to President Honeycutt from Paul Simmons. "Early Retirement," 7 January 1993.

Paul Simmons's "Letter to Board of Trustees," Fall, 1992.

Paul Simmons's "Unpublished Response to Board of Trustees," 1990, n.p.

Simmons, Paul. "The Grace of God and the Life of the Church: Ephesians." *Review and Expositor* (fall 1979): 495–506.

———. "NO: The Human Life Amendment Denies the Biblical Teaching of Human Personhood." *Word and Way*, 15 January 1987, 7.

———. "A Personal Reflection on Theological Education and the Politically Correct." *Baptists Today*, 18 March 1993, 9.

———. Review of Bishop John Spong's *Living in Sin. Review and Expositor* (winter 1989): 138.

———. "A Theological Response to Fundamentalism on the Abortion Issue." Published by Religious Coalition for Abortion Rights, n.d.

Warner, Greg. "Southern Trustees Appear Headed for Heresy Hearings on Simmons." Associated Baptist Press, 23 December 1992.

Wilkinson, David. "Trustees Approve Response to Glorietta Statement during Annual Session." *Towers of the Southern Baptist Theological Seminary*, 4 May 1987.

Wolfe, Bill. "Probe Clears Baptist Professor of Student's Charges of Heresy." *Courier Journal*, 26 January 1990, A-1.

Robert S. Alley

Henry Preserved Smith
(1847–1927)

Henry Preserved Smith was born on 23 October 1847 in Troy, Ohio. He came from Puritan ancestry, with persons in the ministry being found on both sides of the family. His parents were New England Congregationalists, but upon moving to Ohio, they joined the New School Presbyterians, meaning that they raised their son in what was for their day a moderate form of Presbyterianism. In essence, the New School softened the interpretation of some of the harsher doctrines of the Westminster Confession and the Catechisms, for example, affirming a general rather than limited Atonement and making humanity's ability to do right a product of moral rather than of natural ability. Essentially, Smith imbibed his early Christianity from his home and environment, becoming a communicant member of the Presbyterian Church at 16 years of age.

Smith graduated from Dayton High School in 1864, attended Marietta College for two years, and then went to Amherst, from which he graduated in 1869. At that time he was elected to Phi Beta Kappa. Both Marietta and Amherst had a religious atmosphere in which Smith was comfortable. As a product of that atmosphere, 20 out of Smith's graduating class of 56 went on to study theology.

In 1869 Smith returned to Ohio to study for the ministry at Lane Theological Seminary,* a seminary of the New School Presbyterians located in Cincinnati. However, the Old School Presbyterians, although reunited with their New School counterparts, were still very much in evidence in southern Ohio. Thus, the Seminary sought to demonstrate that it was theologically responsible to its neighboring Presbyterians of the previous Old and New Schools. Perhaps as a product of this, Smith later reflected, his seminary education was principally carried out within the boundaries the church had set for persons desiring to enter the pastorate, and little knowledge outside the dogmatic realm was sought. The study of the Scriptures was carried out with the preunderstanding that they were without error, a position that Smith did not question, and higher criticism of the Bible was not considered. Smith was licensed to preach in 1871 and served two small churches in northern Ohio. He graduated from Lane in 1872 and then, through the beneficence of his father, was able to spend two winter terms studying in Berlin, with trips to Palestine, Italy, and Switzerland between them. From this, he gained a knowledge of German and an insight into conservative German biblical scholarship.

Upon his return to the United States, he was invited to teach church history at Lane Seminary for a year, because an unexpected vacancy had occurred in the faculty. A year later, there was another vacancy. This time Smith was asked to teach Hebrew with the indication that if all went well, he would be invited to continue. He agreed, but with the understanding that if he were successful, he would be given a year's leave to study abroad to improve his skills. Between the two appointments at Lane, he was ordained to the Presbyterian ministry in the summer of 1875.

Smith chose to spend his year abroad at the University of Leipzig because of the orthodox reputation of its scholars, particularly Franz Delitzsch. Even with their conservatism, however, his teachers were beginning to make some concessions to the new criticisms as a result of their historical studies. Upon returning to Lane, Smith sought to teach his students enough Hebrew to pass examinations for ordination and to read the Old Testament commentaries intelligently. To this end, he published a small pamphlet covering the Masoretic text and the versions of the Old Testament, thus introducing his students, on a small scale, to textual criticism. In his teaching of the Old Testament, however, he primarily tried to give the students a sense of the content of the books.

Writing in 1925 and thus in retrospect, Smith recognized that he was developing in his early years at Lane a gradual separation between his understanding of the role of the exegete and that of the dogmatic theologian. For the exegete the meaning of the Bible was to be found through the use of linguistic and historical tools. The function of the exegete was not to confirm the dogma of the church but rather to let the Bible speak for itself. The more he listened to the Old Testament, the clearer it became to Smith that the copyists of the texts were far from infallible. Thus, the received text could not be said to be inerrant. With the growing knowledge of the biblical world derived from archeology and other historical disciplines, it gradually became clear to Smith that even the "original autographs" of the biblical literature could not be held to be inerrant on issues of historical or scientific fact. The dates when the documents were written had to be considered, and this consideration led directly to the tools of higher criticism with their questions about the inerrancy of the text. Smith never doubted, however, that both the original and received texts were inerrant on issues of faith and practice.

Smith's reading of Julius Wellhausen's *Geschichte Israels*, Volume 1, was the pivotal experience that solidified his thinking on the need for a historical examination of the biblical texts. While he was not prepared to accept all of Wellhausen's ideas, he did feel that he was bound to make some concessions to the historical methodologies. Those concessions were: "1. Differences of style imply difference of author. 2. The historical circumstances in which an author wrote are apt to be reflected with more or less definiteness in his work. 3. The ethical and religious conceptions of his time will also influence his work" (Smith, *The Heretic's Defense*, 67). Thus, the historical methods of inquiry were essential to the study of the Bible.

Many Presbyterians in the last half of the nineteenth century held a doctrine of the absolute inerrancy of scripture as it came from the pens of the original authors. Charles Hodge and Benjamin B. Warfield were champions of this position, although even they had to admit errors in transmission, thereby permitting room for the discipline of textual criticism that worked to restore the original text. Many Presbyterians were militant about inerrancy, and that militancy surfaced at the 1881 General Assembly. The Revised New Testament had just been released, and copies of it were on sale at the Assembly. Many felt the new text challenged the Word of God, which they uncritically equated with the King James Version.

At almost this same time, *The Presbyterian Review* was founded. The coeditors were Charles Augustus Briggs* and Charles Hodge. Briggs saw the *Review* as a vehicle for discussion, while Hodge saw it in an apologetic vein. Among the earliest articles to appear were one written by Hodge and Warfield on the issue of the verbal inerrancy of the Scriptures and another by Briggs that suggested that historical views of the Scriptures did not conflict with the Westminster Confession and that Christians should be careful in the manner in which they challenged others' views. Smith was in sympathy with Briggs.

Following the 1881 General Assembly, Smith was invited by Briggs to write an article for the *Review*. Smith suggested a review of Wellhausen's book, the result being deep concern among some in the church that German rationalism was beginning to appear in America. The 1882 General Assembly's response was to pass resolutions that warned against the teaching of higher criticism in the seminaries or the teaching of anything else that called into question the complete sufficiency of the Scriptures on all matters. Apart from one paper read in the Cincinnati Ministerial Association aimed at Smith, there was little condemnation of him at that time. He was even elected moderator of the Presbytery.

The events that were to sweep Henry Smith toward trial and ultimately the loss of his ministerial standing were precipitated on 20 January 1891 by Charles A. Briggs's inaugural address at the time of his installation as

Edward Robinson Professor of Biblical Theology at Union Theological Seminary in New York. Briggs's subject was the authority of the Scriptures. However, he cited certain barriers to the Bible's authority, among them dogmatic systems that had replaced the authority of the Word of God. Some of those dogmatic barriers were "superstition, verbal inspiration, authenticity, and inerrancy" (Smith, *The Heretic's Defense*, 79). Based solely on the newspaper reports of the address and without benefit of the full text, a great hue and cry were raised among the conservatives who began to demand that Briggs's appointment to the chair of biblical theology not be ratified. Smith's home Presbytery of Cincinnati joined in the condemnation of Briggs, but since none of the Lane professors were present at an adjourned meeting on 16 February, action on the resolutions was deferred. However, at a meeting on 2 March, the resolutions against Briggs were reintroduced that petitioned the General Assembly to take such action as was necessary to maintain the peace and purity of the church. In essence, it was a demand to veto Briggs's appointment. Smith and Llewelyn J. Evans opposed the action, terming it hasty—since there was still no full text available—and unconstitutional—because it pronounced judgment on a member of another Presbytery (Smith, *Inspiration and Inerrancy*, 21). In addition, they challenged the assertion of some that critical investigation of the Scriptures was solely for the purpose of vindicating the doctrines of the church, a stance they felt was a mark of Roman Catholicism and something against which the Protestant movement had revolted. Despite their opposition, the resolution passed on a vote of 54 to 17, but some Presbyters were angry that there should have been any opposition. Smith's retrospective comment was, "Looking back at the event, I do not see how we could have done anything other and still have remained honest men" (Smith, *The Heretic's Defense*, 84).

Both Evans and Smith were invited by the Presbyterian Ministerial Association in Cincinnati to address them on the topic of inspiration. They spoke on successive Monday afternoons. Evans first addressed the Association from the standpoint of a New Testament exegete, and Smith then spoke from the Old Testament exegete's perspective. Both found it impossible on the basis of their studies to affirm inerrancy in all aspects of the Scriptures. The addresses were printed in a pamphlet entitled *Biblical Scholarship and Inspiration*.

Smith was elected a commissioner to the May General Assembly held in Detroit. The main issue was the appointment of Briggs to the chair of Biblical Theology at Union. Smith spoke on behalf of Briggs, sustaining Briggs's "liberty and duty to oppose Bibliolatry if he discovered it" (*The Heretic's Defense*, 89) and asking for charity toward the man. The vote was 449 to 60 against Briggs. The logical result of Briggs's condemnation was that those who had opposed Briggs were now compelled to prosecute

Smith and Evans. Evans, however, accepted a position in Wales, but he died two months after returning to his native land.

A resolution was introduced on the floor of the Presbytery of Cincinnati essentially condemning Smith. He responded that there was an orderly way to bring such an accusation through the judicial processes of the church. Consequently, a Committee on Erroneous Teaching was appointed, ostensibly (1) to find out what the doctrine of "errancy" was and to what degree it was being taught in the seminaries and (2) to draft some resolution on the issue. There was no general intent that the Committee initiate a judicial process against Smith. However, some seemed to see the Committee as a way of pronouncing Smith unorthodox without judicial process. The Committee sought to elicit from Lane Seminary a pledge that the doctrine of errancy would not be taught by Smith and that the professors would take a pledge every three years not to teach such a doctrine. Some persons encouraged Smith to comply. Since he had never taught *errancy* as a doctrine but rather had asserted that the doctrine of *inerrancy* did not coincide with the facts of the Scriptures, he did not feel he could make such a statement without denying what he had written or going beyond the boundaries laid down in the Westminster Confession. In response to the Committee, the Seminary indicated that affirmation of the Westminster standards was sufficient for professors at the Seminary, and declined to pass the resolution. As a consequence, the Committee recommended that a committee of prosecution be appointed to draw up charges against Smith and report at the 17 October 1892 meeting of the Presbytery. Their recommendation was accepted.

There were three charges lodged against Professor Smith: (1) that he had taught in two articles in the *New York Evangelist* that ministers could abandon the system of doctrine to which they had assented at the time of ordination and still retain their standing as ministers; (2) that he had taught in his pamphlet *Biblical Scholarship and Inspiration* that the Holy Spirit did not guide the authors of the Scriptures in such a way that all their words were absolutely truthful—that is, "free from error when interpreted in their natural and intended sense"; and (3) that he had stated in the same pamphlet that while the Scriptures are the infallible rule of faith and practice, he denied the sense of inspiration attributed to the Scriptures by the Scriptures themselves and the Confession of Faith (the Westminster Confession). Under each charge were specifications. Smith responded to the charges and specifications on 14 and 15 November 1892. However, by the time he appeared to give his response, the General Assembly had declared it to be doctrine of the church that the original autographs as they were delivered by God were without error and any ministers who disagreed with that stand should leave the church or, failing that, the Presbytery should cite them for violation of their ordination vows. By this statement, the hand of the conservatives was immensely strengthened. Smith would object in his defense that he was not bound by a pronouncement of the General Assembly but only by those statements contained in the Westminster Confession and the Scriptures that bore on the issue, neither of which supported the doctrine of inerrancy.

The trial was held in the First Presbyterian Church of Cincinnati, the same church in which Lyman Beecher* was tried. As a beginning, Smith questioned whether three members of the Presbytery who had already written articles pronouncing him guilty of heresy should be allowed voting privileges. After assuring the Presbytery that they felt they could be objective, they were permitted to retain their seats. All three ultimately voted against Smith.

Smith's responsibility before the Presbytery was twofold: (1) to argue whether the charges were factually true and whether they supported the allegations of heresy and (2) to argue whether the facts were supported by competent testimony. Initially, he dealt with matters of due process. He argued that the Committee on Erroneous Teaching was not empowered to consider ministerial standing, that the Committee was prejudiced against him from the beginning, that the Presbytery did not inquire whether the judicial proceedings were really necessary, and that there had been no private conference with the accused as prescribed by the polity of the church. He then challenged the charges themselves, asserting that they were general and not specific and that they were based on someone else's interpretation of his words and not on his own understanding of what he meant. In other words, he could not be charged with meaning something that he didn't mean. These comments led to a revision of the charges on 29 November 1892 to make them more specific.

Since Charge I, which accused Smith of stating that persons could abandon essential elements of the church's doctrine following ordination while maintaining their ministerial standing, was not sustained by the Presbytery, it will not be examined here. Suffice it to say that Smith never espoused such a position. In his response and argument against Charges II and III, Smith pointed out that the charges were essentially the same; that is, they accused him of denying the inerrancy of the Scriptures. Smith's defense was meticulous from the standpoint of biblical literature, church history, theology, and the Confessions.

One of Smith's first challenges to the charges against him asked whether the doctrine of inerrancy was fundamental to the faith, something that it was necessary for the Presbytery to prove if they were to convict him. Smith pointed out that the doctrine of inerrancy could not be found in the Westminster Confession, and therefore the Committee was unable to shape the charge in the language of the Confession. All the Confession stated was that scripture is "given by inspiration of God, to be the rule of faith and life" (*Westminster Confession*, 6.002). It affirmed that everything necessary for human salvation was given in the Scriptures and that scripture was made plain by the inward illumination of the Spirit. Nowhere did it mention inerrancy. Thus, argued Smith, if the Confession did not deem inerrancy to be of sufficient merit to treat it clearly, it could not be held to be a fundamental doctrine of the faith.

Smith charged that the Committee was reading its own dogmatic interpretation into both the Confession and the Scriptures. First, the doctrine of inerrancy was purely speculative, because there were clearly contradictions in the Scriptures as they had been received by the church. Even Hodge and Warfield had admitted that the biblical text in its present form was not inerrant. It was for that reason that both theologians gave a place in their thought to textual criticism, because both believed that inerrancy would be found in the original texts before errors in transmission had occurred. Thus, inerrancy was a theological dogma, not supportable from scripture itself, and meaningless in the face of the current state of the scriptural text. In addition, it was a doctrine about which there had been no unity among theologians of the church, and Smith gave a masterful summary of the divergent stands of the Church Fathers, the Schoolmen, and the Reformers.

He continued his argument by noting that the logical conclusion of the doctrine of inerrancy was that it based salvation on an inerrant text rather than upon Christ. If, as some asserted, the mission of the church was dependent upon an inerrant scriptural text, then no salvation was currently available, because all admitted that the text was corrupt. However, if God preserved inerrantly that which was *necessary* for salvation or, in the words of the Confession, that which was essential for "faith and life," then scripture could contain errors of fact on issues of history or science without contaminating that for which scripture was given in the first place, that is, "all things necessary for his [God's] own glory, man's salvation, faith, and life" (*Westminster Confession*, 6.006). Thus, amidst the human elements of scripture, and the natural errors and biases that humans bring to all endeavors, was to be found the inerrant Word of God concerning the critical issues of life, that is, those issues that bear on faith and practice. Consequently, an original inerrant autograph was as unnecessary theologically as a current inerrant text. Salvation was not dependent upon either but, rather, upon Jesus Christ, who was, and is always to be, met in the very human words of the scriptural text.

As a part of his argument, Smith articulated, as already noted, a distinction between the role of the theologian and that of the exegete. He said, "As an exegete it is my duty to deal with the facts of Scripture, and state them. It is the duty of the theologians to make their theory accord with these facts, and if the theory is not in accord with the facts, the fault does not lie with the facts" (Smith, *Response*, 145). Thus, when it is clear that the Chronicler used the same narrative that the author of Kings was using, but made selections of material and even modified material to suit his own purposes, it is not the exegete who is on trial but the theologians who must modify their theories to fit the facts of the Scriptures.

Smith summarized the points of agreement between himself and the Committee. All agreed that the Bible contained the revelation of God, that it contained other material that was not revealed that was important for historical purposes, that the material was arranged by human beings, and that "the result is a book which in its totality is the Church's permanent and infallible rule of faith and life" (158). The essential point of difference was over the *extent* of the activity of the Holy Spirit on the writers in the production of the texts. In summary, Smith made the following statement:

> The evidence shows that I admit a bias in the inspired writers some-times affecting their statements of fact. Your committee have [sic] failed to show that this is contrary to the Scriptures or the Confession of Faith. Your committee have [sic] failed to show that I deny the infal-libility of the Scriptures as the rule of faith and life. Your committee has failed to show that my doctrine of inspiration is in any way con-trary to that affirmed in the Scriptures and the Confession. Your com-mittee has failed to show that I advocate *anything* out of harmony with the facts of Scripture or with the statements of Scripture rightly inter-preted. Your committee has failed to show that I have in any way impugned the essential and necessary articles of the Westminster sys-tem. (160)

The Presbytery was not convinced. They voted 31 to 26 to suspend Smith from the ordained ministry "until such time as he shall make manifest, to the satisfaction of the Presbytery, his renunciation of the errors he has been found to hold, and his solemn purpose no longer to teach or propagate them" (*Response*, 166–167).

Smith appealed first to the Synod of Ohio and then, when the Synod refused his appeal, to the 1894 General Assembly. There he was forced to argue his case mostly on procedural issues rather than those issues at the heart of the question. As expected, the General Assembly refused his ap-peal, but Smith related that he made the appeals to "help some minds to a better, that is a more historical, view of the Bible" (*The Heretic's Defense*, 112). One person who spoke on his behalf was Professor George Foot Moore of Andover Theological Seminary,* one of the outstanding biblical scholars of the day. Following the verdict, Moore felt he could no longer remain a Presbyterian and thus resigned his ministerial standing and mem-bership.

While the case was being appealed, Lane Seminary was willing to keep Smith on the faculty but would not permit him to teach. Thus, he resigned his appointment in 1893. For the next five years, he held no permanent position but used the time to write his commentary on Samuel for the *International Critical Commentary*. In 1897 he was invited by Union Theological Seminary to give the Ely Lectures. Smith delivered his addresses on *The Bible and Islam*, which gave him an opportunity to examine the Islamic attitude toward the inspiration of the Qur'an. Because Smith's conviction included a ban against preaching, he dutifully refused to preach even in non-Presbyterian churches. However, in 1897 he was offered a joint appointment as professor of biblical literature at Amherst and associate pastor of the College Church. Even when he pointed out that he could not bring a letter certifying his good standing, the association of Congregational ministers welcomed him. From 1907 to 1913, Smith taught the general history of religion at Meadville Theological School. From 1913 to 1925 he served as chief librarian at Union Theological Seminary, and in 1917 he was also appointed professor of Hebrew and related languages. However, his principal work continued to be with the library. Upon retirement, he moved to Poughkeepsie, New York, where he died on 26 February 1927.

In summary, Henry Preserved Smith's story is one of a man caught in the theological whirlpools of his day. His case was decided before it ever went to trial. However, his arguments are still instructive for those who wrestle with the question of the relation between the divine and human elements to be found in the texts of the sacred Scriptures.

SELECTED BIBLIOGRAPHY

Evans, Llewelyn J., and Henry Preserved Smith. *Biblical Scholarship and Inspiration: Two Papers. With Preface on How It Came About, and an Appendix Containing Two Articles from the New York Evangelist on Ordination Vows, Also the Charges and Specifications Presented in the Presbytery of Cincinnati, October 17, 1892.* Cincinnati: Robert Clarke & Co., 1892.

Smith, Henry Preserved. *The Bible and Islam; or, The Influence of the Old and New Testaments on the Religion of Mohammed: Being the Ely Lectures for 1897.* New York: Scribner's, 1897.

———. *The Heretic's Defense: A Footnote to History.* New York: Charles Scribner's Sons, 1926.

———. *Inspiration and Inerrancy: A History and a Defense. Containing the Original Papers on Biblical Scholarship and Inspiration.* Cincinnati: Robert Clarke & Co., 1893.

———. *Response, Rejoinder, and Argument.* Cincinnati: Robert Clarke & Co., 1893.

Roger R. Keller

Egbert Coffin Smyth
(1829–1904)

Andover Theological Seminary* was America's first seminary, founded in 1808 amid theological controversy, its first patrons wrapping themselves in a mantle of trinitarian orthodoxy. For generations after the school's inception, certain alumni appointed themselves responsible for monitoring questions of doctrine and for setting acceptable limits to expressions of belief. This attitude remained vigorous up to the 1880s when alarms once again swirled across the Massachusetts campus, calling a diverse group of participants to join the fray.

The individual most often singled out in accusations of heresy during this period was Egbert Coffin Smyth, who at the time served as president of Andover's faculty in addition to occupying his post as Brown Professor of Ecclesiastical History. Smyth had been born in Brunswick, Maine, on 24 August 1829, the son of a Congregationalist minister who taught mathematics and natural science at Bowdoin College for 45 years. In due course Smyth graduated from Bowdoin (1848) and for a while taught public school and tutored in Greek at his alma mater. Deciding on a ministerial career, he studied at Bangor Theological Seminary (1851–1855), remaining a year beyond the B.D. for further study. He taught rhetoric at Bowdoin for 2 years and after his ordination in 1856 served as Collins Professor of Natural and Revealed Religion for 6 years. In 1862 he followed a growing trend among American scholars by traveling to Germany for graduate work, absorbing a host of determinative ideas at universities in Halle and Berlin. Upon his return in 1863 he accepted appointment as church historian at Andover Seminary, a position held for the rest of his career and one wherein he drew hostile attention from disgruntled alumni.

Classroom lectures provided small opportunity for Smyth to disseminate his views. He seems to have regarded book-length publications as similarly restrictive because most of his public expressions appeared as printed essays of modest length. He published lectures on the religious history of Bowdoin College, on the value of historical study to ministerial education, on the development of doctrines about Christ and the Trinity during the first three centuries of ecclesiastical history, plus studies of eighteenth-century religious thought, particularly that of Jonathan Edwards. In addition to lectures and books, Smyth chose a third avenue as a professional outlet, one that touched a vitally interested audience. In 1884 he became a founder and principal editor of the *Andover Review*, a new monthly journal that announced its determination to interpret old theological standards in the light of modern scholarship. Besides Smyth, the other editors were William J. Tucker, professor of sacred rhetoric, John W. Churchill, professor of elocution, George Harris, professor of Christian theology, and Edward Y. Hincks, professor of biblical theology. These men were also included in ensuing debates over heterodoxy and permissible standards for Andover faculty, but Smyth was singled out as the chief advocate of new ideas and therefore as the primary heresiarch.

Using the *Review* as their platform, Andover's professors articulated a bold policy through editorials and the essays they accepted for publication. In the very first issue Smyth set the tone for subsequent religious writing with a cogent prolegomenon. There he characterized the monthly's viewpoint that was sustained in all its later activities. Basic to his perspective was a recognition that change through time was inevitable and usually beneficial. "Many dogmas have become extinct," he observed, serving notice, too, that "others must go" because "not all is genuine which wears the garb of orthodoxy" ("Theological Purpose," 3). This attitude was meat and drink to historians with modern training, of course, but Smyth also used it on a theological plane to legitimate revisionism. Religious systems eventually needed revising, he held, because they eventually lost touch with the life experience that gave them root. The Greek church, for example, had come to substitute orthodoxy for piety; the Latin, legalism for spirituality; the Reformation, scholasticism for justification by faith alone. Another reason given for imperfect theologies was the fact that the pure gospel had to be filtered through the impure medium of human language. This imperfection made wise men modest in regard to the worth of extant statements and hopeful for progress in revising them to produce better vehicles of faith.

In his discussion of changes throughout history, Smyth was optimistic about contemporary revisions. He was more than a relativist who acknowledged the adequacy of bygone ideas for their own time while insisting on freedom to seek new articulations of his own. By pointing to changed religious expressions as a necessary consequence of altered circumstances, he thought that such changes were generally improvements over what preceded them (Williams, *Andover Liberals*, 27, 65, 74). This was the case when theologians pursued their true task, that is, reflecting in their own contexts on the truth that was revealed in Christ. Improved theology resulted from "revealed truth interpreted, applied, logically developed, formally stated, by Christian minds." Revised theology was not something to be equated with revelation itself, but it increasingly approached "a reproduction and development of Apostolic teaching according to the laws which govern human thought" ("Theological Purpose," 6). Genuine improvement in theological utterance depended on living faith, on "regenerated consciousness" as a wellspring of new insight. This dynamic perspective allowed Smyth to hold that "the true theologian is not a mere collector and classifier of proof-texts, but a reproducer of the divine testimony. Truth thus received and wrought out is . . . friendly to the soul, commending and attesting itself in life and conduct" (2).

It is crucial to a proper understanding of Smyth's viewpoint, and to a proper adjudication of later events, to see that he thought theological change could achieve "real growth . . . genuine and admirable progress." The vital factor in such improvement was that its proponents had "become more and more Christian in their conceptions of honor and right, of justice and grace, of creation and its laws, of government and its prerogatives." A great many serious errors could have been avoided in the past, and the present as well, if people had been more "intelligent and resolute to think according to Christianity," especially if guided by such important conceptions as "persons with their correlative duties and rights . . . God and man . . . this life and the life beyond" (11). Open and frank exchange of views elicited candor and hopeful anticipation among the editors. The result of this expected theological growth would be greater understanding among the Seminary's students as well as the journal's general readership. Smyth faced future theological updating with confidence, speaking for all his colleagues, "We seek to promote large-minded, large-hearted discussions of Christian truth, recognizing our own limitations and the many-sidedness and growing proportions of the truth as it is in Jesus" (12).

The general heading Smyth used for aligning theology with modern concepts was "Progressive Orthodoxy," something that claimed both contemporary relevance and ancient authenticity. It is important to note his operational viewpoint before treating any specific doctrine because this perspective undergirds everything he did in theological discussion. In his mature thought, Smyth distanced himself from those who confined themselves to extant orthodoxy because, in the end, they lacked faith in the source of redemption, the vital root that allowed new growth and affirmations. "We much prefer," he said, "to be recognized as disciples of Him who is the Truth than to be credited with conformity to standards of belief of human construction." With the assurance of one convinced that his faith was securely grounded in the proper source, Smyth went on to enumerate advances in contemporary scholarship that furthered improvements in theological revisions of his day. Such changes did not reject the core truths held since earliest times, of course, but with the help of evolutionary philosophy, historical criticism, and new findings in biblical hermeneutics, he was convinced that present-day doctrinal formulations were definite improvements over preceding ones ("Progressive Orthodoxy," 466–468).

Subsequent charges of heterodoxy must have come as a shock to Smyth since he maintained that advances in Christian thought during his time possessed "a fuller knowledge of the purpose of God respecting the extension of Christianity to human history than it was possible to communicate to the early church." He saw this possession especially pronounced in the linked topics of Incarnation and Atonement. These categories had loomed large in the early days of New England Theology and had remained the driving force behind Andover's founders. As heir to those movements, he felt that while moving beyond previous definitions, he was consistent with them. Progressive Orthodoxy still gave the doctrine of divine sovereignty what he called "a formal ascendancy." Beyond that, however, he viewed sovereignty not so much as judgment but "as administered on the basis of universal atonement." Balancing this broader soteriology was a conception of Christ's work as "exalted to a position of dignity and power never before so adequately and scientifically represented."

Some mildly skeptical responses to the new theological slogan were voiced by a few like Nicholas Gilman, who quipped that the Andover editors claimed to have "safely harnessed the 'wild filly Progress' and the sober nag Orthodoxy to one and the same carriage." It remained to be seen if the mismatched team could pull together in the same direction (Hutchison, *Modernist Impulse*, 108). But more serious were those stung by what they regarded as departures from a comfortable creed, and they feared that Smyth might be drifting toward Andover's original enemies. Echoing prior squabbles, those who cried heresy thought his Christology smacked of Unitarianism, while his thoughts on redemption tended dangerously toward Universalism. Such backward-looking fretfulness, mild or full of dread, did not dismay Smyth and his colleagues because they were convinced that their updated theology drew strength from a proper orientation. Theirs was a broader view where the person of Christ was central not only to redemption but to all of "Creation, Revelation, and the universal knowledge of God" as well. Their theology went beyond mere pietistic eulogies. It strove to be nothing less than "a systematization of religious doctrine through . . . knowledge of God's ethical nature, communicated by Him who is the beginning and end of all divine revelations" ("Progressive Orthodoxy," 470–472).

On 7 July 1886 Andover's Board of Visitors met in Boston and voted to act upon a petition submitted by a small "committee of certain of the alumni." Later that summer accusations against Smyth and his four editorial colleagues were specified and enumerated at length. Responses followed. Legal counsel was retained on both sides. Argumentation expanded, running to hundreds of printed pages. Turmoil and confusion abounded. This entry will attempt to streamline the welter of sallies and ripostes, filtering out verbose flourishes and winnowing the grain from a great deal of chaff that was generated over the next few years.

The main conservative salvo made a formidable display. Touching four broad headings and then listing 16 particulars, the Visitors charged, first, that Smyth and colleagues had "taught doctrines and theories . . . not in harmony with, but antagonistic to, the Constitution and Statutes of the Seminary, and 'the true intention' of its Founders." A second broadside found them "not men 'of sound and Orthodox principles' as summarily expressed in the Westminster Assembly's Shorter Catechism . . . and . . . the Creed of the Seminary." As if the point were not yet clear enough, a third charge accused the professors of not being "Orthodox and Consistent Calvinists." There followed a ponderous list of particulars that, if proved against these lightning rods of conservative wrath, would suffice to "remove or admonish" everyone who had strayed from the comfortable confines of traditional New England orthodoxy (Tucker, *My Generation*, 188).

Looking at the list of objectives, one can readily see that the charges fall into four categories. One cluster faulted Andover's faculty for holding that "the Bible is not the only perfect rule of faith and practice but is fallible and untrustworthy even in some of its religious teachings." This charge had little direct application to Smyth, but it created an atmosphere of suspicion for all that followed. A second group of tenets pertained to various Christological affirmations regarding historicity and modality, echoes of earlier logomachies and of marginal application here. More relevant was the third area covering the largest number of specifics. In short, it denounced Smyth for believing that men without knowledge of Christ are not lost forever. Ignorance of the historic Christ afforded no opportunity for repentance, and if His proffered salvation were not deliberately rejected, there could not be eternal damnation through default. This led to a final disputed area that was for Smyth consistently humane but one that was monumentally perturbing to those steeped in Calvinistic rigor. The last blanket charge was that Smyth believed there would be "probation after death, for all men who have not in this world had knowledge of the historic Christ." This extra chance for salvation was possible because modern theology saw Atonement as possible essentially through the means of an incarnated Christ who identified with the whole human race, propitiating God to men and thus endowing all of humanity with the power to repent (Tucker, *My Generation*, 189). Incarnation and Atonement clearly meant widely different things within each of the different theological positions.

If Progressive Orthodoxy was objectionable simply for presuming that modern ideas were superior to earlier thought, the Visitors sought to sway campus opinion in their direction by applying subtle pressure of another sort. Not only did they feel obliged to uphold "the good name of the Seminary" and "the honor of Evangelical religion"; they felt required to provide "honest administration of trust funds given by devout and generous donors." Battling for truth employed hints of boycott and tightened purse strings to gain added advantage in this struggle over disputed theses. But all told, there was no mistaking the Visitors' summary judgment: "[T]he said Professors hold and teach many things which cannot be reconciled with that Orthodox and consistent Calvinism which the Statutes require of them . . . and that in repeated instances these Professors have broken solemn promises made when they subscribed the Creed" (Tucker, *My Generation*, 190).

There followed a plethora of responses from those accused of teaching the above-mentioned "errors." Their rejoinders consisted essentially of denials or arguments from premises quite different from the Visitors' position. Here lies the heart of the matter. The two sides began from different positions, proceeded with different methods, honored different priorities, and reached different conclusions—each consistent within themselves, each opposed to the other. It may be inaccurate to say that Smyth did not understand his antagonists, but they certainly never understood him. In November of 1886 the Visitors again rejected sophisticated responses offered by the accused and pronounced once more that each professor "holds, maintains and inculcates, doctrines not according to the terms and conditions prescribed by the Statutes of the Foundation of said Seminary, but antagonistic to the same" (Tucker, *My Generation*, 194).

Mention of "terms and conditions" in the statutes allows us to notice a side issue of some interest. Many of the conservatives were anxious to avoid the witch-hunting stereotype of bygone days. So they tried to finesse the issue by characterizing their investigation as merely a matter of contractual obligation, not a reversion to "the odious methods of the fifteenth century." Claiming to be fastidious rather than pugnacious, Visitor Henry M. Dexter insisted that "the only suit against those gentlemen to which I am a party . . . is a friendly one, to determine whether or not they are guilty of . . . *breach of trust*." Then, attempting to squelch vilification in the daily press, he added: "One would think that in a community of high-minded merchants . . . such an endeavor would be received with a decent candor" rather than the misrepresentations against which he wrote in protest. But few were fooled by this high-sounding pretense. Even counsel for the complainants argued that if professors were charged with violating their contractual obligations by departing from the founders' creed, then the crux of inquiry lay with whether their beliefs were heterodox or not. Nonconformity to a creed might be regarded as a breach of trust, but one first had to prove nonconformity (Tucker, *My Generation*, 196–197). So the tactic of denouncing heterodoxy from behind a gentlemanly facade fell through.

If conservatives were interested in rooting out heretical tendencies, they would have to declare themselves openly as watchdogs of orthodoxy and acknowledge their charges for what they were: attempts to impose standards of religious affirmation on everyone.

A formal trial—a merely formal enactment of the preceding *guerre de plume*—took place between 28 December 1886 and 3 January 1887. It was convened in the dining hall of Boston's United States Hotel, and large crowds attended every session. There they learned through lengthy exchanges that the two sides entertained basic differences over biblical criticism, trinitarian theory, and soteriology. Alongside those perennial issues there were questions of more immediate application regarding the theological intention of the Andover Creed: what transpired when one subscribed to it, and the nature of obligations assumed by subscribing to it or that of any religious institution. The complainants argued for a literal creedal interpretation, stringently and explicitly applied to unchangeable documents. Anyone departing from such high standards was obviously subversive to the plain requirements of professional duty. The principal respondents countered with arguments that there should be latitude in subscribing to creeds—enough to permit modernized interpretations in light of new knowledge. Smyth held (predictably) that he did not betray Andover's confessional statement because that creed was a progressive affirmation, "not an antiquated or reactionary document, but rather one of the landmarks in the history of theological progress." He maintained that the Seminary's founders wrote a creed only to prevent retrogression from perceived truth, not to stifle further improvement. The Andover Creed was neither an obstacle to change; those who relied thereafter on literal interpretations were impediments to healthy growth because they utilized the faulty assumption of unchangeableness (Tucker, *My Generation*, 197–200).

Five months later, the Visitors announced their findings. Again without repeating their convoluted and tedious semantics, the gist of their ruling was a condemnation of Smyth, with no judgment at all passed on his four colleagues. Stated more formally, the Visitors found (not surprisingly) that Smyth "maintains and inculcates beliefs inconsistent with, and repugnant to, the Creed of said Institution, and the Statutes of the same, and contrary to the true intent of the Founders thereof." Furthermore, they did "adjudge and decree" that the accused "hereby is removed from [his professorial chair] and said office is hereby declared vacant" (*Andover Case*, 191). Thus did the conservatives drive out devils that loomed in their own imaginations. But what consequences followed their pronunciamento?

On the practical level, very few. On the theoretical side, several, including a reaffirmation of Andover's professoriate and a defense of their freedom to continue exploring Progressive Orthodoxy. This support came from the Seminary's Board of Trustees, a separate body of overseers charged with more immediate responsibility for administering institutional affairs. The

Trustees regarded Visitors as filling only supervisory and appellate roles, and for them to overstep those stated bounds violated both propriety and the original intention of the Seminary's founders. In a surprising aside never publicly mentioned until the end of the trial, Trustees disclosed the fact that Visitors had first asked them (the Trustees) to pursue the case. Only when Trustees declined to act, refusing to allow them to proceed as well, did certain Visitors seize the initiative and make public their private disgruntlement. So the Trustees condemned all subsequent maneuvers on procedural as well as conceptual grounds. They expressed sympathy with the professors' views, found the Visitors' charges not sustained, and refused to remove anyone from his academic position. Incorporating language now familiar to those on campus, the Trustees upheld those striving for theological progress, saying that the real question was not whether contemporary views were contrary to historic creeds but whether they clashed with the core of faith upon which those creeds depended. In a ringing affirmation of liberal men and ideas, the Trustees averred that "this Creed is to be interpreted according to the ordinary rules of creed interpretation and to the liberal usage which began in the lifetime of the Founders [and] has continued to this day" (*Andover Case*, 193–194).

The matter might have ended there. Conservative alumni had employed a minor administrative cadre to voice their complaints against faculty whose views differed from their own. They claimed victory in ensuing debate by pronouncing Smyth a heretic from their own vantage point. Such a self-centered triumph proved hollow, though, because those more directly in control of Seminary life defended the faculty and protected their tenure. No one lost his job, and the case was never pursued through any kind of denominational machinery—of which Congregationalists had little to begin with.

Nevertheless, Smyth chafed under the Visitors' findings, and he refused to let the question fade into deserved obscurity. Insisting that the public assertions of a kangaroo court be publicly reversed in turn, he brought suit in the Massachusetts Supreme Court. Andover's constitutional provisions (Article XXV) allowed such a move, and he took advantage of it. In this second phase of the trial, there were again a great many specifications, only a few of which need be mentioned. In aid of Smyth the Trustees once again entered the fray, asserting that the Visitors had refused to let them appear as a party to the trial, thus usurping power and invalidating visitorial rights. Smyth concentrated his appeal on one W. T. Eustis, secretary to the Board of Visitors, charging him with "partiality and prejudice" and having consequently "openly prejudiced" the trial's first phase. Many witnesses subsequently verified overt prejudice in Eustis's attitudes. The court's final decision (1891) rested not so much on Smyth's complaint against prejudiced indictment as on the Trustees' claim for equitable jurisdiction. The rendered opinion used language similar to that of the Visitors' original complaint, but this time the conclusion contrasted to those inquisitorial impulses with striking irony. It found that the Visitors had been wrong from the beginning because their action "was not in accordance with the statutes which they were trying to maintain" (*Andover Case*, 204–208). A complaint charging professors with violating principles laid down by the Seminary's founders was ultimately rejected because it violated those very principles themselves. In a never-say-die frame of mind, the Visitors considered launching a third phase of litigation. But this never happened for two reasons: W. T. Eustis and H. M. Dexter, principal antagonists, had died, and because of routine rotation of appointments, the Board of Visitors consisted of almost entirely new personnel. These later committee members feared that appeal to federal courts might result in nullifying all the Board's visitorial powers. So they decided to let bygones be bygones, leave Smyth with his vindication, and bury the past (209–213).

Another small irony in the Andover case is that until it occurred, Smyth had been regarded as rather conservative. But when defending his position on questions related to the history of doctrine, the divine and human in Christological affirmations, and hope for all humanity in Christian heritage, he rightly emerged as properly the central figure in the whole controversy. Thus singled out, he faced adversity undaunted, confident that his perspective was the only one ultimately beneficial to faith in future times. Some of his concluding words are worth quoting here, not as an epitaph for foreshortened exploration but as a principle for the next generation of theologians to use in search of religious vitality. Assuring liberals and conservatives alike that he had never betrayed the truth contained in historic confessions, he declared creeds to be "a summary of principles which are to be applied and developed from generation to generation." Working within that perspective, he claimed to "have done something far better and more faithful than a literal interpretation" of any creed. The work that dignified his efforts was nothing less than having "confronted present great and important questions of religious thought and life" (Tucker, *My Generation*, 215).

So the Andover case ended with a frustrated attempt by conservatives to apply early nineteenth-century categories to late nineteenth- and/or early twentieth-century theology, with a victory for academic freedom on at least one campus of some stature and with a ringing affirmation of human questing after religious truth as perceived within contemporary cultural contexts. It would be a faulty historical interpretation to see these events as the death knell of heresy hunting in American life, however much one might wish for such a state of affairs. But Smyth's experience at Andover helps delineate the course of modern circumstances wherein people are free to explore religious truth and to offer their ideas for others to share. Censure may come from petty officials who control denominational machinery, but the open marketplace for ideas in American culture offers opportunity for alternate outlets so that variant ideas can in these times see the light of day. Then their success depends on whether people will accept them in the light of reason, charity, and faith in search of understanding.

BIBLIOGRAPHY

The Andover Case: With an Introductory Historical Statement; a Careful Summary of the Arguments of the Respondent Professors; and the Full Text of the Arguments of the Complainants and Their Counsel, Together with a Decision of the Board of Visitors: Furnishing the Nearest Available Approach to a Complete History of the Whole Matter. Boston: Stanley and Usher, 1887.

Hutchison, William R. *The Modernist Impulse in American Protestantism.* Cambridge, MA: Harvard University Press, 1976.

Smyth, E. [Egbert] C. *The Andover Defense: In the Matter of the Complaint against Egbert C. Smyth and Others, Professors of the Theological Institution in Phillips Academy, Andover. Defense of Professors Smyth, Arguments of Professor Theodore W. Dwight, with Statements of Professors Tucker, Harris, Hincks, and Churchill.* Boston: Cupples, Upham and Co., 1887.

———. "Progressive Orthodoxy, Criteria of Theological Progress." *Andover Review* 3, no. 17 (May 1885): 466–472.

———. "The Theological Purpose of the Review." *Andover Review* 1, no. 1 (January 1884): 1–13.

Tucker, William Jewett. *My Generation: An Autobiographical Interpretation.* Boston: Houghton Mifflin Company, 1919.

Williams, Daniel Day. *The Andover Liberals: A Study in American Theology.* New York: King's Crown Press, 1941.

Henry Warner Bowden

Newman Smyth
(1843–1925)

From beginning to end, the informal heresy trial of Newman Smyth was largely an episode of unanticipated consequences. "It was entirely accidental," wrote Smyth of the controversy over his appointment at Andover Theological Seminary,* "so far as at the beginning my responsibility for the initiation of it was concerned. Without previous intimation or desire, I found myself chosen by the Andover Trustees to the chair of theology which Professor Park had left vacant. Nothing could have been more foreign to my own purpose or expectation" (quoted in Buckham, *Progressive Religious Thought*, 268–269). To be sure, Smyth did not seek the Abbot Chair of Christian Theology vacated by Edwards Amasa Park in 1881; nor had he intended that a comment regarding the future probation of the impenitent would create a stir; and certainly, he did not anticipate that the furor raised over his own candidacy would become the catalyst for the much larger "Andover Controversy" from 1882 to 1892.

Perhaps because Smyth did not go looking for trouble, the heated controversy over his appointment to the faculty of Andover never became—as suspicions of heresy did for so many of the subjects of this volume—a defining moment in his life. While Smyth considered the incident of signal importance to the freedom of theological inquiry at Andover, he considered it of minor importance to his own career. As circumstances would have it, he had little to lose. When the controversy arose, he felt little pressure from his Presbyterian Church in Quincy, Illinois, or from the local Presbytery. Moreover, when Andover's Board of Trustees and faculty urged him to challenge the Board of Visitors' vote of rejection, Smyth refused to make himself the center of a potential heresy trial and legal imbroglio.

The author of 15 books, Smyth is recognized as the leading pioneer of the New Theology, a nineteenth-century Protestant attempt to adjust theology to Darwin's theory of evolution and to the new biblical criticism (Averill, *American Theology*, 23; Hutchison, *Modernist Impulse*, 77). His *Old Faiths in New Light* (1879) represented the first clear statement of the New Theology, whose advocates included Theodore Munger, George Gordon, Washington Gladden, William Newton Clarke, and William Adams Brown. According to Roland Bainton, Smyth made two significant contributions to the New Theology: He was one of the first Americans to recognize that the New Testament contained more than one theology, and he integrated the concept of scientific evolution into his theology (Gowing, "Newman Smyth—New England Ecumenist," 80).

BACKGROUND

Some knowledge of Smyth's personality and the years of his formative development provide an appropriate context for understanding not only the New Theology but, more specifically, the controversy over his appointment at Andover. "I often think," he noted in his autobiography, "that two elements must have been combined in my heredity—that I was a born mystic and a born sceptic—and that my intellectual life has been for me, more or less consciously, the assertion and reconciliation of both" (Smyth, *Recollections*, 3). Smyth's penetrating self-disclosure of faith as a subrational feeling (his mystical side) and the acceptance of critical and scientific methods (his skeptical side) reveal those tendencies of thought that would eventually expose him to charges of perverting traditional Christian teaching.

Samuel Phillips Newman Smyth was born to William and Harriet Smyth in Brunswick, Maine, on 25 June 1843. By all accounts, his upbringing in this "Eden" was evangelical but not dogmatic or intolerant (14, 25). His father was professor of mathematics at Bowdoin College and a community leader and evangelical activist who supported the temperance movement and opposed slavery, even opening his home to fugitive slaves as a station of the underground railway to Canada. As in so many New England evangelical homes of the nineteenth century, Newman's mother profoundly influenced her son's religious sensibilities. Smyth acknowledged that his captivation with Frederick Schleiermacher's notion of religion as feeling of "absolute dependence" was traceable to his mother's pious influence on his early spiritual development. Newman was barely 12 when he entered Phillips Academy in Andover, Massachusetts, and 16 when he graduated from Bowdoin in 1863. In the fall of 1864, after a year as assistant librarian and assistant professor of mathematics in the United States Naval Academy (then in Newport, Rhode Island), Newman joined the Union Army's 16th Maine Volunteers Infantry Regiment as a first lieutenant. His Civil War experience proved determinative in the choice of a vocation.

"I think my year of service in the army," Smyth recalled, "was one of the best years of preparation for my ministry,—and of theological preparation for it. It formed the habit of thinking in contact with the realities of life. I came to doubt any thinking that was not thought out in the midst of men, in daily and close contact with human life. It was probably this instinct that made me adverse to accepting any academic chair." (Quoted in Buckham, *Progressive Religious Thought*, 263)

Following the end of the war, Smyth immediately enrolled at Andover Theological Seminary, where he entered as a junior, graduating in 1867. During Smyth's sojourn, the Seminary was in a state of transition, if not transformation. On the one hand, biblical professors such as Joseph Henry Thayer and Charles Marsh Mead, fresh from studies in Germany, introduced students to recent critical methods of studying the Scriptures, including the uncertainties of documentary evidence. On the other, theologians such as Edwards Amasa Park continued to work within the orthodox Calvinistic paradigm of inductive argument. Park regarded theology as a science, placing reason in control of the theological enterprise. He recognized a place for the feelings, but appeals to emotion and sentiment were more appropriately made from the pulpit, not from the lectern (Vanderpool, "The Andover Conservatives," chaps. 7–8). Such an academic environment exposed Smyth simultaneously to new, pathbreaking ways of approaching scripture and the older, more familiar avenues of traditional theology. By his own admission, his most influential teachers (for better and for worse, respectively) were Austin Phelps in homiletics and Park in theology (*Recollections*, 77). Given Smyth's proclivity toward ministry, he was stricken by Phelps's insistence (and example) that good preaching include polished English. Park convinced most students, but not Smyth and a handful of others, that the study of theology was the continued codification of the New England Theology. Fathered by Jonathan Edwards in the mid-1750s and comprehensively developed and "improved" by such devotees as Joseph Bellamy, Samuel Hopkins, Timothy Dwight, Nathanael Emmons, and Leonard Woods, the New England Theology reached its most systematic articulation under Park during his years as Abbot Chair of Theology (1847–1881) (Conforti, *Jonathan Edwards*, chap. 5). Park's lectures, Smyth recalled, were never dull but left him disappointed: Park "shaped Edwards to conform to his system of New England theology rather than leading us to understand Edwards' thought. . . . It seemed to be Professor Park's ambition to become the final exponent of the New England theology. As a formal system it may almost be said that he did finish it; and," concluded Smyth with a tone of smug satisfaction, "it was buried with him" (*Recollections*, 79–80).

Smyth found Park's thoroughgoing rationalism stultifying and methodologically wrongheaded. "The prevalent New England theology . . . seemed to me . . . to be an orthodox rationalism; and rationalism of any kind did not satisfy me" (*Recollections*, 80). Clearly, Smyth's seminary experience was marked by cognitive dissonance. While Park taught a kind of proof-text, static, scholastic theology, biblical professors approached the Scriptures from a critical, historically rooted perspective, albeit with apologetic purposes in mind. Moreover, Smyth's brother, Egbert Coffin Smyth,* a professor of church history, emphasized the living and expanding development of theology through his lectures on the Ante-Nicene Fathers (*Recollections*, 80–81). Smyth, then, left Andover convinced that Park's approach was increasingly irrelevant in a new era of scientific advances and that, consequently, the Christian faith was rapidly losing its intellectual integrity. Dissatisfied with old ways of knowing, he would soon embark on a voyage to the source of the new learning.

After leaving Andover, Smyth served as a part-time pastor of a mission chapel of the High Street Congregational Church in Providence, Rhode Island. His ministerial qualities blossomed, and when the High Street Church vacancy occurred a year later, he was offered the position. By now, however, Smyth's continued frustration with the state of American theology led him on a pilgrimage to Germany. And so it was that during the winter of 1868–1869 he experienced the turning point in his understanding of Christian faith and theology. At the University of Berlin, Smyth fell under the spell of Isaak A. Dorner, "the greatest living theologian" (Smyth, *Orthodox Theology of To-day*, 54), and read his *Geschichte der protestantischen Theologie* (1867; *History of Protestant Theology*, Engl. trans., 1871). He then went on to the University of Halle, where he met Julius Müller and came under the influence of Friedrich August Tholuck, a critical scholar of formidable learning and evangelical piety. Upon Tholuck's recommendation, Smyth read Willibald Beyschlag's "The Biblical Theology of the New Testament"—a work that opened up a new approach toward biblical study in comparative, independent, and critical methodologies. Smyth's brief exposure to this *Vermittlungstheologie* (mediating theology)—the school of nineteenth-century German Protestant theologians who endeavored to combine traditional Protestantism with modern science, philosophy, and theological scholarship—yielded the much-sought-after tonic.

Returning home with a "restored assurance of faith," Smyth embarked upon a career of notable scholarship joined to fruitful parish ministry (quoted in Buckham, *Progressive Religious Thought*, 267). From 1870 to 1875 he pastored the First Congregational Church of Bangor, Maine. Seeking a new experience in a different part of the country, he traveled west to Quincy, Illinois, where he served the First Presbyterian Church from 1876 to 1882. Smyth then returned to his native New England and pastored the venerable and prestigious Center Church (First Church of Christ Congregational) in New Haven, Connecticut, from 1892 to 1907. His years of retirement were among his most active: He authored six more books and championed the cause of ecumenism before his death in 1925.

ROOTS OF THE CONTROVERSY

Smyth's first three books, written prior to the controversy over his appointment at Andover, reflect his profound indebtedness to modern German scholarship and established him as the earliest explicator of the New Theology. These early works particularly reflect the influence of Schleiermacher and Dorner on Smyth's theological formulations. His first book, *The Religious Feeling* (1877), was a "garland for Schleiermacher" (quoted in Ahlstrom, *Religious History*, 782). Schleiermacher, wrote Smyth, "led the thought of his age into the true way of approach toward God. . . . He met the vulgar rationalism of his day by compelling reverence to the immediate revelation by the Divine through the religious feeling" (*Religious Feeling*, 33). Smyth, too, located the source of religion in feeling, "the feeling of absolute dependence"—a prerational intuition that "is both before and after knowledge" (34). Smyth considered this work "my first attempt to formulate what from childhood had been my instinctive desire and later my dominating conviction: that in some way we are in touch with realities" (quoted in Buckham, *Progressive Religious Thought*, 267). *Old Faiths in New Light* (1879) explored traditional ways of understanding Christianity "in the light of modern thought" (vii). Smyth interpreted the Bible as a living book, containing the historical, evolutionary, and progressive unfolding of God's plans. He supported the historical veracity of the Gospels but understood them in a more symbolic than literal way. Jesus "appeared as the end of a supernatural evolution"; his miracles were evidence of a "higher consciousness" (245); and the literal resurrection of the flesh was an "unapostolic blunder" (369). Smyth's third book, *The Orthodox Theology of To-day* (1881; new ed., 1883), was a compilation of sermons given before a club of skeptics in defense of the Christian faith. Arguing that "the best defense of orthodox theology involves to some extent its dogmatic reconstruction" (iv), Smyth laid bare the reconstructive principles of the New Theology in his preface to the 1883 edition: (1) a personal and ethical conception of religion; (2) the historical and scientific interpretation of the Scriptures; (3) a more careful recognition of the limits of knowledge and the admission of mystery; and (4) a moral interpretation of the nature of God and the Atonement—a view summarized in the phrase "God is love" (vii–x).

With the publication of *Old Faiths in New Light* and *The Orthodox Theology of To-day*, Smyth emerged as a prominent advocate for Protestant liberalism. By 1881, he had published two important books and a number of equally important articles, earned a reputation as a broadminded and critical scholar and a proven pastor, and distinguished himself as an apologist of the faith. At the age of 38, Smyth was a recognized rising theological star within the small but growing Protestant liberal galaxy. His status was not lost on the faculty at Andover Theological Seminary, who invited Smyth to replace the retiring Park. For the first (and last) time, Smyth was tempted to dedicate himself to an academic career.

Since December 1881, Smyth had been in correspondence with the Andover faculty and Trustees. In February 1882, his brother Egbert informed him that he had been elected by the faculty and Trustees to fill Park's vacated Abbot Chair of Theology and that the action was being reviewed by the Board of Visitors. It was with this latter group that Smyth encountered resistance and eventual rejection. That a controversy ever arose over Smyth's appointment was in large measure owing to the peculiar arrangement of Andover Seminary as a corporate body. If indeed Smyth was unanimously and enthusiastically elected by the faculty and 11 of the 12 Trustees (1 abstained), then how was it that the Board of Visitors, composed of only 3 members, could overrule these other faculty-appointing bodies?

The founding of Andover Seminary in 1808 represented the joint efforts of Old Calvinists at Phillips Academy and New Divinity Hopkinsians (the followers of Jonathan Edwards whose theology was explicated further by Samuel Hopkins) of the Andover Foundation (also called "Associate Founders") to defend the Calvinist tradition against the corrosive effects of Harvard's Unitarianism. The incorporation of Andover Seminary reflected the interests of these two groups. While the Board of Trustees acted as the governing body of the academy and Seminary, it did so along with a board of oversight, the Board of Visitors. This latter self-perpetuating body of three members represented the interests of the Associate Founders of the Seminary who had contributed funds for the establishment of three chairs (including the Abbot Chair). The Board of Visitors "were to be the guardians, overseers, and protectors of our Foundation," ensuring that current and prospective faculty agreed with the Seminary's doctrinal position as expressed in the "Associate Creed of Andover"—a document that combined the Westminster Shorter Catechism and the New Divinity "improvements" of doctrines. The Board had power to approve or reject the appointment of any professor. Over the years the lack of coordination between the boards became a potential source of friction and, in the case of Smyth's nomination, a realized source of division (Tucker, *My Generation*, 102–104; Williams, *The Andover Liberals*, 2–7).

With the public announcement of Smyth's election in March 1882, what had been a private and smooth process quickly met public resistance. Dr. E. K. Alden, secretary of the American Board of Commissioners for Foreign Missions (ABCFM), scrutinized Smyth's book *The Orthodox Theology of To-day*, especially those pages in which Smyth intimated the possibility of some redemptive grace for those after death who had never known Jesus

Christ in their earthly life. Disturbed by Smyth's position, Alden, Park, and others mounted opposition. *The Congregationalist*, the conservative voice of Congregationalism, came out against the Board of Visitors' confirmation of the Trustees' election.

What precisely had Smyth written that so offended the conservatives? Smyth remarked that the controversy centered on a point that he considered "quite secondary and merely incidental in its presentation." He had taken up the apologetic task of defending the Christian faith in light of his own critical views. "I had been challenged," he wrote, "by a group of unbelievers, and in response had invited them to hear me speak concerning some of our chief Christian doctrines. They constituted the audience primarily to whom a series of sermons was addressed, taken down by a stenographer and subsequently published under the title, 'The Orthodox Theology of To-day' " (quoted in Buckham, *Progressive Religious Thought*, 269). For Smyth, the issue of the fate of the lost or impenitent was related less to systematic theology and more to the concerns of theodicy: "Annihilation" (the view that the impenitent perish at death) seemed "like a confession of divine inability to overcome evil with good" (*Orthodox Theology of To-day*, 92). Smyth acknowledged that various texts of scripture "do not teach explicitly a second probation, or mean without doubt that there shall be a final reconciliation of evil to God." But, he continued in what became the flash point of the controversy,

> so long as such expressions have been left in the Bible, our theology ought, at least, not to be over-confident that it has learned the whole mind of the Spirit concerning God's work and purpose in the interval— we know not how long it may be—between death and final judgment; and these Scriptures are sufficient to give us a needed, though too often overlooked, intimation that the Lord has his own administration of the regions of the dead until the Messianic kingdom shall be delivered up to the Father; and of what the Father and the Christ are working there we need to know far more than has been disclosed to us before we are competent to judge the ways of God to men, or have reason to doubt that the awards of the last great assize shall be in accordance with truth, justice, and mercy. I feel that I have a moral right—a right guaranteed by these Scriptures—to take refuge from the perplexities of the final issues of evil in my own ignorance and in the silence of God's Word; to find peace, comfort, and hope in the merciful obscurities of revelation. (125–126)

Clearly, Smyth did not explicitly defend, but only suggested the possibility of, what his detractors quickly dubbed as a "second probation." Nor was he the first Congregationalist to broach such views. Ferment over eschatological questions had been brewing since the latter 1870s. Rev. James Whiton in *Is Eternal Punishment Endless?* (1876) contended that the future punishment of the impenitent might not be endless; and Rev. James Merriam at his installation council in 1877 proposed that the Bible left open the question of the eternal punishment of the impenitent (Foster, *Modern Movement*, 17–20). While these views created alarm in some quarters, they were not seen by critics as potentially damaging as Smyth's might become if circulated year after year among Andover's students.

From the perspective of Alden and the ABCFM, a "second chance" for the spiritually lost undercut the raison d'être of missions. As William Jewett Tucker, a Smyth partisan and Andover professor, noted: "There are 'vested interests' in dogmas as there are vested interests in property. The dogmas of the universal decisiveness of this life, involving the perdition of the heathen, was a vested interest of incalculable value in the judgment of certain managers of missionary boards. To question this dogma was in their language, 'to cut the nerve of missions' " (Tucker, *My Generation*, 109). Of course, those who disagreed with Smyth's views did not merely have vested interests at stake: To them, the very suggestion of a second chance contravened the plain teaching of the Scriptures.

Because the Andover Creed was silent on the issue of an indeterminate state of the lost, Smyth could not be accused of outright heresy. Yet *The Congregationalist* judged that the authors of the creed would have condemned the theory in question, had it been broached. Such a judgment, noted Tucker, "was to deal in that most dangerous of all creations of the human mind—'constructive heresy' " (Tucker, *My Generation*, 110). Indeed, *The Congregationalist* affirmed that anyone who embraced Smyth's hypothesis could not in good conscience subscribe to the creed; moreover, anyone who did subscribe would subject the Seminary to the charge of misuse of funds.

In the context of the emerging paper war and while Smyth's election was still in the hands of the Visitors, the Andover faculty issued its own letter to the public (published in *The Independent* on 13 April 1882), outlining the profound significance of the issue:

> While the election of a Professor at Andover is in the hands of the Visitors, it would ordinarily be improper for either the Board of Trustees or the Faculty to engage in a public discussion of it. If we exceed the customary rule in the present instance, it is because the discussion has swept into its current questions far broader and more vital than that of the confirmation or rejection of the Professor-elect—questions that touch not only the life of Andover Seminary, but the perpetuity as well of all trusts conditioned by a creed, and even the possibility of an orthodoxy at once stable and progressive. (Quoted in Tucker, *My Generation*, 110–111)

This statement anticipated the trouble that lay ahead, for the Andover Controversy that followed in the wake of the Smyth episode turned on the very issue of creedal interpretation.

At this juncture in the Smyth affair, the Board of Visitors sought to avoid further controversy. They suggested that the Board of Trustees "unelect" Smyth by withdrawing their vote. The Visitors declared their satisfaction with Smyth's doctrinal views, noting they were "in substantial agreement with the characteristic doctrinal position of this Seminary." At the same time, they raised concerns that Smyth seemed "to conceive of truth poetically rather than speculatively" and feared that this "rhetorical quality would interfere with his precision as a teacher" (quoted in Tucker, *My Generation*, 114–115). Clearly, the Visitors did not wish to tackle the central issue head on—namely, to render judgment on Smyth's views. Was Smyth's New Theology in agreement with the founders' "old theology"? In point of fact, Smyth (and even some faculty at Andover) repudiated Calvinism (and hence, the original meaning of the Andover Creed), considering its tenets not static but temporal expressions that now, in light of new discoveries and new methods, required wholesale reconstruction. The Visitors' reference to Smyth's understanding of truth as poetic, not speculative (or doctrinal), went more to the heart of the issue, for Smyth's understanding of truth was based on feeling or intuition, not on the more rational, propositionally based truth revealed in the Scriptures. Smyth knew precisely what was at stake. As he observed in his autobiography, "The real Andover issue . . . was between the finality of the prevalent orthodoxy and the liberty to be granted to the new theology" (*Recollections*, 107).

The Board of Trustees was in no mood for the Visitors' temporizing and rejected the request to withdraw its election of Smyth. Once again, the case reverted to the Visitors, who in their second communication formalized and finalized their decision. Reiterating that Smyth's views were "in substantial agreement with the doctrinal position characteristic of this Institution," the Visitors rejected Smyth because of his tendency "to use language more as expression of his feelings than of his thoughts, and to conceive truth sentimentally and poetically rather than speculatively and philosophically" (quoted in Tucker, *My Generation*, 115–116). This final decision did not deter the Trustees, who tried to secure another position for Smyth (in apologetics or comparative theology) that was free of visitorial jurisdiction—despite the obvious legal challenge to the Visitors' authority. One Trustee urged Smyth to accept the Abbot Chair and to use the appointment as a test case to question the full authority of the Visitors. Smyth carefully considered the offer but declined, thus officially terminating his candidacy—and his informal heresy trial.

THEOLOGICAL ISSUES AND THE AFTERMATH

As narrated in another entry in this volume ("Andover Theological Seminary"), the controversy surrounding Smyth's election blew up in the faces of the Visitors, resulting in a prolonged dispute. The critical issue involved subscription to the Andover Creed. Was the creed to be read strictly or loosely, literally or freely? Did faculty have the right to personal liberty? At stake was the fundamental issue of theological freedom within a creed-affirming institutional setting.

As for Smyth, he accepted an invitation to become pastor of the Center Church in New Haven, Connecticut, where he continued as a popular preacher and prolific author. Of special note was his English translation, with notes and introduction, of the section on eschatology of Dorner's *System of Christian Doctrine*, entitled *Dorner on the Future State* (1883). Dorner, of course, had inspired Smyth's controversial speculations on future probation (Hutchison, *Modernist Impulse*, 84–87). Now, on the heels of the Andover affair, Smyth made available the source of his questionable views. In his lengthy introduction, he repudiated the New England Theology and defended the freedom of theological inquiry. "Men like the fervent Tholuck, the profound Müller, and the learned Dorner, may be good enough Christians for Germany," he wrote, "but not for New England" (1). Smyth offered perfunctory respect for the now-passé New England Theology and then urged "the need to assimilate to our own thought, and to transform in our own life, the most Christian thought, and the best life, of other countries, or we shall be hopelessly hardened in provincialism. Especially should we be willing to turn with a teachable spirit to a Christian theology which has grown up and shown its power to survive in the midst of an atmosphere of scepticism and rationalism" (22–23). The intellectual survival of Christianity necessitated rejection of the orthodox rationalism of the New England Theology and the embrace of the New Theology. It was not enough to modify Calvinism; rather, modern faith required "a thorough Christian reconstruction of theology" (34).

The remainder of Smyth's career was dedicated to this reconstruction. He engaged in a long and successful ministry, spent countless hours at Yale's laboratories conducting experiments seeking to better understand evolutionary science, and then, in retirement, championed ecumenism. The brief controversy over his Andover appointment became a forgotten issue— primarily because Smyth turned to other interests and, consequently, never mentioned the issue of a second probation in his preaching. "I was both amused and gratified," he recalled, "when one day one of my parishioners said to me, . . . : 'We hear a good deal said now about future probations, but I have never heard our pastor express his views on the subject; I wish you would preach to us a sermon on it' " (*Recollections*, 120).

BIBLIOGRAPHY

Ahlstrom, Sydney E. *A Religious History of the American People*. New Haven: Yale University Press, 1972.

Averill, Lloyd J. *American Theology in the Liberal Tradition*. Philadelphia: Westminster Press, 1967.

Buckham, John Wright. *Progressive Religious Thought in America*. Boston: Houghton Mifflin Co., 1919.

Conforti, Joseph A. *Jonathan Edwards, Religious Tradition, and American Culture*. Chapel Hill: University of North Carolina Press, 1995.

Foster, Frank Hugh. *The Modern Movement in American Theology*. New York: Fleming H. Revell Co., 1939.

Gowing, Peter Gordon. "Newman Smyth—New England Ecumenist." Th.D. diss., Boston University, 1960.

Hutchison, William R. *The Modernist Impulse in American Protestantism*. 1976. Reprint, New York: Oxford University Press, 1982.

Smyth, Newman. *Dorner on the Future State: Being a Translation of the Section of His System of Christian Doctrine Comprising the Doctrine of the Last Things, with an Introduction and Notes*. New York: Charles Scribner's Sons, 1883.

———. *Old Faiths in New Light*. 2nd ed. New York: Charles Scribner's Sons, 1879.

———. *The Orthodox Theology of To-day*. New ed. New York: Charles Scribner's Sons, 1883.

———. *Recollections and Reflections*. New York: Charles Scribner's Sons, 1926.

———. *The Religious Feeling*. New York: Scribner, Armstrong & Co., 1877.

Tucker, William Jewett. *My Generation: An Autobiographical Interpretation*. Boston: Houghton Mifflin Company, 1919.

Vanderpool, Harold Young. "The Andover Conservatives: Apologetics, Biblical Criticism and Theological Change at the Andover Theological Seminary, 1808–1880." Ph.D. diss., Harvard University, 1971.

Williams, Daniel Day. *The Andover Liberals: A Study in American Theology*. New York: King's Crown Press, 1941; reprint, New York: Octagon Books, 1970.

David Kling

Southeastern Baptist Theological Seminary
(1985–1994)

Southeastern Baptist Theological Seminary opened its doors to students for the first time in the fall of 1951. The institution had been created to fill a need for a Southern Baptist theological school in the geographical heart of the Southern Baptist Convention (SBC), both historically and in terms of membership. Its first Board of Trustees included numerous leaders from the more progressive part of the Convention, individuals who believed in education and reason as absolutely necessary to an effective clergy. On 15 February 1951, that Board elected Sydnor L. Stealey as the first president.

Stealey was the son of one of the most vigorous antievolutionist ministers in the Convention. During the 1920s the elder Stealey harassed President E. Y. Mullins of the Louisville Seminary for his willingness to tolerate discussion of evolution on the campus. It was to that institution that the young Stealey found his way to become a student at the height of his father's crusade. Stealey rejected the narrow fundamentalism espoused by his father while observing firsthand the bitter fruits of heresy hunting.

Following receipt of his doctorate, Stealey served four churches as a minister before joining the Southern Seminary faculty in 1942 as professor of church history. In that capacity, he was to become one of the most popular teachers on the campus, noted for his intellectual curiosity, humor, freedom, and tolerance for differing views.

With the Seminary's goal of becoming an intellectual center for a new generation of Baptist clergy, Syd Stealey was a visionary choice. Many college graduates from Baptist-affiliated colleges in Southeastern's geographic area chose the school because of the promise of openness and announced willingness to explore biblical criticism, literary and historical. Those who knew him recall Stealey's pride in his new faculty, which included New

Testament scholars Harry Oliver and Robert C. Briggs.* He encouraged his faculty to explore the newest forms of criticism and to become familiar with scholars such as Rudolf Bultmann. Fear of repercussions from the distant Western climes was not in evidence as the school matured.

The early rumblings of trouble for the school, beginning in the 1960s, are detailed in another entry in this volume (Robert C. Briggs*). But even as some of its best and ablest faculty departed in those years, the school sought to retain the Stealey legacy. Sadly, the Seminary, with that heritage, is now a stumbling corpse of a school, laid low by the fundamentalist mentality that engulfed the Convention and the Seminary by 1987.

THE DEATH OF A SEMINARY

Southern Baptists have been electing fundamentalists as presidents of their Convention since the late 1950s. Among them, all but one serving two terms, were Ramsey Pollard, K. O. White, R. G. Lee, Homer Lindsey, and W. A. Criswell. The Convention was a place of uneasy peace in those years. The bureaucrats at the Nashville headquarters were not driven by dogma, and the seminaries in Louisville and Wake Forest sent hundreds of graduates into churches. In addition, the inerrantist wing of the Convention had no obvious political agenda aside from the pomp of holding the presidency. Even Criswell did not often use his extensive appointive power over the Committee on Committees to load seminary boards with ideologues of a single persuasion. Even so, he gave fair warning in his writings that a new strategy might be on the horizon. For no apparent reason, the decade of the 1970s saw presidents less bombastic in their public demeanor, more like the Nashville bureaucrats who were typical organization men.

One disturbing trend had, however, been under way since 1958 when President Duke K. McCall created the debacle at Southern Seminary with the consequent loss of 13 bright scholars (see "Professors without Classrooms," 19 June). While most found places of service in the denomination, all the seminaries became more vulnerable to attacks on their faculties.

The skirmishes and battles with rigid inerrantism after 1958, experienced at all six SBC seminaries, weakened the leadership in the schools and generally removed their faculties from prominent roles of leadership in the Convention, a leadership quite common in the first half of the century. The word seemed to be out: "Keep the faculty under wraps." When the Convention most needed its scholars, the seminaries were successively embroiled in theological controversy. Indeed, when Dean Morris Ashcraft resigned from Southeastern in 1987, it was the third time, at three different seminaries, that he had been faced with Trustee anti-intellectualism.

From the election in 1979 of Adrian Rogers as president of the SBC, the clock began ticking for Southeastern. Its particular tradition of respect for ideas and new scholarly approaches made it the most attractive target for an activist brand of fundamentalism that seized control of the Convention governance machinery and put it to use to impose rigid dogma in all the denomination's agencies.

Newsweek reported in 1981, "The storm clouds began gathering two years ago when fundamentalist pastor Adrian Rogers captured the SBC presidency and set about replacing moderates on Baptist governing boards with officials who believed in Biblical inerrancy" (Contreras, "Battling Baptists," 88). It was further noted that traditionally Southern Baptists "have upheld the right of each believer to interpret the Bible for himself—and most theologians at SBC seminaries are Biblical conservatives who uphold the authority of Scripture. But few teach that the Bible must be interpreted literally, especially on matters of a scientific or historical nature, and that is what irks fundamentalists. 'I call it Dalmatian theology,' says Dallas pastor Paige Patterson. 'They're saying the Bible is inspired in spots. A person becomes God over the Bible when he chooses what he believes in.' "

In 1981 the Convention elected Bailey Smith as president, and he was, according to *Newsweek*'s interpretation at the time, expected to root out seminary professors whose "theology does not include Biblical inerrancy." At the time, President Randall Lolley of Southeastern Seminary stated, "He can leave [the denomination] in shambles if he wants to."

Firmly in control of the denominational machinery by 1985, fundamentalists created the "Peace Committee" to look into the causes of controversy within the denomination and to make recommendations concerning them.

When Southeastern was founded, it adopted a statement of principles identical to the one by which Southern Seminary had been governed since 1858. This Abstract of Principles was to be signed by all faculty upon receiving tenure. There were two articles therein of primary concern as the seminaries faced the Peace Committee. The first one declares both the Old and New Testaments to be inspired and "the only sufficient, certain and authoritative rule of all saving knowledge, faith and obedience." The eighteenth article is an affirmation of individual liberty of conscience. There is not a single word about biblical inerrancy in the first article, and coupled with the "liberty of conscience" affirmation in article eighteen, the two provide a wide latitude for interpretation by faculty.

On 4 February 1986, four members of the Peace Committee visited the Southeastern campus. A daylong meeting was held with President Lolley, Dean Morris Ashcraft, and Trustee chairman Charles Horton. They talked about the nature of the Bible, faculty accountability, and women in the clergy. The Committee members also "took part in a nearly four-hour meeting with a group of students belonging to the Conservative Evangelical Fellowship, a meeting of which President Lolley was unaware until late the next morning" (Committee A, "Academic Freedom," 36). The students had 27 complaints. Among these there was concern with historical authenticity of the burning bush and the virgin birth, the authorship of biblical books, homosexuality, liberation theology, and authority of the Bible. These concerns involved 15 of the faculty members. No formal charges were made, and President Lolley was forced to go on a "fishing expedition," asking each faculty member to reply to the relevant concerns. Some were mystified, others freely admitted to having made some statements quoted but sought to convey intent and meaning. Lolley was satisfied and reported his findings in March to his Trustees and to the Peace subcommittee of four who had come to the campus. In August the subcommittee asked for additional clarifications of some replies to the 27 concerns. On 18 September Lolley forwarded additional information to the subcommittee. He expressed concern that three other seminaries were freed from any further investigation by the Peace Committee. The president wrote that this "extraordinary situation" was "[p]erilously near to the greatest of all ironies—being held hostage, without information, responses, or charges, in of all things, a process seeking peace" (37). The Peace Committee never responded. With hindsight, it is clear that the end of Southeastern's existence as a scholarly institution was quite near.

But the Peace Committee had to play out its sham. It met with seminary presidents in Glorietta, New Mexico, in October 1986. They issued a joint statement that danced around the inerrancy question, using theological double-talk easily manipulated to satisfy those in power.

The Southeastern Board of Trustees was slightly shy of a majority of inerrantists when "the drift of things was apparent." The American Association of University Professors (AAUP) report notes, "In February 1987, following a faculty search, President Lolley recommended the appointment" of Roy De Brand in preaching and Elizabeth Barnes in theology. The Trustee committee on instruction, led by James DeLoach and Robert Crowley, interviewed the two candidates. "It was clearly their intention to determine the stand of the two nominees on the question of inerrancy." The Instruction Committee recommended De Brand for appointment by a vote of 5 to 0. Barnes was approved 4 to 1. On 9 March the Instruction Committee met again just prior to a full Board meeting. The issue was Barnes's theology. "Considerable pressure was brought to bear to change votes." No votes were changed, and the two professors were voted on by the full Board. De Brand was approved 25 to 2; Barnes, 13 to 12. "One trustee was heard to say, however, that Professor Barnes would never get tenure" (38).

In May 1987, the Peace Committee reported to the SBC, calling for cessation of political maneuvering, lobbying, and appeals to the press. The Committee proposed to pull out an ill-advised chestnut from the 1960s, the "Baptist Faith and Message" adopted by the Convention in Kansas City in 1963. It was recognized in that year as probably innocuous but conceivably dangerous by those who opposed it. By 1987 it took on the shape of a creed that is antithetical to Baptist tradition. At the 1963 Convention there were warnings that the section on the Scriptures, while not intending to convey adherence to inerrancy, could easily be corrupted to mean exactly that.

Editor Reuben E. Alley of the Virginia Baptist journal *The Religious Herald*, commenting on the "Baptist Faith and Message," wrote, "The statement received scant consideration for a document of this kind. The speed with which the Convention approved its creedal statement put the early church councils to shame." The editor went on, referring to remarks made by the late William O. Carver, longtime professor at Southern Seminary. Of the Convention's adopting a faith statement in 1925, Alley wrote, "Dr. Carver could see no reason for a creedal statement, nor did he think that the Convention should engage in that kind of business. He warned that such a statement might be used as a club to force free Christians, their churches or institutions into conformity" (Editorial, 10). One other note from that year. Referring to the seminaries, newly elected Convention president K. O. White stated, "There are still areas within our schools that have liberal tendencies."

And so it came to pass. The Peace Committee in 1987 assumed the "Baptist Faith and Message" to be a doctrinal norm for the seminaries. And the statement on the Bible was taken to mean inerrantism. "Trustees were encouraged to investigate the theological positions of faculty and administrators in order to guide them; and the institutions were called upon to bring their faculties into conformity with 'majority opinion' among Southern Baptists" (Committee A, "Academic Freedom," 37). So much for "soul competency."

In October 1987 the *New York Times* reported that Southeastern's Board of Trustees had been taken over by fundamentalists who "promised to hire only those who believe the Bible is literally true" (Smothers, "Baptists War," A18). This was made possible because the Convention directly elects members to all institutional boards at its annual meeting, dominated by fundamentalists since 1979. Prior to that year, a Convention Committee on Committees appointed by the president with two members from each state had allowed for diverse points of view according to the thinking of each region. That diversity ended when the president began to appoint only inerrantists even from those states whose majority had no patience with such irrational thinking.

On 12 October 1987, the Board appointed Robert Crowley as the new Trustee chairman at Southeastern. He quickly announced a new hiring policy. The Trustees "were determined that henceforward only inerrantists would be appointed to the faculty" (Committee A, "Academic Freedom," 39). On 19 October, President Randall Lolley and Dean Morris Ashcraft, joined by the Seminary attorney and three assistants to the president, informed the Trustees that they intended to resign.

In a chapel address on 22 October, Lolley stated, "I cannot fan into a flame a vision which I believe to be contradictory to the dream which formed Southeastern in 1951 and which has nourished me as a student and alumnus of the school." The same day, Ashcraft said he was resigning as dean of the faculty because he could not implement the new Trustee mandate (Associated Press, "Baptist Seminary Officials Quit," 34). There was an immediate reaction by the North Carolina Conference of the American Association of University Professors, which passed a resolution of support for the faculty. Professor Richard Barnett told the AAUP, "What is taking place at Southeastern is an offense against all liberal education." Outcries of indignation against the Trustee tactics were heard from innumerable Baptist groups in the region.

On 17 November 1987, President Lolley made his resignation official. He predicted other resignations would follow. "He said newly elected conservative trustees . . . took office with a 'pre-packaged agenda' for sweeping changes" (McLaughlin, "Lolley's Resignation"). Lolley noted that the new Trustees "have never set foot on this campus before becoming trustees. Yet upon arrival they seem to know precisely what needs to be done and who needs to be disciplined." Lolley also noted that biblical inerrancy is "a code word for power politics." Ashcraft made his resignation official and stated, "The real issue is, as I see it, not theological at all. It is conservative takeover and power. . . . I will not be a party to some of the actions now taking place and injuring persons, nor will I hold the coats of those who do."

A presidential search committee was appointed in December and "steady pressure was put on President Lolley, who was accused of disruptive and wrecking tactics, to resign before the agreed date of July 31, 1988, a step Dr. Lolley refused to take unless his successor were chosen earlier" (Committee A, "Academic Freedom," 39). On 12 February the search committee announced its selection of Lewis A. Drummond, professor of evangelism at Southern Seminary and associate of Billy Graham, and "following a series of interviews and strongly stated faculty opposition, he was elected by the board (20 to 6) at its meeting on March 14 and 15, 1988" (39). He took office on April Fool's Day, promising to hire as faculty members only those who accept the Bible as inerrant (Religious News Service, "Fundamentalist Shift Succeeds," B6).

On 16 March Lolley addressed the Trustees for the last time. He vowed to work to return control of Southeastern to moderates. He confronted the Trustees with these words: "I declare eternal hostility against every tyranny over the minds and hearts of God's people anywhere on this earth. I commit from this day forward every moment of my time and every millibar of my energy to restoring this school into the hands of her friends and out of the hands of her foes, so help me God!" ("Seminary President Blasts Conservatives").

In December the Southern Association of Colleges and Schools declared Southeastern deficient in three of the four categories used to accredit schools and facing "institutional ineffectiveness" in the fourth area. The Association cited investigation of the theological convictions of faculty "without due notification and faculty participation," intrusion of the Board of Trustees "into traditional areas of faculty prerogatives," and interrogation by Trustees of prospective faculty "concerning their views on biblical inerrancy" (Hyer, "Report Assails N.C. Baptist Seminary," G12).

Two adjunct positions became a point of focus in 1989 when the Board of Trustees refused to reappoint Janice Siler as visiting instructor of pastoral care and her husband Mahan Siler as visiting professor of pastoral care. The cause of this decision appears to have rested on the contention that Mahan Siler believed homosexuality is an acceptable lifestyle and that materials promoting a homosexual conference were seen in Siler's church, Pullen Memorial Baptist. Janice Siler did not take part in the conference and has taken no public stand on the question of homosexuality. "It is her feeling that throughout this transaction she was not judged on her own merits but merely as an appendage of her husband" (Committee A, "Academic Freedom," 40).

The faculty of the Seminary remained, seeking to retain the character of the school in spite of the Trustee actions. A major confrontation occurred over the appointment of L. Russ Bush as dean of the faculty. The faculty voted unanimously to reject Bush on the grounds of academic shortcomings, lack of administrative experience or evidence of capacity for leadership, narrowness of view (e.g., his being inordinately concerned to advance the idea of creationism), and the divisiveness his appointment would bring (41). The Board of Trustees voted in March, 22 to 8, to elect Bush.

The newly elected Dean Bush then attacked the moderate faculty and said, "[I]t is absolutely essential that a conservative majority on the faculty be achieved as soon as possible" ("Seminary Trustees"). In the midst of this chaos, in early March 1989 the Southern Baptist Alliance voted to found a new, "exclusively moderate seminary in Richmond, Virginia" (Niebuhr, "Fundamentalists").

In May the American Association of University Professors published in *Academe* its censure of Southeastern. In January 1990 the Southern Association of Colleges and Schools placed the Seminary on warning for its academic deficiencies ("Southeastern Seminary on 'Warning,' " F15). By 1991, *Time* reported a fierce struggle at Southeastern where "unhappy moderates dominate the faculty, while fundamentalists run the administration and board" (Ostling, "Fundamental Disagreement"). That majority quickly evaporated during the year as resignations of faculty became numerous in 1991. The administration said the "voluntary departures" would help the financial picture and make it easier to fashion a completely conservative faculty (Turner, "Faculty Reported Fleeing," 3E). By the close of the year, the Southern Association placed the Seminary on probation, the severest ranking possible short of loss of accreditation.

In early 1992 Lewis Drummond announced his retirement as president. The Seminary had seen its faculty shrink from 34 to 17 since 1987. He received $100,000, a car, and furniture from his official house at the hands of the Trustees that had sent the school into a financial tailspin in the previous five years.

Drummond was the stalking horse for the real takeover that was to occur when in April 1992 the Trustees appointed Paige Patterson as president. He had been a primary player in the fundamentalist takeover of the Southern Baptist Convention. When appointed to his new post, he was serving as president of Criswell College in Dallas. In an interview, Patterson said that at Criswell he had been "a Socratic gadfly on the posterior" of the Southern Baptist Convention. He said he would be a "denominational servant" at Southeastern ("Patterson Nominated," 3E). According to published reports by the Religious News Service, Patterson had been given six months by the Criswell Trustees to find another job. They felt he had been inattentive to administrative details ("Criswell's President Planning to Leave," 3).

After serving six months in the job, Patterson delivered himself of these sentiments concerning the Southern Association probation. "Look, when you're in a rodeo, trying to stay on the bucking back of several hundred pounds of irritated bull, which sports a healthy disdain for all human fellowship, and the pickup men don't arrive on time, you don't just fall off and then shoot the animal. You hang on for dear life, pray God's intervention, and ride the critter until he becomes your personal buddy. That's what we'll do here" ("Seminary Leader," B5). Perhaps Patterson was offering an inerrantist interpretation of Matthew 21:5.

Upon arrival at Southeastern, Patterson sought to join the Wake Forest Baptist Church. Minister Tom Jackson and his congregation are far from any type of inerrantist view. The deacons of the church voted 16 to 1 to reject Patterson's request that he and his wife be accepted under the watchcare of the church. Jackson eloquently stated his position. "This church has been wounded in the Southern Baptist war more than any other church in the Southern Baptist Convention. Out of 15 million members claimed by Southern Baptists, he [Patterson] is the one person identified most of all as the source of all that pain" (Cattau, "N. Carolina Church Rebuffs Patterson," 33A).

The Seminary was in academic shambles when Patterson announced in March 1994 the creation of the Bailey Smith Chair of Evangelism with a gift from an anonymous couple. It was Smith who, while president of the Southern Baptist Convention, announced nationally that God does not hear the prayer of Jews.

The destruction of the faculty at Southeastern was accomplished by immunizing it from scholarly inquiry. A loyal faculty persevered for a time, but their commitment to the freedom of the Christian spirit finally convinced them that they must seek other avenues of service. Resignations from the faculty included Samuel Balentine, Elizabeth Barnes, William Clemmons, Robert D. Dale, Roy E. De Brand, Thomas H. Graves, G. Thomas Halbrook, C. Michael Hawn, Richard L. Hester, Randall Lolley, Glenn T. Miller, Alan Neely, Robert L. Richardson, Luke B. Smith, and Richard A. Spencer. Those who retired include Morris Ashcraft, Thomas Bland, Donald E. Cook, Robert H. Culpeper, John Eddins, T. Furman Hewitt, H. Eugene McCloud, Albert Meiberg, Archie L. Nations, Robert Poerschke, and Malcolm O. Tolbert. Among administrators, Morris Ashcraft, Carson Brisson, Rodney Byard, C. Woody Catoe, Donna M. Forrester, C. T. Harris, W. David Lee, Ethel Burton Lee, Randall Lolley, Wayne F. Murphy, Jerry L. Niswonger, and W. Robert Spinks all resigned. Of the 34 members of the faculty at Southeastern in 1987, only 7 remained in 1994. Of the 16 administrators in 1987, only 3 remained in 1994.

Because Southeastern was in an area of the Convention where the vast majority of Baptists rejected the inerrantist approach, the same spirit that brought Southeastern into being in 1951 expressed itself anew in the states of Virginia, North Carolina, and Maryland as well as in large parts of the states of South Carolina and Georgia. Fundamentalism has always been a disruptive burden in Southern Baptist life. Freed from that element the Southeastern heritage is alive, indebted to all those valiant teachers and administrators in Wake Forest, North Carolina, from 1951 through 1989. They provided the bridge to a brighter future with their dogged commitment to freedom.

BIBLIOGRAPHY

Associated Press. "Baptist Seminary Officials Quit; Cite Fundamentalism." *Los Angeles Times*, 24 October 1987, I34.

———. "Seminary Leader to Ride Out Probation." *Los Angeles Times*, 26 December 1992, B5.

Bland, Thomas A., ed. *Servant Songs: Reflections on the History and Mission of Southeastern Baptist Theological Seminary, 1950–1988*. Macon: Smyth and Helwys, 1994.

Cattau, Daniel. "N. Carolina Church Rebuffs Patterson; Ex-Dallas Cleric Agrees to Worship Elsewhere." *Dallas Morning News*, 10 February 1993, 33A.

Committee A on Academic Freedom and Tenure of AAUP. "Academic Freedom and Tenure: Southeastern Baptist Theological Seminary." *Academe* (May–June 1989): 35–45.

"Criswell's President Planning to Leave for Southeastern Post." *Houston Chronicle*, 25 April 1992, 3.

Editorial. *Religious Herald*, 23 May 1963, 10.

Hyer, Marjorie. "Report Assails N.C. Baptist Seminary; Accreditation Study Cites Interference from Fundamentalist-Dominated Board of Trustees." *Washington Post*, 7 January 1989, G12.

McLaughlin, Mike. "Lolley's Resignation Becomes Official at Southeastern." *United Press International*, 17 November 1987.

Niebuhr, Gustav. "Fundamentalists Notch Another Win at Troubled Baptist Seminary." *St. Petersburg Times*, 18 March 1989, 3E.

Ostling, Richard N. "Fundamental Disagreement." *Time*, 13 May 1991, 50.

"Professors without Classrooms." *Religious Herald*, 19 and 26 June 1958, 10.

Religious News Service. "Fundamentalist Shift Succeeds; Seminary President to Hire Only Backers of Inerrancy." *Washington Post*, 19 March 1988, B6.

————. "Patterson Nominated to Head Embattled Baptist Seminary." *St. Petersburg Times*, 25 April 1992, 3E.

"Seminary President Blasts Conservatives in Farewell Meeting." *United Press International*, 16 March 1988.

"Seminary Trustees Pick Dean Over Faculty's Objection." *United Press International*, 15 March 1989.

Smothers, Ronald. "Baptists War Over Hearts and Minds." *New York Times*, 19 October 1987, A18.

"Southeastern Seminary on 'Warning.' " *Los Angeles Times*, 6 January 1990, F15.

Turner, Darrell. "Faculty Reported Fleeing Southern Baptist School." *St. Petersburg Times*, 3 August 1991, 3E.

Woodward, Kenneth L., with Joe Contreras. "The Battling Baptists." *Newsweek*, 22 June 1981, 88.

Robert S. Alley

Frank Stagg
(1911–   )

For two days in April 1956, the instruction committee of the Board of Trustees of New Orleans Baptist Theological Seminary questioned Frank Stagg, who was professor of New Testament and Greek at the Seminary, in order to determine whether or not to dismiss him from his faculty position because of his theological views.

Frank Stagg is a native of Louisiana and a member of one of the first French families who accepted the Baptist message. Frank's grandfather, Etienne Stagg, became a Baptist in about 1870; one of the Baptist associations of Louisiana is named for Etienne's brother, Adolphe Stagg.

Frank Stagg was born in 1911 and graduated from Louisiana College, the only Baptist college in the state, in 1934. He and his wife Evelyn Owen Stagg moved to Louisville, Kentucky, the following year to attend Southern Baptist Theological Seminary.* He received a Ph.D. degree from that institution, and in 1941, he assumed the pastorate of the First Baptist Church of DeRidder, Louisiana. On 1 January 1945, he joined the faculty of the Baptist Bible Institute in New Orleans, later renamed New Orleans Baptist Theological Seminary.

When Stagg arrived at the Seminary, that institution had experienced no theological controversies, but soon after he arrived, several changes occurred in the Seminary. For example, in 1946 Helen E. Falls began teaching missions, one of the first women in America to teach in a graduate school of theology. Shortly thereafter, women students were admitted for the first time to study for a degree in the school of theology. In 1951, along with the other Southern Baptist seminaries, New Orleans began to admit black students. Frank Stagg had been one of the most vocal of the Seminary faculty members concerning racial justice. In fact, one of Stagg's most vigorous critics expressed appreciation for Stagg's "desire for social justice."

Also in 1951, Frank Stagg read a paper on the atoning work of Christ to a group of ministers in South Carolina. The paper, entitled "The Cross— A Rationale," was well received, and Stagg prepared mimeographed copies for many persons who expressed an interest in it. Among its admirers was the president of the Seminary, Roland Q. Leavell, who told the Seminary faculty that it was the finest thing he had ever read on the subject. However, others began to express reservations concerning Stagg's view of the Atonement.

In 1953–1954, Stagg was on sabbatical leave at Edinburgh, where he developed a deepened appreciation for the work of John Baillie. In 1955, Stagg's commentary on Acts was published; it was entitled *The Book of Acts: The Early Struggle for an Unhindered Gospel*. In it, Stagg drew parallels between the struggle of early Jewish Christians to accept Gentiles as equal members of the church and the struggle of white American Christians to accept black Christians as equal members of the church. He wrote, "To be preoccupied with [the geographical factor in Acts] is to miss a greater one—the very one which Luke seemed most concerned to present. The boundaries most difficult to cross—then as now—were religious, national, and racial, not geographical. *It is easier today to send missionaries to Africa than to have fellowship across racial lines at home*" (Stagg, *The Book of Acts*, 36).

In early March 1956, four doctoral students at New Orleans Baptist Theological Seminary wrote to President Leavell to inform him that they believed that Frank Stagg was teaching things that were inconsistent with the doctrinal guidelines of the Seminary, known as the Articles of Religious Belief. Apparently, their action provided an incentive for the Trustees to review Stagg's theology. Over the next few weeks, dozens of letters concerning Stagg's theology were solicited—it is not known who solicited them—from students and also from persons outside the Seminary. These letters were received by President Leavell; they were typed up in his office; each page of the typed copies was marked "Strictly Confidential"; all names were omitted from the typed copies; the typed copies were distributed both to Stagg and to members of the Board of Trustees. Some of the letters contained a defense of Stagg and his theology; most contained criticisms of his theology. The letters make it clear that a coordinated effort had been made to get information concerning Stagg's views.

The accusations in these letters were the focus of the two-day meeting in April in which Frank Stagg replied to questions put to him by members of the instruction committee of the Trustees. President Leavell was present during the proceedings, which took place at a hotel in New Orleans.

In the months leading up to his meeting with the Trustees, Stagg and his family were filled with misgivings. In fact, the Staggs were so sure that Frank would be fired that Evelyn Stagg enrolled in Tulane University (she was already a graduate of Louisiana College and of Southern Baptist Theological Seminary, and she had begun graduate studies at Northwestern University in Illinois before her marriage to Frank) in order to qualify as a teacher, Evelyn wanted to be in a position to support her family so that Frank could return to school to prepare to enter some vocation other than theological education.

The Trustees seem to have been divided into four groups. One group was committed to Stagg and his ideas. A second group was friendly to Stagg but pressed him repeatedly concerning his views. A third group was undecided about Stagg's theology but was convinced by factors other than Stagg's defense of himself. A fourth group urged Stagg simply to tell the other Trustees what they wanted to hear.

No minutes of the Trustee investigation have survived, but some idea of the scope of issues discussed may be gained from the letters that were the focus of the investigation. Six issues were mentioned in the letters.

First, there was the issue of whether Stagg's view of the Scriptures was acceptable. In particular, he seemed to value the New Testament more than the Old, and he emphasized the human element as well as the divine element in the Scriptures. Stagg felt that these positions constituted a positive hermeneutic; his critics felt that they constituted a rejection of the inspiration and infallibility of the Scriptures.

Second, there was the issue of the Trinity. Although Stagg clearly affirmed the deity of Christ and routinely referred to the Father, the Son, and the Spirit, he also pointed out that there is no doctrine of the Trinity in the Bible. He felt that his position was a biblical one; his critics felt that he was rejecting the traditional Trinitarian understanding of God in favor of modalism.

Third, there was the issue of the work of Christ. Stagg rejected an understanding of the work of Christ that he described as "transactional." By that term he meant understandings of the Atonement that were objective and that called people to believe but failed to call them to take up the cross and follow Christ. Stagg thought that his position was true to the New Testament; his critics thought that he was rejecting part of the New Testament teaching that was also an important part of the theological heritage of Baptists.

Fourth, there was the issue of the wrath of God. Stagg emphasized that God's wrath is the inevitable consequence of sin, not a vindictive response God makes to sinners. Stagg felt that he was affirming the teaching of passages such as Romans 1 and Galatians 6:7; his critics felt that he was denying the teaching of passages that speak of God as judge.

Fifth, there was the issue of demons. Stagg affirmed the reality of demons, but he did so in such a way as not to exonerate human beings of their own guilt and sin. Stagg believed that his interpretation of demons was warranted; his critics felt that Stagg's interpretation was too psychological in character.

Sixth and finally, there was the issue of the interpretation of individual passages in the Bible. A good example of this was Numbers 15:32–36, which tells the story of the Israelites' stoning a man who had picked up sticks on the Sabbath. Stagg felt that Jesus rejected such violence, and he said that no one today really believes that it was God's will for the man to be stoned, since no one today is prepared to stone anyone for such conduct; Stagg's critics felt that Stagg was rejecting the clear teaching of the passage.

After the meeting, the Trustees of the Seminary voted unanimously not to dismiss Stagg from the Seminary faculty. For his part, Stagg agreed to provide a clarification of his theology for the Seminary at one of its chapel services, which he soon did.

Stagg continued as a faculty member at the New Orleans Seminary until, in 1964, he accepted an invitation to become the James Buchanan Harrison Professor of New Testament Interpretation at his alma mater, Southern Baptist Theological Seminary.

The story of Stagg's trial for heresy has an unusual sequel. A few months after the trial, Stagg was visiting President Leavell (Leavell and Stagg remained warm friends until Leavell's death), and Leavell charged Stagg with having been arrested for drunk or reckless driving early in 1956, that is, before the heresy trial. Stagg was astonished, as no such thing had ever happened, and Leavell immediately recognized his error. The story that emerged is as strange as it is fascinating.

An assistant city attorney in New Orleans, Grady Durham, was a Baptist; his father and Stagg's father-in-law were close friends. Sometime early in 1956, Durham had visited a wealthy Trustee of the Seminary, O. J. Farnsworth, and told him that a client had been arrested for drunk or reckless driving in north Louisiana. He then asked Farnsworth to give him (Durham) $2,000 to pay the client's bail. When Farnsworth pressed Durham about who the client was, Durham said that it was Frank Stagg and pledged Farnsworth to secrecy in order, he said, to protect Stagg. Farnsworth then gave Durham the money. Farnsworth related this story to President Leavell and to at least one member of the faculty, but no one had said a word to Stagg about it.

Although it is impossible to be certain, it seems likely that this story, which so slanders the character of Frank Stagg, was on the minds of President Leavell and also of at least one of the Trustees who met with Stagg in April 1956.

In any case, the story was quite untrue, as Leavell learned by bringing Durham and Farnsworth together. Subsequent events in Durham's life suggest that he fabricated the story in order to get the money, for in a story in *The Times-Picayune* of New Orleans dated 1 July 1961, it was reported that Durham had been missing for two weeks, that he was accused of theft, and that Mrs. Durham had asked the Orleans Parish coroner's office to locate her husband and to hold him at Charity Hospital for a mental examination.

Frank Stagg's theology is no secret. He is a prolific author and a forceful speaker. In more than a dozen books and numerous other writings, Stagg has presented his understanding of the New Testament message. In Stagg's theology, the center of gravity is the life and teachings of Jesus. Although Stagg does not like human creeds or confessions, he could with justice claim to have followed consistently a principle offered in the "Baptist Faith and Message," a confessional statement adopted by the Southern Baptist Convention in 1963. That document states: "The criterion by which the Bible is to be interpreted is Jesus Christ."

From the publication of his commentary on Acts in 1955 until his retirement from Southern Baptist Theological Seminary in 1982 and beyond, Stagg was one of the most influential Bible scholars in the Southern Baptist Convention, and his influence continues through his books and through the writing, lecturing, and preaching that he is doing in his very active retirement. Probably his most influential book has been *New Testament Theology* (1962); another very influential book was *The Doctrine of Christ* (1984), which was written to be used as a study book in Southern Baptist Churches and which brought great honor (and no criticism) to its author.

BIBLIOGRAPHY

Sloan, Robert. "Frank Stagg." In *Baptist Theologians*, edited by Timothy George and David S. Dockery. Nashville: Broadman Press, 1990.

Stagg, Frank. *The Book of Acts: The Early Struggle for an Unhindered Gospel.* Nashville: Broadman Press, 1955.

———. *The Doctrine of Christ.* Nashville: Convention Press, 1984.

———. *New Testament Theology.* Nashville: Broadman Press, 1962.

St. Amant, Penrose. "A Continuing Pilgrimage: A Biographical Sketch of Frank Stagg." In *The Theological Educator.* New Orleans: New Orleans Baptist Theological Seminary, 1977.

Tolbert, Malcolm. "Frank Stagg: Teaching Prophet." In *Perspectives in Religious Studies.* Macon: Mercer University Press, 1985.

Fisher Humphreys

James J. Strang
(1813–1856)

James Jesse Strang, son of Clement and Abigail Strang, was born on 21 March 1813 near Scipio, New York. The pastoral New York setting of the childhood of James Strang was anything but tranquil. The warnings of William Miller's millennialism, the Fox sisters' rappings, Charles G. Finney's perfectionism, and the mystic séances of Andrew Jackson Davis disturbed and distorted traditional Christian views in nineteenth-century rural America. James, a descendant of persecuted French Huguenots, seemed particularly vulnerable to these religious extremes. Being reared in a superstitious, fear-ridden religious home influenced his beliefs: "From my infancy I have been taught that mankind were totally depraved, and my own observation and experience have demonstrated that the heart of man is an impure fountain from which bitter waters are perpetually flowing" (27 June 1832 from Strang, *Diary*, 21). (James wrote in a journal from age 18 to 23. Of the original handwritten journal, 122 pages are housed in the Western Americana, Coe Collection at the Yale University Library.)

Although quick to observe the depravity in others, his self-assessment was far above his common station. Being the son of a poor farmer, christened by an itinerate Baptist preacher, and less than five feet four and slight of frame did not deflate his sense of superiority. Andrew Jackson's rise to the presidency signaled for James the triumph of the common man. He was determined to catch the tide and lead the way. But the nagging question was, How?

On his nineteenth birthday he penned, "I am 19 years old and am yet no more than a common farmer. 'Tis too bad, I ought to have been a member of Assembly or a Brigadier General before this time if I am ever to rival Caesar or Napoleon which I have sworn to" (21 March 1832, from

Strang, *Diary*, 17). As the 1832–1833 national issues over the Carolinas rocked the nation with rumors of war, James wrote in his diary, "Amidst all the ev[i]ls of the disturbances of our national affairs there is one consolation: that is if our government is overthrown some master spirit may form another. May I be the one. I tremble when I write but it is true" (27 January 1833, from Strang, *Diary*, 32).

His private megalomania did not manifest itself publicly for a decade, although his personal writings reveal his vaulting ambitions. During the decade, he moved from a conservative rural setting to Randolph, New York, where he accepted a teaching position. (Among the four books purchased for his class was a copy of the *Life of Napoleon* for $1.25.) "School teaching does not agree with my health generally," wrote James, "but this winter my labours have been intolerable" (22 February 1833, from Strang, *Diary*, 39). Feeling much dissatisfaction from his employment, on 1 January 1835 he penned, "[A]nother year. . . . [I]t is gone in the way of the world, and passed as others have passed their days who have died in obscurity. Curse me eternally if that be my fate. I know it is in my power to make it otherwise" (50–51).

At the age of 23 James left teaching and was admitted to practice law by the Court of Common Pleas in Chautauqua County, New York. Respect accorded an attorney led to other positions of trust for him—village postmaster, newspaper editor, and temperance lecturer. As his local reputation increased, he became impatient for greater opportunities: "I have spent the day in trying to contrive some plan of obtaining in marriage the heir to the English Crown. It is a difficult business for me, but I shall try if there is the least chance. My mind has always been filled with dreams of royalty and power" (27 May 1832, From Strang, *Diary*, 19). In 1836, James pushed aside his dream and married a commoner, Mary Perce, the 18-year-old daughter of a Baptist clergy, and settled for a respectable lifestyle and even conventional mediocrity. He joined his father-in-law's Baptist Church and for the next seven years was a model, conservative citizen.

Unexpectedly, on 18 July 1843 he loaded his books and his wife and two children into a spring carriage and journeyed to Wisconsin Territory. It was in Racine County, Wisconsin, that he learned of Mormonism. Curious about the new religious movement, James traveled to Nauvoo, Illinois, to meet Joseph Smith, the Mormon Prophet. He was baptized by Smith on Sunday, 25 February 1844, in the baptismal font of the partially finished Nauvoo Temple. He claimed that while being confirmed by Smith, he heard the Prophet pronounce, "Thou shall hold the keys of the Melchizedec Priesthood; shalt walk with Moses, Enoch, and Elijah, and shalt talk with God face to face" (Shepard et al., *James J. Strang*, 254). This promise began to be fulfilled four months later on the day Joseph Smith was killed in Carthage Jail: "And at the same moment in which Joseph was slain," wrote James, "I was visited by an Angel of God, accompanied by a numerous heavenly train, and anointed and ordained to the Prophetic office, as Moses and Joseph had been before me" (246).

For those who doubted his angelic visitation, a letter of appointment purported to be written by Joseph Smith on 18 June 1844, nine days before the martyrdom, stated, "My Dear Son: . . . I have long felt that my present work was almost done." The letter then named James Strang as the Prophet's successor and announced that the new Zion was to be built in Voree, Wisconsin. Voree "being interpreted, garden of peace, for there shall my people have peace and rest and wax fat and pleasant in the presence of their enemies" (251–252).

On 5 August 1844 James read his letter of appointment to an assembled Mormon congregation in Florence, Michigan. The congregation was confused and stunned. After a heated discussion, it was agreed that selected elders should journey to Nauvoo to announce the letter of appointment and the angelic visitation; "meanwhile, those elders who accepted Strang's appointment were to preach it on their own responsibility, while those who doubted were to maintain silence." An uproar ensued in which James forcefully decreed his opponents could not command "whom God had placed at their head." Opposing local church leaders reacted to his shocking claim as the Lord's anointed by "cutting him off" from the church (VanNoord, *King of Beaver Island*, 9).

Unruffled by this court proceeding, James sent his loyal followers to Nauvoo to spread the news of his prophetic succession, while he returned to Wisconsin to begin building his Zion in Voree. After listening to one disciple of Strangism, Brigham wrote, "Is it not surprisingly strange, that Joseph Smith should appoint a man to succeed him in the presidency of the church some seven or ten days before his death, and yet not tell it to the High Council, nor to any of the authorities of the church. . . . If Mr. Strang had received his appointment from Joseph, why did he not come here upon the death of Joseph and take charge of the church, and lead them to Voree? Because his own guilty heart would not let him come near the Furnace of trial. . . . Joseph Smith never wrote or caused to be written Strang's letter of appointment. It is a lie—a forgery—a snare. And let this testimony be had in remembrance before God, and let it stand against him" (Quaife, *The Kingdom*, 23).

The second church court against James Strang was held on 26 August 1844 in Nauvoo with Brigham Young presiding. The published verdict of the proceedings stated:

> Whereas Elder James J. Strang [has] . . . been circulating a "revelation" (falsely called) purporting to have been received by Joseph Smith on the 18th day of June, 1844; and through the influence of which [has] . . . attempted and [is] attempting to establish a stake, called Voree, in Wisconsin Territory, thereby leading the saints astray: therefore, the

said James J. Strang . . . [is] cut off from the church of Jesus Christ of Latter Day Saints, this 26th day of August, 1844. (Riegel, *Crown of Glory*, 44)

As word of the second court proceeding and verdict reached James, he shrugged and disdainfully remarked, "As if a man could be cut off without being tried, or a prophet could be brought under the yoke of the Twelve!" (46). He added, "I am delivered over to the buffetings of Satan, yet when I pray God answers. I lay hands upon the sick and they recover. I can speak in new tongues. . . . Is it not rather strange if God gave such gifts to men who believe not in him and blaspheme his name continually. . . . If I am not what I profess to be, I am of all men most wicked" (VanNoord, *King of Beaver Island*, 9, 11).

With great energy, James hurled a counterattack. He fought the Twelve with polemic weapons and reported revelations, miracles, and angelic visitations that confused and confounded the Mormon membership. Conjecture over his prophetic succession accelerated, and many lay members of the church recorded in journals their troubled opinions: "[H]is letter of appointment carried on its face the marks of a base forgery, being written throughout in printed characters," wrote Jacob Norton (9). Another diarist penned, "The contents of the thing was altogether bombastic, unlike the work of God, and dishonorable to the name of Joseph Smith" (Jacob, *Autobiography*, 10–11).

Despite widespread rejection of Strang's claim, James did not succumb to mounting religious tumult. He sent emissary Reuben Miller to Nauvoo "bearing a warning from Strang to the Twelve that they desist from further iniquitous procedure and present themselves at Voree before April 7 [1845] to undergo trial upon the charges that would be preferred against them" (Quaife, *The Kingdom*, 22). The Twelve were not awed by the summons but were concerned over the impact Strangism was having among the Mormons. One biographer reported that James was Brigham Young's "most feared contender" (Fitzpatrick, *King Strang Story*, 28).

On 24 January 1846 the Twelve addressed a lengthy letter of admonition and warning to church members. In the letter James was described as an "excommunicated member of the church. His pretended revelations and letter from Joseph Smith were characterized as a base and wicked forgery, and their author a wicked liar." The letter concluded, "[I]f any wish to follow . . . J. J. Strang I say let them go; we will cut them off from the church, and let them take their own course for salvation" (Smith, *History*, 7: 574). About 300 or 400 Mormons ignored the warning and gathered at Voree. As promised, James in April 1846 held a formal trial against the Mormon Apostles who had ignored his summons. They were charged with "abolishing the liberty of speech and the press by command and violence; systematically plundering the church of its property for the use of themselves and their favorites; teaching that polygamy, fornication, adultery, and concubinage are lawful and commendable; that lying, to build up the church of God is justifiable, and that secret wickedness will not be brought into judgment, and carrying out these principles in constant practice" (Quaife, *The Kingdom*, 22, 27).

With all due solemnity, James cut off the Twelve and delivered them over to the "buffetings of Satan in the flesh" and cursed them eternally: "May their bones rot in the living tomb of their flesh; may their flesh generate from its own corruptions a loathsome life for others; may their blood swarm with a leprous life of motelike, ghastly corruption feeding on flowing life, generating chilling agues and burning fevers. . . . [M]ay each gratification turn to burning bitterness and glowing shame" (Riegel, *Crown of Glory*, 69).

The reaction of the Twelve to the court, buffetings, and curse was blistering. Elder Orson Hyde spoke of James Strang as leagued with Judas Iscariot and Lucifer. Elder John Taylor denounced him as an "impostor, a false and wicked man." James became so distraught by the critical comments that he demanded a public debate to defend his position. The Mormon Apostles replied, "After Lucifer was cut off and thrust down to hell, we have no knowledge that God ever condescended to investigate the subject or right of authority with him. Your cause has been disposed of by the rightful authorities of the Church. Being satisfied with our own power and calling, we have no disposition to ask from whence yours came." James countered by labeling the Twelve as "rebels against God, sinners crimsoned with the blood of innocents, forgers moved and instigated by their father, the devil, whose God is their belly and their glory is their shame." When called a fraud himself, he queried, "Would I have survived indignation one day if I had perpetrated a fraud?" (Riegel, *Crown of Glory*, 92, 104, 112).

"Strangism is strangled beyond hope," declared Brigham Young, while others of the Twelve reported that Strangism is dead, but that was too optimistic (VanNoord, *King of Beaver Island*, 76). Angels, brass plates, Urim and Thummim, and coronation were yet to come. On 1 September 1845 James proudly acknowledged:

> The angel of the Lord came unto me, . . . he showed unto me the plates of the sealed record, and he gave into my hands the Urim and Thummim, and out of the light came the voice of the Lord saying: . . . Behold the record which was sealed from my servant Joseph, unto thee it is reserved. . . . [T]he angel of the Lord took me away to the hill in the east of Walworth, against White River in Voree, and there he showed unto me the record, buried under an oak tree. . . . It was enclosed in an earthen casement, and buried in the ground as deep as a man's waist. (Shepard et al., *James J. Strang*, 177–78)

As planned, 33-year-old James miraculously retrieved from under the oak tree the case of slightly baked clay, containing three plates of brass. The plates, each about one and one-half by two and three-fourths inches, had etched engravings and were viewed by residents in the community, curious Mormons and infidels. A newspaper reporter exaggerated the level of interest in the plates: "These occurrences waked up the whole country to a high state of excitement, and several thousand persons came to examine the ground and the plates" (189).

James added to the inciting account by writing his first pastoral letter to Mormons residing in Illinois, "I call upon you to assist me. Let not my call to you be vain. . . . Many of you are about to leave the haunts of civilization and of men to go into an unexplored wilderness amongst savages, and in trackless deserts, to seek a home in the wilds where the foot-print of the white man is not found. The voice of God has not called you to this. . . . Let the oppressed flee for safety unto Voree" (Riegel, *Crown of Glory*, 55–56). This type of propaganda increased as James Strang began a newspaper called *The Voree Herald.*

As summoned, a few gullible Mormons gathered to Voree. There James was acknowledged president of the Church of Jesus Christ of Latter-day Saints and translator of the plates of brass, containing the two tablets that were written by the finger of God in the days of Moses.

After a home was built for him by his followers, he succeeded in translating the purported ancient scripture in five days. Examples of the doctrine he introduced follow:

> All the animals, or, at least, all the domestic animals, and many not domesticated, all the superior kinds of animals, and many of the inferior, have a natural language; a language of the passions. (*Book*, 68)

> [O]ver the graves of persecutors and blasphemers, and they who shed the blood of the innocent, and at the places of their abominations shalt thou pile rough stones, with muttered curses, against the day of the resurrection of damnation. And thou shalt teach thy children to add a stone to the pile as they pass by, and to curse him that removes the stones, and cleaves unto their wickedness. (*Book*, 111)

Despite these unconventional teachings, his religious movement grew. The confines of Voree proved too small for the Strangites. To alleviate the housing shortage, James conveniently received a revelation, "I have appointed the Islands of the Great Lake for the gathering of the Saints, saith the Lord God. . . . And I have appointed my servant James the anointed Shepherd of my flock, to apportion unto every one his portion, for a perpetual inheritance" (*Book*, 298). It was on Beaver Island, the largest island in the archipelago, that his grandest childhood wish of becoming a king was realized: "He hath chosen his servant James to be King; . . . above the Kings of the earth; and appointed him King in Zion," saith the Lord (169).

On 8 July 1850 James was crowned king of Zion, king of the Earth, and set upon his throne. Nearly 300 attended his coronation and watched him stroll from the "King's cottage" on the "King's highway" clad in a "flowing, floor-length robe of red flannel, trimmed with white flannel with black specks. Strang held a wooden scepter. On his breast was a large metal star. On his head was a miter ornamented with metal stars." The coronation began with prayer, and then James proudly announced his true identity. He was a Jew, a pure descendant of the House of David, and had inherited the throne of Israel through the lineage of David. After his speech, those gathered shouted, "Long live James, King in Zion!" (VanNoord, *King of Beaver Island*, 106–7).

In royal fashion, he predictably began issuing imperial edicts. "Of all the fruit of your fields, and the increase of your flocks, a tenth shall you render to the house of the Lord your God, and the treasury of the King." For those who failed to give the royal tribute, an additional edict announced, "[T]he King shall take your goods and your substance from you, to recompense what you have defrauded the house of the Lord, and the treasury of the King, with increase. And if ye obstinately defrauded in these things, ye shall be beaten with stripes" (*Book*, 331, 334).

A more centralized autocracy, within the democratic republic of the United States, would be difficult to devise. James, through revelation, had pronounced himself king of the Earth by direct appointment from God. For the support of his reign, a system of tithing, with sweeping provisions for enforcement, stuffed his coffer. Property in the archipelago was apportioned to the saints, referred to as subjects, at his whimsical discretion. With subjects giving homage and royalty stemming from God, James confidently wrote, "I have made my mark upon the times in which I live which the wear and tear of time in the unborn ages shall not be able to obliterate" (Strang, *Diary*, xxx).

Yet the trouble with his unmitigated ambition was that James never arrived at a plateau worthy of his sojourn. On 2 November 1852 he pronounced himself a candidate for the state assembly from Newaygo district, a district comprising over 20 counties, consisting of one fourth of the state of Michigan. He was elected to office and reelected in 1854, almost without opposition. In writing to his brother after the landslide election, he boldly confessed, "Frankly, brother, I intend to rule this country; and it will be a hard struggle if I do not make myself one of the judges of the Supreme Court within one year" (VanNoord, *King of Beaver Island*, 180).

The one blind spot in his vision of absolute domain was his faith in his own invulnerability. He never seriously considered the rising discontent or rebellion of his subjects. Assassination was not in his plans. Yet James Strang was shot on 9 July 1856 in the head, the back, and the right eye, then beaten with a pistol in full view of several men at a general store on Beaver Island and the crew of a nearby government boat anchored in the harbor. None of the witnesses made any attempt to stop the brutality.

James lived for 11 days after the attempted assassination. His removal from the island to Voree, to be with extended family members, rendered him little relief. In character until his last breath, he refused to admit defeat and relinquish his ordination or crown to another. When asked by a loyal follower to name a successor, he deliberately refused, stating, "I do not want to talk about it" (Quaife, *The Kingdom*, 180). James Strang was buried at Voree in an unmarked grave.

CONCLUSION

Failure to name a successor did "strangle Strangism," as Brigham Young had predicted. The majority of his loyal followers soon scattered, and his claims of revelation and scripture seemed for not. Yet today 120 Strangites still profess that James J. Strang was a prophet and the king of the Earth. They believe that to judge James by the failure of his disciples to perpetuate his teachings widely would be folly. They continue, "[A]ll the prophets that ever stood on the earth and spoke in the name of God, are all rejected and their works and revelations and testimonies are become of no moment to mankind; for many prophets have been slain in the past, and their flocks were scattered and led into bondage" (Shepard et al., *James J. Strang*, 185). For these few believers in the 1990s, James Strang no more failed in his ministry than John the Baptist, Elijah, or Elisha.

Although this argument has validity when speaking of the ancient prophets and their disciples, in the case of James Strang, it is unconvincing. His own writings reveal early in life his disturbing, possibly pathological megalomania. External evidence supports contemporary claims that James was a forger, liar, and deceiver. His claims of divine intervention were absurd in the extreme. His curious mark in history is but a footnote today in the annals of Mormonism.

SELECTED BIBLIOGRAPHY

The Book of the Law of the Lord, Consisting of an Inspired Translation of Some of the Most Important Parts of the Law Given to Moses, and a Very Few Additional Commandments, with Notes and References. St. James, MI: Royal Press, 1948.

Fitzpatrick, Doyle C. *The King Strang Story, a Vindication of James J. Strang, the Beaver Island Mormon King.* Lansing, MI: National Heritage, 1970.

Jacob, Norton. *The Life of Norton Jacob.* Provo, UT: Harold B. Lee Library, Special Collections, Brigham Young University, 1937. (Typescript).

Quaife, Milo M. *The Kingdom of Saint James, a Narrative of the Mormons.* New Haven, CT: Yale University Press, 1935.

Riegel, O. W. *Crown of Glory: The Life of James A. Strang, Moses of the Mormons.* New Haven, CT: Yale University Press, 1935.

Shepard, William, Donna Falk, and Thelma Lewis, comps. and eds. *James J. Strang: Teaching of a Mormon Prophet.* Burlington, WI: Church of Jesus Christ of Latter-day Saints (Strangite), 1977.

Smith, Joseph, Jr. *History of the Church of Jesus Christ of Latter-day Saints.* 7 vols. Salt Lake City: Deseret Book Company, 1976.

Strang, Mark A. *The Diary of James J. Strang—Deciphered, Transcribed, Introduced and Annotated.* Ann Arbor: Michigan State University Press, 1961.

VanNoord, Roger. *King of Beaver Island, the Life and Assassination of James Jesse Strang.* Urbana: University of Illinois Press, 1988.

Susan Easton Black

Julian M. Sturtevant
(1805–1886)

Julian Monson Sturtevant was born on 26 July 1805 in the farming community of Warren in Litchfield County, Connecticut. A direct descendant of Samuel Sturtevant, who arrived at Plymouth Colony in 1642, Julian's heritage was of solid New England Protestant stock: hardworking, pietistic, and literate. Under the influence of Dr. Lyman Beecher* of Litchfield, Sturtevant early in his life became devoutly religious, schooled in the Calvinism of the Shorter Catechism and the Congregationalism of his native New England. He was accepted as a communing member of the Warren Congregational Church at the age of nine upon a statement of faith (the kind of "personal relation" typical of Reformed churches and New England Puritanism). This particular congregation, however, was markedly anti-creedal, giving the young Julian a sense of individualism and universalism that would mark his faith and ministry throughout his life.

Due to economic disasters throughout the Connecticut Valley caused by the Napoleonic Wars and the War of 1812, many farmers were forced to emigrate to the Western Reserve, and the Sturtevants were no exception, moving to Tallmadge, Ohio, in 1816. Julian entered the academy at Tallmadge in 1817, studying Latin and Greek in preparation for entrance to Yale in 1822. In 1825, to help alleviate the financial strain of attending college, he briefly withdrew from Yale and became headmaster at the academy in New Canaan, Connecticut, eventually graduating from Yale in the spring of 1826. While at New Canaan, he met his future wife, Elizabeth Maria Fayerweather, and continued to court her after his return to Yale. In October of 1827 he entered Yale Seminary under the tutelage of Nathaniel W. Taylor.

While at Yale, Sturtevant participated in the "Society of Inquiry," a meeting of seminarians at which papers were read primarily concerning home and foreign missions. In December 1828 a group of seminarians led by Theron Baldwin, Mason Grosvenor, Asa Turner, Jr., Sturtevant, and others formed an association for the purpose of cooperating in a mission work in a frontier state or territory likely to become a state. Their aim was to establish an institution of higher learning that would assist all the evangelical churches in the region. They decided to cast their lot with the work begun by the Rev. John M. Ellis of the American Home Missionary Society (at that time the home mission arm of the Congregational, Presbyterian, and Dutch Reformed Churches of New England and the Middle Atlantic states) in Jacksonville, Illinois, becoming known thereafter as "the Illinois Band" from Yale. By moving to Illinois as a "band," they hoped to "secure cooperation" among the Christian groups already there and to avoid what Sturtevant described as "that peculiar isolation which is among the greatest disadvantages of a home missionary on the borders of the wilderness" (Sturtevant, *An Autobiography*, 136; hereafter *AY*). On 21 February 1829, they signed a "compact" at Yale outlining their proposed mission:

> Believing in the entire alienation of the natural heart from God, in the necessity of the influences of the Holy Spirit for its renovation, and that these influences are not to be expected without the use of means; deeply impressed also with the destitute condition of the western section of our country and the urgent claims of its inhabitants upon the benevolent at the East . . . and believing that evangelical religion and education must go hand in hand in order to the successful accomplishment of this desirable object; we the undersigned hereby express our readiness to go to the State of Illinois for the purpose of establishing a Seminary of learning such as shall be best adapted to the exigencies of that country—a part of us to engage in instruction in the Seminary—the others to occupy—as preachers—important stations in the surrounding country. (*AY*, 138–139)

In September 1829, Sturtevant, now an ordained Congregationalist minister, and his new bride left Connecticut to begin a 56-year ministry at Illinois College in Jacksonville, Illinois. The college commenced operations on 4 January 1830, with Sturtevant as head administrator and professor of mathematics, natural philosophy, and astronomy. In autumn 1830 the Rev. Edward Beecher,* pastor of Park Street Church in Boston and the son of Lyman Beecher, accepted the position as president of Illinois College, commencing his duties in January 1832. Sturtevant would eventually succeed Beecher as president in 1844, a position he retained until 1876.

Sturtevant was not long in Illinois before he was confronted by what for him would be "the most distressing and perplexing problem" of his ministry—a sharp sectarianism among the various Christian groups present in Jacksonville combined with a latent distrust of a learned clergy. Obvious differences existed between "the Band" from New Haven and the frontier Methodists led by the likes of Peter Cartwright, whose sermon before Sturtevant and the others in the "shared" assembly hall in Jacksonville in December 1829 attacked both Calvinism and intellectualism. Cartwright boasted that he had "never spent four years in rubbing [his] back against the walls of a college" (*AY*, 162). Nor did the "revivalist" spirit of the local Cumberland Presbyterians incline its followers toward an appreciation of the culture and intellectual stimulation proffered by Sturtevant and the new Illinois College. The ecumenical spirit of cooperation Sturtevant had absorbed at New Haven was now beset by hatred, on the one hand, and "a shower of emptiness and stupidity," on the other. He now found himself in a "realm of confusion and religious anarchy" where "every man's hand was against his brother" (*AY*, 163). "Those were crude times," he writes in his *Autobiography*,

> and the introduction of New England ideas of education and theology in a community largely southern in its opinions and prejudices, and accustomed to an uneducated ministry, could not have been accomplished without some pretty sharp conflicts. . . . In Illinois I met for the first time a divided Christian community, and was plunged without warning or preparation into a sea of sectarian rivalries which was kept in constant agitation, not only by real differences of opinion, but by ill-judged discussions and unfortunate personalities among ambitious men. (*AY*, 160–161)

Yet even within the very denomination and missionary organization from which he had been sent, "sectarian rivalries" and "ambitious men" were present. Much division occurred in the 1820s and 1830s within the Presbyterian Church throughout the Frontier West and south of Hudson River Valley between those who favored the teachings of Sturtevant's mentor at Yale, Dr. Nathaniel Taylor (the leader of the New Haven Theology that had much preponderance among Congregationalists and Presbyterians in New England), and those who still held closely to the church of John Knox and the teaching of John Calvin and Jonathan Edwards (the Old School Presbyterians). The former group consisted largely of transplanted New Englanders of Congregationalist origin (like Sturtevant) who had been absorbed into the Presbyterian Church by the "Plan of Union" proposed by Jonathan Edwards the Younger and negotiated between the General Assembly of Philadelphia (Presbyterian) and the General Association of Connecticut (Congregationalist) in 1801. The Plan declared that all missionaries to the frontier states were "to promote mutual forbearance, and a spirit of accommodation" among members of both churches. Although the original intent of the Plan was designed to maintain equality between the churches, the aggressiveness of the Presbyterian Church as it moved west (dominated as it was by the Old School) and the meekness of the Congregationalists themselves (many of whom came to believe that the Presbyterian form of church government might be more advantageous to missionary activity in the frontier states) created a situation that effectively limited the spread of Congregationalism in the western states. The Old School Presbyterians, convinced that matters of church government were part of divine law and hence articles of faith, had never been receptive to what they considered a blasphemous and clearly deformed Plan of Union. Keenly distrustful of most religious ideas imported from New England, they feared that the evangelical awakening occurring in New England and exemplified by the Illinois Band from Yale would only increase the influence of the New England party over their own. Thus, efforts were soon under way to "arrest the progress" of Sturtevant's group and "strengthen the bands of ecclesiasticism" (AY, 183) within the Presbytery of central Illinois.

The American Home Missionary Society, headquartered in New York City and under whose authority Sturtevant and the group at Jacksonville had been commissioned, reflected the New England plan of union and cooperation. Those who sought a more rigid Presbyterian ecclesiastical control worked through the Presbyterian General Assembly's Board of Missions in Philadelphia. Sturtevant became more and more convinced that these two groups "could not co-exist . . . without unceasing strife" (AY, 187). Yet Sturtevant, like most of those associated with the New School, was so committed to the Plan of Union that he resisted the initial formation of a Congregational Church in Jacksonville in 1832, convinced for the moment that the original compact between the General Assembly of the Presbyterian Church and the General Association of Connecticut intended for Congregationalism to remain in New England, with the territory west and south of the Hudson, "even to the going down of the sun," reserved for the Presbyterians. Within a short time he would realize how such a view of the "compact" weakened both his ability to find some means of relief from the tension within the Presbyterian Church in Illinois at that time and the future of Congregationalism as a viable alternative to frontier sectarianism.

The tension between the conservative Old School ministers and the more "liberal" New Schoolmen increased dramatically in early 1833, led by the efforts of the Rev. William J. Fraser. Fraser had been commissioned by the General Assembly's Board of Missions in 1827 and joined the Illinois Presbytery in 1831, pastoring several churches close to Jacksonville. As a Board of Missions man, he was naturally suspicious of the missionary efforts of the American Home Missionary Society in Illinois; he was equally opposed to any effort on their part in promoting New School theology on the frontier. A "very unscrupulous man," Sturtevant once noted (AY, 183), in February 1833 Fraser harbored four ministerial students in his home who had been dismissed from Illinois College. He assisted them in criticizing the school in the *Illinois Herald*, an action that produced two consequences: Charges of heresy were placed against President Beecher, Sturtevant, and the Rev. William Kirby, a fellow teacher at the college, who then placed a countercharge of slander against Fraser. On 28 March 1833, the regular annual meeting of the Illinois Presbytery convened oddly enough in Fraser's home, at which time Fraser was to be tried for slander and the other three men for heresy. Fraser was found guilty and suspended from the ministry until he could demonstrate true repentance. His charges against Sturtevant and the others, however, for "*carving* and *dissecting* the *old doctrines and discipline* of the Church" (Fraser, *Facts*, 6–7) remained before the Presbytery.

Sturtevant has little to say about the trial in his *Autobiography*, describing it as a "great annoyance" that "shocked [his] tastes and humiliated and disgusted [him]" (*AY*, 199), for he was convinced that no "human tribunal" had a right to try him for his "religious opinions" (199). The charges against the men were twofold: that they held "doctrines contrary to the standards of the Presbyterian Church" and that they held "doctrines contrary to the Word of God" (199). Sturtevant offered no defense to the first charge, for he admitted that he had never formed his opinions "with reference to the standard of the Presbyterian Church" (199) and that he never would. "I stated that I had never given my assent to those standards, and that I did not intend to do so. Whether I was constitutionally a minister of the Presbyterian Church or not, I left it for them to decide, I myself having nothing to say on the subject" (199–200).

Sturtevant had arrived in Illinois, he said, with "absolutely no opinions about church government" (169). His basic position was always a Congregationalist one. Admission to the church was based on the evidence of one's Christian character, not adherence to a creed; in matters of discipline, liberty of conscience must be allowed in all areas not essential to the Christian faith and among which believers held differing opinions. This, he believed, would eliminate excessive dogmatism and contentious sectarianism. This position was immediately put to trial in Illinois, for shortly after arriving there he was faced with the reality of joining the Presbyterian Church, as previously agreed upon by the Band and the American Home Missionary Society. His initial understanding, as an ordained Congregationalist minister, was that he would be immediately received into the Presbyterian Church in Jacksonville without question, but that was not the case. He found that the Illinois Presbytery requested that he "accept the Confession of Faith and the Catechisms of the Presbyterian Church as containing the system of doctrine taught in the Holy Scriptures" and that he "approve of the government and discipline of the Presbyterian Church in the United States" (*AY*, 170). He was not prepared, or even of a mind, to give his full assent to the statement that the Westminster Confession contained "the system of doctrine taught in the Holy Scriptures"; to do so would have been a violation of his conscience, he contended. His friends, however, advised him to assent, even with reservations, accepting the Confession only "for substance of doctrine" but not in every particular. To Sturtevant, such a compromise was "an indefensible violation of good faith" (171). He was convinced that "he who publicly commits himself to a form of words which he does not in his heart believe, wrongs himself and the community in which he seeks to exert an influence. . . . Few errors can be more harmful than the insincerity involved in a solemn utterance made with a mental reservation" (206). Since refusal on this issue would have ended his mission in Illinois, he had little choice but to agree with the Presbytery on the Confession, not point by point but "for substance of doctrine" only. He did so and, ironically, opened the door whereby the heresy trial was made possible.

The second charge, that he held "doctrines contrary to the Word of God," stemmed directly from the first. Since Sturtevant could not assent completely to the entire Westminster Confession as equivalent to biblical doctrine, then it was believed that he must be teaching something contrary to the Confession and hence contrary to the Bible. What some of the ministers were convinced of was that Sturtevant and others were spreading not only Congregationalism within the Presbytery but also "Taylorism," or New Haven Theology. Nathaniel Taylor had broken with the generally accepted theological position held by New England Congregationalism (as well as that of the Presbyterian Churches in the West and South)—a theology originating with Augustine, codified by John Calvin, and institutionalized in eighteenth-century America by Jonathan Edwards, Joseph Bellamy, Samuel Hopkins, Timothy Dwight, and others. His primary point of departure concerned the freedom of the will. What to Edwards was a mere "illusion," simply a name for that aspect of human volition that always pursues the strongest motive, was to Taylor a very real ability on the part of all men to choose among various motives. Human beings have the power to choose because they are not born totally depraved (the beginning point of the Calvinist TULIP [Total depravity, Unconditional election, Limited attonement, Irresistible grace, and Perseverance of the Saints]); they are simply born with certain sinful inclinations. Sin was not the result of a sinful *nature* (original sin) but of certain sinful *acts* all men commit. These acts are not causally necessary, but they are inevitable, even though man, as a free, rational, and moral entity, has the "power to the contrary," as Taylor would put it. To turn men away from sin and toward God, one needed only to appeal to man's natural desire for happiness, which Taylor equated with "self-love," a love that would ultimately become in the mind and life of the regenerate man an unselfish love of God. As Sturtevant put it in his *Autobiography*, "The selfish man is the man who is determined to secure his own happiness without regard to the welfare of others; while the benevolent man is he who deliberately determines to seek his own highest good by promoting the greatest good of the whole" (*AY*, 127). This was essentially a reversal of the emphases of Calvinism upon man's inability to effect spiritual good apart from a preordained supernatural work of God. In fact, to the Old School Presbyterians, this was at best Arminianism, at worst Pelagianism, and they would have none of it.

> Sturtevant acknowledged his debt to Taylor without apology, claiming that no other mind [had] exerted so great an influence on my thinking as his. He did not teach us to follow his instructions blindly, or to accept anything upon his authority, but cultivated in us the habit of self-reliance. He had arrested my attention, awakened my enthusiasm, and impressed his system indelibly upon my mind. His teachings became the starting point, not the end of my religious thinking, and they greatly assisted me in constructing the theologic house in which I have since lived. (*AY*, 131)

What Sturtevant and the others in the Band had brought to central Illinois was not Pelagianism but an ecumenical spirit of cooperation and a belief in the human capacity for benevolence that stood in stark contrast to the rabid sectarianism and dogmatic Old School Calvinism of the frontier. In this, Sturtevant was convinced he and his coworkers had been "misjudged":

> We were not propagandists of Taylorism or of anything else save the Gospel of Christ. We were not seeking to gain an influence in the Presbyterian Church. Our only purpose was to do an earnest and honest work in laying foundations for the kingdom of God. Most of us had then no thought of ever organizing Congregational churches in Illinois. We had no fear that Presbyterians would oppose such plans as ours. On the contrary we took it for granted that we should have their sympathy and help. (*AY*, 183)

Sturtevant, of course, pled "not guilty" to the second charge and defended himself by attacking the theology of his prosecutor, Rev. Fraser, rather than appealing to Taylorism. One such point of contention was the Atonement. To Sturtevant, the Old School position needed amending:

> It has long seemed to me a great defect in our theology that we seem to assume that a moral governor may rightly administer his government by mere rewards and punishments without a proper remedial system. There is nothing either in the Scriptures or outside of them to justify such an assumption. The authority of any moral governor over his subjects depends on the confidence which he inspires that his whole heart and character are in harmony with a righteous law. It is quite as necessary in order to such confidence that he should devise and carry into execution appropriate measures for reforming the fallen as that he

> should show his displeasure against the incorrigibly guilty. The idea of a government administered over a race of fallen subjects, propagated through unnumbered generations and yet not hopelessly beyond the reach of reform, without any reformatory system is to my mind utterly revolting. A government so administered cannot inspire the confidence of its subjects in the perfect rectitude of the governor. (*AY*, 129)

What was to Sturtevant a defense of God's benevolence was to men like Fraser a defense of man's ability to reform himself according to his desire for self-love and happiness. Given the nature of their differences, it is not surprising that after Sturtevant's "attack" the good reverend "broke out, as I expected he would, in a storm of angry passion which so revealed his own character and spirit as to render a long defense on my part unnecessary" (*AY*, 200). By an overwhelming majority, the Presbytery voted the men "not guilty."

Fraser was not content by any means with such a vote and, accordingly, took the matter by way of appeal to the Synod, which was to meet the following October. Neither Beecher nor Sturtevant attended these hearings, but for whatever reason, the cases were not prosecuted before the Synod. Sturtevant believed that if they had been tried for heresy before the Synod, the vote would have gone against them, which would have forced them to defend themselves before the General Assembly in Philadelphia. In Jacksonville, however, the forces opposed to the College had been greatly chastened for the moment.

Sturtevant, despite his overt Congregationalism, would retain his connection to the Presbyterian Church throughout most of his career in Illinois. He made it clear, however, that he was not at heart a Presbyterian. "I came among you as a Congregationalist," he told them, "and as such I have continued with you. My connection here is fraternal rather than ecclesiastical" (*AY*, 273). He expressed these views most eloquently in his pamphlet "The Unsectarian Character of Congregationalism" in 1855 (an enlarged version appeared in 1880 as *The Keys of Sect*). This was his overriding concern throughout his 56 years of ministry in Illinois. As he wrote to Mrs. Theron Baldwin in 1885:

> I mourn that our Congregationalism is still to a very great extent unconscious of its strength and knows not the function which God hath raised it up to perform. It tries me that many consider it only almost as good as other sects, especially as Presbyterianism, instead of recognizing it as God's own instrumentality for breaking all the bands of sect and fusing the whole Christian brotherhood into that spiritual kingdom which the Son of Man came to establish. . . . Sect is too mean and hateful a thing to last forever under the government of God. (*AY*, 339)

BIBLIOGRAPHY

Barton, C. E. *The Founders and Founding of Illinois College.* Jacksonville, IL: John K. Long, 1902.

Fraser, William J. *Facts, in Reference to the Suspension of the Rev. W. J. Fraser, from the Office of the Gospel Ministry.* Jacksonville, IL, 1833.

Hedrick, Travis Keene, Jr. "Julian Monson Sturtevant and the Moral Machinery of Society: The New England Struggle against Pluralism in the Old Northwest, 1829–1877." Ph.D. diss., Brown University, 1974.

Heinl, Frank. "Jacksonville and Morgan County: An Historical Review." *Journal of the Illinois State Historical Society* 18 (1926): 5–38.

Norton, A. T. *History of the Presbyterian Church in the State of Illinois.* St. Louis: W. S. Bryan, 1879.

Rammalkamp, Charles H. "Fundamentalism and Modernism in a Pioneer College." *Journal of the Illinois State Historical Society* 20 (1928): 395–408.

Sturtevant, Julian Monson. *An Autobiography.* Edited by J. M. Sturtevant, Jr. New York: Fleming H. Revell, 1885.

Timothy David Whelan

David Swing
(1830–1894)

Chicago between the Civil War and the Great Fire exuded energy and optimism. Not yet the big-shouldered city of Carl Sandburg's vision, Chicago
toddled through the 1870s. It grew rapidly but clung firmly to much of its
robust, if rustic, past. Chicagoans often found themselves pulled between
two worlds. One, the world of progress, change, and complexity, appealed
to those who foresaw a great destiny for the city by the lake. The other,
the world of pastoral simplicity and eternal verities, appealed to those who
foresaw greatness for the city only if it retained its commitments to those
eternal verities.

Two ambitious men drawn into the maelstrom that was Chicago in the
1870s contended earnestly for those competing views. The one, Francis
Landey Patton, hoped to make Chicago safe for Presbyterian truth. The
other, David Swing, wanted to ensure the continuing relevance of Presbyterianism in a progressive city. The competing visions of those two men
resulted in a sensational trial when Patton accused Swing of heresy. While
the trial immediately involved Presbyterian doctrine and polity, its implications for the rapidly changing religious climate in the United States must
not be overlooked.

That a heresy trial in a particular denomination not involving some sensational sexual or financial scandal commanded national attention casts
light upon the social structure of the United States in the nineteenth century.
The trial of David Swing captured such national attention. The newspapers
of the major northeastern cities sent reporters to Chicago who provided
dispatches detailing the charges, the specifications, the testimony, and such
other pertinent data as they could. Quite literally, reporters sought all the
news that was fit to print. Swing's trial compelled attention because it was,

as William R. Hutchison put it, "of signal importance in announcing and augmenting the presence of modernist ideas within the evangelical churches" (Hutchison, *Modernist Impulse*, 48). In short, Swing's trial marked a preliminary skirmish in the war eventually labeled "the fundamentalist-modernist controversy."

Patton received his theological training at the nineteenth-century bastion of Presbyterian orthodoxy, Princeton Theological Seminary. Patton learned from Charles Hodge that the truth once received superseded any innovation or rethinking that might be entertained. For Patton the Westminster Confession was a nonnegotiable compendium of biblically ordained truth.

David Swing received a different sort of education. Swing learned the value of human creativity. He received training in classical studies at Miami University in Oxford, Ohio, near his boyhood home in Cincinnati. After his schooling at Miami, he studied theology at Lyman Beecher's* Lane Theological Seminary* in Cincinnati. After a stint as a teacher in classical studies at Miami, during which time he occasionally preached at local churches, he accepted a call to preach in 1866 at Westminster Presbyterian Church in Chicago. Three years later, Westminster merged with North Presbyterian to form Fourth Presbyterian Church.

Swing quickly gained a reputation as a riveting "poet-preacher." He displayed his erudition in his sermons, extolling the creative power of human beings as evidence of the great goodness of God. Another evidence of God's great goodness Swing located in human freedom and ability. Congregations numbering in the thousands came to hear Swing's sermons. Thousands more read them in published form, either in the Chicago *Pulpit* or the Chicago *Alliance*, where Swing offered written musings in addition to his sermons.

Such a highly visible figure attracted critics as well as worshippers. Foremost among those critics was Francis Landey Patton. Patton moved into Chicago from Princeton in 1872 to teach theology at McCormick Seminary. Like Swing, he edited a newspaper, *The Interior*. Unlike Swing, he refused to believe that the creed needed modernization or that worshippers needed aesthetically pleasing sermons. What they needed, from Patton's perspective, was solid doctrinal exposition as directed by the Westminster Confession of Faith.

In 1874 Patton moved to silence Swing. He lodged a complaint against Swing, charging him with heretical teachings. More specifically, Patton filed two charges of heresy supported by numerous specifications. The first charge stated that Swing "had not been zealous and faithful in maintaining the truths of the gospel and has not been faithful and diligent in the exercise of his public duties of his office as minister." The second charge alleged that Swing did not "sincerely receive and adopt the Confession of Faith of this Church as containing the systems of doctrine taught in the Holy Scripture" (Johnson et al., *The Trial*, 8–14).

Citing procedural considerations, the judicial committee of the Chicago Presbytery found some of the specifications excessively vague (a great irony since one of Patton's main objections to Swing's preaching was its vagueness). Patton amended his specifications, bringing forward 24 specifications in support of his first charge and another 4 in support of the second. Even then, many of the specific allegations amounted to little more than an attempt to condemn Swing for his associations. The tenor of the charges is such that they provide Swing ample justification to complain of Patton's small-mindedness. Despite Patton's fine-tuning (at the insistence of the committee), many of the allegations appear childish, permitting Swing to cast himself as the victim of an overly suspicious, peevish little man. While Patton was actually neither of those things, the construction of his complaint against Swing trivialized the substance of his charges. Patton also might have noted the concerns manifested by the committee when they insisted on the revisions. In fact the moderator warned Patton that a decision in Swing's favor might augur ill for the accuser (Johnson et al., *The Trial*, 4–7).

Patton attempted to craft most of the specifications so that Swing implicated himself in writing or orally. The first specification accused Swing of employing "equivocal language" to discuss such "fundamental" matters as the person of Christ, the fall of humanity, and the like. To Patton's Princeton-trained ears, Swing's commentary on those matters sounded Unitarian (8).

The second specification charged that Swing's remarks received great praise from Chicago's Unitarian ministers, who affirmed that Swing's teachings were "substantially Unitarian." Worse, when Swing learned of such Unitarian approval, he took no action to clarify his own position. Drawing from Swing's writings, Patton charged that Swing offered too much praise to John Stuart Mill, "a man known not to have believed in the Christian religion." The fourth specification returned to the Unitarian theme, Patton arguing that in at least 14 published sermons or writings Swing had "spoken disparagingly of the doctrine of the Trinity" (Johnson et al., *The Trial*, 8–9).

Patton objected to Swing's failure (in Patton's view) to preach "the doctrines commonly known as evangelical," among which Patton included propitiation, redemption, justification by faith alone, the deity of Jesus, and the inspiration of the Scriptures. He attacked one of Swing's sermons, "Christianity and Dogma," because in it Swing taught that dogma had value only insofar as it could be experientially verified. The seventh specification indicted five sermons for approving of, even applying, Darwinian evolution (9).

Patton pointed to Swing's 1873 sermon "Influence of Democracy on

Christian Doctrine" as containing "false and dangerous" remarks regarding the value of standards of faith and practice. Patton's disapproval extended especially to Swing's assertion that Christians must throw off the "old garments" of the past and conform Christianity to modern times and tastes (10).

The support for Patton's first charge goes on in this vein with another 15 specifications to support the first allegation of heresy. Patton accuses Swing of Sabellianism, of denying Presbyterian ideas concerning baptism, and of repudiating the notion of a special calling to the ministry. On the latter point, Patton cites Swing's sermon on the occasion of the installation of one Arthur Swazey as pastor of Ashland Avenue Presbyterian Church in Chicago in January 1872. On that occasion, Swing purportedly argued that the ministry was simply a profession like any other that anyone could freely choose to join (Johnson et al., *The Trial*, 11, Specification 14).

Patton finally ended his litany (as to the first charge) and produced a list of witnesses he intended to call in support of the first count of heresy. There are 23 individual names on Patton's list, along with that name of a Chicago printer, Carpenter & Sheldon. Significantly, but perhaps not surprisingly, all of Patton's individual witnesses were males.

As to the second charge, that Swing denied the doctrinal veracity of the Westminster Confession, Patton produced but four specifications. Patton again tried to convict Swing with Swing's own words. He believed he could prove that Swing had publicly stated his essential theological agreement with a Chicago Unitarian minister, Robert Laird Collier. Patton stated that he could prove Swing's rejection of such venerable Presbyterian doctrines as predestination, perseverance of the saints, and total depravity by the testimony of one George A. Shufeldt, Esquire. Patton's "smoking gun" in that regard happened to be a letter from Swing to Shufeldt in which Swing allegedly said that he had long before abandoned the five points of Calvinism as announced by the Synod of Dort. Thus, Patton argued, Swing denied three specific points in the Westminster Confession. Finally, Patton alleged that Swing's sermon of 12 April 1874 contained "statements, which by fair implication, involve a disbelief in one or more of the leading doctrines of the Confession of Faith" (Johnson et al., *The Trial*, 13–14).

Swing's reply to Patton's charges illustrates the growing chasm within Presbyterian circles that would eventually divide all denominations of the Protestant mainstream in the United States. After simply asserting his innocence, Swing elaborated on each of the charges in some detail. Significantly, his responses showed a confidence in his position before the Presbytery despite apparently overwhelming evidence of "guilt." Swing undoubtedly knew the temper of the Chicago Presbytery better than did his zealous young accuser. In any event, Swing began his statement by asserting that Patton took his remarks out of context. More important, Swing pointed to his New School Presbyterian roots and denied any conflict between his teachings and "any of the Evangelical Calvinistic doctrines of the denomination with which I am connected" (Johnson et al., *The Trial*, 17). The reunion of Old School and New School Presbyterians took place only five years before, and Swing's defense made clear that the reunion "papered over" differences that tenaciously persisted within the denomination.

Beyond the assertion of his New School background, Swing further suggested that his apparent embrace of "liberal churches" (read Unitarians) amounted to nothing more than a showing of "good will towards [sic] all men." By no means, Swing argued, did he intend to advance or promote such groups. He simply seized upon opportunities to display love impartially to those outside his own group. In a barbed reference Swing noted that Charles Hodge might more clearly apprehend the truth than did the Liberals but that nowhere did the Bible suggest that only those with the clearer apprehension of truth inherit the kingdom of heaven. In another pointed reference, Swing reminded his auditors that the beloved hymn writer Isaac Watts had been accused of Unitarianism in his lifetime as well (Johnson et al., *The Trial*, 17).

Swing took great pains to point out that the Confession must be reformable to keep it relevant in ever-changing social settings. Patton accused him, said Swing, of being a bad Presbyterian. Swing countered by asserting that Patton showed more interest in defending a statement of historic Christianity than in presenting actual Christianity to nineteenth-century audiences. "The Presbyterian Church," said Swing, "permits its clergy to distinguish the church *actual* from the church *historic*" (18, emphasis in the original).

In short, Swing refused to be tried by the standards of the Westminster Assembly of Divines. Those standards belonged to the ages. Swing had no intention of quietly submitting his ministry to a tribunal more than 200 years absent. Swing reminded the Presbytery (and Patton and the gathered reporters) of the changes of mood that had taken place in the two centuries since the Assembly did its work. Swing argued that Presbyterians gradually moved away from harsh doctrines such as infant condemnation and away from the fatalistic overtones of predestination toward a recognition that a loving God created humanity in God's own image and with free will. God sought our loving response, not our adherence to formal statements. Only God, not the Westminster Confession, was timeless and immutable.

Swing concluded his remarks with a positive statement of that which he believed. Along with the "general creed as rendered by the former New School theologians," Swing announced that he was "willing to meet the educated world, the skeptical world, and the sinful world" with a number of affirmations. He affirmed the inspiration of the Bible (assiduously avoiding the term "plenary"), the doctrine of the Trinity, the divinity (though not the deity) of Jesus, the office of Christ as mediator, conversion of the unbeliever by the Spirit, human sinfulness (perhaps thinking of Patton and

Hodge as examples), and a "final separation of the righteous and the wicked" at the end of time (Johnson et al., *The Trial*, 20).

The theological positions thus staked out, the trial commenced and Patton set out to prove his fidelity to Princeton orthodoxy if not his case against Swing. Sixty-one members of the Chicago Presbytery sat for a month listening to Patton's arguments, to his witnesses, and to readings of the sermons that Patton believed demonstrated Swing's guilt. They also heard Swing's responses and protestations of his innocence. The record of proceedings reflects Patton's persistence and the patience of the Presbytery. More than 300 pages of small type record the evidence that Patton amassed against Swing. As William R. Hutchison observed, Patton did move away from the rather vague charge that Swing failed to preach "evangelical Christianity" ("Disapproval of Chicago," 43). Patton stood firm, however, on the charge that Swing refused to preach the Westminster Confession, and the evidence he produced showed precisely that.

For Patton it was unfortunate that merely proving Swing's refusal to preach the letter of the Westminster Confession was insufficient evidence of guilt for the Chicago Presbytery. Chicago Presbyterians championed the New School teachings in the antebellum period and had little taste for Patton's brand (or any other flavor) of Princeton orthodoxy before or after the Civil War. Members of the judicial committee pressed Patton to show how his allegations proved Swing an unfit pastor. That line of questioning provided more than a small hint to Patton that he was not preaching to the congregation. Swing pastored a happy, healthy flock in Chicago. More ominous for Patton, the Chicagoans accepted Swing's interpretation of the Confession as a statement of historical interest, asserting not only their willingness to adapt the creed to nineteenth-century exigencies but also their refusal to acknowledge the authority of Princeton theology.

With passionate insistence, Patton asserted that the trial implicated more than one popular minister's career. The Chicago Presbytery faced a grave responsibility in judging "whether the Presbyterian Church has a creed, or whether broad churchism without limit is to be the policy of the future." Assuring the Presbyters that the eyes of the denomination were on them, Patton cautioned that "the Presbyterian Church expects every man to do his duty" (Johnson et al., *The Trial*, 185–186).

The recorded vote of the Presbytery indicates that those men perceived their duty differently than did Patton. Forty-eight men voted to acquit Swing of Patton's charges. Only 13 agreed with Patton. At the end of the day, one of the city's longtime New School ministers, Robert W. Patterson, provided the rationale for the vote. Patterson noted that neither Swing nor Patton required an absolute literal reading of the Confession. On that basis, Patterson reasoned, there was no cause to allow Patton his interpretations without granting the same latitude to Swing. Though he did not speak for the entire Presbytery, Patterson's logic showed that the distance between

Chicago and Princeton was far greater than the distance between Illinois and New Jersey (Hutchison, "Disapproval of Chicago," 44).

The Swing trial ended, finally, with Swing vindicated and Patton rebuked. The story might have ended at that point with Swing continuing his work in Chicago and a chastened but unbowed Patton returning to his post at McCormick Seminary, clicking his tongue over the sorry state of Presbyterianism in Chicago. The respective temperaments of the two men conspired to prevent that result. Patton doggedly stood by his conviction that Swing's preaching was heretical. He determined to press his case against Swing by appealing the decision of the Chicago Presbytery to the Northern Illinois Synod. Patton apparently felt that Swing's popularity led to a decision contrary to the evidence and that a larger body not as directly under the spell of his charisma (and not as cognizant of the size of his congregation) would render the proper verdict. Given the relative size and importance of the Chicago Presbytery in the Northern Illinois Synod at that time, however, the likelihood of a different result seems remote. As Hutchison supposes, Patton would most likely have lost again at the Synod level. He would then have pursued his case to the General Assembly (Hutchison, "Disapproval of Chicago," 44).

Swing's disposition differed from Patton's. Vindicated in his adopted home city, Swing had no intention of allowing Patton to persist in his role of the ant at the picnic. Instead, Swing resigned from the Presbyterian pulpit. Many of his parishioners "resigned" with him—when their leader left, they followed. Swing moved into an independent ministry, preaching regularly to large, adoring crowds at the Chicago Music Hall. For another 20 years, until his death in 1894, Swing preached his poetic sermons emphasizing the love of Jesus, only occasionally pausing to point out the folly of binding oneself to some historical statement of faith, especially in 1889 and 1890 when his former Presbyterian brethren wrestled with the idea of revising the Westminster Confession. Throughout his life, David Swing remained an enormously popular clergyman in Chicago, rivaling the great revivalist Dwight L. Moody in public esteem.

Patton probably felt some sense of vindication upon Swing's resignation. Convinced of the correctness of his position and the hopeless bias of the Chicago Presbytery in judging Swing, Patton realized part of his goal. David Swing no longer preached against the Westminster Confession from a pulpit bound to uphold it. Any sense of triumph that Patton experienced, however, would have been tempered by his knowledge that Swing's ministry continued unabated, perhaps even enhanced, in the wake of the trial. Patton eventually returned to Princeton, becoming president of Princeton College in 1888. Later he served as president of Princeton Theological Seminary and as moderator of the General Assembly. He remained a steadfast adherent to and defender of the Westminster standards during denominational discussions on creed revision in 1889 and 1890. Predictably, Patton opposed the revision effort. Later in life he supported the archconservative J. Gresham Machen* in his battles at Princeton in the 1920s.

The Chicago Presbytery spoke with a clear voice in 1874. The group cleared Swing of the charges against him, rejecting in the process a rigid, propositional orthodoxy. Fittingly, however, the trial of David Swing failed to destroy the careers of either of the principal figures. David Swing and Francis Patton went on to enjoy long and distinguished careers. Each believed he was correct and the other sadly mistaken. Presbyterians wrestled with the questions raised in Swing's trial for an additional 50 years until finally even Princeton accepted a position more near that of Swing than that of Patton. Therein, perhaps, lay Swing's final vindication.

BIBLIOGRAPHY

Hutchison, William R. "Disapproval of Chicago: The Symbolic Trial of David Swing." *Journal of American History* 59 (June 1972): 30–47.

———. *The Modernist Impulse in American Protestantism*. New York: Oxford University Press, 1976. Esp. 48–68.

Johnson, David, Francis L. Patton, and George C. Noyes, eds. *The Trial of the Rev. David Swing: Before the Presbytery of Chicago*. Chicago: Jansen and McClurg, 1874.

Newton, Joseph Fort. *David Swing: Poet-Preacher*. Chicago: Unity Publishing Company, 1909.

Swing, David. *David Swing's Sermons*. Chicago: W. B. Keen, Cooke and Company, 1874.

———. *Truths for Today*. Chicago: Jansen, McClurg and Company, 1874.

W. Russell Congleton

John H. Tietjen
(1928–)

One perceptive observer has suggested that in the 1960s the Lutheran Church–Missouri Synod was "an explosion waiting to happen." Long a bastion of conservative Lutheranism and Germanic culture, a degree of both theological and cultural diversity had nonetheless come to the Synod after World War I. By the 1960s, two fairly well-defined parties were contending for the leadership of the Synod. The conservatives desired to maintain the traditions of the Synod as they had been defined by its earliest leaders—especially C.F.W. Walther (1811–1887) and Franz Pieper (1852–1931). The liberals, who preferred to be called "moderates" since there were no real liberals in the Missouri Synod in the usual Protestant sense of the word, were ready to modify both the theological stance and certain practices of the Synod. Central to the deepening division were different approaches to the interpretation of the Scriptures; also of great importance were differing views on the nature of authority in the church.

Viewed against the larger background of American church history, the emerging conflict in the Missouri Synod can be seen as yet another chapter in the ongoing fundamentalist-modernist controversy that has been characteristic of American Protestantism in the twentieth century. This generalization fails, however, to do justice to the particularity of the Lutheran situation, which encompassed not only the Missouri Synod but most other Lutheran churches in America as well.

"Old Lutheranism," a movement that arose in Germany in the early nineteenth century, lay behind many Lutheran conflicts in America in the nineteenth and twentieth centuries, including the one that erupted in the Missouri Synod in the late 1960s. Reacting against rampant rationalism and the perceived doctrinal indifference of pietism, many Lutheran pastors and laypeople called for a return to the pure faith and practice of the "old Lutheran Church" of the sixteenth and seventeenth centuries. This happened within the context of a widespread revival of evangelical faith in Germany, known as the *Erweckungsbewegung*, that led to a renewed commitment to the historic Christian faith.

The revival did not necessarily lead to a renewed commitment to the theological and liturgical particularities of Lutheranism, however. On the contrary, King Frederick Wilhelm III of Prussia, greatly influenced by the *Erweckungsbewegung* and believing that there were no fundamental differences between them, became an ardent proponent of merging the Lutheran and the Reformed Churches in his land, so that together they might advance the evangelical faith more effectively. In 1817 he decreed an administrative union of these churches, and by the 1830s he was mandating their full unity in doctrine and worship. A common liturgy for the united church was written by the king himself. Other German principalities soon copied these developments.

Many "awakened" Lutherans accepted the territorial union churches and were satisfied to worship and witness within them. Others, however, were deeply disturbed by this turn of events. Already in 1817, Pastor Claus Harms of Kiel published 95 theses on the state of faith and of the church in Germany that included several statements critical of the Prussian Union. After the promulgation of the king's liturgy, Lutheran opposition to the united church intensified. Many Lutheran pastors refused to use the rite, which they believed conceded far too much to the Reformed understanding of the Lord's Supper. The charge of "unionism" was leveled at the government and at the supporters of the union within the church; the critics meant that a superficial unity had been imposed on churches that still differed from one another in fundamental doctrines. Many called for a return to the confessional standards of the *Book of Concord* (1580) and consequently were dubbed "confessionalists." In Prussia, the king decided to use the police power of the state to bring the recalcitrant Lutherans into line. Fines were levied, pastors were barred from their parishes, and some were even jailed for continuing to conduct traditional Lutheran services. At the height of the conflict in the mid-1830s, significant numbers of Lutheran pastors and laypeople began to emigrate—first to Australia and then to the United States—to escape unionism and the oppression of their rulers. These "Old Lutherans" came to their new homes with a strong sense of having been deeply wronged and with an avowed intent never again to allow unionism or the power of the state to corrupt pure Lutheranism. When the Missouri Synod was founded in 1847, it included a large and influential component of Old Lutherans, led by young pastor and professor C.F.W. Walther; it was they who largely determined the shape of the new organization. Disputes over the doctrine of the church and its ministry, and various issues pertaining to biblical and confessional interpretation, were all settled along Old Lutheran lines as determined by Walther. As late as the 1880s, during a controversy over the doctrine of predestination, Walther and his allies triumphed easily over opponents within the Synod who had challenged their theological leadership. After his death, Walther's authoritarian style of leadership in the St. Louis seminary and the Synod was continued by his successor, Franz Pieper.

Theologically speaking, Old Lutheranism was not synonymous simply with adherence to the confessions of the sixteenth century. It was equally (critics said, more) devoted to a Lutheran version of scholastic theology that had been developed in the late sixteenth and seventeenth centuries. The chief characteristics of this theology, apart from its loyalty to the doctrinal standards of the confessions, were its attempt at comprehensiveness and its use of Aristotelian categories to provide a framework for doctrinal expression. Like earlier scholasticism, it aimed to supply the highest possible degree of certitude on almost every conceivable theological topic. In order to accomplish this, Lutheran scholasticism was based on the premise of an inerrant and infallible Bible. After almost a century of Old Lutheran leadership, most pastors and members of the Missouri Synod were well imbued with its scholastic understandings of Bible, church, ministry, and the paramount importance of doctrine in the life of the believer and in the church.

To outsiders, the Synod's most obvious characteristic was its refusal to engage in any form of fellowship with other Christians, including most other Lutherans. This stance was rooted in its long-standing fear of unionism; by the late nineteenth century, the Synod understood unionism to include even prayer with Christians with whom one had not previously established doctrinal unity. It was simply taken for granted that pastors could not exchange pulpits with pastors from other traditions and that intercommunion was impossible even with most other Lutherans, since the Lutheran Churches in America had not been able to reach doctrinal unanimity on a number of issues.

The first challenges to Old Lutheranism in the Synod came in connection with the fellowship issue, beginning in the 1920s and 1930s. A maverick pastor, Otto Hermann Pannoke, associated freely with other American Lutherans and went so far as to propose that all American Lutherans should unite into one church as soon as possible. Even more important for the future, a respected missionary to India, Adolph A. Brux, was charged with heresy for praying with other Christians; his censure became something of a cause célèbre both within the Synod and in wider missionary circles.

The clearest sign that some attitudes were changing came in 1945, when a group of 44 Missouri clergy—some of them prominent—wrote "A Statement" in which they took the Synod to task for its spirit of harsh, judgmental lovelessness. They called on the Synod to exhibit instead a greater measure of a truly evangelical spirit on such matters as the interpretation of the Scriptures, prayer fellowship, and relationships with other Lutherans. While "A Statement" had little immediate impact, and indeed was soon withdrawn as a basis for further discussion by the 44 themselves, historians have generally seen the publication of this document as the beginning of a more liberal or progressive party within the Missouri Synod. While Missouri liberals might seem pretty tame to outsiders—"A Statement" reaffirmed the doctrine of biblical inerrancy, for example—they represented a significant new force in the formerly almost monolithic organization.

Another critical development after World War II was the decision of many bright young pastors to undertake graduate study in institutions outside the Synod. John Tietjen, a graduate of Concordia Theological Seminary* in St. Louis, did his doctoral work at Union Theological Seminary in New York in the 1950s. He later recalled that this experience had raised many theological problems for him in the light of his scholastic heritage, although it made him "if anything, more of a confessional Lutheran." Exposed for the first time in a positive way to historical-critical methodologies, Tietjen and his colleagues struggled with fundamental questions of biblical interpretation, historical analysis, and doctrinal formulation. And, as Tietjen put it, most of them came to a "profound appreciation for the convictions of other Christians." They were convinced that the Missouri Synod must become an active participant in the very ecumenical Christianity that it had so long shunned.

By the late 1950s and early 1960s, many of the new breed of scholars had joined the faculties of the Missouri Synod's seminaries and colleges. At several schools, including the flagship Concordia Seminary in St. Louis, they became a potent force for change. Their way into these positions was eased by the fact that most of them had impeccable Missouri Synod credentials, including having come up through the Synod's comprehensive educational system. A few, like John Tietjen, remained in parish ministry beyond the obligatory first appointment or took up other nonacademic tasks. Others, like Jaroslav Pelikan (who taught at Concordia Seminary from 1949 to 1953) and Martin Marty, left the Synod for appointments in secular universities.

As the rank and file in the Missouri Synod gradually became aware of these developments, a decided reaction began. Organized opposition to what some traditionalists called "the liberal takeover" took several forms. One center of opposition was at "the other Concordia," Concordia Theological Seminary then located at Springfield, Illinois. This seminary had long served as a "practical seminary" to train those who for one reason or another (age, marital status, academic deficiencies) could not follow the Synod's prescribed preseminary path to St. Louis. Although the academic differences between the two Concordias had lessened by the 1960s, the Springfield school still tended to enroll a more diverse student body than its sister school. Fewer of the new breed of faculty served there, and most important, the president of the school after 1962 was an avowed conservative, J.A.O. ("Jack") Preus, who had previously served on the faculty. He was determined to make the seminary a bastion of orthodoxy as the Missouri Synod had traditionally understood the term. Even before his presidency, the seminary's periodical, *The Springfielder*, had become a major organ of the conservative party.

Another important center of opposition to any and all forms of theological or political liberalism beginning in the early 1960s was the private publication *Christian News*. Edited by Herman Otten, a St. Louis graduate who had been denied ordination in the Synod, its antiestablishment and antiliberal rhetoric was sometimes considered shrill, overstated, or untruthful even by some conservatives. But Otten's yellow journalism caught the attention especially of many laypersons who otherwise might have been largely unaware of the emerging dispute in the Synod. After a while *Christian News* was joined by other publications with a similar message; Jack Preus and his brother Robert, who was a professor at St. Louis, named their paper *Balance*, to indicate that theirs was a more responsible conservatism than that of Otten.

As conservative opposition to liberalism grew, tensions between liberals and conservatives surfaced repeatedly in Missouri Synod conventions. As early as 1959, a convention passed a resolution binding all pastors, teachers, and professors to a doctrinal statement, written by Franz Pieper and first adopted by the Synod in 1932, that was scholastic and even fundamentalistic in its approach to the Bible. When Professor Martin Scharlemann of St. Louis continued to teach that the term *inerrancy* as applied to the Scriptures needed reinterpretation, a resolution was offered at the 1962 convention to relieve him of his position; only his confession of guilt before the assembled body prevented this. He assured the convention that he was fully committed to "the doctrine of the verbal inspiration of the Sacred Scriptures" and that he would "withdraw" essays that seemed to call this into question. The humiliation of Scharlemann, who thereafter threw in his lot with the conservatives, infuriated and worried the "moderates," with good reason.

The moderates were encouraged, however, by the election of Oliver Harms to the Synod's presidency in 1962. Harms was no theological liberal, but he was known to favor an openness to other Lutherans, and he was willing to allow the young professors in the Synod a certain degree of latitude in expressing their theological opinions. The moderate faculty at St. Louis was encouraged that their reforming program would go forward, albeit cautiously.

Organized opposition to the Harms administration began immediately after his election. *The Springfielder, Christian News*, and other publications were particularly alarmed at Harms's ideas about establishing fellowship with The American Lutheran Church (TALC, another conservative midwestern group) and about establishing a pan-Lutheran council in the United States, moves that were viewed by conservatives as unionistic. Harsh words were hurled at "neo-Lutherans" both within the Missouri Synod and in other Lutheran bodies, charging that they had abandoned the authority of the Bible. The seminary's attempt to pour oil on these troubled waters by assuring its critics that nothing of importance had changed in its theology was met with disbelief by conservatives, who charged the moderates with conscious duplicity.

In spite of growing conservative opposition, the Missouri Synod followed its moderate leadership by approving membership in the Lutheran Council in the USA (LCUSA) in 1965. It also approved participation in a joint service book and hymnal project with the other large Lutheran bodies that year. Attempts to charge certain St. Louis professors with teaching "false doctrine" were turned aside. In 1967, however, the moderate leadership in the Synod was unable to consummate the hoped-for fellowship with TALC. And as the 1969 convention approached, conservatives campaigned actively to unseat Oliver Harms, who was a candidate for reelection.

The climax of the growing conflict came at the 1969 convention when Jack Preus of the "other Concordia" was elected president of the Missouri Synod. Perhaps in order to maintain a sense of balance, the convention then approved the fellowship with TALC that it had postponed in 1967. Conservatives were jubilant, in spite of the fellowship vote, for they now expected to purge the Synod of all expressions of liberalism and unionism.

President Preus saw his election as a mandate to do just that. Although he did not immediately press such issues as withdrawing membership in LCUSA or rescinding fellowship with TALC, he moved swiftly to deal with what he saw as the heart of the crisis in the Synod—the theology being taught at the St. Louis seminary. From Preus's point of view, the crisis in the Missouri Synod was primarily a theological crisis, which was caused directly by the false teachings of the majority of the faculty at St. Louis. To make matters worse, the Board of Control of Concordia Seminary had recently elected a new president of the seminary with strong moderate credentials—John H. Tietjen. Tietjen had published his views on Lutheran unity, which were unionistic by Old Lutheran standards, in a book entitled *Which Way to Lutheran Unity?* He had further compounded this affront to the conservatives by service on the staff of LCUSA, from which he was called to the seminary.

President Preus's first major challenge to the faculty majority at St. Louis came in September 1970, when he appointed a synodical Fact Finding Committee to investigate the allegations of doctrinal aberrations. The faculty participated under protest in this process, which consisted of a review of their published writings and individual interviews. John Tietjen insisted that any information developed in this way must ultimately be judged by the seminary's own Board of Control. He also opposed Preus's determination that the criteria by which the faculty would be judged would include synodically adopted doctrinal statements, in addition to the Bible and the *Book of Concord*. Tietjen's response began several years of procedural haggling between himself and Preus. From Preus's point of view, the issues lay within the purview of his constitutional authority to supervise the doctrine of the Synod. He also believed that the Synod's doctrinal statements clarified biblical and confessional issues in an authentic way (a position that had often been articulated during Missouri's unbroken Old Lutheran period). From Tietjen's point of view, the investigation was both an unwarranted intrusion into the internal affairs of the seminary (which continued to assert an unqualified allegiance to the confessions) and a definitive move to elevate synodical statements to confessional status (which was a violation of the confessions themselves).

The 1971 synodical convention gave some comfort to the moderates when it declined to endorse Preus's view that the Synod's doctrinal statements could be used to discipline faculty and referred the fact-finding report to the seminary board. On the other hand, beginning with this convention, moderate board members began to be replaced with conservatives. The complexion of the board would thus shift over a period of time, although moderates remained in the majority for the time being.

When the Board of Control formally received the fact-finding report, it took its time analyzing and responding to its charges. As it contemplated these, Preus urged it not to renew the contracts of several younger untenured members of the faculty, at least until their doctrinal soundness could be determined by the conservatives. Most were eventually continued, although Arlis J. Ehlen of the Old Testament Department became the first faculty casualty of the dispute when his reappointment failed on a four to five vote. In the midst of this tense situation, Preus authored *A Statement of Scriptural and Confessional Principles*, which was a restatement of traditional scholastic doctrine on several subjects; it was intended to influence wavering pastors and laypersons. When the board finally issued a progress report regarding the fact-finding document in June 1972, it told Preus that it had not yet found any evidence of false doctrine in the faculty.

Preus responded to the still-moderate Board of Control by issuing a report of his own. Acting according to one provision of the Synod's 1971 resolutions, which called for him to report the progress of the Board of Control in this matter to the next convention, he published his lengthy *Report of the Synodical President to The Lutheran Church–Missouri Synod*, popularly known as "the Blue Book." In it, he reaffirmed his belief that false doctrine was being taught at the seminary and took John Tietjen to task for putting procedural roadblocks in the way of a full and fair resolution of the issues. Within a week of the publication of the Blue Book, Tietjen defended the faculty in *Fact Finding or Fault Finding? An Analysis of President J.A.O. Preus' Investigation of Concordia Seminary*. From this point on, the parties to the dispute were clearly irreconcilable. One observer has aptly noted that the ensuing battle "had the bitterness and humorlessness of a fierce family quarrel."

The moderates steadily lost ground to the increasingly powerful forces of conservatism. In January 1973 the Board of Control formally cleared all faculty of the charges against them, but this was a hollow victory. Efforts by several district presidents to mediate the dispute went nowhere. Failing to elect sympathetic delegates in sufficient numbers, the moderates approached the 1973 convention with a sense of dread. At this convention, dubbed by some "the Second Battle of New Orleans," the Synod reversed itself, declaring all of its doctrinal statements binding on its teachers, and then adopted Preus's *Statement* as such. At the urging of Preus, the convention resolved further that the majority of the faculty at St. Louis were guilty of denying the historicity of key events described in the Bible, such as Adam and Eve as real persons, and that they were therefore teachers who "cannot be tolerated in the church of God, much less be excused and defended." The transition to a conservative majority on the Board of Control was completed; the convention instructed the reconstituted board to deal with Tietjen's future as president of Concordia.

John Tietjen and his faculty were clearly at a crisis point in the summer of 1973. Their protests that they had been condemned without a hearing at New Orleans (indeed, that those on the Board of Control who had actually given them a fair hearing had exonerated them) fell on the increasingly deaf ears of the triumphant conservatives. At this point, the moderates began to organize more formally; by September they had formed Evangelical Lutherans in Mission (ELIM), which Tietjen later described as "a mutual defense league." In August, the new Board of Control suspended John Tietjen from office, for "allowing and fostering false doctrine." Although it soon had to reverse its action for procedural reasons, it was clear to everyone that John Tietjen's days at Concordia Seminary were numbered. For its part, the faculty majority stressed its solidarity with Tietjen, identifying his cause completely with its own. The board responded by ordering the retirement of several of the older faculty, by refusing to renew the contract of Paul Goetting, and by involving itself in several day-to-day management matters. It also offered John Tietjen a deal whereby charges against him would be dropped, Goetting would be reemployed, and a one-year cooling-off period relative to the faculty would be observed, if he would accept a call to another ministry. Tietjen angrily rejected the deal, seeing it as proof that the conservative majority was unprincipled in the exercise of its power.

In January 1974, having gotten its procedural ducks in a row, the Concordia Seminary Board of Control suspended John Tietjen as president on a vote of six to five; Martin Scharlemann was named acting president. The big question for moderates, which had been discussed for some time, was what to do when this event actually occurred. On 21 January, students and faculty each made a crucial decision. The majority of the students decided that they had to do something to demonstrate solidarity with the faculty majority; their decision was to declare a "moratorium" on classes, presumably until Tietjen should be reinstated. The faculty reacted similarly, declaring that the suspension of Tietjen was de facto a suspension of them as well; they promised not to return to the classrooms until a positive resolution was reached. With the suspension of most classes (a faculty minority of five persons supported Preus and the Board of Control), students and faculty engaged in intense discussions about their future and engaged in a major effort to communicate their position to the members of the Synod.

On 17 February 1974, the Board of Control resolved that the faculty must return to the classrooms by 19 February or be held in breach of contract. Ignoring this ultimatum, a large majority of faculty and students decided to leave the seminary and establish "Concordia Seminary in Exile," or "Seminex." In a well-orchestrated media event, hundreds of students and faculty marched from the Concordia campus to a nearby park, where they announced their intentions to the Synod and to the world. The next day, classes resumed at Eden Seminary and at St. Louis University, which had agreed to make the former Concordia professors adjunct faculty. If the faculty or students in exile thought they could bring President Preus to the bargaining table by this tactic, they soon learned otherwise. Preus stood firm and instructed the Board of Control to proceed with the termination of the faculty. As one observer has noted, "[W]ith one stroke the faculty under Tietjen's leadership accomplished what Preus could not have done within his lifetime: empty the seminary of its troublesome faculty."

Faced with the reality of permanent exile, Seminex (later renamed Christ Seminary–Seminex) was soon a viable seminary in its own right. Once John Tietjen had been formally removed from the presidency and the faculty of Concordia Seminary—a process that took until October 1974—he became president of Seminex. With the support of ELIM and later of the Association of Evangelical Lutheran Churches (AELC, a group of breakaway Missouri congregations), it existed as a separate institution until 1988, when it was merged into three existing seminaries at the time of the formation of the Evangelical Lutheran Church in America.

The resolution of the seminary issue in this way did not fully resolve John Tietjen's personal situation within the Missouri Synod. Some conservatives, furious at the part he had played in the dispute, were determined to make an example of him. In the spring of 1975, an attempt was made to remove Tietjen from the Synod's clergy roster, on the grounds that he had already been proven to teach false doctrine. When the Synod's Missouri District refused to do so, Preus referred the matter to Theodore Nickel, third vice president of the Synod, for further adjudication; it was a foregone conclusion that Nickel would suspend Tietjen from the ministerium of the Synod, an action that finally occurred in September 1977. Tietjen's expulsion was anticlimactic, as he had already entered the clergy ranks of the AELC.

The experience of the Missouri Synod in the case of John Tietjen and the Concordia Seminary faculty majority illustrates one of the most troubling issues that has faced contemporary Protestantism, that of the proper exercise of its teaching authority. While the conflict in the Synod was ostensibly over the interpretation of the Bible, the attention of both parties was soon focused on questions of authority and power. In effect, the faculty of Concordia Seminary, St. Louis, had functioned as the teaching magisterium of the Synod since its inception. The question that conservatives believed they faced in the 1960s and 1970s was: What shall we do when our acknowledged (albeit informally) center of theological authority departs from many of the traditions of our church? Jack Preus's answer was that the Synod as a whole had to assert its authority and bring the erring institution back into line. The moderates often charged that Preus rode roughshod over constitutional procedures and basic notions of fairness, as he undoubtedly did at times. His attitude seems to have been that nothing less than the fundamental theological integrity of the Synod was at stake, a situation that the authors of bylaws and institutional policies had hardly foreseen. Procedural niceties should not be permitted to stand in the way of a resolution of the fundamental issues. Taking the heroic stance of one called to thwart the forces of evil (a stance also not unknown among the moderates), he asked the Synod to give him the extraordinary powers to do the job that needed to be done, and the Synod complied.

For their part, John Tietjen and the faculty majority seemed to believe that by virtue of their office they had not only the right but the duty to instruct the Synod in truth, even if that truth was unpalatable to many. Consistently underestimating the strength of the conservative perspective among the rank and file, the moderates seemed not to recognize the enormity of the task of theological reconstruction that they had undertaken. When their program began to unravel, they turned to the mass media to assist them in getting their message across not only to the Synod but to the larger public. While this generated considerable sympathy for them, it hardly helped resolve the fundamental issues of biblical interpretation and authority in the church that were at stake.

In the end, Old Lutheran conservatism tinged with American fundamentalism triumphed in the Missouri Synod; the moderates were forced out of all positions of influence or authority. That the conservatives represented the majority in the Synod became clear during the course of the controversy; the purge of Tietjen, the faculty majority at St. Louis, and of many others was thus in some sense a victory for democratic processes. Whether it was a victory for Christian truth was a question that continued to trouble thoughtful observers, who wondered if politicized church conventions and packed committees are any better equipped than fallible seminary faculties to determine the will of God for the life of the church.

BIBLIOGRAPHY

Adams, James E. *Preus of Missouri and the Great Lutheran Civil War*. New York: Harper and Row, 1977.

Danker, Frederick. *No Room in the Brotherhood: The Preus-Otten Purge of Missouri*. St. Louis: Clayton Publishing, 1977.

Marquart, Kurt E. *Anatomy of an Explosion: Missouri in Lutheran Perspective*. Fort Wayne, IN: Concordia Theological Seminary Press, 1977.

Meilaender, Gilbert. "How Churches Crack Up: The Case of the Lutheran Church–Missouri Synod." *First Things*, no. 14 (June–July 1991): 38–42.

Tietjen, John H. *Memoirs in Exile: Confessional Hope and Institutional Conflict*. Minneapolis: Fortress Press, 1990.

———. *Which Way to Lutheran Unity?* St. Louis, MO: Concordia Publishing House, 1966.

Donald L. Huber

Crawford Howell Toy
(1836–1919)

It is possible to argue that the story of Crawford Howell Toy should not occupy a place in a book with the title *Dictionary of Heresy Trials in American Christianity*. The chairman of the Board of Trustees of Southern Baptist Theological Seminary, which accepted Toy's resignation, stated afterwards, "It was in no sense a trial of Dr. Toy. He was held in the highest estimation for his scholarship and piety by all the trustees" (*Religious Herald*, 22 May 1879, 2). Furthermore, Toy was never pronounced a heretic, only that there was a "divergence in his views from those generally held by supporters of the Seminary" (2).

Nevertheless, it is clear that many in his denomination (the Southern Baptist Convention) believed that his views on inspiration were heretical. Furthermore, a long "conference" with Dr. Toy by a committee of Trustees may well be regarded as an informal trial. And there is no doubt that his resignation came as a result of considerable pressure on him.

Toy was born in Norfolk, Virginia, in 1836. His father, a druggist, continued his own intellectual growth by extensive reading and the study of languages, including Hebrew. He was active as a founding member of the Freemason Street Baptist Church in Norfolk and became a student of the Scriptures. Thus, young Toy, the first of nine children, was reared in a family where learning was greatly valued, where a knowledge of languages was a proficiency one needed to acquire, and where the Scriptures were highly valued.

After graduating from the University of Virginia in 1856, Toy taught English at the Albemarle Female Institute in Charlottesville. When the Southern Baptist Theological Seminary was founded at Greenville, South Carolina, in 1859, he followed his scholar-pastor, John A. Broadus, to that institution—Broadus as professor and Toy as student. Later, when Toy was ordained in Charlottesville in June 1860, Broadus journeyed from Greenville to deliver the "charge."

Toy had planned to be a missionary, but these plans were interrupted by the outbreak of the Civil War in 1861. In time, after joining the Confederate Army, he became a chaplain in Lee's army but continued his study of languages even after he was captured at Gettysburg. In 1864 he was appointed professor of natural philosophy at the University of Alabama, then a military training school for the Confederacy. After the war, he taught Greek at the University of Virginia during 1865–1866. Toy then spent two very important years studying in Berlin—theology with Dorner, Sanskrit with Weber, and Semitics with Roediger and Dieterici.

After teaching Greek at Furman University in Greenville, South Carolina, for a year, 1869–1870, he was elected professor of Old Testament interpretation and Oriental languages in the Southern Baptist Theological Seminary where he had once studied. Broadus's health was poor, and Toy's appointment was designed to give his revered teacher some relief.

Since the Old South was so thoroughly bankrupt as a result of the war, the Seminary moved to Louisville, Kentucky, in 1877, where it was thought it could have a brighter financial future. After two years there, the event occurred that may be designated as the informal heresy trial leading to Toy's leaving the Seminary.

At the time of Toy's appointment to the faculty of the Southern Baptist Theological Seminary, there was great enthusiasm expressed about the future of this young scholar and teacher. The 20 May 1869 issue of the *Religious Herald* reported the following: "[H]is eminent lingual attainments, his sound judgments, amiable manners, and earnest piety will qualify him for the post of which he has been selected. Should his life and health be spared and circumstances favor the prosecution of his studies, it is confidently expected that he will, at no distant day, rank among the foremost Biblical scholars of the world."

His inaugural address at the Seminary, "The Claims of Biblical Interpretation on Baptists," was well received. Although the address brought no criticism and considerable praise, it contained an element that would later contribute to his resignation. Briefly stated, it was that he believed the Scriptures had both an external and internal element. The external element was one that would necessarily be examined as any other document by the use of grammatical, historical, and logical investigation. It was this type of investigation that led to Toy's problems.

Toy had increasing difficulty with the prevailing orthodoxy of his time as he began to make an effort to harmonize the first chapter of Genesis and the findings of modern science. At first, he tried to do this by saying that the word *day* in the Genesis account referred to a long period of time rather than a single day of 24 hours. However, he soon became dissatisfied with this approach. He was very interested when the evolutionary theory of Darwin with respect to man and those of Keuenan and Wellhausen with respect to the history of Israel appeared. (He even gave a popular lecture while the Seminary was still located in Greenville favorable to Darwin's view of man.) The views of the latter scholars helped him in his own reconstruction of the Old Testament material. He came to believe that the proper approach was to "take the kernel of truth from its outer covering of myth" (Toy, "A Bit of Personal Experience," in Lindsay, Scrapbook, 3). Although he reached this conclusion about two or three years before the Seminary moved to Louisville, he did not incorporate it to any extent in his teaching until after the move.

It was during the first session of the Seminary in Louisville, 1877–1878, that there was evidence of alarm on the part of his colleagues, notably, his great teacher, John A. Broadus, and his president, James P. Boyce. Broadus thought that Toy was teaching a view of inspiration that questioned the accuracy of the Old Testament. Boyce opposed such views, and he was especially concerned that these teachings might make it very difficult to raise an endowment, which would endanger the Seminary's future.

Boyce, "anxious to avoid anything that looked like an official inquisition" (Robertson, *Life and Letters*, 262), used Broadus to transmit his concerns to Toy. Toy tried to leave the "theoretical questions" alone. Yet he felt it necessary to answer and to answer truthfully his students' persistent questions, and this necessitated the statement of his own views.

The concerns about Toy's orthodoxy at this time seem to have been limited internally to the Seminary, for the Baptist papers of the day raised no question about the teachings of Toy.

The real crisis began to brew as a result of critical and exegetical notes written by Toy for the *Sunday School Times* in 1879. In the 12 April 1879 issue, the lesson for 28 April 1879 was presented. Based upon Isaiah 42: 1–10 and entitled "The Coming Savior," Toy stated that the section Isaiah 40–66 had as its purpose the consolation and promise of deliverance of the exiles in Babylon. He further stated that the "Servant of Yahweh" made primary reference to Israel, not to Christ directly. In the very next lesson, carried in the *Sunday School Times* issue of 18 April 1879, he repeated essentially the same idea as it appeared in Isaiah 53: 1–12. He said that the immediate reference was to Israel throughout the passage, though he did see a final complete fulfillment in the Messiah.

There was an immediate outcry against Toy and his views by several papers. The *Christian Intelligencer*, a publication of the Reformed Church in America, and two Presbyterian papers, the *Christian Statesman* and the *United Presbyterian*, led the attack.

This assault was soon taken up by Baptist papers in the North, the *Central Baptist*, published in St. Louis, and the *Journal and Messenger*, with offices in Cincinnati, Indianapolis, and Parkersburg, West Virginia. This latter paper was especially concerned because such teaching was coming from one who was teaching others. The only Southern Baptist paper to attack Toy prior to his resignation, and that on the very day of his resignation, was the *Biblical Recorder*, the North Carolina Baptist publication. The *Biblical Recorder* went so far as to call for the dismissal of Professor Toy from the faculty of the Seminary. It declared that Toy was "teaching error," an error that strikes at the very foundation of the Christian religion (*Biblical Recorder*, 7 May 1879, 2). The article also implied that unless Toy resigned or was dismissed, support for the Seminary would stop.

After the publication of the articles in the *Sunday School Times* in April, events moved very rapidly. The Board of Trustees of the Seminary began its annual meeting on 7 May 1879 in the First Baptist Church of Atlanta, Georgia. It should be noted that although Atlanta was also hosting the annual meeting of the Southern Baptist Convention at this time, the Convention was never asked to consider the action that the Board took, nor did it take any direct part in the events that transpired within the Board. Toy's resignation was not even announced to that body by the Board.

In the afternoon session of the first day of the meeting, President James P. Boyce told the Trustees that he was transmitting a statement that Dr. Toy wished to present to the Board. (The original copy of this statement is in the Library of the Southern Baptist Theological Seminary. A printed copy is in Duncan, "Crawford Howell Toy," 79–84). After Dr. Boyce had read the statement, the meeting was adjourned until 8:30 the following morning.

As the founding president of the Seminary, Dr. Boyce had been responsible for three basic principles he believed should guide the institution. Two were that it should seek to provide the highest quality of theological education possible to those prepared for it and that it should provide education for those numerous young men who had not had the advantage of a college education. The third was crucial. It was that the orthodoxy of its teachers should be preserved through an Abstract of Principles that each should sign. This document, which all professors, including Toy, had signed, was rather general and generous in its doctrinal statements. Its assertion with regard to the Scriptures was that "the Old and New Testament were given by inspiration of God, and are the only sufficient, certain, and authoritative rule of all saving knowledge and obedience."

In his eloquent declaration presented to the Trustees, Toy first was emphatic in stating that he did not believe nor teach contrary to the Abstract of Principles. He then proceeded to present his conclusions regarding the Scriptures and the result he perceived of teaching and holding those views. He asserted his belief that the Scriptures were inspired by God but that they are silent with regard to the manner of God's action. "Nothing is said of the mode of operation of the Divine Spirit, . . . of the relation of the divine influence to the ordinary workings of the human intellect. . . .

Against facts, no theory can stand, and I prefer, therefore, to have no theory, but submit myself to the guidance of the actual words of Holy Scripture." He enlarged upon his views by asserting

> that the Bible is wholly divine and wholly human; the Scripture is the truth of God communicated by Him to the human soul, appropriated by it and then given out with free, human energy, as the sincere, real conviction of the soul. To undertake to say what must be the outward forms of God's revelation of himself to man, seems to me presumptuous.

He proceeded to say that the authors of the Scriptures received messages from God but wrote them "under purely free, human conditions. The inspired man speaks his own language, not another man's, and writes under the conditions of his own age, not under those of some other age." He wrote:

> I find that the geography, astronomy and other physical science of the sacred writers was that of their times. It is not that of our times, it is not that which seems to us correct, but it has nothing to do with their message of religious truth from God. . . . The message is not less divine to me because it was given in Hebrew and not in English, or because it is set in the framework of a primitive and incorrect geology. . . . If our heavenly Father sends a message by the stammering tongue of a man, I will not reject the message because of the stammering. . . .
>
> The early history of Israel was for a long time not committed to writing but handed down by oral tradition, under which process it was subject to a more or less free expansion. In the expanded form it was received at a comparatively late time by the Prophets and Priests who put it into shape, and made it the vehicle of religious truth.

He said that the same principle applies to the New Testament:

> I will not lightly see a historical or other inaccuracy in the Gospels or the Acts, but if I find such, they do not for me affect the divine teachings of these books. The centre of the New Testament is Christ himself, salvation is in Him, and a historical error cannot affect the fact of His existence and His teachings.

In his final section, Toy offered his resignation and concluded with these words:

> I beg leave to repeat that I am guided wholly by what seems to me the correct interpretation of the Scriptures themselves. If an error in my interpretation is pointed out, I shall straightway give it up. I cannot accept *a priori* reasoning, but I stake everything on the words of the

Bible, and this course I believe to be for the furtherance of the truth of
God.

And now, in conclusion, I wish to say distinctly and strongly that I
consider the view above given to be not only lawful for me to teach as
Professor in the Seminary, but one that will bring aid and firm stand-
ing-ground to many a perplexed mind, and establish the truth of God
on a firm foundation.

But that I may relieve the Board of all embarrassment in the matter,
I respectfully tender my resignation as Professor in the Southern Baptist
Theological Seminary.

At the evening session, Toy's communication was again considered by
the Trustees. Dr. J. C. Hiden of South Carolina, at the request of Toy,
brought some additions and changes made to his original communication.
An addition that somewhat toned down the original statement was as follows: "I should add that in the majority of the cases I hold that the New
Testament quotations correctly represent the sense of the Old Testament,
and that there is always a true spiritual feeling controlling them." This and
other evidence support the view that Toy did not want, nor expect, the
Trustees to accept his resignation.

In submitting the extensive document stating his views, including his
argument that the teaching of these views was beneficial, Toy handed in
his resignation in order to bring the whole matter to a head. He surely
knew there was a chance they might accept his resignation, but he most
likely thought his argument would carry the day and he would receive
vindication. There is no question but that the Board was now faced with
a rather complicated set of issues. Should they seriously consider the question of whether or not his view of inspiration violated the Abstract of
Principles? If Toy's views were not technically in conflict, they were more
advanced than those of most Southern Baptists. Was this deserving of dismissal? If he were dismissed on this ground, did it not make the Seminary
simply an institution to teach the majority view of Southern Baptists rather
than one of creative theological research and instruction? The immediate
way out of the dilemma was to appoint a committee. The five members
were chaired by James C. Furman, the president of Furman University, an
old friend and acquaintance of Toy. In fact, the chairman of the Board,
J. B. Jeter, later reported that all members of the committee were Toy's
"personal friends" (*Religious Herald*, 22 May 1879, 2).

The committee proceeded to have a period of consultation with Toy,
who was in Atlanta as a delegate of his home church, the Broadway Baptist
Church of Louisville. There is no record of what was said on either side,
though Jeter spoke of "an anxious consideration of the subject" (2). The
report of the committee was heard on the morning of 10 May 1879. It was
as follows:

They have had under protracted and serious consideration the matter committed to them. They sought a conference with Professor Toy, and in addition to the carefully expressed paper presented to the Board along with his resignation, they had a very free and candid expression of his opinions on some of the points less fully expressed in his written communication.

While deeply impressed with the beautiful Christian spirit of our beloved brother, they cannot but recognize what he himself asserts; that there is a divergence in his views of inspiration from those held by our brethren in general. In view of this divergence, your committee feel constrained to recommend to the Board the acceptance of Professor Toy's resignation. In this recommendation they concur unanimously. (From manuscript report held in the library of the Southern Baptist Theological Seminary)

It is reported that there was a "full discussion" by the entire Board. There is no record of what was said in that discussion, although Chairman Jeter reported in the *Religious Herald* of 22 May 1879:

The report was adopted by the Board, after earnest discussion, with only two dissenters, who deemed the action hasty. It was in no sense a trial of Dr. Toy. He was held in the highest estimation for his scholarship and piety by all the trustees. There was however a conceded divergence in his views from those generally held by supporters of the Seminary; and the trustees deemed it inexpedient to subject it to the disadvantages which would inevitably arise from a protracted controversy on an important theological subject, especially while efforts were being made to obtain an endowment. (2)

So the committee and the Board declined to enter into the question of Toy's orthodoxy or even to consider whether his teaching was in conflict with the Abstract of Principles. Essentially, they determined that the Seminary would be an institution that would mirror the current preponderant views of the denomination.

On Monday morning, 12 May 1879, two members of the Board sought to have their opposition to the action entered into the record of the meeting. These dissenters were D. W. Gwin, pastor of the First Baptist Church of Atlanta, Georgia, and J. A. Chambliss, pastor of the Citadel Square Baptist Church of Charleston, South Carolina. They felt that there had been no evaluation of what Toy had said in the document he had presented to the Board. It seemed to them that the acceptance of his resignation should not have occurred until the Board had come to some conclusions concerning these stated views. They wished the Board to postpone the decision for several months until it was possible to deal fairly with the issue. There had been no effort to determine whether or not Toy's views were hurtful to the progress of Christianity, and since there was no distinctive Baptist principle involved in the subject of inspiration, his views had done no violence to Baptist principles. However, the motion to reconsider was laid on the table. Thus, the decision reached was irrevocable.

The Board now elected Basil Manly, Jr., a member of the Board who had voted to accept Toy's resignation, to the position that Toy had held. Thus, the Board was able to announce the vacancy and the fact that it had been filled at the same time.

Toy's colleagues at the Seminary appeared pained by the whole episode. In a letter to his wife, Broadus wrote from Atlanta:

> Alas! The mournful deed is done. Toy's resignation is accepted. . . . I learned that the Board were all in tears as they voted. Poor bereaved three; we have lost our jewel of learning, our beloved and noble brother, the pride of the Seminary. God bless Toy, and God help us, sadly but steadfastly to do our providential duty. (Robertson, *Life and Letters*, 313)

When Toy was ready to leave Louisville, both Boyce and Broadus accompanied him to the railway station. There, Boyce threw his left arm about Toy's neck and lifting his right arm said, "Oh, Toy, I would freely give that arm to be cut off if you would be where you were five years ago, and stay there" (263–264).

Toy's closest colleague was William Heth Whitsitt,* the Seminary's church historian. To Whitsitt the whole episode was an academic calamity and a denominational blunder that had been created by ignorance and lack of appreciation. He would later be forced to resign his professorship and presidency because he stated a view of Baptist origins that was not current.

Some of Toy's friends and former students carried on the long battle through the Baptist papers during the months that followed. J. A. Chambliss was especially outspoken. He noted that the Trustees never dealt with the real question of whether Toy's views were "sensible and Christian." He and many others dreaded the thought of the Seminary "becoming a manufactory of theological music boxes, all shaped and pitched alike to give forth an invariable number of invariable tunes" (quotations from articles appearing in the *Courier* and *Herald*, in Lindsay, Scrapbook, 67, 68).

The Toy case was the subject of numerous newspaper accounts. It was through such an account that President Elliot of Harvard first heard of Toy. W. Robertson Smith was Elliot's first choice to occupy the chair of Hebrew and other Oriental languages. Smith, himself, was undergoing a trial for his teachings at the Free Church College, Aberdeen. When the Assembly in May 1880 refused to condemn him, Smith decided to remain in Scotland. Elliot then wrote Smith that the "Governing Body had appointed an American heretic, whose views on Isaiah had offended the Baptist communion to which he had belonged" (Black and Chrystal, *The Life of William Robertson Smith*, 375).

Toy quickly built up the Semitic department at Harvard and rapidly gained a reputation as one of the truly great scholars and teachers in his field. He published extensively, including books, articles, and reviews.

Toy's *History of the Religion of Israel* went through numerous editions and had tremendous influence in bringing even conservative seminaries into teaching the historical development of the Old and New Testament religions. The historical approach to the biblical period was not common among American biblical scholars when Toy began to advocate such.

Since the Toy episode, Southern Baptist scholars have been very cautious in their expression of the results of the critical study of the Bible, and the course of Southern Baptist theological education has continued to be disturbed.

Toy's loss to Southern Baptists surely became a gain for the whole Christian scholarly community.

BIBLIOGRAPHY

Black, J. S., and George Chrystal. *The Life of William Robertson Smith*. London: Adams and Charles Black, 1912.

Duncan, Pope A. "Crawford Howell Toy: Heresy at Louisville." In *American Religious Heretics*, edited by George H. Shriver. Nashville: Abingdon Press, 1966.

Hurt, Billy Grey. "Crawford Howell Toy: Interpreter of the Old Testament." Th.D. diss., Southern Baptist Theological Seminary, 1965.

Lindsay, Pauline. Scrapbook composed of newspaper clippings, in the library of Southern Baptist Theological Seminary. Contains many items relating to the Toy controversy.

Lyon, David G. "Crawford Howell Toy." *Harvard Theological Review* 13 (January 1920): 1–22.

Moore, George F. "An Appreciation of Professor Toy." *American Journal of Semitic Languages and Literature* 26 (October 1919): 1–17.

Robertson, Archibald Thomas. *Life and Letters of John Albert Broadus*. Philadelphia: American Baptist Publication Society, 1901.

Toy, Crawford Howell. *History of the Religion of Israel*. Boston: Unitarian Sunday School Society, 1882.

Pope A. Duncan

William Heth Whitsitt
(1841–1911)

In May 1899, Trustees of the Southern Baptist Theological Seminary accepted the resignation of William Heth Whitsitt, professor of ecclesiastical history and president of the institution since 1895. The resignation had been submitted in July 1898, culminating three years of bitter controversy and revealing deep divisions among the Trustees and Southern Baptists. Some Baptists questioned Whitsitt's presidential leadership because they rejected conclusions he had reached in his historical research. In a series of articles published anonymously in 1880, Whitsitt had argued that Baptists in England had practiced immersion as the mode of baptism only since 1641. After his accession as president in 1895, the controversy steadily gained momentum, threatening the viability of Southern Seminary. Whitsitt realized that only his resignation would halt the erosion of support for the Seminary that could deprive Baptists of the means to establish an educated ministry. W. O. Carver, his colleague and supporter, viewed Whitsitt as a martyr in the maturation of Southern Baptists, a necessary but regrettable sacrifice that the events and scholarship of the future would vindicate (Carver, "William Heth Whitsitt," 467–469).

William Whitsitt was born near Nashville, Tennessee, in 1841. His Scots-Irish ancestors moved from Virginia in 1788 after having abandoned their native Presbyterianism for the enthusiasm of Baptists in a local frontier revival. William's grandfather was a Baptist preacher of considerable reputation in Tennessee and a powerful influence on the youngster. After early education at a local academy, William received his baccalaureate in 1861 from Union University in Murfreesboro, where he established a reputation for conscientious study and graduated with distinction. He served with the Army of Tennessee under Nathan B. Forrest, first as a private and, after ordination by his grandfather's church in 1862, as a chaplain. In 1866, Whitsitt studied for a year at the University of Virginia, then for two more at the Southern Baptist Seminary in Greenville, South Carolina. He again impressed the faculty, particularly John A. Broadus. His formal preparation was completed with two years in Germany at the Universities of Leipzig and Berlin, where he imbibed deeply from the scientific orientation in scholarship that characterized continental studies. In the fall of 1872, Whitsitt became professor of ecclesiastical history at Southern Seminary in Greenville. He taught polemical theology, history of doctrine, and special classes in reading theological works in German. According to a contemporary colleague, his course in church history was characterized by the patient methods of German investigative scholarship and the incorporation of careful research into class presentations. By his own admission, Whitsitt was more comfortable in individual research, and only with effort could he impart his conclusions to students and challenge them to think creatively on another's collected data. But he treated students as fellow searchers and set for them an example of careful methodology, keen insight, and creative communication of conclusions. "In pointing out the significance of movements and of men, Doctor Whitsitt was at his best. With him history was philosophy teaching by example" (Pollard, "The Life and Work of William Heth Whitsitt," 164). Influenced by his thorough training in the classical languages and literature, his lectures frequently included uncommon expressions or utilized ordinary words in their classical rather than contemporary meanings. In lectures and preaching, such usage dramatized the word picture that he created; in written scholarship, however, only fellow scholars fully appreciated the nuances that he intended. For others, especially critics, unusual language was the fuel for misunderstanding and the means for misrepresentation.

In 1880, Whitsitt spent a sabbatical leave in England, studying documents in the British Museum and the Bodleian Library on the origins of English Baptists. As a historian, he was well aware that Baptists bridged the gap between the authoritative New Testament period and the contemporary existence of the church with undocumented historical generalizations. For the most part, Baptists saw nothing of real importance in the institutional church, both Roman Catholic and Protestant, that was not also preserved in an independent stream allegedly stretching unbroken from the time of Jesus to a contemporary Baptist congregation. Moreover, the historic church had abandoned many identifying marks and practices of the true New Testament church including, most notably, the immersion of believers upon their personal confession of faith. The resulting Baptist individualism troubled Whitsitt deeply. He wanted Baptists to study and to understand their history and their true relationship with the larger fellowship of Christians. He believed that documentary study using the scientific methods of German scholarship could begin that task in his own time and would strengthen the denomination that he loved. In the late nineteenth century, that denomination was in danger, Whitsitt believed. Baptist individualism frequently precluded interdenominational cooperation in the important tasks of evangelism and missions. Even ministerial education received less than full support from the churches. Whitsitt's fears and frustrations in this regard even led him to consider uniting with another denomination. In his personal diary, he wrestled with his own soul: "[W]hither can I go? Ah, whither alas!" (quoted in Carver, "William Heth Whitsitt," 454). He did not dare discuss his personal doubts with colleagues or friends, confining his struggle to his own mind. Only on the idea of the exclusivity of the local church did Whitsitt question the doctrines held dear by Baptists. But in that area, Whitsitt believed that individualism threatened the vitality and continuing existence of Baptists and hence the wholeness of the gospel ministry.

From documentary evidence, Whitsitt became convinced while studying in England that an unbroken line of immersion baptism from New Testament times could not be reliably demonstrated. His research established that English antecedents of American Baptists had introduced immersion into their congregation only in 1641 and practiced that mode consistently only afterward. Whitsitt published his findings anonymously in 1880 in an independent religious periodical; his authorship remained unknown for 15 years. He submitted his research to recognized Mennonite, Congregational, and Baptist scholars, including A. H. Newman and Henry S. Vedder, and all had accepted his methodology and his conclusions. Whitsitt therefore incorporated this material into his lectures at the Seminary and in 1893 contributed an article on Baptists for *Johnson's Universal Cyclopedia* in which—under his own name—he set forth his startling conclusions of the 1880s. Immediately, opposition of Baptists appeared in the periodical press. In the ensuing exchange, Whitsitt contended that his earlier anonymous authorship was not an attempt to hide his identity but to establish the priority of his research in relation to other Baptist historians who by the 1880s were advocating similar ideas. Amid calls for his resignation, Whitsitt published the full elaboration of his scholarship in *A Question in Baptist History* (1896). According to the standards of his time, it was an admirable piece of historical writing. He carefully reviewed recent historical work on the subject, giving full documentation. He briefly sketched the Christian usage of baptism on the continent and in England, showing the predominance of infant baptism generally and the almost complete acceptance of pouring or sprinkling even among the Anabaptists of Reformation times. No Anabaptists in England or Holland, from whom English Baptists received the ordinance, immersed. Mennonites in Amsterdam, who accepted John Smyth, Thomas Helwys, and their small English congregation, baptized adults by sprinkling and pouring. None of the primary documents of this church prescribed immersion, and records after the congregation returned to England do not include immersion until 1641.

Whitsitt analyzed and critiqued other theories advocating an earlier immersion of Smyth and immersions of Anabaptists, which were accepted by historians Thomas Crosby and Thomas Armitage. He then moved to the documents of the 1630s and 1640s relating to the Jessey Church and the William Kiffin Manuscript. These authenticated materials of the earliest English Baptists clearly demonstrated that the congregations known as Particular Baptists reintroduced the mode of immersion in 1641, and thereafter it rapidly became mandated practice among these churches. Whitsitt buttressed his conclusion with reviews of pamphlets published immediately after 1641 that testified that immersion was unknown in England prior to that time and that themselves argued for or against the restoration of the practice. All together, the evidence for restoration at this time was convincing, both for Whitsitt and for modern scholarship.

The presentation was weakened when Whitsitt appended a brief summary of the evidence concerning whether Roger Williams* was immersed in 1639. He thought not, but a clear conclusion was impossible. Whitsitt again was faithful to his documents and admitted that the question remained open. But his decision to include this appendix was probably a mistake, since it clearly antagonized his opponents unnecessarily.

Whitsitt also complicated the situation when he stated in early writings that Baptists "invented immersion" in 1641 in England without clarifying that immersion had been employed in other times and places but not in England itself. He used the term *invented* in "its strictly etymological sense of having 'come upon' and adopted" (Carver, "William Heth Whitsitt," 465). The critics exploited the archaic usage and misled less-educated Baptists on Whitsitt's true intent.

Despite these weaknesses, Whitsitt's writing was a sound historical presentation, even by modern standards. Primary and contemporary materials were carefully explored and major points precisely documented. Whitsitt's conclusions appear consistent with the data. But the publication did not silence Whitsitt's critics. Instead, the opposition increased, and many fully expected the Seminary Trustees quietly to remove this erroneous professor who now led Baptists' most prominent institution for the preparation of young ministers.

Since Baptists had no procedure regarding the formal removal of persons for deviation or heresy, Whitsitt's "trial" was conducted publicly in the periodical press and in discussions in associations, churches, and conventions (Beck, "The Whitsitt Controversy," 260–261). It can best be reviewed briefly through the ideas and motivations of his critics.

In another time and place, William Whitsitt's research conclusions would have made little difference to Baptists in America. The churches viewed their mission in terms of contemporary evangelism, and its success validated their emphasis. As the denomination flourished in the nineteenth century, it became more programmatic and self-conscious, and an earlier indifference to the past Baptist witness gave way to a new awareness of history. Several Christian groups competed with Baptists on the American frontier, and Presbyterians, Methodists, and Disciples of Christ were equally successful. These groups undergirded their contemporary message with clear reference to their place in the unfolding of God's kingdom in this world. Presbyterians could point to John Calvin and the Protestant Reformation, Methodists to their birth within Anglicanism, and Disciples to their restoration of pure New Testament Christianity. A young America needed to connect the excitement of new democracy and religious enthusiasm to the deeper traditions of classical civilization and Christianity. In this context, Baptists by midcentury sought to emphasize their distinctive preservation of local congregational autonomy and believer's baptism by immersion. The historical continuity of that tradition grew more and more important in the competitive environment of the American frontier.

Among Baptists, that movement became known as Landmarkism. At an association meeting in 1848, Tennessee Baptists led by J. R. Graves questioned the long-standing tradition of inviting non-Baptist ministers to a final session to strengthen the spirit of Christian cooperation in the task of evangelizing the frontier. Later, Graves presented a series of ideas that defined the true church as totally local in character, having a ministry directly commissioned by Jesus and composed exclusively of believers who had been immersed upon their profession of faith. No universal church existed in the New Testament, he contended, and through the centuries, other Christian groups were societies or movements, not churches. Only the local Baptist Church could correctly use that designation. Graves advocated that true churches had existed in an unbroken chain that extended from Jerusalem to the smallest Baptist congregation on the American frontier. The preservation of the true witness forced Landmark Baptists to deny the valid ministerial ordination of other Christians, to reject any baptism except of believers immersed by a true minister, and to disallow any observance of the Lord's Supper except by members of a particular congregation. Graves publicized his ideas through his position as editor of *The Tennessee Baptist*, while Kentuckian J. M. Pendleton wrote a pamphlet entitled *An Old Landmark Reset* (1857), and A. C. Dayton popularized the movement in a two-volume novel called *Theodosia Ernest* in the late 1850s.

This localism gave immediate and exclusive standing to the individual Baptist congregations and rapidly grew in popular acceptance on the American frontier. Older Baptist Churches in the coastal states, which were well established in the mainstream of American religious life and needed no such exclusiveness to promote their evangelism, viewed the Landmark ideas as a break with historic Baptist perceptions, as a discouragement of cooperation with other denominations, and as a dangerous threat to the organizations of churches that had been founded to promote and manage Baptist educational and evangelistic efforts. Indeed, according to Graves, the Southern Baptist Convention, founded in 1845, was unnecessary. He believed that it confused the gospel mission of the true Baptist Church; a local Baptist Church should commission and support its own missionaries in the task of preaching the gospel to the world.

Periodicals, pamphlets, and sermons debated the meaning of New Testament *ecclesia* relative to the local and universal church and simply assumed that the correct translation of *baptizo* could be no other than immersion of believers. The controversy raged in the 1850s and resumed in more muted tones after the Civil War. A substantial majority of Southern Baptists accepted the Landmark interpretation, and most of them lived west of the Appalachians. As the frontier states gained more and more Baptists, power shifted into these strongholds of Landmark ecclesiology. When the Seminary was moved from Greenville, South Carolina, to Louisville, Kentucky, it was surrounded by the Landmarkist mode of thought. It was not surprising, therefore, that local opposition to Whitsitt's interpretation of Baptist history was immediate and intense. The most prominent critic was Thomas T. Eaton, Whitsitt's pastor at the Walnut Street Baptist Church in Louisville.

According to many of his contemporaries and Charles B. Bugg's research of the entire controversy, Eaton was an outspoken, aggressive, and ambitious Baptist leader. He disagreed with the results of Whitsitt's research, and the long friendship between the two men showed strain as early as 1894. For Eaton, Baptists were to maintain the purity of the faith "once and for all time delivered to the saints." As pastor of Walnut Street, his opinion carried weight among Baptist laymen. Moreover, Eaton was editor of the *Western Recorder*, the state Baptist paper of Kentucky, which gave his ideas even wider circulation. Rosalie Beck has documented that state papers were potent means of influencing Baptist thinking, and the Kentucky editor did not hesitate to use that forum to advocate his perspective. Finally, Eaton had aspired to be president of the Seminary when Whitsitt was elected in 1895 and apparently even sought to delay the election for a year in hopes of strengthening support for himself among the Trustees. When that failed, he publicly praised the choice of Whitsitt, but the breach was substantial and became evident when the Whitsitts transferred their membership from Walnut Street to the McFerran Memorial Baptist Church in 1896. Eaton consistently maintained that his concern was solely for Baptist ecclesiology, but many contemporaries and modern scholars believe that his presidential ambitions contributed substantially to his criticism of Whitsitt.

Franklin H. Kerfoot, a faculty colleague of Whitsitt, also aspired to the presidency. As treasurer of the Seminary, he had experience in financial matters and, according to W. O. Carver, was deeply disappointed when his candidacy failed to gather support in 1895. He was unpopular with students, and some believed that personal experience too frequently substituted for scholarship in his courses. While Kerfoot also professed public support for Whitsitt throughout the controversy, the beleaguered president believed Kerfoot to be the source of subtle opposition and the primary influence in undermining the positive support of faculty colleagues A. T. Robertson and John Sampey during the final days of the controversy. According to Whitsitt papers studied by Charles Bugg, Kerfoot's knowledge of the financial circumstances of the Seminary was used to frighten Robertson into believing that only Whitsitt's resignation would save the Seminary (Bugg, "The Whitsitt Controversy," 106). In 1899, the Trustees failed again to respond to Kerfoot's candidacy, and soon thereafter, he left the institution.

John T. Christian, a Louisville pastor, countered Whitsitt's conclusions with his own research published in *Did They Dip?* and *Baptist History Vindicated*. Whitsitt's opponents frequently cited both, but historians recognized that Christian's writings were flawed. Regarding Roger Williams's baptism, Henry M. King, pastor of First Baptist of Providence, wrote books and articles defending the tradition of Williams as an immersed Baptist. King believed that Whitsitt misread the English evidence, but his own demonstrations were clearly inconclusive.

As the controversy spread throughout the Southern Baptist Convention, the most articulate and influential opponent of Whitsitt was Benajah H. Carroll of Texas, pastor of the First Baptist Church of Waco and a Seminary Trustee during Whitsitt's tenure. During the early stages of the controversy, Carroll remained quiet, believing that the Trustees would correctly deal with what he considered to be Whitsitt's flawed conception of the church. Carroll was essentially a Landmarkist, praising Graves, Pendleton, and Dayton as denominational leaders and using Pendleton's *Church Manual* in his Waco church as a text in ecclesiology. Carroll rejected the idea of a universal church; the only true church was the local group of baptized believers. He affirmed Baptist succession in theory and needed no extensive documentation of the chain from John "the first Baptist" to the present. He did not, however, follow Landmarkism in its rejection of denominational organizations in support of missions and other causes of evangelism. He was a tireless worker for the Boards of Home and Foreign Missions and strongly supported efforts to educate Baptist ministers for Texas churches. Carroll's opposition to Whitsitt surfaced after the 1897 convention seemed to allow Whitsitt's interpretation of Baptist history to stand unchallenged and the Seminary Trustees appeared ready to leave the matter alone. Carroll then expressed his views editorially through the *Western Recorder* and reignited the controversy. He rejected Whitsitt's conclusions and voiced the concern that Baptists would cease to support the Seminary financially because of Whitsitt's leadership. Hence, he suggested, it might be necessary to separate the Seminary from official Baptist support in order to preserve its viability. Carroll perceived Whitsitt as a threat to Baptist unity in support of education and missions. The Texan's editorial triggered a chain of events, ostensibly to save the Seminary, that culminated in Whitsitt's resignation.

Many Baptists defended the scholarship and leadership of the Seminary president. William E. Hatcher, an influential Virginia pastor and Seminary Trustee, campaigned tirelessly. A. T. Robertson, professor of New Testament, supported President Whitsitt until convinced that the Seminary was in mortal danger. George Loftin, a pastor in Nashville, wrote articles and published four books defending Whitsitt's conclusions on the recovery of immersion in 1641. The Seminary faculty and students in general supported Whitsitt both as a scholar and as an able administrator.

Both sides believed that the Southern Baptist Convention meeting in Wilmington, North Carolina, in May 1897, would debate the matter and establish a trend for or against Whitsitt. But discussion was limited to a closed meeting of the Trustees. Whitsitt apologized for the manner in which he presented his research in anonymous publications but held firm to the conclusions he had reached. Carroll wanted the matter forwarded to the convention floor for debate, but the Trustees defeated his proposal. It appeared to be a victory for Whitsitt supporters, but the activities of critics intensified. By fall, the battle raged in state periodicals and local associations while Whitsitt worked to maintain the Seminary enrollment and financial stability. He succeeded despite an outbreak of yellow fever in the South that hurt enrollment and a general economic depression that threatened contributions. The 1898 convention meeting in Norfolk, Virginia, left the Whitsitt controversy untouched once again, but a June meeting of the Kentucky General Association voted 198 to 26 to request Whitsitt's resignation. This grassroots opposition fueled Carroll's earlier contention that the Seminary must become independent because Whitsitt's presidency would destroy Baptist support.

When the Trustees met in July 1898, the trial conducted in the Baptist fashion was over; his resignation was tendered, effective in May 1899, giving ten months for the jury of Southern Baptist opinion to crystallize. Efforts of Whitsitt's supporters during that year never gained momentum, handicapped by fear for the Seminary's future. Even A. T. Robertson and John Sampey quietly urged their friend and colleague not to resist what appeared inevitable. Whitsitt's resignation from the presidency was accepted in May 1899 with little opposition; his resignation as professor was accepted by a vote of 22 to 20. After a year of rest and further research in England, Whitsitt returned to Louisville, then accepted a teaching position at Richmond College where he completed his professional career.

An article by Rufus Weaver, citing George W. Lasker's *Baptist Ministerial Directory* (1899), revealed the educational experience of Baptist ministers who led the judgment on Whitsitt's scholarship and leadership (Weaver, "Life and Times of William Heth Whitsitt," 121–123). Of those answering a survey, 49 percent had no training beyond elementary school; almost 60 percent had no college experience. Less than 6 percent of all Southern Baptist ministers had theological training. Of over 10,300 active ministers, 313 had attended Southern Seminary and 60 had earned a degree. In 1895, 58 graduates of Southern were in pastorates in the South, half of them in Virginia and South Carolina. Therefore, few ministers knew Whitsitt except through the periodical press. These editors likewise had little theological training, but they knew that emotional issues filled churches and controversy sold subscriptions. The jury appeared ill-equipped for judgment.

The teaching of Baptist history in the twentieth century has resoundingly vindicated the scholarship of William Whitsitt. His immediate successor in the Southern Seminary classroom taught the Whitsitt interpretation that English Baptists reintroduced immersion baptism in 1641 (Carver, "William Heth Whitsitt," 468). Baptist institutions of higher education and professional training have consistently accepted both Whitsitt's scholarship and his conclusions.

It therefore appears that Whitsitt's trial and forced resignation involved more than issues of academic freedom and scholarship. While critics would have attacked Whitsitt's interpretations in publications and in the classroom, it was his position as leader of Southern Seminary that sufficiently armed critics with powerful weapons in the Baptist press. And Whitsitt's nonaggressive personality, which endeared him to students and faculty, did not equip him for public battle. His convictions in scholarship never wavered, but he clearly would not risk Southern Seminary's future in order to solidify historical conclusions that his scholarly peers had readily accepted and had confirmed on their own research. Powerful personalities using demagogic tactics were determined to scuttle Whitsitt's leadership. Some likely desired the Seminary presidency for themselves; others enjoyed their roles as king makers. Baptists cherish the radical democracy in which leaders flourish or wither according to popular acclaim. It is a heavy price that sometimes batters the truth unmercifully. In William Whitsitt, however, truth ultimately triumphed—but not without the pain of personal tragedy.

SELECTED BIBLIOGRAPHY

Beck, Rosalie. "The Whitsitt Controversy: A Denomination in Crisis." Ph.D. diss., Baylor University, 1985.

Bugg, Charles B. "The Whitsitt Controversy: A Study in Denominational Conflict." Th.D. diss., Southern Baptist Theological Seminary, 1972.

Carver, W. O. "William Heth Whitsitt: The Seminary's Martyr." *Review and Expositor* 51 (October 1954): 449–469.

Pollard, E. B. "The Life and Work of William Heth Whitsitt." *Review and Expositor* 9 (April 1912): 159–184.

Weaver, Rufus W. "Life and Times of William Heth Whitsitt." *Review and Expositor* 37 (April 1940): 115–132.

Whitsitt, William H. *A Question in Baptist History.* Louisville, KY: Charles T. Dearing, 1896; reprint, New York: Arno Press, 1980.

Jerry L. Surratt

Roger Williams
(c. 1603–1684)

As part of the Great Migration of Puritans leaving England in the 1630s, Roger and Mary Williams boarded a sailing vessel in Bristol in December 1630 and two months later arrived off the coast of the tiny Massachusetts Bay Colony. The Williams party, like the John Winthrop party that had departed eight months earlier, fled England only with reluctance and sadness. But convinced as these earnest Christians were that the Church of England had no interest in becoming a pure and truly reformed church, conforming to the New Testament as closely as possible, their consciences compelled this daring and risky venture into the unknown. Old England had failed to set a sterling example of what the Protestant Reformation was all about; a new England, without bumptious bishops or arrogant kings, could put things right and become an example to a spiritually hungry and waiting world.

Roger Williams shared this grand vision for the future even as he shared the grim assessment of old England's stubborn failures and ecclesiastical corruption. The Church of England concerned itself with fashion, not faith; with Parliament, not piety. And if it would not listen to its own reformers but only stifle and silence them, then those reformers must seek another land where the gospel could be freely proclaimed and triumphantly lived. "Behold," said the apostle Paul, "all things are become new."

For Williams and a few others, this meant starting afresh, with an entirely new church, with a slate cleansed of all tired traditions and liturgical encumbrances, with a New Testament unalloyed and uncompromised. For Winthrop and many others, the newness only required a reformation from within: One need not forsake the venerable national church, only purify and perfect it. What may have seemed to be only a difference in emphasis quickly became an unbridgeable difference in principle. In healing the Church of England of its many ills, the Puritans believed that medicines and gentle therapies could cure. Williams took a stand in favor of radical surgery; if one does not cut himself off wholly from that which is corrupt and unclean, the corruption will continue to fester, poison, and ultimately destroy.

Standing in the more radical ranks of Puritanism as well as with such early English Baptists as John Smith, Thomas Helwys, and John Murton, Roger Williams as Separatist advocated a complete break with the Church of England. Anything less was temporizing, compromising, hypocritical. It was, said Williams, like trying to walk down a road with one foot on the path and the other in the ditch. Or, in another figure, it was like trying to build a square house on the keel of a ship. The result would be an architectural joke; more seriously, it would never prove to be a "soul saving Ark or Church of Christ Jesus." One must, as the Scriptures made clear, separate the "holy from unholy, the penitent from impenitent, the godly from ungodly." "My conscience was persuaded," Williams wrote, "against the national church and ceremonies." The greatest insult to divine majesty was to pretend to pay homage to the true God with a false worship. Such was equivalent, declared Williams, "to a spirit and disposition of spiritual drunkenness and whoredom, a soul sleep and a soul sickness" (Gaustad, 25ff.).

Once Williams began looking at Winthrop's "New England Way" more critically, he found much to denounce and reject. Puritans had happily left politically powerful and spiritually corrupt bishops behind, but they had failed to leave behind the fatal alliance between politics and religion. In Massachusetts the civil magistrates did not distinguish between duties purely "civil," on the one hand, and intrusions into affairs properly ecclesiastical or spiritual, on the other. Like bishops before them, the magistrates punished heresies, enforced church discipline, made laws for the Sabbath, and required even unbelievers to take religious oaths in court. Civil authority, Williams argued, had no "commission from Christ Jesus" to declare what was a true church or a false one, what was a true ministry or a false one. Only the church could make such judgments, he asserted, and only the church might punish (but never by the sword) the spiritual offender.

Massachusetts was fond, Williams pointed out, of comparing itself to the nation of Israel in the Old Testament where church and state were mixed together or—in Williams's language—where the wilderness of the world invaded the garden of the church. New England was still hung up on Moses, forgetting that there was now a new covenant, a new testament, a new Israel that is not a state or a nation but only a Christian community—a spiritual, not a political, entity. If one takes the New Testament seriously, Williams explained, one sees that Jesus made no appeal to civil authorities, nor did He seek help from them in advancing His cause. In fact, the light of Christianity never burns so brightly as when it is persecuted rather than "protected," just as stars shine the brightest on the darkest nights, and spices smell the sweetest when ground, pounded, and crushed.

When civil authorities behave like spiritual rulers, then the church—that garden or bride of Christ—is corrupted, ravished, ruined. And history testifies to the horror and folly of such mixing of power that should always be kept separate. The blood of innocent men, women, and children has been repeatedly shed, "oceans of blood," because civil authorities did not confine themselves to civil matters. Rather, over and over, the tender consciences of all humankind have been violated as persons have been forced to support a church they did not attend, to perform a ritual in which they did not believe, to heed a ministry they did not call. Wars have been fought, heads have been severed, tongues have been burned—all in the name of God of peace and love. Christ Jesus, said Williams, came into the world not to destroy men's lives but to save them.

Roger Williams also expressed his dismay over the treatment of the American Indians, especially the greedy appropriation of their land. By what right did English Puritans occupy Boston and surrounding areas, Williams asked. By royal right and explicit stipulations of the founding charter, the Massachusetts Bay authorities quickly replied. King Charles I had granted to these settlers "all that part of America" from 40 to 48 degrees northern latitude "from sea to sea," together with "all the firm lands, soils, grounds, havens, ports, rivers, waters, fishing, mines, and minerals." Could anything be clearer? That matter, at least, was firmly settled. Yes, that was settled, Williams agreed, if only we can find out who gave all that expanse, from sea to sea, to Charles I in the first place. Certainly not the native Americans who were already here; certainly not Moses who was, otherwise, the favorite lawgiver of the Puritans.

Sounding very modern, Williams protested that English colonization was nothing less than a "sin of unjust usurpation upon other's possessions." The land was initially theirs and would remain theirs unless purchased or acquired through mutual agreement. Sounding very defensive, Winthrop explained that land that "lies common, and hath never been replenished or subdued is free to any that possess or improve it" (Gaustad, 32ff.). Besides, Winthrop added, the Indians were not suffering: "If we leave them sufficient for their use, we may lawfully use the rest, there being more than enough for them and us" (Gaustad, 32ff.). The real question, however, gradually intensifying, was whether Massachusetts had enough land to contain both Williams and the Bay Colony leaders—"him and us."

For if Williams was growing ever more dissatisfied with Puritan behavior and belief, the spokesmen were growing ever more weary and wary of this noisy dissenter in their midst. To hear him, said the authorities, we must conclude that our worship is false, our government tyrannical, our charter null and void. Godly patience could not be infinite. In the early 1630s, the Bay Colony was fighting for survival in an inhospitable wilderness. The last thing that it needed, the last thing that it could endure, were threats to its fragile hegemony, challenges to its still-forming authority. Williams, it appeared, could not be ignored, for the moment one controversy began to die down, he quickly provoked another. Could he be silenced? or intimidated? or somehow persuaded to change his destabilizing opinions?

In December of 1633 the General Court decided to fire a warning shot across Williams's bow. The Court, which really was a court but also the legislative and executive arms of the infant colony, gathered unto itself all the civil authority that could be brought to bear on any problem of equity or law—or dissent. When the leaders heard Williams question the charter that King Charles had granted, they decided that any attack on the charter was also an attack on the king. Could Williams be found guilty of treason? If so, then that troubler of Israel might be brought to heel with some finality and force.

At this juncture, the Court proceeded with commendable caution. They consulted with the two leading ministers of Boston's first and only church to see if the charge of treason could be made to stick. The ministers (John Wilson and John Cotton) concluded that the language that Roger Williams had employed was somewhat obscure and ambiguous; perhaps no traitorous rhetoric was intended. If Williams would acknowledge that Charles I was his king, too, and that he was a loyal son of the crown, perhaps this unpleasant matter could, just now, be set aside. Williams assured the Court that no treason was intended. He sought justice for the Indians, not destruction for England. The result of this first encounter with the General Court was a standoff, but Williams was not through with the Puritans, nor they with him.

In 1634 Williams continued to roil the waters, joining others in a demand that women wear veils in church (as some thought was implied by I Corinthians 11:13) and with still others in demanding that the cross, a papal cross at that, be removed from the English flag. These, however, were minor matters compared with his challenge to the charter, his efforts to limit the scope of the civil magistrates, and his call for radical surgery with respect to England's national church. These positions threatened the very foundations on which Governor Winthrop and others sought to erect an enduring and godly commonwealth. By March 1635, some on the General Court were prepared to go after Williams once again, being dissuaded from doing so by the assertions of John Cotton (later Williams's more voluble antagonist) that the hard questions that Williams raised were fundamentally theological rather than political. Another standoff, but the inevitable crept closer.

Meanwhile, after a brief stay in Plymouth Colony, Williams returned to his original place of settlement in Salem. There, to the surprise and con-

sternation of Boston authorities, the church in the summer of 1635 elected
Roger Williams as the official teaching elder of the congregation. This could
be seen as a defiance of the Winthrop forces, a strengthening of the Williams party, and a hint of civil and debilitating strife between the young
settlements of Boston and Salem. The General Court decided it was time
to show some muscle. In July, Williams was summoned to appear once
more, this time to be informed that his opinions were "erroneous and very
dangerous" and that he should be removed from his church office. The
Court recognized that it did not have authority to effect that removal; it
did have the authority, however, to delay acting on a Salem petition for a
grant of land—to delay until the town and its church came to their collective senses.

Over the next three months, positions on both sides hardened. Williams
urged the Salem church to separate itself from all other churches in the Bay
Colony, a proposal so radical that many in his congregation declined to
follow his lead. For its part, the Court concluded that every concession
made to Williams resulted only in his making more uncompromising demands and in his advancing more unnerving opinions. By October the
Court stood ready to deal with Williams once more, this time without
ambiguity or evasion or doubt. The Puritan colony, a mere five years old,
was still on trial in the minds of Parliament and the king, if not in the
minds of many Massachusetts settlers as well. Virginia, after all, had been
deemed a failure in less than two decades after the founding of Jamestown
and so was taken over by the king in 1624. If Massachusetts could not
keep its own house in order, others stood ready to do it for them.

So on 8 October 1635, Williams would be given one final chance to
recant those "dangerous opinions" and one final chance to be convinced
of his error by the learned arguments of Thomas Hooker, founder of the
Connecticut colony. When the next morning the Court learned that Williams had neither recanted nor repented, that august body was ready with
its pronouncement.

> Whereas Mr. Roger Williams, one of the elders of the church at Salem,
> hath broached & divulged diverse new & dangerous opinions, against
> the authority of magistrates, as also written letters of defamation, both
> of the magistrates & churches here, & that before any conviction, &
> yet maintaineth the same without retraction, it is therefore ordered,
> that the said Mr. Williams shall depart out of this jurisdiction within
> six weeks . . . which if he neglect to perform, it shall be lawful for the
> Governor & two of the magistrates to send him to some place out of
> this jurisdiction, not to return any more without license from the Court.
> (Shurtleff, *Records*, 1: 160–161)

Exile: unequivocal, undebatable, unpostponable. Roger Williams who had
arrived in Massachusetts less than five years before, filled with vision and

dedication, now stood condemned and despised by those with whom he had once bravely joined in the battle for a purified church and an emancipated gospel.

Boston officialdom granted Williams six weeks to put his affairs in order and prepare his young family for departure (his second child was born that very October). Williams was granted this time period only, however, if he did not go about trying to draw others toward those new and dangerous opinions. The dissenter kept his part of the bargain, at least as he interpreted it, by not engaging in any public preaching or exhorting. But those who called at the family home found that Williams had changed his mind not one whit. Word inevitably seeped back to Boston that Williams had not maintained a perfect silence—such would have been beyond the power of most men, certainly of this voluble radical.

The General Court ordered Williams back for a hearing, but the latter begged off on the ground of illness. Hardly mollified, the Court decided that it had been lenient enough. It would seize Williams, immediately put him aboard a ship bound for England, and thus prevent the heretical plague from spreading any farther. But whispers could spread from Boston to Salem just as well as in the opposite direction. Williams resolved to frustrate the Court one more time, leaving home before the officers of the law arrived. When the Court's deputies did show up, "they found he had been gone three days before; but whither they could not learn." The "whither" was a mystery to Williams himself, for he knew better what he fled from than what he fled to. He fled from his fellow countrymen from whom he now expected no charity; he fled from the prospect of a persecuting English church that would salivate over the thought of getting its hands on a dissenter so uncompromising that even the Puritans could not tolerate him. He fled toward the Indians, concluding that he would find more hospitality among the wild "savages" than among the civilized English. He also fled for refuge into the arms of God, as his modest poetic effort made clear.

God makes a Path, provides a Guide,
And feeds in Wildernesse!
His glorious name while breath remaines,
O that I may confesse.

Lost many a time, I have had no Guide,
No House, but Hollow Tree!
In stormy Winter night no Fire,
No Food, no Company:

In him I have found a House, a Bed,
A Table, Company:

No Cup so bitter, but's made sweet,
When God shall Sweet'ning be.
(Williams, *A Key into the Language*
of America, 153–154)

He trudged through January's bitter snow and cold, "exposed to the mercy of an howling Wilderness," not knowing for 14 weeks what bread or bed did mean. At length, he escaped beyond the bounds of the Bay Colony, moving slowly southward to the headwaters of Narragansett Bay. There he purchased some land from the Indians and named his settlement Providence "in a Sense of God's merciful Providence to me in my distress." And there in the spring, he would welcome family, friends, and neighbors into the new colony of Rhode Island and Providence Plantations.

When the Massachusetts General Court in 1635 banished Roger Williams from its territory, John Cotton explained that Williams had not been exiled so much as "enlarged" to the whole country beyond. Cotton spoke better than he knew. Williams had indeed been "enlarged," as he published back in London works that would do two things: first, give his side of the controversy with the Bay Colony authorities; and second, make the case as passionately and persuasively as he possibly could for a full freedom of conscience in all matters of religion. This he did notably in his *Bloudy Tenent of Persecution for Cause of Conscience* (1644), a book burned in London, despised in Massachusetts, honored in Rhode Island, and eventually vindicated in a new nation that in 1791 gave the "free exercise of religion" its most powerful legal expression.

Williams was also "enlarged" so far as his denominational impact was concerned. Though a Baptist only briefly, he helped bring America's first Baptist Church into existence in Providence, Rhode Island, in 1638. Beyond that, however, he gave to the Baptists a cause—"soul liberty"—that provided them with an identity and a rallying point for generations to come. Although the Baptists grew quite slowly in the seventeenth and the first half of the eighteenth century, they made Rhode Island a haven for dissenters of all stripes, especially the harshly persecuted Quakers. By the time of the Great Awakening in the 1740s and of the Revolution in the 1770s, Baptists began their dramatic march across the North American continent, always keeping before them the clear-eyed vision of him whom Massachusetts rejected.

In 1936, just over 300 years after the sentence of exile was pronounced against Roger Williams, the legislature of Massachusetts formally revoked its earlier action. Long before that time, however, Williams had been exonerated by an American public determined to keep the calloused hands of government far, far away from the tender sanctuary of the soul. The heresy trial of 1635 had helped to determine the meaning and shape of all subsequent American history.

BIBLIOGRAPHY

Gaustad, Edwin S. *Liberty of Conscience: Roger Williams in America*. Grand Rapids: Eerdmans Publishing Co., 1996.

LaFantasie, Glenn W. *The Correspondence of Roger Williams*. Hanover, NH: University Press of New England, 1988.

Morgan, Edmund S. *Roger Williams: The Church and the State*. New York: Harcourt, Brace, 1967.

Shurtleff, Nathaniel G., ed. *Records of the Governor and Company of the Massachusetts Bay in New England*. 5 vols. Boston: William White, 1853.

Williams, Roger. *A Key into the Language of America*. 1643. Edited by V. V. Teunissen and E. V. Hinz. Detroit: Wayne State University Press, 1973.

Winslow, Ola E. *Master Roger Williams: A Biography*. New York: Macmillan & Co., 1957.

Edwin S. Gaustad

Alexander Winchell
(1824–1891)

Alexander Winchell was an author, teacher, geologist, and publicist whose termination as professor of geology and zoology at Vanderbilt University in 1878 for his views on evolution attracted widespread attention. This event provided a major example of the hazard of teaching the "new science" without adequate protection and reasonable safeguards for academic freedom within the academy.

Born in Dutchess County, New York, on 31 December 1824, the son of Horace and Caroline (McAllister), Winchell entered Stockbridge Academy, South Lee, Massachusetts, where he studied for two years. At first he was fascinated by mathematics and astronomy, but later his interest turned to medicine. From 1841 to 1842, at age 16, he taught school. Teaching then captured his interest, and he entered Amenia Seminary in 1842. Here he started a natural history collection, which he later continued to develop. In 1844, he entered Wesleyan University, Middletown, Connecticut, and graduated in 1847. As a faculty member at Pennington Male Seminary, he continued his interest in natural history. Returning to Amenia Seminary to fill the chair of natural history, he gave his initial public lecture on geology. On 5 December 1849, he married Julia F. Lines of Utica, New York.

In 1850, Winchell and his wife moved south because he had been chosen to head a new academy at Newbern, Alabama. The next year he accepted a post to open the Mesopotamia Female Seminary in Eutaw. He accepted the presidency of Masonic University in Selma, Alabama, in 1853 but, due to an outbreak of yellow fever, departed that same year. Having received an offer of the chair in physics and civil engineering at the University of Michigan, he moved to Ann Arbor. A new chair in geology, zoology, and botany at the same university was offered to him in 1855, which he accepted and held until 1872. Throughout this period, he continued to enlarge his natural history collection, began publishing materials, and continued public lectures. By 1859 he was successful in organizing the state geological society. Although the society was suspended during the Civil War, it was revived in 1869 with Winchell as director. From 1872 to 1874 he held the post of chancellor of Syracuse University, and from 1875 to 1878, he served as professor of geology and zoology at newly created Vanderbilt University in Nashville, Tennessee. Returning to Ann Arbor in 1879, he was unanimously recalled to the chair of geology and paleontology at Michigan, where he taught until his death on 19 February 1891. Here he added to his accomplishments by leading in the organization of the Geological Society of America and serving as its president in 1891.

During his service in Alabama, Winchell had forwarded part of his natural history collection to the Smithsonian Institute in Washington, D.C. Here Spencer Fullerton Baird, one of the preeminent naturalists of that day, and other researchers were impressed with Winchell's work. Concurrently his activities as teacher, public lecturer, and popular writer on science brought him increased recognition. Eventually credited with nearly 250 articles and books, his discernible theme throughout his career was the reconciliation of the supposed conflict between science and religion. *Sketches of Creation: A Popular View* (1870), *Geological Chart* (1870), *The Doctrine of Evolution: Its Data, Its Principles, Its Speculations, and Its Theistic Bearings* (1874), *Reconciliation of Science and Religion* (1877), *Preadamites; or A Demonstration of the Existence of Men before Adam* (1880), *Sparks from a Geologist's Hammer* (1881), *World Life* (1883), a textbook entitled *Geological Studies* (1886), *Walks and Talks in the Geological Field* (1886), and *World-Life or Comparative Geology* (1889) all expressed the author's commitment to the theme of reconciliation.

In his *Sketches of Creation*, he stated, "[S]cience interpreted is theology. Science prosecuted to its conclusions leads to God" (vii). And in his *The Doctrine of Evolution*, he wrote, "[S]hall these doctrines [evolution] become proven even in their extreme phases, there will be no proof of the absence of immediate divine agency from any of the operations of life; and, having seen organization emerge from inert matter, we can believe more easily than before, 'God made man of the dust of the earth.' In any development of truth, Christian Theism has nothing to fear, but only new truth to gain; and should entertain a gratitude above all other interests for being placed in possession of new, solid material to incorporate into its system" (121–122). In his last major work, *World-Life*, he continued to assert "the omnipresence and supremacy of One Intelligence" that provides unity and interdependence of the "grand system of the universe" (v–vii).

In his work, Winchell was strongly influenced by Asa Gray, a Harvard botanist and correspondent of Charles Darwin, who reviewed *Origin of the Species* (1859) for the *Atlantic Monthly* magazine. Natural selection, he concluded, did not exclude the doctrine of "design" nor did it identify with skepticism and materialism. Gray, a devout Christian, was convinced "that Omnipotent fiat did not exclude the development theory and secondary causes." Indeed, this view and variations of it were shared by noted scientists, for example, James Challis, Michael Faraday, John Herschel, James P. Joule, James Clerk Maxwell, Charles Pritchard, G. G. Stokes, William Thomson, T. G. Bonney, J. W. Dawson, Joseph LeConte, Charles Lyell, Roderick Murchison, William North Rice, George Frederick Wright, David Brewster, Philip Henry Gosse, and St. George Mivart.

In sharp contrast with this group were Thomas Huxley and John Tyndall who stressed conflict between science and religion. Tyndall sought to claim ground for science at the expense of religion; Huxley believed his mission was to challenge clericalism in all its forms. Together they endeavored not only to remove science from the control of religion but to project scientific thinking into other areas of life. In this view the supernaturalistic interpretation of life was outmoded; scientific naturalism or scientific humanism was the alternative philosophy. Others who espoused these views in varying degrees were Herbert Spenser, W. K. Clifford, Leslie Stephen, John Morley, and George Eliot. That Charles Darwin, however, had no interest in attacking religion directly is stated in *The Life and Letters of Charles Darwin*. For example:

> [T]here is a great deal of talk and not a little lamentation about the so called religious difficulties which physical science has created. In theological science, as a matter of fact, it has created none. . . . The doctrine of Evolution . . . does not even come into contact with Theism, considered as a philosophical doctrine. That with which it does collide, and with which it is absolutely inconsistent, is the conception of creation, which theological speculators have based upon the history narrated in the opening of the book of Genesis. (5:2: 203–204)

It was his book *The Descent of Man* (1871), however, that was popularly interpreted to mean that man had descended from the apes. This popular image came to symbolize the debate between science and religion.

In this period of intellectual transition in the nineteenth century, Daniel D. Whedon, editor of *The Methodist Quarterly Review* (1856–1884), maintained a tradition of covering a broad range of theological and philosophical subjects. Reviews and essays by Victor Cousin, Henry L. Mansel, William Hamilton, John P. Lange, Karl Ullman, and Daniel Schenkel were published. Contributions by Theodore Parker, Horace Bushnell,* Charles Hodge, George P. Fisher, Laurens P. Hickok, Edward A. Park, and Henry Preserved Smith* were printed. Articles by Methodists William F. Warren, B. F. Cocker, Alexander Winchell, and Borden Parker Bowne* treating doctrinal, scientific, and ethical topics were frequently featured. Indeed, in the 1870s within American Protestantism, and American Methodism specifically, the respective positions between defenders of biblical theism and revisionists of traditional thought were openly presented in print. Winchell, for example, between 1870 and 1881 contributed, reviewed, or was cited 14 times in the *Quarterly*. His effort to reconcile science and religion is evident in two of his earliest essays included in this journal: "Sketches of Creation" (1870) and "Geology of the Stars" (1872).

It was in 1872 when Bishop Holland N. McTyeire of the Methodist Episcopal Church, South, received a gift of $500,000 from Cornelius Vanderbilt that the arena was constructed where six years later an event involving Alexander Winchell and the future of academic freedom was dramatically performed. With this gift, Bishop McTyeire was able to convert Central University, in Nashville, Tennessee, into Vanderbilt University. Elected bishop in 1866, McTyeire was noted as a champion of lay representation within the church, longer stays for ministers in pastoral appointments, and the organization of a Colored Methodist Episcopal Church. Recognizing the need for a more formally educated clergy, he was instrumental in organizing Vanderbilt to fill that purpose. As president of the Board of Trustees with veto power, he judiciously deflected criticism from a fellow episcopal colleague. Bishop George F. Pierce announced that "every dollar invested in a theological school" would prove damaging to Methodism. Although Pierce's words were harsh, they did reflect a widely held suspicion of higher learning among many American Methodists. Hence, McTyeire's effort on behalf of a Methodist-related university was remarkable for its time.

In 1875, Vanderbilt University formally opened, and Bishop McTyeire was determined to recruit a well-qualified faculty. To head the biblical department, the foremost theologian in southern Methodism, Thomas O. Summers, was appointed. In the department of science, a professorship of geology and natural history was to be shared between James M. Safford and Alexander Winchell. With his reputation as a scientist, Winchell was expected to add prestige and recognition to the university. He was to spend one half the year at Vanderbilt, while the other half was shared with Syracuse. In addition to his publications, his travel abroad and wide-ranging contacts with other scholars enhanced Vanderbilt's reputation. In 1875, no one expected that in just three years Winchell would be abruptly terminated and a journalistic battle over the event would highlight the profound distrust a segment of the religious community had for Darwinism and a fraction of the scientific fraternity had toward dogmatic religion.

Although Winchell's position on science and religion was publicly known, it was a series of articles published in the *Northern Christian Advocate* in 1878 entitled "Adamites and Preadamites or a Popular Discussion Concerning the Remote Representation of the Human Species and Their Relations to the Biblical Adam" that drew particular attention. In 1880 the ideas expressed in these articles were elaborated in *Preadamites*, but in the meantime, Winchell's contention that the Bible does not claim that Adam had no progenitor and his argument that Preadamites did not void the divine creation of Adam nor impair the unity of humankind became points of controversy. These assertions, he argued, did not preclude Preadamites and their descendants from the benefit of the "plan of redemption," nor did it diminish Adam by simply making him the starting point of humanity. Man, he claimed, did not rise from the organic level of a brute but merely was in existence before the "firstman" of the Hebrew popular tradition. A related view was that Negroes were racially too inferior to have stemmed from the biblical Adam, but this was not a new idea in the literature of race mythology. The claim that evolution provided the best proof for theism and that environment and natural selection were simply efforts to describe God's "instrumental means of accomplishing a certain premeditated result" aroused opposition.

It was these views that brought Winchell into conflict with Thomas O. Summers, dean of the Theological Department at Vanderbilt and editor of the Nashville *Christian Advocate*. Editor of an edition of John Wesley's *Sermons*, Richard Watson's *Theological Institutes*, and other Methodist classics, commentaries on the Gospels and Epistles of Paul, and an anthology of hymns, Summers was highly regarded in Methodist circles. His mission at Vanderbilt, as stated by Edwin Mims in *History of Vanderbilt University*, "was to champion orthodoxy; he was in every sense a defender of the articles of religion and an expositor of creeds" (50). He, too, knew what heresy was and where it lurked, and warned his audiences against it. His attitude toward science and evolution in particular became evident after a visit of Thomas Huxley to Nashville in 1876. To Summers, evolution was contrary to the plan of redemption. The fact that Winchell's views were publicized at a time when Summers believed Methodism was losing ground due to the decline of class meetings, family devotions, and knowledge of the Twenty-Five Articles of Religion served to intensify his opposition to Winchell's ideas.

Accused in the Nashville *Christian Advocate* of attempting to destroy the truths contained in the Gospels, Winchell was informed of this minutes before delivering a lecture at the university on the subject "Man in the Light of Geology." In Winchell's account of this event published in the Nashville *Daily American* on 16 June 1878 and entitled "Science Gagged in Nashville," it was Bishop McTyeire who informed him that he was charged with challenging the idea of Adam as a special creation and hence the theory of Atonement. Pressed by Winchell for an explanation, the bishop cited the pamphlet *Adamites and Preadamites* (1878) and added, "[O]ur people do not believe those things; they object to evolution. . . . Our people are of the opinion that such views are contrary to the 'plan of redemption.' " Noting that criticism was likely to increase, the bishop requested Winchell to relieve the Board of Trustees of the embarrassment by declining reappointment. Twice adamantly denying that evolution was professed in the pamphlet, Winchell asked if professors were subject to annual appointment. In special cases, he was told, this was true. Protesting "I have had no opportunity to explain or defend," he was subsequently informed that the professorship he held had been abolished for financial reasons.

The Nashville *Daily American, Northwestern Christian Advocate,* and *New York Christian Advocate* supported Winchell, and the Nashville *Christian Advocate, Wesleyan Christian Advocate,* and the *Southern Christian Advocate* endorsed the actions of the Board of Trustees. "Professor Winchell is determined to be a martyr. He appeals to the public against what he calls 'medieval proscription for opinion's sake,' 'the heel of priestly authority,' 'dismissal from office on account of heresy,' etc.," declared the editor of the Nashville *Christian Advocate* on 13 July 1878. Then he added, "Vanderbilt University is safe . . . [T]hose who are in charge of it know what they are about." Both the *Wesleyan Christian Advocate* and the *Southern Christian Advocate* editorialized the Trustees' decision. The *Southern Christian Advocate* on 6 August 1878 stated, "[T]he Professor is responsible to the Board, and the Board is responsible to the Church. . . . It seems to us an easy question, which should have the benefit of the doubt, the Church or the Doctor? Conservatism is not likely to be a fatal mistake in this fast age."

A vigorous critique of Vanderbilt's action came in the August 1878 issue of *Popular Science Monthly,* edited by Edward L. Youmans, entitled "Religion and Science at the Vanderbilt University." Defending Alexander Winchell and his work, Youmans declared, "Vanderbilt University decides not to take its old traditions out of the way but to fight the progress of science by the same policy of bigotry, intolerance, and proscription, that has been employed for centuries by the same party in doing the same." Emphasizing that Winchell was not antagonistic to religion or the authority of the Bible but one who attempted "to harmonize the teachings of Scripture with the conclusions of science" did not spare him from "the 'weak' foolishness" of the sort of Methodist theologians who have the institution in charge. That this happened to one whose position was previously published in his book *Reconciliation of Science and Religion* compounded the affront to Winchell and science. Reporting on this article, the Nashville *Christian Advocate,* on 17 August 1878, asserted that the learned editor of the *Popular Science Monthly* was speaking for Darwin and Huxley, insisting the conflict between science and religion is profound and goes to the root of human belief. Scientists of this persuasion should not be interfered with in their pursuit of truth. Vanderbilt is fighting "the progress of Science." Then the editor stated the paper's position that "the bearing of all these things upon Bible history and doctrine, and upon Church enterprise, are unmistakable."

In October 1878, the Tennessee Conference of the Methodist Episcopal

Church, South, one of the conferences with a vested interest in the university, recorded its approval of the action of the Trustees. In its published *Journal*, 5 October 1878, it stated "science we must have, science we intend to have, but we want only science clearly demonstrated, and we have great cause to rejoice in this, for it deals a blow, the force of which scientific atheism will find it exceedingly difficult to break." To this the *Popular Science Monthly* replied in December 1878, in an editorial entitled "Vanderbilt University Again." Recalling its previous article of August, it stated, "[W]e gave an illustration not long ago of the bigotry and intolerance exhibited by the authorities of Vanderbilt University in abruptly dismissing . . . an able professor of science." As a result of the Tennessee Conference's action last October, "Dr. Winchell is thus branded with a false and libelous charge by a body of religious teachers which pretends to commend the university as a protector of morals!"

The December 1878 *Popular Science Monthly* editorial was not the last to cite and call to the public's attention the case of Alexander Winchell. In *History of the Warfare of Science with Theology in Christendom* (1896), Andrew D. White, president of Cornell University, was struck by the number of heresy cases involving the teaching of evolution. Among those cited for stifling intellectual freedom were a number of denominational colleges and seminaries. The dismissal of Winchell from Methodist-controlled Vanderbilt was one of several cases noted and elaborated. President White also included the expulsion of Crawford Howell Toy* from Southern Baptist Seminary in Louisville, Kentucky, and the forcing out of James Woodrow* from Presbyterian Seminary, Columbia, South Carolina. But this type of case was not limited to the South. Dr. E. P. Gould resigned from Newton Theological Institute in Massachusetts in 1882; five professors at Andover Theological Seminary* were charged with theological liberalism and one convicted; and Professor Charles Augustus Briggs* of Union Theological Seminary in New York City was suspended from the Presbyterian ministry in 1893 on a charge of heresy.

The impact of these events on higher education in the United States provoked an academic revolution that brought together like-minded people to protest unfair and improper treatment. Alexander Winchell in Nashville telling his story to the press, Egbert Coffin Smyth* and friends at Andover taking their case to the Supreme Court of Massachusetts, and William Graham Sumner at Yale sharing his concern for academic freedom by letter with colleagues all helped to bring together teachers, scholars, scientists, and philosophers. Increasingly society was made aware of the difficulties with which college faculty were faced in the discharge of their responsibilities, especially in denominationally related institutions. To those well read, John W. Draper's recently published *History of the Conflict between Religion and Science* (1874) could have been describing these cases.

Bishop Holland McTyeire and the Trustees of Vanderbilt University were severely criticized for their failure to show understanding and leadership for academic freedom and fair treatment in the Winchell case. Reexamining this event years later, with persons who were at Vanderbilt at the time, Hunter D. Farish in his book *The Circuit-Rider Dismounts* (1938) concluded that McTyeire was motivated solely by a concern for the welfare of the young university and that his action was in no sense personal opposition to the teaching of science. That the bishop did succumb to executive expediency rather than measure up to his established principled approach to issues is evident (295–298). In a sense, it is not unlikely that Winchell's dismissal in 1878 from Vanderbilt did the image of religion more harm than his views expressed in the pamphlet *Adamites and Preadamites*.

In a letter dated 24 July 1878, Andrew D. White wrote to Daniel C. Gilman, president of Johns Hopkins University and an advocate of intellectual freedom, "I have been rather interested of late in the Winchell imbroglio at Nashville. What an idea of a University those trustees must have! What was tragical in Galileo's case is farcical in this. It appears that Bishop McTyeire took great pains to show to Winchell that there was no similarity between the two cases. Neither of them was aware that the Bishop used precisely the same argument to Winchell indeed, virtually, *verbatim*— which Cardinal Bellarmin used to Galileo" (Hofstadter, *American Higher Education*, II, 848). Acknowledging Winchell's superior reputation as a scientist, White suggested Gilman appoint Winchell to his university and added that he would if his university could afford it. Although Winchell was not offered a position at either Johns Hopkins or Cornell, he did receive a unanimous appointment to the chair of geology and paleontology at the University of Michigan in 1879.

In his last major publication, *World-Life or Comparative Geology* (1889), he noted, "[S]ome of these [my critics] have honored me by very special attentions. They have challenged me to controversy, and their abettors have sometimes jeered me over my assumed inability to rise from the pile of ruins which has been made of me and my theory. I need not disguise the satisfaction I feel in the arrival of the convenient time when these gentle gladiators shall discover themselves battering their blades against a wall" (vii). While Winchell had earned an excellent reputation in the scientific community, it should not be forgotten that among educated and well-to-do persons his efforts to reconcile science and religion via Darwin's theory had reduced an irrational and absolutist interpretation of life and human existence to more comprehensible and meaningful forms. The supposed loss of the importance of the supernatural was balanced by a new sense of perception and understanding.

BIBLIOGRAPHY

Chiles, Robert E. *Theological Transition in American Methodism: 1790–1935*. New York: Abingdon Press, 1965.

Cosslett, Tess, ed. *Science and Religion in the Nineteenth Century*. Cambridge: Cambridge University Press, 1984.

Darwin, Charles. *The Descent of Man*. New York: D. Appleton and Co., 1871.

———. *The Life and Letters of Charles Darwin*. New York: D. Appleton and Co., 1888.

Draper, John W. *History of the Conflict Between Religion and Science*. New York: D. Appleton and Co., 1874.

Farish, Hunter D. *The Circuit-Rider Dismounts*. Richmond: The Dietz Press, 1938.

Harmon, Nolan B., gen. ed. *The Encyclopedia of World Methodism*. 2 vols. Nashville: United Methodist Publishing House, 1974.

Hofstadter, Richard, and Walter P. Metzger. *The Development of Academic Freedom in the United States*. New York: Columbia University Press, 1955.

Hofstadter, Richard, and Wilson Smith, eds. *American Higher Education: A Documentary History*, 2 vols. Chicago: University of Chicago Press, 1961.

Mims, Edwin. *History of Vanderbilt University*. Nashville: Vanderbilt University Press, 1946.

Schlesinger, Arthur M. *A Critical Period in American Religion 1875–1900*. Philadelphia: Fortress Press, 1967.

White, Andrew D. *History of the Warfare of Science with Theology in Christendom*, 2 vols. New York: D. Appleton and Co., 1896.

Winchell, Alexander. *Preadamites*. Chicago: S. C. Griggs and Co., 1880.

———. *World-Life or Comparative Geology*. Chicago: C. C. Griggs and Co., 1889.

Frederick V. Mills, Sr.

The Witchcraft Trials in Salem
(1692)

The witchcraft trials in Salem Village, Massachusetts, may be the most notorious of all heresy trials in North American history. From May through September of 1692, more than 100 people accused of witchcraft were crammed into jail; 13 women, 6 men, and 2 dogs were hanged for witchcraft; and 1 accused man, Giles Cory, was pressed to death for his refusal to participate in the trials, even by pleading innocence.

The Salem trials were the most dramatic and far-reaching episode of witchcraft accusation in New England but not the only one. More individualized episodes pepper the histories of seventeenth-century New England villages, and at least 15 persons were hung for the sin and crimes of witchcraft before 1692. But the Salem trials were atypical in the number of people incarcerated and executed within a short time and also in their late date in comparison with witchcraft trials in English and European societies. In those societies, preoccupation with witchcraft spanned a 150-year period from 1500 to 1650. When the Salem trials drew the attention of all of New England in 1692, accusations of witchcraft in England, Germany, and France were largely a thing of the past.

ACCUSATIONS MADE BY SALEM VILLAGE GIRLS

Accusations of witchcraft began in Salem Village after Betty Parris, the nine-year-old daughter of minister Samuel Parris, her cousin Abigail Williams, and two of their friends experimented in fortune-telling and other forms of magic. When Betty and Abigail were seized by fits, the West Indian occultist and slave Tituba, who lived with the Parris family, attempted to cure the girls with a cake made with their urine. When Samuel Parris discovered this recourse to what he viewed as the Devil's own means, he condemned Tituba and attributed the spread of affliction among other Salem Village girls to her action. Accusations multiplied as girls and young women in Salem Village claimed they were being persecuted by the Devil's witches for refusing to become witches themselves.

The physical contortions and anguish of these young women was so convincing that even relatively liberal-minded Puritans believed the young women were actually experiencing diabolical tortures. After the trials, the minister of nearby Beverly, John Hale, explained that the suffering the girls endured was so horrible that, coming in the wake of certain other troubles New England was experiencing, authorities were led to condemn many innocent people: "[S]uch was the darkness of that day, the tortures and lamentations of the afflicted, and the power of former presidents [precedents], that we walked in the clouds, and could not see our way." Hale described how the girls "were bitten and pinched by invisible agents; their arms, necks, and backs turned this way and that way, and returned back again, so as it was impossible for them to do of themselves, and beyond the power of any Epileptick Fits, or natural Disease to effect." Through these "cruel Sufferings," the girls "were taken dumb, their mouths stopped, their throats choaked, their limbs wracked and tormented so as might move an heart to stone, to sympathize with them, with bowels of compassion for them" (Hale, *Modest Inquiry*, in Burr, *Narratives of the Witchcraft Cases*, 427, 413).

The girls and young women afflicted by witchcraft seemed to have been not only pinched, pulled, and bitten but also prevented from eating. Thus, after Mercy Short cursed the accused witch Sarah Good, who begged Short to bring her tobacco while she was incarcerated in Boston, Short underwent "extreme Fasting for many Days together." Occasionally, she would be able to take a little fruit, a chestnut, and "some Hard Cider," but if anything else were offered her, "her Teeth would bee sett, and Shee thrown into hideous torments." According to Short, her tormentors sometimes brought her "a little Cup" of "Whitish Liquor" that "They would pour down her Throat, holding her Jawes wide open in spite of all [her] Shriekings and Strivings." Cotton Mather "saw her swallow this Poison" and reported that she "swell[ed] prodigiously . . . like one poisoned with a Dose of Rats-bane" (Boyer and Nissenbaum, *Salem Witchcraft Papers*, 1:115; Cotton Mather, "A Brand Plucked Out," in Burr, *Narratives of the Witchcraft Cases*, 265–266).

The afflicted girls were preoccupied by bizarre images of biting, sucking, and other forms of physical invasion. Five young women accused Bridget Bishop, a tavern keeper whose economic life revolved around her supply of food and drink, and the first person to be hanged as a witch in Salem, of practicing "witchcraft in and upon the[ir] bodyes." Susanna Sheldon claimed that on one occasion Bishop and her fellow witches "all set to biteing mee." Sheldon also claimed that she had seen "a streked snake creeping over [Bishop's] shoulder and crep into her bosom" and that, on another occasion, she had seen "the blak man" give Bishop a hairless black pig, which she took first to one breast and then the other, before returning it to its owner. As a result of these allegations, Bishop's body was examined in a "dilligent search" by nine women who found "apreternathurall Excrescence of flesh between the pudendum and Anus much like to Teets." Bishop was only the first of the accused witches to be subjected to such a search for physical evidence of an unholy relationship with the Devil and his familiars.

WITCHCRAFT AS HERESY

New England Puritans considered witchcraft both a crime and a sin. As a crime, witchcraft involved *malificarum*—actions harmful to the health and property of other persons. As a sin, witchcraft constituted rebellion against God—willing alliance with the Devil was the most heinous form of opposition to God. Like many Christians in England and Europe, New England Puritans believed that Satan entered into relationships with some persons in which he ceded extraordinary powers in exchange for possession of their souls and their dependence on his will. English and American Puritans placed special emphasis on the covenant, or legal-like contract, between the Devil and his witches, which they viewed as antithetical to the covenant of grace between God and his saints, to which all true Puritans aspired. While the covenant of grace enabled men and women to live according to God's will, the covenant between the Devil and his witches unleashed evil and harm.

While conceptualization of the Devil and his witches as antagonists of God involved a sharp contrast between Good and Evil, New England Puritans did not attribute ultimate power to the Devil. They believed that God was ultimately in control of everything, including the Devil and his witches, and allowed evil to flourish through them as a way of punishing others for their sins. Thus, New England Puritans took any appearance of witchcraft in their midst as a sign that they and other New Englanders had failed in their obedience to God and were being punished for their sins. This self-referential aspect of Puritan belief in witchcraft may help explain why the Salem villagers and the judges at the Salem trials were so avid in their accusations and prosecutions. Since the appearance of witchcraft was a sign of the religious decline of New England, brought on by the failure of the Puritan community to obey God, then the identification and punishment of individuals believed to perpetrate that witchcraft was a means of declaring one's commitment to God and contributing to the reversal of that decline.

Like Europeans who believed in witchcraft, Puritans also understood the heretical nature of witchcraft in terms of the unholy physical relationship supposed to exist between Satan and his witches. A number of women pressured to confess to witchcraft at the Salem trials claimed to have given themselves "body and soul" to the Devil as part of their covenant relationship with him. In the context of Puritan culture, these claims suggested a demonic inversion of the covenant of grace, which was often described by Puritans as a marriage relationship between God and his saints. An even more prominent aspect of the Salem confessions involved claims of participating in a diabolical eucharist. For example, Sarah Bridges "owned She had been to the witch Meeting" at Andover with "@ 200 Witches" where they all "Eat bred & Drank wine." Abigail Hobbs confessed that "She was at the great Meeting in Mr Parris's Pature when they administered the Sacram'tt, and did Eat of the Red Bread and drink of the Red wine at the same Time." Her mother Deliverance Hobbs confessed that she had seen the former Salem minister, George Burroughs, who was also accused of witchcraft, in the Parris pasture, that he had "administered the sacrament" consisting of "Red Bread, and Red Wine Like Blood," and that several women subsequently jailed on charges of witchcraft "distributed the bread and . . . filled out the wine in Tankards." Elizabeth Johnson claimed that "20 or 30" witches had been at the meeting she attended and that the wine she tasted there was bitter and had probably come from Boston (Boyer and Nissenbaum, *Salem Witchcraft Papers*, 1:140; 2:410, 423, 501).

These fantasies of not enough or more than enough bread and wine and the details of earthen cups and filled tankards reveal a preoccupation with eating and drinking and with the relationship between meals and community. Descriptions of the Devil's eucharist were reminiscent of the boisterous May Days enjoyed in England and also of a supper party brought by wicked merchants to Salem Village. In noting that the Devil's wine had probably come from Boston, Elizabeth Johnson expressed the resentment Salem villagers felt toward mercantile townspeople, as well as the tension between town life and Salem Village, where community life was simpler, less individualized, and less sophisticated.

THE SOCIAL CONTEXT

As Paul Boyer and Stephen Nissenbaum argue, charges of witchcraft made by village girls against upstanding widows, merchants, and their wives expressed the hostility many rural New Englanders felt toward the merchant families of New England whose economic well-being flourished at the expense of their own and whose comparatively sensual and individualistic lifestyles seemed to epitomize the power of the Devil and the demise of Puritan community. The accused witches included Mary Bradbury, the wife of a ship's captain; Rebecca Nurse, a prominent member of the Salem Town church that for many years had denied Salem Villagers a church of their own; Philip English, one of the richest shipowners in New England and the merchant responsible for introducing trade between New England and France, Spain, and Portugal; and Bridget Bishop, who represented the relaxation of Puritan morality in her "Red paragon Bodys," which she wore at her tavern on the road between the landlocked farm lands of Salem Village and the commercial center of Salem Town. Villagers passed by her tavern when they traveled to exchange their produce at the poor rate commanded by Salem merchants.

Many of those accused of witchcraft, both at Salem Village in 1692 and in other New England villages earlier in the century, represented a possibility of female autonomy that seems to have fascinated and angered the servant and farm girls who accused them. As Carol F. Karlsen argued in her study of witchcraft in New England from the 1630s through 1692, those most vulnerable to accusation and to execution were widowed women who had inherited their husband's wealth and women who stood in a position to inherit enough money to live with some independence. In contrast to these objects of accusation, the accusing girls of Salem Village faced bleak futures. With marriageable young men more able than they to leave the village for better economic prospects, the servant girls, farmers' daughters, and child of the village's failed-merchant-cum-preacher who composed the accusing group looked forward to lives as spinsters, servants, beggars, or, at best, wives of poor farmers. The episode of fortune-telling that precipitated things reflected their sense of a dismal future. While gazing into an egg and a crystal ball, the girls asked for a sign of "what trade their sweet harts should be of." They saw a "spectre in likeness of a Coffin" (Karlsen, *Devil in the Shape of a Woman*, 101).

As Alan MacFarlane argued about witchcraft in sixteenth-century Essex, England, accusations of witchcraft occurred when the social system in which individuals functioned collectively was deteriorating but when individuals were still so invested in those systems that they were unable to fully accept personal autonomy. According to MacFarlane, when a housewife eager to establish an independent identity but still tied to her collective identity turned away an older woman begging at her door, she coped with her guilt by attributing her own hostility to the beggar and suspected her of witchcraft when a cow died or a child fell ill.

While MacFarlane's theory that older, impoverished women were especially vulnerable to witchcraft accusation describes some of the women accused in Salem—especially Sarah Good, a querulous old woman reduced to begging, the "Rampant Hag" Martha Carrier, and the impoverished Susanna Martin, whose sharp tongue contributed to her reputation as "one of the most Impudent, Scurrilous, wicked creatures in the world"—others accused of witchcraft in Salem were more prosperous and sophisticated than their accusers. Lashing out against the group ultimately responsible for their poverty and marginalization, one might say that the young women of Salem Village reversed the process of social change for a summer.

In addition to reflecting the stress of social change and the role of women as victims in Puritan society, the Salem trials also reveal the roles of women as agents of Puritan social order. As John Demos argued, the accusations of witchcraft at Salem reflect hostility on the part of the younger women toward older women. Because the afflicted girls wreaked revenge against the group most responsible for surveillance of their behavior, the Salem trials point to the control older women generally exercised over younger women in Puritan culture (Demos, *Entertaining Satan*, 63–64). At another level, the trials suggest the importance of women in Puritan culture by demonstrating the profound concern the girls' suffering elicited in the larger Puritan community. The girls' ability to send many people to jail and some to death is evidence of the considerable, if twisted, power available to them through the exercise of suffering, which New England Puritans regarded as a form of chastisement from God and potential means of sanctification.

Ten years before the Salem trials, the image of a woman sanctified by suffering had represented New England's historic and religious identity. First published in 1682, Mary White Rowlandson's *Narrative of Captivity* linked the integrity of New England during the difficulties of King Philip's War with a woman's sufferings, obedience to God, and eventual redemption from Indian captivity. In contrast, the bizarre and apparently demonic sufferings of the afflicted young women of Salem made it difficult for them, or anyone else, to forge a link between suffering and sanctity or to represent the integrity of New England in terms of such a link, as Mary Rowlandson had done.

The uncontrollable suffering of the Salem girls coincided with widespread anxiety about the political and religious integrity of New England and expressed the disarray of the Puritan social order as well as a frantic and ineffective attempt to reestablish that order. Puritan control of New England was undermined in 1684, when Charles II annulled the charter held by the Puritan government of Massachusetts. Although the colony received a new charter in 1691 after William of Orange's ascension to the English throne, its terms were considerably less favorable to Puritanism than the terms of the old charter. No longer were Massachusetts Puritans free to ban competing forms of Protestant worship, make church membership a prerequisite for voting in civil elections, or elect their own governor. In this moment of religious and political crisis, the phenomenon of female suffering lost its earlier association with personal and collective sanctity.

THE PROBLEM OF EVIDENCE

In their hurry to identify and punish witches, the Salem judges exerted considerable pressure on defendants to confess they were witches. Several persons accused of witchcraft did confess, perhaps in desperate efforts to quiet their accusers and please the judges. The judges sought confessions because they often corroborated accusations against other defendants, as well as those lodged against the confessor herself, and because they were the most solid form of evidence available. But the judges did not rule out more indirect forms of evidence, such as accidents or other instances of misfortune that were preceded by an angry interchange between the victim of misfortune and an accused witch. Unusual physical attributes in an accused witch were treated similarly; the remarkable physical power of George Burroughs became indirect evidence of a covenant between him and the Devil, through which the former minister of Salem Village was alleged to have received superhuman strength. Protuberances discovered on the bodies of female defendants, especially around the genitals, were admitted as possible signs of the defendant's means of suckling a pet demon and therefore as circumstantial evidence of witchcraft.

The most problematic form of evidence involved the accuser's claim that she saw the specter of the accused witch actively tormenting her, even as the accused witch, in her physical form, was sitting still in the court room before dozens of witnesses. This claim involved the belief that the witch's covenant with the Devil allowed him to use her specter, or spirit form, in his efforts to harm others. After the trial was over, Cotton Mather argued that in admitting spectral evidence the judges had not taken the Devil's power seriously enough—surely the Devil was powerful enough to use the specter of an innocent person for his malevolent ends. But during the trial, many were condemned on the basis of being seen as tormenters in the mind's eye of their accusers.

CONCLUSION

The outbreak of accusations and executions subsided as quickly as it had emerged. The Court of Oyer and Terminer responsible for trying and sentencing defendants was dissolved in early October of 1692 after Increase Mather, the president of Harvard College and one of New England's most influential ministers, condemned several forms of evidence allowed in the trials in an address, published soon after as *Cases of Conscience Concerning Evil Spirits Personating Men*. This denunciation of the legal proceedings at Salem, along with Mather's claim that "[i]t were better that ten suspected witches should escape, than that one innocent person should be condemned," had a chilling effect on public support for the trials, and those accused of witchcraft and still awaiting trial were quickly acquitted.

The religious extremism of the Salem trials exposed the perversity of the Puritan devotion to suffering and gave some New Englanders an opportunity to leave that devotion behind. While many New England women continued to derive authority from the association between suffering and sanctity, for many men, the transformation from Puritan to Yankee culture during the eighteenth century involved a new appreciation of manhood and its virtues of independence and self-confidence, and the collective hysteria and religious extremism of the Salem trials contributed to this development.

The Salem trials proved an embarrassment for New England leaders, who prided themselves in their capacity for moral judgment and rationality. After 1692, New England writers avoided mention of the trials, perhaps out of reluctance to draw further attention to the embarrassing event. Eventually, the trials came to epitomize the inhumanism of Puritan culture. Thus, when they became the subject of numerous poems, novels, and plays in the nineteenth century, the accused were depicted as innocent and beautiful young women unjustly accused of witchcraft by cruel and lascivious rogues whose sexual attentions they had rebuffed, and the judges were depicted as twisted and life-hating authorities who epitomized the narrow-minded, moralistic, and authoritarian nature of Puritan culture. In these revisionist interpretations, the Puritans responsible for the trials were clearly malevolent, in sharp contrast to their victims, who were portrayed as sweet and young. By the mid–twentieth century, the Salem trials had come to function so effectively as a symbol of the repressive and puritanical aspect of American culture that Joseph McCarthy's congressional investigations of suspected Communists in the 1950s were routinely characterized, by their liberal critics, as witchcraft trials.

BIBLIOGRAPHY

Boyer, Paul, and Stephen Nissenbaum. *Salem Possessed: The Social Origins of Witchcraft*. Cambridge: Harvard University Press, 1974.

———, eds. *The Salem Witchcraft Papers: Verbatim Transcripts of the Legal Documents of the Salem Witchcraft Outbreak of 1692*. 3 vols. New York: Da Capo Press, 1977.

Burr, George Lincoln, ed. *Narratives of the Witchcraft Cases, 1648–1706*. New York: Charles Scribner's Sons, 1914.

Demos, John. *Entertaining Satan: Witchcraft and the Culture of Early New England*. New York: Oxford University Press, 1982.

Hale, John. *A Modest Inquiry into the Nature of Witchcraft*. Boston, 1702.

Karlsen, Carol F. *The Devil in the Shape of a Woman: Witchcraft in Colonial New England*. New York: W. W. Norton, 1987.

Mather, Cotton. "A Brand 'Plucked Out of the Burning,' Being an Account of Mercy Short Who Was Supposed to Suffer by Witchcraft." Boston, 1692.

Mather, Increase. *Cases of Conscience Concerning Evil Spirits Personating Men*. Boston, 1693.

Porterfield, Amanda. *Female Piety in Puritan New England: The Emergence of Religious Humanism*. New York: Oxford University Press, 1991.

Amanda Porterfield

James Woodrow
(1828–1907)

James Woodrow, a seminary professor and center of the evolution controversy in the Presbyterian Church in the United States (1884–1889), was born in Carlisle, England, on 30 May 1828 to Reverend Thomas and Marion Williamson Woodrow. He graduated from Jefferson College (now Washington and Jefferson College) in 1849, studied at the Lawrence Scientific School, Harvard, in the summer of 1853, and received an A.M. and a Ph.D. in chemistry from the University of Heidelberg in 1856. He married Felie S. Baker in 1857. Over his long career, Woodrow held various distinguished positions: teacher/principal of academies in Alabama, 1850–1853; science professor, Oglethorpe University, Georgia, 1853–1861; ordination to ministry, 1860; editor and proprietor of *Southern Presbyterian Review* (quarterly), 1861–1885; editor and proprietor of *Southern Presbyterian* (weekly), 1865–1883; treasurer of Foreign Missions and Sustenation, Presbyterian Church, United States, 1861–1872; Confederate States of America (C.S.A.) chief of Columbia, South Carolina, Laboratory, 1863–1865; professor, 1869–1872, 1880–1897, president, 1891–1897, of South Carolina College (now University of South Carolina); professor, Columbia Theological Seminary, 1861–1886; banker; and businessman.

In 1861, Woodrow inaugurated a unique chair in theological education at Columbia Theological Seminary, The Perkins Professorship of Natural Science in Connection with Revelation, designed "to evince the harmony of science with the records of our faith, and to refute the objections of infidel naturalists" (Gustafson, *James Woodrow*, 58). Young ministers would have such enlarged views of science and its relationship to revealed religion that they would not act with indiscrete zeal in defending the Bible against the supposed assaults of true science but expound science in its relationship to the Bible and unfold and illustrate the truths of the Bible through an understanding of the knowledge of science.

Woodrow's announced approach was to find harmony between science and the Scriptures. A careful study of the principles of science and of biblical interpretation would inevitably lead to the discovery of harmony or at least the absence of discord.

He acknowledged that when one studied what the Bible said of God's relation to the universe, the biblical meanings were clear and could be understood, but when one turned from these broad tracks of light, a diversity of views appear on every subject. The Bible could impart a knowledge of the fact and moral bearing of Creation as they affect us but did not intend, and was not intended, to teach science as to the mode and details of Creation (66–67).

The Civil War intervened, closing the immediate needed discussion of his address. Columbia Theological Seminary, closed during the war, was reopened in September 1865. Woodrow resumed his teaching.

In 1884 he was asked to reveal his views on evolution. Dr. J. B. Mack, an influential secretary of the Board of Trustees, claimed that he had heard complaints that Woodrow was teaching evolution. Although Woodrow denied that he had taught evolution and his friends alleged that enemies were attempting to have him removed (155–161), Woodrow agreed to present his views at the annual meeting of the Alumni Association of the Seminary on 7 May 1885.

Woodrow's position was within the framework outlined in the 1861 address with two modifications: With proper interpretations, the Bible and science were noncontradictory rather than harmonious, and a form of evolution could be noncontradictory with the Bible. The Bible did not teach science, and science was incompetent to answer theological questions such as who or what was the power behind Creation. His description of the methodology of the work of the scientist—namely, the systematic observation and conclusions from observations—were hospitable to the prospect of evolution. He had delineated the province of science and the province of religion so as to avoid improper questions being asked of either discipline.

A proper definition of evolution excludes all references to the origin of the forces and laws by which it works, and therefore it is neither Christian or non-Christian and it does not affect the belief in God or in religion.

Accordingly, reasonable interpretations of the Bible do not contradict anything taught by science regarding the earth, the lower animals, and man as to his being. He suggested that the "dust" referred to in the Genesis story of Adam's creation could be "organic dust" as well as inorganic dust, and he cited the Scriptures. To admit this possibility was to admit the possibility of a form of evolution (151–152).

Woodrow stated that he had never once from 1 January 1881 to 10

December 1884 referred to the doctrine of evolution, even in its limited application, as probably true. He had taught for many years before 1880 that even if true (and he did not think it was), it did not contradict or in any way affect the truth of the Scriptures. His students concurred. Since it did not affect the Scriptures, it was a matter of indifference to believers in the Bible whether it was true or not. He acknowledged that in preparing for the address, the numerous facts with which he had become acquainted convinced him personally that evolution as he defined it was probably true, even though he had not taught it as true (155).

The Board of Directors of Columbia Seminary meeting on 16–18 September 1884 was under pressure from the religious press and from a statement made by the General Assembly commending the Board's efforts to determine that no "insidious errors are taught in our institution" (161–162). The statement was prompted by an unofficial report by Dr. Mack to the General Assembly's Committee on Theological Seminaries that the Board had requested Woodrow to make his views on evolution known.

By an eight to three vote, the Board approved Woodrow's views of the relations between the teachings of the Scriptures and natural science. While not concurring with Woodrow's view as to the probable creation of Adam's body, it believed that nothing in the doctrine of evolution as defined and limited by Woodrow was inconsistent with perfect soundness in the faith.

The minority report of the three disagreed: Evolution was an unproved hypothesis; the Seminary was not the place for such teachings; belief in evolution changes the interpretation of many scripture passages that are now received by the Church (164). The reaction to the Board's decision by Woodrow's enemies was swift in demanding his dismissal.

There were four Synods controlling the Seminary. At the meeting of the Synod of South Carolina, Woodrow complained that he was being charged with heresy and denied the safeguards of a trial. He demanded a trial.

In the various controlling Synod meetings, Woodrow and/or his supporters contended he had the right to adjust the method of approach regarding the relation between science and the Scriptures from harmony to noncontradiction and that the church had placed him in the chair to study—the very thing Woodrow had done. They argued that the Bible was not a textbook for science, resisted attempts to condemn him without trial, and attacked the move to stifle free inquiry in a theological seminary. Woodrow had been faithful to his trust, had rendered invaluable service to the church, and had not betrayed the Scriptures or the beliefs of the church.

The anti-Woodrow faction maintained that the chair ought to evince the harmony of science and religion, that the Bible was supreme in revelation and in science, and where science impugned on revelation, science must be rejected. The Confession of Faith, their arbiter on matters of science and the received (agreed upon by leading theologians) interpretation, was authoritative in the absence of statements from the Assembly on how the Bible should be interpreted in the face of scientific matters touching on the Bible.

The Synod of South Carolina, meeting first, was willing to allow evolution to be taught in an expository manner (193). The other Synods responded that evolution was not to be taught in the Seminary in any form, and the Board was instructed to take necessary steps to see that it was not taught. There was no directive that the Board dismiss Woodrow or that he be tried.

The Board of Trustees reconstituted to reflect the minority report met on 10 December 1884 and, by a vote of eight to four, requested Woodrow's resignation (198).

Woodrow refused. To do so would acknowledge the action of the Synods, which he regarded as illegal in form and incorrect in fact. He charged that their resolutions condemning his teaching as being unscriptural and contrary to the standards had been made without judicial investigation, by which alone such matters must be authoritatively determined. He affirmed that his teachings, so far as they were expositions of the Sacred Scriptures, accorded perfectly in every particular with the teachings of the Confession of Faith and Catechisms; and so far as they related to natural science, did not on any point contradict the Sacred Scriptures as interpreted by the church's standards (199). He demanded a trial.

The Board, acting with questionable procedures, refused his request for a trial and dismissed him. Without being lawfully charged with the commission of any offense, without the legal trial provided for in the constitution, Woodrow was treated as though he had been found guilty, condemned, and sentenced to deposition from office (201 [Constitution, Article 11]).

In April 1885, Dr. Woodrow requested that Augusta Presbytery try him, claiming that for the last eight or nine months he had been repeatedly charged in public journals with heresy and that the Synods had declared his teachings on a certain subject to be in conflict with the teachings of Sacred Scriptures. If the trial found him guilty, he requested that they institute process against him, in accordance with the provisions of the Book of Discipline. If not, he would be cleared of the false accusations (202–203).

Augusta Presbytery met on 23 April 1885 and found nothing that warranted a trial for heresy. Since no one appeared or offered to make charges, no process could be instituted. Woodrow gave notice that he would make a complaint to the Synod of Georgia. He believed that while the Presbytery did not find anything warranting a trial for heresy, it had taken the position, in failing to endorse the substitute motion, that there were possible grounds for a judicial process against him (202–203).

He appealed his removal at the 1885 Synods' meetings, claiming that it was based on erroneous information that he would hereafter teach as probably true the hypothesis of evolution (203). He did acknowledge that in teaching evolution, as defined and limited by him, he would be obliged to say he believed that it was probably true. But he never expressed any intention to disregard the wishes of the Synods that he not teach on the subject. The Board of Directors never asked him or intimated any desire to know if he would obey the wishes of the Synods (204). He acknowledged the right of the Synods to prescribe the subjects to be taught or not taught, and if he could not comply, he would feel duty bound to withdraw from the professorship at once. He charged that the Board had violated the covenant between the controlling Synods and a professor, ignoring the stipulated rights and obligations of the professor and the Synod (204).

The Synod had ruled that he should not be removed except for unfaithfulness to his trust or incompetence in the discharge of his duties; but it allowed for temporary suspension by the Board, the Synod's agent, until the case could be fully tried (204). Having been removed without the benefit of the trial guaranteed him in the covenant, he requested the Synods to withhold approval of the Board's action.

Some intrigue was evident in the strategy to remove Woodrow without a trial. John L. Girardeau, a leading proponent and colleague of Woodrow, wrote in a letter: "A formal trial of Dr. Woodrow was impossible. . . . [N]o offence was, or could have been charged against him, for the simple reason that he had committed none" (205).

The Synods of South Carolina and South Georgia and Florida disapproved the Board's decision, claiming that it had failed to ascertain from Dr. Woodrow if he would obey the voice of the Synods. The Board had executed a judicial sentence without having first given him a trial as provided in the constitution of the Seminary. The Synods of Georgia and Alabama approved the Board's decision. The Synods had split.

The Synod of Georgia sustained Woodrow's complaint against the Presbytery of Augusta, stating that while the Presbytery declined to say that there were no grounds for judicial process, it had refused to prefer charges against the complainant and try him. It returned the case to Augusta Presbytery, directing it to reopen it and either to declare that there were no grounds for judicial process or to proceed to trial (206).

One year after having removed Dr. Woodrow, the Board recognized him to be still the legal incumbent of the chair and asked if he would comply with the Synod's wishes in his teachings on evolution. Woodrow acknowledged the right of the Synods to prescribe what subjects should be taught and stated he would omit evolution from the subjects taught. Even with Woodrow's promise of compliance, the Board by a vote of eight to five requested him to resign in order to stop the agitation and promote the highest interests of the Seminary. He said he was not ready to answer the request. The Board's vote to remove him lost seven to six (206–207).

Since the Synod of Georgia upheld Dr. Woodrow's complaint, Augusta Presbytery reopened the case. The Reverend William Adams drew up an indictment for a trial to occur at the August meeting of the Presbytery—strategically after the May meeting of the General Assembly of the Presbyterian Church, United States.

Dr. Adams charged Woodrow with "[t]eaching and promulgating opinions and doctrines in conflict with the Sacred Scriptures as interpreted in the Confession of Faith and the Larger and Shorter Catechisms of the Westminster Assembly" by citing his May 1885 Alumni Address given before the Association and published in the 21 and 28 August and 15 October 1885 *Southern Presbyterian* newspapers and citing speeches before the three Synods. He also referred to the January 1885 *Southern Presbyterian Review* article that he claimed also taught and promulgated opinions of a dangerous tendency "calculated to unsettle the mind of the Church respecting the accuracy and authority of the Holy Scriptures as an infallible rule of faith." That dangerous opinion was that "the body of Adam was probably not made or created of the dust of the ground, as is universally understood by the Church to be the declaration of the word of God, but of organic matter preexisting in the body of a brute" (208–209).

With the trial delayed until after the General Assembly's meeting, the way was cleared for the General Assembly delegates to be led to state that the Scriptures, expounded in the Confession of Faith and Catechisms, taught that "Adam and Eve were created, body and soul, by immediate acts of Almighty Power, thereby preserving a perfect race unity; That Adam's body was directly fashioned by Almighty God, without any natural animal parentage of any kind, out of matter previously created from nothing" (209–210). Any doctrine at variance with this statement was a dangerous error leading to the denial of fundamental doctrines of the faith.

Woodrow tried, in vain, to keep the Assembly from making any statements regarding Creation that were not expressed in the Scriptures.

> The question before us is, shall this Assembly inject into the word of God something that is not there? You are asked to prescribe the time occupied by God in the creation of man, when God has not told you. The Bible tells us that God created man of dust, but it doesn't say how long he was in doing it, and you are adding your own petty notions to his ever glorious and true word. You will be violating the sacred truth imposed on you. You will be saying what he has not authorized you to speak. I beseech you, therefore, not for my sake, but that you may be true servants of the high God, that you do not drive away those who cannot subscribe to such a declaration. There is nothing in the Bible that will authorize you to say the creation was "immediate," and if you do so, you go in the face of the Word of God. (210)

His plea fell on deaf ears.

The General Assembly's action was in essence an *in thesi* deliverance since a trial was pending before Augusta Presbytery and actions by the

Assembly would influence these deliberations. The safeguards assuring a Presbyterian minister of a lawful hearing by Presbytery without a higher court's prejudicial actions weighing in the balance had not been preserved. The Assembly, assuming immediate jurisdiction over seminaries, recommended that the Synods dismiss Dr. Woodrow from the chair and appoint another professor in his place (211).

As Presbyterians waited for Woodrow's first and only trial in Augusta Presbytery, there were troubling questions raised: Did the Assembly have this much power? Was it wise for the Assembly to handle and to conclude questions on the issue in a trial pending before Augusta Presbytery when its actions might prejudice one way or another the results of the trial? Another surprise came from the trial in Augusta on 14 August 1886.

Augusta Presbytery found Woodrow not guilty. A stunned Adams—who had earlier indicated his willingness to drop all charges and avoid a trial if Woodrow would promise not to teach his views and resign his position—appealed the verdict to the next meeting of the Synod of Georgia (217).

Expressing reluctance to teach in the Seminary until the appeal was settled, on 16 September 1886 Woodrow requested and was given a leave of absence. The Synod of Georgia sustained Dr. Adams's complaint and annulled the action of Augusta Presbytery, giving as its reasons "that the findings and judgment of the Presbytery are contrary to the evidence of the said defendant . . . [whose stance] as to the origin of the body of Adam, was contrary to the word of God as interpreted in the standards of the Church" (220). It ordered his dismissal from the Seminary. The other controlling Synods concurred in the dismissal. The Board removed him at its December 1886 meeting.

Dr. Woodrow protested the actions to the May 1887 General Assembly, but illness kept him from attending. He did attend the 1888 General Assembly and made an impassioned plea for the church not to decide a scientific question on scriptural grounds. To do so would reveal that the church had assumed the false principle that the Bible teaches science. Historically, every mistake so made by the church had become an additional barrier in the ways of acceptance of the gospel of salvation through Jesus Christ, which the church was commissioned to preach to every creature (224).

By a vote of 109 to 34, the Assembly did not sustain Woodrow's complaint but did adopt a statement containing some of Woodrow's thinking.

> Now, therefore, it is the judgment of this General Assembly, that Adam's body was directly fashioned by Almighty God, of the dust of the ground, without any natural parentage of any kind. *The wisdom of God prompted him to reveal the fact, while the inscrutable mode of his action therein he has not revealed.* Therefore, the church does not propose to touch, handle or conclude any question of science which

belongs to God's kingdom of nature. She must by her divine constitution, see that these questions are not thrust upon her to break the
silence of scriptures, and supplement it by any scientific hypothesis concerning the mode of god's being or acts in creating, which are inscru-
table to us. (225)

Woodrow's advocates claimed this confusing statement raised several
questions. How could the Assembly affirm "that Adam's body was directly
fashioned . . . of the dust of the ground without any natural parentage of
any kind" and then state that God in his wisdom did not reveal the "in-
scrutable mode of his action" (227)? Where the Bible is silent, may not
Christians who make it the supreme rule of faith and morals hold either
theory without determent to their orthodoxy? If the Bible did not declare
the mode of Creation, the decree of the Assembly left the mode an unsettled
matter for the Presbyterian Church. If this were so, then why couldn't Dr.
Woodrow and his advocates believe and teach evolution without violating
any laws of the church?

When the resolution mentioned words such as *directly* and *dust of the
ground* and *without animal parentage*, though it made no reference to evolution as a mode of Creation, the terms in the first sentence seemed to
preclude evolution as a mode. Was the first sentence a concession to the
opponents of Dr. Woodrow?

The General Assembly recognized that Dr. Woodrow's ministerial status
was not affected by its decision since he was not on trial at the Assembly,
nor did it give new instructions for another trial. He had been removed
from the Perkins Chair. He had been found not guilty in a trial before
Augusta Presbytery. The Synod of Georgia annulled the actions of Augusta
Presbytery. Woodrow lost his appeal of the Synod's actions at the General
Assembly. No further trials were ordered. His ministerial status was never
questioned, and he was elected and appointed to positions of honor and
responsibility by the Presbytery, Synod, and subsequent General Assemblies. In all of this, he maintained his scientific and religious views as articulated throughout the long ordeal.

In 1967 (60 years after Woodrow's death), the General Assembly of the
Presbyterian Church in the United States requested its Permanent Theological Committee to study the question of the relationship of evolution to the
Bible and to report to the next succeeding General Assembly whether the
position stated by the General Assemblies of 1886, 1887, 1888, 1889, and
1924 should be reviewed (Presbyterian Church, *Minutes*, 49, 102; Gustafson, *James Woodrow*, 233).

The committee's report "Evolution and the Bible," presented and
adopted in 1969, was a two-part document. The first part listed the stated
positions of each of the five Assemblies, and the second part consisted of

conclusions and recommendations. The position of Dr. James Woodrow was favorably recognized, footnoted, and endorsed in their conclusion. "We conclude that the true relation between the evolutionary theory and the Bible is that of noncontradiction and that the position stated by the General Assemblies of 1886 [1887], 1888, 1889, and 1924 was in error and no longer represents the mind of our Church. We affirm our belief in the uniqueness of man as a creature whom God has made in His own image" (Gustafson, *James Woodrow*, 234). These twentieth-century Presbyterians echoed Dr. Woodrow's views:

> Neither Scripture, nor our Confession of Faith, nor our Catechisms, teach the creation of man by direct and immediate acts of God so as to exclude the possibility of evolution as a scientific theory. . . . Nowhere is the process by which God made, created or formed man set out in scientific terms. . . . If the Confession of Faith, or the Catechisms, appear in some manner to support the position of the General Assemblies of 1886 [1887], 1888, 1889, and 1924 this is not because of Scripture itself but rather because Scripture was interpreted with 17th. Century perspectives and presuppositions. . . . Our responsibility as Christians is to deal seriously with the theories and findings of all scientific endeavors, evolution, included, and to enter into open dialogue with responsible persons involved in scientific tasks about the achievements, failures, and limits of their activities and of ours. (235)

In 1909 Thornton Whaling (president of Columbia Theological Seminary, 1911–1929) in the John Calvin McNair Lectures at the University of North Carolina in Chapel Hill prophetically anticipated the significance of the 1969 Assembly's actions: "[S]lowly and imperceptibly the Church has come to the platform which he [Woodrow] so carefully and completely constructed, and will doubtless rest therein until the end of time. The only original contribution made by our Church to the world's scholarship is found in the signal service which this learned professor thus tendered by giving what is practically a demonstration that there can be no contradiction between God's word rightly interpreted and God's works rightly understood" (235).

Before his death on 17 January 1907, Woodrow was honored by a resolution from the Board of Directors of Columbia Theological Seminary "removing any and all aspersions or implications upon his character, standing, or theological orthodoxy which might be drawn from this or other actions of the Board" (262). Unfortunately, he was not alive to hear the vindication of his views by the General Assembly of 1969.

BIBLIOGRAPHY

Gustafson, Robert K. *James Woodrow (1828–1907): Scientist, Theologian, Intellectual Leader.* Lewiston, NY: The Edwin Mellen Press, 1995.

Presbyterian Church in the United States. *General Assembly Minutes*, 1861–1944, 1969.

Woodrow, Marion, ed. *Dr. James Woodrow as Seen by His Friends; Character Sketches and His Teachings*. Columbia, SC: R. L. Bryan, 1909.

Robert K. Gustafson

Unscientific Postscript

Affirmation and deep commitment are at the heart of religious heresy. Heretics have certainly been "true believers," although those who have tried them would have us believe otherwise. Their positive affirmations have been couched in tentative yet qualitative terms, for they have drunk deeply of the spirit of religious concern in Christianity that acknowledges that throughout life's pilgrimage one must remain open to the judging and renewing activity of God made known in Jesus the Christ. Let the records of these formal and informal trials speak for themselves in this regard.

Values and truths are often lost when they are taken for granted and/or simply forgotten. These trials are strong reminders of the importance of religious and academic freedom at the lectern, in the pulpit, and in the pew. This kind of responsible freedom becomes an offensive rather than a defensive tool. The heretics described in this volume did not play hide-and-seek with this idea. Their maneuvers were affirmative, offensive, and responsible.

The great new fact of the twentieth century in religious circles has often been said to be the ecumenical movement—confessionalism rising above denominationalism and sectarianism. Neo-orthodoxy has taught us well that we are finite creatures on pilgrimage. And in our better moments we have become humble and teachable in the relationships we have with our fellow human beings. This is a positive relativism that leads to more genuine humility and tolerance that is understanding and accepting. That kind of faith that necessitates absolute dogma and propositional truth for its support certainly senses anarchy in such relativism. But heirs of the faith can be brought to finite submission before God in the context of this kind of relativism. Most of the entries in this volume vividly illustrate the major role that ecumenism played in the careers of these particular heirs of the Christian faith.

Rufus Jones's *The Church's Debt to Heretics* expressed an insightful description of heretics: "A heretic in one generation would have been a saint if he [she] had lived in another, and a heretic in one country [or denomination] would often be a hero in another" (24). Again, these entries spell out this truth in numerous illustrations. Many of the theological positions of the heretics here have become either the normative standpoint of most schools and pulpits or at least a tolerated view. In a sense, these heretics have often come home. Others who have not have actually become political, sociological, and ecclesiastical victims but rarely theological victims alone. Some heretics have come home, then, but others have left or been pressured out by insensitive hierarchies and power structures that will not allow "insubordination." These heretics' interests in the critical and correlating tasks of the schools and churches have been avoided. Some contemporary heretics have been better satisfied with the Sunday newspapers than with the institutional churches due to this kind of avoidance of issues.

Fortunately, some of the heretics in this volume reflected on their experiences by means of autobiographical writings. Henry Preserved Smith, for example, wrote his story in 1926 in *The Heretic's Defense*. Still relevant, the conclusion of his book summarily gives the central issues of criticism and correlation:

> And now the reader who has had the patience to follow me may ask the question that others have asked: "Was it worth your while to unsettle the faith of the simple-minded Christian believer by your discussion of critical questions?" The answer must be the answer to the general inquiry whether education has any value. It would be possible to argue that the *sancta simplicitas* of the peasant woman who brought her fagot to the fire that burned John Huss should not be disturbed. In like manner the good lady who complained to Doctor Roberts that the Lane Seminary professors were taking her Bible away from her might conceivably be let alone in her belief in every statement of the sacred book; or the member of the Assembly of 1894 who protested that he accepted the whole Bible "from Generations to Revelations" might be spared by the scholars. But it is plain that in these cases the remedy is in their own hands. No one can take the Bible from them. All they have to do is to let the higher criticism alone. But the teacher [and preacher] has others to consider. The minds of our young people are keen to know all that has been discovered. Set them to read the bible, assuring them that it is the inerrant Word of God—that God is "inverbate" in it as He was incarnate in Christ—and they will at once raise questions that you will find difficulty in answering. A minister asked me once whether he ought to give his people some information concerning the higher criticism. My reply was: "Better for them to get it from you than from the Sunday newspapers." (123–124)

At his own trial, Algernon Sidney Crapsey at one point briefly spoke the same ideas: "I have the right to think, and my generation has the right to think in terms most apt to make these great truths real to our souls. To me God is not a definition; He is a living Being, and no definitions can confine or fully describe His nature or my relation to Him" (*Arguments*, 133–34).

Amid the negative developments in some denominational circles in relation to heresy and heretics, there are certainly numerous hopeful signs in contemporary Christianity. With so much pluralism and denominational options, heretics continue to come home, and as they do, they put out the welcome mat to those outside the churches by means of fresh and creative experiments in renewal, always committed to the spirit of ecumenism. To be involved in the business of criticism and correlation means many different things to many different people; a variety of exciting developments in church life are taking place.

The tradition of the heretics offers one of the finest opportunities of renewal that the churches have. Heretics must be able to find "place" in the churches; their rejection by especially fundamentalist traditions is at the same time a rejection of part of the essence of the Christian tradition. Where "place" is offered, however, the churches must not expect worldly and popular success or even absolute correctness and peace from their "dissenters come home." They will occasion mistakes. The heretics have never claimed infallibility. Chandler Davis in *The New Professors* observes a cogent truth:

> But in the nature of things a really significant innovation is likely to be hard to appreciate, or even understood, in the old terms. Its advocates themselves may not understand it too well. Their easily stated tenets may seem self-exposing falsehoods to normal people (particularly if they deny something economically or emotionally [or religiously] precious), and may, indeed be wrong. The new generally resembles the old in one respect anyhow: not being perfect. ("From an Exile," 184)

Dissenting heretics should be welcomed *and* heard—even though some of them will never make a unique contribution. Truly, their best contributions may simply be to prod other persons to contribute more creative contributions than they were able to give.

The far greater threat to free inquiry is illustrated in the cocksureness of the orthodox position rather than that of the dissenter. *The New Professors* notes correctly that "diehard adherence to a heresy is in general less menacing to free inquiry than matter-of-course adherence to orthodoxy; because the heretic, being constantly challenged, is deprived of the illusion that his rut is the whole road" (192).

The context for the heretics' homecomings is not one of suspicions, accusations of insubordination, rigidity, or the threatening of coercive power. It is, rather, one of trust—mutual trust and collegiality. Effective creativity is certainly not nurtured in an atmosphere of distrust that breeds suspicion. This only leads to a spirit of fear, frustration, and despair. Mutual trust involves a spirit of love, dialogue, and appreciation that leads to a creative witness.

Hopefully, let the glaring exceptions among American Christian denominations put away for good their formal and informal heresy trials in the relic trunk. Let them do some serious history homework in their own traditions. Any continued use of the trial tactic does serious damage to the *koinonia* (church community) and leaves many members in a state of loneliness, depression, and demoralization. The would-be-heretic who remains within that particular communion is stifled, and the tradition itself is infeebled due to depriving itself of the self-criticism and renewal that might result from the confrontation of the heretics. May these denominations welcome their twentieth-century heretics home so that they may in turn cope creatively with the more serious issues posed to the churches by the twenty-first century.

Christianity must recover the heresy of Jesus the Christ if it is to speak and minister effectively to the contemporary world. Part of this recovery is not only allowing but also nurturing its amateur or incidental as well as its professional heretics. A new kind of "heresy hunt" is needed—one that actively engages and enlists the heretic for service. Christianity, especially since the sixteenth century, has had a great deal to say about the priesthood of every believer. This priesthood most definitely involves the principle of nonconformity to idolatry in whatever form, institutional or otherwise. In a vital way, then, all of the poor priests of God are called to be obedient heretics at some time or another in their pilgrimage of life. If only one lesson is taught by these entries concerning American Christian heretics, let it be this one above all others.

BIBLIOGRAPHY

Arguments for Presenters and Defense of Reverend A. S. Crapsey before the Court of Review of the Protestant Episcopal Church upon His Appeal from the Judgment of the Court of the Diocese of Western New York. New York: Thomas Whittaker, 1906.

Davis, Chandler, "From an Exile," *The New Professors*, compiled by Robert O. Bowen. New York: Holt, Rinehart, and Winston, 1960.

Jones, Rufus. *The Church's Debt to Heretics*. New York: George H. Doran Co., 1924.

Smith, Henry Preserved. *The Heretic's Defense: A Footnote to History*. New York: Charles Scribner's Sons, 1926.

Appendix:
Identification of Trials
by Denominational Family

BAPTIST

Briggs, Robert C.

Clark, Theodore R.

Elliott, Ralph H.

Foster, George Burman

Louisville Thirteen, The

Marshall, Molly

Mercer Heresy Trials

Moody, Dale

Simmons, Paul D.

Southeastern Baptist Theological Seminary

Stagg, Frank

Toy, Crawford Howell

Whitsitt, William Heth

CHURCH OF JESUS CHRIST OF LATTER-DAY SAINTS

Brodie, Fawn McKay

Godbe, William S., and Elias Lacy Thomas Harrison

Johnson, Sonia

Strang, James J.

CONGREGATIONAL

Andover Theological Seminary
Beecher, Edward
Bushnell, Horace
Hutchinson, Anne
Smyth, Egbert Coffin
Smyth, Newman
Williams, Roger (Puritan, Baptist, unaffiliated)
Witchcraft Trials in Salem, The

EPISCOPALIAN

Crapsey, Algernon Sidney
Pike, James A.
Righter, Walter

GERMAN REFORMED

Schaff, Philip

LUTHERAN

Concordia Theological Seminary
Gotwald, Luther A.
Tietjen, John H.

METHODIST

Bowne, Borden Parker
Mitchell, Hinckley Gilbert Thomas
Winchell, Alexander

PRESBYTERIAN

Barnes, Albert
Beecher, Lyman
Briggs, Charles Augustus
Kenyon, Walter Wynn
Lane Theological Seminary

Machen, J. Gresham
McCune, William Clement
McGiffert, Arthur Cushman
Smith, Henry Preserved
Sturtevant, Julian M.
Swing, David
Woodrow, James

QUAKER

Dyer, Mary

ROMAN CATHOLIC

Curran, Charles E.
Hodur, Francis

Selected Bibliography

AAUP Bulletin (now *Academe*) 61 (April 1975): 49–59.

Academe 75 (May–June 1989): 35–45.

Adams, James E. *Preus of Missouri and the Great Lutheran Civil War*. New York: Harper and Row, 1977.

Adams, Robert L. "Conflict over Charges of Heresy in American Protestant Seminaries." *Social Compass* 17, no. 2 (1970): 243–260.

Ahlstrom, Sydney E. *A Religious History of the American People*. New Haven: Yale University Press, 1972.

Allison, C. Fitzsimons. *The Cruelty of Heresy*. Harrisburg, PA: Morehouse Publishing, 1994.

Ammerman, Nancy Tatom. *Baptist Battles*. New Brunswick, NJ: Rutgers University Press, 1990.

The Andover Case: With an Introductory Historical Statement; a Careful Summary of the Arguments of the Respondent Professors; and the Full Text of the Arguments of the Complainants and Their Counsel, Together with a Decision of the Board of Visitors: Furnishing the Nearest Available Approach to a Complete History of the Whole Matter. Boston: Stanley and Usher, 1887.

Andrews, Theodore. *The Polish National Catholic Church in America and Poland*. New York: Macmillan, 1953.

Averill, Lloyd J. *American Theology in the Liberal Tradition*. Philadelphia: Westminster Press, 1967.

Baird, Robert. *Religion in America*. New York: Blackie and Son, 1844.

Barnes, Albert. *Life at Three-Score*. Philadelphia: Parry and McMillan, 1859.

———. *Life at Three-Score and Ten*. Philadelphia: Henry B. Ashmead, Book and Job Printer, 1869.

Battis, Emery. *Saints and Sectaries: Anne Hutchinson and the Antinomian Controversy in the Massachusetts Bay Colony*. Chapel Hill: University of North Carolina Press, 1962.

Beck, Rosalie. "The Whitsitt Controversy: A Denomination in Crisis." Ph.D. diss., Baylor University, 1985.

Beecher, Edward. *The Conflict of Ages; or, The Debate on the Moral Relations of God and Man.* Boston: Phillips, Sampson, and Co., 1853.

Belloc, Hilaire. *The Great Heresies.* London: Sheed and Ward, 1938.

Berger, Peter L. *The Heretical Imperative.* Garden City: Anchor Press/Doubleday, 1979.

Bland, Thomas A., ed. *Servant Songs: Reflections on the History and Mission of Southeastern Baptist Theological Seminary, 1950–1988.* Macon: Smyth and Helwys Publishing, 1994.

Bowden, Henry W., ed. *A Century of Church History.* Carbondale: Southern Illinois University Press, 1988.

———. *Church History in the Age of Science.* Chapel Hill: University of North Carolina Press, 1971.

———. *Dictionary of American Religious Biography.* Westport, CT: Greenwood Press, 1977.

———. "Liberal Theology and the Problem of Continuity in Church History: A. C. McGiffert as a Case Study." *Union Seminary Quarterly Review* 27 (winter 1972): 67–79.

Bowen, Robert O., ed. *The New Professors.* New York: Holt, Rinehart and Winston, 1960.

Bowne, Borden Parker. *Studies in the Christian Life.* Boston: Christian Witness, 1900.

———. *Theism.* New York: American Book Co., 1902.

Boyer, Paul, and Stephen Nissenbaum, eds. *The Salem Witchcraft Papers: Verbatim Transcripts of the Legal Documents of the Salem Witchcraft Outbreak of 1692.* 3 vols. New York: Da Capo Press, 1977.

Briggs, Charles Augustus. *Authority of Holy Scripture: An Inaugural Address.* New York: Charles Scribner's Sons, 1891.

Briggs, Robert C. *Interpreting the Gospels.* Nashville: Abingdon Press, 1969.

Brodie, Fawn M. *No Man Knows My History: The Life of Joseph Smith, the Mormon Prophet.* New York: Alfred A. Knopf, 1945.

Brown, Robert M. *The Spirit of Protestantism.* New York: Oxford University Press, 1961.

Bushnell, Horace. *Christian Nurture.* Introduction by John M. Mulder. Grand Rapids, MI: Baker Book House, 1979.

Chiles, Robert E. *Theological Transition in American Methodism: 1790–1935.* New York: Abingdon Press, 1965.

Christie-Murray, David. *A History of Heresy.* New York: Oxford University Press, 1989.

Chu, Jonathan M. *Neighbors, Friends, or Madmen: The Puritan Adjustment to Quakerism in Seventeenth-Century Massachusetts.* Westport, CT: Greenwood Press, 1985.

Clark, Theodore R. *Saved by His Life.* New York: Macmillan Co., 1959.

Coalter, Milton J., John M. Mulder, and Louis B. Weeks, eds. *The Organizational Revolution: Presbyterians and American Denominationalism.* Louisville: Westminster John Knox Press, 1992.

Conforti, Joseph A. *Jonathan Edwards, Religious Tradition, and American Culture.* Chapel Hill: University of North Carolina Press, 1995.

Coser, Lewis. *The Functions of Social Conflict.* New York: Free Press, 1956.

Cosslett, Tess, ed. *Science and Religion in the Nineteenth Century.* Cambridge: Cambridge University Press, 1984.

Crapsey, Algernon S. *The Last of the Heretics.* New York: Alfred A. Knopf, 1924.

———. *Religion and Politics.* New York: Thomas Whittaker, 1905.

Cross, Barbara M. *Horace Bushnell: Minister to a Changing America.* Chicago: University of Chicago Press, 1958.

———, ed. *The Autobiography of Lyman Beecher.* 2 vols. Cambridge, MA: Harvard University Press, 1961.

Curran, Charles E. *Faithful Dissent.* New York: Sheed and Ward, 1986.

Danker, Frederick. *No Room in the Brotherhood: The Preus-Otten Purge of Missouri.* St. Louis: Clayton Publishing, 1977.

Demos, John. *Entertaining Satan: Witchcraft and the Culture of Early New England.* New York: Oxford University Press, 1982.

Dowell, Spright. *A History of Mercer University, 1833–1953.* Atlanta: Foote and Davies Co., 1958.

Elliott, Ralph H. *The "Genesis" Controversy and Continuity in Southern Baptist Chaos: A Eulogy for a Great Tradition.* Macon, GA: Mercer University Press, 1992.

———. *The Message of Genesis: A Theological Interpretation.* Nashville: Broadman Press, 1961.

Erwin, Robert. "The Concept of Heresy: Sorting Out the Confusion." *Christian Century* 98, no. 29 (23 September 1981): 930–934.

Evans, Llewelyn J., and Henry Preserved Smith. *Biblical Scholarship and Inspiration: Two Papers. With Preface on How It Came About, and an Appendix Containing Two Articles from the New York Evangelist on Ordination Vows, Also the Charges and Specifications Presented in the Presbytery of Cincinnati, October 17, 1892.* Cincinnati: Robert Clarke & Co., 1892.

Fletcher, R. S. *A History of Oberlin College.* 2 vols. Oberlin: Oberlin College, 1943.

Fosdick, Harry E. *The Living of These Days.* New York: Harper and Row, 1956.

Foster, Frank Hugh. *The Modern Movement in American Theology.* New York: Fleming H. Revell Co., 1939.

Foster, George Burman. *Christianity in Its Modern Expression.* Edited by Douglas Clyde McIntosh. New York: Macmillan Company, 1921.

———. *The Finality of the Christian Religion.* 2nd ed. Chicago: University of Chicago Press, 1909.

———. *Friedrich Nietzsche.* Edited by Curtis W. Reese, with an Introduction by A. Eustace Haydon. New York: Macmillan Company, 1931.

———. *The Function of Religion in Man's Struggle for Existence.* Chicago: University of Chicago Press, 1909.

Gallin, Alice, ed. *American Catholic Higher Education: Essential Documents, 1967–1990.* Notre Dame: University of Notre Dame Press, 1992.

Gaustad, Edwin S. *Dissent in American Religion.* Chicago: University of Chicago Press, 1973.

———. *Liberty of Conscience: Roger Williams in America.* Grand Rapids: Eerdmans Publishing Co., 1996.

Gotwald, Luther A. *Testimony and Trial—An Autobiography*. Edited by Luther A. Gotwald, Jr. Davidsville, PA: Editor, 1973.

Gotwald, Luther A., Jr. *The Gotwald Trial Revisited*. Davidsville, PA: Author, 1992.

Handy, Robert. *A History of Union Theological Seminary in New York*. New York: Columbia University Press, 1987.

Henry, Stuart C. *Unvanquished Puritan: A Portrait of Lyman Beecher*. Grand Rapids, MI: Eerdmans Publishing Co., 1973.

Hillis, Bryan. *Can Two Walk Together Unless They Be Agreed: American Religious Schisms in the 1970s*. Brooklyn, NY: Carlson Publishing, 1990.

Hofstadter, Richard, and Walter P. Metzger. *The Development of Academic Freedom in the United States*. New York: Columbia University Press, 1955.

Howe, Claude L., Jr. *Seventy-five Years of Providence and Prayer: An Illustrated History of New Orleans Theological Seminary*. New Orleans: NOBTS, 1993.

Hurt, Billy Grey. "Crawford Howell Toy: Interpreter of the Old Testament." Th.D. diss., Southern Baptist Theological Seminary, 1965.

Hutchison, William R. *The Modernist Impulse in American Protestantism*. Cambridge, MA: Harvard University Press, 1976.

James, Rob [Robison B. James], and Gary Leazer, eds. *The Takeover in the Southern Baptist Convention: A Brief History*. 2nd ed. Decatur, GA: Baptists Today, 1994.

Johnson, David, Francis L. Patton, and George C. Noyes, eds. *The Trial of the Rev. David Swing: Before the Presbytery of Chicago*. Chicago: Jansen and McClurg, 1874.

Johnson, Sonia. *From Housewife to Heretic*. Garden City, NY: Doubleday & Company, 1981.

———. *The Ship That Sailed into the Living Room: Sex and Intimacy Reconsidered*. Estancia, NM: Wildfire Books, 1991.

Jones, Rufus. *The Church's Debt to Heretics*. New York: George H. Doran Co., 1924.

Karlsen, Carol F. *The Devil in the Shape of a Woman: Witchcraft in Colonial New England*. New York: W. W. Norton, 1987.

Kephart, William M. *Extraordinary Groups: The Sociology of Unconventional Life Styles*. New York: St. Martin's Press, 1976.

Krumm, John M. *Modern Heresies*. Greenwich, CT: Seabury Press, 1961.

Kuzniewski, Anthony J. *Faith and Fatherland: The Polish Church War in Wisconsin, 1896–1918*. Notre Dame: University of Notre Dame Press, 1973.

Laeuchli, Samuel. *The Serpent and the Dove*. Nashville: Abingdon Press, 1966.

LaFantasie, Glenn W. *The Correspondence of Roger Williams*. Hanover, NH: University Press of New England, 1988.

Lang, Amy Shrager. *Prophetic Woman: Anne Hutchinson and the Problem of Dissent in the Literature of New England*. Berkeley: University of California Press, 1987.

Lindsay, Pauline. "Scrapbook Composed of Newspaper Clippings." Library of Southern Baptist Theological Seminary. (Contains many items relating to the Crawford H. Toy controversy)

Loetscher, Lefferts A. *The Broadening Church: A Study of Theological Issues in the Presbyterian Church since 1869*. Philadelphia: University of Pennsylvania Press, 1954.

Longfield, Bradley J. *The Presbyterian Controversy: Fundamentalists, Modernists, and Moderates*. New York: Oxford University Press, 1991.

Mack, Phyllis. *Visionary Woman: Ecstatic Prophecy in Seventeenth-Century England*. Berkeley: University of California Press, 1992.

Mahan, Asa. *Autobiography*. London: T. Woolmer, 1882.

Marquart, Kurt E. *Anatomy of an Explosion: Missouri in Lutheran Perspective*. Fort Wayne, IN: Concordia Theological Seminary Press, 1977.

Marshall, Molly Truman. *No Salvation outside the Church? A Critical Inquiry*. NABPR Dissertation Series, no. 9. Lewiston, NY: Edwin Mellen Press, 1993.

————. *What It Means to Be Human*. Macon: Smyth and Helwys, 1995.

May, William W., ed. *Vatican Authority and American Catholic Dissent: The Curran Case and Its Consequences*. New York: Crossroad, 1987.

McConnell, Francis John. *Borden Parker Bowne, His Life and His Philosophy*. New York: Abingdon Press, 1929.

Merideth, Robert. *The Politics of the Universe: Edward Beecher, Abolition, and Orthodoxy*. Nashville: Vanderbilt University Press, 1963.

Mitchell, H. G. *For the Benefit of My Creditors*. Boston: Beacon Press, 1922.

Moody, Dale. *Apostasy, a Study in the Epistle to the Hebrews and in Baptist History*. Macon: Smyth and Helwys, 1991.

————. *The Word of Truth*. Grand Rapids: Wm. B. Eerdmans, 1981.

Mueller, William A. *A History of Southern Baptist Theological Seminary*. Nashville: Broadman Press, 1959.

Newton, Joseph Fort. *David Swing: Poet-Preacher*. Chicago: Unity Publishing Company, 1909.

Nichols, James H. *Romanticism in American Theology*. Chicago: University of Chicago Press, 1961.

Nigg, Walter. *The Heretics*. New York: Alfred Knopf, 1962.

Norton, A. T. *History of the Presbyterian Church in the State of Illinois*. St. Louis: W. S. Bryan, 1879.

Nuesse, C. Joseph. *The Catholic University of America: A Centennial History*. Washington, D.C.: Catholic University of America Press, 1990.

Nutt, Rick. *Contending for the Faith: The First Two Centuries of the Presbyterian Church in the Cincinnati Area*. Cincinnati: Presbytery of Cincinnati, 1991.

Oden, Thomas C. "Can We Talk About Heresy?" *Christian Century* 112 (12 April 1995): 390–403. (Counterpoint by Lewis S. Mudge)

Pelikan, Jaroslav. *Obedient Rebels*. New York: Harper and Row, 1964.

Penzel, Klaus. *Philip Schaff*. Macon: Mercer University Press, 1991.

Pestana, Carla Gardina. *Quakers and Baptists in Colonial Massachusetts*. New York: Cambridge University Press, 1991.

Pike, James A., and Dianne Kennedy. *Search: The Personal Story of a Wilderness Journey*. Garden City: Doubleday, 1970.

Porterfield, Amanda. *Female Piety in Puritan New England: The Emergence of Religious Humanism*. New York: Oxford University Press, 1991.

Prentiss, G. L. *Union Theological Seminary, Its Design and Another Decade of Its History*. Asbury Park, NJ: M. W. & C. Pennypacker, 1899.

Rahner, Karl. *On Heresy*. New York: Herder and Herder, 1964.

Rian, Edwin H. *The Presbyterian Conflict*. Grand Rapids, MI: William B. Eerdmans, 1940.

Richards, W. Wiley. *Winds of Doctrine*. Lanham, MD: University Press of America, 1991.

Robertson, Archibald Thomas. *Life and Letters of John Albert Broadus*. Philadelphia: American Baptist Publication Society, 1901.

Rowe, Henry. *History of Andover Seminary*. Newton, MA: Andover-Newton, 1933.

Rudnick, Milton L. *Fundamentalism and the Missouri Synod: A Historical Study of Their Interaction and Mutual Influence*. St. Louis: Concordia Publishing House, 1966.

Schaff, Philip. *America*. New York: Scribner's, 1855.

————. *The Principle of Protestantism*. Chambersburg: Publication Office of the German Reformed Church, 1845.

————. *The Reunion of Christendom*. New York: Evangelical Alliance Office, 1893.

Schlesinger, Arthur M. *A Critical Period in American Religion 1875–1900*. Philadelphia: Fortress Press, 1967.

Shriver, George H., ed. *American Religious Heretics*. Nashville: Abingdon Press, 1966.

————. *Philip Schaff*. Macon, GA: Mercer University Press, 1987.

Shurden, Walter B. *The Life of Baptists in the Life of the World*. Nashville: Broadman Press, 1985.

————. *The Struggle for the Soul of the SBC*. Macon, GA: Mercer University Press, 1993.

Shurtleff, Nathaniel G. *Records of the Governor and Company of the Massachusetts Bay in New England*. 5 vols. Boston: William White, 1853.

Smith, George D. *Religion, Feminism, and Freedom of Conscience*. Buffalo: Prometheus Books, 1994.

Smith, H. Sheldon. *Horace Bushnell: A Library of Protestant Thought*. New York: Oxford University Press, 1965.

Smith, Henry Preserved. *The Bible and Islam; or, The Influence of the Old and New Testaments on the Religion of Mohammed: Being the Ely Lectures for 1897*. New York: Scribner's, 1897.

————. *The Heretic's Defense: A Footnote to History*. New York: Charles Scribner's Sons, 1926.

————. *Inspiration and Inerrancy: A History and a Defense. Containing the Original Papers on Biblical Scholarship and Inspiration*. Cincinnati: Robert Clarke & Co., 1893.

————. *Response, Rejoinder, and Argument*. Cincinnati: Robert Clarke & Co., 1893.

Smyth, E. C. *In the Matter of the Complaint against Egbert C. Smyth and Others, Professors of the Theological Institution in Phillips Academy, Andover. The Andover Defense. Defense of Professor Smyth, Arguments of Professor Theodore W. Dwight, with the Statements of Professors Tucker, Harris, Hincks, and Churchill*. Boston: Cupples, Upham and Co., 1887.

Smyth, Newman. *Old Faiths in New Light*. 2nd ed. New York: Charles Scribner's Sons, 1879.

———. *The Orthodox Theology of To-day*. New ed. New York: Charles Scribner's Sons, 1883.

———. *Recollections and Reflections*. New York: Charles Scribner's Sons, 1926.

Stagg, Frank. *The Book of Acts: The Early Struggle for an Unhindered Gospel*. Nashville: Broadman Press, 1955.

Stonehouse, Ned B. *J. Gresham Machen, a Biographical Memoir*. Grand Rapids, MI: William B. Eerdmans, 1954.

Stowe, Lyman Beecher. *Saints, Sinners, and Beechers*. Indianapolis: Bobbs-Merrill, 1934.

Stringfellow, William, and Anthony Towne. *The Bishop Pike Affair: Scandals of Conscience and Heresy, Relevance and Solemnity in the Contemporary Church*. New York: Harper and Row, 1967.

Sturtevant, Julian Monson. *An Autobiography*. Edited by J. M. Sturtevant, Jr. New York: Fleming H. Revell, 1885.

Swing, David. *David Swing's Sermons*. Chicago: W. B. Keen, Cooke and Company, 1874.

Tietjen, John H. *Memoirs in Exile: Confessional Hope and Institutional Conflict*. Minneapolis: Fortress Press, 1990.

Tucker, William Jewitt. *My Generation: An Autobiographical Interpretation*. Boston: Houghton Mifflin Company, 1919.

Turner, H. E. W. *The Pattern of Christian Truth*. London: A. R. Mowbray, 1954.

Walker, Ronald W. "When the Spirits Did Abound: Nineteenth Century Utah's Encounter with Free Thought Radicalism." *Utah Historical Quarterly* 50 (fall 1982): 304–324.

Whitsitt, William H. *A Question in Baptist History*. Louisville, KY: Charles T. Dearing, 1896; reprint, New York: Arno Press, 1980.

Williams, Daniel Day. *The Andover Liberals: A Study in American Theology*. New York: King's Crown Press, 1941; reprint, New York: Octagon Books, 1970.

Williams, Selma R. *Divine Rebel: The Life of Anne Marbury Hutchinson*. New York: Holt, Rinehart and Winston, 1981.

Wrodlowski, Stephen. *The Origins and Growth of the Polish National Catholic Church*. Scranton, PA: Polish National Catholic Church, 1974.

Index

Boldface page numbers indicate the location of main entries.

About the Contributors

ALLEN, WILLIAM LOYD. Ph.D., Southern Baptist Theological Seminary. Associate Dean and Professor of Church History and Spiritual Formation, Mercer University School of Theology.

ALLEY, ROBERT S. Ph.D., Princeton University. Professor of Humanities Emeritus, University of Richmond.

BLACK, SUSAN EASTON. Ed.D., Brigham Young University. Associate Dean of General Education and Honors and Professor of Church History and Doctrine, Brigham Young University.

BOWDEN, HENRY WARNER. Ph.D., Princeton University. Chair and Professor, Department of Religion, Rutgers University.

BRINGHURST, NEWELL G. Ph.D., University of California, Davis. Instructor of History and Political Science, College of the Sequoias (CA).

COCHRAN, BERNARD H. Ph.D., Duke University. Chair and Professor, Department of Philosophy and Religion, Meredith College.

CONGLETON, W. RUSSELL. A.B.D., Duke University. Has practiced law for five years.

DAVIS, THOMAS J. Ph.D., University of Chicago. Assistant Professor of Religious Studies, Indiana University–Purdue University at Indianapolis.

DUNCAN, POPE A. Ph.D., Southern Baptist Theological Seminary. Chancellor, Stetson University.

FISHER-OGDEN, DARYL. Ph.D., University of Notre Dame. Instructor in Historical Theology and Presbyterian Studies, Fuller Theological Seminary.

GAUSTAD, EDWIN S. Ph.D., Brown University. Professor of History and Religious Studies Emeritus, University of California, Riverside.

GRAGG, ALAN. Ph.D., Duke University. Vice President for Academic Affairs and Dean of the College, Brewton-Parker College.

GRAHAM, STEPHEN R. Ph.D., University of Chicago. Dean of Faculty and Associate Professor of American Church History, North Park Theological Seminary.

GUSTAFSON, ROBERT K. Th.D., Union Theological Seminary (Richmond). Professor Emeritus, University of North Carolina at Pembroke. Deceased, November 1995.

HENRY, STUART C. Ph.D., Duke University. Professor of American Christianity Emeritus, Duke University.

HUBER, DONALD L. Ph.D., Duke University. Professor of Church History, Trinity Lutheran Seminary (Columbus, OH).

HUMPHREYS, FISHER. Th.D., New Orleans Theological Seminary. Professor of Divinity, Beeson Divinity School, Samford University.

JAMES, ROBISON B. Ph.D., Duke University. Professor of Religion, University of Richmond.

KELLER, ROGER R. Ph.D., Duke University. Associate Professor of Church History and Doctrine, Brigham Young University.

KIRKLEY, EVELYN A. Ph.D., Duke University. Assistant Professor of Theological and Religious Studies, University of San Diego.

KLING, DAVID. Ph.D., University of Chicago. Associate Professor of Religious Studies, University of Miami (FL).

LOWE, EUGENE Y., JR. Ph.D., Union Theological Seminary (New York City). Associate Provost for Faculty Affairs and Senior Lecturer in Religion, Northwestern University.

MARKHAM, COLEMAN C. Ph.D., Vanderbilt University. Professor and Chair, Department of Religion and Philosophy, Barton College (NC).

MCCARTHY, DAVID B. A.B.D., Graduate student, Duke University.

MCDANIEL, REVEREND SUE ELLEN MOODY. M. Div., Southeastern Baptist Theological Seminary. "Currently and hopefully forever unemployed," as she states.

MCGEE, DANIEL B. Ph.D., Duke University. Professor of Religion, Baylor University.

MCKEOWN, ELIZABETH. Ph.D., University of Chicago. Associate Professor, Department of Theology, Georgetown University.

MILLER, GLENN T. Ph.D., Union Theological Seminary (New York City). Professor of Church History, Bangor Theological Seminary.

MILLS, FREDERICK V., SR. Ph.D., University of Pennsylvania. Professor of History, La Grange College (GA).

PORTERFIELD, AMANDA. Ph.D., Stanford University. Professor of Religious Studies, Indiana University–Purdue University at Indianapolis.

POTTMYER, ALICE ALLRED. B.A., Brigham Young University. Freelance writer, Washington, D.C.

ROGERS, MAX GRAY. Ph.D., Columbia University. Professor of Old Testament, Southeastern Baptist Theological Seminary. Deceased, February 1996.

SHAW, STEPHEN. Ph.D., University of Chicago. Adjunct Professor, Joliet Jr. College (IL).

SHRIVER, GEORGE H. Ph.D., Duke University. Professor of History, Georgia Southern University.

SHURDEN, WALTER B. Th.D., New Orleans Baptist Theological Seminary. Callaway Professor and Chair, Department of Christianity, Mercer University.

SMITH, HARMON L. Ph.D., Duke University. Professor of Moral Theology (Divinity School) and Professor of Community and Family Medicine (Medical School), Duke University.

SURRATT, JERRY L. Ph.D., Emory University. Homer V. Lang Professor of History and Religion and Dean of the College of Arts and Sciences, Wingate University.

VANDALE, ROBERT L. Ph.D., University of Iowa. Professor of Religion, Westminster College (PA).

WALKER, RONALD W. Ph.D., University of Utah. Senior Research Associate, Joseph Fielding Smith Institute for Church History and Professor of History, Brigham Young University.

WESTERKAMP, MARILYN J. Ph.D., University of Pennsylvania. Associate Professor of History, Merrill College, University of California, Santa Cruz.

WHELAN, TIMOTHY DAVID. Ph.D., University of Maryland. Assistant Professor of English, Georgia Southern University.

ISBN 0-313-29660-X

90000>

EAN

9 780313 296604

HARDCOVER BAR CODE

Dictionary of heresy trials
in American Christianity